THE *Atlanta Daily Intelligencer*
COVERS THE CIVIL WAR

STEPHEN DAVIS & BILL HENDRICK

THE *Atlanta Daily Intelligencer* COVERS THE CIVIL WAR

The University of Tennessee Press / Knoxville

Copyright © 2022 by The University of Tennessee Press / Knoxville.
All Rights Reserved. Manufactured in the United States of America.
Cloth: 1st printing, 2022.
Paper: 1st printing, 2023.

Library of Congress Cataloging-in-Publication Data

Names Davis, Stephen, 1948- author. | Hendrick, Bill, author.
Title The Atlanta Daily Intelligencer covers the Civil War / Stephen Davis & Bill Hendrick.
Description First edition. | Knoxville : The University of Tennessee Press, [2022] | Includes bibliographical references and index. | Summary: "This book investigates how Atlanta's most important newspaper, the *Daily Intelligencer*, covered the Civil War in its news articles, editorial columns, and related items in its issues of April 1861–April 1865. Authors Stephen Davis and Bill Hendrick show how the *Intelligencer* reported the war's important events based on the news it received, at what points the paper (and the Confederate press, generally) got the facts right or wrong, and how the paper's editorial columns reflected on the war from a distinctly pro-Confederate point of view. While focusing on the *Intelligencer*, Hendrick and Davis also contribute to the scholarship on Confederate newspapers, emphasizing their role as voices of Confederate patriotism and Southern nationalism and as contributors to wartime public morale" —Provided by publisher.
Identifiers LCCN 2022005545 (print) | LCCN 2022005546 (ebook) | ISBN 9781621907367 (hardcover) | ISBN 9781621907374 (pdf)
Subjects: LCSH: Daily intelligencer (Atlanta, Ga. : 1858) | Patriotism—Confederate States of America. | Nationalism—Confederate States of America. | United States—History—Civil War, 1861–1865—Press coverage—Georgia—Atlanta. | United States—History—Civil War, 1861–1865—Press coverage—Confederate States of America.
Classification LCC E609 .D38 2022 (print) | LCC E609 (ebook) | DDC 973.7/8—dc23/eng/20220214
LC record available at https://lccn.loc.gov/2022005545
LC ebook record available at https://lccn.loc.gov/2022005546

Ad nostros dulces uxores | BILLIE AND LAURA

Contents

A Look at Our Chapters *xi*

Prologue. Approaching the *Intelligencer* *1*

1. The *Intelligencer* Goes to War *5*
2. Operations of the *Intelligencer*: A Look Inside the Office *19*
3. After the Smoke Cleared *38*
4. Manassas *45*
5. Settling into War *61*
6. The *Trent* Affair *71*
7. Reporting Defeat: Mill Springs *78*
8. The Fall of Fort Donelson and Nashville *85*
9. Atlanta Becomes a Hospital Center *96*
10. "DEFEATED BUT NOT CONQUERED" *109*
11. Yankees in Atlanta *119*
12. The Fall of New Orleans *131*
13. Death in Atlanta *140*
14. The War in Virginia by Telegraph *158*
15. Lee versus McClellan: The Seven Days' Battles *176*
16. The War Turns Harder *193*
17. A "Great Victory in Maryland" Turns Sour *209*
18. "Our Prospects Bright" *223*
19. "Clio" Writes of Fredericksburg *235*
20. "Glorious Victory at Murfreesboro" *245*
21. The Press Association of the Confederate States of America *259*
22. Plant Corn, Not Cotton *266*
23. Chancellorsville: Piecing Together a Battle Narrative *274*

24. The Running Down of Streight *285*
25. Vicksburg *296*
26. Gettysburg *306*
27. Charleston Is Shelled *315*
28. Chickamauga *322*
29. President Davis Visits Atlanta *330*
30. "290" Is Joined by "A. S. A." *338*
31. The Editors Speak *346*
32. The Dahlgren Raid *353*
33. "Glorious Victories" *359*
34. The Story Behind an Editorial *370*
35. "General Johnston Is Falling Back" *377*
36. Kennesaw Mountain *389*
37. The Newspapers Leave Town *396*
38. A City Under Shellfire *405*
39. The Fall of Atlanta *413*
40. The *Intelligencer* Takes on President Davis *421*
41. Hood Moves North *432*
42. Lincoln is Re-Elected *443*
43. The *Intelligencer* Returns to a Ruined City *447*
44. The Debate to Arm the Slaves *457*
45. Nearing the End *463*
46. Surrender *473*

Epilogue. After the War *485*
Works Cited *487*
Index *513*

Illustrations

FOLLOWING PAGE 250

The Car Shed, Looking East
Federal Wagon Train Going Up Peachtree Street
Gustavus Bull
Alfred Waud, "The Battle of Resaca"
Joseph Emerson Brown
Fighting at Shiloh
Intelligencer Office in the Autumn of 1864
Alexander St. Clair Abrams' Booklet Title Page
Rallying the Troops of Bee, Bartow, and Evans at Manassas
When the *Intelligencer* Returned to Atlanta
Jared Irwin Whitaker
Intelligencer Front Page, April 20, 1861
Intelligencer Second Page, May 19, 1864

A Look at Our Chapters

1. THE *INTELLIGENCER* GOES TO WAR Early days of the *Atlanta Daily Intelligencer*—Jared Whitaker buys in—the presidential election of 1860—the paper supports secession—other dailies in the city—Fort Sumter—Archibald Gaulding, editor and William Bassford, associate editor.

2. OPERATIONS OF THE *INTELLIGENCER*: A LOOK INSIDE THE OFFICE The telegraph and American newspapers—layout of the *Intelligencer*—the importance of exchanges—employees and their roles—telegraphic news service—"special" correspondents in the field.

3. AFTER THE SMOKE CLEARED Lincoln calls for 75,00 troops—Gaulding and Whitaker buy out James Miller—the Confederate government calls for volunteers—Atlantans form companies.

4. MANASSAS Virginia secedes—Col. Lucius Gartrell and the 7th Georgia—the *Intelligencer*'s typesetter volunteers—President Davis calls for a day of fasting and prayer—Georgians write from Virginia—"GLORIOUS VICTORY!!"—Editor Gaulding warns of rumors, but prints them anyway.

5. SETTLING INTO WAR Promoting Southern literature—victory in Missouri—the *Intelligencer* supports Governor Brown's re-election—Dr. Westmoreland writes from Virginia——the Whitaker Volunteers—Ball's Bluff.

6. THE *TRENT* AFFAIR Atlantans vote for Davis and Stephens—Jared Whitaker named Georgia commissary general—tension between the United States and Great Britain—Gaulding reviews the year's end.

7. REPORTING DEFEAT: MILL SPRINGS The editor brags about his paper—slow telegraphic news service—Zollicoffer's force routed in Kentucky—living with the blockade—wartime difficulties for newspapers.

8. THE FALL OF FORT DONELSON AND NASHVILLE Federals push up the Tennessee and Cumberland Rivers—Fort Henry surrenders, February 6—"CONFEDERATE VICTORY AT FORT DONELSON!"—the truth sinks in—Nashville falls.

9. ATLANTA BECOMES A HOSPITAL CENTER Jefferson Davis' inauguration—Confederate conscription boosts volunteering—hospitals for sick and wounded soldiers—contributions for the hospital charities.

10. "DEFEATED BUT NOT CONQUERED" The *Virginia* at Hampton Roads—"GREAT VICTORY IN ARKANSAS!"—the fall of Island No. 10 and New Madrid—"The Reign of Terror in Nashville"—Gaulding editorializes against "Lincoln's minions."

11. YANKEES IN ATLANTA The *Intelligencer* calls for martial law in Atlanta—disagreement with the *Southern Confederacy*—Fort Pulaski captured—reported victory at Shiloh—the *Intelligencer* euphoric—Andrews' train thieves.

12. THE FALL OF NEW ORLEANS Costs of printing a newspaper—more complaints against the Southern Associated Press—newspaper editors meet in Atlanta—McClellan lands at Virginia's Peninsula—"Yankee subjugation!"—Federals capture the Crescent City.

13. DEATH IN ATLANTA The *Intelligencer* suggests arming slaves—"YANKEE LIES"—John Steele joins the *Intelligencer*, April 1862—pen names—Butler's "woman order"—the paper publishes lists of soldiers who died in the city.

14. THE WAR IN VIRGINIA BY TELEGRAPH The *Intelligencer* warns of the enemy's designs on Atlanta—"Stonewall" Jackson's victories in the Shenandoah Valley—McClellan advances on Richmond—the threat of subjugation by the North—the battle of Seven Pines—Gaulding on Yankee newspapers' "whoppers."

15. LEE VERSUS MCCLELLAN: THE SEVEN DAYS' BATTLES Gaulding views the situation optimistically—Lee attacks McClellan—victory at Gaines' Mill—Uncle Henry, a patriot—one of the slain, Maj. Eli Hoyle—Gaulding sells his share to Whitaker—John Steele becomes editor.

16. THE WAR TURNS HARDER Massachusetts Colonel Lee writes Virginia General Lee—John Pope's proclamations—Richmond threatens no quarter—Lincoln's slow embrace of emancipation—slave prices in Atlanta—Jackson's "foot cavalry" marches to Manassas—Lee and Longstreet rout Pope's army.

17. A "GREAT VICTORY IN MARYLAND" TURNS SOUR Smith's victory at Richmond, Ky.—the *Intelligencer* announces a price increase—Bragg declares martial law in the city—decree annulled—Lee's march into Maryland—conflicting news from Sharpsburg.

18. "OUR PROSPECTS BRIGHT" Steele reflects optimistically—Lincoln's preliminary Emancipation Proclamation—battle at Corinth—sluggish telegraphed news—Perryville and Bragg's retreat—Steele advocates for a destitute soldier's wife.

19. "CLIO" WRITES OF FREDERICKSBURG "Clio" begins to send articles from Richmond—in Northern elections, Democratic gains—the battle of Fredericksburg.

20. "GLORIOUS VICTORY AT MURFREESBORO" Bragg's premature declaration of victory, December 31—his army retreats, and Steele struggles to explain—hospitals in the city—the president passes through Atlanta—a 25 percent hike in subscription prices.

21. THE PRESS ASSOCIATION OF THE CONFEDERATE STATES OF AMERICA The *Commonwealth*, Atlanta's third daily—a Press Association CSA is formed in Augusta, Feb. 4-5, 1863—John Thrasher hired as superintendent.

22. PLANT CORN, NOT COTTON Governor Brown presses the legislature for agricultural legislation—Steele compliments his correspondent, "290" (Samuel Chester Reid)—the Richmond and Atlanta bread riots—the Bath, S.C., paper mill burns—the *Intelligencer* announces another price hike.

23. CHANCELLORSVILLE: PIECING TOGETHER A BATTLE NARRATIVE Review of the campaign and battle, May 1-4, 1863—what Steele in his sanctum learned—"More Glorious News"—"THE DEATH OF GENERAL T. J. JACKSON."

24. THE RUNNING DOWN OF STREIGHT *ADI* reports capture of Union raiders, May 5 near Rome—Grierson's Raid—Crawford, Frazer advertises negroes for

sale—Van Dorn's Holly Springs raid—Grant launches his Vicksburg campaign—Federals take Jackson and besiege Vicksburg.

25. VICKSBURG The *Memphis Appeal* arrives in Atlanta—Grant's army invests Vicksburg—the ADI reports the fall of Vicksburg.

26. GETTYSBURG Brandy Station—Lee's army fords the Potomac—battle at Gettysburg—"40,000 prisoners!"—the *Intelligencer* deals with the news.

27. CHARLESTON IS SHELLED "290" reports the Union attack on Battery Wagner, July 18, 1863—another *ADI* price increase—the Federals bombard the city.

28. CHICKAMAUGA "290" reports from Tunnel Hill—fall of Knoxville and Chattanooga—Bragg attacks at Chickamauga—reports of Confederate victory—Atlanta hospitals receive many wounded soldiers.

29. PRESIDENT DAVIS VISITS ATLANTA "Cousin Nourma" at the battlefield—General Bragg's officers balk—the President travels through town—Governor Brown's re-election—Yankee preachers.

30. "290" IS JOINED BY "A. S. A." Steele cloaks Sam Reid's identity—"290" reports rout at Missionary Ridge—Bragg is relieved—Alexander St. Clair Abrams reports as "St. Clair"—Abrams' history of the Vicksburg siege.

31. THE EDITORS SPEAK "Clio," "290" and A. E. Marshall—the newspaper office likened to an infantry corps—Alexander Abrams' "Review of the War"—Sam Reid joins the Knoxville/Atlanta *Register*.

32. THE DAHLGREN RAID Col. Ulric Dahlgren leads Union cavalry toward Richmond—he is ambushed and killed—papers found on his body disclose intent to murder Davis and cabinet members—the *Intelligencer* voices shock—Northerners accuse Rebels of planting the papers—historians side with the Southern version.

33. "GLORIOUS VICTORIES" The *Hunley* sinks the *Housatonic* at Charleston—"Clio" fades from the *Intelligencer*—the Atlanta printers' strike, April 1864—the *Atlanta Daily Press* and *Reveille*—St. Luke's, the new Episcopal church in town—Hoke captures Plymouth, N.C.—Kirby Smith beats Banks

at Mansfield, La.—Bedford Forrest takes Fort Pillow, Tenn.—large loss of life among the garrison—the *Intelligencer* defends the general.

34. THE STORY BEHIND AN EDITORIAL How could John Steele remain optimistic about the Confederacy's future?—a review of the facts, early 1864—reasons for Southerners' sustained hopes.

35. "GENERAL JOHNSTON IS FALLING BACK" Grant's plan for a five-front advance, May 1864—failure of Banks, Butler and Sigel—Grant vs. Lee in the Wilderness, May 5-6—Sherman moves against Joe Johnston at Dalton—Federals' flanking maneuver forces Johnston's retreat, May 12-13—battle of Resaca, May 14-15—another flanking move, another retreat—Steele writes about "long faces" in Atlanta—the aborted attack at Cassville, May 19—Confederate victories at New Hope Church and Pickett's Mill—Atlanta's fortifications.

36. KENNESAW MOUNTAIN Johnston's Lost—Pine—Brush Mountain line, early June—General Polk is killed, June 14—Sherman's flanking tactics—the *Intelligencer* reports battle at Kennesaw Mountain, June 27—an *Intelligencer* printer falls in battle.

37. THE NEWSPAPERS LEAVE TOWN Grant and Lee settle into semi-siege at Petersburg—Sergeant Collier's bravery—the *Intelligencer* complains of downtown "stink k k k"—"Olla Podrida"—Johnston retreats across the river, July 9-10—citizens panic—the *Rebel, Register, Confederacy, Appeal* and *Intelligencer* all clear out.

38. A CITY UNDER SHELLFIRE President Davis decides to relieve General Johnston—Gen. John B. Hood succeeds to army command—his attacking battles, July 20-28—Sherman's plan to take the city—the *Intelligencer* moves to Macon—foreman Isaac Pilgrim reports the Federal bombardment of Atlanta.

39. THE FALL OF ATLANTA Bombardment casualties—Sherman's semi-siege—the *ADI* relates the Confederate evacuation of Atlanta—Dr. I. E. Nagle, "our ASSOCIATE"—President Davis comes to Palmetto.

40. THE *INTELLIGENCER* TAKES ON PRESIDENT DAVIS The *Intelligencer* criticizes the president—Davis speaks in Macon—"The man who uttered this is a scoundrel"—Steele confesses that the "scoundrel" was Dr. Nagle.

41. HOOD MOVES NORTH —Hood launches an offensive—*ADI* to a half-sheet—a sample of the paper's material—"the maniac gaze" of a rape victim—Hood moves into north Alabama.

42. LINCOLN IS RE-ELECTED Lt. Bennett Young's raid on St. Albans, Vt.—Confederates reckon with Lincoln's victory.

43. THE *INTELLIGENCER* RETURNS TO A RUINED CITY The *ADI Extra* of December 10 is printed in Atlanta—Yankees' damage to the city before marching to the sea—The *Intelligencer* reports Sherman's march—the bloody battle of Franklin.

44. THE DEBATE TO ARM THE SLAVES News of Hood's rout at Nashville—the *Intelligencer* announces its eighth rate increase of the war—the Confederate Congress debates arming slaves.

45. NEARING THE END The Hampton Road Conference steels Confederate resolve—Sherman's troops wreak revenge in South Carolina—"Burnwell"—Atlanta rebuilding—Johnston faces Sherman in North Carolina—the fall of Richmond—Steele voices Confederate optimism—subjugation and its consequences.

46. SURRENDER Wilson's raid—rumors of Lee's surrender dismissed—irrefutable confirmation—Abraham Lincoln's assassination—Steele bemoans the tragedy—Johnston surrenders his army to Sherman—the *Intelligencer* editor offers words of consolation and advice to his readers.

EPILOGUE What happened to the *Intelligencer* and its principals after the war.

Prologue

IN THIS WORK WE DEMONSTRATE how Atlanta's most important newspaper, the *Daily Intelligencer*, covered the Civil War in its news articles, editorial columns and related items from April 1861 to April 1865. Our main themes will be to show 1) how the *Intelligencer* reported the war's important events, based on the news it received; 2) whether the paper got the facts accurately, according to our study of the historical literature; and 3) how the paper's editorial columns reflected on those events from a distinctly pro-Confederate point of view.

We quote the paper liberally, as our intent is to let the *Intelligencer* speak for itself, allowing our readers in turn to see how Atlantans learned about the war from its pages. At the outset we determined to let the paper take our narrative where it would; therefore our text chronologically follows the course of the war and how the *Intelligencer* reported it. Often that reporting was sketchy, at times misleading, if not downright wrong (as when the paper hailed Shiloh as a Southern victory). Nonetheless, as related by J. Cutler Andrews' *The South Reports the Civil War* (1970), other Confederate newspapers demonstrated the same shortcomings.[1] The *ADI*, in other words, was in good company.

The *Intelligencer*'s two wartime editors, Archibald Gaulding and John Steele, were staunchly pro-Confederate in their outlook and writing. "Confederate journalism became almost a nationalistic venture," as Drew Gilpin Faust puts it.[2] We emphasize the *Intelligencer*'s functions as a propaganda organ. Historians agree on them: 1) fix blame for the war on the enemy; 2) confidently predict victory for the cause; 3) vilify the enemy's war leaders; 4) accuse the foe of committing atrocities; and 5) stoke the people's morale.[3] We will assert that in fulfilling these roles, the *ADI* had few peers in the Confederate press as it sought to shape the views of its readers. Its denunciations of Yankees could be both colorful and vicious: "cerulean abdomens"—a highfalutin' term for bluebellies—had been "gathered from all the purlieus of effete Europe and the North" and were thus second-rate soldiers: "Dutch immigrants, cheated Irishmen, bamboozled mongrels, miserable contrabands, miscegenating adults and brigades of silly youths with cerulean abdomens, and a sufficiency of Yankees to leaven the whole mess with their accursed principles of injustice and wrong." By the summer of 1864, hatred of the enemy could appear in grotesque manifestation, as when the *Intelligencer* celebrated all the Yankees dying at Andersonville, the notorious prisoner of war camp southwest of Atlanta, boasting of the considerable labor and material it would take to bury them.[4]

One thing we've noticed is how historians speak of *Confederate* newspapers, not Federal ones. Partly this is a temporal device, referring to the four-year period of Southern nationhood. But it is also a reflection of the nationalistic fervor one sees in almost all papers operating in Confederate held-territory.[5]

In this connection, we regard our work as paralleling that of recent students of Confederate cultural nationalism, such as Jason Phillips, who writes, "To demonize the enemy, Rebels elicited savage and racist monikers, including 'barbarian,' 'vandal,' 'abolitionist' and 'miscegenator.'" We see all of these terms—and plenty more—in the pages of the *Intelligencer*. Michael T. Bernath quotes the editor of the *New Orleans Daily Delta* to make his point that Confederates believed their separation from the North had to be cultural, not just political.[6] The *Intelligencer* emphasized the same, advising readers to read only Southern journals, and to hire Southern-born schoolmarms for their children.

WHY WE CHOSE THE *INTELLIGENCER*

As recently as 2015, George C. Rable, in *Damn Yankees!: Demonization & Defiance in the Confederate South*, has written, "the whole topic of the Civil War-era press deserves much more study."[7] In such a collective effort we believe our work fits, in good measure because the *Atlanta Daily Intelligencer* was so representative of Confederate newspapers as a whole. For example, it faced the same troubles that beset other Confederate newspapers: paper shortages, high ink prices, printers striking for higher pay, faulty telegraphic news service. To stay afloat during the war, it had to raise subscription rates eight times.

Yet by several indices the *Intelligencer* was an exceptional publication. It was one of Georgia's prominent newspapers, having been founded as a weekly in 1849, converting to a daily five years later. It was rivaled only by the *Atlanta Southern Confederacy*, another daily. In July 1864, as Sherman's forces approached, both papers fled the city and relocated to Macon, there resuming publication. While less is known about the relocated *Southern Confederacy*, the *Atlanta/Macon Intelligencer* continued its war reporting until the paper returned to the city after Sherman's departure in mid-November. The *Intelligencer* then resumed operation in Atlanta through the end of the war and afterward.[8]

The *Intelligencer* was also politically powerful, so closely allied with Georgia governor Joseph E. Brown that the editor felt he had to defend it against the charge that it was "Gov. Brown's organ." Circulation is obviously a benchmark; in 1860 the U.S. Census posted 3,000 subscribers for the *Daily* and *Weekly Intelligencer*, thus ranking it among the top three papers in the state. Another index is paid advertising, which appeared abundantly in the paper's pages. Moreover, in the economically straitened Confederacy, the *Intelligencer* was able to increase its ad rates five-fold during the war.[9] This reflected wartime inflation, of course, but it also reflected the *Intelligencer*'s appeal to regional businessmen.

An incident further illustrates the *Intelligencer*'s political clout. When editor John Steele was away in September 1864, associate editor Dr. I. E. Nagle penned an editorial criticizing President Davis for his apparent negligence of Georgia's safety, with Sherman's army ensconced in Atlanta. In a speech delivered in Macon, Sept. 23, 1864, Davis called an unnamed newspaperman "a scoundrel." Southerners at the time and historians since then have wondered to whom the president was referring. We cracked the code: it was Nagle of the *Atlanta Intelligencer*, based on an admission by editor Steele after he had returned to his *sanctum* and noted all the hubbub about the "scoundrel" in the Southern press.[10] When your paper comes to the attention of the President of the Confederate States, that's definitely saying something.

Finally, there is the issue of accessibility. A virtually complete run of the *Intelligencer* reposes in microfilm at the Atlanta History Center, which also owns original copies, something that cannot be said for a lot of Confederate newspapers.

WHAT LIES AHEAD

One last word about our content and style. When we quote the *Intelligencer* we relate its spelling directly (*e.g.*, rumour, centre). A newspaper, particularly a popular one, is nothing if not eclectic. In addition to reporting war news and bucking up the people's morale, the *ADI* also offered colorful stories and vignettes, such as the execution of deserter Jacob Adams in Charleston (front page!). We feature these, as well as items of local news, such as the editor's protest over the noxious odor of the city's filthy streets ("stink k k k").[11]

Reflecting our respective careers as historian (Davis) and journalist

(Hendrick), we have composed our book as a metaphorical newspaper: short chapters written in a breezy style, inviting readers to select any of them as one would choose articles of particular interest in the morning newspaper. Hence our two purposes in writing this book: to contribute to the scholarship, as well as to offer an enjoyable read.

Along the way, we remember the words of Mark Twain: "The difference between the *almost* right word and the *right* word is really a large matter. 'Tis the difference between the lightning bug and the lightning."

NOTES

1. J. Cutler Andrews, *The South Reports the Civil War* (Princeton NJ: Princeton University Press, 1970), 538–39.

2. Drew Gilpin Faust, *The Creation of Confederate Nationalism: Ideology and Identity in the Civil War South* (Baton Rouge: Louisiana State University Press, 1988), 8.

3. Louis Turner Griffith and John Erwin Talmadge, *Georgia Journalism 1763–1950* (Athens: University of Georgia Press, 1951), 66; J. Cutler Andrews, "The Confederate Press and Public Morale," *Journal of Southern History*, vol. 32, no. 4 (November 1966), 448; Carl R. Osthaus, *Partisans of the Southern Press: Editorial Spokesmen of the Nineteenth Century* (Lexington: University Press of Kentucky, 1994), 111.

4. "The Situation," *ADI*, May 23, 1864; "Dead Yankees in Andersonville," *ADI*, Aug. 19, 1864.

5. Richard M. McMurry, "The Confederate Newspaper Press and the Civil War: An Overview and a Report on Research in Progress," *Atlanta History*, vol. 42, nos. 1–2 (Spring-Summer 1998), 59–75.

6. Jason Phillips, *Diehard Rebels: The Confederate Culture of Invincibility* (Athens: University of Georgia Press, 2007), 53; Michael T. Bernath, *Confederate Minds: The Struggle for Intellectual Independence in the Civil War South* (Chapel Hill: University of North Carolina Press, 2010), 14.

7. George C. Rable, *Damn Yankees!: Demonization & Defiance in the Confederate South* (Baton Rouge: Louisiana State University Press, 2015), 195.

8. Henry T. Malone, "Atlanta Journalism During the Confederacy," *Georgia Historical Quarterly*, vol. 37, no. 3 (September 1953), 210–12; Henry T. Malone, "The Weekly Atlanta Intelligencer as a Secessionist Journal," *Georgia Historical Quarterly*, vol. 37, no. 4 (December 1953), 278–86; Alan Bussel, "The Atlanta Daily Intelligencer Covers Sherman's March," *Journalism Quarterly*, vol. 51, no. 3 (Autumn 1974), 405–10.

9. "Gov. Brown and the Intelligencer," *ADI*, Aug. 13, 1861; Kenneth W. Rawlings, "Statistics and Cross-Sections of the Georgia Press to 1870," *Georgia Historical Quarterly*, vol. 23, no. 2 (June 1939), 179; Debra Reddin van Tuyll, *The Confederate Press in the Crucible of the American Civil War* (New York: Peter Lang, 2012), 194.

10. Michael B. Ballard, "Breakdown in Macon," *Civil War Times Illustrated*, vol. 19, no. 6 (October 1980), 31–33; "The President's Speech in Macon—His War Policy," *ADI*, Oct. 4, 1864.

11. "Execution of Jacob Adams," *ADI*, May 22, 1863; "The City," *ADI*, July 2, 1864.

1. The *Intelligencer* Goes to War

THREE DAYS AFTER CONFEDERATE FORCES fired on Fort Sumter, the *Atlanta Daily Intelligencer* declared in a fiery editorial, "We are determined not only to achieve our independence at whatever the cost, but we will teach these Northern Goths and Vandals a lesson, before this war is over, which they will never forget."

The *Intelligencer* (a popular name for 19th century newspapers, meaning "conveyor of information") had become Atlanta's leading paper during the 1850s, the turbulent decade of mounting hostility between the North and South. The *Atlanta Weekly Intelligencer* had been established in 1849, after local businessmen, Joseph Clapp and Frederick Bartlett, had bought a weekly, the *Southern Miscellany*, and renamed it the *Intelligencer*. Several papers had already failed in the fledgling city (renamed Atlanta from Marthasville in 1845). But the *Weekly Intelligencer* showed staying power, and in 1850—among a population counted in that year's census as just over 2,000 whites, 2,058 enslaved African Americans plus 18 free blacks—it could boast a circulation of about 700. The paper demonstrated its strength when it became a daily in August 1854. At that time Atlanta's population numbered about 6,000. The young city had grown enough to support two daily papers, the *Intelligencer* and its rival, the *Examiner*. The two publications prudently combined in September 1857. The *Atlanta Daily Intelligencer and Examiner* then held forth until the *Examiner*'s name was dropped in the spring of 1858. Like most dailies, the paper came out in the morning, six days a week. (The staff was given Sunday off, so there was usually no Monday issue.) Meanwhile, a weekly edition continued to be published, serving subscribers of lesser means, or those living outside the city. "DAILY INTELLIGENCER. DAILY & WEEKLY," was its self-description, for instance, in its issue of Oct. 7, 1858. Publisher was named as "A. A. GAULDING & CO.," the firm of Archibald Alexander Gaulding. Born in Virginia in 1808, Gaulding moved to rural middle Georgia, Pike County, from which he was elected to the state legislature in 1847. In 1855, at Griffin, Georgia, he became an owner and the editor of *The Empire State*. A few years later Gaulding moved to Atlanta.

He also held political posts, surveyor-general of the state as well as auditor of the state-owned Western & Atlantic Railroad. Gaulding was evidently a learned man. Beneath the *Intelligencer*'s title in its front-page nameplate ran a famous quotation that the paper attributed to President Thomas Jefferson, but which actually came from John Milton's polemic of 1644, *Aereopagetica*: "Error ceases to be dangerous when reason is left free to combat it." The statement had been added to the front page sometime during 1857–58, a variant of Jefferson's observation in his First Inaugural Address, "error of opinion may be tolerated where reason is left free to combat it."[1]

Several months later, the same masthead informed readers that editors for the newspaper were Archibald A. Gaulding and Varney A. Gaskill. One sees that advertising on the front page of the *Intelligencer* at that time, in January 1859, was the law firm of Whitaker and Gaskill. From this listing we learn that Gaskill, Gaulding's editorial partner, earned his primary income as an Atlanta attorney, sharing his downtown office at Whitehall and Alabama Streets with lawyer Jared I. Whitaker, the prominent grandson of a former governor of Georgia.

In 1859 business interests published Atlanta's first "Directory, City Guide, and Business Mirror." Prospering enterprises took out full-page ads in the booklet, and "Atlanta Intelligencer, Daily and Weekly" was one of them. A. A. Gaulding & Co. was named as publisher, with Gaskill and now Whitaker listed as Gaulding's other principal; it is apparent that Gaskill had brought his law partner into the paper (the ad posted a subscription rate of $6 a year for the daily, $2 for the weekly). Whitaker purchased Gaskill's interest in November 1859.

James I. Miller was also associated with the paper, apparently as a partial owner. An advertisement for the *Intelligencer*'s auxiliary business, "Book and Job Printers, and Book Bindery," boasted that Miller's "reputation as a practical printer . . . is favorably known in this State." The job office, according to the city directory of 1859, was operated in a downtown building at the southwest corner of Whitehall and Alabama Streets—the heart of the city's business district. The directory also listed "Whitaker & Gaskill, Attorneys at Law" as continuing their law practice, suggesting that owning a daily newspaper could be a sideline to one's main vocation.[2]

In the 1850s, American newspaper operation was such that a couple of lawyers could at least venture into, if not double as both journalists and jurists. To own or edit a newspaper required education and considerable wealth, providing prestige and influence in return. Of those associated with the *Intelligencer*, Jared I. Whitaker's was the most prominent name in its entire lifespan.

A grandson of Jared Irwin, Georgia's governor for several terms during 1796–1809, Whitaker, as practicing attorney in the custom of the day, was bestowed the honorary title of "Judge." His up-and-coming status was confirmed by his election to the City Council in July 1853. At the time, his business involvements included positions as charter founder of the Atlanta Medical College, director of the Bank of Fulton, and incorporator of an early railroad company, the Georgia Air Line Railroad. Election to the Georgia State Senate followed in 1857, which propelled Whitaker to Atlanta's political front rank.

The two major proprietors of the paper, Archibald Gaulding and Jared Whitaker, were not only slaveowners, but large ones at that, at least by the norms of slavery in Southern cities, in which most owners seldom had more than three or four slaves. By the census of 1860, Gaulding owned nine persons: five females, aged six to thirty-five, plus four males, aged three to fifteen. The youth of Gaulding's "property" suggests that the females may have been primarily assigned to routine household tasks. The oldest male, fifteen, could have been hired out by Gaulding in Atlanta's many businesses, but a logical surmise is that he may also have been employed in the *Intelligencer*'s print shop.

Jared Whitaker's eight enslaved African Americans were considerably older. Four women ranged between eight and fifty years old. The men in 1860 were also of the age of adulthood (50, 50, 40 and 18). Here, too, the readiest assumption is that Whitaker profited by hiring out his males to Atlanta's burgeoning industries and manufacturing shops. Then again, we may guess that they could have been experienced pressmen at Whitaker's and Gaulding's newspaper plant.[3]

In early 1860, with "Gaulding, Whitaker & Miller" remaining as proprietors of the *Intelligencer*, Editor Gaulding listed as his Associate Editor one J. Edmund Burke. By that time Whitaker and Gaskill had split up their law practice; Whitaker was practicing solo, while Gaskill shared offices with Marcus A. Bell in the Concert Hall Building, at the south end of Peachtree Street across from the Georgia Railroad Bank Agency. By mid-year, Whitaker had taken a partner (E. P. Watkins) into his law practice. Meanwhile, at the paper, associate editor Burke was gone; in his place had come John W. Leonard. In their opinion columns, amidst the increasingly heated acrimony with the North over slavery, editors Gaulding and Leonard voiced full-throated defense of the South and its "institution." In an editorial in January 1860, for instance, the *Intelligencer* expressed opposition to the very presence of free black men in the state. "Every negro in Georgia should have a master," it asserted.

The nation's political crisis intensified in 1860 with the coming of national presidential elections. The two main parties nominated their candidates. Republicans offered Abraham Lincoln of Illinois on a platform opposing the extension of slavery into the western territories. Democrats rallied behind Sen. Stephen A. Douglas, also of Illinois. But his position on slavery in the territories—allowing the people of each to decide for themselves, or "popular sovereignty"—was deemed too tepid by ardent pro-slavery activists, so Southern Democrats split off and nominated their own candidate, John C. Breckinridge of Kentucky.

Pro-Breckinridge Atlantans organized, and Jared Whitaker was chosen chairman of their executive committee. When Douglas visited the city on October 30, 1860, just a week before the election, Whitaker and his committee posed a series of questions for the candidate. "Has not each State the sovereign right to decide for itself what shall be sufficient cause for a withdrawal from the Union?" topped the list, signaling Southern Democrats' fears of Lincoln's impending election, and the possibility that slaveholding states would have to secede from the Union if it had become inimical to their interests.

If a state so seceded, the committee asked, "would the Federal government have a right to coerce her back into the Union, and would you assist the Federal government in so coercing her?" Whitaker and his colleagues objected to Douglas' answers as "evasive." The committee explained its perspective the next day in the *Intelligencer*: "States Rights men of Georgia, will you sustain the abominable Federal government? Are freemen of the South slaves of the Federal government?"[4]

The presidential election was held on November 6, 1860. The next day the paper was able to report how Atlantans voted. Despite the editors' appeal to "freemen of the South," it became apparent that more Atlantans favored some sort of compromise with the North. John Bell of Tennessee, who ran on a third party "Constitutional Union" platform offering vague promises of conciliation, got 1,070 votes in the city. Breckinridge, Whitaker's favorite, came in second with 825; Douglas followed with 334. Abraham Lincoln's name was not even on the ballot, as the Republican Party had no organization in the South. Statewide, Georgians went more for Breckinridge (51,893), then Bell (42, 855) and finally Douglas (11,580).[5]

Breckinridge had carried most of the South, but Lincoln had swept all of the North and with it the electoral majority needed to win the presidency. On the night of November 8, a hastily assembled group, the "Minute Men of Fulton County," met downtown to discuss what should be done next. Convening the meeting was no less than the editor of the *Intelligencer*, Archibald Gaulding (a Minute Man colonel), assisted by William B. Bassford (also a Minute Man officer who would soon join the paper's editorial staff). Bassford put forth a resolution condemning Lincoln's election as promising "the destruction of our constitutional rights, and eternal hostility to our domestic institutions" (meaning, of course, slavery), and affirming support for Georgia leaving the Union. Amidst hot-blooded seconding speeches, the measure carried handily.

The paper kept up its drumbeat for secession. A week after the Minute Men's meeting, on November 15, the *Intelligencer* denounced those who would seek to compromise with the North, as Lincoln's administration portended for the South only "the yoke of Black Republican rule, unless we rise up to our defense." There was no middle ground for the South, according to the *Intelligencer*. "The naked question to be decided by the people," it declared on November 27, "is secession or submission." Within a month, on Dec. 20, 1860, a convention of South Carolinians passed an ordinance announcing the severance of ties between their state and the federal union. A few days later, to those who worried that Southern secession could lead to war with the North, editors of the *Intelligencer* predicted confidently that the departure of more Southern states would be effected without "the shedding of a drop of blood."[6]

Georgia's political leaders evidently shared the sentiment. On November 17 the legislature unanimously voted to hold a state convention to debate secession. By the time it convened in the capital of Milledgeville on January 16, 1861, Mississippi, Florida and Alabama had also voted to leave the Union, joining South Carolina. Georgia's convention delegates followed suit on January 19.[7]

Amidst this tumult, Atlantans in January 1861 also held their annual election for mayor, whose one-year term filled the calendar year. Three-term incumbent mayor William Ezzard offered himself for re-election, but dissenters put forth Judge Whitaker's name, after another candidate backed out. In the election held on January 17, Whitaker won by a vote of 695 to 452. The *Intelligencer* warmly greeted the news about its co-owner, declaring, "Judge Whitaker bids fair to make an honest, upright and efficient mayor." Indeed, two weeks after the election, the paper confided that the new mayor was so busy, "we seldom are favored with 'the light of his countenance.'"

This meant that Gaulding had more to do in running the paper. Under any circumstance, newspaper finances could be challenging. On January 4, 1861, the *Intelligencer* printed an editorial to its patrons. "*Dunning* is not in our line," it complained, so it requested subscribers to pay their overdue bills. Employees expected to be paid every Saturday afternoon, the editors explained, and costs of paper were onerous. "We hope this hint will be enough," they concluded. The senior editor's workload worsened when his associate editor, John W. Leonard, announced that he was quitting. In a signed editorial printed on January 18, Leonard declared that his physician had recommended that he leave the job for reasons of health, and "seek a business that will give me more exercise than editing a daily paper." Gaulding followed with a sympathetic piece of his own, commending Leonard as "a scholar and a gentleman," wishing him all the best, including "improved health." This latter, however, would not come to be. Three months later, the *Intelligencer* sadly announced that Leonard had died on March 14.

By the first of February, seven states of the Deep South—South Carolina, Mississippi, Florida, Alabama, Georgia, Louisiana and Texas—had seceded, with political leaders calling for their organization into a confederation. Such a government was organized by a convention assembled in Montgomery, and on February 9 elections were held for national offices. Jefferson Davis of Mississippi and Alexander H. Stephens of Georgia were chosen as president and vice president.

Davis was in Mississippi at the time, having resigned his U. S. Senate seat on January 21. Summoned to Montgomery by the convention, the president-elect chose a roundabout train route that would allow him to give a score of whistle-stop speeches to the people. After travel through Tennessee, on February 16 Davis arrived in Atlanta, where he spoke at the Trout House, the city's largest downtown hotel, to several thousand citizens who had gathered outside. Mayor Whitaker introduced the chief executive to the crowd, declaring, "Your election to the Presidency of the free, sovereign and independent Confederate States of America, meets the entire approbation of our fellow citizens." The *Intelligencer* opined that "President Davis responded in one of the most eloquent, patriotic and thrilling appeals to which we ever listened," and in the article quoted Davis' remarks. "The North has driven us to this step [secession] by the repeated aggressions made upon our rights, and we are determined to maintain and defend ourselves and our institutions," he declared. "If the North attempt to coerce us," the president-elect warned, "we will strike for our right, as our fathers did in 1776. . . . We have taken a proud position among the nations of the earth, and we intend to maintain it."

The writer was thrilled that a crowd estimated at 5,000 people, in spite of rain, escorted the president to the city's stately downtown train station, officially termed Union Depot but more commonly called the "Car Shed," and saw him off on the train to Montgomery. "It was a demonstration which not only reflected credit to our city," he concluded, "but which was due the President of a new Republic." Davis, a hero of the Mexican War and a former U.S. representative, senator and secretary of war, was "a man who is acknowledged on all hands to be one of the ablest statesmen, purest patriots, and chivalric soldiers of the age," Gaulding gushed.[8]

Archibald Gaulding was clearly a Southern Rights man. In its issue of March 7, the paper declared that "Col. A. A. Gaulding, the senior editor," was "swearing vengeance against Fort Sumter." Yet the *Intelligencer* was not the only voice of Confederate patriotism in Atlanta. A few years before, longtime businessman Cornelius R. Hanleiter founded a competing daily, the *National American*, which was published also as a weekly and tri-weekly. After Georgia's secession, the title seemed less than appropriate, so owner Hanleiter changed the paper's name to the *Gate City Guardian* (reflecting the bestowal of Atlanta's nickname "Gate City" a few years before). In February '61 Hanleiter sold a half-interest to businessman George W. Adair. A month later Hanleiter and Adair bought the name and presses of another Atlanta paper, the weekly *Southern Confederacy*. The daily *Guardian* thus became the daily *Southern Confederacy* on March 4, 1861— the same day Lincoln was being inaugurated in Washington. Two weeks later, James B. Hambleton, an Atlanta physician who had doubled as editor of the *Southern Confederacy*, then assistant editor for Hanleiter and Adair, announced his connection with the paper was at an end. Dr. Hanleiter was eventually appointed surgeon of a Georgia infantry unit. Meanwhile, another paper had started in Atlanta; the *Commonwealth*. The *Intelligencer* on March 9 announced its debut; the *Commonwealth*, edited by J. S. Peterson, however, would prove short-lived, folding in 1863.

On March 6, the *Intelligencer* printed the text of Lincoln's inaugural address along with its editorial commentary. "Upon one point he is perfectly plain," the paper observed: "he decides for war." Lincoln had announced that "he will use all the Federal Power, for the purpose of coercing the South." Such a prospect was cause for no fear at all, declared the editors, who welcomed the coming conflict. "We say, then, to Lincoln and his myrmidons, come on! . . . We are fighting for our rights and our liberties, for justice, truth and honor. . . . we place our trust in the GOD OF BATTLES."

The *Intelligencer* promoted itself in a declaration that ran repeatedly on page three. "Our paper," the editors proclaimed, "has a large and growing city and country circulation and commends itself as a safe and reliable medium for advertisers." In another reference, printed in mid-February, the paper advised, "those wishing a first class political, commercial . . . newspaper, would do well to subscribe for the Intelligencer." It complimented itself as "the oldest journal published in the City of Atlanta," but studiously avoided providing any numbers for its circulation or subscriber base.

During the early, heady days of Confederate independence, the *Intelligencer* touted Atlanta as a prominent city of the new republic, if not as its very capital. Georgia had not yet even left the Union when, in mid-January, the City Council sent invitations to Southern governors, suggesting Atlanta as a convention site for delegates of the seceding states. When those representatives met instead in Montgomery, Atlantans on January 31 agreed to send Mayor Whitaker and four other citizens to Montgomery to personally lobby the city's case for consideration as capital. The *Intelligencer* voiced its own boosterism, promoting Atlanta as a city well-connected by railroads, with sufficient downtown hotel space, and possessing a healthful climate, free from the scourge of yellow fever. In addition to plentiful meats and vegetables for visitors, the *Gate City Guardian* in early February boasted of Georgia's peanut crop, yielding "goobers, an indispensable article for a Southern Legislator." On March 5, the day after it became the *Southern Confederacy,* the same paper even hailed the local geologic eminence, Stone Mountain, as a civic asset. The huge granite outcropping, it declared, could "furnish material enough to construct the public buildings of a thousand Confederacies."

Not to be outdone, the *Intelligencer* on March 5 argued for Atlanta as the Southern capital, claiming the city "offers peculiar advantages over any of her competitors." On the 7th it printed the laudatory column of a traveler passing through town. "This is indeed the Gate City of the South," the visitor exclaimed, as he remarked upon "its picturesque beauty." A walk downtown led the observer, who signed himself as "Model," to comment on "the improvement and rapid growth of one of the most enterprising cities in the Southern Confederacy." The business district, with its attractive merchandise beckoning through storefront windows, "will vie with any of the most favorable marts of the Union." Hundreds of shoppers, tradesmen and visiting farmers thronged the sidewalks. The four railroads linking up downtown chugged in with their goods and passengers, "giving life and activity" to the entire scene. "Atlanta is destined to be a great city," "Model" concluded. Its healthful climate and important railroads alone entitled it to consideration as capital for the new nation. In addition to all of these benefits, the City Council on March 8 voted to add one more: free use of City Hall and other buildings for Confederate officials and bureaucrats if they should come.

Alas, Montgomery was selected as the Confederate capital, but even this did not stop the *Intelligencer* from continuing to advocate Atlanta as the would-be seat of government for the new republic.

Though he was obviously a major booster of his city, it is apparent that Mayor Whitaker scrupulously separated his political duties from his role at the *Intelligencer*. On April 12, 1861, Whitaker and the City Council voted that the Southern Confederacy Publishing Company—not his own *Intelligencer*—would serve as the city's public printers. This nod to the *Southern Confederacy* allowed the chief rival to the mayor's own paper the privilege of publishing municipal ordinances, charging the city the same as it would to advertisers.[9]

That very day—April 12—for all intents and purposes, war broke out between the Northern and Southern states. Atlanta's two daily newspapers, the *Intelligencer* and *Confederacy*, would henceforth vie with each other to report news of America's civil war to their readers.

Everyone knew by this time that a United States garrison, commanded by Maj. Robert Anderson, held Fort Sumter, an imposing brick bastion on a man-made island in the middle of Charleston harbor. The Confederate government, organized at Montgomery just two months before, had demanded that President Lincoln remove the offending bluecoats from Confederate territory. Brig. Gen. Pierre Gustave Toutant Beauregard was dispatched to command Confederate forces fortifying and placing artillery batteries around Fort Sumter in Charleston harbor. In the weeks after Lincoln's inauguration on March 4, high-level discussions had taken place with three "commissioners" sent to Washington by Davis to seek the peaceful removal of the Federal garrison at Sumter. Lincoln would not meet with them, as doing so would be conferring some form of recognition to the Rebel "government." Neither would his Secretary of State, William H. Seward. But through go-betweens, Seward seemed to pledge to the Southern commissioners that the garrison would soon be removed. At the same time, Lincoln authorized a naval expedition to take supplies to Anderson's men, who were running out of rations. The administration so informed the Rebels. Southerners felt betrayed, and the Davis government ordered Beauregard to seek Anderson's surrender before the Northern expedition arrived. When the Union commander refused on April 11, Confederate artillery opened on Sumter at 4:30 a.m. on the 12th.[10]

The next day, April 13, the *Intelligencer* reported at the top of page two that "from dispatches from Augusta received in this city, we learn that Gen. Beauregard opened his batteries on Fort Sumter, yesterday morning at half-past 4 o'clock. Later dispatches from the War Department at Montgomery confirmed the previous news." That was it: the full telegraphic reporting on the tumultuous events that had started the nation's civil war. After this wire dispatch, the *Intelligencer* had to wait for other papers to arrive with their news from the coast. Fortunately, a train arriving in the city around midnight of April 12–13 brought confirmation of the day's sketchy telegram, allowing the *Intelligencer* on the 13th to run this article:

LATEST NEWS

WAR! WAR!! WAR!!!

By the twelve o'clock train, last night, we received the following news in regard to the operations at the seat of the war.

The bombardment of Fort Sumter progressed rapidly, and telling blows were given, which was [*sic*] returned by Anderson from the Fort. Several war vessels were reported off the bar.

The Cabinet at Montgomery have [*sic*] called an extra session, to convene on the 29th inst. The city of Montgomery is in great excitement and rejoicing.

Then it devoted several inches of the column to related news that was considered urgent, including a false report that President Davis had assembled an army of 25,000 men "to make an onslaught on Washington City, and to take Lincoln and Scott as prisoners." The article closed with the statement, "All telegraphic news of a war-like character has been cut off."

Thus it was the train from Augusta bearing dispatches that brought the first word to Atlantans of Sumter's bombardment. "Every mail and every arrival of the trains . . . are expected to bring the news that blood has been shed," the *Intelligencer* editors wrote excitedly.

They obviously wanted to report more details from Charleston harbor, but were hobbled by the inadequacy and delay of timely news reports. The issue of April 13, under "LATEST NEWS," printed a short item datelined "Charleston, April 11—P.M.," stating that General Beauregard that night had demanded Fort

Sumter's evacuation—a story that was already two days old. Gaulding, editor, and Bassford, associate editor (as of February 15), conveyed their frustration at the limitations, asserting that "everybody seems to be on tip toe to know the news. The question meets us every where, 'What is the war news?'" They complained that their sources of information were few, including "'sensation' telegrams and newspaper correspondents from the *North*."[11]

The *Intelligencer* issued no edition on Sunday, April 14, which was the day that Anderson and his garrison formally surrendered, but it did on Monday (ordinarily the weekday when no paper was issued). Most observers realized the impact of the Sumter news when they glanced at the *Intelligencer*'s "By Telegraph" column; it began with the headline, "LINCOLN INDIGNANT!" In the journalistic style of the day—in which "bank" or "deck" headlines could run for a dozen, separate short lines—the *Intelligencer* synopsized the recent days' momentous events.

BY TELEGRAPH
Expressly for the Atlanta Intelligencer.
LINCOLN INDIGNANT!
75,000 Men ordered out.
The South to be coerced back
Pennsylvania, New York, and Ohio
Furnish 13,000 each.
Extra Session of the Congress.
War Department Busy.
Arrival of Federal Troops in Washington City.
Departure of Anderson and his Men.
Government Fleet still off the bar at Charleston.
The North Indignant.
Anderson denounced as a Traitor at the North.

The telegraphic column, dated April 14, 9:30 p.m. from Washington, announced ominously that President Lincoln's call for 75,000 men was to help the federal government "suppress all the combinations made in the seceding States, and cause all the laws of the Federal government to be duly enacted." Such troops would be directed to enter the rebellious territory and repossess the government forts, arsenals and other property that had been seized by the "combinations."

Gaulding and Bassford declared in a bitter editorial on page two, titled "Our War Policy," that "the aggressive policy of the Black Republican party of the North, has culminated in war, as we long since predicted it would." They went on to forecast "the bitter disgrace, overthrow and annihilation of the whole batch of abolition conspirators who planned this infamous revolution, and plunged a free, happy and once united people in all the horrors of civil war."[12]

At the time, however, the *Intelligencer* could only report the news as it came into its editorial offices. A second telegraphic dispatch was received on the night of April 14, announcing that Pennsylvania, New York and Ohio were being requisitioned for 13,000 men each, "to coerce the South." The balance of Lincoln's requisition would come from the "free states."

Another bulletin, also from that night, summarized the particulars blared in the headline: Anderson and the Sumter garrison, having surrendered, were put on a steamship headed for New York (there was no official war yet, hence no need for "prisoners of war"). Anderson's capitulation had "created tremendous excitement and indignation at the North," the paper declared. Some people in the North apparently thought that the major had given in too easily, as "the people denounce Anderson as a traitor."[13]

The telegraphic news ended there. With that, the *Intelligencer* column shifted to a report on crops and weather in nearby Gwinnett County.

Even so, the editors announced that they had delayed this daily edition of April 15 "for the purpose of giving to our readers the very latest intelligence from Charleston." As disappointing as they had been in their length and content, "we published all the dispatches received."

Fortunately, there was telegraphic correspondence issued by the Confederate War Department in Montgomery, reprinting the missives exchanged between General Beauregard and Confederate Secretary of War Leroy P. Walker, April 8–12, as the government inched toward its decision to authorize bombardment of the Federal fort and garrison in Charleston harbor, and Beauregard learned from Major Anderson that he would not yield to demands for surrender.

In all likelihood the Confederate commander did not know that he was about to fire the first shots of what would be the bloodiest war in American history. Nonetheless, his final note to Major Anderson virtually dripped in gentlemanly manners: "Fort Sumter, S.C., April 12, 1861, 3:20 A.M. Sir: By authority of Brigadier General Beauregard, commanding the Provisional Forces of the Confederate States, we have the honor to notify you that he will open the fire of his batteries on Fort Sumter in one hour from this time. We have the honor to be very respectfully, Your obedient servants, James Chesnut, Jr., Aide-de-camp. Stephen D. Lee, Captain C.S. Army, aide-de-camp."

After Confederate artillery ringing the harbor opened fire, Beauregard notified the secretary of war in Montgomery by telegram, published by the *Intelligencer* in all its terseness:

Charleston, April 12, 1861.
To L. P. Walker:
We opened fire at four, thirty minutes.
G. T. Beauregard[14]

NOTES

1. "Our War Policy," *Atlanta Daily Intelligencer* (hereafter *ADI*), Apr. 15, 1861; William E. Ames, *A History of the National Intelligencer* (Chapel Hill: University of North Carolina Press, 1972), 3; Debra Reddin van Tuyll, *The Confederate Press in the Crucible of the American Civil War* (New York: Peter Lang, 2012), 81; Henry T. Malone, "The Weekly Atlanta Intelligencer As a Secessionist Journal," *Georgia Historical Quarterly*, vol. 37, no. 4 (December 1953), 278; Franklin M. Garrett, *Atlanta and Environs: A Chronicle of Its People and Events*, 2 vols. (New York: Lewis Historical Publishing Co., 1954), vol. 1, 224–25, 233–34, 251, 279, 377, 385, 401 (hereafter, *A & E*); Ruth Elaine Feldman, "A Checklist of Atlanta Newspapers, 1846–1948," master's thesis, Emory University, 1948, 17–18; Donald S. Hart, "The Mood of Atlanta 1850–1861," *Atlanta Historical Bulletin*, vol. 15, no. 2 (Summer 1970), 24; J. Ford Risley, "Georgia's Civil War Newspapers: Partisan, Sanguine, Enterprising," Ph.D. dissertation, University of Florida, 1996, 29; *ADI*, Oct. 7, 1858; David W. Bulla and Gregory A. Borchard, *Journalism in the Civil War Era* (New York: Peter Lang, 2010), 90; Adrienne Koch and William Pederson, *The Life and Selected Writings of Thomas Jefferson* (New York: Modern Library, 1944), 322. The most complete collection of the *Daily Intelligencer* on microfilm is to be found in the Kenan Research Center of the Atlanta History Center, which has served as our research touchstone.

2. "DAILY INTELLIGENCER," *ADI*, Jan. 27, 1859, Mar. 5, 1859; "DAILY INTELLIGENCER BOOK AND JOB OFFICE," *ADI*, Mar. 29, 1861; Williams' *Atlanta Directory, City Guide, and Business Mirror* (Atlanta: M. Lynch, 1859), 102, 120, 145; "C. R. H." [Cornelius Redding Hanleiter], "A History of Newspaper Enterprises in Atlanta," *Atlanta Southern Confederacy*, July 14, 1861.

3. Richard C. Wade, *Slavery in the Cities: The South 1820–1860* (New York: Oxford University Press, 1964), 28 ("most commonly a few slaves"), 29–30, 33, 38; 1860 U.S. Federal Census Slave Schedules, courtesy Atlanta History Center.

4. Ralph Benjamin Singer, Jr., "Confederate Atlanta," Ph.D. dissertation, University of Georgia, 1973, 90; Garrett, *A & E*, vol. 1, 353, 376, 399, 406, 408–409, 424, 473; vol. 2, 85; [Louis L. Parham, ed.], *Pioneer Citizens' History of Atlanta 1833–1902* (Atlanta: Byrd Printing Co.,

1902), 38, 53; Hart, "Mood of Atlanta," 26; "Jared I. Whitaker Attorney at Law," *ADI*, Jan. 4, Mar. 21, 1860; 'DAILY INTELLIGENCER," *ADI*, June 6 and July 25, 1860.

 5. Singer, "Confederate Atlanta," 40–41.

 6. Singer, "Confederate Atlanta," 42–43, 51, 55; Hart, "Mood of Atlanta," 35.

 7. T. Conn Bryan, *Confederate Georgia* (Athens: University of Georgia Press, 1953), 3–4, 6, 9.

 8. Garrett, *A & E*, vol. 1, 496; "Our New City Authorities," *ADI*, Jan. 31, 1861; "A Word to our Patrons," *ADI*, Jan. 4, 1861; "Parting Words" and "Mr. John W. Leonard," *ADI*, January 18; "Death of John W. Leonard," *ADI*, March 15; William C. Davis, *Jefferson Davis: The Man and His Hour* (New York: HarperCollins, 1991), 296, 305; Lynda Lasswell Crist, *et al.*, eds., *The Papers of Jefferson Davis*, 14 vols. (Baton Rouge: Louisiana State University Press, 1992), vol. 7, 44; Singer, "Confederate Atlanta," 68; "Reception of President Davis in Atlanta, *ADI*, February 18.

 9. "The Atlanta *Intelligencer* of yesterday morning . . . ," *ADI*, Mar. 7, 1861; Henry T. Malone, "Atlanta Journalism During the Confederacy," *Georgia Historical Quarterly*, vol. 37, no. 3 (September 1953), 211–12; Garrett, *A & E*, vol. 1, 251, 305, 398, 432, 454, 488, 510; Singer, "Confederate Atlanta," 65–67, 88, 89; "Dr. James B. Hambleton," *ADI*, Mar. 22, 1861; Lillian Henderson, comp., *Roster of the Confederate Soldiers of Georgia 1861–1865*, 7 vols. (Hapeville GA: Longino and Porter, 1959–64), vol. 3, 844; "The Commonwealth," *ADI*, Mar. 9, 1861; Richard Barksdale Harwell, "Atlanta Publications of the Civil War," *Atlanta Historical Bulletin*, vol. 6, no. 25 (July 1941), 194; [Hanleiter], "History of Newspaper Enterprises"; "Inaugural of President Lincoln," *ADI*, March 6; "Our Paper," *ADI*, February 15, 22, 27, March 1, 4 and 5; "The Intelligencer," *ADI*, February 16; "Capital of the Southern Confederacy," *ADI*, March 5; "Dear Dispatch" and "Atlanta," *ADI*, March 7, April 3; Singer, "Confederate Atlanta," 67; Wendy Hamand Venet, *A Changing Wind: Commerce and Conflict in Civil War Atlanta* (New Haven: Yale University Press, 2014), 35; [Parham, ed.], *Pioneer Citizens' History*, 77; Williams, *Directory*, 117; Stephen Davis, *What the Yankees Did to Us: Sherman's Bombardment and Wrecking of Atlanta* (Macon: Mercer University Press, 2012), 7.

 10. W. A. Swanberg, *First Blood: The Story of Fort Sumter* (New York: Charles Scribner's Sons, 1957), 220, 236, 280, 285, 291–98; Maury Klein, *Days of Defiance: Sumter, Secession, and the Coming of the Civil War* (New York: Alfred A. Knopf, 1997), 357–402 *passim*.; David Detzer, *Allegiance: Fort Sumter, Charleston, and the Beginning of the Civil War* (New York: Harcourt, 2001), 214–49 *passim*.

 11. "Telegraphic"; "Railroad Guide"; "War! War!! War!!!"; "The News! The News!! The News!!!"; and "The Evacuation of Fort Sumter Demanded," *ADI*, Apr. 13, 1861.

 12. "LINCOLN INDIGNANT!" and "Our War Policy," *ADI*, Apr. 15, 1861; J. Cutler Andrews, *The South Reports the Civil War* (Princeton: Princeton University Press, 1970), 25; Avery Craven, *The Coming of the Civil War* (Chicago: University of Chicago Press, 1957 [1942]), 432.

 13. "2d Dispatch" and "3d Dispatch," *ADI*, Apr. 15, 1861.

 14. "Crops, Weather, &c.," *ADI*, Apr. 15, 1861; Robert N. Rosen and Richard W. Hatcher III, *The First Shot* (Charleston SC: Arcadia Publishing, 2011), 17; "From the Seat of the War," *ADI*, Apr. 15, 1861.

2. Operations of the *Intelligencer*

A LOOK INSIDE THE OFFICE

THANKS TO SAMUEL MORSE'S INVENTION of the telegraph in 1844, the *Intelligencer* was able to get timely news reports on events at Charleston harbor and elsewhere. Before then, mail, as slow as it was, served as editors' chief news source. But because most newspapers in the early decades of the republic were weeklies, timeliness was not a special concern. The federal government helped in 1792 by permitting editors to exchange papers throughout the country free of charge; most agreed to lift each other's material so long as attribution was made. Twenty years later, newspapers accounted for ninety percent of mailed volume in the country. With improvement of the old hand press of colonial days, the number of newspapers in the United States reached 1,200 in the 1830s (of which, however, only about ten percent were dailies).

Morse's "magnetic telegraph" had been developed for business and economic reasons, but newspaper editors soon realized the benefits of the new electrical contraption. Before long 23,000 miles of telegraph line stretched across the country, linking all major American cities except San Francisco. "By the eve of the Civil War," writes J. Cutler Andrews, noted journalism scholar, "telegraph mileage exceeded railroad mileage, with some fifty thousand miles of line in successful operation throughout North America, over fourteen hundred stations, and a telegraph force of nearly ten thousand operators and clerks."[1]

Telegraphic communication meant that even out-of-the-way newspapers had access to national news. The earlier scarcity of such content had meant that in the days of the young republic, American papers offered their readers advertisements—the main income source, with subscription fees, for owners—essays, poetry and literary excerpts for their reading entertainment—but not much national news. (And how could they? At the end of the Revolution, it took six days for a letter from Boston to reach New York; nine in bad weather.)

But non-local news could now be had, especially if readers called for it—as they did when war broke out with Mexico in 1846.²

The telegraph arrived in Atlanta in early 1849, in time to serve the *Weekly Intelligencer* when it began to roll out shortly thereafter. In 1860, the telegraph allowed the *Daily Intelligencer* to announce the "doleful news" of Lincoln's election within two days. "Lincoln is elected and we are destined to wear the yoke of Black Republican rule, unless we rise up in our defence," the paper warned on November 8, using the derisive phrase for Lincoln's party that had taken hold in the South from the mid-1850s (as well as an arcane spelling of *defense*).³

Atlanta's telegraph office during the war was located in the Gate City Hotel, at Pryor and Alabama Streets, not far from the train depot. News dispatches were received by the telegrapher, who wrote out their text. Sometimes, however, his handwriting was hard to read. At the end of one wartime article in his "BY TELEGRAPH" column, Gaulding had to insert, "[The remainder of the telegraphic dispatch is so badly written, that after a vain effort to decipher it, we are forced to let it pass.—ED. INT.]"⁴

So when dramatic events began to unfold in Charleston harbor in April 1861, the *Intelligencer* had a technological hook-up to the news scene. What it did not have, in today's parlance, was boots on the ground: a staff reporter at Charleston to draft news accounts of what was happening, and to send them back to Atlanta for setting into print.

The events in Charleston during the spring of 1861 had been simmering for so long that at least nine papers had had time to send reporting correspondents there. No acts of violence had yet occurred between Anderson's garrison and Beauregard's besiegers, so when newsmen from New York arrived, they were not prevented from reporting. The *New York Times* had even had a man on the scene, George Salter, for more than two months. The competing *New York Herald* had two representatives. Charleston papers, of course, enjoyed the hometown advantage, shared by the *Courier* and the *Mercury*. From nearby Savannah, the *Morning News* and *Savannah Republican* were fed reports from their correspondents. Other Georgia papers—the *Columbus Times*, the *Macon Telegraph*—also had reporters in Charleston ready to relate the collapse of negotiations and the Confederates' bombardment. The *Intelligencer*, however, had no correspondent on-site. When the firing commenced, it would have to rely upon the telegraph for news to relay to its readers.⁵

On April 12, 1861, there appeared a short piece, "Charleston Affairs," clipped from the *Charleston Courier* of April 10, announcing the arrival of various troop units. Besides the telegraph, the *Intelligencer*, like all papers of the day, relied upon "exchanges" for news: editors agreed to swap their papers and borrow news and features from each other, so long as attribution was made as to the source. As stated above, the U. S. Congress had granted free use of the mail by newspapers (the Confederate Congress continued the practice). Copyright law had not yet extended to American newspapers, so reprinting was commonplace as well as necessary. These "lifts" were free of charge among cooperating editors, and certainly much less expensive than telegraphic dispatches, for which the telegraph companies could charge dearly. And they could be much longer, helping editors fill otherwise empty pages.

The obvious disadvantage of exchanged news, however, was its datedness. Savannah and Charleston papers took at least a day to travel to Atlanta by train. Nevertheless, Gaulding drew more often on the *Charleston Courier, Savannah Republican* and *Montgomery Advertiser* than he did other papers, at least in the month of April 1861. A survey of the *Intelligencer* issues that month shows that fully fifty-eight out-of-town newspapers were quoted at length or summarized by the editor with attribution to the exchanging paper. Lifts were drawn from three Richmond dailies in April 1861; more would be used after the Confederate capital moved there from Montgomery a month later. Gaulding even drew from the *New York Times* and a few other Northern papers (just as Northern editors were not shy about quoting the *Intelligencer* and other Rebel papers). Sometimes Gaulding summarized Yankee items, but without naming his sources. "Late News Items from our Exchanges," for instance (front page, April 30), included mention of pro-Union sentiment in Hagerstown, Md., news from Philadelphia ("twenty thousand men are drilling"), and other tidbits from Boston, New York and Cairo, Illinois. Closer to home, the *Intelligencer* lifted from four Augusta papers, chiefly the *Constitutionalist* and the *Chronicle and Sentinel*, both because they were strong papers, but also because, by way of the Georgia Railroad, they were only 171 miles away, and could be received relatively quickly after they were put upon the Atlanta train. Gaulding occasionally clipped from distant papers as well; his issue of April 3, reprinted an article from the *Gilmer* (Texas) *Patriot*, outlining why Atlanta should be made the capital of the Confederacy.[6]

The farther away the exchanging paper, the longer it took for anything it sent out to be reprinted. Example of this is to be seen on the front page of the *Intelligencer* on April 15. Reprinted from the *Mesilla Valley* (Arizona) *Times* was a long article describing the proceedings of a meeting of Southern sympathizers in Mesilla, not quite fifty miles northwest of El Paso, Texas, in the territory that had been purchased from Mexico by James Gadsden (hence the "Gadsden Purchase"). As for this cut-and-paste journalism editors were not only unembarrassed, but actively supportive. As one writer in the *Memphis Daily Appeal* acknowledged, "it was better to reprint good material from the exchanges than to write bad material."

As the war lengthened, however, the quantity of material obtainable from exchanges dramatically diminished. In June 1862, *Intelligencer* editor Gaulding complained that "our exchange newspapers reach us very irregularly," though he refrained from blaming the Confederate postal service or the papers themselves. "We rarely receive more than three issues of our Richmond and Charleston exchanges per week," he groused; even papers published within Georgia arrived sporadically. The problem worsened with enemy conquest of major Southern cities, such as Nashville, New Orleans and Memphis, all of which fell in the first half of 1862; Confederate newspapers from those points could no longer be had. Gaulding thus issued a self-defense: "whenever, therefore, our readers are about to complain at our supposed 'short-comings' in giving the news, or in supplying the demand for 'interesting reading matter,' let them reflect a little upon the deprivations to which the Georgia press had been subjected."

The typical editor's late-night work has been described by historian Debra Reddin van Tuyll thus: "the editor seated on the editorial tripod in an office lit by gas lamps, scribbled his words on scrap newsprint with pencil and paper." The nocturnal nature of the editor's labors has led another historian to claim that the invention of the kerosene lamp itself was a milestone in the development of American journalism, allowing editors and printers to work well into the night for their morning editions.[7]

Clearly the editor was the commander of the paper's operations. It was he who selected the exchanged material for printing; in this the telegraph helped, and not just by bringing distant stories more quickly than the mails. Telegraphic dispatches allowed updates on ongoing stories; they also tipped the editor off to important developments, for details of which he could scan his exchanges. Most importantly, the editor or an associate wrote the paper's editorials, which at times could be the most important items in an issue. Larger papers assigned editorial work to several individuals. Running the five Richmond dailies, for instance, were men designated as editor, co-editor, senior editor, joint editor, editor-in-chief, contributing editor and news editor. At the *Richmond Examiner*, Edward Pollard, according to Andrews, "was variously identified as editor, co-editor, associate editor, editorial writer, and contributor."

A competent editor, as we say today, had to be a good multi-tasker. Because the *Intelligencer* did not have a staff of reporters, the editor and sometimes his assistants occasionally worked as reporters, especially of local news. Archibald Gaulding, as example, after attending a concert at the Atheneum, given for the benefit of an Atlanta infantry company heading off to war, could write about it the next day. Much more vocationally varied was the newspaperman reported by a Mississippi paper in December 1861: "Down on the Eastern Shore of Virginia there is an editor, who is also his own compositor and pressman, and makes occasional voyages along the coast of Norfolk as Captain of the Schooner Polly; who preaches on Sunday, teaches school on weekdays, and still finds time to take care of a wife and eighteen children!"

But the editor obviously could not put out a paper by himself. In her study of four newspapers publishing in Augusta, Georgia in 1861, Debra Reddin van Tuyll counts ten different employee positions. Below the proprietor and editor would be the assistant editor and a local editor; these made up the editorial staff. Bookkeeper and assistant bookkeeper comprised the business office. In the backshop staff was obviously the printer, but sometimes a foreman, who oversaw the printer's work, a pressman and apprentice. The total number of individuals in these positions hovered at a dozen; the *Augusta Constitutionalist* and *Augusta Chronicle and Sentinel* employed fourteen and twelve respectively. This confirms the observation of Henry Timrod, the famed Southern poet who worked awhile at the *Columbia South Carolinian*, that Confederate newspaper staff numbered around fifteen men. In 1865 the *Constitutionalist* could actually name eighteen men on its staff, including a mail clerk and clerk.[8]

Keeping these workers, given the ordeals of wartime, proved a challenge, especially in the first months of the war. During the heady period of volunteerism, editors, pressmen, reporters and newsboys rushed off to war like Southerners in other professions and vocations. For example, Nathaniel Tyler and Jennings Wise, editors of the *Richmond Enquirer*, both left their paper to join the army early in the war. Georgia editors followed suit. The editors of the *Sandersville Central Georgian* and *Rome Courier* left their newspapers to go off to war. Other offices were decimated in the volunteering surge after Sumter. The *Waynesboro* (Georgia) *News* lost its editor, press foreman and typesetter by the end of April 1861. Within days of Fort Sumter, the *Macon Telegraph* reported that nine of its twenty employees had resigned in order to volunteer. By the end of April 1861, more than a dozen editors of South Carolina papers had left for military service, according to the *Abbeville Press* (which lost its editor, too).

Two-thirds of the newspapermen in Mississippi volunteered in the conflict's first year. The workforce drain continued throughout the war. By June 1864, fully three-quarters of the 800 printers in the Confederacy were, or had been, in the army—one may guess ten printers for every editor.

The *Intelligencer*, for example, was advertising in May 1863 for a printer to run its steam press. Some papers hired young apprentices who could learn various skills in the pressroom and assume more central roles in a paper's operation, especially if experienced workers went off to war. A typical ad in a Southern paper announced that "a smart, industrious, good boy can get a good home, and learn a good trade." In August 1862, the *Intelligencer* sought an apprentice with an ad reading, "WANTED. An industrious lad, 14 or 15 years old, to become an apprentice to the printing business. Apply at this office." Apprentices offered the additional benefit of being below the usual age at which Southern men were volunteering for the army.

The *Intelligencer* did not print a staff directory in 1861, so we do not know the number of its employees—ten to a dozen in total would be a good assumption. After Jared Whitaker and Archibald Gaulding, proprietors, in February 1862, John F. Buchanan held the office of treasurer and John T. Smith that of cashier. The *Intelligencer* also employed a "book-keeper" who in the spring of 1862 was charged, as the paper announced, with enforcing its policy of not giving away free issues to people wandering into its office. In 1863 one W. L. Bloodworth also worked in the paper's financial office. The National Archives in Washington has a file of miscellaneous documents related to the *Atlanta Intelligencer*. Among them is a receipt signed by Bloodworth for payment from the Confederate quartermaster's office in the city (the *Intelligencer* was running its advertisements offering reward for the return of deserters). In 1864, another employee, R. C. Fitts, was signing subscription receipts for papers going to Atlanta-area Confederate hospitals.

Every now and then, the *Intelligencer* signed on a writer. In late June 1861, the paper announced its hire of C. G. Baylor, "widely known in the Southern States as an accomplished writer and able political economist." Baylor, termed "our new Associate," assumed a role in the *Intelligencer*'s "editorial department." Beyond this notice, his name is not seen elsewhere in the pages of the paper, suggesting that newspaper "employment" in the Confederate South was a very ephemeral thing.

Under the editor there was likely to have been a clerk or assistant, to take papers to the post office or train station, although most papers' lean budgets did not allow for many such positions. Among the employees were also a few hired slaves. In an article published in mid-June 1861, the *Intelligencer* mentioned the "operatives of this establishment, both old and young, and I may say white and black." African Americans in the newspaper office were usually employed to operate the steam-powered press and perform other heavy labor. Georgia law had for decades prohibited slaves from setting type, as that function would have required a level of literacy. The *Intelligencer* also employed African American lads as newspaper carriers. In April 1862, for instance, the paper announced its intention to hire "a smart negro boy, about 15 or 16 years old."[9]

Like so many other nineteenth-century American industries, steam power revolutionized the production of newspapers. Traditional hand presses, which a number of Southern papers were still using at the start of the war, could turn out a few hundred copies an hour. A German inventor had made a steam press as early as 1814 that could print more than a thousand papers in the same period of time. In 1830 an Englishman had improved the German two-cylinder machine so that it could produce 3,000 papers per hour. Finally, in 1843, New Yorker Richard M. Hoe invented a rotary press that quadrupled the output of its English predecessor.

Some Southern papers used a steam press that bore the name of Adams, but the *Intelligencer* printed with a Hoe. In its issue of Aug. 24, 1862, the newspaper advertised for a Hoe job press, "for which a liberal price will be paid." An advertisement in its issue of May 8, 1863 read: "TO PRINTERS—A Pressman wanted to run a Hoe Cylinder press. Inquire at this Office." Whitaker and Gaulding could not have operated their side enterprise, a job and book printing firm, had they not possessed an efficient steam press. So equipped, Gaulding's backshop could have produced all the papers needed for morning distribution in less than an hour. In its issue of April 21, the editor confided that his circulation was averaging "upwards of eight hundred copies." "The circulation of our edition is constantly on the increase in the city and in the country contiguous to Atlanta," he continued. Moreover, Gaulding informed his readers that the *Intelligencer* was always seeking to be "fully equal to any paper in the State in all the interesting news of the day." Even before Beauregard's bombardment of Fort Sumter started the war, the paper informed its subscribers that, by telegraphic dispatch, they "will be furnished with the news from the Seat of War, at any hour of the day, by calling at our office."[10]

The war brought about a change in the telegraphic news service on which Southern newspapers had depended. The *Intelligencer* on April 16 had already announced, "We are informed that all communication by mail, is cut off with the North, by the Lincoln Government. So we will have no letters or papers from the North for some time to come." The telegraphic service was severed when Northern troops occupied the Washington office of the American Telegraph Company on April 19. Three weeks later the company informed William S. Morris, its only Southern director, that it would henceforth cease to serve the Southern states. The Northern telegraphic news sources were thus lost to newspapers in the Confederacy. Morris and another Virginian quickly organized the Southern Telegraph Company.

The American Telegraph Company's trunk line ran from New York through Washington to the capitals of the South Atlantic states. Another firm, the Southwestern Telegraph Company, extended from Louisville thorough Tennessee and Mississippi to New Orleans. Its line from Louisville was also cut. A new headquarters for the Southwestern Company still serving the Confederacy was established in Nashville.

So the wires were in place across the South, but who would provide the telegraphic news dispatches for newspapers? William H. Pritchard of Augusta, who had been an agent for the New York Associated Press, stepped in and organized a service to wire subscribing papers a brief summary of the day's events. As we will see, editors became dissatisfied with Pritchard's firm, and several other newsgathering organizations would be started in the Confederacy.[11]

Besides news, it took a lot of material to fill up an issue of four pages, which was the size of most Southern newspapers at the start of the war. A welcome source of text, which came frequently to an editor's desk, were the letters sent home by Atlanta's soldiers in the field. The war, as the *Intelligencer* acknowledged in an editorial of June 1862, had "bred prolifically, legions, as it were, of letter writers to home," servicemen who were afflicted with "cacoethes scribendi"—the incurable desire for writing. Not only did the soldiers want to write, the letters' recipients back home wanted to see them printed in the *Intelligencer*. With so many requests, Gaulding frankly declared it a chore to have to decide which letters merited publication. "To separate 'the chaff from the wheat,' even in this correspondence," he sighed, created work that was frankly fatiguing. "When will these labors cease, as we sit in our editorial chair, we have often exclaimed!" he confessed.

Thus were a newspaper's pages filled. The pages themselves were not small;

the *Intelligencer*'s issue of April 4, 1861, possessed by the Boston Atheneum, measures 21.65 by 14.96 inches. The *Richmond Dispatch,* as another example, measured 14 inches wide by 20 inches tall (today's papers are about as wide and a little longer). The *Intelligencer* occasionally reminded readers of its layout, as in its issue of April 30 it stated, "See First and Third Page for Telegraphic News."[12]

Putting all of this material together made for a long day. The *Intelligencer* released its afternoon edition at 5 p.m. (not on Sundays). The morning issues were printed by one o'clock in the morning, giving delivery boys time to pick up their papers and start distributing them. Occasionally, receipt of some sensational news item might compel, on top of all this labor, the printing of an "extra," a third edition of the day. Yet that process would be exceptional, as the *Intelligencer* reminded its readers in September 1862. "We shall issue no 'EXTRA' save when news of *importance* is received," the editor announced, adding, "we shall also, on our Bulletin Board, give brief announcements during the day, of any *important* events that have occurred, as soon after we receive them as possible."

Indeed, given the mounting difficulties and pressures of running a newspaper, the question of why editors stayed on deserves addressing. Dedication both to the mission of keeping their readers informed and of supporting the Confederate cause was one altruistic reason. More personal ones included the lack of other vocational options or, after 1862, the exemption from military service that Confederate law gave newspapermen, white- and blue-collar alike. For Archibald Gaulding, the answer may have involved money. As co-owner of the *Intelligencer* with Jared Whitaker, Gaulding was entitled to at least half of the paper's profits. If so—as with most Confederate newspapers, account books and business records for the *Intelligencer* no longer exist—this arrangement would have served as incentive to Gaulding to put out the best paper he could, draw subscribers and advertisers, and make money. (One may ask how he found the time to do it all, with his law practice on the side; in late March 1862 the front page of the *Intelligencer* advertised "A. A. GAULDING ATTORNEY AT LAW ATLANTA, GA.")

But it was a tough business. Historians of journalism have concluded that daily newspapers were far from easy profit centers. When the *Raleigh Standard* made a profit of $8,000 in 1860, Debra Redden van Tuyll notes that this was "not bad for a daily published in a town with barely 5,000 people." This also explains, as J. Cutler Andrews has observed, why newspapers generally ran their operations in rented space; they did not own their buildings. When the *Savannah Republican* compiled a list of its assets—presses, paper, ink, type and even office furniture—a physical building was not among them (everything listed, when the war began, was valued at $25,000).

Income from subscription fees and advertising revenue were a paper's chief financial supports, and editors were always seeking to increase both. Circulation—the number of paid subscribers—was obviously an important gauge of a paper's financial well-being. Southern newspapers could not match the formidable circulation numbers of, say, the New York dailies. Still, a respected Southern paper might boast of "upwards of ten thousand subscribers," as did the *Charleston Mercury* in July 1861. The *Intelligencer* did not publicize its circulation numbers; as Pennsylvania State University Prof. Ford Risley notes for Georgia newspapers, "most of the state's papers had circulations in the hundreds rather than the thousands." Indeed, of the 105 Georgia newspapers listed by the U.S. Census Returns of 1860, fewer than half (51) reported circulation figures of 1,000 or more. Only seventeen had a circulation of 3,000-plus. And of these seventeen, only two papers in the state were dailies: one was the *Intelligencer* (3,000); the other was the *Atlanta Southern Confederacy*. (Not bad for a city in whose five wards the census in 1860 counted 7,741 whites.)

At the same time, circulation figures usually underplayed the extent of a paper's readership. Not only did non-subscribers drop in on newspaper offices to scan the headlines, but paying subscribers, particularly in the countryside, would often pass an issue around to friends. The *Augusta Chronicle and Sentinel* boasted of 6,000 subscribers in 1864, but estimated that its "reach" should be calculated at two and half times that number. The *Raleigh State Journal* went even further, claiming that an issue of 11,000 copies would be seen by 55,000 individuals. One North Carolina lady recorded that a newspaper would be passed "from house to house until utterly worn out." Moreover, during the war, strong papers saw their subscriber base increase, as the public demand for war news surged. For a while after Fort Sumter, the *Chronicle and Sentinel* received seventy-five new subscriptions a week. In March 1862, the *Intelligencer* editor thanked the paper's "hundreds of new subscribers," especially for accompanying their subscriptions with cash. Because of such support, Gaulding confirmed that "the INTELLIGENCER, both DAILY and WEEKLY, is upon a solid foundation," adding his pledge that it would continue to appear "as long as paper and ink can be procured."

Some papers enjoyed contracts for government printing, which for these fortunate journals provided another source of income. While Jared Whitaker and Archibald Gaulding strongly supported Georgia governor Joseph E. Brown in the pages of the *Intelligencer*, generally only papers in Milledgeville, the capital, got lucrative printing jobs from the state government.

The *Intelligencer*, like a number of other papers, had a third source of revenue: its job and book printing and binding business, which boasted "all the latest improvements in Printing, Binding, &c." according to one ad. Another advertisement for this enterprise ran in the paper's issue of April 23, 1861, proclaiming that the *Atlanta Intelligencer*'s Book and Job Office could "do all kinds of work in the best style of the Art. We have an experienced man at the head of this department, and we are prepared to print and bind, in the best and most substantial manner, Books, Pamphlets, Catalogues, Diplomas, Bank Checks, Posters, Hand-Bills, Programmes, business, wedding, and visiting Cards, Way-Bills, and every sort of printing and binding done at a first class office." This was no idle boast. One book produced by the Intelligencer Steam Power Presses in 1863, *The Angel Daughter*, is termed by Confederate bibliographer Richard Barksdale Harwell as "one of the most elaborately printed books of the period."[13]

At some point in the war, the *Intelligencer* moved from Parr's Building (at Whitehall and Alabama) to a brick structure at the foot of Whitehall Street near the railroad. According to the few photographs we have of the area, the paper was quartered on the second story of a building whose bottom floor housed Wittgenstein's wholesale liquor store. Out front on the sidewalk, the paper's staff hung a bulletin board on which they pinned announcements of the latest important events. For instance, when the office received word on the evening of April 18, 1861, that Virginia had seceded, the editor (as he wrote the next day) "immediately announced the same on our Bulletin Board in front of our office, free to all!" In addition, the *Intelligencer* welcomed readers (both subscribers and nons-) to drop in at its reading room to scan the day's edition and sample the out-of-town papers that had arrived as exchanges. Other papers had their reading rooms, too; that of the *Charleston Mercury* even had Northern newspapers, mailed by its Richmond correspondent, Dr. George Bagby.

The editor had his office, his "sanctum," where he composed his editorial columns. Nearby was the composing room in which the typesetter, sometimes called a compositor, with his composing stick laid out the type for printing. A "counting room" served as the paper's business office, where readers could purchase papers and buy advertising space. It was also the place where news boys hawking the paper on the streets, or running them to subscribers' homes, could pick up their issues. "News boys can have their orders filled," one notice read, "by applying at the counting room."

Largest space at the paper's office was given over to the press room, where the printing and folding of each day's issue took place. It was a hot place, especially in the summer, when the wood-fed steam engine added to temperatures. The press room was also large, if only because the printing machinery was, too; the larger model of the Hoe cylinder press measured 7' by 13'.

Perhaps a half-dozen workers labored away in the back shop, most importantly pressmen running the printing machinery. At the start of the war, the *Intelligencer* employed one "journeyman printer," George Hathaway, whom it lost in August 1861 when he volunteered for the army. (The *Macon Telegraph*, for example, employed six backshop men, including one to tend the steam engine.) A foreman was on hand as well, to lay out page content and generally oversee production. In the spring of 1862, the *Intelligencer*'s foreman was Isaac B. Pilgrim, who had come to Atlanta from Lawrenceville, Georgia, where he had served as editor of the *Lawrenceville News*. As for salaries, a foreman could expect a minimum wage of $25 a week, although the weeks were long: six days, each of twelve hours' duration. Working such hours, a printer, the man who put the ink to the page, as van Tuyll writes, "could expect to bring home about $27 a week in 1860, or $647 in 2010 dollars.") Obviously, newspapers needed printers, and journalists often tried to help one another out. When the *Macon Citizen*, for instance, advertised for "two good, steady printers" in April 1861, the *Intelligencer* reprinted the ad. At many Southern papers, the backshop was integrated; enslaved black men, rented from their owners, performed much of the hard work in the press room. In June 1864, for instance, the *Intelligencer* announced that "our negro pressmen," who had been temporarily drafted by military authorities to work on the city's fortifications, had been allowed to return to the newspaper's back room.

Compositors or typesetters were generally paid according to how much type they set, as measured in ems—typographical measurement units. An experienced compositor could set a thousand ems of type in an hour. In Richmond, January 1862, the typographers' union set salaries for their tradesmen at thirty-five cents per thousand ems. Ten months later, in Knoxville, Tennessee, the going rate was forty cents for a thousand ems. When the *Intelligencer* advertised for "a good compositor" in December 1863, it called for a worker "who does not keep 'fashionable hours.'" It pointedly added, "those that are in the habit of getting intoxicated need not apply."[14]

The *Intelligencer*, like newspapers across Georgia, maintained a six-day work week. A scan of its issues for June 1861 indicates that Sunday was employees' day off, meaning that no paper came out on Monday. Only once during the month was this schedule thrown off, and that was because the *Intelligencer* closed its offices on Thursday, June 13, which President Davis had proclaimed as a national day of fasting and prayer. "In accordance with ancient usage," it also announced that it was giving its printers a day off on Thursday, July 4.

Typesetters, printers and pressmen were thrown out of work, though, if they ran out of the one staple upon which they depended: paper. In 1861, of 555 paper mills in the United States, only 24 (four percent) were located in the Confederacy. Professor Risley counts four paper mills in antebellum Georgia. At least two of these were near Atlanta, at Roswell and Marietta, thus conveniently located close by for the operations of the *Intelligencer*; the Marietta mill was sited at the convergence of Sope Creek and the Chattahoochee, a dozen miles north of downtown Atlanta.

Yet at the start of the war, all Southern paper mills together could not produce enough to serve the needs of regional newspapers. Their combined output was 75,000 pounds a year, when Southern presses demanded twice that amount. In the antebellum years, the shortfall had been made up by paper imported from abroad or purchased from Northern mills. The latter source obviously was cut off after Sumter, and Lincoln's blockade made obtaining European product much more difficult.

The war was barely begun before Southern journals began running short of paper. The technology of the time relied on cloth rags for paper's raw material; wood-pulp paper would not begin to be used in the South till after the war. Textile mills were focused on producing uniforms as well as bandages for Confederate hospitals; cartridge factories also required wadding. Anxious editors began proposing ways to improve the situation; one way was obviously to build more paper mills. "The press throughout the Southern Confederacy is made to suffer severely for the want of paper," declared a Vicksburg paper as early as June 1861. "There are several manufactories in Georgia," the editor observed, but they "turn out daily about half the amount consumed in the same length of time." To meet the need, he concluded, "a number of places are urging the importance of erecting paper mills."

As it turned out, very few paper mills were built in the war-torn Confederacy. So when one important mill went down, even temporarily, newspapers were dramatically affected. After the Marietta Paper Mill in September 1863 lost a number of its employees to home guard duty, the plant was compelled to suspend operation, sending to the *Intelligencer* "just a few bundles of paper," according to a report at the time. Appeals to the government soon returned enough workers to resume operation at the mill on at least a limited basis.

The Marietta manufactory, along with the other paper mill in nearby Roswell, were both burned by Sherman's troops in the summer of 1864. Tragedy could strike in other forms. On August 2, 1863, the paper plant in Bath, South Carolina, accidentally burned to the ground. "The loss of this 10-year-old mill threatened to shut down the entire Confederate newspaper industry," van Tuyll writes. Less catastrophic was the simple wearing out of the very machinery used to make the product. The *Southern Confederacy* in January 1862 was forced to reduce the size of its weekly edition, it announced, because "the Mill which makes our paper is unable, on account of recent damage to the machinery which cannot be repaired or replaced till the blockade is ended." "We may find it impossible, for love or money, or both combined, to get paper from any other mill," the editorial concluded.[15]

The *Atlanta Commonwealth* was similarly beset. Unable to procure newsprint, according to early Atlanta historian Wallace Reed, it resorted to the use of "book paper, pure white news, straw colored, manilla, common brown wrapping paper, and even wall paper." When Joel Chandler Harris, then a fourteen-year-old working for a middle Georgia weekly newspaper, wrote the editor of the *Commonwealth* in 1863, he closed his note by "hoping that you receive a thousand reams of nice paper." Harris' wish was not fulfilled; the *Commonwealth* folded in 1863.

Besides paper, another essential ingredient was ink. An ink factory located in Augusta helped Georgia papers, but one in Marietta did, too. In July 1862, the *Intelligencer* started running an advertisement for the firm, B. A. Randall. Yet as with all commodities in the Confederacy, prices rose to painful levels during the war. Ink priced at eighteen cents a pound before rose to eighty cents during—more than a 400 percent increase.[16]

The price of war news in the Confederate South was literally going up. In addition to the cost of raw materials for printing were the expenses of getting the news in the first place. Telegraphic dispatches, for example, became more expensive the longer they were. In Southern newspaper offices, rarely were more than fifteen hundred words a day received by wire. The demand for war news led to more money spent on telegraphic reports. In the early stage of the war, the *Intelligencer* dodged another expense: paying reporters or field correspondents—"specials," as they were called—who sent back stories from the front line. (Most were men; only seven women have been identified as specials—three for Southern newspapers, four for Northern.) These writers were sometimes paid by the piece; George W. Bagby earned $5 per story from the *Nashville Union and American*. Others were salaried, such as Henry Timrod; in 1862 the *Charleston Courier* paid him six dollars a day plus expenses. Their dispatches became front-and-center as public demand for war news increased. "Nearly all the more prominent Confederate daily newspapers at the beginning of the war," J. Cutler Andrews explains, "used the first page for the display of advertisements and notices, and published editorials and war news on the later pages. As the war progressed, war news and even editorials took over the first page, while the amount of advertising diminished and was relegated to the back of the newspaper."[17]

Through it all, Jared Whitaker and Archibald Gaulding carried on with their enterprise. The paper's front page in May 1861 virtually screamed for subscribers in a vertical ad that ran the entire length of the page. Moreover, like many newspapers, they had agents selling advertising space. In the fall of 1861, the *Intelligencer* announced it had an agent for subscriptions and ads in Newnan, about forty miles southwest of Atlanta. In early 1862, one W. T. Beall was serving in Atlanta as agent for the paper, "duly authorized . . . to receive subscriptions and make collections."

Because pages needed to be filled and bills needed to be covered, editors favored their advertisers by giving over half of every four-page issue to paid ads. The *Intelligencer*'s rates were printed on the front page of every issue. In mid-June 1861, the paper offered a ten-line square, one insertion, for a dollar; after that, it was fifty cents per each insertion for up to a month. But a table presented rates for the same sized ad to run up for two, three, four, six months, even a year. The math was apparent. An advertiser could run an ad for three months in every daily issue for less money ($10) than it would cost for the ad to run twenty days ($10.50).

No wonder, then, that so much of the paper's advertising appeared on the same page, day after day. "Advertisements often ran for weeks or even months with no changes except their position on a page," journalism historian Ford Risley notes. In the *Intelligencer*'s pages during January 1861, advertisers ranged from local grocers, hardware stores, clothiers and insurance agents to vendors of more specific items: shoemakers, jewelers and distillers. There were plenty of ads for personal health items: "Cephalic Pills CURE Sick Headache" trumpeted one prominent ad. Another announced that Mrs. Winslow's Soothing Syrup would help children teething. One efficacious vegetable medicine addressed "female obstructions." Male baldness could be treated with "Heimstreet's Inimitable Hair Restorative"; and, yes, there were male virility aids ("Manhood.—How Lost.—How Restored").[18]

Thus was the business of running a Southern newspaper. It can be summarized in a few lines. The work called for an industrious editor, experienced typesetters and sturdy printers. Dispatches received at the downtown telegraph office, coupled with exchanges gotten through the mail, provided the *Intelligencer*'s most important content. Subscription and advertising revenue were the paper's mainstays, but the *Intelligencer* also had a Book and Job Office for other work. Faced with paper shortages, freeloading readers and other vexations, the *Atlanta Daily Intelligencer* proudly pursued its mission of reporting the war for its readers. And behind it all lay an emergent Confederate patriotism that the *Intelligencer* shared with the majority of them. On May 1, 1861, students of the Atlanta Female Institute put on a program that included a *faux* bombardment of Fort Sumter. The newspaper covered the event. "It became necessary for one of the smallest of the girls to hoist the United States flag, and to keep it standing until the close of the bombardment," it reported. William P. Howard, teacher at the institute who directed the event, apparently had trouble finding a volunteer. One girl of about ten told him, "No, it is not our flag, and I will never hold it." Two more young ladies also refused. A reluctant flag bearer was finally found, and held the Stars and Stripes, though crying as she did so, saying that she hoped she was not disgracing herself. "Our enemies should learn wisdom from this little incident," Gaulding concluded. "Our enemies talk of coercing us! When the last man, woman and child in the South is no more, our cities destroyed and our fields laid waste, and the last vestige of civilization entirely blotted from the face of our fair land, then we will be a coerced people, and not till then."[19]

NOTES

1. Bernard A. Weisberger, *The American Newspaperman* (Chicago: University of Chicago, 1961), 34–35, 40, 51–53, 62, 65–67; Frank Luther Mott, *American Journalism: A History of Newspapers in the United States Through 250 Years, 1690 to 1940* (New York: Macmillan, 1941), 160–61, 194, 216, 247–48; Daniel Walker Howe, *What Hath God Wrought: The Transformation of America, 1815–1848* (New York Oxford University Press, 2007), 691; Russel Blaine Nye, *Society in America, 1830–1860* (New York: Harper & Row, 1974), 265; J. Cutler Andrews, "The Southern Telegraph Company, 1861–1865: A Chapter in the History of Wartime Communication," *Journal of Southern History*, vol. 30, no. 3 (August 1964), 319.

2. Lorman A. Ratner and Dwight L. Teeter Jr., *Fanatics and Fire-eaters: Newspapers*

and the Coming of the Civil War (Urbana: University of Illinois Press, 2004), 16; Brayton Harris, *Blue & Gray in Black & White: Newspapers in the Civil War* (Washington: Brassey's, 1999), 6–8; James Melvin Lee, *History of American Journalism* (Boston: Houghton Mifflin, 1923), 273–74; George Henry Payne, *History of Journalism in the United States* (New York: D. Appleton, 1920), 138; David E. Markle, ed., *The Telegraph Goes to War: The Personal Diary of David Homer Bates, Lincoln's Telegraph Operator* (Hamilton NY: Edmonston Publishing, 2003), 1; Louis M. Starr, *Bohemian Brigade: Civil War Newsmen in Action* (New York: Alfred A. Knopf, 1954), 13; Richard A. Schwarzlose, *The Nation's Newsbrokers. Volume 1: The Formative Years, from Pretelegraph to 1865* (Evanston IL: Northwestern University Press, 1989), 62, 65, 106; Menahem Blondheim, *News over the Wires: The Telegraph and the Flow of Public Information in America, 1844–1897* (Cambridge: Harvard University Press, 1994), 108.

3. Garrett, *A & E*, vol. 1, 277–79; Venet, *Changing Wind*, 25–26; Bulla and Borchard, *Journalism in Civil War Era*, 92.

4. Mary Hubner Walker, *Charles W. Hubner: Poet Laureate of the South* (Atlanta: Cherokee Publishing, 1976), 31; "From Missouri," *ADI*, May 18, 1862.

5. Andrews, *South Reports*, 9–21.

6. "Charleston Affairs," *ADI*, Apr. 12, 1861; Carl R. Osthaus, *Partisans of the Southern Press: Editorial Spokesmen of the Nineteenth Century* (Lexington: University Press of Kentucky, 1994), 4; van Tuyll, *Confederate Press*, 109, 112–13, 243–44; *ADI*, Apr. 1–30, 1861, *passim.*; Andrews, *South Reports*, 26; "Late News Items from our Exchanges," *ADI*, April 30; Valentine T. Barnwell, *Barnwell's Atlanta City Directory* (Atlanta: Atlanta Intelligencer Book and Job Office, 1867), 109; "Atlanta," *ADI*, April 3.

7. "Proceedings of a Convention of the People of Arizona, held in the City of Mesilla, March 16, 1861," *ADI*, Apr. 15, 1861; "OUR EXCHANGES," *ADI*, June, 13, 1862; Debra Reddin van Tuyll, "Essential Labor: Confederate Printers at Home and War," *Journalism History*, vol. 31, no. 2 (Summer 2005), 76; Schwarzlose, *Nation's Newsbrokers*, 163.

8. Osthaus, *Partisans of Southern Press*, xiii, 2–3; Schwarzlose, *Nation's Newsbrokers*, vol. 1, 165; van Tuyll, *Confederate Press*, 147, 157; Andrews, *South Reports*, 24, 27–31; Alfred McClung Lee, *The Daily Newspaper in America: The Evolution of a Social Instrument* (New York: Octagon Books, 1973), 611; "Concert for the Benefit of the Atlanta Grays," *ADI*, May 21, 1861; Ellen Gay Detlefson, "Printing in the Confederacy, 1861–1865: A Southern Industry in Wartime," Ph.D. dissertation, Columbia University, 1975, 7; van Tuyll, "Esssential Labor," 77–79.

9. Andrews, *South Reports*, 27, 43; Ford Risley, *Civil War Journalism* (Santa Barbara CA: Praeger, 2012), 109; Risley, "Georgia's Civil War Newspapers," 63; E. Merton Coulter, *The Confederate States of America 1861–1865* (Baton Rouge: Louisiana State University Press, 1950), 494; "TO PRINTERS," *ADI*, May 8, 1863; "WANTED," *ADI*, Aug. 5, 1862; Detlefson, "Printing in the Confederacy," 4–5; *Atlanta Intelligencer*, Confederate Citizens' File, Business Document no. 3, M346, Roll 28, National Archives and Records Administration; "CITY SUBSCRIBERS," *ADI*, May 21, 1862; Lee, *Daily Newspaper in America*, 611; van Tuyll, *Confederate Press*, 222; "A little incident . . . ," *ADI*, June 12, 1861; van Tuyll, "Essential Labor," 82; "All persons are requested . . . ," *ADI*, May 3, 1863; "WANTED," *ADI*, Apr. 6, 1862.

10. B. G. Ellis, *The Moving Appeal: Mr. McClanahan, Mrs. Dill, and the Civil War's Great Newspaper Run* (Macon: Mercer University Press, 2003), 3; Andrews, *South Reports*, 25–26;

Bulla and Borchard, *Journalism in the Civil War Era,* 90; van Tuyll, *Confederate Press,* 210; "WANTED," *ADI,* Aug. 24, 1862; "TO PRINTERS," *ADI,* May 8, 1863; "THE INTELLIGENCER," *ADI,* Apr. 21, 1861; "TAKE NOTICE," *ADI,* April 11.

11. "ALL CORRESPONDENCE CUT OFF," *ADI,* Apr. 16, 1861; Andrews, "Southern Telegraph Company," 321; D. G. Duncan to L. P. Walker, Apr. 25, 1861 and Duncan to Walker, May 10, U. S. War Department, *The War of the Rebellion: A Compilation of the Official Records of the Union and Confederate Armies,* 128 vols. (Washington: Government Printing Office, 1880–1901), ser. 1, vol. 51, pt. 2, 33, 77 (further references to the *OR* will be to series 1 unless noted); Ford Risley, "The Confederate Press Association: Cooperative News Reporting of the War," *Civil War History,* vol. 47, no. 3 (September 2001), 224; Quintus C. Wilson, "Confederate Press Association: A Pioneering News Agency," *Journalism Quarterly,* vol. 26 (June 1949), 160; Andrews, *South Reports,* 55.

12. "CACOETHES SCRIBENDI," *ADI,* June 13, 1862; G. B. Buchanan, "RICHMOND CORRESPONDENCE," *ADI,* June 10; "See First and Third Page," *ADI,* Apr. 30, 1861. For the measured dimensions of the *Intelligencer* issue of Apr. 4, 1861, we express our appreciation to Carolle R. Morini, Caroline D. Bain Archivist and Reference Librarian at the Boston Athenaeum.

13. "INTELLIGENCE FROM THE ARMY AND ARMY INCIDENTS," *ADI,* Sept. 13, 1862; Van Tuyll, *Confederate Press,* 14, 30, 33, 149, 157, 183, 185, 188–90, 212; Andrews, *South Reports,* 7; "The following article we copy from the Charleston *Mercury* . . . ," *ADI,* July 10, 1861; Risley, "Georgia's Civil War Newspapers," 27; Kenneth W. Rawlings, "Statistics and Cross-Sections of the Georgia Press to 1870," *Georgia Historical Quarterly,* vol. 23, no. 2 (June 1939), 181–84; Garrett, *A & E,* vol. 1, 488; "THE INTELLIGENCER," *ADI,* Mar. 18, 1862; "Daily Intelligencer Book and Job Office," *ADI,* Mar. 29, 1861; "The Atlanta Intelligencer Book and Job Office," *ADI,* April 23; Harwell, "Atlanta Publications," 168.

14. Michael Rose, *Atlanta: A Portrait of the Civil War* (Charleston SC: Arcadia Publishing, 1999), 111; "Virginia Has Seceded!," *ADI,* Apr. 19, 1861; "Personal," *ADI,* Apr. 17, 1861; van Tuyll, *Confederate Press,* 115, 199, 204, 210, 212, 223, 228–29, 232, 239–40; 'THE INTELLIGENCER—LATE NEWS," *ADI,* Apr. 17, 1861; van Tuyll, "Essential Labor," 77; B. Kimball Baker, "The Memphis Appeal," *Civil War Times Illustrated,* vol. 18, no. 4 (July 1979), 32; "THE DEAD AND BURIED SOLDIERS," *ADI,* May 11, 1862; "A CORRECTION," *ADI,* Dec. 3, 1863; Joseph P. Byrd IV, *Confederate Sharpshooter: Major William E. Simmons* (Macon: Mercer University Press, 2016), 7; "PRINTERS WANTED," *ADI,* Apr. 1, 1861; "OUR READERS . . . ," *ADI,* June 22, 1864; Davis, *What the Yankees Did to Us,* 62, 67; Detlefson, "Printing in the Confederacy," 7–8; Risley, *Civil War Journalism,* 110.

15. "FOURTH OF JULY," *ADI,* July 3, 1861; Van Tuyll, *Confederate Press,* 204–206; Risley, "Georgia's Civil War Newspapers," 30; Louis Turner Griffith and John Erwin Talmadge, *Georgia Journalism 1763–1950* (Athens: University of Georgia Press, 1951), 67; Risley, *Civil War Journalism,* 109; Sarah Blackwell Gober Temple, *The First Hundred Years: A Short History of Cobb County, Georgia* (Atlanta: Walter W. Brown Publishing Co., 1935), 154; Detlefson, "Printing in the Confederacy," 75–77, 80.

16. Wallace P. Reed, *History of Atlanta, Georgia* (Syracuse NY: D. Mason, 1889), 186; Wayne Mixon, "Joel Chandler Harris," in Kenneth Coleman and Charles Stephen Gurr,

eds., *Dictionary of Georgia Biography*, 2 vols. (Athens: University of Georgia Press, 1983), vol. 1, 400; Bryan, *Confederate Georgia,* 201; Harwell, "Atlanta Publications," 194; Van Tuyll, *Confederate Press,* 185, 189, 208–209; "PRINTER'S INK," *ADI,* July 2, 1862.

17. J. Cutler Andrews, *The North Reports the Civil War* (Pittsburgh: University of Pittsburgh Press, 1955), 6; Andrews, *South Reports,* 47–48; van Tuyll, *Confederate Press,* 190; Risley, *Civil War Journalism,* 2; Debra Reddin van Tuyll, "Beyond the Household Gate: Women War Correspondents in the Confederacy," in David B. Sachsman, ed., *A Press Divided: Newspaper Coverage of the Civil War* (New Brunswick NJ: Transaction Publishing, 2014), 164.

18. "ATLANTA INTELLIGENCER BOOK AND JOB OFFICE," *ADI,* May 4, 1861; Van Tuyll, *Confederate Press,* 192; "Agent for the Intelligencer," *ADI,* Oct. 19, 1861; "Mr. W. T. Beall," *ADI,* Feb. 4, 1862; "Rates of Advertising," *ADI,* June 15, 1861; Risley, "Georgia's Civil War Newspapers," 30; "JONES & WOOD, WHOLESALE AND RETAIL GROCERS," "Hardware . . . by Hawson, Gilbert & Burr," "BRYSON AND BEAUMONT'S Clothing & Tailoring Establishment," "FIRE AND LIFE INSURANCE AGENCY," "R. S. DUNNING . . . BOOTS AND SHOES," "ER LAWSHE . . . CLOCKS, WATCHES, JEWELRY," "FREEMAN AND SIMPSON'S OLD MAGNOLIA WHISKEY," "Cephalic Pills CURE Sick Headache," "CHILDREN TEETHING," "Dr. J. Bovee Dods' Celebrated VEGETABLE MEDICINES," "YOU CAN'T FIND . . . HAIR RESTORATIVE" and "Manhood.—How Lost.—How Restored," *ADI,* Jan. 1, 2 and 3, 1861.

19. "Children's Patriotism," *ADI,* May 4, 1861.

3. After the Smoke Cleared

SO, FOR ALL INTENTS AND PURPOSES, a war was on, and to judge from reports in the *Intelligencer*, Southerners welcomed it.

The *Intelligencer* had already slipped comfortably into its role as an organ of Confederate propaganda. Three aspects of this function were 1) to pin blame for the war on the enemy, 2) to confidently predict victory and 3) to personalize the foe, then excoriate him. These points were on full display in Gaulding and Bassford's long editorial, "Our War Policy," published on April 15. In it they made clear Southerners' view that it was the North that had brought on the conflict. "The aggressive policy of the Black Republican party of the North, has culminated in war, as we long since predicted it would," the editors began. They accentuated the hypocrisy of "Lincoln and his Cabinet advisers" attempting to reinforce forts within the Confederate nation, while "at the same time" communicating to Southerners that "they have no hostile intention and their policy is to be entirely peaceful." The editors stressed, "war is at all times a great evil, but in the present case, our people have been patient and long suffering, we have exhausted every means in our power, to preserve the peace, done everything consistent with our sense of right, honor and justice to avert the dire calamity, but all to no purpose."

While Confederate commissioners sought a peaceful resolution to the crisis, Gaulding and Bassford continued, "the Lincoln government has displayed a double-dealing and treachery, for which the world furnishes no example." "The first gun has been fired in the war of Southern Independence," they declared, giving the coming conflict a name which Confederates would soon embrace.

"We predict," the editors concluded, "the utter disgrace, overthrow and annihilation of the whole batch of abolition conspirators who planned this infamous revolution, and plunged a free, happy and once united people in all the horrors of civil war."[1]

Foretelling Confederate victory even before the war was fairly begun, the *Intelligencer* manifested the dissonance between editorializing with propagandistic opinion on the one hand and reporting with factual news on the other. On April 16 news items filled a full column on the paper's front page—such placement of news was a rarity at the time. Lincoln's proclamation calling for 75,000 troops—issued the day before and conveyed by telegraph to the various state governors—was printed in full. The administration's first aim, President Lincoln proclaimed, would be to "repossess the Forts, places and property which have been seized from the Union" in the seven states of Alabama, Florida, Georgia, Louisiana, Mississippi, South Carolina and Texas. Predictably, the *Intelligencer* had a lot of fun with this in its opinion column, "Lincoln's Proclamation," on page two; it found the ostensibly solemn proclamation "laughable in the extreme." If Northern troops intended to repossess seized property, "let them commence on Fort Sumter," which was now securely under Confederate control. "By the help of God," the paper averred, "we intend to hold and maintain it." As for Lincoln's demand that the insurrectionists retire peaceably back into their homes, "we will do so," the *Intelligencer* affirmed, "when we have driven the invader from our soil, and not till then." "So bring on your seventy thousand Black Republicans," the editors taunted. The half-million soldiers soon to be raised by the Confederacy, they vowed, would vanquish Union forces in battle. "We have room enough for them all," the editorial concluded, "to enrich the red fields of our worn out lands with their dead carcasses."

The difference in timeliness between exchange and telegraph, when readers demanded the very latest news, placed even more importance on wire dispatches. Then, as now, competing newspapers worked to "scoop" each other, which meant that the paper printing the latest telegraphic news won. The *Atlanta Southern Confederacy*, for example, bragged that it was the only journal in north Georgia that offered readers regular, reliable telegraphed news. The *Intelligencer* countered on April 16 that the contention was "entirely without foundation." The editors emphasized their practice of providing readers with the latest telegraphic reporting, reminding all that "no trouble or expense will be spared by the conductors of this paper, to set the very earliest and most reliable news by telegraph before our readers."

The very next day the *Intelligencer* promised, "in order to satisfy the general interest felt by all classes of our citizens, in the exciting facts occurring in all parts of the country, we have made arrangements to be amply and fully supplied with the latest news by telegraph from every quarter." Editor Gaulding and Associate Editor Bassford further promised to print a special evening edition at 1 p.m. "when the news is of special interest." The issue would be available for sale at the paper's office for the usual price of five cents; newsboys would assist in its circulation.²

At the same time, the newspapermen politely reminded Atlantans that they had a business to run. Heretofore, they explained in an announcement on April 17, they had given away extra copies "to our subscribers and others who might ask for them." Such generosity, however, "has been a very large tax on us." Henceforth, single numbers would be available to everyone at five cents each. They explained their logic (and pricing) thus: "a paper not worth *five cents* is not worth asking for."

Then there were the freeloaders; the *Intelligencer* management addressed them, too. During the day citizens were welcome to visit the paper's offices, both subscribers and not. These latter, however, would come to read the morning issue without paying. Worse, sometimes they walked off with the exchanged papers from which the editors drew their lifted columns. This practice had to stop, they explained. "Persons who are too penurious to subscribe and pay for a paper, and yet whose consciences will allow them to read our paper and carry off our exchanges, we have no respect for." The announcement, headlined "Personal," made no mention of corrective measures that might be implemented to address the moochers. Rather, the article closed simply with, "A word to the wise is sufficient."

As the proprietors sought ways to trim costs and improve efficiency, the owners themselves changed. The issue of April 18 announced that Gaulding and Whitaker had bought out their third partner, J. I. Miller. No reason was given; Miller was wished success "in any enterprise in which he may engage." In the days ahead, Gaulding and Whitaker pledged their continuing efforts to make the *Intelligencer* "what it ought to be, the leading Journal in this section of the country."³

It was evident that the people wanted news, and wanted it fast. But not all news was taken from the telegraph or clipped from other papers. Much was obtained from local sources in the city itself. As Atlantans responded to Fort Sumter, to Lincoln's proclamation and to predictions of war, there was indeed much to report as the city's citizens—meaning, white males of military age—rallied to take up arms.

Well before the first shot was fired, martial units had already existed in Atlanta, across Georgia, and, indeed, the whole South. Large communities had volunteer companies, elite units in which membership was accorded to gentlemen in the manner of club memberships. Colorful uniforms and convivial gatherings attracted these holiday soldiers, who elected their officers, passed their bylaws and adopted warlike-sounding names for their units. Atlanta claimed four volunteer military companies: the Atlanta Grays, City Light Guards, Fulton Dragoons and Gate City Guards.[4]

The officers and men of the Gate City Guards, to take one unit as example, represented "the best element of Atlanta's citizenship," in the words of local historian Franklin Garrett. Organized in January 1858, the company distinguished itself with dark blue uniforms marked by shoulder epaulets and gold trim. Tall black shako hats with white plumes topped off the colorful get-up.[5]

Secession furor brought about more volunteers forming new companies in Atlanta, such as the Georgia Volunteers a week after the state left the Union. The *Intelligencer* reported that on the morning of January 25 a number of men gathered at City Hall to hear about the new company; thirty-two signed up "as volunteers to serve the State of Georgia, in her present emergency," as the paper stated. Election of officers was held; for captain there was chosen George Washington Lee of nearby Stone Mountain, whose vocations included millwright, grocer and bartender.

Within another month, two more units had formed, the Atlanta Cadets and Fulton Blues. And more were coming. The paper reported, "young gentlemen" gathered to elect officers for the Davis Infantry, named for the nation's new president. A chief organizer of all this activity was Capt. Alexander M. Wallace of the Atlanta Grays. When Wallace announced that he wanted to start still another company and resigned from the Grays, the members held another election, in which Thomas L. Cooper was chosen as captain.

The *Intelligencer* did more than report the news; at times it helped to create it. After G. W. Lee's Volunteers organized, another enrollment meeting was held (sixty-one more men signed up). Associate Editor Bassford delivered the address, and it was a stemwinder. According to Wallace Reed, early historian of Atlanta, he "reviewed the rise and progress of the slavery agitation, the repeated violations of the Constitution by the Abolitionists of the North, and the final culmination of Abolition fanaticism in the election of Abraham Lincoln as president, on principles hostile to the South by a sectional majority." Southern secession had rightly ensued; Bassford predicted that all fifteen slave states would unite, "fighting for their rights, their liberties and their independence." If war came with the North, he welcomed it and predicted Southern victory. "Stand by the flag of Georgia, stand by one another," the associate editor exclaimed, "and if our independence has to be bought with blood, I yet say to you, as the Spartan mother said to her son, 'Go forth to battle, my son, for your country, take this shield, and return with it or upon it.'"[6]

As they had during the visit of President-elect Davis on February 16, Atlanta's volunteer soldiers got a chance to show off when Vice President Stephens came to town on March 12. "The entire Military force of our city," the paper announced, "the Fire Department, and an immense concourse of citizens" greeted Stephens at the train station and escorted him to a downtown hotel. In the course of the reception, the Atlanta Grays fired a seven-gun salute.[7]

For a while, the impression prevailed that Atlanta's volunteer soldiers were getting all dressed up with nowhere to go. They were not alone, as troops were being raised throughout the state. Then the Confederate government stepped in. On March 9 Secretary of War Leroy P. Walker issued a call from Montgomery to the seven governors for 2,000 men from each state as the basis for a Confederate provisional army. Half of Georgia's allotment would be sent to Fort Pulaski, the imposing fort guarding Savannah, which had been seized by Georgia state troops on January 3 from U.S. forces. The other thousand would head for Pensacola to bolster the Confederate forces warily watching the Federal garrison inside Fort Pickens.[8]

Atlantans acted with alacrity to the calls for troops. George W. Lee's volunteers, a full-fledged company of one hundred strong, were mustered into Confederate service, and by March 17 were ready to entrain for Pensacola. The Gate City Guards (Capt. William L. Ezzard plus seventy-five men) left April 1, also for the Florida coast. The Guards' sending-off proved to be a big event. Despite a drizzling rain, a crowd gathered on Alabama Street in front of the Franklin Printing House to see Ezzard's company form ranks with others in the city. Then they heard a dignitary hold forth on the current crisis. The North was pushing the notion of racial equality, the speaker asserted, but Southerners knew that "the Black Race are, and should be, our Slaves." The Union had effectively been dissolved by these radicals; Georgia had been compelled to "resume our sovereignty." After this speechifying, Josephine Hanleiter, daughter of Cornelius Hanleiter (owner of Franklin Printing) presented Captain Ezzard with a Confederate "stars and bars." The banner, with seven white stars in its blue corner, and three red-white-red horizontal bars, was inscribed with *In Hoc Signo Vinces*—the Latin for "in this sign you shall conquer."

A few hours later the scene shifted to the train depot, where the Guards boarded a southbound train with other companies from north Georgia. About

7,000 people gathered at the station, the *Intelligencer* judged, adding "we never saw so much enthusiasm manifested on any other occasion." The paper took particular notice of the large number of women in the cheering crowd. Among them were a hundred young ladies, students of the elite Atlanta Female Institute, who had come to the station "to bid good-bye to the gallant soldiers, who were going to fight the battles of their country."[9]

Women were summoned to perform patriotic duties as well. The paper printed the call from a citizen that Mayor Whitaker convene the ladies of the city for the purpose of preparing lint and bandages for the troops being sent to Pensacola. The women did indeed quickly gather at the home of Mrs. Maria Westmoreland, wife of the physician Willis F. Westmoreland. They committed to bandage-making, but soon broadened their purpose to sewing clothing for Confederate soldiers, taking on the name of the Ladies' Soldiers' Relief Society.[10]

Everyone was trying to help. Although exempt from militia duty, all four of the city's volunteer fire companies offered themselves for local guard duty. In its statement, Mechanics' Fire Company No. 2 affirmed that "Washington should be rescued and our flag put upon it." The firemen's services were accepted by Mayor Whitaker on April 26. Atlanta physicians met and resolved to provide medical care for poor families in the city whose men had gone off to fight. The *Intelligencer* pitched in with a call for all citizens to help the cause. It complimented one resident, though "a poor man," who promised to donate a load of wood each week for the next three months for families whose heads were in the service. This gesture prompted an appeal from the paper: "Let all do something, no matter how little, to help the cause along."

More Atlanta companies formed in late April: the Confederate Volunteers (Capt. Lucius J. Gartrell); the Stephens Rifles, named for the vice president; the Silver Grays. This latter troop accepted only men over forty-five years old, hence the name. Most, if not all, of these exuberant volunteers had seen no prior military service, as in the Mexican War or campaigns against the Seminoles. In early May the *Intelligencer* therefore published a column of helpful tips submitted by "An Old Soldier." "Remember," the veteran began, "that in a campaign more men die from sickness than by the bullet." This sobering warning was consequently followed by advice on healthful habits for green recruits. Hygiene was important; soldiers should try to wash themselves daily. The veteran suggested that men grow beards "so as to protect the throat and lungs." Felt slouch hats were recommended, as they could be turned up on sunny days and turned down on rainy ones. It was very important to line one's blanket and procure a rubber one on which to lie at night. "Chilly or night air," the old soldier solemnly admonished, "often causes fever and death."

By late May the paper could report that four companies raised in the city and Fulton County had been sent into the field: Lee's Volunteers and the Gate City Guards at Pensacola; another company in Savannah; and the Atlanta Grays "have just left us for the soil of the Old Dominion" (the Grays left for Richmond on the 24th, after a big parade downtown). Thus four hundred men were away and under arms. Moreover, the editors boasted, "we have fully one thousand more, who are organized into companies," and were ready for the call.[11]

It would come soon.

NOTES

1. "Our War Policy," *ADI*, April 15.
2. "By Telegraph," "Lincoln's Proclamation" and "Telegraphic Dispatches," *ADI*, April 16; "The Intelligencer—Late News," *ADI*, April 17.
3. "Our Extra Papers" and "Personal," *ADI*, April 17; "The undersigned . . . ," *ADI*, April 18.
4. John Hope Franklin, *The Militant South 1800–1861* (Cambridge: Harvard University Press, 1956), 171–72; William R. Scaife and William Harris Bragg, *Joe Brown's Pets: The Georgia Militia, 1861–1865* (Macon: Mercer University Press, 2004), 185–88.
5. Garrett, *A & E*, vol. 1, 440–41, 497.
6. Reed, *History of Atlanta, 109–110*; Robert Scott Davis, *Civil War Atlanta* (Charleston: History Press, 2011), 24, 30; "Enlistments in Atlanta," *ADI*, February 28; "Capt. Wallace," *ADI*, February 27; "Atlanta Grays," *ADI*, March 8.
7. "Arrival of Vice-President Stephens, *ADI*, Mar. 13, 1861.
8. Joseph H. Parks, *Joseph E. Brown of Georgia* (Baton Rouge: Louisiana State University Press, 1977), 128, 134, 136; "First Draft from Atlanta," *ADI*, Feb. 26, 1861.
9. "Lee's Volunteers," *ADI*, Mar. 13, 16, 19, 1861; Garrett, *A & E*, vol. 1, 508; Reed, *History of Atlanta*, 113–14; "Gate City Guards! Flag Presentation! Grand Military Display!," *ADI*, April 2; Venet, *Changing Wind*, 38–39; "Departure of the Military" and "Atlanta Female Institute," *ADI*, April 2.
10. "M.," "Aid to Our Soldiers," *ADI*, April 17; Reed, *History of Atlanta*, 113–14; Venet, *Changing Wind*, 49.
11. Garrett, *A & E*, vol. 1, 508; Reed, *History of Atlanta*, 114–15; "Blessed is the Giver," *ADI*, May 25, 1861; "Advice to Volunteers," *ADI*, May 2; "Atlanta Grays," *ADI*, May 24.

4. Manassas

ABRAHAM LINCOLN'S CALL for volunteers in mid-April had at least two dramatic effects. It roused the Northern states to prepare for war, and it prompted states of the upper South to choose between staying in the Union, or joining the Confederacy.

Virginians made their decision quickly. A secession convention assembled in Richmond and in just two days was ready to vote, which it did on April 17 in favor of disunion. A week later, the Old Dominion officially joined the young Confederacy.

Even though Virginia shared no borders with the Confederate States—and would not until North Carolina seceded a month later—the secession of Virginia was cause for huge celebration in the South. The *Intelligencer* staff received the news by telegraphic dispatch on the 18th, and immediately posted an announcement on the bulletin board that it kept in front of its office. "The news was received by our citizens with the wildest manifestations of joy," the paper reported. Church bells started tolling, people filled the streets, shouting and cheering. Downtown businesses closed and as darkness approached, people set bonfires in the streets and shot fireworks into the air. The main buildings (hotels, stores on Peachtree, Whitehall and Alabama Streets, even the *Intelligencer* office) "were brilliantly illuminated." The local military companies, such as the Fulton Blues and Atlanta Cadets, came out in force, so that, as the article reported, "the sound of martial music and the heavy tread of dense masses of men was heard on every hand." Only the secession of Georgia three months earlier, the paper reckoned, had stirred such a level of palpable excitement "among all classes of our population."[1]

The very propinquity of the Confederacy's northernmost state to the capital of Yankeedom—Richmond and Washington were just a hundred miles apart—meant that Virginia quickly became the new front of impending war. This dubious status was confirmed when the Congress in Montgomery voted on May 20 to move the national capital to Richmond. Virginia Governor John

Letcher had begun to raise his own state army when the War Department issued orders for Confederate troops to start heading for Virginia.[2]

The Confederate concentration in Virginia beckoned those Atlanta volunteer companies that had not left town. One of them was the Atlanta Grays, for whom a benefit concert was given at the Atheneum by the city's recently organized musical troupe, the Atlanta Amateurs. The Amateurs had been formed by twenty-seven men and women expressly to perform entertainments raising money for the troops. Officers were elected for the ensemble, including William H. Barnes, the downtown dry goods merchant, as manager. On the day of the Amateurs' event, May 21, the *Intelligencer* urged the citizenry to come out and show support for the Grays before they departed for "the seat of the war," which was now Virginia. "Let the Hall be crowded by the elite of our city," the editors harkened, to honor the men "who are going forth to battle for our altars and our firesides."

The Atheneum was indeed crowded that night and the entertainment colorful. The Amateurs opened the show with a sham battle between a Yankee Doodle character and one who personified Dixie. Needless to say, Dixie won the fight and the defeated Doodle slunk offstage. This brought a triumphant waving of the Confederate Stars and Bars before the cheering audience. The mood grew somber and hushed as Mark Cooper, owner of the Etowah Iron Works north of Atlanta—and father of the Grays' captain, Thomas Cooper—presented a Bible to each member of the company. The *Intelligencer* reported that Cooper's remarks, "touching and pathetic in the extreme . . . went home to the hearts of his hearers." Captain Cooper spoke as well, after he was given a flag stitched lovingly by local ladies. "We go to defend the same rights, principles and laws," he affirmed, "that were consecrated and made sacred by the blood of the Revolution." The next day, as the Grays boarded the train for Virginia, the *Intelligencer*'s effusions continued. "We are not very much inclined to pay compliments," the editors declared, "but we will venture the assertion that the Atlanta Grays present the finest *personnel*, which we have ever seen."[3]

Rules of military organization prescribed that ten companies of up to a hundred officers and men each were to be grouped together to form a regiment. Such had been done with the 1st Georgia Volunteer Infantry, dispatched to Pensacola. Given the speedy recruitment happening in Georgia (and throughout both North and South) in the spring of '61, by early May a half-dozen regiments of Georgia infantry had been formed. Thus on May 8 was the 7th Georgia Infantry organized. This regiment, unlike its predecessors, was comprised mostly of men from Fulton, DeKalb and Cobb counties. Two companies, the Davis Infantry and the Confederate Volunteers, represented Fulton County. The latter had been recruited by Atlanta attorney, state court judge and former U.S. congressman Lucius J. Gartrell. After Gartrell was elected colonel of the regiment, the *Intelligencer* extolled him as "a champion of Southern rights, of Southern Honor and Southern Independence, at home, and in the Halls of Congress" (it did not seem to matter that Gartrell was innocent of military experience). Upon Gartrell's promotion, Green J. Foreacre took charge of the company; Foreacre had been a real estate agent in Atlanta, further proving the point about inexperience. As the 7th prepared to depart for Virginia, Governor Brown reviewed the regiment at Atlanta's Fair Ground, the area southeast of downtown that had hosted agricultural fairs in the 1850s.

Other Atlanta companies also headed for Virginia, such as the Confederate Continentals. Its captain, E. M. Seago, made it clear to Atlantans that his men did not object to being sent so far away. "The war in Virginia is our war," Seago wrote in a column in the *Intelligencer* on June 5, "and the defence of the homes of her citizens is the defence of our homes; their success is our success." A week later, the paper printed Captain Seago's announcement that the Continentals expected to leave for Virginia on the 16th. The men were drilling daily near the Concert Hall downtown (the south end of Peachtree Street at the railroad); uniforms were being furnished; and volunteers were still being enrolled. "Our ranks are fast filling up," Seago announced, hinting there were still openings in the company roster for last minute recruits.[4]

Such appeals tugged at the military-eligible men in the city, and continued to bring forth volunteers. Those joining the army, of course, left behind not just their families but their jobs, forcing employers to adjust. Newspaper offices were not immune, as when the *Intelligencer* announced that it was losing one of its typesetters, George Hathaway. Hathaway had signed up with a new company, the Georgia Volunteers, and the newspaper staff resolved to send him off in style. "The boys concluded to present him with a handsome silk sash," the paper reported on June 12. Apparently everyone had gathered in the office the previous Saturday afternoon for the gift presentation and some remarks by one of the staff, F. S. Stoy.

"In behalf of your fellow operatives of this establishment, both old and young, and I may say white and black," Stoy began—with remarks that inform us that the *Intelligencer* employed leased slaves in its work force. He observed that Hathaway was "a Northern man" who had come South and had learned to "appreciate the nature of our Southern institutions" (a nineteenth century euphemism for *slavery*) to the point of signing up to fight for them. Stoy then bestowed the silken sash, "this humble testimonial of our esteem," to Hathaway. According to the paper, the typesetter was taken by surprise. He nonetheless expressed his thanks and affirmed his love for the South. "As regards the present difficulties between the two sections," he explained, "I believe the South is right"; hence he was taking up arms, "even though I should meet my [Northern] brothers on the battle field."

Hathaway, "journeyman printer" for the *Atlanta Intelligencer* (as he was described in June 1862), would survive the war. After enlisting on June 11, 1861, in the Georgia Volunteers, he became second sergeant when his unit became Company A of the 19th Georgia Infantry. Sergeant Hathaway served in the regiment throughout the war as part of Brig. Gen. Alfred Colquitt's brigade in the Army of Northern Virginia. In 1865 the unit was in North Carolina, fighting with Joe Johnston and contesting the advance of Sherman's army. Hathaway surrendered with Johnston's forces at Greensboro, April 26, 1865.[5]

The *Intelligencer*'s reporting of Hathaway's farewell observances in the paper's office on June 8 made for an interesting, even touching story. But it was not, as we say today, front page news. Indeed, following American newspapers' practice of the times, the front page of a four-page daily was the one part in which the reader would rarely find any news of importance. If there were a noteworthy item, it would be printed in the far right of the page's customary six columns—the only one typeset differently each day.

A perusal of the *Intelligencer*'s front page, say, for the last half of May 1861, shows that all but the right column appeared virtually the same for the entire two weeks. This allowed the front page to be typeset several days in advance of printing. The leftmost column carried information about the paper, schedules for the four railroads serving the city, and a few ads. Second from left one saw "professional cards" from law firms, an ad for McPherson's book store, and one from Dr. J. Bovee Dods' vegetable medicines ("Beware of Mineral Poisons"). To its right were notices from insurance companies. Third column from the right was filled entirely by a large promotion for the Intelligencer Book & Job Office & Book Bindery. Second from right were listed officers of the C.S.

government (president, cabinet, members of Congress) plus ads for lotteries and men's clothing.

All of this did not change; the same content appeared every day. New material appeared only in the far-right column, but it was hardly scintillating, able to be considered as filler, and generally lifted from other papers: "Maryland Legislative Caucus" (*Baltimore Sun*); "Virginia News from the Charleston Courier"; the *Raleigh Register* on a percussion cap factory; "Views of the English Press" (*Manchester Guardian*). A bit of rare relief came from an occasional poem. Northern newspaper items were reprinted on such topics as "Why Irishmen are not with the North." On May 30, the entire right column was given over to an account of the Mexican War battle of Buena Vista of February 1847 (and Jefferson Davis' role in it).

Occasionally a major presidential proclamation or governmental announcement would grace the front page. Such was the case in the *Intelligencer*'s issue of June 2, which printed an unusual proclamation from President Davis: the designation of a day for all the people to engage in religious fasting and prayer. "When a people who recognize their dependence upon God, feel themselves surrounded by peril and difficulty," the order began, "it becomes them to humble themselves under the dispensation of Divine Providence." Providence had thus far extended its blessings upon the Confederate States, Davis acknowledged, a beneficence that called for the people to demonstrate "devout and heartfelt gratitude." Moreover, the people should pray that the country continue in its godly ways: "we would implore the Lord of Hosts to guide and direct our policy in the paths of right, duty, justice and mercy."

For all of these purposes, the president called upon the people to fast, pray and attend religious services on Thursday, June 13, that the Almighty should "bless us with His favor and protection, and . . . bestow His gracious benediction upon our government and country."[6]

Davis' designation of a special day was not an idle instance. During the course of the war, as it turned out, the president called for fasting and religious observances on ten days, as late as March 10, 1865. "Congress, state legislatures, and denominational bodies designated so many more," quips James W. Silver, historian of Confederate church propaganda, "that a strict compliance with all might have saved enough food to feed Lee's hungry army."

The *Intelligencer*, like many other Confederate newspapers, published the presidential proclamation (June 2 and again on June 4), with the editors voicing their support. "We hope that this day will be generally observed by our people," they declared in a statement on June 9; "let us *all* kneel to the God of battles and ask His blessing upon our cause." The day before the designated occasion, the paper printed the proclamation issued by Mayor Whitaker and the City Council, asking businesses to close and asking people to "observe the 13th inst., as a day of Thanksgiving and Prayer."

Atlantans complied. All the churches held services and businesses were generally closed, as the paper reported afterward. The soldiers encamped around the city participated, too. The editors evidently attended the service conducted by a local cleric for the 9th Georgia Infantry, quartered west of downtown at Walton Spring: "one of the most eloquent and patriotic sermons it was ever our pleasure to listen to," they attested.[7]

Reliant upon the telegraph and swapped papers for news, the *Intelligencer* soon got another reportorial source: actual letters written by soldiers at the front, mailed back to the paper for the edification of the homefolk. Editor Gaulding and associate editor Bassford had dispatched no staff correspondent to mail back publishable letters from Virginia. Like so many other editors, they consequently welcomed contributions from literate soldiers who composed missives for hometown readers and through the Confederate postal service mailed them back, relating the details and drama of army life. Soldier-correspondents were amateurs—only the larger newspaper operations could afford to send a paid journalist into the field—yet their letters were mostly crisp and honest, allowing local readers to connect with their loved ones. The system worked great for the newspapers: they got first-hand reporting, their readers were pleased, and (best of all) the soldier correspondents did not cost the paper.

These amateur reporters almost always used *noms de plume,* but at times gave a clue to their identity by signing columns with their initials. One such was Pvt. Vardy Sisson of the Atlanta Grays, who sent a letter to the *Intelligencer* dated June 4 over his initials, "V.P.S." The Grays and its regiment, the 8th Georgia, were then in Richmond, but they had just gotten word from the regimental adjutant that they would be headed for Harpers Ferry in northwestern Virginia. The prospect was exciting. "The men are all eager of a fight," Sisson declared; "they didn't come here to rusticate in a beautiful pine grove." No, they were "all anxious to get a glimpse at the elephant." Sisson had been in camp long enough to have learned some soldier-slang, and "seeing the elephant" was one such popular phrase. Like much of American slang, its origins are multiple, but an accepted one comes from the nineteenth-century travelling circuses that roamed the land. A small show might only boast of performing dogs and ponies—hence another popular idiom today—but the real deal, we might say, was when a big circus could bring exotic animals to town—like elephants. To thus "see the elephant" was an initiation into the big-time, a rite of passage for the many nineteenth-century Americans who lived rather uneventful lives in small towns or rural settings.

The men of the 8th Georgia heard the adjutant, Lt. John Branch, announce the order for the departure to Harpers Ferry, and cheered. The troops also saw and heard no less than the president of the Confederacy address some of them on the evening of June 3. "Jeff Davis was in camp last night incog.," Private Sisson told the *Intelligencer,* "or rather we were not aware of his presence until he had gone." Others in the regiment were not thrown off by President Davis' alleged *incognito.* Pvt. Hamilton Branch, brother of the adjutant and also in the 8th Georgia, wrote his mother on June 4 (the same day Sisson wrote the *Intelligencer*), "the President says we are a fine body of men and he will rely on our courage strength and rediness [*sic*] to go, as a safeguard against defeat."

Soldiers will always grouse, and Private Sisson chose to do this too, in his letter to the *Intelligencer.* For one thing, their arms were deficient. Before entraining, the Grays had been ordered by Governor Brown to hand in their state-owned rifled muskets; on reaching Richmond they had been handed old-fashioned smoothbores. "We intend to shoot these old smooth bore muskets," Sisson grumbled, "and if they don't hit anything it will be no fault of ours." Then there was the loneliness felt by soldiers a long way from home. They felt like orphans, yet Sisson proudly declared, "we glory in our orphanage." Still, the lack of hometown newspapers increased their feelings of isolation. "We have received no papers since our arrival here," the private complained, "and are rather disposed to censure our friends in Atlanta." He further could not predict what kind of mail service they would get once at Harpers Ferry, "so if I do not write again you know the reason why."[8]

Letters from the field were always welcomed by the editors, but they could not be counted upon for daily news content. Hence the importance of telegraphic items, which the *Intelligencer* usually stacked up on page three. Headlining them itself took up a good portion of a column, as this deck from June 12 demonstrates:

BY TELEGRAPH.
Expressly for the Intelligencer.
Result of the Tennessee Election.
Apprehensions at Washington.
Burning Bridges by the Confederate Troops.
Fight Still Progressing.
Activity of the War Department.
Refusal of Virginia Bank Bills.
Four Thousand Secessionists in Baltimore.
Gov. Hicks in Trouble.
Fight at Bethel Church.
300 Federalist and one Confederate killed.
Capture of Jackson's Brother.
Surprise of Scouting Parties.
Capture of 18 Secessionists.
News from Washington.
Affair in Louisville.
&c., &c., &c.

This represented a broad swath of news, including events big (Tennesseans' vote to secede, June 8) and small (fight at Big Bethel, Virginia, June 10, with its comparatively modest toll of 87 casualties, both sides—18 Federals killed, 53 wounded and 5 captured; eleven Confederates wounded, including one mortally).

Just as the war was taking hold of the *Intelligencer*'s news features, so too was it seeping into the paper's advertising. In the spring of '61 one started to see notices for various militaria. James McPherson, the downtown bookseller, announced the availability of "Military Books" starting with *Hardee's Tactics* (published in 1855 by William J. Hardee, a U. S. Army officer who had resigned and by late June was already a Confederate brigadier general). J. M. Holbrook's Hat Manufactory offered "military hats or cap, made to order" for all the companies being formed. H. Braumuller on Whitehall Street announced that he was in the business of making bass and kettle drums for the musicians of any troop. Occasionally the editors would plug a particular vendor, as when they commended "Mr. A. H. DeWitt of this city" as a manufacturer of swords. "We visited his establishment yesterday," they explained, and found both the place and the product "fully equal to the purpose."[9]

Gaulding and Bassford, the editorial "we" of the *Intelligencer,* became singular in mid-June, when the paper announced that the latter was leaving as associate editor. No explanation was given, only that the proprietors, Gaulding and Whitaker, had made "arrangements which they conceived would be advantageous to the paper." They wished Bassford well, and even endorsed him for an editorial position with another paper. "As he is eminently qualified for the duties of Editorial life," they wrote, "we hope to see him again engaged in the Editorial chair"—just not at their daily.[10]

Down one in senior staff (Bassford) and at least one trained hand in the press room (Hathaway), with his co-owner tending to other matters (Mayor Whitaker), editor Gaulding needed all the help he could get in procuring war news for the *Intelligence.* Doubtless Gaulding was cheered to receive a letter from the Virginia front sent to him not by a soldier (Sisson), but by an unexpected contributor: Atlanta attorney Amos W. Hammond.

The *Intelligencer* announced to readers on June 29 that "Col. Amos W. Hammond, of this city," had written from Winchester, in the Shenandoah Valley. At fifty-three years Hammond was too old to volunteer for the army, and there is no record of him having served in a Georgia unit during the war. (Southern custom of the day bestowed "colonelcies" very liberally.) Yet for some reason he had set out on June 16 for Virginia, apparently to visit the camps of the 7th and 8th Georgia Regiments. By the 21st he had reached them at Winchester, and sent back to the *Intelligencer* an account of his trip. "Dear Gaulding," his letter began, "when I promised to write you, I could see you did not think I would do it. But you see I have." Hammond had travelled by train through east Tennessee to Manassas, only to learn that the Georgia boys had been sent off to Winchester. Once there he encountered the Atlanta Grays and Davis Infantry, and even spent the night in the tent of Col. Lucius Gartrell, commander of the 7th. As for the troops, "they want to fight more than ever you saw a set of men in your life." Based on what he had been hearing, Hammond predicted a big battle in a matter of days.[11]

In his prediction of a big battle, Hammond would be proven wrong, as the *Intelligencer* followed news from Virginia. Telegraphic dispatches from Richmond reported developments in "the seat of the war," but details were skimpy. Confederate Brig. Gen. P. G. T. Beauregard commanded forces at Manassas Junction, less than thirty miles west of Washington. Around the Northern capital Union Brig. Gen. Irvin McDowell had a larger army, widely rumored to be about to advance on Manassas. Fifty miles to the northwest, near Winchester, Confederate Brig. Gen. Joseph E. Johnston led a second Southern army (including the 7th and 8th Georgia), that was warily watching enemy forces under Pennsylvanian Robert Patterson to its north.

The big battle that many had anticipated finally took place at Manassas on July 21, but it was not till Tuesday morning, the 23rd, that the *Intelligencer* could report the event:

GLORIOUS VICTORY!!
Frightful report of the Battle from Washington.
The Carnage Tremendous on both sides.
The Dead and Wounded of the Enemy strewn on the ground for miles.
Four of the Enemies Batteries taken.
Great Fright in Washington.
Large amount of Stores, Munitions, arms and
a vast number of slain left on the field.
The New York Fire Zouaves cut to pieces.
Report of the Battle by President Davis.
&c., &c., &c.

To be sure, the headline trumpeting "Glorious Victory" was correct, but editor Gaulding had to be careful in patching his story together. The first telegraphed dispatch came from Richmond on the night of the battle: fighting broke out near Manassas early in the morning of July 21, and by evening "the federalists retired, leaving the Confederates in possession of the field." "This was a terrible battle," the terse report closed, "with great slaughter on both sides."

More details came in the next day: having given Patterson the slip, General Johnston's troops had arrived from the Shenandoah Valley in time to help drive McDowell's army from the battlefield. President Davis had even ridden from the capital by special train to watch the fighting. Among Confederates slain were Col. Francis Bartow and Brig. Gen. Barnard Bee, the paper correctly reported; "McDowell reported severely wounded" (not true).

Bare-boned reports were limited, however, to these bits of news. Subsequent messages added background on Bartow, Bee and other matters. In the days following the battle, the *Intelligencer* printed correspondence from Atlantans who had fought with the 7th and 8th Georgia Infantry Regiments.[12]

But because of its focus on the role of Georgians at Manassas, one story that the *Intelligencer* missed was the famous "Stonewall" incident during the battle.

On July 25, the *Charleston Mercury* printed a letter sent by its correspondent in Virginia, Leonidas W. Spratt. At Manassas on the day of the battle, Spratt had afterward conversed with the Confederate Brig. Gen. Barnard Bee's principal aide and had taken down the officer's account of what Bee had shouted during the fight: "Look men, there is Jackson standing like a stone wall! Let us determine to die here, and we will conquer! Follow me!" The *Mercury* story was reprinted in the *Richmond Dispatch* on July 29 and the *Lexington* (Va.) *Gazette* two weeks later—but not in the *Intelligencer*. Over time, Bee's "stone wall" allusion would be applied to General Jackson as a nickname. This incident is an example of how, as the saying goes, newspapers write the first draft of history.[13]

After a major engagement, perhaps the press' most important responsibility was to report casualties from local units; on the 24th the *Intelligencer* listed casualties among the officers and men of the Atlanta Grays. Telegraphed by two members of the company, Messrs. McGuire and Adair, the Grays' list counted thirteen killed and seventeen wounded, from severely to slightly. "The wounded are in Richmond," McGuire and Adair added, "attended with God like kindness and affection, and a God bless them should be uttered by every tongue in the South." Two-thirds of a column on the 25th listed the wounded and killed of the 7th Georgia; Colonel Gartrell, himself wounded in the leg, counted 118 wounded and 22. Confederate authorities were beginning to calculate the losses among Beauregard's and Johnston's forces. A tally published in the paper put the killed at 500 plus a thousand wounded and missing. This early count of Confederate casualties has been confirmed by historians of the battle of Manassas: 387 killed, 1582 wounded and 13 missing (William C. Davis); 382 K, 1465 W, 13 M (John Hennessy).

One of the slain was Colonel Gartrell's own son, sixteen-year-old Henry Clay Gartrell. According to Joseph T. Derry, author of the *Georgia* volume in *Confederate Military History*, young Henry "had insisted on following his father to the field and was killed in this battle." Actually, Henry had enlisted in Capt. Greenberry J. Foreacre's Atlanta Confederate Volunteers on May 31, and went with the unit to Virginia when it became Company B of his father's regiment, the 7th Georgia Infantry. Gartrell's agony over the fate of his son was magnified by his uncertainty as to it. In a report on his regiment's casualties dated four days after the battle, the colonel wrote, "Puckett and six of Capt. Foreacre's men were killed—my son among them." Yet another report, published by the *Intelligencer* on the 24th, claimed that the son had not been killed in action: "his son is severely wounded, and it is believed, has since died." This, too, was wrong. Following the battle, Henry had at least been strong enough to have been transported to Warrenton, a dozen and a half miles from Manassas battlefield, where townspeople took in many ailing soldiers. According to a South Carolinian, hundreds were in residences. Private Gartrell was received into the home of a gentleman named Rice W. Payne. But, alas, the young soldier succumbed to his wounds on July 28, a week after the battle. The *Intelligencer* on August 4 printed a brief notice, taken from the *Charleston Mercury*, which mentioned that Henry Gartrell's burial in a Warrenton cemetery had been "with military honors."[14]

Beyond Colonel Gartrell's loss, the list of Georgians fallen on the field was headed by Colonel Bartow, leader of the 8th Georgia, who had been elevated to brigade command before the battle (and who for this reason some believed had been promoted to brigadier general). Bartow's original company, the Oglethorpe Light Infantry of Savannah (Company B of the 8th), suffered five killed and thirty-eight wounded at Manassas; the *Intelligencer* named the casualties on July 26. The issue for that day reported that after Governor Brown called for public flags in the state to be lowered and for cannon-salutes to be fired, Mayor Whitaker took steps in compliance. "All the flags of the city were hoisted at half staff," the paper related, and "guns were fired every hour from sunrise to sunset." Because there was no artillery in the city, Whitaker appealed to the governor for a gun. One from the Cherokee Artillery (from Rome in northwestern Floyd County) was sent. Sgt. Max Van Den Corput was among the gunners serving the piece in its ceremonial firing—Van Den Corput would later command the Cherokee battery when it came again to Atlanta three years later.

The *Intelligencer*, to be sure, was less concerned with enemy casualties, but it kept track of reports of the Federal prisoners bagged in the battle and in the Confederate pursuit of McDowell's routed army. "650 prisoners were brought here to-night," it declared, citing a missive from Richmond, dated July 23. That day, in a little snippet at the end of a page-column, the *Intelligencer* offered its partisan opinion: "It is proposed to set the Yankee prisoners to work making shoes for our troops. Most of them are said to be fit for nothing else." That led the editor to lift the comment from the *Charleston Mercury* entitled "The Great Battle yesterday," which added another term of aspersion for the enemy. "The hireling hosts of our ruthless foes," it began, "after a desperate fight of ten hours, have been routed, at the point of the bayonet, by the Southern troops."[15]

The paper's battle reporting shrank alongside the dramatic letter of a member of the 7th, which it published on July 31. It was written by a private in Company B

("Confederate Volunteers"), James A. Bennett to his wife, relating his role in the recent battle. Apparently Mrs. Bennett shared it with the paper; editor Gaulding printed it in full. More, he added a very appreciative preface. "The following letter," he enthused, "from a Georgia volunteer to his wife in Atlanta, we conceive to be worthy of a place in every newspaper in the South." Gaulding was not just moved by Bennett's narration of the battle, but also by his manifest patriotism, devotion to duty and his sacrifice—he had been seriously wounded in the fight. "I received a shot just above the left hip, passing *through me*," the private informed his wife, dismissing it as "only a flesh wound." But Gaulding took it seriously (italicizing *through me*), declaring Bennett "a wounded, perhaps a dying soldier of the ranks."[16]

Gaulding was so moved by Bennett's account that at the end of the soldier's letter he remarked that he had created a fund for Bennett and his wife ("by this time she is on her way to Richmond," where her husband lay in hospital). "Think of the battle of Manassas—read the unaffected narrative of this brave soldier, and if only ten cents, send in your subscriptions," he urged. "Contributions should be marked, 'For J. A. B., of the Georgia 7th,' care *Intelligencer*, Atlanta, Georgia."

After such a dramatic letter, the editor apparently had little need of more. In a note printed beneath Private Bennett's letter, Gaulding acknowledged receiving letters from four other Atlanta soldiers, "corroborating the various accounts we have received by telegraph and from private sources."[17]

Telegraph and private sources could only provide so much news, and even then could not be counted on as consistently correct. Rumors were transmitted so freely that editors learned to print them with a standard caveat, "if true." Such was the case with an article in the *Intelligencer* of August 3, "Important if True." "There is a rumor that Beauregard has crossed the Potomac and cut off the supply of water between the water works and the City of Washington," it began. Gaulding relished the prospect of Northern troops in the city having to drink "the unhealthy (and sometimes) brackish water" of the Potomac River. The editor went further still, speculating on military possibilities based upon this unsubstantiated report. "If this rumor is confirmed," he declared, "it indicates that we are crossing the Potomac above Washington with the view of cutting off the retreat of Lincoln, his cabinet, congress, officers and army."

Beauregard's army in Maryland!? Gaulding let his Southern partisanship get the better of his journalistic judgement with the thought of Confederates bagging Lincoln—"one of the greatest captures ever known." "The idea of taking Lincoln, [Gen. Winfield] Scott and the entire brood, is too good to be realized," he admitted, especially since the idea came from unproven rumor. This would not be the last time that Gaulding and the *Intelligencer* let imagination race into print before confirmation could be had.[18]

The *Intelligencer*'s reporting of the war's first big battle tells us a lot, especially how difficult it was for editor Archibald Gaulding to patch together a cohesive narrative of what had happened in Virginia on July 21. We also observe the paper's duties to report casualties in regiments raised in the locality; to print letters from soldiers who had seen the elephant; and to trumpet the whole thing as a great feat of Confederate arms.

NOTES

1. James I. Robertson, Jr., *Civil War Virginia: Battleground for a Nation* (Charlottesville: University Press of Virginia, 1991), 8–9; "Virginia Has Seceded!" and "Virginia Seceded—Atlanta Jubilant," *ADI*, Apr. 19, 1861.

2. Robertson, *Civil War Virginia*, 18, 23.

3. "Concert" and "Concert for the Benefit of the Davis Infantry," *ADI*, June 1, 1861; "[By Request.] Dixie As Sung by the Atlanta Amateurs," *ADI*, May 29; "BRILLIANT OVATION!," *ADI*, June 9.

4. Reed, *History of Atlanta*, 115–16; Derry, *Georgia*, 31, 419; Garrett, *A & E*, vol. 1, 486, 500; "Seventh Regiment Georgia Volunteers," *ADI*, June 4, 1861; "Election of Officers," *ADI*, April 19; "Seventh Regiment," *ADI*, June 1; "To Arms! To Arms!!," *ADI*, June 5; "The Confederate Continentals . . . ," *ADI*, June 12.

5. "A little incident . . . ," *ADI*, June 12, 1861; Garrett, *A & E*, vol. 1, 501; Derry, *Georgia*, 40–41; "G. L. H.," *ADI*, June 5, 1862; Henderson, *Roster Confederate Soldiers*, vol. 2, 699–700.

6. Van Tuyll, *Confederate Press*, 78; "Proprietors," "Rates of Advertising," "Railroad Guide," "Professional Cards," "Go to McPherson & Co's Book Store," "Beware of Mineral Poisons," "Atlanta Intelligencer Book and Job Office," "Provisional Government of the Confederate States of America" and "Maryland Legislative Caucus," all in *ADI*, May 15, 1861; "Virginia News. From the Charleston Courier," *ADI*, May 17; "Raleigh Percussion Cap Factory" and "The Season of Love", *ADI*, May 18; "Views of the English Press," *ADI*, May 19; "Why Irishmen are not with the North," *ADI*, May 22; "The Battle of Buena Vista," *ADI*, May 30; "Proclamation to the People of the Confederate States," *ADI*, June 2, 4.

7. James W. Silver, *Confederate Morale and Church Propaganda* (Tuscaloosa: Confederate Publishing Co., 1957), 64; Harry S. Stout, *Upon the Altar of the Nation: A Moral History of the American Civil War* (New York: Viking, 2006), 85; "Day of Fasting and Prayer," *ADI*, June 9; "Mayor's Proclamation," *ADI*, June 12; "The Thirteenth," *ADI*, June 15.

8. Singer, "Confederate Atlanta," 90; van Tuyll, "Crucible of War," 7–10; "V.P.S.," "Our Virginia Correspondence," *ADI*, June 12, 1861; Warren Wilkinson and Steven E.

Woodworth, *A Scythe of Fire: A Civil War Story of the Eighth Georgia Infantry Regiment* (New York: William Morrow, 2002), 19, 27, 28; Henderson, *Roster Confederate Soldiers,* vol. 1, 961; Gerald Conti, "Seeing the Elephant," *Civil War Times Illustrated,* vol. 23, no. 4 (June 1984), 19; Joseph Allan Frank and George A. Reaves, *"Seeing the Elephant": Raw Recruits at the Battle of Shiloh* (Westport CT: Greenwood Press, 1989), 82, 84, 98; Mauriel Phillips Joslyn, ed., *Charlotte's Boys: Civil War Letters of the Branch Family of Savannah* (Gretna LA: Pelican Publishing, 2010), 15.

9. "By Telegraph," *ADI,* June 12, 1861; Stanley F. Horn, comp., *Tennessee's War 1861–1865 Described by Participants* (Nashville: Tennessee Civil War Centennial Commission, 1965), 18; *OR,* vol. 2, 82, 97; "Rates of Advertising," *ADI,* June 15; "Military Books," *ADI,* June 12; "To Military Companies," *ADI,* February 22; "Drums! Drums!!," *ADI,* June 15; "Georgia Made Swords," *ADI,* June 12.

10. "W. S. Bassford," *ADI,* June 19, 1861.

11. "Our Virginia Correspondence" and "A. W. H.," "Letter from Virginia," *ADI,* June 29, 1861.

12. James M. McPherson, *Battle Cry of Freedom: The Civil War Era* (New York: Oxford University Press, 1988), 339–45; "Battle at Manassas," *ADI,* July 23, 1861; "The Battle of Manassas," *ADI,* July 24; "VIRGINIA CORRESPONDENCE," *ADI,* July 30 (Letter of "N.B.W.").

13. [Leonidas W. Spratt], "Our Special Accounts from Richmond," *Charleston Mercury,* July 25, 1861; Andrews, *South Reports,* 83–84; James V. Murfin, "How Stonewall Got His Name," *Civil War Times Illustrated,* vol. 1, no. 4 (July 1962), 39–40; John Hennessy, "Stonewall's Nickname: Fact or Fable?," *Civil War,* vol. 8, no. 2 (March-April 1990), 10–17.

14. Richard Michael Allen, comp., *The 7th Georgia Volunteer Infantry Regiment, 1861–1865: A Biographical Roster* (El Dorado Hills, CA: Savas Beatie, 2018) 53, 261; "Prisoners and Losses," *ADI,* July 26; William C. Davis, *Battle at Bull Run: A History of the First Major Campaign of the Civil War* (Garden City NY: Doubleday, 1977), 245; John Hennessy, *The First Battle of Manassas: An End to Innocence July 18–21, 1861* (Lynchburg VA: H. E. Howard, 1989), 133–35; Joseph T. Derry, *Georgia,* vol. 6 of Clement A. Evans, ed., *Confederate Military History,* 12 vols. (Atlanta: Confederate Publishing Co., 1899), 419; L. J. Gartrell, "From the 7th Georgia Regiment," *ADI,* July 25; Terry L. Jones, "Lucius Jeremiah Gartrell," in William C. Davis, ed., *The Confederate General,* 6 vols. (Harrisburg PA: National Historical Society, 1991), vol. 2, 174; "List of the Killed and Wounded of the Atlanta Grays," *ADI,* July 24; "The Wounded and Killed," *ADI,* July 25; Horace H. Cunningham, *Field Medical Services at the Battles of Manassas (Bull Run)* (Athens: University of Georgia Press, 1968), 33–34; Henderson, *Roster Confederate Soldiers,* vol. 1, 846; "DEATH OF A YOUNG SOLDIER," *ADI,* August 8.

15. Lindsey P. Henderson, Jr., *The Oglethorpe Light Infantry: A Military History* (Savannah: Civil War Centennial Commission of Savannah and Chatham County, 1961), 17–18, 20; "List of Killed and Wounded," *ADI,* July 26, 1861; "Respect to the Honored Dead," *ADI,* July 26; "It is proposed . . . ," *ADI,* July 23; "The Great Battle Yesterday," *ADI,* July 24.

16. "Georgia and Virginia," *ADI,* July 31, 1861; George G. Kundahl, *Alexandria Goes to War: Beyond Robert E. Lee* (Knoxville: University of Tennessee Press, 2004), 305. The

Intelligencer signed the Atlanta private's missive to his wife, "J. A. B—t.," allowing one to confirm his identity as James Alexander Bennett from Henderson, *Roster Confederate Soldiers*, vol. 1, 844.

17. "News from Manassas," *ADI*, July 31, 1861.
18. "Important if True," *ADI*, Aug. 3, 1861.

5. Settling into War

THE *INTELLIGENCER* DID ITS PART to help the Confederate war effort in a number of ways. One meant promoting Southern manufactures over Yankee ones. Two months after Georgia's secession, the paper announced, "the time has come when Southern people should patronize Southern institutions." In so doing, it plugged a local hatmaker, J. M. Holbrook, as one who "makes as good hats as can be made in New York City." Holbrook's enterprise was thus commended to the paper's readers.

And in line with its admonition, "read unmistakable Southern newspapers," the editor on June 4 railed against Northern ones. "We hope we have seen the last of Northern journals," it announced; "no Southern man should even permit one of the things to enter his family." Indeed, the mere sale of such trash "ought to be an indictable offense." A week later, when it began serial publication of a novel entitled "The Soldier's Daughter," Gaulding promoted it as something Southern. It really was not, though. The author of this "beautiful romance," the pseudonymic Hendrick Conscience, was actually Flemish, but the translator was "a Southern writer." This made the composition far better than "the miserable cheap trash, heretofore circulated in Southern families by Northern papers." It followed that Northern textbooks were also to be shunned in the education of Southern schoolchildren. "No good English ever came out of New England," the *Intelligencer* asserted, lifting from the *Mobile Tribune*, as it called for qualified individuals to set to work preparing distinctly Southern texts for young readers.

It went without saying that Southern schoolchildren should be taught by Southern teachers. One of them complained to the *Intelligencer* about the salaries that parents were prepared to pay. "Now that the people are awaking from their slumber, and wish to employ southern teachers," the writer declared, "they wish to procure them very cheap." Southern teachers had spent a lot of money on their educations, but now that they were "expected to take the places of discarded Yankees," people expected to pay them less than they had Northern instructors. The writer, who signed himself "Teacher," implored Southerners not to be "blind to your own interest. . . . Give your deserving people the same opportunity . . . that you have given your Yankee teachers."[1]

To promote Southern literature, the *Intelligencer* at least occasionally featured it on its front page. The top right space came to be the spot for Southern war poetry that began to be penned and printed soon after the first guns cooled. American newspapers' practice of publishing poetry and essays as entertaining filler went back to colonial days. Even the most strait-laced journals of commercial news or political opinion found it convenient to leaven their pages with fiction and rhyme. The war prompted versifiers in both North and South to write poems (of wide-ranging quality), based on military victories, army heroes and patriotic themes. The South had only a few publications specializing in the arts, chiefly Richmond's *Southern Literary Messenger,* but also *Southern Field and Fireside* in Augusta. The former, for example, had published before the war much poetry by Edgar Allan Poe and Henry Timrod, the South Carolinian. But lesser poets usually sent their work to local newspapers, which welcomed such content. The better verses, by established writers, were then reprinted in papers across the South.

The *Intelligencer* at times also received compositions from local writers. One of them was Mary A. H. Gay of Decatur, who contributed a poem, "The Stephens Rifles," expressly for the *Intelligencer.* Thirty-three-year-old Mary Ann Harris Gay was a longtime resident of Decatur and a resilient Rebel. Her poetry celebrated the local boys whose company would become part of the Georgia Legion, organized in August 1861 by Col. Thomas R. R. Cobb of Athens. When the paper printed Gay's poem on July 30, the boys had not left for the front. "Go, Soldiers, go!," she thus began; "the time has come/When to linger were a crime/Leave your hearthstones and your homes/Your sires did in olden time." They would meet the enemy: "Death to every foe,/Who dares to provoke a Southern fight . . . and teach the Yankee minions/ that ye know your cause is right. . . . And when the War notes cease to sound/and the Vandals made to flee," the poetess concludes, "then, return with joyous bound/And our hearts will welcome thee."[2]

Publishing patriotic poetry was in keeping with the *Intelligencer*'s role as an organ of Confederate propaganda. Another service was that of providing readers news from the war front. One sees in the paper that the farther away the front, the harder it was to get reliable news. Such was the case with the battle of Springfield, or Wilson's Creek, fought on August 10 in southwest Missouri.

First came this message from St. Louis, which the paper printed on the 14th: "Thousands of rumors from Missouri. . . . Dispatches from Lyon to headquarters report a skirmish on Sunday last. Lyon was probably at Springfield." The message at least touched on the fact that Union Brig. Gen. Nathaniel Lyon commanded a small army based at St. Louis that he had led toward Springfield, two hundred miles to the southwest. There, on August 10, Lyon attacked a larger Southern force commanded by Sterling Price, a major general in the pro-Confederate Missouri State Guard. The Southerners repelled the Federals' assault, then advanced on their own. In the fighting Lyon was mortally wounded and his successor, Franz Sigel, ordered a retreat. More than a fourth of Lyon's 5,000 troops were killed, wounded or missing. The victorious Confederates lost nearly as heavily, some 1,230 casualties.

But this level of information was unknown to the *Intelligencer*. First word of the Union defeat actually came from a telegraphic item out of Indianapolis, where a Northern officer called for reinforcements to help out in Missouri: "a battle has been fought in Missouri. Lyon is slain; our army is in full retreat." The paper printed this on the 16th. Two days later, the *Intelligencer* could report on "our great victory" at Springfield, based on further messages from Little Rock. As usual the casualty numbers were wrong: "the enemy's loss from 2500 to 3000. Our loss from 300 to 400 killed and wound." Moreover, the magnitude of the Confederate victory was exaggerated: "A later dispatch says Segler's whole force captured and brought back." Brig. Gen. Franz *Sigel,* Lyon's second-in-command, in fact had not been captured, much less his "whole force." Still, the article properly conveyed the main message for Southern readers: "a complete rout of the enemy. . . . Gen. Lyon is dead; fell early in the contest. Glorious news."[3]

More reliable information came from Virginia—closer to home, and where many soldiers from Atlanta were stationed. On August 27 the *Intelligencer* printed another letter by "V. P. S." (Pvt. Vardy Sisson of the 8th Georgia) relating how the regiment was faring in Virginia. He mentioned that seven men of his company, the Atlanta Grays, had been captured at Manassas and were prisoners at Washington. When it published a long letter from Gustavus Orr, another member of the 8th Georgia, recounting the battle of Manassas, the paper had a local artisan render a map of the battlefield into a woodcut for printing as accompaniment to Orr's letter. The Manassas map would be a rarity for the *Intelligencer*. Nineteenth century technology allowed the publication of illustrations only after they had been engraved as woodcuts. In the North, *Frank Leslie's Illustrated Newspaper* and *Harper's Weekly* had the artists, engravers and printing supplies to publish woodcuts in every issue. In the Confederacy, only the *Southern Illustrated News* had the resources to print regularly woodcuts of generals, maps and other images (all of them rather crude by Northern standards). The *Intelligencer*, like other Southern newspapers of the time, was thus largely an illustration-less publication.

The *Intelligencer* served as both reporter and eulogizer of Atlantans who had fallen at Manassas. Among them was Dr. Bartley M. Smith, who owned a drug store with William L. Ezzard in the Concert Hall building at Peachtree Street and the downtown railroad. Smith, whom the *Intelligencer* termed one of Atlanta's "most public-spirited citizens," had enlisted in the Atlanta Grays as a lieutenant, and in the battle of July 21 had been wounded, subsequently succumbing in a Richmond hospital. When his remains were brought home, no less than Mayor Whitaker and his councilmen participated in the funeral procession to the City Cemetery on September 5. The Fulton Blues led the way, followed by Masons and firemen (Smith had been a member of the volunteer Fire Company No. 1). The paper even published a small diagram of how the six pallbearers would flank and carry the casket (another rare instance of its printing a woodcut illustration).[4]

Dr. Smith's funeral even had a marshal, C. R. Hanleiter—the same Cornelius Hanleiter who, with George Adair, had launched the *Southern Confederacy* in March 1861. By this time, Hanleiter had sold his half-interest to J. Henly Smith; Adair and Smith shared both ownership and editorship of the *Intelligencer*'s rival. Atlanta's two leading dailies—the *Commonwealth* limped behind as third—vied in reporting the war news, but in the midst of it was politics: Georgians were about to elect a governor. It soon emerged that the *Intelligencer* and the *Confederacy* backed different candidates. Whitaker and Gaulding favored Governor Brown's re-election; Adair and Smith supported Brown's opponent, Eugenius Nisbet, an attorney from Macon.

The *Intelligencer* voiced its support so strongly that on August 13 it ran an editorial denying that it was "Gov. Brown's organ." Most newspapers across the state threw their support behind Nisbet, criticizing Brown for his disagreements with the Davis administration over state rights. In fact, among the major dailies in Georgia, only the *Intelligencer* and the *Milledgeville Southern Federal Union* backed the governor. Just before election day, on October 1 the *Intelligencer* ran a rare front-page editorial, "To the Independent Voters of Georgia," laying out the reasons they should re-elect Governor Brown.

On Wednesday, October 2, election day, the governor took 46,493 votes,

Nisbet 32,802. Brown's victory allowed the *Intelligencer* on October 9 to chortle and congratulate itself about its political positions not only in this but also in previous elections, both state and national. "In 1850, it [meaning the newspaper] was a Southern Rights journal," Gaulding boasted, supporting a like-minded gubernatorial candidate then, and in 1853 and 1855. The paper had supported Joseph E. Brown in 1857, 1859 and '61. All of its picks were "men, who, like its present proprietors [Whitaker and Gaulding] were of the old Southern Right school."[5]

As war governor, Joseph E. Brown had an obligation to inform Georgians of their contributions to the cause. In early September he reported that so far, Georgia had raised more than thirty-two regiments and three battalions, totaling 30,000 "gallant Georgia troops." Two-thirds of them were serving at the time in Virginia. The governor professed his intent to send them clothing, shoes and blankets, but warned that the men would need more.

Echoing Brown's statement, the paper on September 10 printed an announcement from one N. J. Hammond that he had been informed by Capt. J. T. Lewis, commander of the Atlanta Grays, that his company in Virginia needed blankets for the coming cold weather. If family and friends of the soldiers pitched in, Hammond offered to forward the goods to Virginia. The *Intelligencer* published his notice in the interest of supporting the troops, which it did constantly. Earlier, for instance, it had lauded one "Mrs. W. T. Wilson, of our city, whose husband is now in the service of the Confederate States, in Virginia," for offering to knit socks for the soldiers if other ladies donated thread to her. "This may be considered by some as a very small thing," Gaulding commented, "but when cold weather comes on, it will make a poor soldier's heart glad to receive a good warm pair of home knit socks." "Who of our patriotic countrywomen," the editor asked, "will aid in this benevolent enterprise?"

In similar vein, the paper publicized the efforts of Mrs. Maria Westmoreland and her Ladies' Soldiers' Relief Society when they responded to the Atlanta Grays' need for winter clothing and sent 75 shirts, 75 pairs of pants and 75 pairs of socks. The men in Virginia were most grateful to get them. V. P. Sisson, who had written to the paper as "V. P. S.," was secretary of the Atlanta Grays when near Manassas, September 7, the company assembled in formal meeting. Captain Lewis read to the men the letter sent by Mrs. Westmoreland accompanying the donated apparel. "The letter was received with much enthusiasm," Sisson wrote, "and elicited from the company three hearty cheers for the noble women of our State who have anticipated our wants and so generously supplied them."

After the clothing was distributed, the officers and men passed resolutions of thanks and appreciation to Mrs. Westmoreland and the ladies of the relief society, making motion that they be sent to the Atlanta papers for publication. The *Intelligencer* readily complied.[6]

Maria Westmoreland was the spouse of Dr. Willis Westmoreland, who had volunteered in a company that became part of Col. Lafayette McLaws' 10th Georgia Infantry. Willis became regimental surgeon. His brother John, also a physician, had joined the Fulton Dragoons "as a private soldier" and gone to Virginia, as he explained in a letter to the *Intelligencer* in early September. By that time his medical skills had been recognized, and after his commission as a surgeon, Westmoreland had been sent to Williamsburg to take charge of the hospital which had been set up on the campus of the College of William and Mary. "My task before breakfast is to see the whole number of patients," he wrote in his missive, published on September 13, "which range from 100 to 150 or 160, and prescribe for them"—almost all of the cases involved sickness.

Readers of the paper learned that disease, more than enemy bullets, had laid low many Southern soldiers. "B.," an officer with a Georgia regiment in Johnston's army near Manassas, wrote to "Col. Gaulding" on October 2, mentioning "the great number of sick" in his regiment. Measles, mumps and typhoid fever were the ailments that had hospitalized 362 men—more than a third of the regiment. The officer explained how typical childhood diseases, measles particularly, prostrated rural soldiers who in childhood had never experienced them, but now as adults had been rendered dangerously ill. "It is astonishing the number of men that grow up to manhood without having measles and mumps," he observed sadly.[7]

With Southern soldiers dying in hospitals and preparing themselves for winter's cold, clearly this would not be a short war. The *Intelligencer* addressed the prospect in an editorial on October 5. "Appearances indicate that the war will be a protracted one," Gaulding ventured. Even though McDowell's army had been thrashed and driven back to Washington, the Yankees—driven by Republicans' thirst for vengeance and continued political power—now seemed committed to "a long, protracted, harassing, ignoble war." Confederates were ready, the editor asserted in another column a week later. The South's abundant agricultural resources would feed her armies for as long as the contest lasted. It did not even matter that the North had twenty million people and a military manpower exceeding the South's; "the South will never yield," even if the war lasted four more years. By that time, Gaulding predicted on October 11,

Lincoln and his Cabinet would be driven from power, probably replaced by "some military Chief" whose first task would be to sue for peace with the South, ending the war with recognition of Confederate independence.[8]

It was not agricultural richness alone that would provide for Confederate victory, but industry as well, even though Gaulding the previous May had had to concede that manufacturing was "in embryo" in the South. Still, the paper listed cotton manufactories across Georgia alone. It mentioned iron foundries in Atlanta and a woolen factory in Roswell "which is now making clothing for our soldiers." Cannon, shot and shell were being cast; percussions caps were being turned out in Macon. Atlanta herself had a large rolling mill making cannon; railroad cars were also being built in the city. "Holbrook's Hat Manufactory, in Atlanta, is doing its best and increasing rapidly," it declared, giving another little plug for one of the paper's advertisers. Across Georgia, tanneries and shoe factories "are full of work and increasing their capacity." Mark Cooper's Etowah Works was "constantly turning out the best quality of iron." "With these aids to independence, a climate and rich soil that will produce cotton, grain, sugar, molasses, and all kinds of fruit, in abundance, with cattle to supply our wants without stint," the editor proclaimed, "with an industrious and thriving population, what need have we of dependence on the Northern fanatics, our bitterest foes—our would be master and tyrants." Gaulding answered himself by declaring, "And who doubts our success?"[9]

Producers of military goods supported the paper with their paid advertising. "Drums! Drums!!" was the banner for an ad by H. Braumuller, offering brass and kettle drums "to any Military Company"; his enterprise was on Whitehall Street. McNaught, Ormond and Company made metal buckles "suitable for knapsacks, bridles, &c." The editors gave their own infomercials, as when they plugged Winship's Iron Works. "We had the pleasure yesterday, of looking through this magnificent establishment. It is going on admirably," the paper chirped, as it manufactured metal castings of all kinds. "Best of all, notwithstanding the increased demand for their manufactures," Gaulding added, "prices instead of being increased have been reduced. Patronize Southern enterprize and Southern capital. That is our motto."[10]

A longer war called for more men to volunteer, and Atlantans continued to step forth. In mid-October another infantry company was formed in the city, and this one took as its name that of the mayor (and co-owner of the *Intelligencer*). The paper of course hailed the formation of the Whitaker Volunteers, boasting that such patriotic service would entitle Atlanta to a nickname not only of the "Gate City," but of the "Volunteer City" as well. On October 28, Mayor Whitaker was present at the rail depot to send the company off with "a handsome stand of colors," as the *Intelligencer* reported the next day. The flag featured a lone star, with "The Whitaker Volunteers" around it on one side, and "Georgia Forever" around it on the other. The mayor's wife, Nannie, however, was not on hand to view the proceedings. She had given birth nine days before to the couple's son, "which event," Gaulding quipped, "was evidence that they had both not been neglectful of one duty which is incumbent upon fathers and mothers to raise soldiers for the service of the State."[11]

The *Intelligencer,* among the numerous urban and rural newspapers serving the Southland, prided itself on the speed with which it could deliver the news. In a self-promoting item offered in mid-October, the editor boasted that readers would always find "the *very latest telegraphic news*" in its pages. Each night the last wire dispatches were picked up at the city's telegraph office (just a few blocks away) and laid out in press for the morning issue. "Those who desire the *latest news,*" the paper claimed, "will not be disappointed if they seek for it under our telegraphic head" on the third page of each issue.[12]

The limitations of that telegraphic news were nonetheless to be seen in how the *Intelligencer* reported the Confederate victory in the battle of Ball's Bluff, Virginia, fought on October 21. First word came by wire from Richmond on Wednesday, the 23rd, which the paper published the next morning. Details were sparse: a fight had occurred near Leesburg on Monday; three Confederate regiments (8th Virginia, 17th and 18th Mississippi) had been engaged. The enemy had lost 1,000–2,000 men, including 600 captured. Gaulding inferred from these brief particulars that the battle had involved a "brilliant repulse," and "slaughter of the enemy."

Another telegram from Richmond on October 24 only provided information on some of the Union officers who had been captured in "the Leesburg battle on Monday." Total number of Federals captured ranged from 650 to 1,000; 525 prisoners had arrived in Richmond Thursday morning. The Confederates' toll of killed and wounded could not be determined.

A second wire that day added particulars. "The fighting was terrible on both sides"; the 8th Virginia had charged, captured a battery, and put the Federals to flight. The enemy panicked as they fled to the river; they "were slaughtered" and "the battle field was thick with the killed and wounded of the federals"; "hundreds were drowned" trying to get away. Col. Burt of the 18th Mississippi had been badly wounded. Still another telegram from Richmond on the 24th mentioned the name of the Confederate commander, "Col. Evans," and put the battle's casualties as 2,000 Federals killed, wounded and captured, as opposed to "not over two hundred" Southerners. More prisoners were arriving in Richmond, as well as Confederate wounded. "They say it is impossible to describe the scene, or to estimate the number of the drowned," according to the report telegraphed from the capital; "hundreds of the enemy were shot while swimming and struggling in the water . . . many of them drowned each other in their efforts to escape."

"Additional particulars" about the battle near Leesburg came from the *Richmond Dispatch,* one of five wartime dailies published in the capital, and one from which, along with the *Richmond Enquirer,* the *Intelligencer* drew news from exchanges. Yet in the end, informational details paled beside the battle's bottom line. As the *Dispatch* put it, "truly, Providence had once more prospered our cause. Our victory is glorious and complete."

Truly could the Confederate faithful believe that Providence was prospering their cause. In this spirit President Davis issued a proclamation setting Friday, November 15 as "a day of Fasting, Humiliation and Prayer throughout the Confederate States," the *Intelligencer* announced on November 7. Then, as with the president's first fast day proclamation in June, "virtually every Confederate paper" reprinted it, according to historian Harry S. Stout. Thus did the *Intelligencer* quote Davis' declaration: "I do hereby invite the Reverend Clergy and the people of the Confederate States, to repair on that day to their usual places of public worship, and to implore the blessing of Almighty God upon our arms."[13]

Whether the people's imprecations would indeed lead to Confederate successes was a question yet be resolved, but the Southern victories at Springfield, Mo. (August 10) and Ball's Bluff, Va. (October 21), coming on the heels of the "glorious victory" at Manassas, gave the *Intelligencer* editor good reason to be confident.

NOTES

1. "Hat Manufactory," *ADI,* Feb. 2, 1861; "Northern Papers," *ADI,* June 4; "Southern Literature," *ADI,* June 12; "The Mobile Tribune says . . . ," *ADI,* September 13; "Teacher," "Southern Inconsistencies—Education," *ADI,* December 28; "To the Authors of the South," *ADI,* August 10; Richard W. Iobst, *Civil War Macon: The History of a Confederate City* (Macon: Mercer University Press, 1999), 7, 102.

2. Mott, *American Journalism,* 55, 201, 391; Jay B. Hubbell, *The South in American Literature*

1607–1900 (Durham: Duke University Press, 1954), 464–66, 468, 523, 533; "M. A. H. G.," "For the Intelligencer. To the Stephens' Rifles," *ADI*, July 30, 1861; Mary A. H. Gay, *Life in Dixie During the War* (Atlanta: Charles F. Byrd, 1897 [3rd ed.]), 23.

3. "St. Louis, Aug. 13," *ADI*, Aug. 14, 1861; Albert Castel, *General Sterling Price and the Civil War in the West* (Baton Rouge: Louisiana State University Press, 1968), 41–47; William Riley Brooksher, *Bloody Hill: The Civil War Battle of Wilson's Creek* (Washington: Brassey's 1995); 236; "Indianapolis, Aug. 15," *ADI*, August 16; "Advices from Springfield via Little Rock," *ADI*, August 18.

4. "V. P. S.," "Our Virginia Correspondence" and "G. H. B.," "Richmond Correspondence," *ADI*, Aug. 27, 1861; Gustavus J. Orr, "The Eighth Georgia Regiment" and "Map of the Battle Field Near Manassas," *ADI*, August 18; Risley, *Civil War Journalism*, 31–32, 41; W. Fletcher Thompson, Jr., *The Image of War: The Pictorial Reporting of the American Civil War* (New York: Thomas Yoseloff, 1959), 20–23; "Dr. B. M. Smith," *ADI*, September 3; Williams, *Directory*, 136; "Funeral of Dr. B. M. Smith," *ADI*, September 3, 5.

5. Parks, *Joseph E. Brown*, 157–63; Louise Biles Hill, *Joseph E. Brown and the Confederacy* (Westport CT: Greenwood Press, 1972 [1939], 67–72; "Governor Brown and the Intelligencer," *ADI*, Aug. 13, 1861; "To the Independent Voters of Georgia," *ADI*, October 1; "The Atlanta Intelligencer," *ADI*, October 9.

6. "To the People of Georgia," *ADI*, Sept. 7, 1861; "The Atlanta Grays," *ADI*, September 10; "A Patriotic Lady," *ADI*, June 28; "Ladies Relief Society," *ADI*, September 12; Venet, *Changing Wind*, 49–50; "From the Atlanta Greys," *ADI*, September 13.

7. J. G. Westmoreland, "College Hospital. Williamsburg, Va., Sept. 8, 1861," *ADI*, Sept. 13, 1861; Derry, *Georgia*, 33; "B.," "Virginia Correspondence," *ADI*, October 15; Frank R. Freemon, *Gangrene and Glory: Medical Care during the American Civil War* (Madison NJ: Fairleigh Dickinson University Press, 1998), 37.

8. "The War," *ADI*, Oct. 5, 1861; "The Duration of the War," *ADI*, October 11.

9. "South," "Items of Southern Independence," *ADI*, May 22, 1861.

10. Venet, *Changing Wind*, 51; "Drums! Drums!!," *ADI*, July 30, 1861; "Manufacture of Buckles," *ADI*, September 1; "Winships' Iron Works," *ADI*, May 17.

11. "The 'Whitaker Volunteers,'" *ADI*, Oct. 22, 1861; "The Whitaker Volunteers—Flag Presentation," *ADI*, October 29: "MRS. NANNIE WHITAKER DEAD. Wife of Late Judge Jared I. Whitaker Passed Away Last Night. Funeral Tomorrow," *Atlanta Constitution*, Oct. 21, 1901.

12. "The Telegraphic News of the Intelligencer," *ADI*, Oct. 17, 1861; Davis, *What the Yankees Did to Us*, 89.

13. "BY TELEGRAPH. Expressly for the Intelligencer" and "The War News," *ADI*, Oct. 24, 1861; "BY TELEGRAPH. Expressly for the Intelligencer," "Further details of the Leesburg fight," and "One hundred and sixty more Federal prisoners," all in *ADI*, October 25; "From the Richmond Dispatch. Battle of Leesburg," *ADI*, October 27; Venet, *Changing Wind*, 47; "Day of Fasting and Prayer," *ADI*, November 7; "By the President—A Proclamation," *ADI*, November 7; Stout, *Upon the Altar*, 85.

6. The *Trent* Affair

SIX MONTHS INTO WAR, the *Atlanta Intelligencer* seemed to be faring well financially. Not only had advertising rates not been increased, but by early October front-page advertising had even been reduced to a column and a half. On October 4, the paper began devoting more than half of its first page to a long article printing the full text of a law recently passed by the Confederate Congress, the Sequestration Act. In it the C.S. government announced that it would sequester the property of "any alien enemy" of the Confederacy and use proceeds from its sale to reimburse C.S. citizens whose property had been damaged or destroyed by enemy forces. The paper reprinted the long text daily well into the month. Soon it gave over another big section of page one to a long letter addressed "To the Voters of the 8th Congressional District" by Col. Lucius Gartrell of the 7th Georgia Infantry, in which he discussed his possible candidacy for Congress. That letter, too, began to run daily. Meanwhile, though actual numbers are hard to find, the paper's circulation seemed to remain at least steady, as evidenced by the *Intelligencer*'s announcement that it had procured an agent in Newnan (thirty-five miles southwest of Atlanta) who would sell subscriptions and paid advertising to residents of Coweta County and vicinity.

Colonel Gartrell eventually decided to resign his commission and stand for election. Indeed, Wednesday, November 6 was a national election day for the Confederate Congress. The Confederate Constitution prescribed the number of representatives to serve from each state: Georgia was allotted ten seats (the largest number in the then-seven-state confederation). The Congress in May had set the first Wednesday in November 1861 for the election, in which also the people would have the opportunity to vote in confirmation of Jefferson Davis and Alexander H. Stephens as president and vice president. Because no political parties had emerged in the young republic, Davis and Stephens faced no electoral opposition.

Nevertheless, the prospect of even an uncontested plebiscite gave the

Intelligencer opportunity to voice enthusiasm for the Confederacy's two leaders. On July 6 the paper had on page two inserted a card reading,

FOR PRESIDENT,
JEFFERSON DAVIS,
FOR VICE PRESIDENT,
ALEX H. STEPHENS

And with it Gaulding editorialized, "we throw our banner this day to the breeze." The paper implied that it was among the first to recognize the two candidates' forthcoming election: "the initiative had to be taken by some one, and as well we as any body else." "We nail the flag to the head of our columns," the editor proudly declared, "having inscribed upon it the names of JEFF. DAVIS for President, and A. H. STEPHENS for Vice President." Indeed, until the election, the *Intelligencer* ran Davis' and Stephens' names regularly on its second page. It added others, as in its issue of September 29, under Davis' and Stephens' names it listed "FOR GOVERNOR, JOSEPH E. BROWN," as well as candidates for the Georgia House and Senate.

When election day neared, the *Intelligencer* reminded citizens to get out and vote, as all Georgia papers were doing. Nevertheless, most expected a small turnout, and some were even voicing negativism about it. Gaulding objected to the inference that "a *small vote* will be indicative of loss of interest in the cause of the Southern Confederacy, or a waning of united and determined purpose on the part of the South to achieve its Independence." On the contrary, the editor predicted that a diminutive turnout in Georgia would reflect the absence of a contested presidential election as well as the absence of 40,000 male citizens away from home in the army. And to those nabobs who equated small voter numbers with presidential unpopularity, the *Intelligencer* had words for them, too: "the great WASHINGTON himself, after the old Revolution, could not claim to have possessed more of the confidence of our fathers than do DAVIS and STEPHENS possess of our fathers' sons of the present day." For good measure, on Tuesday, November 5, the paper published one more reminder for the voters of Georgia to go to the polls on the morrow "and deposit their votes for the ticket pledged to the support of 'Davis and Stephens.'"

As it had done with the voting results for governor in October, the *Intelligencer* published tallies after November 6: Atlantans had cast 837 votes for Davis and Stephens. General Gartrell handily won his seat from Georgia's 8th Congressional District, defeating John A. Jones; among votes cast in the city, the margin was 625 to 97. Gartrell would serve only one term in the House, however, before returning to the army in 1864 as brigadier general.

The paper did not comment on the fact that more Atlantans had voted for a presidential slate that was unopposed than they had for a congressional race that was. The important consequence occurred on December 5 in Milledgeville. There, assembled before Governor Brown and both houses of the legislature, the state's twelve electors cast their votes for President Davis and Vice President Stephens.[1]

The co-owner of the *Intelligencer* and wartime mayor of Atlanta, Jared Whitaker, took on another job after Governor Brown's re-election: he was appointed commissary general for the "Georgia Army," with the rank of lieutenant colonel. The appointment may have been a patronage award for Whitaker's support in the recent political campaign; Archibald Gaulding, the *Intelligencer*'s editor, had been appointed by Brown as state surveyor general the previous August, to fill a death-caused vacancy. The *Intelligencer* was relatively mum on Whitaker's appointment—it announced the co-owner's new position in a one-sentence statement on November 5—perhaps to avoid chatter among other newspapers that had supported Judge Nisbet. But Whitaker's position was no sinecure; he resigned as mayor on November 25 to take on his new responsibilities. In his resignation letter to the City Council, Whitaker explained that he was leaving office "believing it inconsistent and contrary to true policy and true principle of Government to hold more than one office of profit at the same time." (A special election was held on December 11; Thomas F. Lowe was elected to succeed Whitaker.)

Chief among the new commissary general's duties was that of overseeing the distribution of such prized commodities as salt. Without refrigeration, both the civilian population and the army needed salt for packing and preserving meat. Salt prices were rising so fast in the autumn of '61, to twenty and twenty-five dollars a sack, that Governor Brown ordered Whitaker on November 20 to confiscate salt supplies in Atlanta, Columbus and Macon for use by Georgia troops, paying no more than $5 per sack. Accordingly, Whitaker on the 23rd issued an order to railroad agents in the city that they should not ship any salt "held or owned by speculators and traders," without permission. How the agents were to identify speculators' salt from any other was not prescribed, so when authorities prevented a farmer from obtaining salt for his personal use, the *Southern Confederacy* got editorially involved, "pouring the vials of his [the editor's] wrath upon the devoted head of the Commissary General," as the *Intelligencer* phrased it. This led to both Whitaker and Brown issuing clarifications that their orders were not intended to apply to "small lots for family use in the State." Needless to say, the *Intelligencer* defended Whitaker's and Brown's position against the criticism of "our neighbor of the Confederacy."[2]

While the former mayor of Atlanta was dispensing salt to Georgians, the company named after him was standing guard on the coast near Brunswick. The *Intelligencer*, still half-owned by Whitaker, published a list of the officers of the Whitaker Volunteers, which under Governor Brown's authority was helping to protect the state's borders as part of the 4th Regiment, 2nd Brigade, Georgia State Troops. Capt. M. W. Rasberry and 61 men from Atlanta were among them as Company C, according to the paper's reporting on December 12.

Whitaker's and Gaulding's paper voiced its support for distant journalistic colleagues when, in early December, it addressed "The Militia Law and the Newspapers." Tennessee legislators had introduced a bill exempting newspaper printers from compulsory militia service. The *Nashville Banner* endorsed the exemption in an opinion piece reprinted by the *Intelligencer*. So many printers had left their jobs to volunteer, the *Banner* explained, that "barely enough are left in this city to supply the actual need on our local papers." If further printers were taken away, papers in Tennessee's capital would suffer "embarrassment, to say the least." The *Intelligencer* closed the *Banner*'s article with the obvious: "the people must have the papers, and the papers must have printers."[3]

News came from elsewhere in the Southland. Telegraphic notices reported that a huge fire had broken out in downtown Charleston on the night of December 11, as the *Intelligencer* related on the 14th. "Towards midnight, the fire assumed an appalling magnitude," the paper stated. Whole blocks had been consumed; "great distress prevails among the poor families." Atlantans formed a committee to raise money to send to Charlestonians who had suffered as result of the big fire. By the day after Christmas, the committee was able to report $268.06 raised in donations from both businesses such as W. R. Herring & Co., the clothing manufacturers ($25) and individuals like Edward E. Rawson, the prosperous hardware merchant ($20). The paper printed a list of all contributions, including those of just 25 cents.

Atlanta had its own blaze shortly thereafter, when fire destroyed a small wooden building downtown between the Trout House hotel and Masonic Hall, just north of the railroad and the train depot. A visitor in the city, staying at the Trout House, lectured "the wealthy men of this city" in a column submitted to the *Intelligencer* and published on December 29. "Let every old combustible wood and pitch pine building around and about the Trout House, be torn down and brick ones in their place erected, and other parts in danger." The public-spirited suggestion was made so as to reduce fire-risk among the wooden structures downtown, but it fell flat. No such urban renewal project was undertaken in Atlanta until General Sherman's fires of mid-November 1864.[4]

News turned international when "the *Trent* affair" gripped both those in the North and South. The event pitted the United States against the British government over the rights of neutral vessels on the high seas. In the fall of 1861 the Confederate government sought to establish diplomatic relations with England and France. It thus dispatched James M. Mason, ex-U.S. senator from Virginia, and John Slidell, former Louisiana senator, to London and Paris as commissioners. Their trans-oceanic route began with a blockade runner from Charleston and passage to Havana. From there on November 8 a British steamer, *Trent,* was carrying them to the British West Indies when a U. S. warship, the *San Jacinto,* stopped the *Trent* and the Northern captain, Charles Wilkes, demanded that the two Southerners be handed over. The British reluctantly complied, and Mason and Slidell were taken to Boston.

Her Majesty's government, outraged, instructed Lord Richard Lyons, its minister in Washington, to demand the return of the two Confederate envoys, along with an apology. The British Cabinet was so worked up that Lyons was told to withdraw his embassy should Lincoln and his secretary of state, William H. Seward, refuse.

Lyons conveyed the British demand to Seward on December 19—the day after the *Intelligencer* broadcast its headline, "GOOD NEWS FROM EUROPE! ENGLAND INDIGNANT." Telegraphed news related that the British government regarded the seizure of Mason and Slidell to be an insult demanding reparations; "a dispatch dated Liverpool the 28th ult., says the excitement here over the stoppage of the *Trent* has been most intense, exceeding anything since the Crimean War."

On December 19, the paper opined on the diplomatic crisis, agreeing with the English that "a grosser outrage indeed was never perpetrated on the high seas, save in piratical cases."

Gaulding worried that the British would be taken in, somehow, by the Lincoln government, which it deemed "an enormous cheat, a great swindler and liar, and a curse to the civilized nations of the world."

In the end, Lincoln agreed to give up the jailed diplomats, the British accepted the concession, and the crisis which Confederates hoped would precipitate a war between Yankee Doodle and John Bull evaporated. The *Intelligencer*, reprinting a column on December 22 from the *Charleston Mercury*, would be proven wrong in prognosticating, "the capture of the Commissioners of the Confederate States from the deck of the British steamer *Trent*, on the 8th of November last, bids fair to be the turning point of the present war."[5]

Governor Brown's re-election, the Confederate victories at Springfield and Ball's Bluff, the Federals' seizure of Confederate diplomats and the prospect that the North and Britain might go to war—all of this pressing news justified the announcement by the *Intelligencer* on December 21 that its daily issue would henceforth appear in two editions a day. "The morning edition is kept open till 12 o'clock, at night, and contains all the Telegraphic Reports up to that hour," it announced. The evening edition would be held till 6 p.m. to catch all the available telegraphed news. Indeed, wired dispatches became all the more important as the national postal service began to sag in efficiency. The editors complained on December 13 that the exchanges with other papers on which it depended for timely news were arriving by mail irregularly: "our *daily* exchanges sometimes come to us in *showers*, three or four from the same office, at one time. Fault lies somewhere." For its part, the *Intelligencer* placed blame all the way to the top, upon the head of the C.S. postal service, John H. Reagan: "Postmaster General Reagan, in our opinion, is utterly deficient."[6] Nevertheless, the establishment of an evening edition in December 1861 showed that eight months into the war, the *Atlanta Daily Intelligencer* was thriving.

NOTES

1. "The Sequestration Act," *ADI*, Oct. 4, 1861; "To the Voters of the 8th Congressional District," *ADI*, October 11; Venet, *Changing Wind*, 51–52; "Agent for the Intelligencer," *ADI*, October 19; Marshall L. DeRosa, *The Confederate Constitution of 1861: An Inquiry into American Constitutionalism* (Columbia: University of Missouri Press, 1991), 136; Wilfred Buck Yearns, *The Confederate Congress* (Athens: University of Georgia Press, 1960), 42, 223; "We throw our banner . . . ," *ADI*, July 6; "For President . . . ," *ADI*, September 29; "The Election for President and Vice President of the Confederate states," *ADI*, November 1; "The Election on To-Morrow," *ADI*, November 5; "The Election on Wednesday," *ADI*, November 8; Ezra J. Warner and W. Buck Yearns, *Biographical Register of the Confederate Congress* (Baton Rouge: Louisiana State University Press, 1975), 99; "Milledgeville Correspondence," *ADI*, December 10.

2. Hill, *Brown and the Confederacy*, 68n.; "Appointment by the Governor," *ADI*, Nov. 5, 1861; "Executive Appointment," *ADI*, August 18; "To the City Council of Atlanta," *ADI*, November 27; Garrett, *A & E*, vol. 1, 496; Bryan, *Confederate Georgia*, 40; "Col. Whitaker—Salt and the Confederacy," *ADI*, Dec. 5, 1861; Ella Lonn, *Salt as a Factor in the Confederacy* (University: University of Alabama Press, 1965), 111, 214–16, 265n.2; Parks, *Joseph E. Brown*, 212.

3. "List of the Staff and Company Officers of the 4th Regiment, 2d Brigade, Georgia State Troops, Encamped at Wayneville, near Brunswick," *ADI*, Dec. 12, 1861; "The Militia Law and the Newspapers," *ADI*, December 6.

4. "Further from the Fire in Charleston," *ADI*, Dec. 14, 1861; Robert N. Rosen, *Confederate Charleston: An Illustrated History of the City and the People During the Civil War* (Columbia: University of South Carolina Press, 1994), 86; "[Communicated.] Atlanta, Dec. 26th, 1861. Messrs. Gaulding & Whitaker," *ADI*, December 27; "Fire!," *ADI*, December 29; "For the Intelligencer. Trout House. Atlanta, December 28, 1861. Messrs. Editors," *ADI*, December 29.

5. Norman B. Ferris, *The Trent Affair: A Diplomatic Crisis* (Knoxville: University of Tennessee Press, 1977), 3, 5, 8, 21–29, 44, 50; D. P. Crook, *Diplomacy During the American Civil War* (New York: John Wiley and Sons, 1975), 48, 50; Alfred P. Grant, *The American Civil War and the British Press* (Jefferson NC: McFarland, 2000), 67–69; "By Telegraph. Expressly for the Intelligencer. Good News from Europe! England Indignant," *ADI*, Dec. 18, 1861; "Excitement in England," *ADI*, December 19; "From the Charleston Mercury. Notes of the War. The Mason-Slidell Embroglio," *ADI*, December 22.

6. "With a View to Meet the Earliest Possible Mail Arrangements, from Atlanta, Two Editions . . . ," *ADI*, Dec. 21, 1861; "Post Office Department," *ADI*, December 13.

7. Reporting Defeat

MILL SPRINGS

ON THE FIRST DAY OF 1862, the paper gave its printers New Year's Day off, so there was no issue for January 2. The next morning, though, the *Intelligencer* announced that it was now commencing its eighth year as a daily newspaper in Atlanta. "Other enterprises of a similar character have been attempted in this city," editor Gaulding explained, "but with the exception of the recently established '*Confederacy,*' they have all failed to survive." The *Intelligencer*, on the other hand, had shown its staying power through the past seven years, and predicted that it would weather the next seven, even in time of war. "Here, as well as in every other city of importance in the South, newspaper expenditures have been largely increased," Gaulding continued, and "even the most prosperous journals have had to curtail their expenses and proportions." The *Intelligencer* had not trimmed back its size, nor would it, the editor pledged; "what it has been it still will be, and no effort will be spared to make it ever acceptable to its old and its tried friends."[1]

With the opposing forces in Virginia stationed in their winter quarters, war news from that front was in short supply. The *Intelligencer*'s "Telegraphic News" column for January 3 included several items from Richmond, but they pertained to the release of Mason and Slidell, the Confederate diplomats who had been seized and jailed by the Federals. Even for these slim dispatches, Gaulding and his typesetters had had to wait till midnight to receive them from the telegraph office, and it was not till almost 3 a.m. on the 3rd "before they could be deciphered, '*set up,*' by the compositor and put to press." This brought complaint from the editor the next day. "It is not very pleasant to be sitting in an office from eight to twelve o'clock at night," he groused, "waiting the slow performance of the wires, or rather of those who control them." With this latter poke, Gaulding was referring to William H. Pritchard.[2]

Pritchard had organized a limited telegraphic news service after the Confederacy had been cut off from Northern wire services in the spring of 1861. But editors soon found fault with Pritchard's operation, as did Gaulding in January 1862. "We are satisfied that our friend PRITCHARD, at Richmond, closed his work early enough for us to receive his favors between the hours of nine and ten," the editor assumed, but not to get Pritchard's wire dispatches till after eleven o'clock was just too late. This, he concluded, "we do not exactly understand, and must complain at, until we hear some good reason given for it."

Other papers were complaining as well. Several weeks after Gaulding criticized Pritchard for his delayed telegrams from Richmond, the *Intelligencer* reprinted from the *Charleston Courier* its criticism of the slothful pace of news telegraphed from Nashville. So slow were the wired dispatches it received, the paper claimed, that sometimes the mail actually beat them. It made the point by reporting that on the previous Tuesday, January 21, its office had received by mail Nashville newspapers dated the 19th; mail had taken two days to reach Charleston from the Tennessee capital. "About five hours later, the *Courier* continued, "we received a dispatch giving Nashville reports and rumors of the 18th inst." In other words, it had taken *three* days for telegraphed news to arrive. Needless to say, the *Courier* did not use this old dispatch, as its editor punned, "we have endured enough of this sort of *dispatch*."

Editors across the Confederacy agreed that something had to be done. The *Charleston Mercury* called for a meeting whose purpose would be "making arrangement for a permanent, extended, better organized, and, at the same time, more economical news agency." Other papers signed on to the idea of this editorial convention, which it was decided would be held in Atlanta in mid-March. Both the *Intelligencer* and the *Southern Confederacy* pledged their participation, as did eleven other newspapers: two in Savannah; both of Augusta's dailies; two from Nashville; and one each from Memphis, Columbus, Montgomery, Selma and as far away as Vicksburg. Gaulding promised to do his part to "make their stay here as agreeable as possible."[3]

Hastening the transmission of telegraphic news could not change the situation when that news reported Confederate defeat, or even forebode it. Such was the ominous tone of an anonymous correspondent in Nashville who composed a short report on January 13, published in the *Intelligencer*'s "Telegraphic" column two days later. It warned, "A private dispatch received here this evening states that a large Federal force is marching on Burkesville to flank Gen. Zollicoffer. Reliable intelligence received which excites much anxiety for the safety of

Zollicoffer's command." The item was correct. Union Brig. Gen. George H. Thomas was leading 5,000 troops against some 4,000 Confederates quartered near Logan's Cross Roads and Somerset, in southeast Kentucky. Brig. Gen. Felix K. Zollicoffer, their commander, warned his superiors that a quarter of his men had no weapons and that many of the rest were armed with ancient flintlocks and shotguns.

With good reason, then, the *Intelligencer*'s source for this telegraphic report confessed "much anxiety for the safety of Zollicoffer's command." Things turned worse when Zollicoffer's superior, Maj. Gen. George B. Crittenden, ordered an attack on Thomas for January 19. The Federals held, General Zollicoffer was killed early on, and a Union counterattack broke the Confederate line. Thomas' troops pursued the retreating Rebels for ten miles, overrunning their camp, capturing a thousand horses and mules, more than a hundred wagons and a dozen cannon. Casualties in the three-hour battle came to 40 killed, 207 wounded and 15 missing for Thomas; 125 killed, 309 wounded and 95 missing for Zollicoffer. General Crittenden was subsequently accused of drunkenness on the battlefield, and was allowed to resign from the army.

There was little way to varnish this disaster, but the *Intelligencer* tried it anyway. Telegraphic dispatches printed on January 24 reported "Zollicoffer's defeat and death"; the Confederates' repulse "with heavy loss"; and the fact that they had been "utterly routed, losing all their artillery, baggage, equipments, &c." Editor Gaulding nevertheless added at the end of this article, "Our readers will see that the foregoing is the *Federal* account of the whole affair. It is doubtless greatly exaggerated.—Ed. INT."

January 19, 1862, the day of the battle at Mill Springs, happened to be the anniversary of Georgia's secession from the Union. The *Intelligencer* observed the occasion by forecasting Southern victory in its war for political self-determination. "We see foreshadowed our Independence won" at some point in the future, Gaulding affirmed, with "the 'Confederate States of America' freed from Yankee thraldom, Yankee domination, Yankee trade, and Yankee associations, but at peace, and in fraternity with the rest of mankind."[4]

Such a prospect was certainly blissful to Archibald Gaulding, but in the meantime there were other matters to tend to, including the choosing of a new city executive. The mayoral election, held on January 15, pitted attorney James M. Calhoun against Thomas L. Thomas, Methodist minister and former city councilman. In the Calhoun-Thomas contest the *Intelligencer* took no side, editorializing the day before the election that "they are both well qualified for the office." Election day was a rainy one, and voter turnout was low. The paper published the tallies on the 17th: Calhoun, 530; Thomas, 256.[5]

The *Intelligencer* had barely taken note of Lincoln's announcement, April 15, 1861, that the Union navy would establish a blockade of Southern seaports. Indeed, most Southerners were not worried about it. Many Confederates were convinced that England, starved for Southern cotton, would intervene on their side, demanding free and open trade. (The *Intelligencer* opined on January 22 that Southerners would have to plant less cotton and raise more foodstuffs "unless the blockade is raised.") Moreover, they reasoned, how could the small, outdated U. S. Navy cover a coastline from Virginia to the Rio Grande—3,500 miles, the distance from New York to Liverpool?

Gradually, however, Confederates came to conclude that the blockade was real, and was having an effect. Union warships hovered outside Charleston, Mobile, New Orleans and as far away as Galveston, blocking vessels from entering or leaving. After Federal troops landed on Tybee Island, Savannah was effectively closed as a port. Other harbors, however, especially on the South Atlantic coast such as Wilmington, bustled with blockade runners. The Confederate government encouraged private ship-owning companies to carry out cotton to relatively nearby ports in Bermuda, and bring back munitions and commercial goods demanded by the public. Because profits from the sale of such items were so high, investor-owned companies took considerable risks for the fabulous returns that even one successful run could bring.

With time, the Union navy added more blockaders outside key ports, gradually pinching the availability of importable goods. After Northerners sank a number of old ships loaded with rock at the entrance to Charleston harbor in an attempt to obstruct the shipping channels (the "Stone fleet" as it was called), the *Intelligencer* denounced the action as "work of the Northern barbarians," earning "the anathemas of the civilized world." "A just retribution," the editor hoped, "will soon overtake the dastardly wretches." But such aid would probably not come from England, as Gaulding cautioned in an editorial, "Self-Reliance of the South," printed on January 30. Observing that many Southerners "look with a longing eye to help from England, trusting that she will soon come to our aid, remove the blockade, and make war with Lincoln," the editor warned that such hopefulness was misplaced and possibly harmful to the Confederate cause. "Let us have no more of this," he asserted, "but let us be self-reliant and we will prove invincible and victorious."[6]

Beyond the lofty virtues espoused in Confederate propaganda—a poem on page one of the *Intelligencer*'s issue of January 15 urged the South's "gallant heroes [to] go and fight,/In honor for our virtuous right"—there always lurked the unseemly shadow of slavery and racism. On that same page, the paper ran an editorial complimenting a recent issue of the *Southern Literary Messenger*, the Richmond-based journal. Among the articles singled out for mention was that by William H. Holcombe, entitled "Characteristics and Capabilities of the Negro Race." Dr. Holcombe's essay, the paper declared, "should be read by every man" as it "would satisfy all that 'the negro is not a white man with a black skin,' but 'a permanent variety of the human race,' with 'physical, ethnical, and psychological peculiarities which differentiate him from all other races of man.'" The *Intelligencer* closed its endorsement of the *Literary Messenger* by mentioning its Richmond publisher (Macfarlane & Ferguson), its editor (George W. Bagby) and adding "the subscription price is only $3 per annum."[7]

Prices mattered, as newspaper publishers throughout the Confederacy battled rising costs and struggled to maintain subscribers and advertisers. Editor Gaulding took note of this in mid-January when he extended well-wishes to the *Charleston Courier* as it entered its sixtieth year of operation. But there was a cautionary message, too, as he commented that the *Courier* was beginning the year "with a reduced size—the result it says of 'constantly increasing difficulties and expenses attending the issue of a newspaper.'"

"Increasing difficulties and expenses," indeed. In addition to loss of labor when printers and other staff members volunteered for the army, newspaper publishers faced rising prices for the one product it had to have: paper. At the start of the war, according to an early history of journalism, the South had all of fifteen paper mills, whose combined output could furnish enough newsprint to fill the needs of only half of its papers. A more recent scholar, Ford Risley, counts at least twenty-five paper plants. The shortfall in product had once come from the North, which was no longer possible; now it could be brought through the blockade, but that was increasingly difficult. The only remedy was to reduce the size of the printed pages. The *Charleston Courier* began doing this in September 1861. Its sister publication, the *Mercury*, complained two months later that the war "has made paper scarce and dear." One reason had to do with the country's railroads. Demands of military transport occupied the Southern train network, such that paper which the *Mercury* expected from North Carolina could not be shipped. Other papers were similarly affected. In late September the *Macon Telegraph* announced that it was shrinking its page size due to shrinking revenue. "For several months," explained editor Joseph Clisby, "the demand for advertising has diminished, and must continue to diminish with the diminishing amount of merchandise soliciting a market."

The problem hit home when the *Intelligencer*'s competitor, the *Southern Confederacy*, announced in early October '61 that it was not only reducing in size by half, but was being forced to print on brown paper. Other newspapers were even more colorful. The *Charleston Mercury*, pinched for regular newsprint, started appearing in January 1862 on sheets of "a lovely fuschia paper," as described by Mary Elizabeth Massey, chronicler of Confederate shortages and substitutions; "later the color was toned down to a dusty salmon."

For the time being, Gaulding and Whitaker were able to resist resorting to such measures. But the paper warned its readers, "newspapers have more to contend against now to keep up appearances . . . than any other branch of business in the South." "Subscribers in arrears should bear this in mind," it concluded, "as well as advertisers."[8]

Despite the ever-tightening blockade, the failure of England and France to come to the South's aid, and battlefield reverses such as Mill Springs, confidence voiced in ultimate Confederate victory remained unshaken in the *Intelligencer*. Similarly, paper shortages and a clunky telegraphic news service did not diminish the paper's determination to stay afloat.

In the midst of all this, editors could always find some jollity, especially in the pages of exchanged newspapers. On January 31 the *Intelligencer* reprinted from the *Athens Banner* a little story entitled "A GOOD BEGINNING." The *Banner* told how "a young boy from the country" had come to the paper's office and shelled out, in nickels and dimes saved up for nearly a year, enough money to subscribe to the newspaper. The Athens staff was impressed; lads often used their money, the *Banner* judged, for candy, or (worse) tobacco and alcohol. Instead, this one wanted to read his local newspaper; he told the staff that after working all day, he read it "by a light-wood knot fire at night." "We conversed with him a few minutes," the article explained, "and were astonished at the knowledge he displayed of the history of the present war." "If we both live long enough," the writer forecast, "we expect to see him President of the Confederate States. Hurrah for the light-wood knot boy!"[9]

NOTES

1. "The New Year," *ADI,* Jan. 1, 1862; "The Daily Intelligencer," *ADI,* January 3.

2. "Landing of Federals—Mason and Slidell," *ADI,* Jan. 3, 1862; "Our Telegraphic News," *ADI,* January 4.

3. Wilson, "Confederate Press Association," 160; "Our Telegraphic News," *ADI,* Jan. 4, 1862; "The Telegraph," *ADI,* January 24; "Editorial Convention," *ADI,* January 26.

4. "By Telegraph. Expressly for the Intelligencer. Kentucky News," *ADI,* Jan.15, 1862; Lowell H. Harrison, *The Civil War in Kentucky* (Lexington: University Press of Kentucky, 1975), 16–17, 24–27; "By Telegraph. Terrible Battle in East Tennessee [*sic*]. Second Dispatch," *ADI,* January 24; "The Day of Secession," *ADI,* January 19.

5. "Our City Election," *ADI,* Jan. 14, 1861; "Our City Elections," *ADI,* January 17.

6. Stephen R. Wise, *Lifeline of the Confederacy: Blockade Running During the Civil War* (Columbia: University of South Carolina Press, 1988), 13, 25, 28, 51, 612, 63; "The Cotton Crop," *ADI,* Jan. 22, 1862; Rosen, *Confederate Charleston,* 86; "Lincoln's 'Stun Fleet'" and "Self-Reliance of the South," *ADI,* January 30.

7. "TO THE SOUTHERN SOLDIERS OF GEORGIA," and "THE SOUTHERN LITERARY MESSENGER," *ADI,* Jan. 15, 1862.

8. "The Charleston Courier . . . ," *ADI,* Jan. 15, 1862; Griffith and Talmadge, *Georgia Journalism 1763–1950,* 67; Risley, *Civil War Journalism,* 109; Andrews, *South Reports,* 42; van Tuyll, *Confederate Press,* 9; William Herbert Wilken, "As the *Telegraph* Saw It: A Study of the Policy of the Macon *Daily Telegraph (And Confederate),* 1860–1865," master's thesis, Emory University, 1964, 11; Mary Elizabeth Massey, *Ersatz in the Confederacy: Shortages and Substitutes on the Southern Homefront* (Columbia: University of South Carolina Press, 1952), 140.

9. "A GOOD BEGINNING," *ADI,* Jan. 31, 1862.

8. The Fall of Fort Donelson and Nashville

IN THE WINTER LULL before the start of the 1862 military campaign season, *Intelligencer* editor Archibald Gaulding had an opportunity to reflect on the news he had been receiving in a column entitled, "REPORTS! RUMORS!" In brief, this experience invited skepticism. "The reports from 'reliable gentlemen,' passengers on railroads, and from other sources, that reach us in the quiet of our *sanctum*," Gaulding explained, "absolutely confuse and astonish us.... We have learned to be patient, and wary of such reports, and would advise our readers to be so too." He proceeded to cite some of the "news" that had turned out to be false and incorrect. "It may be that *St. Louis* has been taken by the gallant Price." (Rumor!) By the end of January 1862, Sterling Price, commander of the Missouri State Guard, had been pushed out of Missouri into northwestern Arkansas. "It may be that the enemy have been defeated at Bowling Green," Gaulding continued. No, the enemy had not. After the Confederate defeat at Mill Springs in southeast Kentucky, Gen. Albert Sidney Johnston had far too few troops to launch an offensive at Bowling Green, in south central Kentucky.

"It may be that other victories have been won," Gaulding conjectured, "but our telegraphic 'News Agent' tells us nothing about it, nor do our exchanges from the localities of the point at which the victories have been won say anything about them." In the absence of confirmable news, what was an editor to do? *Print the rumor.* "Rumor confirms rumor," Gaulding complained, "and yet, we of the press still remain indebted to nothing but rumor for all these reports." Clearly the *Intelligencer*—and probably the rest of the Southern wartime press—was in a predicament. His paper, Gaulding related, had "an earnest desire to be considered a *reliable* newspaper, in the communication of news to our readers." Yet the best he could do, given the uncertain flow of reliable news, was to remain "incredulous and wary" about the war "news" that he received.[1]

These problems worsened in the winter of 1861–62, when long-distance news channels were challenged to report events in northwest Tennessee. The nature of telegraphic reports—brief to the point of skimpiness, due to cost of every word transmitted—meant that readers in Atlanta were denied background information for such items as that which ran in the *Intelligencer* on January 19: "private dispatches report that the Federals are in force this morning between Fort Henry and the Tennessee river. There was some firing, but the Federal balls did not reach the fort." A short second paragraph added, "Advices from Fort Donelson say that Gen. Tiergham feels confident of his ability to defend Forts Donelson and Henry."

Where were Forts Henry and Donelson, and how were the Federals moving against them? And who was "Gen. Tiergham"? For this story on page three, the *Intelligencer* could not offer contextual information, for it had none.

The Mississippi, running through the heartland of the Confederacy, was a logical invasion-route for Union forces, but there were other rivers, too. The Tennessee and Cumberland both flowed out of the Great Smoky Mountains, traversing Tennessee, north Alabama and western Kentucky before emptying into the Ohio River. To forestall the obviously impending Union advance up the two rivers, Tennessee governor Isham G. Harris had ordered engineers to find sites for fortifications and water batteries. On the Cumberland, eleven miles south of the Kentucky line and 75 miles downriver from Nashville, a steep bluff on the west bank was chosen for a large earthwork. It would take the name of Donelson, after Brig. Gen. Daniel S. Donelson, who helped supervise its construction. A dozen miles to the west flowed the Tennessee northward; on its eastern bank Confederates selected a site for another fort, this one named for Tennessee senator Gustavus A. Henry.[2]

Most observers knew that the Federals would soon move on the twin river forts. Union Maj. Gen. Henry Halleck, commanding at St. Louis, in late January ordered Brig. Gen. Ulysses S. Grant and Flag Officer Andrew H. Foote to advance together and capture Fort Henry. Grant commanded at Cairo, Illinois, where the Ohio River joined the Mississippi; Foote commanded the Federals' Western Flotilla.

As Grant and Foote's expedition neared its objective, news was slow to come in to the *Intelligencer* offices. A brief telegraphic report, dated "Nashville February 5," indicated that "the enemy fired about 40 shots" at Fort Henry, "but no damage was done." Another item, sent from Memphis on the 6th, reported that 20,000 Federals were landing near Henry, eight gunboats were coming upriver, and the water was rising rapidly. Still another, also from Memphis on February 6, gave the first inkling of fighting at Henry: "Dispatches from

Danville at 2 o'clock, P.M., state that firing had commenced at Fort Henry at 12 o'clock M. [Noon]. One hundred and fifty guns had been fired—the result was unknown. The firing had ceased."

Then came the bad news by a wire from Clarksville, Tenn., dated February 7: the report stated that "Fort Henry has fallen into the hands of the enemy, and that our forces were retreating to Fort Donelson—gunboats at Danville— The Tennessee River Bridge has been destroyed by the Federals—no further particulars." Another brief telegraphed item mentioned that the Federals had taken the fort after two hours' fighting.[3]

A later dispatch from Nashville, "Further Particulars of the Fort Henry Fight," filled in a few more details for the *Intelligencer* on the 9th. "It is reported that Fort Henry is inundated," the report declared. This was not only true; it proved to be decisive. The fort had been built on low ground to begin with, and now the Tennessee was at flood stage. On the morning of February 6, a Confederate artillery officer actually entered the fort by boat. As Northern gunboats were steaming closer to bombard the fort, Brig. Gen. Lloyd Tilghman concluded it could not be held, so he sent most of his men marching for Fort Donelson. Tilghman stayed behind with a few men to fire some cannon shots at the seven enemy ships. After just a few hours' artillery fire (during which Confederates actually disabled one of Foote's vessels), Tilghman lowered the fort's flag in surrender.

"Not many lives lost at Fort Henry," the *Intelligencer*'s report continued, which was true, both because of the brevity of the "battle" and because there were comparatively few lives within the fort to be lost. The action had ended so quickly that Grant's infantry, landed at a distance, had not even gotten into position when Tilghman struck his colors.

"Gen. Tilghman, Maj. Gilmer, Capt. Miller, and about 80 officers and men surrendered with the Fort." Which was also true—partly. Maj. Jeremy Gilmer, Confederate engineer with the garrison, had escaped before the fort's capitulation (albeit on foot). There was no "Capt. Miller"; rather, Capt. Jesse Taylor was among the surrendered garrison. Writing after the war, Taylor judged that "the number captured, including Tilghman and staff, hospital attendants and some stragglers from the infantry, amounted to about seventy." Flag Officer Foote, who accepted Tilghman's surrender, captured not only the fort's seventeen mounted guns, as a recent chronicler of the battle, Timothy Smith, has written, but "an entire Confederate field battery of six guns, Culbertson's Tennessee battery, captured when the miry roads and need for haste caused the artillerymen to abandon their cannon," as they raced for the safety of Fort Donelson.⁴

The Confederates' bad news from Tennessee had to be digested, and commented on. This the *Intelligencer* attempted to do in an editorial titled, "The War Cloud," printed on February 11. Gaulding acknowledged the fact that Fort Henry had indeed fallen to the enemy. "Well, what of that?" he asked, in the developing pattern of Southern newspaper editors minimizing reports of Confederate defeats. He asked the question of whether the fort could have been successfully defended. "It could not," he answered, "and we shall show why. . . . We only wonder that it was defended at all." "Far better would it have been," the editor concluded, "had it been destroyed by our own forces, and its guns and ammunition removed to some point, where they could have been of more service."

Despite the infelicitous intelligence concerning Fort Henry, the *Intelligencer*'s editor remained upbeat. "We are not discouraged by these successes of the enemy," he reasoned, as "they will rouse our people to action—to a more determined resistance." "The war-cloud is lowering on the South," Gaulding declared, "and recent events demand resolution, *courage,* ACTION! . . . the time to 'try men's souls' is not coming, but *has come,* and we *feel* that all true Southern men are ready, now, to 'dare all that man dares do' for liberty, and life, and freedom of Yankee tyranny."

As if that were not enough, the editor followed up with another column of exhortation and reassurance the very next day. "Reverses have recently come upon us," he repeated. People were becoming despondent, but Gaulding urged them to be strong in spirit. "We cannot expect in the conflict in which we are now engaged, to be victorious in every battle," he reasoned; therefore, "let not our faith be shaken." "Our cause is just," he counseled; "no reasonable man can doubt this. It may cost treasure, it may cost blood, but Southern arms must ultimately triumph."⁵

Yet the enemy was approaching Fort Donelson. From Nashville, dated the 12th, came telegraphic word that a Northern gunboat had neared the fort and lobbed some shells. "The Federals have landed in force," the report read, "and a battle with light artillery commenced this evening." This was not quite true; on February 12 Northern vessels had been seen approaching the fort, but they did not commence firing. And Grant's infantry had not "landed"; they were marching overland from Fort Henry. The Union column, fifteen thousand strong, neared Donelson by the end of the day.

Inside the earthen fortification were seventeen thousand Southerners under the command of Brig. Gen. John B. Floyd, a former United States Secretary of War with no military experience. The "Engagement at Fort Donelson," as the battle was announced in the *Intelligencer*'s "BY TELEGRAPH" column on February 15, began heating up two days earlier, on the 13th. Only one Northern warship, the ironclad *Carondelet*, had arrived, and it spent the day trading long-distance shots with the Confederates' water batteries. Ashore, General Grant's infantry moved into position along the length of the Rebels' line of entrenchments. At places, Union troops probed the strength of those works, and at one point an attack not authorized by Grant was repulsed with considerable loss to the Federals. For his part, General Floyd was content to stay in his defensive works as the two sides exchanged artillery and sharpshooter fire. By the end of the day Fort Donelson was effectively surrounded by Grant's infantry. A bolder Southern commander might have counterattacked before the Federals dug in and got stronger. And this they did during the day: steamers brought fourteen fresh infantry regiments to join Grant's army. Flag Officer Foote was likewise bringing three more ironclads and two wooden gunboats, which arrived late that night.

The *Intelligencer*'s telegraphic reports, however, were far from ominous in reporting these developments. "The enemy keeps at a respectful distance," read one wire from Nashville on the 13th, bearing the time of 11:30 a.m.; "the field artillery is engaged all along the lines at Fort Donelson." An update came three hours later: "we have so far repulsed the enemy on the points of our line. Our loss is small. The gunboats have retired—we think they are severely injured. Our men are in fine spirits."

A final dispatch on the 13th cheerily announced, "the day is almost past, and we still hold our own—have repulsed the enemy; driven back his gunboats; and whipped him by land and by water." "He still lies around" it added, "and will probably attack us to-morrow again."[6]

Journalists should know the reportorial danger of pronouncing judgement on a story still unfolding, but that is what occurred when the *Intelligencer* on February 16, in its "BY TELEGRAPH" section, ran an article that began with the bold headline, "CONFEDERATE VICTORY AT FORT DONELSON." Then followed the details that brought on the premature jubilation, as "reported" from Nashville (dated February 15): "The victory at Fort Donelson is ours.—We have whipped the enemy by land and by water. The enemy's loss was tremendous. Their force is 50,000." (No numbers were given for the size of the Confederate garrison at

Donelson.) A separate item related that Union gunboats had shelled the fort on the afternoon of the 14th. "Not a man or gun on our side was hurt" in the two-hour battle, while "two gunboats of the enemy were badly injured, and a third was crippled."

Another dispatch that day was dated "Nashville, Feb. 15th, 11 ½ A.M.," reporting that at seven o'clock that morning the enemy had attacked and "was driven back from the Fort to his camp . . . with great slaughter on both sides. . . . We have captured two of the enemy's batteries." At the time the message was written, it declared that "our troops are still driving the enemy back with cold steel."

At the end of the article came an item from Richmond, also dated the 15th, which concluded cautiously, "the Confederate victory was complete; but it is probable the Federals will renew the attack to-day."[7]

The *Intelligencer*'s issue of February 16 came out on a Sunday; the paper put forth no issue on Monday, the 17th. When it appeared again on Tuesday, the news was more or less still the same. Fighting had continued on Saturday, the 15th, "for nine hours. Five hundred Confederates were killed and wounded. We took 3,000 prisoners, six of the enemy's guns, and killed and wounded 1500 of the enemy." This was all rather cheering, except for the reporter's conclusion: "It is expected the battle will be renewed on Sunday. The final result in a great battle is yet uncertain."

The next day, uncertainty was compounded by anxiety. A dispatch from Richmond, dated the 18th, explained that "the wires connecting to Nashville are covered with ice and icicles for the past two days, and great difficulty is experienced in transmitting messages." There was, it concluded, thus "great anxiety to hear particulars from our own men." Without those, Southern newspapers had to turn to their most resented news sources: the Northern press. The *Intelligencer*'s telegraphic news section of the 19th included an unsettling statement: "At Norfolk Northern papers to the 17th have been received. The *Baltimore Sun* of the 17th states that at 2 o'clock P.M., of the 16th, Fort Donelson surrendered with 15,000 prisoners." Gaulding printed this, but added at the end, "*A lie.* ED. INT."

Printed below it was another Northern telegraphic item, this one from Chicago, February 17: Federal forces had stormed Donelson's fortifications, "over which the stars and stripes are now floating." This update bore the *Intelligencer*'s headline, "Northern Reports and Lies." Still a third, titled "More Yankee Lies"

(Cincinnati, February 17), repeated that "Fort Donelson was taken yesterday, with 15000 prisoners."[8]

Clearly, events had transpired quickly since the telegraphic reports of "Confederate victory." On February 14, Foote's vessels had shelled Donelson; in doing so they took numerous hits from the Confederates' cannon. Two of the Northern vessels were eventually disabled, and Foote had to retire.

General Floyd finally realized that, hemmed in by Grant's army, it was time to attempt a breakout. He planned it on the night of the 14th with his second-in-command, Brig. Gen. Gideon J. Pillow, and his third-, Brig. Gen. Simon Bolivar Buckner. Accordingly, the Confederates attacked the right of the Union line at dawn of the 15th, but failed to break through and withdrew back into the fort. That night, the Confederate generals conferred and reluctantly decided that surrender was their only option. Floyd and Pillow announced that they would try to sneak out, leaving Buckner the responsibility of capitulation. He dutifully did so on the morning of February 16.[9]

In Atlanta, Gaulding and the *Intelligencer* had a hard time realizing that the rumors of Fort Donelson's surrender were not "Yankee lies," as the paper had declared on February 19. From the Confederate capital itself that same day was issued a twenty-six-word telegraphic statement reading merely, "Advices received in reliable quarters, state that the Confederates will make a stand at Nashville, having an effective force. Brigadiers Pillow, Johnson and Floyd are there." The paper offered no comment on this report, printed on the 20th, because the only inference that could have been drawn from it was that Fort Donelson no longer stood as Confederates' main defensive position on the Cumberland River; Nashville, 75 miles upstream, had become the new place to make a stand.

Instead, the editor seized on the best inferences he could glean from the telegraphed news so far received. In an editorial entitled, "Not Impregnable," published on February 20, the *Intelligencer* dwelled on the success of Donelson's river batteries in damaging and driving off Foote's gunboats. "*Iron-clad* though they are, or may be, still Southern shot and shell can penetrate their bulwarks and scatter death among the crews." Because of the river batteries' success, "the dreaded gunboats of the enemy," predicted the editor, "will soon have done their work, and cease to be a terror to our people"[10]

In this frame of mind, when Gaulding on February 21 printed a distillation of the *New York Herald*'s reporting of Donelson's surrender, he once more titled the story "Northern Lies." Under an item, "Nashville," on the same page, ran a statement that Federals had captured Nashville. The editor added his dismissive comment, "[We have had similar dispatches here for several days. We doubt the truth of the foregoing, as we did the others.—ED. INT.]"

Finally, there came a bit of reporting that both acknowledged the surrender of the Confederates' fort and garrison and offered Southerners a modicum of consolation. "The latest Northern accounts of the battle at Fort Donelson, received at Norfolk," it began, "admit that the Federal Army was cut to pieces. The dead lay in heaps. The scene of the battle beggars all description. . . . The dead were thickly strewn across. The artillery of the Confederates did fearful work." "It was a deadly bought victory," the article concluded—meaning a victory "dearly bought" by the Federals, the only concession that the battle had ended in Confederate defeat.[11]

The statistical dimensions of the Donelson disaster were unknown to Archibald Gaulding and his journalist colleagues, even as they finally came around to its reality. On February 22, the *Intelligencer* printed an article, "From Fort Donelson," based on the statement made by a Confederate officer who had arrived in Augusta on the 20th. On Saturday, February 15, he explained, "a desperate fight" began between the Federals, who one prisoner said "were fifty thousand, and were reinforced by thirty thousand." Against this overwhelming host, Generals Pillow, Floyd, Buckner and Bushrod Johnson could only muster some 13,000 to 15,000 troops. When Buckner heard of the size of the enemy force—thus far in the telegraphic reporting Ulysses S. Grant's name had not yet appeared—"Buckner raised the White flag and proposed to capitulate." Thus the garrison surrendered, although "stragglers in squads, companies and battalions escaped during Saturday night, under the cover of the darkness." "Our loss in killed and wounded is estimated from 3000 to 5000," the article declared; some 1,200 to 1,500 wounded were said to have been removed by boat.

Then, the next day, the *Intelligencer* printed a letter written to an Atlantan by none other than W. S. Bassford, Gaulding's former associate editor. On the 19th Bassford was in Chattanooga, where already a number of residents of Nashville had begun to seek refuge. From them Bassford learned that Fort Donelson had indeed been surrendered on Sunday morning, February 16, giving up 9,000 prisoners. "Generals Pillow and Floyd escaped," he learned, but Buckner had been taken captive. "I fear Tennessee is lost to us," he ruefully concluded.[12]

Chief threat now to Nashville, the Tennessee capital, came from Union gunboats, which after the fall of Fort Donelson were free to steam up the Cumberland toward the city.

On Friday, February 28, under its "BY TELEGRAPH" section, the *Intelligencer* announced, on authority from a wire from Richmond two days before, "a dispatch from Chattanooga states that the Federal gunboats reached Nashville on Tuesday morning," the 25th. Then, two days later on March 2, the paper printed another telegraphed news item confirming Confederates' evacuation of Nashville, adding, "the Governor burned all the State Documents and retreated to Murfreesboro."

This latter part was off in several respects. As early as the afternoon of February 16, the day of Donelson's surrender, Governor Isham Harris in Nashville had been advised by General Johnston to remove the state archives, as the evacuation of the capital appeared imminent. Harris quickly complied and that very day saw that the state's papers were packed onto a special train to Memphis; they were not burned, as the *Intelligencer* stated. Further, Murfreesboro, thirty miles southeast of Nashville, was not the governor's first place of refuge. On the 16th he issued from his office in the capitol a notice to members of the legislature that they were to re-assemble in Memphis on the 20th.

Rumors of Donelson's surrender were already flying about the capital as legislators were seen packing up and getting out. On that morning, too, Confederate troops from Bowling Green began marching through in their withdrawal farther south. Johnston had determined not to try to defend the capital against the advance of Don Carlos Buell's forces, which were slowly approaching Nashville from the north. With many residents in panic and preparing to flee, Mayor Richard Cheatham announced that he would surrender the city to the first Federals arriving. But they took their time in doing so, allowing Confederates opportunity to remove ordnance, rations and supplies out of the city to places of safety. The last Southern troops evacuated Nashville on February 23; two days later, Federal soldiers disembarked from steam boats and occupied the city.[13]

Aside from clinging upon early rumors of "Confederate victory at Fort Donelson" and challenging "Northern lies"—willful responses of an inveterate Confederate propagandist—Archibald Gaulding missed the opportunity to comment on war news that we can see today only with hindsight: the admittedly arguable assumption that the surrender of Forts Henry and Donelson, with the loss of Nashville, portended the eventual collapse of the Confederate war effort in the trans-Appalachian west.

But then again, that's what we are able to see today, just as we know that

Nashville, the first Southern state capital to fall to Union forces, would not be the last.

NOTES

1. "Reports! Rumors!," *ADI*, Feb. 2, 1862; Castel, *General Sterling Price*, 65, 82; Charles P. Roland, *Albert Sidney Johnston: Soldier of Three Republics* (Austin: University of Texas Press, 1964), 283; Nathaniel Cheairs Hughes, Jr., *General William J. Hardee: Old Reliable* (Baton Rouge: Louisiana State University Press, 1965), 89.

2. "Western News," *ADI*, Jan. 19, 1862; Benjamin Franklin Cooling, *Forts Henry and Donelson: The Key to the Confederate Heartland* (Knoxville: University of Tennessee Press, 1987), 14, 46–47.

3. "Western news," *ADI*, Jan. 21, 1862; Stephen D. Engle, *Struggle for the Heartland: The Campaign from Fort Henry to Corinth* (Lincoln: University of Nebraska Press, 2001), 40–41; Cooling, *Forts Henry and Donelson*, 88–89; "The Firing at Fort Henry" and "Memphis, Feb. 6," *ADI*, Feb. 7, 1862; "Capture of Fort Henry," "Further from Fort Henry" and "The Capture of Fort Henry" (editorial), *ADI*, February 8.

4. "Further Particulars of the Fort Henry Fight," *ADI*, Feb. 9, 1862; Edwin C. Bearss and Howard P. Nash, "Fort Henry," *Civil War Times Illustrated*, vol. 4, no. 7 (November 1965), 10–11; Timothy B. Smith, *Grant Invades Tennessee: The 1862 Battles for Forts Henry and Donelson* (Lawrence: University Press of Kansas, 2016), 124.

5. "The War Cloud," *ADI*, Feb. 11, 1862; "The Prospect Before Us," *ADI*, February 12.

6. "Nashville, Feb. 12," *ADI*, Feb. 14, 1862; Engle, *Struggle for the Heartland*, 67–70; "Engagement at Fort Donelson" (Nashville, Feb. 13, 11:30 A.M.), *ADI*, Feb. 15, 1862; Kendall D. Gott, *Where the South Lost the War: An Analysis of the Fort Henry-Fort Donelson Campaign, February 1862* (Mechanicsburg PA: Stackpole Books 2003), 159–60; "Still Later from Fort Donelson" (Feb. 13, no time given), *ADI*, February 15.

7. "Confederate Victory at Fort Donelson" (Nashville, Feb. 15), "From Fort Donelson" (Nashville, Feb. 14), "Important from Fort Donelson" (Nashville, Feb. 15, 11:30 A.M.) and "From Richmond" (Feb. 15), *ADI*, Feb. 16, 1862.

8. "BY TELEGRAPH. The Battle at Fort Donelson" (Richmond, Feb. 16), *ADI*, Feb. 18, 1862; "News from Richmond" (Feb. 18), "Northern Reports and Lies" (Chicago, Feb. 17) and "More Yankee Lies" (Cincinnati, Feb. 17), *ADI*, February 19.

9. Stephen E. Ambrose, "Fort Donelson: A 'Disastrous' Blow to the South," *Civil War Times Illustrated*, vol. 5, no. 3 (June 1966), 8, 10–13, 42–43.

10. "BY TELEGRAPH. From Richmond," *ADI*, Feb. 20, 1862; "Not Impregnable," *ADI*, February 20.

11. "Northern Lies," "Surrender of Fort Donelson," "Nashville" and "More Northern Accounts," *ADI*, Feb. 21, 1862.

12. "From Fort Donelson," *ADI*, Feb. 22, 1862; "Interesting Correspondence," *ADI*, February 23.

13. "From the West," *ADI*, Feb. 26, 1862; "Gun Boats at Nashville," *ADI*, February 28;

"From the West," *ADI*, March 2; John Miller McKee, "The Evacuation of Nashville," in Edwin L. Drake, ed., *The Annals of the Army of Tennessee and Early Western History* (Nashville: A. D. Haynes, 1878), 226–28, 264–65; Horn, comp., *Tennessee's War*, 62–69.

9. Atlanta Becomes a Hospital Center

ON FEB. 26, 1862, the *Atlanta Intelligencer* published President Jefferson Davis' inaugural address, delivered on February 22, in the nation's capital. "With humble gratitude and adoration, acknowledging to Providence which has so visibly protected the Confederacy during its brief, but eventful career," Davis had intoned, "to Thee, Oh God! I trustingly commit myself, and prayfully invoke Thy blessing on my country and its cause. [Continued and enthusiastic cheering.]"

It was actually the president's second such speech; the first he had delivered a little more than a year before (Feb. 18, 1861) after he had been elected provisional president of the Confederate States of America by the convention of delegates at Montgomery (the Confederacy's first capital), where the representatives had ratified the creation of a new nation. The Constitution they drafted and approved stipulated that a general election was to be held that November for the people to ratify by vote the delegates' selection of the Confederacy's two highest officers. Davis and Stephens, of course, had won the election (they "ran" unopposed). Thus when Davis formally assumed office in February 1862, he began serving the six-year term that the Confederate Constitution had instituted.

When it printed the president's text on the 26th, the editor pronounced it as "admirable," adding, "as most productions from his pen, the PRESIDENT has been happy in this one." Gaulding praised Davis as "the great leader who is to work out Southern Independence."[1]

Confederate officials had chosen February 22 as the date of Davis' inaugural because it was George Washington's birthday. The president referred to "our Revolutionary forefathers" in his speech as patriotic, resolute heroes who could serve Southerners as models in their own fight for independence. The president even gave his address outside the statehouse in Richmond under the imposing equestrian stature of Washington, even though it was raining (someone held an umbrella over him as he read his speech).

The *Intelligencer* took notice of all this in its issue of Saturday, the 22nd. The presidential inauguration, it commented, was being conducted "while a dark cloud appears to lower over the Confederacy"—allusion not to the weather in Richmond, but to the recent defeats in Tennessee. The editor, as was his practice, sought to be optimistic when he concluded, "It should be every patriot's trust that the influences which the day itself—Washington's Birth Day—should exercise over every Southern man, will soon dissipate the cloud, and restore the brilliant sunshine that for months cheered our gallant troops on to victory upon victory."

In contrast to the sunny summer of '61, with the Confederate triumphs at Manassas and Springfield, the winter of '62 was indeed clouded and somber. President Davis recognized this when on February 20 he issued a proclamation to the people for another national fast day—his third of the war so far. The *Intelligencer* took these occasions seriously. On the 21st Gaulding ended the paper's "BY TELEGRAPH" section by stating, "with the foregoing we have received the Proclamation of President Davis, setting apart a day of humiliation and prayer—which we shall publish to-morrow.—ED. INT." (Gaulding did.)[2]

Jefferson Davis was not the only one issuing proclamations: Joseph E. Brown was, as well. Issued from the Executive Mansion in Milledgeville on February 11, the governor called for more volunteers to join the Confederate army. The *Intelligencer* printed the document in full on page two in its issue of the 14th, and again the next day on its front page. Gaulding praised it in an accompanying editorial, deeming it "one of the most able and patriotic productions that we have seen during the war." In his proclamation, the governor reviewed the causes of the war ("the outrageous usurpations of power and aggressions upon our rights, committed by the Federal Government"); the enemy's prosecution of the conflict ("Northern troops have been permitted to disregard all the rules of civilized warfare"); the consequences of possible Confederate defeat ("we . . . lose all the lands and all the other property we possess"); and what it would take for victory ("thousands more from Georgia must immediately fly to arms"). For all of these reasons, the national government, Brown explained, had called upon Southern governors for more men to serve for three years or the duration of the war.

Georgia's share of the requisition totaled twelve regiments. This amounted to 15,715 troops, according to a listing for the eleven Confederate states prepared by Secretary of War Judah P. Benjamin (Kentucky and Missouri were not included). In the state-by-state breakdown, Georgia's allotment ranked as seventh in size, between Virginia's (64,342, or 47 regiments) and Florida's (4,614—2½ regiments). The War Department in Richmond would arm, clothe and equip all volunteers, plus pay each a bounty of $50. (This was a considerable sum; for most of the war, Confederate soldiers received pay of eleven dollars a month.) Volunteering units could also elect their own officers. The governor announced that the new recruits would be dispatched to training camps near Savannah, Griffin and Marietta (Camp McDonald).

Brown appealed to every man's patriotism to come forth in service to the cause. If they did not, he threatened to draft them. The *Intelligencer* approved of the governor's mix of appeal and demand. "He invites, and he warns," Gaulding observed, adding his hope that enough volunteers for the twelve regiments would come forth, instead of waiting to be drafted. The paper did its part to help implement the call for volunteers by printing the governor's proclamation on its front page every day for the rest of the month. On February 21 it listed the specific occupations in which men could be exempted from service, beginning with clergymen and including telegraph officers, railroad workers and factory superintendents. The editor advised those in the exempted groups to comply with stated registration procedures, "so that future embarrassments may be avoided" in case of a draft. Then, when the local state militia general, William P. Howard, called for officers to provide "the name of every white male citizen, as well as alien, between the ages of eighteen and forty five years," the paper printed that announcement, too.

In his proclamation of February 11, Governor Brown entertained the unpleasant prospect that some of Georgia's men might actually shirk volunteerism and await a draft. In such cases, he declared, "I cannot believe that the noble women of the State, who have done so much for the cause, would ever tolerate such delinquency."

All of these appeals seemed to work, as evidenced by the militia muster held in Atlanta on March 4. Col. Robert F. Maddox, commanding the Fulton County Regiment of Georgia Militia, oversaw a robust turnout; Gaulding afterward declared that most of his staff was present (although he did not offer a number), delaying printing of the next day's issue. Also on hand was Brigadier General Howard, commander of the 1st Brigade, 11th Division, G. M., as well as Confederate colonel Thomas R. R. Cobb, who was in town seeking volunteers for his legion. The editor reported the next day that Cobb addressed the assemblage with "enthusiastic eloquence." Gaulding proudly announced that not only did enough men volunteer for the army to meet Fulton County's quota, but two additional companies were also raised. "We are proud of her," he added, referring to Fulton, and praised as well the folk of Atlanta. "Our Rail Road city," he concluded, "will never tire, we feel confident, in doing her part in the pending struggle for Southern independence."[3]

On Wednesday, February 19, the *Intelligencer* announced a "Citizen's Meeting": "The citizens of Atlanta are requested to meet at the City Hall this, Wednesday, afternoon, at 3 o'clock. Business of importance to transact. Let none fail to attend, who feel an interest in the affairs of our country. Businessmen of Atlanta—close your doors for an hour or two, and attend this meeting. All we hold sacred in life, depends on our action at this time." The editor did not explain the purpose of this meeting, or why such dire language was being used concerning it. The agenda may have had to do with the city's military preparedness; Fort Donelson had fallen, Nashville would surely be next, and the Federals' further advance into Tennessee threatened north Georgia. The paper later announced what had happened: evidently not much. Mayor Calhoun had presided, and a committee had been appointed. The *Intelligencer* of Thursday, the 20th, announced another citizens' meeting to be held that morning, this time at the Atheneum, the city's largest auditorium. For this gathering, Gaulding's explanation showed a limited agenda. Confederate military equipment was being shipped out of Nashville; much of it was apparently headed for Atlanta. Citizens were being called together "for the purpose of devising measures for the safe keeping of the Government stores, now being shipped to this city, and for enquiring, if there be any good reason, why the *new fire proof* Macon Depot cannot be used for that purpose," and also how the Macon & Western Railroad running south from Atlanta would be put to use in hauling it. Still another "citizen's meeting" was held at the Atheneum on Friday afternoon, February 21, when the Committee would offer a report. Apparently the outcome was undramatic, for the *Intelligencer* ceased to report on the entire matter.[4]

Army supplies and munitions removed from Nashville might be sent farther south to Macon, but sick and wounded Southern soldiers evacuated out of Nashville hospitals could not, as Atlanta began its emergence as a Confederate hospital center.

The *Intelligencer* had already begun to address sundry medical topics. It had printed Dr. John Westmoreland's letter the previous fall, when he reported on the large number of disease cases he was treating at the army hospital in Williamsburg, Virginia. Reports of the most common "camp diseases" had led the paper to publish an article on how to prevent them. Diarrhea could be avoided if soldiers did not drink bad water. As for rheumatism, caused by continuous exposure to rain and cold weather, "wear flannel and keep the digestion sound." (By commenting, "hard drinkers are particularly liable to bed attacks," the paper was essentially advising soldiers not to go to sleep drunk.) Prevailing medical lore still stressed the unhealthfulness of noxious vapors and miasmatic effluvia; to avoid fevers, the *Intelligencer*'s medical sources suggested that "good food and active exercise will generally keep a man well unless the air is uncommonly deleterious."

Disease, however, ran rampant in soldiers' encampments. One Atlantan, unnamed, wrote "Col. J. I. Whitaker" from Manassas on February 10, complaining about poor medical care that the men were receiving. "There is some little sickness in camp," the correspondent stated; Virginia offered colder temperatures than they were used to, and this with the ongoing rainy weather contributed to illnesses that regimental physicians seemed unable to treat effectively. "We suffer more here for the want of good, sober, steady, well-informed Physicians, than for any thing else," he explained. "Sir," the writer added emphatically, "believe me we have lost more men by disease than we have in battle. Yes, sir, ten to one."[5]

Thus well-informed Atlantans knew that among Confederate troops there were a lot of sick soldiers. And they would have assumed that when Nashville was evacuated, many army hospital patients would be sent to places south, including Atlanta. This is exactly what the *Intelligencer* announced on February 21, printing a message sent from the Medical Director of the Army of Tennessee to Mayor Calhoun. "Five hundred sick soldiers will be sent this day. Provide for them."

The physicians who, with Calhoun, received this warning were Dr. Willis Westmoreland, who had returned to the city from Virginia and opened an obstetrical practice, and probably Dr. Benjamin O. Jones, longtime Atlanta physician. Medical director of Gen. Albert Sidney Johnston's army was Dr. David W. Yandell, but surgeon in charge of Nashville hospitals was Dr. Lewis T. Pim; it was the latter who supervised the evacuation of patients from Nashville. At the time, General Johnston and his troops were at Murfreesboro, thirty miles southeast of the capital.

The promised 500 sick and wounded arrived Saturday night, February 22.

Atlanta then had no large hospital. The Atlanta Medical College, which had suspended classes the previous summer, now was turned into a surgical center, with laboratories as operating rooms and classrooms fitted out with beds. Within just a few days, other public buildings had taken in patients. The *Intelligencer* of February 25 listed them as places where citizens could deliver clothing for soldiers in need: the Medical College, the Gate City Hotel (on Alabama Street, a block south of the train depot), and three "halls," including Hayden's, an office building on Peachtree. In addition, physicians were turning their offices and other spaces into small wards. Drs. Thomas Denny and Daniel Heery established what they called the "Lady Davis" Hospital over R. C. Gaines' grocery store on Peachtree, two blocks northwest of the depot.

The paper also reported that "a large number of the poor fellows have been taken to private houses." The editor thanked the mayor and city authorities for seeing to the patients' care, and especially complimented "the Medical Fraternity of the city" for springing into action. Special mention was made of the women who were serving in various helpful roles. All were doing their part, the editor concluded, in "this sudden advent upon us, for which we were prepared only by a brief telegraphic notice." And more patients were on the way. A young Atlantan, Susan Lin, wrote her brother on February 28, "Atlanta is completely run over with them," she explained; "there is [*sic*] six or eight hundred here now and more are coming every day."[6]

"Atlanta, it appears," the *Intelligencer* opined on February 27, "has been made 'Medical Head Quarters' for the army of the West," referring to General Johnston's forces. This meant that medical officers and other personnel were arriving, increasing the city's population. "Outside of the sick and wounded, numbering several hundred," the editor judged, "the officers and attendants upon them swell to a considerable extent the transient population of our city." The "transients" also included civilians from Kentucky and Tennessee who had been driven from their homes by advancing Federal forces. Displaced mechanics and artisans were also arriving, ready to go to work in Atlanta producing military goods. The paper encouraged city authorities and the citizenry in general to make these newcomers feel welcome and "to extend all the protection and hospitality they can."

Most prominent among the newly arrived medical personnel was Dr. Pim, Assistant Medical Director for Johnston's army. On February 27 he wrote a long open letter addressed to "Fellow Citizens of the Confederate States," which the *Intelligencer* printed on March 2. Dr. Pim announced that he had been sent to Atlanta to set up and organize hospitals for sick and wounded Confederate soldiers. As part of this work, Pim asked citizens to contribute money, bed linen, clothing, bandage-making materials, even intoxicating beverages for the patients under his care. He named Mrs. Maria Westmoreland, president of the Ladies' Soldiers' Relief Society and Mrs. E. B. Walker, Directress of the St. Philip's [Episcopal Church] Hospital Society as the individuals to whom such donations could be delivered.

As he customarily did, editor Gaulding reinforced Pim's appeal with his own supporting commentary. "The eloquent appeal made by the Medical Director here," he declared, "we trust will reach the hearts and purses of our citizens. . . . We look confidently to an early and generous response to this appeal from all parts of the Confederacy."[7]

"Wounded and sick soldiers belonging to the army of the West, continue to arrive in our city by hundreds," the *Intelligencer* reported on March 4. The paper thanked the city's physicians for rendering their compassionate care and "all classes of our citizens" for generously responding to Pim's request for donations of goods. Gaulding, mindful of the exchanges being sent and received by newspapers across the state, urged other editors to reprint Dr. Pim's appeal.

Women in the city were especially active. Maria Westmoreland, head of the Ladies' Soldiers' Relief Society, arranged for all goods donated to her group to be put in a storeroom on Decatur Street, and invited physicians to visit it for supplies; "there will be some one in attendance at all hours of the day." And indeed there was. The *Intelligencer* published minutes of the Society meeting held on March 4, in which two women were assigned to tend the storeroom each day, Monday through Saturday. There was, to be sure, a lot of stuff in the L. S. R. S. storeroom; a listing of contributions received in the first part of March allowed Mrs. Westmoreland to report that 204 shirts, 130 pairs of drawers, 80 pairs of socks, plus bed linen, towels and even 36 bottles of wine had been distributed among the city's hospitals. Martha Winship, president of a newly formed Atlanta Hospital Association, also obtained a storeroom near Silvey and Dougherty's dry goods store at Marietta and Whitehall; on March 22 the paper published her invitation for surgeons to come and help themselves to "all kinds of Wines, Brandies, Cordials, Whiskey" and various edibles.

More women's relief groups were forming. Just as the parishioners of St. Philip's Episcopal had organized, so too did the congregants of Wesley Chapel, the Methodist church near Peachtree Street a few blocks from the train depot. When the "Wesley Chapel Ladies Hospital Association" met, Gaulding published its meeting minutes, along with an editorial praising Maria

Westmoreland for her "patriotism and benevolence," likening her to an "Angel of Mercy."

The paper's editor found various ways to assist in all of the activities taking place in the city. The *Intelligencer* on March 4 reminded women that every day at City Hall a group gathered to "make comforts for the sick soldiers." "Come with needles, thimbles, and a strong will," the notice read; "Come! Come!! Come!!!" Gaulding also sought to stimulate public donations to the hospitals by publicizing particular instances of largesse. On the 4th he printed an article in which he openly thanked the wife of Maj. John Rowland of Cass County (renamed a few months later to honor Francis Bartow, the martyr of Manassas) for having brought in "a large number of bedsteads, matrasses, sheets, pillow-slips and feathers, bed quilts, towels, chairs, pants, drawers, shirts, socks, bottles of catsup, pepper, sage, &c." Such items were "most valuable, indeed," he added, "because such articles were most needed." Moreover, the Ladies' Society in Atlanta was receiving gifts from similar groups elsewhere. In her society's meeting on March 4, Mrs. Westmoreland announced donations received from the Ladies' Relief Societies of Macon and as far away as Lafayette, Alabama.[8]

When a few residents of Big Shanty (now Kennesaw) observed a train passing through town bearing ailing soldiers, they chipped in thirty-two dollars, which sum (enough to buy five years of the *Daily Intelligencer*, at the prevailing rates) eventually made its way to Mayor Calhoun. The mayor also asked the *Intelligencer* to publicize his receipt of a bale of sheeting generously donated for the city's hospitals by the Roswell Manufacturing Company, the cotton and woolen goods mill operating along the Chattahoochee north of Atlanta. The *Intelligencer* on March 20 publicized the various goods received by Mrs. Winship and Westmoreland, as well as Mrs. Walker of the St. Philip's Hospital Society. In that same issue, Gaulding commended the patriotic citizens of Eatonton (a town some sixty miles southeast of Atlanta) for having sent in a lot of stores, plus $150 in cash.

An equal amount—$154.25—was acknowledged by Maria Westmoreland as having been received from the Atlanta Amateurs, the city's popular entertainment troupe. A concert they gave on the night of March 15 was performed for the benefit of the Society. "Long may they live to continue in their acts of mercy," wrote Mrs. Westmoreland in a letter printed by the paper on the 22nd, "and may their exertions send comfort to many a desponding heart."

But as many generous donations as were proffered, more still were requested. The *Intelligencer* regularly published the appeals of the Rev. Andrew F. Freeman, rector of St. Philip's and president of the church's Hospital Aid Society. In his statement appearing on March 13, Father Freeman estimated that there were "some 3,000 sick soldiers here now," and asked the citizenry to "send us anything they can spare, that would be useful to the sick and suffering."

With St. Philip's and other Atlanta aid societies willing to take just about anything, they did indeed receive just that. Cash, of course, was always welcome. In a long listing of donations received that took up fully half a page of the *Intelligencer*'s issue of March 30, Mrs. Winship acknowledged monetary gifts to the Atlanta Hospital Association totaling $988.25 from as far away as Cuthbert, in extreme southwest Georgia, and from such diverse donors as the "servants of Mrs. Kendall" ($1.50). As for goods themselves, clothing and bedding topped the list; among the individuals named by Mrs. Winship for contributing them was "Miss Laura V. Danielly (9 years old) 1 pair socks." Other frequent donations were rags, bandages and lint, sent to help with surgical patients.

Food and related sundries made for a bewilderingly broad range of items. From a Mrs. Ellis in Upson County: "1 sack flour, 1 parcel coffee, 3 doz. eggs, 2 bottles honey, 1 piece dried beef, butter, potatoes, homony, pickles and dried peas." Lest the men be served bland-tasting victuals, a number of persons contributed pepper, sage and catsup. Salt and ginger were other items; Mrs. Robert Adams and a few others sent in something called "slippery elm."

Already wartime privation was visible in the hospital association listing; two ladies donated a quantity of "Confederate coffee," although its exact composition was not disclosed. "The ladies of Campbell co., through Mrs. Bessent," sent "1 box of eggs, 7 chickens, 2 bags of fruit, 1 bundle sage, 1 crackers, 5 pair socks, butter, a large jug of milk." More than with milk, however, did the A. H. A.'s benefactors see to the men's spirits in the category of potables. While a number of donors gave unspecified quantities of wine, one could count more than seventy bottles of it, plus several gallon-jars and jugs. Cordials and brandies there were aplenty. Not to be overlooked were five bottles of corn whisky contributed by the Soldiers' Relief Society of Forsyth, Georgia. How much of all this alcohol actually made it into patients' gullets is unknown, but its contributors commendably had in mind the comfort of the distressed in Atlanta's hospital wards.

Women gave as their means allowed. Mrs. Ellen Ponder, who owned a hundred acres with sixty slaves northwest of the city, sent in $50; a Mrs. Ann Truitt modestly contributed "fruit, sage, old clothing." In addition to individuals, Mrs. Winship acknowledged gifts from eight different relief societies, mostly in

Georgia, but as far away as Selma, Alabama. From the Soldiers Relief Society of Athens, a multitude of gifts included eight bibles and twelve other books.

Altogether, nearly 150 persons or organizations had given to the Atlanta Hospital Association—a bountiful display of benevolence, indicating that people far and wide were moved by the thought of patriotic Confederate soldiers suffering from want or need in hospital.[9]

If 3,000 soldier-patients were in fact in Atlanta at the end of March, as Father Freeman had stated, they were strewn across the city in a variety of facilities. Private homes continued to hold a large number of men. After dispatching her husband Isaac and children downstairs, Martha Winship converted the upper story of her house on Harris Street into a hospital ward; cots filled all six rooms and the hallway. Other citizens had similarly opened their homes when the first five hundred patients arrived on February 22. On March 17, Dr. Pim issued an order for soldiers convalescing in residences to come forward to be registered. Homeowners were requested to assist in the effort, which suggested that the city's medical director probably did not know exactly how many patients were in home-care. The *Intelligencer* published Pim's order the very next day.

At the time, at least ten public buildings were serving as hospitals, according to a "List of Confederate Soldiers buried at Oakland [Cemetery] arranged by Hospital." Despite the ministrations of Pim and his medical officers, some fifty-six patients were said to have died in Atlanta as of March 21, according to a report reprinted in the *Intelligencer* from the *Macon Journal & Messenger*. The first such unfortunate, who perished at the Gate City Hospital, was interred in the City Cemetery on February 25. Between March 2 and 11, soldiers were interred from the Medical College (three blocks east of the train depot), Hayden's Hall, Hindman's Hall, the Bank Hospital, Holland's Hall and Howell's Hall (all on Peachtree), plus the Empire House Hotel on Whitehall, the City Hotel Hospital (Decatur and Loyd Streets) and even the clinic established at the African Methodist Church, three blocks northeast of the depot.

All of these facilities required not just physicians and surgeons, but nurses and "matrons," the usual title for white female hospital workers. Some of these women were paid, but often they volunteered their time in order to aid the cause. At another level, Southern army hospitals employed a whole host of cooks, laundresses and stewards. For these positions, enslaved African Americans were often employed. Such was the case in Atlanta. On March 7, the *Intelligencer* began printing Dr. Pim's announcement that "We need quite a number of negroes—able bodied men, and women without children—to serve in our Hospitals." Slaveowners in Fulton and surrounding counties were asked to contact the medical director's office if they had "negroes to spare." "Liberal wages will be paid," Pim promised.

Gaulding reinforced the call for black laborers with an editorial, also printed on the 7th. "We do earnestly hope that there will be a prompt response to this call," he stated, "for the lives of the soldiers must not be sacrificed for the want of proper and indispensable attention."[10]

The patients receiving Gaulding's "prompt and indispensable attention" were obviously grateful. One of them, a soldier from Arkansas by the name of Walter L. Bragg, was somehow chosen to speak for all Atlanta patients in a program set at the Atheneum for March 27. The *Intelligencer* advertised the event, declaring that Bragg's speech "will thank the citizens, the ladies, and the different Societies of this city . . . for the kindness which they have extended to the sick soldiers of the army."

The medical officers were grateful, too. After Dr. Pim was assigned elsewhere, John M. Johnson became medical director in the city. To Mary Gay, a Decatur resident who offered to help provide for the soldiers, Dr. Johnson wrote a letter which the paper printed on March 28. Johnson readily accepted, thanking "your noble sex" for their patriotic services, as well as their unflinching optimism for the success of the cause. "Clouds have gathered over us, and many hearts are failing," Johnson acknowledged, but "I know of not one lady who desponds. There is no need of it," the doctor concluded, "for as certain as God lives and reigns, we will triumph."[11]

Historians list the several ways in which Atlanta became so important to the Confederacy during the war years: 1) an important railroad terminus for four lines radiating the state; 2) a significant manufacturing center, with one of the South's crucial rolling mills; and 3) a supply/warehousing complex for the army. When the *Intelligencer* boasted, "Atlanta, it appears, has been made 'Medical Head Quarters' for the army of the West," it added a fourth reason as well.

NOTES

1. "INAUGURAL ADDRESS OF PRESIDENT DAVIS," *ADI,* Feb. 26, 1862; James M. McPherson, *Embattled Rebel: Jefferson Davis as Commander in Chief* (New York: Penguin Press, 2014), 16, 18, 64; "Inaugural Address of President Davis," *ADI,* February 25 and 26.

2. "The Confederate Congress," *ADI,* Feb. 22, 1862; George C. Rable, *God's Almost Chosen*

Peoples: A Religious History of the American Civil War (Chapel Hill: University of North Carolina Press, 2010), 148; "BY TELEGRAPH," *ADI*, February 21; "Proclamation by the President, to the People of the Confederate States," *ADI*, February 22.

3. "A PROCLAMATION," *ADI*, Feb. 14, 1862; J. P. Benjamin to John Gill Shorter, Governor of Alabama, February 2 (same to governors of other ten states), *OR*, Ser. 4, vol. 1, 902–903; "The Governor's Proclamation," *ADI*, February 15; "State of Georgia. Adjutant and Inspector General's Office, Milledgeville, February 18" and "The Exempt," *ADI*, February 21; "Special Orders. Headquarters. Atlanta, Ga., Feb. 18, 1862," *ADI*, February 20; "RESPONSE—NO DRAFT," *ADI*, March 5; "Major R. F. Maddox," *ADI*, Feb. 27, 1861; "Candidates," *ADI*, Apr. 15, 1861.

4. "Citizen's Meeting," *ADI*, Feb. 19, 1862; Venet, *Changing Wind*, 57–58; "The Citizen's Meeting of Wednesday," *ADI*, February 21; "Citizen's Meeting," *ADI*, February 20; "The Meeting of Thursday," *ADI*, February 22.

5. J. G. Westmoreland, "College Hospital. Williamsburg, Va., Sept. 8, 1861," *ADI*, Sept. 13, 1861; "Camp Disease—How to Avoid Them," *ADI*, Feb. 12, 1862; Alfred Jay Bollet, M.D., *Civil War Medicine: Challenges and Triumphs* (Tucson: Galen Press, 2002), 17; "ARMY CORRESPONDENCE," *ADI*, February 20.

6. "BY TELEGRAPH," *ADI*, Feb. 21, 1862; Garrett, *A & E*, vol. 1, 768; Glenna R. Schroeder-Lein, *Confederate Hospitals on the Move: Samuel H. Stout and the Army of Tennessee* (Columbia: University of South Carolina Press, 1994), 48, 53; Roland, *Albert Sidney Johnston*, 301; "The Sick and Wounded," *ADI*, February 25; Davis, *What the Yankees Did to Us*, 22–23; "Wanted for the Sick Soldiers" and "Soldier's Hospital," *ADI*, February 25; Williams, *Directory*, 87.

7. "The Influx to Atlanta," *ADI*, Feb. 27, 1862; L. T. Pim, "Fellow Citizens of the Confederate States" and "The Wounded and Sick," both in *ADI*, March 2.

8. "Editorial Summary" and Maria J. Westmoreland, "Hospital stores. . . ." *ADI*, Mar. 4, 1862; "Contributions to the Atlanta Hospitals, Received by the Soldiers' Relief Society," *ADI*, March 13; Mrs. Isaac Winship, "A Card," *ADI*, March 23; Williams, *Directory*; "Atlanta Hospital Association," *ADI*, March 9; Davis, *What the Yankees Did to Us*, 22; "The Ladies of the Wesley Chapel," *ADI*, March 4; "More Aid for the Soldiers," *ADI*, March 6; "The Wesley Chapel Ladies Association," "Atlanta, Ga., March 4th, 1862" and "Mrs. M. J. Westmoreland," *ADI*, March 16; "The Ladies! The Ladies!" and "The Ladies Responding," *ADI*, March 4; "Ladies' Soldiers' Relief Society," *ADI*, March 6; Keith S. Hebert, *The Long Civil War in the North Georgia Mountains: Confederate Nationalism, Sectionalism, and White Supremacy in Bartow County, Georgia* (Knoxville: University of Tennessee Press, 2017), 95.

9. "Patriotic Citizens of Big Shanty," *ADI*, Mar. 6, 1862; Tammy Harden Galloway, ed., *Dear Old Roswell: The Civil War Letters of the King Family of Roswell, Georgia* (Macon: Mercer University Press, 2003), 3–4; "Handsome Donation," *ADI*, March 7; "A Liberal Donation" and "Help for the Sick Soldiers," *ADI*, March 20; "The Atlanta Amateurs," *ADI*, March 22; "To the Citizens of Georgia and of the Other States of the Southern Confederacy," *ADI*, March 13; "Contributions to the Atlanta Hospital Association," *ADI*, March 30; Richard B. Harwell, "Civilian Life in Atlanta, 1862," *Atlanta Historical Bulletin*, vol. 7, no. 29

(October 1944), 214–15; Marc Wortman, *The Bonfire: The Siege and Burning of Atlanta* (New York: Public Affairs, 1999), 80, 139.

10. Davis, *What the Yankees Did to Us*, 23; "Special Order, No. —," *ADI*, Mar. 18, 1862; "Hospitals in Atlanta," *ADI*, March 21; Robert E. Zaworski, *Confederate Sections at Oakland Cemetery Atlanta, Georgia: History and Restoration*, 2 vols. (privately printed, 1996), vol. 2, 198, 211, 219, 227; Williams, *Directory*, 23; Mildred Jordan, "Georgia's Confederate Hospitals," master's thesis, Emory University, 1962, 46, 73–76; Libra R. Hilde, *Worth a Dozen Men: Women and Nursing in the Civil War South* (Charlottesville: University of Virginia Press, 2012), 5; Clarence L. Mohr, *On the Threshold of Freedom: Masters and Slaves in Civil War Georgia* (Athens: University of Georgia Press, 1986), 128; "A CARD" and "Negroes Wanted," *ADI*, March 7.

11. "THANKS," *ADI*, Mar. 27, 1862; Johnson to Gay, March 24, *ADI*, March 28; Gay, *Life in Dixie*, 42.

10. "Defeated but Not Conquered"

ON MARCH 27, 1862, barely a year after it had exulted over the conquest of Fort Sumter, the *Intelligencer* had to reflect on a lot of bad news: two key Tennessee forts had fallen to Federal forces, and a state capital, Nashville, had been occupied by the enemy. These were, obviously, defeats of enormous consequence. Yet editor Archibald Gaulding affirmed, "Defeated, we have not been conquered. . . . Our people know that an hundred Northern victories, cannot subdue the South. Less than a half dozen won by the South, of any magnitude, on the contrary, will drive the invader from our soil, in shame and disgrace."[1]

The role of the *Intelligencer,* and indeed all Confederate newspapers, was to bring information to the people about their war for independence. In just the month of March 1862, at least four different events or specific areas of military operations would find reporting in the pages of Jared Whitaker's and Archibald Gaulding's paper: 1) the naval battle at Hampton Roads, March 8–9, between the Confederate ironclad gunboat *Virginia* and Federal warships; 2) the battle fought at the same time, at Pea Ridge, in northwest Arkansas; 3) the Confederates' loss of several defensive positions on the upper Mississippi River; and 4) the battle fought in New Mexico Territory, Feb. 21, 1862, by Confederate forces advancing into the parched area from west Texas.

The *Intelligencer* reported on the naval battle in southeast Virginia as the news came in. The first telegraphic report, sent from Richmond on March 8, appeared in the *Intelligencer* the very next day: "Reliable intelligence received in official quarters states that the ironclad steamer Merrimac, now known by the name of Virginia, engaged the Federal frigate Cumberland and sunk her, and drove the Federal frigate Congress on shore." Another dispatch, also wired from Richmond on March 8, appeared in the paper on the 11th. It explained that the Confederate steam-propelled armored warship had attacked the two Union frigates at Hampton Roads. A third vessel, the U. S. S. *Minnesota*, approached the *Virginia* and exchanged fire with her before running aground.

On the basis of this news, Gaulding editorialized that the "Great Naval Victory.... equals any naval achievement on record.... Truly we have cause to rejoice over it!"[2]

The *Intelligencer* of March 12 offered more telegraphed particulars of the naval battle of March 8, plus something new. Two-thirds down in this article, sent from Richmond on March 10, a new vessel entered the narrative: the "Erricson Battery," which was not described, and referred to by the misspelled name of its inventor, John Ericsson. "The Erricson Battery engaged the 'Virginia' at a distance of 30 or 40 yards," the article explained. "The 'Virginia' ran aground. The 'Erricson' took advantage of this and poured shot after shot with no effect. After getting off the 'Virginia' ran into the 'Erricson' with her bow, when she fled," according to the account. "The enemy loss in killed and wounded was very great," the article continued, adding that on the *Virginia*, two men had been killed and five wounded in the battle.

So much for Confederate press reporting of the first battle between armored warships in naval history. Because both ironclads had only been battered, the engagement was considered a draw.[3]

On March 15, the *Intelligencer* reprinted an editorial from the Richmond *Enquirer* that summarized the historic engagement. "The Victory at Hampton Roads," it exclaimed, "is without a parallel in the annals of naval achievements.... We rejoice in this result." The article reviewed the destruction of the *Congress* and *Cumberland*, and the damage to the *Minnesota*, but barely mentioned the second day's fight. In articles appearing in the *Intelligencer* nearly two weeks afterward, the Union ironclad was still being called the "Ericson Battery" and the "Erricson" (not the *Monitor*).[4]

It would require much more journalistic alchemy to turn into a Confederate victory the battle fought a thousand miles west of Hampton Roads at Pea Ridge and Elkhorn Tavern, Arkansas. Like that of the ironclads, this engagement took two days, but it resulted in many more Southern casualties, and in its second day was most certainly not a draw between the opposing sides.

By the end of February 1862, the Confederate forces of Generals Sterling Price and Ben McCulloch had abandoned Missouri and moved into northwest Arkansas. Maj. Gen. Earl Van Dorn took command of these troops, who numbered 16,000 (including a thousand Cherokee Indians). On March 3, Van Dorn began leading his army toward the Federal forces that had been pursuing him. First contact was made on March 6 near Elkhorn Tavern, just below the

Missouri border. The Union troops, under command of Brig. Gen. Samuel R. Curtis, prepared for attack the next day.

The Confederates began advancing after dawn of March 7, and during the morning made headway. At 2 p.m. General McCulloch was shot in the chest and killed. Taking charge on the field was Brig. Gen. James McIntosh, who soon also fell dead. A renewed Confederate attack in the afternoon pushed the Federals back. On Pea Ridge Elkhorn Tavern, which had been General Curtis' headquarters in the morning, now became Price's.

With darkness, both sides prepared to resume battle on March 8. The day began with a Union artillery bombardment. Curtis then ordered his infantry to attack. The Southerners began running out of ammunition, and at 10 a.m. Van Dorn ordered his troops to start withdrawing. The Federal pursuit was not vigorous, and by noon the Confederates had retreated from the field.

Curtis' victory cost his troops 1,384 casualties (203 killed, 980 wounded, 201 missing) of some 10,250 engaged (13 percent). Van Dorn had 12,000–13,000 men in the fight; their losses of at least 2,000 meant a casualty rate of approximately 15 percent.[5]

Intelligencer editor Archibald Gaulding, who had earlier warned readers that military rumors could prove to be false (but that he would be forced to publish them anyway), did that very thing with the first telegraphed communication about the battle in Arkansas. From the *Memphis Appeal*, Gaulding summarized the account "that a battle had occurred between the Confederates under General Van Dorn and Price, and the Federals, in which the latter were routed, 5000 killed, wounded and prisoners—our forces being still in pursuit of the retreating enemy." The news was evidently too good to be true, as the editor concluded, "the *Appeal* gives no credit to the report."

The *Intelligencer*'s skepticism proved merited. In the battle of Elkhorn Tavern, as it reported on March 13 from a telegraphic dispatch sent from Memphis on the 12th, "our loss [was] heavy, including Generals. McCulloch and McIntosh killed." Yet there was a hopeful note: "Our forces were in the rear of the Federals driving them Southward, sanguine of success." Still another wired report acknowledged that General Van Dorn's troops were "badly armed, but are fighting like devils, and will eventually defeat the enemy."

Editor Gaulding wisely avoided making such a prediction about the battle, especially since a Northern dispatch, dutifully printed by the *Intelligencer* on March 13, stated that Curtis' Union forces had won at Pea Ridge. On the 13th he merely editorialized on the "sad news" of the deaths of McCulloch and McIntosh.

The truth began to seep in with a telegraphed report, datelined Richmond, March 12 and printed in the *Intelligencer* on March 14, that related news received from General Van Dorn. "He states that he was victorious on the 7th and slept on the field of battle," it began. Then came the sugarcoating: "On the morning of the 8th, in consequence of the death of Gen. McCulloch and others on the right wing of the army, he deemed it judicious to alter position, and withdrew his command to the West of Fayetteville 12 miles from the battle field." "The army retired in good order," the report concluded. "The loss on both sides was heavy. This is reliable."

Then came the *Intelligencer*'s journalistic alchemy. On March 15, based on a report from the *Knoxville Register*, the paper printed a short article bearing the headlines,

GREAT VICTORY IN ARKANSAS!
Confederate Loss, 2,000.
Gens. McCulloch, McIntosh and Hebert, Killed.
6,000 Yankees Killed.
&., &., &c.

"It is a complete victory," the *Register* concluded. Against such exaggeration, small errors really didn't matter; Confederate Brig. Gen. Louis Hebert had been captured, not killed.[6]

A newspaper's ability to turn a judicious altering of position (General Van Dorn's euphemism for retreat) one day into a "complete victory" the next demonstrates Confederate journalism's elasticity when handling bad news from the front. That elasticity was tested anew in short order by the loss of several key positions on the upper Mississippi.

After the fall of Forts Henry and Donelson, Confederates on March 2 had to abandon their strong defensive position at Columbus, Kentucky, overlooking the Mississippi, twenty miles north of the Tennessee state line. Downriver, the next fortification built by Southerners to block Federal gunboats was at Island No. 10—so named as the tenth island south of the confluence of the Ohio and Mississippi Rivers. There, Confederates had mounted nineteen guns on the island, plus two more on a floating battery and two dozen more on the Tennessee shore. In addition, eleven miles downstream at a town called New

Madrid on the Missouri side, Confederates had constructed two forts with twenty-one pieces of artillery.

Maj. Gen. Henry Halleck, the Federal commander at St. Louis, ordered New Madrid and Island No. 10 to be taken, and put Brig. Gen. John Pope in charge of doing it. With 8,000 men Pope started out for New Madrid on February 28, and on March 3 began a siege that would last a week and a half. On the 13th, Pope ordered an infantry demonstration against the Rebel defenses and an artillery barrage that damaged Confederate gunboats offshore. The Confederate commander, Brig. Gen. John McCown, determined that his position was untenable and ordered his 3,000 troops to evacuate New Madrid that night. General Beauregard later relieved McCown for this act; he was replaced by Brig. Gen. William Mackall.

Two days later, on March 15, Union Flag Officer Andrew Foote's gunboats and mortar boats began a bombardment of Island No. 10 that would continue daily for the rest of the month and beyond. On the island, the Confederate garrison endured the shelling with equanimity, according to the *Intelligencer*'s sources. A dispatch from Memphis, dated March 25, claimed, "our soldiers on the Island are in good spirits, and declare they can hold it against the world." (They could not; when Pope's infantry approached Island No. 10, General Mackall saw no means of evacuating his garrison and surrendered on April 8. Pope took in 4,410 prisoners and 109 cannon, with the loss of only thirty men killed, wounded and missing.) [7]

On March 19 the *Intelligencer* printed a telegraphic dispatch stating correctly that New Madrid had been evacuated on the night of the 13th. Yet hope sprang eternal in Confederate propaganda. On March 21, the *Intelligencer* published an editorial of the *Memphis Avalanche* declaring, "We do not believe it practicable for the enemy to descend the Mississippi river," given the firm defensive positions of "New Madrid, Island No. 10 and Fort Pillow"—the latter an earthwork built on the Tennessee shore of the Mississippi, forty miles north of Memphis. As we have seen, though, New Madrid had already fallen the week before. On March 22, the *Intelligencer* reprinted from the *Memphis Appeal* of the 15th an opinion piece declaring, "the evacuation of Madrid was not to us a matter of surprise," and that "there is little in this evacuation of Madrid to discourage us."[8]

Fortunately, there was an occasional Confederate triumph on the battlefield whose reporting could offset dispiriting news from other quarters. On March 29, the *Intelligencer* reprinted an article from the *Augusta Chronicle & Sentinel* that began, "Whilst we have been lamenting our reverses near home, a grand success has attended our arms away off in New Mexico." The report put forth that "twenty-five hundred gallant Southerners have met, defeated and captured thirty-five hundred of the enemy."

The story got better with its next telling. On the 30th, the *Intelligencer* carried an account dated March 28 from Houston. On March 21, it related that at Valverde, in what is today New Mexico (but back then the "Confederate Territory of Arizona"), Confederate General Sibley's force of 2,300 reportedly defeated 6,000 Union troops under a General Canley. The Southerners charged and captured a nine-gun battery. Three hundred of the enemy were killed and wounded; Sibley's command lost 36 killed and 106 wounded. "2500 of the enemy have returned to Fort Craig," the article concluded; "we have surrounded them, and they must surrender."

As usual, the hyperbole clashed with reality. Confederate Brig. Gen. Henry H. Sibley set out from Fort Bliss, at the extreme west end of Texas, with some 2,000 men, following the Rio Grande toward the Union-held Fort Craig. Federal Col. Edward Canby, commanding 3,800 troops, prepared to meet him a few miles from the fort at Valverde, on the west bank of the river. On February 21, after several hours' fighting, a Confederate charge overran a six-gun Federal battery. Sibley's Texans turned the cannon on the enemy, who began retreating back to Fort Craig, leaving Sibley to claim victory. When Canby refused Sibley's demand to surrender the fort, the Confederates moved northward, toward Albuquerque and a hoped-for cache of supplies.

Confederate casualties, about ten percent of some 1,750 engaged, totaled 36 killed, 150 wounded and 1 missing. Canby's forces lost 110 killed, 240 wounded and 35 missing, sixteen percent of some 2,400 engaged. Little wonder that the *Intelligencer* pronounced Valverde a "great victory in the West."[9]

All of this military news had come to Archibald Gaulding *via* telegraph. Another major source of page-filler was the helpful correspondence sent to him for publication. In an advisory "To Correspondents," he announced that the paper could not publish everything it received. "We therefore must in future exercise our right to reject all productions not of general interest," and "publish . . . what, in our judgment, will best please our readers." The paper announced that it was always willing to print, free of charge, announcements submitted to it by "patriotic or charitable institutions," so long as they came in a timely fashion. In an advisory appearing on March 6, the editor reminded readers that such notices had to be received by 3 p.m. if they were to appear in the *Intelligencer*'s evening edition. "At 6 o'clock P.M. of each day we issue our evening edition, and by 3 o'clock '*Copy*' is always in hand and abundant at that."

One announcement the paper definitely chose to publish was Governor Brown's call for "a day of Fasting and Prayer," on Friday, March 7. On February 21, the *Intelligencer* printed Brown's proclamation, along with an editorial commending public observance. "It is meet and proper," the editor declared, "while we shall fearlessly and resolutely dare the enemy to do his worst, proudly bidding him defiance, that we should humble ourselves to the God of battles." Then, the day before the appointed observance, Gaulding repeated his encouragement. "Let us observe the day set apart by our GOVERNOR as a people threatened by subjugation and oppression," he exhorted, "who, though strong and determined, recognize that through GOD cometh the victory!" The *Intelligencer* obligingly announced that its offices would be closed on March 7, resulting in no paper being issued on Saturday, the 8th.

Northerners bent on subjugating and oppressing the South were showing how they would do it in occupied Nashville. Not even a month after taking the city, Federals began to implement a "despotic rule," as the *Intelligencer* reported on March 7. They arrested political leaders, proclaimed that no pro-Rebel speech would be tolerated, shut down newspapers or took them over, and even threatened that citizens would be compelled to take an oath of allegiance to the Union, or be sent to Fort LaFayette, "their property seized, and their families left dependent upon the cold charity of the city." According to the *Intelligencer*, in an article entitled, "The Reign of Terror in Nashville," a Union officer had demanded that an Episcopal priest in the city lead a prayer for President Abraham Lincoln, or be hanged. From the earliest days of the young American republic, the Episcopalian Book of Common Prayer had prescribed in its recited prayers a blessing for the president of the United States. Then, with the formation of the Confederacy, Southern priests had begun leading prayers for the Confederate president, to which practice Federal occupiers of course objected. According to the paper's article, Father George C. Harris, rector of the Church of the Holy Trinity, had received a letter from Union Brig. Gen. Alexander McCook demanding, "You shall pray for the President of the United States or be hung." For all of these reasons, Nashville, Gaulding sadly concluded, "is now, already, from all accounts, a city of despotism and gloom." Yet the people demonstrated a defiance that the *Intelligencer* found most commendable. On March 20, it printed the story of how General McCook, arriving in the capital, sought to strike up his acquaintance with a lady living in the city. When he sent her his card, she wrote on the back of it, "Sir: I do not desire to renew any acquaintance with the invaders of my State." Then there was the lass of fourteen, as the *Intelligencer* reported on April 9, who was playing the piano with a Federal officer present. She made a point of draping a Confederate flag on the piano. When the officer teased her about eventual matrimony, she retorted, "There is not a lady in the Southern Confederacy [who] would have you."

Another "city of despotism and gloom," according to the *Intelligencer,* was Alexandria, Virginia, which on May 24, 1861, became the first city of the Confederacy to have been occupied by Union forces. Ten months later, on March 12, 1862, the *Intelligencer* reprinted an article from the *Richmond Enquirer* that recounted an event in Alexandria's St. Paul's Episcopal Church. On Sunday, February 9, 1862, the rector of St. Paul's, the Rev. K. J. Stewart, as the article explained, omitted the presidential prayer, rather than lead the congregation to pray for Lincoln. A Union officer stood up, read the prayer book phrasing that praised the American president, and walking to the altar, ordered Father Stewart arrested. The priest, as the *Intelligencer* reported, kneeling in prayer, was "dragged from his knees by the soldiers," out of the church, and into the streets "in his surplice." The congregation felt helpless to oppose this indignation.

Alongside this account in his issue of March 12, Archibald Gaulding attached an editorial vilifying "Lincoln's minions" for this "sacrilege." "We want every Southern man to read it," he declared. "When the House of God is invaded, and the ministers of 'HIS WORD' can, with impunity, while addressing their petitions to HIM, be dragged from the sacred altar with pistols at their heads, well may the stern resolve animate every heart, to conquer or die in our Struggle for Southern Independence."[10]

The naval fighting at Hampton Roads, Va., the battle of Pea Ridge, Ark., Union conquests on the upper Mississippi and action way out west in Arizona Territory stretched the *Intelligencer*'s scope of war reporting far and wide. Elevating it to the heavens was only the next step.

NOTES

1. "Defeated But Not Conquered," *ADI*, Mar. 27, 1862.

2. "Richmond, March 8 . . . ," *ADI*, Mar. 9, 1862; "A Grand Naval Battle!," "Further" and "Great Naval Victory," *ADI*, March 11.

3. "Further Particulars of the Naval Battle," *ADI*, Mar. 12, 1862.

4. "The Victory at Hampton Roads," *ADI*, Mar. 15, 1862; "The Balls of the Ericson Battery," *ADI*, March 20; "Congress has passed . . . ," *ADI*, March 21.

5. D. Alexander Brown, "Pea Ridge," *Civil War Times Illustrated*, vol. 6, no. 6 (October

1967), 4–11, 46–48; William L. Shea, *War in the West: Pea Ridge and Prairie Grove* (Fort Worth: Ryan Place Publishers, 1996), 53, 69.

6. "Reports! Rumors!," *ADI*, Feb. 2, 1862; "Reported Battles," *ADI*, March 9, "Battle in Arkansas!," "Further from Arkansas," "Still Later" and "Sad News," all in *ADI*, March 13; "Further from Arkansas," *ADI*, March 14; William L. Shea and Earl J. Hess, *Pea Ridge: Civil War Campaign in the West* (Chapel Hill: University of North Carolina Press, 1992), 167, 366 n.39; "The Fight in Arkansas," *ADI*, March 14; "GREAT VICTORY IN ARKANSAS!," *ADI*, March 15.

7. Larry J. Daniel and Lynn N. Bock, *Island No. 10: Struggle for the Mississippi Valley* (Tuscaloosa: University of Alabama Press, 1996), 4, 6–7, 36, 40, 42, 48, 50, 59, 63, 74–83, 86, 114, 133–34, 145, 159; Peter Cozzens, *General John Pope: A Life for the Nation* (Urbana: University of Illinois Press, 2000), 55–56, 58, 62,64; "News from the West," *ADI*, Mar. 27. 1862.

8. "From Missouri and Tennessee," *ADI*, Mar. 6, 1862; "Evacuation of New Madrid," *ADI*, March 19; "NEW MADRID," *ADI*, March 21; "MADRID," *ADI*, March 22.

9. "Bloody Fight," *ADI*, Mar. 29, 1862; "Battle in Texas," *ADI*, March 30; Christine M. Kreiser, "Showdown in New Mexico," *America's Civil War*, vol. 25, no. 6 (January 2013), 44–47; Martin Hardwick Hall, *Sibley's New Mexico Campaign* (Austin: University of Texas Press, 1960), 73, 98, 101,106; Donald S. Frazier, *Blood & Treasure: Confederate Empire in the Southwest* (College Station: Texas A & M University Press, 1995), 180; "Great Victory in the West!," *ADI*, April 3.

10. "To Correspondents," *ADI*, Mar. 13, 1862; "TAKE NOTICE," *ADI*, March 6; "A Day of Humiliation and Prayer," *ADI*, February 21; "Day of Fasting and Prayer," *ADI*, March 6; "FAST DAY," *ADI*, March 7; "The Yankees in Nashville," *ADI*, March 7; "THE NASHVILLE TIMES," *ADI*, March 21; "A NASHVILLE PAPER," *ADI*, March 21; "THE REIGN OF TERROR IN NASHVILLE," *ADI*, April 15; "Spirit of the Nashville Ladies," *ADI*, March 20; "The ladies of Nashville keep entirely aloof from the enemy . . . ," *ADI*, April 9; Kundahl, *Alexandria Goes to War*, 15; "The Despot's Heel is on Thy Neck," *ADI*, March 12; "Sacrilege," *ADI*, March 12; Rable, *God's Almost Chosen*, 325.

11. Yankees in Atlanta

"LET EVERY TRUE SON OF THE SOUTH look out for Spies and Traitors. That they are in our midst, we have not a doubt," the *Intelligencer* warned its readers in an editorial, appearing on Feb. 11, 1862. "Let every true man look out for Spies and Traitors, and let them be dealt with summarily!"[1]

Atlanta, as a fast-growing business community in the South, had always attracted entrepreneurial Northerners. Its railroad shops and various manufactories employed many workmen and artisans from the North as well. These migrants had for years blended with the city's Southern-born population to make Atlanta the state's fourth-largest city in 1860. For these reasons, the *Mobile Advertiser & Register* in the spring of 1862 commented on a "slight perceptible odor of Yankeedom," hanging about Atlanta.

The people that the *Intelligencer* warned about were those in the current war who actually longed for Northern victory and were willing to take furtive steps to undermine the Confederate cause. "There is another class of person in this and other Southern cities," the paper editorialized on February 16. This group, admittedly small in number, is "disloyal at heart," to the point of uttering "treasonable sentiments."

To these, the *Intelligencer* editor issued a warning: they should leave town. "The men, or women, who have any Northern sympathies, must carry them away from Atlanta. . . . Too much has been tolerated here already of treasonable language, and, in future, *it must cease.*"[2]

It was but a short step in logic from urging that disloyalists should voluntarily leave Atlanta to advocating for a legal administration that would actually enforce such an exodus. The *Intelligencer* broached the subject on March 18, when it reprinted an article from the *Memphis Appeal*, "What is Martial Law?" Its purpose, the article described, "is to place all power, as well as all the resources of the district, in the hands of military authorities, to be used and wielded against the public enemy. . . . It supercedes the ordinary instrumentalities of courts," the essay explained, "such as judges, juries and sheriffs." Indeed, the military commandant enforcing martial law in an area had authority to suspend the writ of *habeas corpus*. Such extraordinary measures could be justified during wartime in the interest of public safety. As example, the *Appeal* pointed out that Gen. Andrew Jackson had enforced martial law in New Orleans for a time in 1814.³

On March 22, a week after publishing this piece, the *Intelligencer* actually took the step of calling for martial law to be imposed in Atlanta. Later, on April 2, the *Intelligencer* repeated its call. "For many wise, patriotic, and useful purposes," the measure should be implemented, the piece argued. It laid out the benefits: "to put down disloyal, and law-breaking practices; to stay the extortioner, speculator, and to rid our city of wandering traitors, who pass to and fro, and stay in it with impunity; martial law should be declared over it." "We do hope that GOVERNOR BROWN will declare it over Atlanta." Gaulding then denounced the current situation in the city: "Atlanta is now made Head Quarters for itinerant speculators in gold, bank notes, Confederate currency, meat and bread."

"Yes, Colonel, meat and bread!" exclaimed a reader who the next day wrote Gaulding. The paper published the letter, penned by "REASON," on April 4. The extortionate practices in Atlanta demanded action, he argued. "For the sake of law and order and the good name of our city, will not the governor come to our rescue?," "Reason" asked. He even echoed the *Intelligencer*'s call for martial law. "As civil law will not remedy our evils," he concluded, "then let us have Martial Law. The people desire it."

The *Intelligencer*'s rival, the *Atlanta Southern Confederacy*, contended that Gaulding had gone too far, arguing on April 4 that the restrictions imposed by martial law would be more onerous than "the yoke of Lincolndom." The editorial jousting continued when the *Southern Confederacy* on April 9 published another editorial voicing opposition to martial law. The piece criticized the *Intelligencer* for "daily advocating martial law, and the most radical and unwarrantable interference with private rights." Gaulding answered the very next day. "The 'Intelligencer' has done no such thing," he countered, charging that "no intelligent reader can be deceived by its sophistry," referring to the *Southern Confederacy*. Gaulding concluded by asking "Will the *Confederacy* have no word of censure for . . . the impudent and avaricious itinerant who with pocket full of money, monopolizes every necessity of life, to extort greedily his gains?"⁴

Presence of Federal troops in Georgia returned to the *Intelligencer*'s telegraphic news column of April 13, with word that Fort Pulaski, downstream from Savannah on Cockspur Island, had been captured by the enemy. The paper on the 11th had reported that Union batteries had started shelling the fort the previous morning. Then the *Savannah Republican* carried the story that the fort had surrendered at 2 p.m. on April 11, after the enemy artillery bombardment had perforated its wall and dislodged many of its cannon. A later account, also printed by the *Intelligencer* on the 13th, explained that Union batteries had fired nearly a thousand rounds at the brick-walled bastion; "the balls were conical and spherical, and propelled with such force as to pass through the wall at nearly every fire." Three balls had dangerously breached the fort's magazine. Col. Charles H. Olmstead had commanded the Confederate garrison inside. One of its members had managed to escape after the fort's colors were struck, and had told the story to the Savannah press. He brought the message from Olmstead, as the *Savannah Republican* reported, "that the garrison had done all that men could do," and that "such was the fire that no human being could stand in the ramparts for even a moment."

In the face of bad news, the *Intelligencer* could only comment that the fall of Fort Pulaski had been practically inevitable, but added hope that the city of Savannah itself would be defended against any enemy attempt at capture.

The paper did not attempt to varnish or miscast the report of Fort Pulaski's fall. Gaulding acknowledged, "it was a delusive hope" that the bastion, on an island menaced by the Union forces that had landed the previous November on Tybee Island, could hold out. Not reported in the news accounts, however, was the key reason for Pulaski's surrender. The brick-and-mortar fort had been constructed by the U.S. corps of engineers during the 1830s and '40s. At the time, its seven-and-a-half-foot thick walls were deemed invulnerable to hostile artillery fire. The heaviest smoothbore cannon placed on Tybee across the waterway from Cockspur, a distance of 1,700 yards, had an average range of 800, too short even to reach the fort. But in the 1850s, rifled artillery had been invented. These new guns had much longer ranges, and greater precision to boot. Federals put such artillery in position for their shelling of Pulaski. Little wonder, then, that after a 36-hour bombardment, with the fort's walls breached and most of his own guns knocked out, Colonel Olmstead was compelled to haul down his colors.[5]

Archibald Gaulding and the *Intelligencer* did not have access to this kind of contextual information; a newspaper can only print the news it receives. This was very much evident in the paper's reporting of the largest battle yet fought in America's civil war, that of Shiloh, Tenn., fought on April 6–7, 1862.

BY TELEGRAPH.
EXPRESSLY FOR THE INTELLIGENCER.
COMPLETE VICTORY!
Great Battle at Shiloh!
Great Slaughter on both Sides.
BEAUREGARD'S REPORT.
Gen. A. S. Johnson Killed.
Gen. Bushrod Johnson Wounded.
Large Number of Federals taken Prisoners.
Gen. Prentiss Captured.
THE YANKEES FLEEING.
&c., &c., &c., &c.

Confederate Gen. P. G. T. Beauregard's telegraphic report to the War Department in Richmond was printed under this exclamatory deck headline in the *Intelligencer* on April 8. Dated April 6, Beauregard's message informed Gen. Samuel Cooper, adjutant general of the army,

> We this morning attacked the enemy in strong position, in front of PITTSBURG, and after a battle of ten hours, THANKS BE TO THE ALMIGHTY, gained a complete victory, driving the enemy from every position. The loss on both sides is heavy, including the loss of the Commander-in-Chief, A. S. Johnston, who fell gallantly leading his men into the thickest of the fight.
>
> G. T. BEAUREGARD,
> Gen. Commanding.

Below this was an article datelined Mobile, April 7. The *Advertiser and Register* of that city had received dispatches from Corinth, Mississippi, sent on the 6th, that added particulars. Confederates had attacked, though incurring heavy casualties. The 21st Alabama Infantry Regiment was said to have captured two enemy batteries; a third fell to the 1st Louisiana. Gen. Bushrod Johnson, who had escaped from Fort Donelson, was reported as wounded.

Thus far, the battle had only been referred to as having occurred at "Shiloh" and "Pittsburg," though the location of these places was not reported. "At night, the enemy is in full retreat," the article continued; "the Confederates in hot pursuit after them."

The writer of this piece in the *Intelligencer* was evidently a special correspondent of the *Mobile Advertiser & Register*, actually present with the Confederate forces. He had composed his account based on what he had seen and heard on April 6: "I write from the enemy's camp, and on Federal paper. A large number of Federal prisoners have already been taken. We expect to capture the greater part of the Federal Army. We are driving them back on to the river, and shall kill or capture the entire army. The battle is still raging with terrible fury. Have captured Gen. Prentiss and a large number of Federal officers."

A cautionary note to this excited report ("large number of Federal prisoners"; "kill or capture the entire army") was the reporter's admission that "the battle is still raging with terrible fury." The downside of the narrative thus far was the death of General Albert Sidney Johnston, which had occurred around 2:30 p.m., according to the *Advertiser and Register*'s special correspondent: "his leg was torn by a shell, and a minnie ball struck him in the body." Despite this loss, General Beauregard, who had then taken over command, was said to have described the day's victorious battle as "a second Manassas fight"—on par with his and Joseph E. Johnston's triumph of the previous summer. The "special" closed his report by stating that General Grant was in command of the Federal army. Rather ominously, he added, "Gen. Buell was not in time to take part in the fight."

Another dispatch from Corinth on April 6, also printed in the *Intelligencer*'s "Telegraphic News" page on the 8th, added that "the Yankees were driven back two miles. Our victorious columns still advancing." "The enemy had eighteen batteries engaged, which were mostly captured," the report claimed; "we have the enemy's camp, all his ammunition, stores, &c.... Two thousand prisoners have already been taken and sent to the rear of the army." The Federal forces were said to have been "driven back to the river, and are attempting to cross on transports." ("The river" had so far remained unnamed, just as the locations of "Pittsburg" or "Shiloh" had not been pinpointed.)[6]

With a continuation of the battle into a second day all but certain, Beauregard was grossly premature to have telegraphed Richmond proclaiming "a complete victory." But the South was starved for some good news (for a change), and Beauregard's incomplete report provided it. Everyone, it seems, fell in line, including the *Intelligencer*. "THANKS BE TO THE ALMIGHTY" headlined Gaulding's editorial on April 8, quoting from General Beauregard's initial report to General Cooper in Richmond. "We reverently echo AMEN to the sentiment," the editor declared, as he noted that "the excitement around and about us has been intense." He promised to give readers "all the additional particulars we may receive of the great 'Battle of Shiloh.'" A telegraphed message, dated April 8 from Richmond, printed by the *Intelligencer* on the 9th, stated that President Davis had announced that in a ten-hour battle, "the enemy was driven in disorder to the Tennessee River" and during the night was trying to get across it on transports. Accordingly, the Congress adopted a resolution of thanks to Beauregard and his army for their "great, complete, and brilliant victory."

Confederate newspapers—so-called today by historians for their editorial support of Southern independence in the 1860s—eagerly broadcast reports of such great, complete and brilliant victories as had been assumed at Shiloh. The *Intelligencer* played this propagandizing role by publishing these items, as well as a short communication from Corinth, dated the 8th, declaring "success to our cause." The paper carried no update of any fighting at Shiloh that occurred on April 7, and thus failed to report that Grant's army, reinforced by thousands of Don C. Buell's troops, had launched a counterattack that day that had forced Beauregard's army to retreat. Moreover, no one seemed to wonder at a later dispatch from Richmond, published by the *Intelligencer* on the 11th, stating that "General Beauregard has carried out his contemplated plan of falling back to Corinth." Instead, the paper on the 12th printed a short piece declaring that a gentleman arriving from Corinth had imparted information that "differs but little from our telegraphed reports."

Intelligencer editor Gaulding, who had more than once cautioned readers about unfounded rumors and unauthenticated news dispatches, not only ignored the implications of Beauregard's retreat back to Corinth, but continued to exult over his initial report from the battlefield. The editor's enthusiasm is palpable in the opinion piece printed on April 12:

THE BATTLE OF SHILOH.

Beauregard calls the battle of Sunday last, the *"Battle of Shiloh."*

Let it be known throughout the length and breadth of the land by that appellation! The word *"Shiloh"* signifies, we are advised, the *"expectation of nations."* From it, we may base glorious expectations indeed—*glorious* as to the future of the Confederate States of America; and *glorious* we feel confident, as to all the nations of the earth, save to that corrupt, fanatical, treacherous, and abominable one, now madly bent upon riveting upon the South the accursed chains of political despotism. *"Shiloh"* let the battle be called! The *"expectations of nations"* let the Southern Confederacy be!

In truth, the *Intelligencer* was not the only Confederate newspaper reporting what it hoped had occurred, rather than what had actually happened. On April 16, the paper published, from the *Savannah Republican* of the previous day, an update on the battle that claimed "we still hold part of the battle field," which was patently untrue. Two days later, the *Intelligencer* reprinted an account taken from the *Richmond Dispatch* of April 14 relating what a Texan, arriving in the capital from the west, had heard while travelling through Corinth about the battle of Shiloh: 8,000 Union soldiers had been captured, along with a huge haul of more than seventy cannon. The *Dispatch* also related that a Confederate congressman had brought from Chattanooga the additional intelligence that the Federals had lost 15,000 men in "the battles of Sunday and Monday"—an acknowledgement of Shiloh's second day of fighting. The *Dispatch* did not elaborate on the congressman's statement that all of the ammunition and supplies captured by Confederates on Sunday had to be left behind by Beauregard "when he retired to Corinth." The *Wilmington Journal* also got swept up in the enthusiasm. In an article appearing in the *Intelligencer* of the 15th, the *Journal* pondered over the names of "three of the most noted battles of the present war and of the most brilliant victories": Bethel, Manassas and Shiloh. The *Journal* found it remarkable that the scenes of these three Confederate triumphs should carry Biblical names. Most significant was Shiloh, fought on a Sunday (April 6) at that; *Shiloh* was a Hebrew name, the paper stated, "by which the Hebrew prophets referred to the coming one, the hope of the nations"—the same point that Gaulding had made in his editorial of the 12th.[7]

This kind of "reporting" continued well after the battle. Northern newspapers' claims of victory at Shiloh were noticed, and dismissed. Reports of fantastic quantities of weapons captured by Confederates ("eighty-six pieces of artillery") were received and credited. As late as April 27, three weeks after the battle, the *Intelligencer* was reprinting from the *Richmond Examiner* an account of the battle that acknowledged the Federals' attacks on the second day, April 7, and Beauregard's retreat back to Corinth. But the article still contended, "the events of both days were considered a thorough victory," given that the Confederate forces had achieved their objective, "to drive the enemy to the river."

It was most ironic, after publicizing and celebrating a Confederate victory that was actually *not* a victory, that editor Gaulding should call for more judicious journalism. In a piece entitled "An Intolerable Evil," printed on April 20, he endorsed the opinion expressed by the *Petersburg* (Va.) *Express* when it termed "the propensity to indulge in fictitious and exaggerated statements about the incidents of the war' an intolerable evil." Gaulding excerpted the *Express* article: "One scarcely knows now what to believe that appears in the public journals. The grossest falsehoods in the shape of sensational reports, flashed through the telegraph, are almost daily afloat. To these may be added continual misrepresentations and exaggerations of actual occurrences"—in other words, that which the *Intelligencer* and other Southern newspapers had done when they took Beauregard's initial telegram of April 6 and transmogrified it into a complete narrative of the entire battle.

Of this, however, Gaulding was innocent of knowledge, as he added his own comment on the *Petersburg Express'* editorial. "We have become tired and disgusted at the newspaper *sensation* paragraphs, which, hourly almost, we read in some of the newspapers," he complained, criticizing especially papers that printed "everything heard on the streets from 'reliable gentlemen' or rather dupes to rumors of all sorts."

There was not much difference between being a "dupe to rumors" and printing them, albeit skeptically. The *Montgomery Advertiser* had picked up a report from the *Mobile Tribune* that claimed, based on statements made by passengers from Corinth, that Confederate generals Kirby Smith and Humphrey Marshall had stormed into Nashville and retaken the city, plus three or four thousand prisoners. The editor of the *Advertiser* had cautioned, "we are not disposed to believe Madame Rumour, but give this for what it is worth, and leave the reader to believe it or not, as he may be inclined." The *Atlanta Intelligencer* reprinted the "Nashville Re-Taken" item in its issue of April 22 without comment.[8]

On the other hand, Gaulding and his newspaper practiced prudent investigative reporting when it covered the sensational story of how, on April 12, Northerners in civilian garb had stolen a train on the Western & Atlantic Railroad north of Atlanta. Within two days, the *Intelligencer* had the written statements of the two railroad employees who had led the pursuit of the train thieves and dogged them eighty-nine miles till they were all captured. Gaulding was able to publish their accounts on April 15, thus preserving invaluable first-hand narratives of the event that would become known as the Andrews Raid.

The two railroad men at the center of the story were Anthony Murphy, the Western & Atlantic's foreman of machinery and motive power, and William A. Fuller, conductor of the *General,* the train hijacked by the Northerners. The day after the event, Murphy and Fuller returned to Atlanta and began telling their story. Staff of the *Atlanta Southern Confederacy* interviewed them, and was able on April 15 to publish a long article, "The Great Railroad Chase." That same day, the *Intelligencer* also carried a long, informative article bearing the headline, "Lincoln's Spies, Thieves, and Bridge Burners." Instead of interviewing Fuller and Murphy, the *Intelligencer* printed their written statements, which had been submitted to E. B. Walker, master of transportation for the Western & Atlantic. Rather than construct its own narrative from the two reports, Gaulding and Whitaker's paper printed them separately. Thus it not only gave a more specific narrative of the event than did George Adair and Henly Smith's *Southern Confederacy*; the *Intelligencer*, because it was a morning paper, could have scooped the story on the 15th.

By that time, the Northern train-thieves had been apprehended, but the Atlanta newspapers had no information about them, or their motive. Today, we know that they numbered twenty: nineteen volunteers from Ohio infantry regiments, led by a civilian, James J. Andrews. Andrews had conceived a plot for the group to slip through Confederate lines toward Atlanta, stealthily board a train heading for Chattanooga, and then at Big Shanty (the stop 28 miles by rail north of Atlanta, now known as Kennesaw), hijack the train while crew and passengers were breakfasting. Their mission, as Andrews conceived it, would be to steam north toward Chattanooga, cut telegraph lines, damage or remove railroad track and burn key bridges, thus crippling the Western & Atlantic's ability to send troops and supplies to Confederate forces in Tennessee. Andrews' timing of his raid coordinated with Union Brig. Gen. Ormsby M. Mitchel's plans to advance from Huntsville toward Chattanooga. General Mitchel liked the plan, despite its improbable chances of success, and gave his approval.

Thus Andrews and his nineteen followers boarded the Chattanooga-bound train at Marietta about 5 a.m. on April 12, dressed as civilians. An hour later they stopped at Big Shanty, so crew and passengers could take their morning meal at a trackside hotel. During the break, Andrews' men uncoupled the train behind the *General* and three empty box cars.

It was at this point that Gaulding set up the narrative. "On Saturday morning last"—April 12—"we were startled by intelligence telegraphed here from Marietta, that the Engine"—eventually identified as the *General*—"with three cars attached to the mail train, from this place [Atlanta] to Chattanooga, had been detached therefrom, while the conductor, engineer, and train hands were breakfasting at Big Shanty, and had been steamed up the Road, by unknown parties."

The conductor was William Fuller; Jeff Cain was the engineer. Anthony

Murphy, the Western & Atlantic foreman, was onboard to inspect an engine at Allatoona. Gaulding turned to Fuller first. "As our readers will be interested in a detailed account of this extraordinary and most audacious attempt of LINCOLN'S SPIES to rob, burn, and destroy the State Road, we give below the statement of Mr. Fuller, the conductor of the train from which the engine and three cars were detached by the Lincoln hirelings." "While at breakfast, I heard the engine 'exhaust' very rapidly and suddenly. I immediately rose up and stated to Mr. A. Murphy, who is Boss of the State Road Shop, but who happened to be a passenger that morning, and Mr. Jeff Cain, my engineer, that something was wrong with the engine. We three then hastened out; and, much to our surprise, discovered that the engine with three cars was out of sight. I, at once, suggested to Messrs. Murphy and Cain, the propriety of following the engine to Chattanooga, if in no other way, on foot, and pursue till we overtook and captured the unknown thieves."

The paper traced the Southerners' breathless pursuit of the train-thieves, quoting Fuller's narrative. "On foot, then, in *double-quick* time, we three started in pursuit. I was the first to reach Moon's Station, some two and a half miles from "Big Shanty." There I found a hand-car and returned a short distance to take in my companions, Messrs. Murphy and Cain, and we then, with a few men whom we got at Moon's Station to push the car along, pursued on to within a half mile of Acworth."

The pursuit party pressed on. Beyond Acworth, their push-car was thrown into a ditch; the train-thieves had pried up and removed a rail. They lifted the car back on the track and resumed the chase. At Etowah Station, Murphy, Fuller and Cain commandeered an engine, the *Yonah*, and a car for their men, who had grown in number to about twenty. "When we arrived at Kingston, we found that the thieves had passed some twenty-five minutes ahead of us," Fuller recalled. They learned that the raiders had told the station agent they were carrying powder and ammunition for General Beauregard. The agent was taken in, and obligingly pulled three southbound freight trains into sidings to let Andrews' band continue north, though after considerable delay. At Kingston the pursuers, blocked by the three freights, changed engines, boarding the *William R. Smith*, "which was already fired up," as Fuller noted.

North of Kingston the raiders pried up another rail and threw it into a box car. They could hear the whistle of the pursuers' train to the south. Halted by the broken track, Fuller and Murphy abandoned the *William R. Smith* and continued again on foot (Cain dropped out) for three miles until they ran into the locomotive *Texas* and engineer Peter Bracken. Bracken uncoupled his freight cars and, chugging in reverse, joined in the chase.

"We reached Calhoun," Fuller continued, "where they had left about five minutes before our arrival there, and when about a mile and a half from that station we came in sight of them." Andrews' men started a fire in their hindmost box car, hoping to uncouple it in the covered wooden bridge over the Oostanaula River near Resaca, eighty-four miles by rail from Atlanta. But they could not get a big blaze going; Fuller, Murphy and Bracken easily pushed aside the smoldering car. They were at this point so close behind the *General* that Andrews, near Tilton, could not fully load up on wood.

Meanwhile, Fuller at Dalton had gotten off a telegram to Confederates at Chattanooga, warning them of the train-thieves' approach. The raiders and pursuers were now in sight of each other; Andrews' men had no time to try to pry up another rail. Worse, the *General* was running out of fuel. Two miles north of Ringgold, Andrews called for every man to jump off and run for it. "Here the rascals jumped off and took to the woods," Fuller explained. The pursuers tried to run them down; Confederate cavalry arrived to help. All twenty train-thieves were rounded up.

Gaulding also introduced Anthony Murphy's account. "Mr. Murphy's statement of the pursuit addressed to Mr. Walker is also before us," he observed; "it differs but little from Mr. Fuller's." The *Intelligencer* printed it; the extended article allowed Gaulding to draw editorial conclusions. "Doubtless these fellows have been up and down the road often, and had acquired an intimate knowledge here and elsewhere of all its operations," he conjectured, reinforcing the editor's previous warnings about Yankees in Atlanta. "Their mission," he added as for the captured train-thieves, "was to spy out the land, to burn and destroy, especially the bridges of the State Road." Lest his admonition not be heeded, Gaulding offered his considered judgment.

> A more daring set than this, we have never been called upon to record. That the parties who committed it, were *emissaries* and *spies* of Lincoln, is admitted by those who have been captured. We have all along believed that Atlanta had been, and is still being visited by disloyal men, spies, and emissaries of our foes. We have warned our people of this; we have appealed to the authorities to look into this matter; we have advocated Martial Law to ensure our safety, and detect the rascals, as well as to rid our community of other evils. We have been taunted in our efforts, with a desire

to interfere with private rights; to interfere with the privileges of our merchants, as though Martial Law would necessarily do this. We now again repeat, that in our judgment, Martial Law is necessary for the security of both *person and property* in Atlanta. We confidently believe that our city has been and is daily being visited by spies and emissaries of the Lincoln government—that the public property here is endangered—and as a consequence private property will share its fate. But to this subject we shall again refer.[9]

Thus far in the *Intelligencer*'s reporting, we have seen how a repetitive series of hindrances weakened the paper's coverage of military events in Virginia, Tennessee and other distant places. Situated in Atlanta, whither Anthony Murphy and William Fuller (the two principal pursuers of the Andrews train thieves) returned, the paper was at just the right place to obtain their written accounts of the exciting event. Archibald Gaulding's decision to publish them in full is an instance of genuinely professional Civil War journalism, one which has not been commented upon by scholars of the subject.

NOTES

1. "SPIES AND TRAITORS," *ADI*, Feb. 11, 1862.

2. James Michael Russell, *Atlanta 1847–1890: City Building in the Old South and the New* (Baton Rouge: Louisiana State University Press, 1988), 39–66; Venet, *Changing Wind*, 15; Dyer, *Secret Yankees*, 95; Russell S. Bonds, *Stealing the General: The Great Locomotive Chase and the First Medal of Honor* (Yardley PA: Westholme, 2007), 93; "OH! YE OF LITTLE FAITH!," *ADI*, Feb. 16, 1862.

3. "What is Martial Law?," *ADI*, Mar. 18, 1862; Coulter, *Confederate States of America*, 337.

4. "Shipment of Cotton to Tennessee," *ADI*, Mar. 22, 1862; "MARTIAL LAW," *ADI*, April 2; "REASON," "SPECULATION," *ADI*, April 4; "SPECULATORS," *Atlanta Southern Confederacy*, April 4; "How It Works," *ADI*, April 10.

5. "Bombardment of Fort Pulaski," *ADI*, Apr. 11, 1862; "Surrender of Fort Pulaski" (Savannah, April 11) and "The Surrender of Fort Pulaski," *ADI*, April 13; Herbert M. Schiller, *Sumter is Avenged! The Siege and Reduction of Fort Pulaski* (Shippensburg PA: White Mane, 1995), 24, 103, 111–12, 133.

6. "BY TELEGRAPH. EXPRESSLY FOR THE INTELLIGENCER. COMPLETE VICTORY!," "MOBILE, April 6" and "From Memphis—The Late Battle," all in *ADI*, Apr. 8, 1862; Grady McWhiney, "General Beauregard's 'Complete Victory' at Shiloh: An Interpretation," *Journal of Southern History*, vol. 49, no. 3 (August 1983), 421.

7. "'THANKS BE TO THE ALMIGHTY,'" *ADI*, April 8, 1862; "Confederate Congress," "From Richmond" and "Special Dispatch," all in *ADI*, April 9; "Later from Corinth," *ADI*, April 11; "THE BATTLE OF SHILOH," *ADI*, April 12; "LATEST FROM

CORINTH," *ADI,* April 16 (from *Savannah Republican*); "From the Richmond (Va.) Dispatch, April 14. THE BATTLE OF SHILOH," *ADI,* April 18; "BETHEL, MANASSAS, AND SHILOH," *ADI,* April 15 (*Wilmington Journal*).

8. "Further Northern News," *ADI,* Apr. 17, 1862; "The Result of the Battle of Shiloh,'" *ADI,* April 22; "From the Richmond Examiner. THE BATTLES OF SHILOH AND PITTSBURG. THE SITUATION IN THE WEST, ETC.," *ADI,* April 27; "An Intolerable Evil," *ADI,* April 20; "Nashville Re-Taken," *ADI,* April 22 (from the *Montgomery Advertiser*).

9. "LINCOLN'S SPIES, THIEVES, AND BRIDGE BURNERS," *ADI,* Apr. 15, 1862; Stan Cohen and James G. Bogle, *The General & the Texas: A Pictorial History of the Andrews Raid, April 12, 1862* (Missoula MT: Pictorial Histories Publishing Co., 1999), 20, 29–32, 35–38; Bonds, *Stealing the General,* xi, 34–35; Stephen Davis, "The Conductor versus the Foreman: William Fuller, Anthony Murphy, and the Pursuit of the Andrews Raiders," *Atlanta History,* vol. 34, no. 4 (Winter 1990–91), 39–40; Wilbur G. Kurtz, Sr., "The Andrews Railroad Raid," *Civil War Times Illustrated,* vol. 5, no. 1 (April 1966), 8–16, 38–43.

12. The Fall of New Orleans

IN THE SPRING OF 1862, Archibald Gaulding, co-proprietor with Jared Whitaker of the *Atlanta Daily Intelligencer,* was supervising a major newspaper in Atlanta, publishing six days a week, essentially by himself as editor with a staff of eight to ten, as best as we can judge (Whitaker, chief of the Georgia Commissary Department, was usually away at Milledgeville). Gaulding's work was not easy. In an open letter to his subscribers, printed on Wednesday, April 9, he explained why. A year into the war, the *Intelligencer* had not raised its prices, which remained $6 a year for the daily, and two dollars for the weekly issue. The co-owner/editor even put forth some of his operating costs. Paper was costing $6.35 a ream of some 425 sheets, about 1 ½ cents each. Then there was the cost to print, after which "there is but a very small margin of profit realized from regular subscribers." Street sales helped a little: "we sell to the newsboys the *Intelligencer* at 2½ cents per copy." But after their sale (for a nickel each), "we are of the opinion that no profit, or but a very insignificant one is made by the sales to the newsboys."

Meanwhile the cost of paper was going up. Gaulding admitted that he had not over a ream on hand, and this had come through the blockade "at advanced prices, varying from 150 to 250 per cent, over the cost of similar quantities of paper anterior to the blockade." These pressures, he declared, had forced other Southern papers to raise their subscription prices.

A few days later, on April 13, Gaulding reinforced his pecuniary point. The *Intelligencer* had not raised its prices since its inception in Atlanta—quite a feat. "We now, in a period of adversity, still exact no more from our subscribers," the editor reminded; "nor shall we do so, till the INTELLIGENCER cannot sustain itself by its present rates." Gaulding nevertheless implored his readers, "all we ask is, that our subscribers will be punctual and prompt in payment." The editor selflessly proclaimed, "in pursuing this course, we may make *no money*, but thousands of our fellow-citizens are in the same condition, and the

INTELLIGENCER can afford to sacrifice to the necessities of the times, as much as they, the subscribers, can, or are patriotically disposed to do."[1]

Then there was the problem of getting the most up-to-date war news, in which newspaper readers were obviously most interested. The problem was especially vexing when telegrams arrived too late for the morning edition. Each night, as Gaulding had earlier explained, the day's last wire dispatches were picked up at the city's downtown telegraph office. The morning edition was held up till midnight so that the latest news could be set and laid out for printing. The *Intelligencer*'s evening edition was similarly held up till 6 p.m.

Sometimes preparing late news made for a long day for the editor and his staff. On Jan. 4, 1862, Gaulding had made a point in an article of criticizing William H. Pritchard, head of the Southern Associated Press. The night before, he complained, telegraphed news did not arrive until midnight, after which typesetting and printing took another three hours. "It was not very pleasant," he declared, "waiting the slow performance of the wires, or rather of those who control them." After the South had been cut off from the New York Associated Press in the spring of 1861, Pritchard (a former agent of the New York A. P.) had organized in Augusta, Georgia, a Southern Associated Press. Southern newspapers paid for his telegraphic news service, but its high cost and inefficient operation sparked criticism from subscribers, including the *Intelligencer*. In his editorial of January 4, Gaulding complained that "our friend PRITCHARD" should have been able to transmit the days' dispatches by 9 or 10 p.m., but he had not gotten them till much later. "We do not exactly understand, and must complain," the editor announced. Other editors felt the same. The *Augusta Chronicle and Sentinel* joined the *Intelligencer* in declaring that Pritchard's service was slow, and even that its dispatches were not newsworthy. The *Columbus* (Georgia) *Enquirer* complained about the cost of the service. By late January 1862 a number of editors had made plans to convene in Atlanta in March to discuss what they could do to address their common problems. To them Gaulding later added the spotty transmission of news that he expected each work day. He read in some of his exchanges about actions of the Confederate Congress that he rightly believed should have been sent to him by Pritchard. "How the same failed to reach this office, we are at a loss to know," he groused on February 22; "for if we are not one of the 'Associated Press of the Confederacy,' to whom such items are due, then we must plead guilty to being caught paying a high price for that which we do not get." And pay they did. A month later, Gaulding offered a reminder: "our readers will, we trust, understand, that we pay for telegraphic news."[2]

The agreed-upon newspapermen's meeting was held March 12–13 in Atlanta, the *Intelligencer* informed its readers, with an attendance "smaller than was expected at the time the very general response was made to the call." Part of the reason, Gaulding explained, was that "the Western papers, which were very deeply interested in the movement, have lately passed into the hands of the enemy." Still, besides the editor of the *Intelligencer,* representatives of the *Memphis Appeal,* the *Atlanta Southern Confederacy,* the *Savannah Republican,* the *Augusta Constitutionalist,* the *Nashville Republican Banner* and the *Charleston Mercury* assembled in Atlanta.

The editorial delegates agreed on a number of actions. The main topic, however, was the need for contracts with the telegraph companies to ensure faster transmission. The *Intelligencer* explained to its readers that a "Committee on Telegraphic News" was appointed on March 12, which met that night. Pritchard, who was present at the convention, attended the committee meeting, and attempted to defend himself in view of the problems that telegraphic services faced in the Confederacy ("the deranged state of the country," in the words of the *Intelligencer*). The next morning the committee put forth a resolution, tabling further discussion until more communication with the several Southern telegraph companies could be had. The committee called for another editorial convention, whose purpose would be to "arrange a plan for an Association of the Press of the Confederate States."[3]

Until that time there was still a war to cover, however flawed was the newspapers' telegraphic news service. Not quite a year after Fort Sumter, the Confederate government acknowledged that it would have to take stringent measures to bolster its military strength. The zealous volunteering of the war's early months was petering away, and if those recruits' period of service was a year, that term was soon to run out. Thus President Davis issued on March 28, 1862, a call for Congress to enact a national conscription law—the first such measure in American history. The *Intelligencer* on April 1 printed the president's message, which declared that all men able for duty, between the ages of eighteen and thirty-five, "shall be held to be in the military service of the Confederate States."

Gaulding followed up with a supportive editorial two days later. "We heartily approve the system," he announced, urging that men eligible to be drafted should quickly enlist, at least to earn the $50 bounty being offered to volunteers, which the proposed law would eliminate ($50 would be more than three times a soldier's monthly pay).

On April 16, Congress passed the conscription act, putting eligible males in the army for three years, and giving soldiers already in it a term of equal length. The *Intelligencer* printed the entire law, as it had appeared in the *Richmond Examiner*. Gaulding suggested that readers keep this issue of his paper and its text of the new legislation, as "reference to it will be constantly made, daily and hourly for some weeks to come."[4]

The conscription law thus addressed the question of whether twelve-months' volunteers would re-enlist. Gen. Joseph E. Johnston, commanding the Confederate army in northern Virginia, had addressed his troops on that issue in a proclamation published by the *Intelligencer* on Feb. 16, 1862. He urged those whose enlistments would soon expire to recommit, "and thus show to the world that the patriots engaged in this struggle for independence will not swerve from the bloodiest path they may be called to tread."[5]

After the battle of Manassas (Bull Run), the Confederate army had held position near the battlefield all during the winter. Commander of the Federals forces near Washington, Maj. Gen. George B. McClellan, won President Lincoln's approval not for a direct advance on Johnston, but a wide-ranging maneuver: moving his immense army by ship down to Fort Monroe, at the tip of the peninsula formed by the James and York Rivers in southeast Virginia. McClellan landed on April 2 with his troops. Against his army, which would eventually number 100,000, Confederate Maj. Gen. John B. Magruder had all of 11,000 men. Magruder had constructed a fortified line across the peninsula, from Yorktown to the James, about ten miles in length. Rather than assault Magruder's works, McClellan cautiously chose to bring up heavy artillery to bombard them, thus commencing his "siege" of Yorktown.[6]

The *Intelligencer* began to cover what has become known as the Peninsula Campaign based on its three principal news sources: exchanges from other papers, telegraphed dispatches, and letters by soldiers writing from the actual front. As example of the former, George W. Bagby, correspondent for the *Charleston Mercury*, wrote a letter to his paper from Richmond on March 29, explaining that General Magruder, aware of McClellan's approach, had called for reinforcements. The *Intelligencer* published Bagby's letter on April 5. Magruder's and McClellan's troops began skirmishing daily, but on April 16, the Federals launched an infantry assault on a sector of the Confederate line. The *Intelligencer*'s "BY TELEGRAPH" column on April 18 carried a short article on the fight, "in which they [Federals] were splendidly repulsed. . . . Our troops behaved nobly," as the paper reported. Dr. John Westmoreland, the Atlanta physician who had written Gaulding from his hospital on the campus of William and Mary, sent another letter summarized by the editor on April 19. "Skirmishing has been going on, on the Peninsula, since the fifth instant, daily," the doctor wrote. Gaulding noticed that Westmoreland was appropriately cautious in reporting the strength of Magruder's forces (using the phrase "no matter what") when he wrote, "prisoners represent the Yankee force at about 80,000. Ours is about—(no matter what)."

The presence of so many enemy troops on Virginia's soil led to allegations in the Confederate press of barbaric behavior. In "INFAMOUS OUTRAGES ON THE PENINSULA," the *Intelligencer* on April 29, quoting the *Petersburg* (Va.) *Express*, reported on what the *Express* had learned from "a gentleman of the highest respectability just from Williamsburg." An elderly resident, Samuel Holley, according to the report, had had his home near Warwick approached by "a lot of Yankee officers and men, who introduced themselves by a brutal proposition to Capt. H's two daughters, both young and beautiful ladies. . . . While endeavoring their designs by force," the *Express* explained, the enraged father had shot one of the soldiers, and was himself immediately shot and killed. There were similar instances, according to the article. A resident of the peninsula, one John Patrick, was killed by Union soldiers "while endeavoring to save an only and beloved daughter from a fate worse than death"—Victorians' delicate phrasing for rape. "Mr. Edward Harwood, who also resided in the vicinity of Warwick Courthouse, the *Express* continued, "was brutally murdered a few days since, while defending his daughter's honor."

Gaulding offered comment on these "horrible outrages of rape and murder perpetrated by the Yankee vandals now on the Virginia peninsula." The editor speculated that perhaps an all-wise God had not struck down "the villains" with providential lightning so that "the *people* of the South might have a foretaste of their doom, should they falter in their struggle for Independence." The editor's conclusion was unmistakable: "Georgians, save your wives and daughters, from the lust and yoke of Yankee subjugation!"[7]

Civil War historians have not come to agreement on the extent of actual rape by Northern soldiers of Southern women—both white and black. The *Intelligencer*'s approach to the subject of "a fate worse than death" and its exhortation for Georgians to save their wives and daughters from Yankees' lust adds a more violent and visceral element to the paper's propagandistic vilification of the enemy.

An enemy "far worse than the Goths and Vandals of historic infamy," as the *Petersburg Express* had cast them, received closer scrutiny when opportunity allowed. From the *Savannah Morning News*, the *Intelligencer* on April 3 drew an article about three Federal prisoners who had recently been confined in the coastal city. One, from New Jersey, according to the report, "is very illiterate and can neither read nor write. He informed us that he was tired of the war, as were many of the regiment to which he belonged." Officers abused the men, food was poor, and "he embraced the first opportunity to make his escape." Two of the captives, the *Morning News* continued, were Germans; one of them said that most men of his regiment had enlisted because "they had no employment in the North." The writer continued: "when asked what they were fighting for, these men promptly and frankly replied, 'For pay.'" The contrast was obvious: ignorant, mercenary Union soldiers had been induced into a war against resolute and principled Southerners fighting for their political independence. The point was emphasized in an article from the *Mobile Tribune* that the *Intelligencer* published on April 22. A lot of Federals recently entering the city appeared "a rough looking set of fellows, and just as filthy as it is possible for men to be," the *Tribune* observed. They were "mostly of foreign birth" who "went into the army for food. . . . They are not able to tell for what they are in arms against us," the article declared; "in this respect they are the antipodes of the men who compose our army."[8]

The tone of the *Intelligencer* turned more somber when reporting the loss of the South's largest city, New Orleans.

In September 1861, the Union navy had taken possession of Ship Island, off Biloxi, Mississippi, and began using it as a base for its blockading operations in the Gulf. In February 1862, Union naval captain David G. Farragut assembled at Ship Island a fleet of a dozen and a half warships. Commander David D. Porter added twenty-one mortar boats and seven side-wheelers.

New Orleans at the time was defended by two brick-and-stone forts, St. Philip and Jackson, seventy miles downriver from the city, and across the Mississippi from each other. Together they mounted more than a hundred cannon of various calibers. Confederates had also put together a flotilla of armed vessels, including the ironclad ram *Manassas* (called the "Turtle" because of its shape), that would add their firepower to that of the forts.

Southern optimists were confident that Federal warships would not be able to get past the forts. If they did, they would have to face two well-armed ironclads being built near New Orleans, the *Louisiana* and the *Mississippi*. But in late March 1862 the machinery of both vessels was yet to be installed. The Confederate commander at New Orleans, Maj. Gen. Mansfield Lovell, had some 3,000 troops in the city's defenses and several other river forts.[9]

On April 18, Porter had his mortar fleet in range of Fort Jackson and that morning opened fire on it. The *Intelligencer* began covering the bombardment of the fort on April 22, with a dispatch sent from New Orleans the day before. "The enemy has fired three hundred and seventy thousand pounds of powder, and over a thousand tons of iron," the paper asserted, with considerable exaggeration. The mortar boats actually fired 1,400 shells on the 18th, dislodging some of the fort's guns and setting fires to buildings.

Porter kept up his shelling of Fort Jackson daily, April 19–23. The *Intelligencer* published a dispatch from Brig. Gen. Johnson K. Duncan, commanding there, dated the 23rd, in which he reported that thousands of shells had fallen in the fort. Nevertheless, casualties were light, and he added that "we are hopeful, in good spirits."[10]

General Duncan and his garrison would be disappointed in their hopefulness. Early on the morning of April 24, Farragut and seventeen Northern warships steamed upriver with the intention of passing by the guns of Forts Jackson and St. Philip before daylight. Confederates spotted the movement and set brush fires on shore and fire rafts in the water to help their artillerymen. The Southerners had brought down more gunboats, including the *Louisiana*, which without power, served as a sixteen-gun floating battery. The battle, however, proved decidedly uneven. Farragut's vessels took some hits, and one was sunk after being rammed. But Porter's mortar boats shelled the forts, Farragut's vessels pounded the makeshift Rebel flotilla, and more importantly succeeded in steaming past Jackson and St. Philip. The crew of the helpless *Louisiana* set her afire; she blew up when flames touched her magazine.

Farragut continued upriver toward New Orleans, notifying Maj. Gen. Benjamin F. Butler, whose 18,000 Union troops were anchored downstream, that he should proceed northward. In New Orleans, as Farragut's ships approached, General Lovell ordered cotton and supplies to be burned, arms and ammunition put on boats heading upriver, and his troops to evacuate the city. The unfinished *Mississippi* was set on fire and sent blazing downstream. On April 25, with his vessels' guns trained on the defenseless city, Farragut sent men ashore to raise the United States flag over the New Orleans customhouse. Downriver, General Duncan surrendered his two forts on April 28. Three days later Butler and fourteen hundred troops landed at the city docks and occupied New Orleans.

Casualties in the campaign were light on both sides. In the Union navy, 39 men were killed and 171 wounded. Confederates in the two forts lost 11 killed,

39 wounded; in their warships, 74 men lost their lives with an equal number of wounded.[11]

Reflecting upon the loss of New Orleans, in an editorial printed on Sunday morning, April 27, Gaulding offered the opinion that as a tactical matter, shore-based forts to block enemy naval expeditions were essentially things of the past: "Modern inventions, it seems, render Forts useless for defence. Iron-clad gunboats destroy, or pass them by with certainty." Then the editor grew darker: "Memphis, we apprehend, will share the fate of New Orleans."[12]

With what prescience Archibald Gaulding was writing, we will shortly see.

NOTES

1. "The Commonwealth seems to think . . . ," *ADI*, Apr. 9, 1862; "THE DAILY INTELLIGENCER," *ADI*, April 13.

2. "The Telegraphic News of the Intelligencer," *ADI*, Oct. 17, 1861; "With a View to Meet the Earliest Possible Mail Arrangements, from Atlanta, Two Editions . . . ," *ADI*, December 21; "Our Telegraphic News," *ADI*, Jan. 4, 1862; Andrews, *South Reports*, 55–56; "Editorial Convention," *ADI*, January 26; Janice Ruth Wood, "John S. Thrasher: Journalistic Revolutionary and Reformer," in Patricia G. McNeely, Debra Reddin van Tuyll and Henry H. Schulte, eds., *Knights of the Quill: Confederate Correspondents and their Civil War Reporting* (West Lafayette IN: Purdue University Press, 2010), 365; "The Confederate Congress," *ADI*, February 22; "Telegraphic News," *ADI*, March 22.

3. "Editorial Convention," *ADI*, Mar. 15, 1862; *The Press Association of the Confederate States of America, Printed by Order of the Board of Directors* (Griffin GA: Hill & Swayze's Printing House, 1863), 5; Wilson, "Confederate Press Association," 160–61.

4. Coulter, *Confederate States of America*, 314; "THE PRESIDENT'S MESSAGE—THE COUNTRY CALLS FOR SOLDIERS," *ADI*, Apr. 1, 1862; "CONSCRIPTION—ITS EFFECTS," *ADI*, April 3; "From the Richmond Examiner. THE CONSCRIPTION BILL," and "THE CONSCRIPT LAW," *ADI*, April 19.

5. "GEN. JOHNSTON'S ADDRESS TO THE ARMY OF THE POTOMAC," *ADI*, Feb. 16, 1862.

6. Stephen W. Sears, *To the Gates of Richmond: The Peninsula Campaign* (New York: Ticknor & Fields, 1992), 18–20, 51; Paul D. Casdorph, *Prince John Magruder: His Life and Campaigns* (New York: John Wiley and Sons, 1996), 142–43, 147, 151.

7. "Richmond Correspondence of the Charleston Mercury. RICHMOND NEWS AND GOSSIP," *ADI*, Apr. 5, 1862; "Battle on the Peninsula," *ADI*, April 18; "FROM WILLIAMSBURG, VA.," *ADI*, April 19; "INFAMOUS OUTRAGES ON THE PENINSULA" (*Petersburg Express*) and "DIABOLICAL OUTRAGES," *ADI*, April 29.

8. "INFAMOUS OUTRAGES ON THE PENINSULA," *ADI*, Apr. 29, 1862; "From the Savannah Morning News. THE YANKEE PRISONERS," *ADI*, April 3; "THE PRISONERS," *ADI*, April 22.

9. John D. Winters, *The Civil War in Louisiana* (Baton Rouge: Louisiana State University Press, 1963), 10, 49–50, 65, 67, 81–82, 84–85, 89; Chester G. Hearn, *The Capture of New Orleans 1862* (Baton Rouge: Louisiana State University Press, 1995), 120, 125–27; Charles Dufour, *The Night the War Was Lost* (New York: Doubleday, 1960), 72, 110, 118–20, 176, 204.

10. Dave Page, *Ships versus Shore: Civil War Engagements along Southern Shores and Rivers* (Nashville: Rutledge Hill Press, 1994), 289–90; "Later from Fort Jackson," *ADI,* Apr. 22, 1862; Hearn, *Capture of New Orleans,* 183–84; "Further from Fort Jackson," *ADI,* April 24; Winters, *Civil War in Louisiana,* 88–89.

11. Hearn, *Capture of New Orleans,* 216; Jack D. Coombe, *Thunder Along the Mississippi: The River Battles That Split the Confederacy* (New York: Bantam Books, 1998 [1996]), 108, 113; Winters, *Civil War in Louisiana,* 90–102.

12. "THE ENEMY AT NEW ORLEANS," *ADI,* April 27, 1862.

13. Death in Atlanta

OVERLOOKED BY HISTORIANS is the fact that the *Atlanta Daily Intelligencer* suggested the arming of African American slaves in the South as early as May 1862.

On May 16, the *Intelligencer*'s astounding editorial appeared, asserting, "we must 'fight the devil with fire,' by arming our negroes to fight the Yankees. There is no doubt that in Georgia alone we could pick up ten thousand negroes, that would rejoice in meeting fifteen thousand Yankees in deadly conflict."

The immediate provocation for the newspaper's bold proposition came from an editorial in the *New York Times,* dated May 1, which the *Intelligencer* reprinted on the 16th. The *Times* called attention to the claims of Southern leaders that Federal troops occupying New Orleans would wither in "the summer heat, malaria, and fevers" that plagued the city. The *Times* acknowledged that "with the coming summer, sickness will very seriously affect the usefulness of our unacclimated soldiery in the South." A solution, the New York paper suggested, would be "the *enrolment and arming of the negroes* in the various cities we may hold on the coast, furnishing them with white officers of skill and accustomed to the climate, who shall drill and discipline them, and exert over them a proper military control."

The *Times* explained that at Port Royal, in coastal South Carolina, Union Maj. Gen. David Hunter had met with blacks from plantations whose owners had fled when the Federals landed. He discerned, according to the *Times,* that they demonstrated "an unexpected alacrity in volunteering to bear arms." (Hunter had actually begun to organize a unit of African American soldiers when President Lincoln on May 20 rescinded the general's proclamation freeing the coastal slaves.) The *Times* nonetheless supported the use of black troops. "They have been employed in the ranks by the Confederates themselves," it argued; "they make good and tractable soldiers . . . and we can safely reckon not only on their fidelity, but on their immunity from climate diseases."

As it turned out, the North would not organize regiments of African American soldiers until 1863. Eventually the Northern war effort enlisted 186,000 black soldiers, an integral contribution to Union victory. The *New York Times* was thus vindicated. In contrast, the call by the *Atlanta Intelligencer* in May 1862 for Georgia slaves to be armed for combat went unheeded. Referring to his claim that 10,000 Southern black men could battle 15,000 Northern whites, Gaulding asserted, "we would be willing almost to risk the fate of the South upon such an encounter in an open field."[1]

The Confederacy never implemented a widespread policy of arming slaves as soldiers, although the Congress passed a law authorizing the practice three weeks before General Lee surrendered at Appomattox. Instead, the South sought to stretch its diminishing white military manpower to meet the many crises occurring at the various battle fronts. One of those loomed uncomfortably close to Atlanta in the spring of 1862, when Federal forces occupied Bridgeport, Alabama, a Tennessee River town some twenty-five miles west of Chattanooga. The loss of Bridgeport was a serious matter indeed. On April 29, Federals drove Confederate Brig. Gen. Danville Leadbetter and his troops from the town back into Chattanooga. Leadbetter came in for considerable criticism for this defeat. In an article from the *Macon Telegraph*, reprinted by the *Intelligencer* on May 6, entitled "THE STAMPEDE AT BRIDGEPORT," the paper reported that when the Federals attacked, "an instant stampede followed, in which Gen. Leadbetter led better than anybody else." (Leadbetter was relieved of duty on July 1.) [2]

The truth of such events as the Bridgeport "stampede" was bad enough, but worse still were false stories being perpetrated by the Northern press. The *Intelligencer* on May 6 spoke out about two "YANKEE LIES" in particular: that the governor of North Carolina had offered to surrender the state to Federal authorities, and that Confederates at Yorktown intended to surrender to McClellan. These phony reports led Gaulding to argue that "the Yankee newspapers *lie* more than ever.... The Yankees are the greatest *liars* on earth." As further example, the *Intelligencer* mentioned another report from the *Louisville* (Kentucky) *Daily Journal*, claiming that Union Gen. Ormsby Mitchel was advancing on Rome, Georgia, aiming to "take that city, burn down the foundries and capture all the arms." Gaulding dismissed such humbuggery by simply countering, "comment upon it ... is needless."

Prevaricating Yankees were just one problem faced by Southern newspapers trying to provide their readers with the most reliable war news. Gaulding had already, in mid-April, warned readers of traitors entering Atlanta and circulating false stories calculated to demoralize loyal Confederates. "We should be a more watchful and vigilant people," he advised, "certainly a less credulous one." But even patriotic Southerners could get their facts wrong. In an article titled "Sensation News," published on May 10, the *Intelligencer* spoke out against the inventors of false rumors "especially if they be 'reliable gentlemen,' or 'passengers by the last train.'" A remedy to this pervasive problem was suggested by the *Petersburg Express*: a law actually enacted two centuries earlier, in colonial Virginia, that prescribed punishment for persons tried and convicted who "forge and divulge false rumors and reports to the greate disturbance of the peace and quiette of his majesties liege persons in this colony."[3]

Because of their unreliability, Gaulding informed readers that "as a rule, the INTELLIGENCER gives but little heed to private dispatches"—meaning telegraphed news stories that did not bear the name of William Pritchard's Southern Associated Press operating out of Richmond. "In the main," he concluded, "they are unreliable, tending to create often undue excitement, and to mislead the people." Nevertheless, in the absence of articles from reliable sources, Gaulding occasionally printed these private dispatches anyway. On the very same page of his issue of April 12, in which he disparaged "private dispatches," the editor related "NEWS FROM HUNTSVILLE. It is reported, by a dispatch to a gentleman in this city," the short article began, that Federal cavalry had occupied Huntsville, Alabama. "If so," it concluded, "then the Memphis & Charleston Railroad is in possession of the enemy." (This "dispatch to a gentleman in this city" turned out to be correct; Union troops captured Huntsville on April 11.)

As for Pritchard's telegraphic news service, its problems continued. A month after the newspapermen's meeting in Atlanta (March 12–13), when Pritchard's operations were openly criticized, the *Intelligencer* on April 12 related that the Southern press had "just cause to complain of the manner in which it has received its telegraphic dispatches, both as to their meagerness and the dates of their reception." After the death of Pritchard on March 24, from diphtheria, Gaulding reported that the son, William H., Jr., had taken over the news service. He expressed hope that under its new management "the Press will have no just cause for complaint in the future." (His hope would not be fulfilled.) [4]

With "private dispatches" sometimes proven false, and with exchanges from other newspapers sometimes delayed in the mail (as Gaulding had complained the previous December), the *Intelligencer* addressed its concerns as many businesses do: it added more staff. On April 27, the paper announced in an article, "PERSONAL," that John H. Steele had joined its editorial operation. Steele himself wrote the piece, signing himself "J. H. S.," describing his new role as "a humble position in the conduct of the 'INTELLIGENCER.'"

Steele was fifty-five years old when he signed on with Whitaker and Gaulding's paper. Born in Charleston, South Carolina in January 1807, he moved to middle Georgia; in the 1830s he was teaching school near Eatonton and winning election to a term in the state legislature. During the administration of Georgia governor George W. Crawford (1843–47), Steele served as a secretary to the governor, following him to Washington when Crawford served as secretary of war in the term of President Zachary Taylor, 1849–50. Returning to Georgia, Steele embarked on a brief career in journalism with the *Griffin Empire State* before being appointed by Gov. Joseph E. Brown as one of his secretaries. After a year in that position, Steele moved to Atlanta. In the spring of 1858, the *Intelligencer* was being edited by a supporter of one of Brown's political opponents; Brown characterized the newspaperman as "not my friend at heart." Steele proposed to the governor that a new paper be established in Atlanta, one that would be presumably more supportive of him. Brown liked the idea, but Steele's new Atlanta paper never got off the ground.[5]

Just as Steele did not define the specific duties of his "humble position" at the *Intelligencer,* so too did Gaulding only hint at how another new hire, William L. Scruggs, would help him with the newspaper. On May 4, he announced that "we have made an arrangement with MR. W. L. SCRUGGS, recently of Chattanooga, by which his services have been secured to the INTELLIGENCER as a regular CORRESPONDENT, and GENERAL AGENT." Scruggs, born near Knoxville in September 1836, had graduated from Strawberry Plains College in Tennessee in 1857. He was admitted to the bar before the Civil War, but never began practice as an attorney. "Mr. Scruggs is a gentleman of education and intelligence," Gaulding wrote. That he would submit articles to the *Intelligencer* was suggested by the editor's comment that Scruggs was "an excellent writer; thoroughly versant in the events and history of the war, and will add much to the interest of the INTELLIGENCER in his correspondence from important points in it." For instance, it may have been Scruggs who from Chattanooga over the name "LOOMIS" wrote an article on May 8 that the *Intelligencer* published on the 11th.[6]

In his wide-ranging letter of May 8, "LOOMIS" described the appearance of "eleven live Yankees" recently captured from Ormsby Mitchel's command; mentioned prices of food items; and related rumors of a battle recently fought at Iuka, Mississippi by General Beauregard's army. "Loomis" stayed busy, and eclectic, as evidenced in the subtitles of three articles written on three consecutive days, from Chattanooga and Knoxville:

Col. Morgan—His Ancestors—Cavalry Scouts—Yankee Bacon—Smuggling—How Things have been Managed, &c.
(May 22)

Who Fired the Bridgeport Bridge—Escape of Morgan's Men—Flag of Truce—Trading in Money—The Markets—Chattanooga, her past, present, and future.
(May 23)

Affairs at Cumberland Gap—Gen. Smith and the Speculators—Money matters—"change"—Pikes—&c., &c.
(May 24)

But "LOOMIS" could wax editorial as well as reportorial. The *Intelligencer* printed his article, titled "CROAKING," on May 18. The frog-throated sound was defined by the writer in his first sentence: "the growing disposition upon the part of the press to grumble at, and find fault with every measure of public policy adopted by our rulers." "LOOMIS" offered the opinion, "it is really wonderful to see how many Solons and Lycurges this revolution has turned up," referring to the brilliant Athenian statesman and the Spartan lawgiver. President Davis, he elaborated, "has suddenly degenerated, in the eyes of these philosophers, from the profound and able Statesman he was twelve months ago, to a mere pigmy." "LOOMIS," of course, argued that the croaking voices should be silenced.[7]

We may not know who "LOOMIS" was, but Archibald Gaulding almost certainly did. On May 24, the editor announced his policy regarding correspondents who used *noms de plume*. "For many reasons," he explained, he adhered to the rule that writers should provide their name with submitted articles if they wanted their work printed; "the exceptions to this rule, with us, have been 'few and far between,' and must continue to be." At least one reason for the *Intelligencer*'s practice had to do with journalistic principle. "The Press has been subject to imposition often for not adhering rigidly to the rule," although the editor did not explain the nature of such "imposition." That the *Intelligencer* carried five articles by "LOOMIS" in the month of May alone suggests that his identity was well known at the newspaper office—indeed, he may have been Bill Scruggs.

One of the "few and far between" instances of the *Intelligencer* printing an article sent in by an unknown involved a writer who signed himself "SENEX" (Latin for "old man"). On May 24, the paper printed a long piece by "SENEX," although alongside it he commented that "'SENEX'... should he favor us with another, will oblige by letting us know who he is." The editor added that he was breaking his rule because of "SENEX's" "well-written communication... trusting when we again hear from him, that he will repose that confidence in us which should exist between correspondent and publisher."

"SENEX" began by discussing potential names for the current conflict. If the South won its independence, he posited, the war would be called the "Second American Revolution"; if the North won, it would bear the name of the "American Rebellion." "SENEX" acknowledged that in recent months the Federals' gunboats had allowed them to make lodgments on Southern coasts and rivers, but he argued that this naval phase of the war "is nearly *played out*." Its final phase—"the last act"—would be fought and decided on land. "On this subject I may write you soon," "SENEX" concluded.[8]

On May 10, the *Intelligencer* asserted in an editorial, "WE ARE WAXING STRONGER AND STRONGER AND THE ENEMY WEAKER AND WEAKER." The paper claimed that so many men were joining the Confederate army that "our effective force will soon approximate, if it does not equal, that of the enemy." This was hopeful indeed. Meanwhile, among Federal troops, more and more Northern soldiers were falling ill, and more would continue to do so as they pushed farther south during the hot summer months. "A mercenary horde of foreigners are now fighting their battles," the *Intelligencer* opined on May 13, "but these will soon be swept away by gunpowder and disease." Moreover, in the North there was evidence of a flagging morale; Democratic electoral victories suggested that Lincoln and his war party were losing support. Senators and congressmen from the Border States, such as Kentucky, where slavery still existed, were denouncing Lincoln and his cabinet for turning the war into one aimed at abolition: "they now begin to see that the entire policy of the administration is to propitiate the Abolitionists and rob the South of the property which was guaranteed to them by the compact of our forefathers." The newspaper concluded, "it is only necessary for the South to put forth all its strength and powers to make our Independence sure." "Courage, then, people and soldiers of the Confederate States!" the *Intelligencer* exhorted in another editorial of May 24; "the North has exhausted its resources. Our work, is thus before us, and we are able to do it!"[9]

With such pronouncements, Gaulding and Whitaker's *Atlanta Daily Intelligencer* was thus fulfilling two of its roles as an organ of Confederate propaganda: "to remind, constantly, both foe and friend that your country is bound to win," in the words of historians Louis Griffith and John Talmadge in *Georgia Journalism,* and "to foster, at all times, among your people the will to win." In the same issue, that of May 24, in which it exclaimed "we are able to do it," the paper also fulfilled another of Griffith and Talmadge's propagandistic roles, "to personalize your people's war hatred in the leaders of the enemy." The immediate provocation came from New Orleans and Maj. Gen. Benjamin F. Butler, the Federal military commander there. As Northern officers and soldiers perambulated the city, women—especially the well-to-do—manifested their dislike and disgust for the intruders in various ways. Some women stitched little Confederate flags on their clothing. "On passing privates," writes James Parton, an early chronicler of General Butler's administration in New Orleans, "they would make a great ostentation of drawing away their dresses, as if from the touch of pollution." If a lady saw approaching Yankees, she would step off the sidewalk so as to avoid having to encounter them. One woman flung herself off the walkway so impetuously that she fell into the gutter. The officers tried to help her up, but she refused, spluttering, according to one source, that "she would rather lie there in the gutter than be helped up by a Yankee."

Other females showed their contempt for the unwanted occupiers in more unsavory ways. When General Butler passed under a balcony, women standing above him whirled their skirts to reveal their *derrieres*. When Captain Farragut walked under a balcony, he found himself doused by the contents of a chamber pot. A favorite means of "expression" soon developed among the citizens, that of actually spitting in the faces of the Yankees.

Butler could not take it anymore. On May 15, he issued an order (printed by the *Intelligencer* on the 24th) declaring that henceforth any lady in New Orleans who insulted a Federal "shall be regarded and held liable to be treated as a woman of the town plying her avocation."

The *Intelligencer* was appalled, calling Butler, in an editorial printed on May 24, a "vile, squint-eyed wretch," "a hyena," "a cowardly hound" and a "malignant viper." The editor put forth his wish, in a veiled way, that the Northern general would be assassinated ("will not some stout heart and strong arm in the Crescent City consign the miserable ruffian to an early destruction?"). Failing that, the editorial stated the hope that maybe yellow fever would strike, "and free the country from so contemptible a wretch."

A month later, the paper went further. On April 26, as they began to occupy New Orleans, Federal soldiers had raised their flag over the U. S. mint. A citizen, William B. Mumford, ascended the building, hauled down the banner and proceeded to City Hall, in front of which he tore it up, handing its shreds to a cheering crowd. General Butler had Mumford arrested and tried. The sentence of death was carried out on June 7, when Mumford was hanged in a public execution. In an editorial two weeks later, Gaulding asserted that the hanging of Mumford, "for pulling down the flag of Yankeedom," rendered Butler into "an outlaw, and any one may kill him at any time hereafter without being guilty of any offence."

In New Orleans, some women refused to conceal their Southern sympathies. The *Intelligencer* reprinted a letter sent by a Crescent City resident to the *Charleston Courier*, dated June 2. "No doubt you have heard of Butler's proclamation concerning the ladies," the correspondent remarked; "our ladies now wear a neat little secession flag on their bosoms, and they plainly show a revolver in the right side of their belt, and a small dirk in the left, and in many cases they are seen turning up their noses, with a peculiar pout, and an insignificant shake of the head—'You nasty Yankee, you,'—and pass on."

But at least the most egregious insults (chamber pots, *derrieres*) ceased. Butler's "woman order" thus actually succeeded in its purpose, when New Orleans women no longer made their most ostentatious shows of disrespect for the occupying Federals. General Butler explained the reason thus: "The order executed itself. . . . All the ladies in New Orleans forebore to insult our troops because they didn't want to be deemed common women, and all the common women forebore to insult our troops because they wanted to be deemed ladies."[10]

News from New Orleans thus figured in the *Intelligencer* in May of 1862, but the paper had to cover military events occurring upriver as well. After the capture of Island Number 10 and New Madrid, Federal vessels had moved downstream to the next Confederate bastion on the Mississippi, which was Fort Pillow, Tennessee. The position was described in an article of the paper, May 1, reprinted from the *New Orleans Delta* of April 14. "About eighty five miles above Memphis," on the east bank of the river, were water batteries that held nineteen 32-pounders and one 11-inch Columbiad. "The channel of the river is within 100 yards of the batteries," the article declared, predicting thus that "no boats, of however light draught, can pass at a greater distance." The *Delta* offered the opinion that Fort Pillow "could hold out against the whole army and navy of the Lincolnites." The "Lincolnites," though, did not have to storm Fort Pillow. In late May, General Beauregard at Corinth, Mississippi reckoned that the position was too vulnerable to attack by Union land forces and ordered it to be abandoned. Confederates did so on June 3; Federals occupied Fort Pillow two days later.[11]

Just as Northern forces were descending the Mississippi, so too were they ascending it. From New Orleans, Flag Officer Farragut sent a warship upriver to Baton Rouge, Louisiana's capital. Gov. Thomas Moore had already evacuated the city and burned its stores of cotton. The capital was thus undefended when Commander James Palmer on May 7 arrived aboard the U.S.S. *Iroquois*. Two days later a Northern contingent landed and took over the Baton Rouge arsenal and barracks. Louisiana thus became the second Confederate state, following Tennessee, to have its capital fall into Union hands.

Farther upriver, Natchez also surrendered, which left Vicksburg, Mississippi as the Federals' next objective. The city was built on high bluffs overlooking the river. On 200-foot heights, Confederates had erected seven artillery batteries, whose plunging fire seriously menaced Union navigation. The *Intelligencer* on May 18 published an article from the *Vicksburg Mississippian* predicting, "this place will be certainly attacked by the Yankee gunboats within a few days." On the 20th the paper printed a dispatch from Mobile stating that five enemy ships had arrived in sight of Vicksburg on May 18, and had sent ashore a surrender demand. "The Mayor replied that the city was unprotected," the report explained, "but he would never surrender it (some words of the dispatch are here unintelligible.—ED. INT.)" The *Mississippian*'s prediction proved correct. The Northern vessels lay quiet for several days after Southerners' refusal to surrender, and then fired some shells into the city on May 26. A few days later, they retired back downriver. A telegram sent from Mobile on June 2 (in the *Intelligencer* four days later) stated, "the Federal fleet which has been threatening Vicksburg has left there for Baton Rouge." Vicksburg was safe, for a while.[12]

Other threats, however, loomed landward. After the battle of Shiloh, Maj. Gen. Henry Halleck, in charge of Federal forces in the western theater, took command of Grant's and Buell's armies, merging them into a huge force of 100,000. In late April he began moving this mass south, toward Corinth. Beauregard resolved to give up his position at Corinth and retreat. On May 28 he informed the government in Richmond of his plan. His army quietly slipped away beginning on May 30, leaving Halleck unaware of the Confederates' withdrawal.

The *Intelligencer* picked up the story on June 5, based on "reports, verbal and otherwise," suggesting that "Gen. Beauregard has fallen back with this army some ten miles South of Corinth." Actually, Beauregard had retreated to Tupelo, closer to fifty miles south. Gaulding had no more information than this. "In our next issue," he pledged, "we shall be more correctly advised as to the true *'situation'* of affairs at and near Corinth, when we shall communicate it to our readers."[13]

The "situation," as it termed the recent events at Corinth, that most troubled the *Intelligencer* was much closer: the menacing Federal presence near Chattanooga. The paper had expressed worry in an editorial of April 22, a week and a half after Ormsby Mitchel's forces occupied Huntsville and Andrews' train-thieves stole the *General*. Tellingly, Gaulding entitled it "IS ATLANTA SAFE?" (For the time being, the editor thought it was.)

Still, the threat of an advance by Union forces into Georgia was quite real. Accordingly, Atlanta mayor James Calhoun called a meeting of concerned residents to convene on Thursday morning, May 8, at City Hall. The *Intelligencer* printed the mayor's proclamation, summoning "the citizens of Atlanta, and surrounding country" to meet and "consider means of defense." The paper voiced its support, adding its hope "that we may all calmly deliberate, and adopt such measures as will ensure *unity of purpose and action* in view of what is threatened by the enemy." On the morning of the meeting, the paper urged "a general attendance," and the next day published its proceedings. "Major" John H. Steele, who had just joined the *Intelligencer* staff, called the meeting to order; William S. Bassford, who had served as Archibald Gaulding's associate editor, was appointed secretary.

Mayor Calhoun, presiding, urged that Atlanta's citizens take vigorous measures "should the enemy march upon us." He proposed that men not already in the service should form companies, be armed and drilled. Participants agreed, and resolved that five local defense companies should be organized. Editor Gaulding found the entire event most heartening. "The meeting," he wrote on the 10th, "was characterized by a display of devoted patriotism, and a stern resolve *never* to compromise one principle for which the South contends, and *never* to yield to the despotism of Lincoln—*never, no, never!*"[14]

After that, the *Intelligencer* tracked events as the city essentially began to put itself on a war footing. It applauded efforts of Western & Atlantic Railroad employees to form a military company. When Confederate Brig. Gen. Alexander R. Lawton, in charge of the Military Division of Georgia, created a "Military Post of Atlanta," he appointed Col. George W. Lee as its commander. Lee in turn appointed a provost marshal, Capt. W. H. Batty, to help him enforce order in the city and issue passes to the citizenry. The *Intelligencer* supported all of this, endorsing the General Order No. 1 that Lee issued on May 14. The measure provided for guards to protect government stores and sentinels to arrest "all suspicious persons." Several prohibitions were announced. For instance, African Americans were not to walk about the city after 9 p.m., and grocers were not to furnish alcohol to soldiers unless directed by a physician.

When Lee was assigned to field command in Virginia, the editor thanked him for his service. "At this point where disorder, riot, drunkenness, and danger disturbed and threatened our city," he wrote with some exaggeration, "in which millions of public property needed efficient protection, previous to COL. LEE's assignment to the command of this post, he has by his energy, firmness, and spirit, restored to quiet, peace, and security, and we, therefore, part from him and his efficient command with regret." When Col. E. P. Watkins succeeded Lee as commander of the military post in Atlanta (himself quickly replaced by Maj. Austin Leyden, who then turned the office over to Col. W. J. Lawton on June 18), the *Intelligencer* published their "General Orders No. 2" (which merely reasserted the points Lee had made earlier). The paper openly commended Colonel Lawton in an editorial printed on June 12. And when Capt. Greenberry J. Foreacre became the new provost marshal, the paper in mid-June printed his announcement regarding location of his office (at first, next to the post office; then to behind Hamilton, Markley and Joyner's drug store). A month later, the *Intelligencer* had reason to express its satisfaction with the public order when it announced the return of George Washington Lee as Atlanta's post commander. Colonel Lee, weakened by "frequent hemorrhage of the lungs," had been forced to resign as commander of a regiment in Virginia and return home to resume his former position. "We welcome him back to Atlanta," the editor declared.[15]

The *Intelligencer*'s concern for public safety extended to public health. In an editorial printed on June 24, it called on the City Council, in conjunction with military officers, "to enquire into the cause of the sickening effluvia, which we are advised by a respectable citizen is caused most probably from the storage cellars on Whitehall Street, of decayed meats." The authorities, it respectfully declared, had a responsibility "in matters pertaining to the removal of all nuisances in the city."

The paper's advocacy did not stop there, but extended to the issue of workers' wages. In an opinion piece published on June 27, the editor related that the day before, one of the co-partners of Lawshe & Purtell, dealers in men's clothing, had come to his office to show how much they paid its ten women workers. "This gentleman brought with him his cash, or day book, and went over many pages with us to show the weekly payments made to each of his female employees, for their labor." Gaulding was impressed both by the business owner's "voluntary exhibition" of his salary scale, and by its evident generosity. The firm was paying one woman as much as $20 a week; others got lesser amounts, with the bottom of the pay grade "always $7 per week, work or no work."

The editor compared Lawshe and Purcell's liberality with the case of another female laborer. While her husband was away in the army, she was responsible for feeding herself and her family. To make ends meet, the mother and a daughter both worked, but together, Gaulding had learned, they made only 40 cents a day—$2.40 for the week. "This lady has a large number of children," he added, "and is suffering for meat and bread—the former is seldom ate in her family."

Gaulding could not conceal his anger: "surely there is something cruelly wrong in this state of things!" Editorial calls for fair pay for women's work were rarely seen in mid-nineteenth-century American journalism. For that reason, when the *Intelligencer* implored the men of Atlanta "to correct, or eradicate this distress," the newspaper was standing as a social beacon.

The editor reinforced this call by occasionally promoting businesses in the city that noticeably helped women and children. In one infomercial for an Atlanta envelope manufacturer, printed in late July 1862, Gaulding declared that he had personally visited the factory of T. S. Reynolds on Whitehall Street, and that he was impressed by its efficient machinery and prodigious output. More, "he employs about 12 hands, composed of females and boys. He has no grown man in the factory except himself," the editor noted, adding, "he is worthy of all praise for his enterprise which gives profitable employment to many who might otherwise be destitute of the means of employment."

New jobs were created when new businesses opened in the city. One such was the H. Marshall sword manufacturing company, which had moved to Atlanta when Nashville was threatened. Gaulding visited the factory, learning its output of 170 edged weapons per week.

The city's growing importance as a wartime supply center was underscored when Jared Whitaker, Georgia's commissary general (and *Intelligencer* co-proprietor) announced in July 1862 that he was moving his office from Milledgeville to Atlanta, "on second floor in Markham's Building, on the corner of Whitehall and Alabama streets." Whitaker was thus barely a block away from the *Intelligencer* office at the foot of Whitehall, by the railroad.

The *Intelligencer* also addressed Atlanta's growing importance as a Confederate army hospital center. In an article printed on May 1, it pointed out that some 500 men were being treated in four hospitals in the city. The editor took it upon himself to visit a facility named "City Hospital," under the supervision of Dr. Thomas S. Powell. He noticed approvingly its clean rooms, comfortable beds, and ample food. Several weeks later the paper reported that the army's medical director in Atlanta, Dr. John Johnson, had begun planning construction of a big hospital complex on the city fairgrounds, a multi-acre tract southeast of the railroad depot that had been the site of antebellum agricultural fairs. The new facility would be able to take more patients arriving in the city, as well as transfer those in the existing downtown hospitals. "This is a most excellent arrangement," the editor observed, "and should have been made, weeks ago."

In this connection the *Intelligencer* commended the three societies rendering aid to the hospitalized soldiers in the city. It further appealed to "our country friends": farmers outside Atlanta who could furnish butter, chickens and eggs for the hospitalized soldiers, and millers who could send them bread. "Let every one lend a helping hand, according to his ability," Gaulding urged, "and we shall have but few cases of mortality among those who are sent to our care."[16]

Unfortunately, there were *many* cases of mortality in Atlanta's army hospitals. The *Intelligencer* announced on May 7 that it had for some time sought listings of soldiers who had breathed their last in the city's medical wards. "We . . . thought it was due to the friends of those, who having breasted the storms of battle, or who had become afflicted with disease, had, far away from home and friends, died, and had been interred in our city cemetery." The paper was therefore pleased when a clerk working at Empire Hospital downtown offered to give it a weekly list of its patient deaths. Before that took place, though, the *Intelligencer*'s foreman, Isaac B. Pilgrim, had obtained a list of the dead from all of the city's hospitals who had been buried in the cemetery. The paper announced its intention to publish the list "in a few days."

It did. On May 11, the *Intelligencer* began printing a list of the names of the unfortunate soldiers who had died in the city's wards from February 25 to May 9. The *Intelligencer* had gotten the list from Pilgrim, although it did not divulge how the foreman had obtained it. Gaulding determined to publish the names of the dead, as well as their company and regiment, so far as they were known, out of "duty to notice their last farewell to earth." The list was incomplete, the editor acknowledged; "the remains of many were removed by, or sent to their relatives or friends." Hence this was a list of Confederate soldiers buried in Atlanta's City Cemetery (now named Oakland).

Because so many makeshift hospitals had been quickly set up after the fall of Nashville, the *Intelligencer*'s mortality list named many hospitals that had been subsequently shut down as Drs. Pim and Johnson imposed order in the city's medical administration. For example, the list showed that four soldiers had died during March 10–17 at "Holland Hall Hospital," established in the three-story brick building at Whitehall and Alabama streets. All told, the paper's list of the dead provided the names of 168 deceased soldiers.

Thanking his foreman, Isaac Pilgrim, for the "mournful record," Gaulding wrote, "we doubt not that the friends of the deceased will also be grateful to him for the self-imposed task, which communicates the death of husbands, fathers, brothers, sons, and the place of their interment." After initial publication of the list on May 11, the *Intelligencer* printed it on the front page in almost every issue throughout May and into June.

No such listing, of course, can even hint at the story behind each soldier's tragic death. Case in point: "Americus C. Davies, 5th Texas Regiment, Co. K" had died on May 6 in City Hotel Hospital. Private Davies was an anomaly among Atlanta's hospital patients, most of whom had come from Gen. Albert Sidney Johnston's western army; the 5th Texas was serving at the time in Virginia, as part of Brig. Gen. John B. Hood's Texas Brigade. How he got to Atlanta is explained by his discharge for disability, Feb. 4, 1862, at Dumfries, Va., where the brigade was wintering. The cause was tuberculosis. We may infer that Private Davies, heading back to Texas by rail, had reached Atlanta when his condition worsened. Hospitalized in the city, he died there on May 6, never getting home.[17]

By mid-June, the *Intelligencer* estimated that some 2,500 men filled the city's hospitals. Five hundred arrived on the evening of June 16, probably from Chattanooga. Confederate army hospitals routinely sent convalescing soldiers home on furlough, both to receive loving care there, but also to free up hospital beds. The men, of course, were expected to return to their commands when sufficiently well. But as a reminder, Dr. John Johnson, medical director in Atlanta, had the *Intelligencer* start running an announcement: "ALL OFFICERS AND SOLDIERS absent on furlough or leave of absence, are required to report at this office by the first day of August next, or be considered as deserters." Johnson thanked "the many true men" who had returned within the specified time of their furloughs or who had submitted "well attested proof of their inability to do so." But then came the warning: "the few who have showed no disposition to keep their word may rest assured that they will be attended to in good time."

The larger number of soldier patients still in the city meant that there were unfortunately more deaths. The *Intelligencer* updated "our Foreman's (Mr. I. B. Pilgrim's)" list of the dead beginning on July 12, naming the soldiers who had perished during late May and June in the city's various hospitals. There were over a hundred names, and these were just the soldiers interred in the City Cemetery. By the length of the listing, the Gate City and Empire House Hospitals were the largest medical facilities; both had been downtown hotels, and in their wards sixty unfortunate patients had succumbed. Private physicians, such as Dr. Daniel Heery, had apparently taken in the sick or wounded into their offices; "Heery's Hospital" ran a notice in the paper about its location, "opposite the Empire House, Whitehall Street." Under its name in Pilgrim's death roster were the names of three men who had died there, June 27–29. The passenger depot remained an improvised care facility, probably for patients too weak to be moved elsewhere in the city. One difference between the foreman's two lists is that the second includes the name of thirteen Federal prisoners who had died at Empire House.

The *Intelligencer*'s listing of the Confederate soldiers who had died in the various hospitals in the city was more than a morbid manifestation of the limits of Civil War medicine. It was an impressive demonstration of alert journalism, providing a public service to the soldiers' families and friends living in the *Intelligencer*'s circulation area and wider, when picked up by other papers. It also showed the value of the newspaper's foreman, Isaac Pilgrim; we still don't know how he got those hospital lists.

A somber consequence of so many soldiers' deaths was that there needed to be so many burials in the City Cemetery (the hospitalized Federal prisoners were interred there, too). The City Council received quarterly reports from the cemetery sexton, and could count the number of graves (157 during January-March 1862; 181 in the second quarter). Thus in late June when the council approved a motion to begin discussions with the military authorities about "purchasing ground for the burial of soldiers," the paper expressed its approval of the solemn necessity.[18]

Death struck closer to the *Intelligencer* when, on May 23, the paper announced the death of the infant son of co-owner Jared Whitaker and his wife Nannie. The notice was somber and brief:

FUNERAL NOTICE

The friends and acquaintances of COLONEL and Mrs. J. I. WHITAKER are invited to attend the funeral of their infant son, JARED IRWIN, at their residence on Houston street, this (Friday) morning, at 9 ½ o'clock.[19]

NOTES

1. "MOVEMENTS AND SPIRIT OF THE WAR," *ADI*, May 16, 1862; "MOVEMENTS AND SPIRIT OF THE WAR, From the N. Y. Times (editorial), May 1. NEGRO MILITARY POLICE FOR SOUTHERN CITIES," *ADI*, May 16; Willie Lee Rose, *Rehearsal for Reconstruction: The Port Royal Experiment* (Indianapolis: Bobbs-Merrill, 1964), 146–50; McPherson, *Battle Cry*, 500, 565; Charles H. Wesley and Patricia W. Romero, *Negro Americans in the Civil War: From Slavery to Citizenship* (New York: Publishers Company, 1967), 110.

2. Arthur W. Bergeron, Jr., "Danville Leadbetter," in William C. Davis, ed., *The Confederate General*, 6 vols. (Harrisburg PA: National Historical Society, 1991), vol. 4, 31; "THE STAMPEDE AT BRIDGEPORT" and "AFFAIRS AT AND ABOUT CHATTANOOGA," *ADI*, May 6, 1862.

3. "YANKEE LIES" and "CAUTION TO THE PRESS," *ADI*, May 6, 1862; "BIG STORIES," *ADI*, April 19; "SENSATION NEWS," *ADI*, May 10.

4. "TELEGRAPHIC NEWS," *ADI*, Apr. 12, 1862; Risley, "Confederate Press Association," 225; "NEWS FROM HUNTSVILLE," *ADI*, April 12; Malcolm C. McMillan, ed., *The Alabama Confederate Reader* (Tuscaloosa: University of Alabama Press, 1963), 127; "HUNTSVILLE AND DECATUR IN THE HANDS OF THE ENEMY," *ADI*, April 17; "Death of Wm. H. Pritchard," *ADI*, March 27.

5. "Post Office Department," *ADI*, Dec. 13, 1861; "PERSONAL," *ADI*, Apr. 27, 1862; Garrett, *A & E*, vol. 1, 869; Kenneth Coleman, ed., *A History of Georgia* (Athens: University of Georgia Press, 1999 [1977]), 154; Parks, *Joseph E. Brown*, 76.

6. "OUR GENERAL AGENT AND CORRESPONDENT," *ADI*, May 4, 1862; "COL. W. L. SCRUGGS DIES SUDDENLY," *Atlanta Constitution*, July 19, 1912; "W. L. SCRUGGS IS DEAD," *New York Times*, July 19, 1912; "WILLIAM L. SCRUGGS," *Roanoke* (N. C.) *News*, May, 16, 1889; "LOOMIS," "FROM OUR SPECIAL CORRESPONDENT," *ADI*, May 11.

7. "LOOMIS," "FROM OUR SPECIAL CORRESPONDENT," *ADI*, May 11, 1862; "LOOMIS," "FROM OUR SPECIAL CORRESPONDENT," *ADI*, May 24; "LOOMIS," "FROM OUR CORRESPONDENT," *ADI*, May 27; "LOOMIS," "Special correspondence of the Intelligencer. FROM EAST TENNESSEE," *ADI*, May 29 (from Knoxville); "LOOMIS," "CROAKING," *ADI*, May 18.

8. "SENEX. . . ." (editorial) and "SENEX," "CORRESPONDENCE OF THE ATLANTA INTELLIGENCER," *ADI*, May 24, 1862.

9. "WE ARE WAXING STRONGER AND STRONGER AND THE ENEMY WEAKER AND WEAKER," *ADI*, May 10, 1862; "THE OLD UNITED STATES," *ADI*, May 13; "GROWLERS AND CROAKERS," *ADI*, May 24.

10. Griffith and Talmadge, *Georgia Journalism*, 66; Chester G. Hearn, *When the Devil Came Down to Dixie* (Baton Rouge: Louisiana State University Press, 1997), 101–103; "BUTLER'S LAST PROCLAMATION," *ADI*, May 24, 1862; Winters, *Civil War in Louisiana*, 98, 134; "YANKEE DISAPPONTMENT," *ADI*, June 22; 'THE FEDERAL FLAG TORN DOWN," *ADI*, May 10; "Butler's Infamous Proclamation," *ADI*, May 21; James Parton, *General Butler in New Orleans* (New York: Mason Brothers, 1864), 325; "FROM NEW ORLEANS," *ADI*, June 13 (from the *Charleston Courier*); Benj. F. Butler, *Butler's Book* (Boston: A. M. Thayer, 1892), 419.

11. "FORT PILLOW," *ADI*, May 1, 1862; John Cimprich, *Fort Pillow, a Civil War Massacre, and Public Memory* (Baton Rouge: Louisiana State University Press, 2005), 32–35.

12. Winters, *Civil War in Louisiana*, 103; Samuel Carter III, *The Final Fortress: The Campaign for Vicksburg 1862–1863* (New York: St. Martin's Press, 1980), 34, 37–38, 54–57; James R. Arnold, *Grant Wins the War: Decision at Vicksburg* (New York: John Wiley & Sons, 1997), 14; "VICKSBURG," *ADI*, May 18, 1862; "From Vicksburg," *ADI*, May 20; "Important from the West," *ADI*, June 6.

13. Williams, *Beauregard*, 150–54; Thomas Lawrence Connelly, *Army of the Heartland: The Army of Tennessee, 1861–1862* (Baton Rouge: Louisiana State University Press, 1967), 177; "CORINTH," *ADI*, June 5, 1862; Andrews, *South Reports*, 156; "THE PRESS COMPLAINING AND DENOUNCING," *ADI*, May 31.

14. "IS ATLANTA SAFE?," *ADI*, Apr. 22, 1862; "A PROCLAMATION," *ADI*, May 7; "THE MEETING TO-MORROW," *ADI*, May 7; "THE MEETING TO-DAY," *ADI*, May 8; "CITIZENS MEETING," *ADI*, May 9; "CITIZENS MEETING ON THURSDAY," *ADI*, May 10.

15. "AN ORGANIZATION," *ADI*, May 14, 1862; Singer, "Confederate Atlanta," 122; Paul D. Lack, "Law and Disorder in Confederate Atlanta," *Georgia Historical Quarterly*, vol. 66, no. 2 (summer 1982), 181–82."MILITARY REGULATIONS IN ATLANTA" and "GENERAL ORDER NO. 1," *ADI*, May 15; "HEADQUARTERS MILITARY POST," *ADI*, May 20; Davis, *Civil War Atlanta*, 51; "COL. G. W. LEE," *ADI*, June 3; "EN ROUTE FOR OLD STONEWALL," *ADI*, June 10; "MILITARY ORDERS " and "OFFICE OF PROVOST MARSHAL," *ADI*, June 11; "HEADQUARTERS MILITARY POST. ATLANTA, June 13th, 1862" and "The Provost Marshal's Office . . . ," *ADI*, June 15; "HEAD-QUARTERS, Military Post of Atlanta, June 19, 1862," *ADI*, June 28; "COL. G. W. LEE," *ADI*, July 27; "THE MILITARY POST," *ADI*, June 12.

16. "BURIAL GROUND FOR SOLDIERS," *ADI*, June 24, 1862; 'THE WAGES OF LABOR," *ADI*, June 27; Williams, *Directory*, 113; "SOUTHERN ENTERPRISE," *ADI*, July 24; "ATLANTA SWORD FACTORY," *ADI*, June 6; "HEADQUARTERS, COMMISSARY GENERAL'S OFFICE, Atlanta, June 30, 1862," *ADI*, July 6; "SICK SOLDIERS," *ADI*, May 1, 1862; "REMOVAL OF CITY HOSPITALS," *ADI*, May 20; Davis, *What the Yankees Did to Us*, 6; "OUR HOSPITALS," *ADI*, May 4.

17. "THE DEAD," *ADI*, May 7, 1862; "THE DEAD AND BURIED SOLDIERS" and "THE DEAD," *ADI*, May 11; Davis, *What the Yankees Did to Us*, 14; Jordan, "Georgia's Confederate Hospitals," 73–76; Harold B. Simpson, *Hood's Texas Brigade: A Compendium* (Hillsboro TX: Hill Jr. College Press, 1977), 245.

18. "SICK SOLDIERS—'FAINT NOT BY THE WAY,'" *ADI*, June 17, 1862; "POST SURGEON'S OFFICE, Atlanta, Ga., July 26, 1862," *ADI*, July 27; "On an outside column of to-day's paper. . . ." and "THE DEAD," *ADI*, July 12; Davis, *What the Yankees Did to Us*, 24, 26; "NOTICE," *ADI*, June 29.

19. "FUNERAL NOTICE," *ADI*, May 23, 1862.

14. The War in Virginia by Telegraph

"THE TRAIN STEALERS.—It will be seen . . . that the Federal rascals who stole the engine and cars at Big Shanty, some weeks ago, have not yet been fully tried for their daring theft."

This was the *Intelligencer*'s update on James Andrews and his nineteen followers, whose locomotive raid of April 12, 1862 it had so thoroughly chronicled. The report, however, appearing in the newspaper on May 28, was inaccurate. The train thieves had been transported to a Chattanooga jail, where Andrews had been tried as a spy (not as a "train stealer"); on May 31, he received his sentence of death by hanging, to be carried out on June 7. By the vagaries of military justice, only seven other spies were tried and convicted after they had been moved to Knoxville. The *Intelligencer* noted the transfer of "the Federal rascals" to Knoxville on May 28, before the trial of the seven, which ended with their having been found guilty.

Then, after Andrews' execution was conducted on June 7 in Atlanta's northern suburbs (today, the corner of Juniper and Third Streets in Midtown), the paper reported the event in its issue of the next day. Before the sentence was carried out, "he confessed his guilt" to the Rev. William J. Scott, who had administered the last rites. "A few moments after these announcements were made to the excited multitude who witnessed the executions," the article continued, "the unfortunate guilty man was launched from Time into Eternity." The editor concluded, "he has paid the penalty of his temerity and on Earth he can suffer no more, to his native South [Andrews had been born in Virginia] he was a *traitor*, and criminal too as a *Spy*, only justice had been meted out to him."

The seven condemned men were hanged on June 18 at a gallows erected near the City (now Oakland) Cemetery. The *Intelligencer*'s notice of the execution, printed on June 19, was much terser than that for Andrews': "Seven of the engine stealers and bridge burners, whose leader was executed here a few days ago, expiated their crimes upon the gallows yesterday evening, in the suburbs of this city."[1]

On the same page carrying the *Intelligencer*'s story about Andrews' demise ("THE DEATH PENALTY PAID," June 8), the paper broadcast another event in headlines more than twice as large: "BOMBARDMENT OF CHATTANOOGA!" The paper printed the dispatch, telegraphed by Brig. Gen. Danville Leadbetter, the Confederate commander at Chattanooga, stating that "a large number of shells were thrown into the city. Very few hurt on our side. The enemy's loss is supposed to be considerable."

How the Union troops of Brig. Gen. Ormsby Mitchel, who shelled Chattanooga on June 7, could have suffered "considerable" losses was not explained by Leadbetter. To be sure, Southern infantry and artillery had fired at the Federals bombarding the city, but the Union commander, Col. H. A. Hambricht, reported that just one of his men had been wounded. The next day, the 8th, the Northerners outside of Chattanooga renewed their demonstration, then withdrew.[2]

Casualty-wise, the fighting at Chattanooga, June 7–8, was not much of an engagement, much less a "battle," but the *Intelligencer* gave the enemy advance much attention. The Federals' shelling of a city a hundred miles from Atlanta augured Northern raids into Georgia, Gaulding warned in an editorial published on June 10; against such threats the paper urged that the state militia be better organized and readied for service. "Chattanooga must be defended and successfully too," the editor warned on the 11th. He could not let the topic go; the very next day, June 12, he again issued predictions of what would happen to north Georgia if the enemy took Chattanooga. "Having occupied *Memphis* and *Chattanooga*," he wrote—the *Intelligencer* had just a few days previous reported on the destruction of the Confederate river fleet near Memphis, which led to the surrender of the city on June 6 (though the enemy had not "occupied" Chattanooga)—"ought not *Atlanta* and Georgia, *wake up* to the danger which threatens the one and the other?"[3]

Fortunately for editor Gaulding's stress level (as we would say today), the *Intelligencer* could look to Virginia, and Confederate victories being won there.

Virginia's Shenandoah Valley in May 1862 became a very active theater of operations. At the time, Maj. Gen. Thomas J. Jackson (who had earned the name "Stonewall" at the battle of Manassas) commanded some 17,000 troops, charged with defending the Valley against Union incursions. The Northern forces in the area were somewhat scattered. As McClellan launched his Peninsula Campaign, Maj. Gen. Nathaniel P. Banks, with some 19,000 men, was directed to push from Maryland into the lower Shenandoah Valley ("lower" as termed by Virginians, because the Shenandoah River flows northward to its confluence with the Potomac). Banks' immediate objective was Winchester, thirty miles south of the Potomac. To the west, Union Maj. Gen. John C. Fremont had 20,000 troops pressing toward Staunton in the upper Valley.

Jackson turned his attention first to the threat on Staunton. On May 7, near the town of McDowell, his troops encountered the advance of a contingent of Fremont's force, some 2,200 troops commanded by Union Brig. Gens. Robert C. Schenck and Robert H. Milroy. The next day, the Federals, though outnumbered, attacked Jackson. After a four-hour fight they were repulsed; Schenck, in overall command, ordered his troops to withdraw from the field. Union losses in this small battle of McDowell numbered 26 killed, 227 wounded and three missing: 256 total casualties. Jackson, who fought with 6,000 troops, lost 45 killed and 423 wounded, for a total of 468.[4]

Stonewall Jackson had delivered to the South a badly needed victory. The *Intelligencer* of May 11 published a dispatch from Richmond, dated May 9, announcing that "Stonewall Jackson's advanced forces"—it is interesting to see how Jackson's nickname had by now become the general's identifier in Confederate newspapers—"engaged the enemy near McDowell's at 5 o'clock, P.M., on yesterday." The short message related that "after four hours hard fighting, he succeeded in driving them back. Our loss is said to be 300." General Jackson waited until noon of May 9 before setting his troops marching after Schenck and Milroy, and then rather slowly at that. He never came into contact with the enemy before the defeated column joined Fremont's main force at Franklin (now in West Virginia). On the 13th, Jackson began retracing his route back toward Staunton.

But in the Confederate press, just about anything Stonewall Jackson did seemed magical. On May 20, the *Intelligencer* printed from its exchanges an article in the *Lynchburg Virginian*, claiming that at Franklin, Jackson's troops had cut off the enemy's retreat. "They are represented as being in the most deplorable condition, utterly broken up, having thrown away their arms and are wandering about in the mountains without either food or arms." Word even had it that 500 Federals had been captured on May 12—which had not happened.

The *Intelligencer* also reprinted from the *Petersburg Express* an exaggerated report on the dimensions of Jackson's victory at McDowell. "The most complete victory of the war," it crowed, entirely without foundation; "the enemy have been utterly routed, losing baggage, ammunition, camp equipage, and everything else of value." The *Express* went on to state that of the enemy's force, "such as have not been killed and captured, are wandering about the mountains in a famished condition, and as all avenues of escape have been occupied by the Confederates, the entire force must eventually fall into our hands." (This, too, would not happen.)[5]

To be sure, when Stonewall actually won another victory, Southern newspapers celebrated all the more exuberantly. In mid-May, Banks cooperated by sending an 11,000-man division off to reinforce McClellan on the Peninsula; this left him with 8,000 troops—half the size of Jackson's command. Banks, positioned at Strasburg, twenty miles south of Winchester, further weakened himself by detaching a thousand men under Col. John R. Kenly to Front Royal, ten miles to the east. On May 23, Jackson fell upon Kenly's garrison in such strength that after an hour's fight the Federals disintegrated. Most of Kenly's troops were taken prisoner. Afterward, Colonel Kenly estimated he had lost 25 to 30 men killed and 40–50 wounded. But this was too low; historians have placed Federal losses at 904: 32 killed, 122 wounded, 750 captured. Against this, Confederate casualties amounted to 36 killed and wounded.

Jackson then moved against Banks, who belatedly ordered his troops to start falling back to Winchester. The Confederates were hard on their heels; panicked Federals left behind weapons and supplies as they raced to Winchester. Banks tried to stem the stampede. "Stop, men! Don't you love your country?" "Yes, by God," cried one of the retreaters, "and I'm trying to get back to it just as fast as I can!" The Northerners did not stop till they had reached Williamsport, on the Potomac.

To an extent, Front Royal and Winchester can be taken as a three days' engagement, May 23–25. During that time, Banks lost 3,030 of his 8,500 men; Jackson lost fewer than 400 (68 killed, 329 wounded, 3 missing). More, the Confederates scooped up 9,300 new muskets, two field pieces, plus tons of supplies and provisions (including 34,000 pounds of bacon) along with several hundred cattle and a few hundred more wagons and teams—so much stuff that Southerners began derisively referring to Banks as "Jackson's commissary."[6]

Needless to say, the Confederate press had a field day with all of this.

GREAT VICTORY.
Front Royal and Winchester Captured.
Over 4,000 Prisoners Taken.
All of the Enemy's Stores
At Winchester Captured.
&c., &c., &c., &c.

"Another victory has been obtained by Stonewall Jackson at Front Royal," the *Intelligencer*'s telegraphed news section reported on May 27. The brief dispatch gave details on captured stores, prisoners and casualties ("our loss is 100 in killed and wounded"). "Our forces are still in pursuit of the enemy who are completely routed," the newspaper gloated.[7]

Thus far, Jackson had held the tactical initiative against Fremont and Banks, but the situation was about to change. No less than President Lincoln got involved in developing a plan to crush Jackson: 1) Banks, reinforced, would push up the Valley (again); 2) Brig. Gen. James Shields, whose division Banks had sent off to join McClellan, would return, approaching the Valley from the east; and 3) Fremont would push in from the west. The three columns would greatly outnumber Jackson, some 64,000 to 16,000, a four-to-one advantage. Moreover, if they were lucky, Banks, Shields and Fremont might converge and trap Jackson, whose troops in late May were spread out from Winchester to Harpers Ferry.

For once, Jackson was caught off guard. He did not order his troops to begin withdrawing up the Valley until May 30; the march began the next morning. By that time Shields had recaptured Front Royal and was pushing on toward Strasburg; Fremont was advancing toward the same point. It looked as if the Confederates' escape route to the south would be blocked. But Jackson's infantry, who were earning the nickname of "foot-cavalry" for their speedy marching, covered thirty miles in fourteen hours. The Southerners passed through Strasburg on June 1, before either Fremont or Shields reached it, and continued their march south.

At Cross Keys, a town twenty miles north of Staunton, Jackson's troops, under the immediate command of Brig. Gen. Richard S. Ewell, had taken a defensive position when Fremont launched an assault on the morning of June 8. The Confederates repulsed it, then counterattacked. Fremont retreated the next day, thus giving Jackson another victory, albeit a small one. Casualties at Cross Keys numbered 684 for Fremont's larger force (including 557 killed and wounded), and 288 for Ewell's—8% of his 3,500 officers and men engaged.

On June 9, Jackson did the attacking, opening battle with Shields at Port Republic, not five miles south of Cross Keys. The Confederate charges eventually broke the Federal lines, and once again Jackson's soldiers were pursuing Union retreaters down the Valley. The cost was dear, though: 800 Confederate casualties out of 5,900 men engaged. Federals lost about 1,000 (half taken prisoner), a quarter of their 4,000 engaged.[8]

Jackson's brilliant finish for his Valley Campaign, as it has come to be called, considerably brightened Southern spirits after a winter of discontent. The *Intelligencer* was swept up in the mania. "Our city is alive with reports and rumors relative to Stonewall Jackson's advance into Maryland," it editorialized on June 3 (enthusiastically but falsely, as Jackson was not advancing into Maryland). As for the rumors, Gaulding declared that "some of these come in 'questionable shape'; others *appear* to have some reliable authority for their circulation." As for the rumors currently afloat, the *Intelligencer* announced that "none of them, however, receive such credit from, as to induce us to make them public through our columns."[9]

Unable to confirm Stonewall Jackson's advance into Maryland, the *Intelligencer* settled for what news it received by wire. That included word of the death of Jackson's cavalry commander, Brig. Gen. Turner Ashby, killed in a fight near Harrisonburg on June 6, which the newspaper reported on the 10th. The *Intelligencer* could also report the news of Port Republic and Cross Keys. The article relating Ashby's death announced, "Glorious Victory of Old Stonewall and General Ewell over Fremont and Shields." The dispatch from Richmond, dated June 9, stated that "Fremont attacked Gen. Ewell. We have driven him back and Ewell is still pressing him hard."[10]

As sensational as the news was from the Shenandoah Valley, those events were really secondary to the movement of the two main armies at the other end of Virginia. "RICHMOND, May 5.—Our forces have retired from Yorktown, a movement highly approved of here." Thus did the "BY TELEGRAPH" column in the *Intelligencer*'s issue of May 6 report the opening movements of the Peninsula Campaign. The campaign itself can be swiftly summarized as a three-week, 65-mile advance by Maj. Gen. George B. McClellan's Army of the Potomac from its base at Fort Monroe to Seven Pines in the outskirts of Richmond, the Confederate capital. For Gen. Joseph E. Johnston's forces (also called the Army of the Potomac by Johnston, but which General Lee had begun calling the Army of Northern Virginia), the Peninsula Campaign represented a three-week, 50-mile retreat from "Prince John" Magruder's lines at Yorktown to behind the Chickahominy River, the only river barrier between the Union army and the capital. During this time McClellan's troops numbered 105,000; Johnston's, 60,000.[11]

The *Intelligencer* handled the Federal army's ominous advance in the most upbeat way it could. Here, as did Southern newspapers in general, Gaulding put Confederate retreats in a positive spin. For example, Johnston's evacuation of the Yorktown lines, conducted in the night of May 3–4, was *not* "highly approved" in Richmond. In a conference in the capital on April 14, when Johnston proposed giving up his Yorktown position and retiring upon Richmond, Secretary of War George W. Randolph had opposed such a retrograde because it would lead to the loss of Norfolk and the valuable ironclad *Virginia*, which because of her draft could not navigate up the James River. General Lee had also spoken against Johnston's proposal, contending that it would bring the enemy's army dangerously close to the capital. President Davis sided with Lee and Randolph. But on May 1, Johnston informed the government that the time had come to give up Yorktown; McClellan's siege guns had begun to lob shells at the town's river wharves. Johnston's message, sent to the capital, stated that he planned to evacuate his lines during the night of May 3–4. Secretary Randolph countermanded it on the spot. He and naval secretary Stephen R. Mallory wanted another week to remove the vast quantity of stores at Norfolk. As he would do at other times, though, the general did as he wished. On May 4, the government received news that Johnston had given up his Yorktown defenses and was withdrawing westward, up the Peninsula and toward Richmond.[12]

After learning on the morning of May 4 that the Southerners had abandoned their lines before him, McClellan ordered a pursuit. Near Williamsburg, the Federals caught up with the Confederate rearguard, which was manning some earthworks that Magruder had constructed. On the morning of May 5, Union Brig. Gen. Joseph Hooker ordered an attack. The Confederate commander, Brig. Gen. James Longstreet, had to hold his position, giving time for the rest of the army to continue its march toward Richmond. This he did, against Federal assaults throughout the day. That night, Longstreet's forces slipped away.

Both sides claimed to have won the battle. Longstreet had repulsed Hooker's assault, but eventually left the Federals in possession of the battlefield. More importantly, he had given the army's wagon trains time to roll westward. Johnston was therefore justified in issuing his general order announcing "an important success" to his troops. McClellan was equally justified in his message to Secretary of War Edwin Stanton in Washington: "every hour proves our victory more complete."[13]

The *Intelligencer* made a brief announcement of the fight at Williamsburg on May 7, based on a telegraphic dispatch from Richmond ("the enemy . . . were easily repulsed by our rear guard"). The newspaper's reporting was only as good as its sourcing. When a subsequent article was received from Richmond, based "on a dispatch . . . received by the Secretary of War from General Magruder," the source seemed credible, even if the article claimed "the loss of the enemy was heavy including nine hundred prisoners, also ten pieces of artillery. Our loss in killed and wounded is reported to be about five hundred." Actually, Union casualties on May 5 came to 2,283 *versus* 1,560 Confederate, and the number of cannon captured in a Southern counterattack numbered four, not ten.[14]

For readers of the *Intelligencer,* bad news came when the port city of Norfolk had to be abandoned because of the Confederate withdrawal from the lower Peninsula. The Southern commander there, Maj. Gen. Benjamin H. Huger, had been ordered as early as April 27 by Johnston to prepare to evacuate Norfolk and move his command toward Richmond. Huger put his men and supplies on westbound trains on May 9, but there was one prize he could not remove: the C.S.S. *Virginia.* The lumbering ironclad could not escape to sea; to lighten her draft for a possible passage of the bar upstream in the James River, Flag Officer Josiah Tattnall had his men throw overboard ballast and everything else heavy. The work was incomplete when warning of the enemy's approach came. Tattnall ordered the vessel set afire, and early in the morning of May 11, the vaunted *Virginia* blew up.

The *Intelligencer* resumed its role as journalistic propagandist when it editorialized on these untoward events. "The evacuation of Norfolk either as a skillful military movement, or one of necessity, ought not to discourage our people," the paper preached on May 14. "Experience has taught us that the enemy is too strong for us on the water," its reasoning went. "The loss of the 'Virginia' is to be deplored," the editorial continued, "but Norfolk evacuated, her draught of water too deep for the York or James Rivers, and her occupation was gone. Commodore Tatnall doubtless was right to blow her up." Indeed, the paper pronounced, the voluntary destruction of a heroic Confederate warship offered a lesson to the Southern people. Just as a priceless naval vessel was destroyed, lest it fall into the hands of the enemy, the paper exhorted, "let us sacrifice all we possess rather than submit to Lincoln's despotism."[15]

The threat of "Lincoln's despotism" joined "Northern subjugation" (from the Latin, "put under the yoke") as a persistent theme in the editorializing of Jared Whitaker's and Archibald Gaulding's *Atlanta Daily Intelligencer.* The concept of political vassalage spoke to nineteenth-century Southerners' ideas of liberty, just three generations after Americans had secured it from the political vassalage they had endured under King George III. "*Subjugation* was the favorite word of Confederate recruits to describe their fate if the South remained in the Union or was forced back into it," writes historian James McPherson. A good case can be made that if Confederate recruits turned frequently to the polysyllabic word *subjugation,* they picked the term up from newspapers. In its issue of May 15, the *Intelligencer* reprinted from the *Western Carolinian* an article addressing the question, "are we to be subjugated by the North?" The author derived his answer by turning back the pages of history. Greece successfully resisted the Persians' attempt at conquest; the Scots vanquished the English at Bannockburn; Portugal seceded from Spain and won the long war to defend her freedom. The Confederate States, the editorial asserted, possessed far more resources than did either Scotland or Portugal. "It follows therefore, as a fact," it concluded, "that if we suffer ourselves to be subjugated it is because we are less brave than either of these kingdoms.—This we do not believe, and therefore utterly discard all apprehension of subjugation."

But there was more, as shown further in the *Intelligencer*'s issue of Thursday, May 15, 1862. That day, one saw a clipping from the *Philadelphia Inquirer* stating that in anticipation of the Union navy's conquest of all Southern coastal cities, Boston and New York merchants were making plans to send southbound ships filled with ice and salt, all vastly marked up in price, to profit from "the demand of the saline staple in the Southern markets." Editor Gaulding could only add his conclusion: "[That is Yankee, all over.]"

In so doing, the *Intelligencer* was playing into one of the most common Southern stereotypes for the Yankee: the greedy sharpster. Fully a generation before the war, a pamphlet circulated that told the imaginary story of a Yankee descended into Hell. The condemned consignee was charged with any number of outrages: selling wooden nutmegs, peddling as "Spanish cigars" those really made of oak leaves, and pawning a well-worn pair of footwear to a pious old lady as the shoes of Saint Paul. Among the Devil's accusations, too, was that of "stealing an old grindstone, smearing it over with butter, and then selling it as a cheese."

Also, in the *Intelligencer*'s issue of May 15, one saw on page three the regular "BY TELEGRAPH" column which was headed by an article, "The Enemy in James River." "Four Federal gunboats are coming up James River," announced the dispatch issued by Richmond, dated the 13th. Actually, there were five: two Northern wooden gunboats and three ironclads, including the famous *Monitor*. After the destruction of the C.S.S. *Virginia*, Union naval officers felt emboldened to steam up the James River, perchance all the way to Richmond, where they might lob some shells into the Rebel capital. This threat justified the *Intelligencer*'s statement that in the capital, "much uneasiness prevails here." (As it would turn out, the Federal flotilla would be turned back on May 15 by the Confederate river battery at Drewry's Bluff, seven miles downstream from Richmond.)

With Northern invasion of the Southland topping the telegraph section on May 15, two columns to the left on that same third page featured another recurrent topic in the *Intelligencer*: national fast days proclaimed by President Davis. So far, the paper had done its part in publicizing the proclaimed days of "fasting, humiliation, and prayer": June 3, 1861, Nov. 15, 1861, and Feb. 28, 1862. So too did it editorially support the one that Davis called for on Friday, May 16. On its first page of May 15, the paper printed the presidential decree, and backed it up with an editorial on the third page. "It is a God adoring, God fearing request," Gaulding observed, further noting, "PRESIDENT DAVIS does not *command*, but *requests* the observance of to-morrow, as a day of fasting, humiliation, and prayer." As it had done before, the *Intelligencer* would do its part by closing its doors on Friday; "therefore no paper will be issued from this office on Saturday."[16]

Sandwiched between "The Enemy in James River" and "FRIDAY A DAY OF FASTING, HUMILIATION, AND PRAYER" was another column that also addressed a major war issue. It was entitled, "THE NEGRO AT HOME—WHAT ONE WHO SAW FOR HIMSELF HAS TO SAY." In a single article, Gaulding and Whitaker's newspaper essentially laid out one of the principal Southern arguments in defense of slavery: that enslaved African Americans in the South actually lived better, in terms of food, clothing and shelter, than did the average working class in the Northern states. "Colonel Gibson of the 49th Ohio, recently wrote a letter from Tennessee, which is attracting some notice," the article began. Gibson claimed that the Negroes he had encountered "are well treated and well provided for. They appear happier and certainly live and dress better than the poor whites or free negroes of Ohio or the North." The Northern officer went so far as to claim, "they love the South and are devoted to their masters."[17]

Subjugation, Yankees, God and slavery: such were the cornerstones of the Southern war for independence. And they were all in the pages of the *Atlanta Daily Intelligencer* on May 15, 1862. It would be hard to find in just one issue of a Confederate newspaper such a full panoply of propaganda, beginning with the dire specter of *subjugation*. Poking fun at stereotypes of *the greedy Yankee* fit in with cultural stereotypes of cavalier and Yankee that were decades in the making. *Invoking God* to buttress people's faith in a cause is an age-old pull on collective belief. During the war President Davis would issue as many as ten proclamations for national fast days; the *Intelligencer* promoted and supported each one with full-throated ardor. (Abraham Lincoln issued three such proclamations.) Finally, white Southerners' belief that their *enslaved people enjoyed a better life* than oppressed wage-earners in Northern factories was also based on years of fearless defense of their peculiar institution.

At the same time, the war in Virginia remained central to the paper's reporting. By mid-May, Johnston had led his army westward across the Chickahominy River to about five miles from the Richmond suburbs. McClellan's was on the other side of the Chickahominy, stationary, as the "Young Napoleon" planned to bring his heavy artillery up from Yorktown to bombard the Confederate capital. Johnston's troops were so nearby that President Davis and General Lee, his chief advisor, rode out to inspect their lines, as the *Intelligencer* reported on May 16.

But what was General Johnston going to do? In an article taken from the *Charleston Mercury*, whose correspondent in the capital, "Hermes" (George Bagby), submitted columns entitled "Richmond News and Gossip," the *Intelligencer* on May 16 printed the talk about town of an impending battle between Johnston and McClellan. The showdown finally came when Johnston on May 31 launched an all-out assault on McClellan at Seven Pines, a crossroads village east of the capital. But the attack that was supposed to start early in the morning did not begin till 1 p.m., after James Longstreet's division took the wrong road in its approach movement. Five hours of bloody battle yielded no advantage for either side. The most important event occurred late in the afternoon, when General Johnston was seriously wounded by a shell fragment to the chest. Immediate command of the army fell to Maj. Gen. Gustavus W. Smith, but President Davis, who was at the field of battle, the next day put the Army of Northern Virginia under the leadership of Gen. Robert E. Lee. On that day, June 1, the Confederates renewed the battle, but their attacks were repulsed. Lee ordered a withdrawal early that afternoon, leaving McClellan's troops in positions they held at the opening of the battle.

It was a costly engagement. The famed English historian Thomas L. Livermore, scrupulously researching reports on the battle from both sides, concluded a generation after the war that Johnston/Smith and McClellan had committed about the same number of men at Seven Pines: 41,816 Southerners against

41,797 Northerners. But the Confederates suffered a higher toll: 980 killed, 4,749 wounded and 405 missing, for a total of 6,134. Federals lost 5,031 officers and men (790 killed, 3,594 wounded and 647 missing). Historians by and large have accepted Livermore's casualty calculations for this, and all major battles of the American Civil War.[18]

News of the battle was slow to get to the *Intelligencer*. Its "BY TELEGRAPH" column of June 1, carrying a dispatch from Richmond dated May 31, stated merely that "there is a fight progressing now on the Williamsburg road, near Chickahominy. . . . No report yet has been received." On June 3, the paper published a longer article, but it made no mention of Johnston's wound, nor of the battle's outcome. In an editorial printed in the same issue, the *Intelligencer* praised General Johnston for his successful conduct of "the great battle at Richmond," but failed to divulge any awareness that the commanding general had been carried from the field wounded. Nor was there report on Johnston's condition in the paper issued on June 4 or June 5. (Eventually the medical reporting would get better. The *Intelligencer* on June 14 announced that "General Johnston is improving every day. He sat up yesterday.")

There was not even an immediate name for the battle of May 31-June 1. An account by Col. Richard Yeadon, printed in the *Charleston Courier* and reprinted in the *Intelligencer* on June 5, referred to "the Great Battle of Chickahominy." "LIST OF WOUNDED GEORGIANS AT THE BATTLE OF CHICKAHOMINY" headlined the roster of soldiers receiving treatment at the 1st Georgia Hospital in Richmond, printed in the newspaper on June 8. "BATTLE OF CHICKAHOMONY" was the title of another article in the paper, June 13. Eventually the engagement came to adopt the name it has today in the military literature: Seven Pines, for the crossroads town, but also Fair Oaks, for Fair Oaks Station, another nearby borough. (By the end of June, the *Intelligencer* was beginning to refer to "the battle of the 'Seven Pines' near the Chickahominy.")[19]

On June 5, the paper took a break from its zealous search for military information about the "battle of Chickahominy" to publish the first letter it had received from George Hathaway, the "journeyman printer" who had resigned from its staff the previous summer to enlist in the army. Hathaway's regiment, the 19th Georgia, had taken part in Johnston's retreat up the Peninsula and the private, writing from "Bivouac near Richmond, May 24th, 1862," wrote a long letter about his experiences. The editor was clearly proud of his former employee's writing, declaring that "his letter, as our readers who may peruse it, will discover, compares most favorably with those of the most popular 'Army Correspondents' for the 'Southern Press.'" Gaulding explained further, "with less educational advantages than most of them, he displays talent in a line that has made money and reputation for many a Newspaper Correspondent, who boasts honors won at College; while those won by 'G.L.H.' thus far have been only with the compositor's stick" (Hathaway had been a typesetter).[20]

Printing letters from Atlanta soldiers guaranteed the *Intelligencer* a ready source of reliable writing from the war fronts. On June 10, it published the letter of James H. Neal, captain in the Jackson Guards (also in the 19th Georgia), written from Richmond on June 3 to his father, John Neal, a prominent Atlanta attorney. The paper stated that "Judge Neal has kindly permitted us to publish the following letter." In it, Neal related his harrowing experiences in the battle of Seven Pines ("several grape shots tore up the ground just at my horse's feet, and cannon balls whistled all the time in close proximity to my head"). At the time of his writing, Neal was convalescing from dysentery "at the house of a Mrs. Howard on Marshall Street." The influx of wounded soldiers into Richmond after Seven Pines had evidently overwhelmed the city's hospitals. As in Atlanta in the winter of 1862, private homes were offered up as patient wards, visited by physicians. "Do not be uneasy about me," he closed, "I am under the treatment of Dr. O'Keefe of our city, and I think I shall soon be well."[21]

In contrast to the private letter from a Confederate soldier to his father, generously offered to the *Intelligencer* for publication by Judge Neal, there was the continuous stream of Northern "reporting" that Gaulding had to deal with. At times he colorfully contradicted its content as untrue. Example is found in the article of June 10, titled by the paper, "The Cannonading near Richmond—Northern Lies." The piece related how the *New York Herald* had handled Seven Pines (*"lying as usual,"* Gaulding inserted). When the *Herald* placed the number of Rebel killed and wounded at 5,500 (with 1,500 captured), the editor interjected, "What a lying sheet!" Then, as for the New York paper's statement that "Gen. Pope is pursuing Beauregard, and has already captured 10,000 prisoners, 15,000 stand of arms, 9 locomotives, &c., &c.," Gaulding could only exclaim, "*What whoppers!*"

A week later the *Intelligencer* published a dispatch from Richmond that again mentioned coverage from the *New York Herald*. As for the *Herald*'s claim that at Seven Pines Confederate casualties included five generals and twenty-three colonels, Gaulding simply added "(*Lie.*)"[22]

Meanwhile, the new commander of the Army of Northern Virginia,

Robert E. Lee, was earning an unflattering nickname among his soldiers, when he ordered them to dig defensive fortifications outside of Richmond: "King of Spades." Union general McClellan also stood on the defensive, intending eventually to open a bombardment of the city with his artillery. The situation was described by an article in the *Richmond Dispatch* that the *Intelligencer* printed on June 17. "Nothing occurred yesterday to break the monotony of the lines on the Chickahominy," it began. "On the enemy's lines it was evident that throwing up entrenchments and the felling of trees was the main occupation of McClellan." (The *Dispatch* article was entitled "The Enemy Digging Dirt Prodigiously.")

Yet Lee was preparing to seize the initiative. McClellan's army was dangerously divided, part south of the Chickahominy, part north. That on the north bank appeared the weaker. On June 11, Lee ordered "Jeb" Stuart, his cavalry commander—so nicknamed from James Ewell Brown Stuart—to lead a reconnaissance raid around the Union army's right flank to pinpoint its position and estimate its strength. Before dawn of the 12th, Stuart had his troopers in the saddle. Quickly he gathered the desired intelligence, but rather than return to the army's main body, Stuart decided on something more daring: a ride completely around McClellan's army, a feat that would bring in even more intel. The Southern cavalry swung wide around, and rode back into the capital on the morning of the 15th, having covered 150 miles in its circuit. The only Southern losses in the daring excursion was one officer killed, Capt. William Latane (in a fight with enemy cavalry near Hanover Court House), several men wounded, and one artillery limber left behind, mired in the Chickahominy swamps.[23]

This was the kind of derring-do that Confederate editors loved to publicize. "Jeb" Stuart was not yet the Southern household name that "Stonewall" Jackson had become, as evidenced by the misspelling of the general's name in the *Intelligencer*'s headline, "Brilliant Exploit of General Stewart," published on June 17. In addition to obtaining the intelligence desired by General Lee ("Brigadier General Stewart has made a circuit through the enemy lines from Richmond"), Stuart's cavalrymen had destroyed three large supply ships on the Pamunkey River, and had brought back with them 175 prisoners, plus 300 horses and mules. On June 20, the *Intelligencer* reprinted the *Richmond Examiner*'s account of Stuart's ride, which added the capture and burning of a hundred Union supply wagons to its accomplishments. (The headline, "A BRILLIANT RECONNAISSANCE BY STUART'S CAVALRY" finally got the spelling right of Jeb's last name).[24]

Confederate newspapers could even have a little fun with Stuart's celebrated ride around McClellan. On June 26, the *Intelligencer* published several vignettes taken from the *Richmond Whig* under the title, "RICHMOND WHIGGERIES."

"Doodle" was an occasional nickname for a Northern soldier (as in "Yankee Doodle"). The *Whig* related that at one point in Hanover, north of Richmond, "as the Yankee cavalry were flying before the gallant Stuart," a lady managed to capture a Federal officer by drawing her pistol on him. "I have the blood of the Washingtons in my veins—I order you to surrender," she demanded. According to the Richmond paper, "the poor 'Doodle' looked hither and thither, and seeing no chance for him, surrendered to the gallant maiden, who held him in durance vile until some of Stuart's boys came up and took him in charge."

Another "Whiggery" was this story, entitled, "How the 'Contrabands' Treat the 'Doodles.'" Early in the war, "contraband" had become a term for African Americans, either enslaved or emancipated. It had originated in the spring of 1861 when, in the area around Federal-held Fort Monroe in coastal Virginia, Union Maj. Gen. Benjamin Butler had taken in slaves who had escaped from nearby plantations. Butler justified the practice, terming the blacks "contraband of war," meaning property rightly taken from the enemy.

In the *Richmond Whig*'s story, the "contraband" was one whom Southerners liked to call a "faithful slave." "A few nights ago a negro entered the Quartermaster's office," the article began, "and said: Mar's 'Arman—here a prisoner."

"Where did you get him?"

"Massa sent him and tole me to see him shot up safe, an de key turned on him."

"Well, Sambo—as you have brought him so far—take him over to jail and see him locked up."

"Thank's Massa—come along, Yankee," and he proudly marched off his prisoner to the jail.[25]

NOTES

1. "THE TRAIN STEALERS," *ADI*, May 28, 1862; Gordon L. Rottman, *The Great Locomotive Chase: The Andrews Raid 1862* (New York: Osprey Publishing, 2009), 12, 53–56; Bonds, *Stealing the General*, 218, 225–26; "THE DEATH PENALTY PAID," *ADI*, June 8; "THE MILITARY EXECUTION," *ADI*, June 19; James G. Bogle, "The Great Locomotive Chase, or the Andrews Raid," *Blue & Gray*, vol. 4, no. 6 (July 1987), 53.

2. "BOMBARDMENT OF CHATTANOOGA!," *ADI,* June 8, 1862; reports of H. A. Hambrecht, June 8, and E. Kirby Smith, June 10, *OR,* vol. 10, pt. 1, 921–22.

3. "GEORGIA AND HER MILITIA," *ADI,* June 10, 1862; "BY TELEGRAPH... Chattanooga, June 10" and "AFFAIRS IN CHATTANOOGA," *ADI,* June 11; "THE ENEMY'S DESIGNS UPON CHATTANOOGA—ITS DANGER," *ADI,* June 12; "YANKEE RULE IN NORTH ALABAMA," *ADI,* June 14; "GEORGIANS TO THE RESCUE" and "THE DESIGNS OF THE ENEMY UPON GEORGIA," *ADI,* June 15; "[From the Mobile Register.] GRENADA, MISS., June 7," *ADI,* June 12.

4. David G. Martin, *Jackson's Valley Campaign November 1861-June 1862* (Conshohocken PA: Combined Books, 1994), 74; Robert G. Tanner, *Stonewall in the Valley: Thomas J. "Stonewall" Jackson's Shenandoah Valley Campaign, Spring 1862* (Garden City NY: Doubleday, 1976), 100–101, 104, 131, 158, 173–74; Jeffry D. Wert, "Battle of McDowell, Va.," in Patricia L. Faust, ed., *The Historical Times Illustrated Encyclopedia of the Civil War* (New York: Harper & Row, 1986), 460.

5. James I. Robertson, Jr., "Stonewall in the Shenandoah: The Valley Campaign of 1862," *Civil War Times Illustrated,* vol. 12, no. 2, (May 1972), 23; "Engagement near Staunton," *ADI,* May 11, 1862; James I. Robertson, Jr., *Stonewall Jackson: The Man, the Soldier, the Legend* (New York: Macmillan, 1997), 378–81; "GEN. JACKSON'S VICTORY" (*Lynchburg Virginian*) and "GEN. JACKSON'S VICTORY" (*Petersburg Express*), *ADI,* May 20.

6. Robertson, "Stonewall in the Shenandoah," 24, 28–32; Vincent J. Esposito, *The West Point Atlas of American Wars,* 2 vols. (New York: Frederick A. Praeger, 1959), vol. 1, map 51; Frederic S. Klein, "Engagement at Front Royal," in Patricia L. Faust, ed., *Historical Times Encyclopedia of the Civil War* (New York: Harper & Row, 1986), 293; Kenly report, May 31, 1862, *OR,* vol. 12, pt. 1, 558; Martin, *Jackson's Valley Campaign,* 22, 109; Burke Davis, *They Called Him Stonewall: A Life of Lt. Gen. T. J. Jackson, C.S.A.* (New York: Holt, Rinehart and Winston), 1964), 56; Donald C. Pfanz, *Richard S. Ewell: A Soldier's Life* (Chapel Hill: University of North Carolina Press, 1998), 197; John H. Worsham, *One of Jackson's Foot Cavalry,* ed. by James I. Robertson, Jr. (Jackson TN: McCowat-Mercer Press, 1964), 47; Webb Garrison, *The Encyclopedia of Civil War Usage* (Nashville: Cumberland House, 2001), 553.

7. "BY TELEGRAPH. GREAT VICTORY," *ADI,* May 27, 1862; "More on the Defeat of Bank's Army," *ADI,* May 28.

8. Robertson, "Stonewall in the Shenandoah," 33–35, 38–40; Martin, *Jackson's Valley Campaign,* 124–39, 170; Tanner, *Stonewall in the Valley,* 275; Darrell L. Collins, *The Battles of Cross Keys and Port Republic* (Lynchburg VA: H. E. Howard, 1993), 82.

9. "RUMORS—STONEWALL JACKSON—AFFAIRS AT RICHMOND," *ADI,* June 3, 1862.

10. "Col. Ashby killed—Glorious Victory of Old Stonewall and General Ewell over Fremont and Shields," *ADI,* June 10, 1862; Thomas A. Ashby, *Life of Turner Ashby* (New York: Neale Publishing, 1914), 187, 209–10.

11. "From Yorktown," *ADI,* May 6, 1862; Esposito, ed., *West Point Atlas,* vol. 1, maps 41–43; Douglas Southall Freeman, *R. E. Lee: A Biography,* 4 vols. (New York: Charles Scribner's Sons, 1934–35), vol. 2, 77n.-78n.

12. Freeman, *Lee,* vol. 2, 21–22, 41–43; George Green Shackelford, *George Wythe Randolph*

and the Confederate Elite (Athens: University of Georgia Press, 1988), 74–75; Charles F. Bryan, Jr., "The Siege of Yorktown Part I," *Civil War Times Illustrated*, vol. 21, no. 4 (June 1982), 14; Symonds, *Joseph E. Johnston*, 152.

13. Charles F. Bryan, Jr., "The Siege of Yorktown, Part II," *Civil War Times Illustrated*, vol. 21, no. 5 (September 1982), 228–29; Mark Grimsley, "Rear Guard at Williamsburg," *Civil War Times Illustrated*, vol. 24, no. 3 (May 1985), 12–13, 27–30; Carson O. Hudson, Jr., *Civil War Williamsburg* (Williamsburg: Colonial Williamsburg Foundation, 1997), 24.

14. "The Battle Begun in Virginia," *ADI*, May 8, 1862; Grimsley, "Williamsburg," 27, 30.

15. Sears, *Gates of Richmond*, 90–92; Jeffrey L. Rhoades, *Scapegoat General: The Story of Major General Benjamin Huger, C.S.A.* (Hamden CT: Archon Books, 1985), 41; R. Thomas Campbell and Alan B. Flanders, *Confederate Phoenix: The CSS Virginia* (Shippensburg PA: Burd Street Press, 2001), 207–208; "THE EVACUATION OF NORFOLK," *ADI*, May 14, 1862.

16. James M. McPherson, *For Cause and Comrades: Why Men Fought in the Civil War* (New York: Oxford University Press, 1997), 21; "ENCOURAGEMENT FOR THE TIMID FROM THE LESSONS OF HISTORY" (*Western Carolinian*) and "We find the following paragraph in the Philadelphia Inquirer . . . ," *ADI*, May 15, 1862; Craven, *Coming of the Civil War*, 173; "The Enemy in James River," *ADI*, May 15; Sears, *Gates of Richmond*, 93–94; Emory Thomas, "The Peninsula Campaign: Part I," *Civil War Times Illustrated*, vol. 17, no. 10 (February 1979),16–17; "PROCLAMATION BY THE PRESIDENT" and "FRIDAY A DAY OF FASTING, HUMILIATION AND PRAYER," *ADI*, May 15.

17. "THE NEGRO AT HOME—WHAT ONE WHO SAW FOR HIMSELF HAS TO SAY," *ADI*, May 15,1862; William R. Taylor, *Cavalier & Yankee: The Old South and American National Character* (New York: Harper & Row, 1969 [1961]), 335; Stout, *Upon the Altar*, 48; Eric L. McKitrick, *Slavery Defended: The Views of the Old South* (Englewood Cliffs NJ: Prentice-Hall, 1963), 57.

18. Emory Thomas, "The Peninsula Campaign, Part II," *Civil War Times Illustrated*, vol. 18, no. 1 (April 1979), 28–29, 33–35; "FROM THE PENINSULA" and "HERMES," "RICHMOND NEWS AND GOSSIP" (from Richmond, May 10), *ADI*, May 16, 1862; Thomas L. Livermore, *Numbers and Losses in the Civil War in America: 1861–1865* (New York: Kraus Reprint Co., 1969 [1900]), 81.

19. "From Richmond," *ADI*, June 1, 1862; "From the Battle near Richmond" and "THE GREAT BATTLE—GEN. JOHNSTON," *ADI*, June 3; "From Richmond," *ADI*, June 4; "From Richmond," *ADI*, June 5; "INTERESTING INTELLIGENCE," *ADI*, June 14; "Dispatch from Col. Richard Yeadon to the Charleston Courier," *ADI*, June 5; "LIST OF WOUNDED GEORGIANS AT THE BATTLE OF CHICKAHOMINY," *ADI*, June 8; Hilde, *Worth a Dozen Men*, 24; "BATTLE OF CHICKAHOMINY,'" *ADI*, June 13; Sears, *Gates of Richmond*, 118; "NEWS FROM THE 'JACKSON GUARDS,'" *ADI*, June 28.

20. "G.L.H.," "ARMY CORRESPONDENCE," and "CAPTURE OF A YANKEE SOLDIER," *ADI*, June 5, 1862.

21. "LETTER FROM CAPT. J. H. NEAL OF THE ATLANTA 'JACKSON GUARDS,'" *ADI*, June 10, 1862; Venet, *Changing Wind*, 79; Alfred Hoyt Bill, *The Beleaguered City: Richmond 1861–65* (New York: Alfred A. Knopf, 1946), 129.

22. "The Cannonading near Richmond—Northern Lies—The Yankees killed and wounded—Gen. Wool Superseded at Fortress Monroe—France and England," *ADI*, June 10, 1862; "BY TELEGRAPH. Northern Lies, &c., &c.—European News. . . . SECOND DISPATCH. RICHMOND, June 14.—The N.Y. Herald . . . ," *ADI*, June 17.

23. Emory M. Thomas, "The Peninsula Campaign, Part III," *Civil War Times Illustrated*, vol. 18, no. 2 (May 1979), 13–16; "THE RICHMOND LINES—THE ENEMY DIGGING DIRT PRODIGIOUSLY," *ADI*, June 17, 1862; Edward G. Longacre, *Lee's Cavalrymen: A History of the Mounted Forces of the Army of Northern Virginia* (Mechanicsburg PA: Stackpole Books, 2002), 88, 92.

24. "Brilliant Exploit of General Stewart" and "BY TELEGRAPH. Northern Lies, &c., &c.,—European News. . . . THIRD DISPATCH," *ADI*, June 17, 1862; "A BRILLIANT RECONNAISSANCE BY STUART'S CAVALRY," *ADI*, June 20 (*Richmond Examiner*, June 16).

25. "RICHMOND WHIGGERIES," *ADI*, June 26, 1862.

15. Lee versus McClellan

THE SEVEN DAYS' BATTLES

Let us, then, arouse and put forth all our exertions in the noble cause in which we are engaged! Let us resolve that the men of Georgia shall never bow their necks to the despotism of the hypocritical Yankee, and that our wives and daughters shall never be insulted by the presence or gibes of the vulgar vandal race! Let us make every preparation to meet the enemy if they should come, and resolve to win such a victory over them as will fill all Yankeedom with mourning, and the Southern Confederacy with rejoicing!

THIS HORTATORY EDITORIAL, with its exclamations ("engaged!," "rejoicing!") and derogations of the enemy ("vulgar vandal race!") appeared in the *Atlanta Daily Intelligencer* on July 17, 1862. Its provocation had come from the *New York Herald*, "whose vermin-like reporters and correspondents," editor Archibald Gaulding wrote, "infest every room in the Departments at Washington, and by sycophancy and flattery, worm out the secrets of the Cabinet, through the Clerks." Apparently the *Herald*, based on whatever sources it could employ, had suggested that Gen. Henry Halleck's Federal army, then at Corinth, would not push farther south into the miasmatic swamplands of Mississippi, but would sidle into eastern Tennessee and northern Georgia. This prospect agitated Gaulding almost as much as the enemy's bombardment of Chattanooga the previous month. He consequently penned an editorial (excerpted above), urging the military authorities, "forewarned, forearmed," to prepare for Halleck's possible push toward Georgia. "Atlanta is the gate to the heart of the Southern Confederacy," the editor repeated from his earlier warnings, "and the country above it should be guarded and defended with the utmost vigilance."[1]

The *Intelligencer* turned its attention as well to the war in Virginia, where the editor was as eager as anyone for a battle that would break the stalemate at

Richmond between Lee and McClellan. On June 20, the editor found cause for an expression of optimism. "Our subjugation is a larger job than they bargained for," he began, asserting, "our prospects were never brighter than at present and the confidence of our people more sure." As an able press propagandist, Gaulding rosily related the situations on both eastern and western fronts: "the delay of the enemy at Richmond, the strategic move of Beauregard from Corinth, leaving Halleck to contend with the malaria of the swamps of Tennessee and Mississippi, and the victories of Stonewall Jackson in Virginia, have . . . inspired our own people with increased confidence." The *Intelligencer* predicted "glorious victories which will excite the admiration of the whole world, and be the theme of the whole human race."

Archibald Gaulding not only chased down Atlanta parents for letters written to them by their sons in Virginia, and wrote regular exuberant columns of Confederate propaganda, but he also selected the poems that his newspaper published every now and then as literary leavening. In its issue of June 25, the *Intelligencer* printed a rhymed composition, "BEAUREGARD." Gaulding prefaced the poem: "The following glorious tribute to one of our illustrious generals, was sent him recently by a lady of Kentucky, whose literary reputation is not confined to this continent. It is a fair index of the spirit that moves the glorious women of Kentucky:—ED. INT." "Our trust is now in thee, Beauregard!," the poem began. "The way that lies before/Is cold and hard;/We are led across the desert by the Lord," the poetess proclaimed, in verse that likened the Confederate people to the chosen ones of Israel. In such an allusion, Pierre Gustave Toutant Beauregard became something of a Moses-figure: "But the cloud that shines by night/To guide our steps aright/Is the pillar of thy might,/Beauregard!"

But the pillar of might's days were numbered. After Beauregard abandoned Corinth to Halleck, President Davis had become critical of the general. When Beauregard took medical leave from his army without informing Richmond, Davis seized on the opportunity to relieve him of command. Gen. Braxton Bragg succeeded him as commander of the Confederate army in Mississippi.[2]

"It is the prevailing belief here that we are on the eve of stirring and decisive events," asserted a dispatch from Richmond, dated June 23. The *Intelligencer*'s edition for the morning of Tuesday, the 24th, reported the situation with a dispatch from Richmond issued the day before: "Nothing of special interest has transpired here for several days. Skirmishing along the lines is of daily occurrence." That was true, but its prediction would not prove to be: "Gen. Joseph Johnston is rapidly recovering, and will soon be able to resume command of the army." That would not happen: Johnston was not ready for field service until November 1862, and by that time Robert E. Lee had led the Army of Northern Virginia in so many illustrious campaigns that Jefferson Davis would never remove him from its command. But the *Intelligencer*'s dispatch was accurate in this augury: "it is the belief here that we are on the eve of stirring and decisive events."

By late June General Lee had strengthened his army with troops from Georgia and the Carolinas, and had ordered Jackson to join him from the Valley. When Stonewall arrived, the Army of Northern Virginia would number some 90,000 officers and men—its largest strength at any time during the war. McClellan, too, had gotten reinforcements, so that the Army of the Potomac had in the field almost 106,000 soldiers. Never again would Robert E. Lee see such parity of strength between his army and his opponents' (who, including McClellan, would number five different generals before the end of the war).

The Northern army was organized as five different corps of infantry, numbered II, III, IV, V and VI (the Federal I Corps had been retained by President Lincoln to protect Washington). Lee had not yet adopted the corps concept for his forces, so that in late June they were organized into eleven divisions. On June 23, Lee assembled the commanders of four of these—Maj. Gens. Stonewall Jackson, James Longstreet, Ambrose Powell Hill and Daniel Harvey Hill (the latter two of no relation, although Harvey Hill and Jackson were brothers-in-law). He announced to them his plan to take the initiative and break the stalemate at Richmond. Stuart's reconnaissance had confirmed that McClellan's army was split by the Chickahominy River, the smaller part of it (the V Corps) on the north bank, the rest on the south. Lee planned to attack the isolated corps when Jackson's troops arrived from the Valley. When Stonewall said they would join the army by June 26, the generals set that day for their attacking battle.[3]

Before then, however, McClellan would strike, albeit in a limited way. On June 25, two Union divisions advanced in their sector, south of the Chickahominy along the road leading east from Richmond to Williamsburg. After some sharp fighting, McClellan, at the scene, ordered his men to withdraw. This engagement, usually named for nearby Oak Grove, would turn out to be the first of a storied series of combats that historians have come to call the Seven Days' Battles. In terms of casualties, Oak Grove would be the lightest of the seven: Union losses numbered 68 killed, 503 wounded, 55 missing (626 total); Confederates lost 66 dead, 362 wounded and 13 missing (441).

The *Intelligencer*'s coverage of the fight on June 25 was brief and inaccurate: "RICHMOND, June 25.—The First Louisiana Regiment engaged this forenoon Sickles's Brigade on the Williamsburg road and drove them back with great slaughter, capturing seventy-five prisoners. Confederate loss comparatively heavy." True, the Union brigade of Daniel E. Sickles was one of the three that ended up doing the attacking. And true, the 1st Louisiana Infantry Regiment played a key role, losing more than a third of its strength in several afternoon charges. The butcher's bill for Oak Grove, though, suggests that the Federals had not been repelled "with great slaughter." And, at least in comparison with the next six days, Confederate casualties on June 25 could not be considered "heavy." Lacking, too, in the *Intelligencer*'s Richmond dispatch was a realistic summation of what the fighting at Oak Grove had accomplished: Federal forces had advanced their picket lines 600 yards. Stephen Sears, chronicler of the Peninsula Campaign, offers an astute observation: "for a fight over advanced picket lines to generate more than a thousand casualties suggested just how intense any fighting between these two armies was likely to be."[4]

The fighting was indeed more intense the next day, June 26, and the *Intelligencer*'s coverage of it more extensive and thorough. It began with publication on the 27th of a telegraphic dispatch:

> RICHMOND, June 26.—The battle which is to decide the fate of Richmond was commenced this forenoon on the left wing of the Confederate army. For three hours the fighting has been rapid and continues in the direction of Mechanicsville. Cannonading [was] heard distinctly in the city, and crowds have repaired to the hills north of the city, from whence bursting of shells were occasionally visible. At eight o'clock firing was still progressing furiously. It is not probable that any particulars will be received from the battle field until morning. There was no fighting of importance on the centre or right to-day. A general engagement to-morrow is considered inevitable.

In this battle of Mechanicsville, June 26, Lee's infantry attacked the sole Union corps, Brig. Gen. Fitz John Porter's V, north of the Chickahominy along Beaver Dam Creek, but the assault did not come off as Lee and his lieutenants had planned on the 23rd. Jackson and his troops were late in their march to the battlefield; at 3 p.m., with Stonewall nowhere in sight, Powell Hill ordered his men to attack. Lee's plan had been to outflank Porter's position, but the Southerners' assaults ended up as costly frontal ones. By the end of the day, they had been repulsed with predictably lopsided losses: 1,475 Confederate,

361 Federal. The next day, June 27, the *Intelligencer* printed a brief article in its telegraphed news column, which stated that in the battle of the 26th, "the numerous field-works and batteries opposed to our advance were assaulted in the coolest manner imaginable and captured with great rapidity"—a claim woefully incorrect.

The reporting was worse in another dispatch coming from Richmond, dated June 27 and printed by the *Intelligencer* the following day: "The firing has not been heard in the city except at intervals for several hours—the enemy having been driven for miles in the direction of the White House on the Pamunkey River." As a matter of fact, McClellan's forces were *not* moving toward White House on the Pamunkey, which was some twenty-five miles northeast of Porter's position (which he still held). Nevertheless, the report stated that Richmonders "are buoyant with the conviction that the God of Battles has vouchsafed a COMPLETE VICTORY over an insolent foe." Another message, also from Richmond on the 27th, declared "all reports from the battle-field confirm the prevailing belief that McClellan's army has been THOROUGHLY DEFEATED, if not routed." The report further stated, "The York River Railroad with the batteries commanding it has been taken by the Confederates." This, too, was a fabrication. The York River Railroad ran eastward several miles south of the Chickahominy, and all the major action on June 26 was north of the river, not to mention that "all the batteries commanding it" had not been captured.

All of this, however, seems not to have been taken in by Gaulding. He appended at the end of this report, "[Glory enough for one day! ED. INT.]"[5]

During the night, General Porter followed McClellan's order to fall back from his Beaver Dam Creek line to a new position, still on the north bank of the river. He chose high ground to the east of a bog called Boatswain's Creek (or Swamp, which it really was), near the gristmill owned by Dr. William Gaines. Lee, wishing to keep up the pressure, ordered a renewed attack on Porter. That afternoon the Southerners' assaults were again repulsed, but Lee was determined to break the enemy line. About 7 p.m., with daylight ebbing, he ordered an advance of his entire front. This time the Confederate charge succeeded, sending the Federals in hurried retreat. The Southerners captured not only many prisoners, but twenty-two artillery pieces—an unusually large haul of ordnance among Civil War battles. During the night Porter and the Union troops north of the Chickahominy managed to get across the river to rejoin the rest of McClellan's army.

The breakdown of casualties for the battle of Gaines' Mill reflects the course of the battle. Porter's corps lost 894 killed, 3,114 wounded and 2,829 captured—this last number from the prisoners taken when Lee's infantry overwhelmed the Northern position. Confederates suffered more bloodily, reflecting their attacking role during the day: only 108 missing, but 1,483 men killed and 6,402 wounded.[6]

Still, the battle of June 27 was an outright Confederate victory, and the Southern press gloried in it. The *Intelligencer*'s "BY TELEGRAPH" column on the 29th began with a printing of General Lee's message to the president, written on the night of the engagement. "Profoundly grateful to Almighty God for the signal victory granted to us, it is my pleasure and task to announce to you the success achieved by this army to-day," he began, explaining that the enemy forces had been assailed "and finally after a severe contest of five hours were entirely repulsed from the field."

Directly below this, the *Intelligencer*, under the title of "The Battle near Richmond," printed a report from the *Richmond Dispatch* of June 28: "The results of yesterday may thus be summed up: we have driven the enemy six miles, beaten them twice in fight, captured 8 or 10 batteries and some 30 pieces of artillery, many stores, much clothing, many prisoners and small arms."

Another short item, "Further from Richmond," informed readers that "about two thousand prisoners were taken last night, including Brig. Gen. Reynolds." This was true: Union brigadier John F. Reynolds was so exhausted by two straight days of fighting that during Porter's nighttime retreat, he slipped out of the line of march to catch some sleep. He was awakened the next morning by Confederate soldiers, who happened to belong to Harvey Hill's division. When presented to Hill, Reynolds expressed embarrassment at being captured in such a way. Reynolds and Hill had served together in the prewar U.S. army; to his old friend, Hill tried to be consoling: "Reynolds, do not feel so bad about your capture; it is the fate of wars."

"Still Later from Richmond" stated that some 3,600 Federal captives were being herded into the city. "The constant arrival of prisoners produces a lively excitement about the streets," the article related, adding, "all reports from the field confirm the thorough discomfiture of the Yankee army, and many expect that McClellan will capitulate."[7]

To be sure, the Young Napoleon had lost his nerve; but not to the point of surrendering. After the battle of Mechanicsville—an engagement that his troops had won—McClellan decided to give up trying to take Richmond. He would withdraw to the safety of Union gunboats on the James River, or as historian

Stephen Sears puts it, "abandon his campaign, cut his losses, and run to safety." When it got out that McClellan had euphemized his timorous retreat from the Chickahominy to the James as a "change of base," Southerners derided him. The *Intelligencer* published a little poem about it: "Henceforth when a scoundrel is kicked out of doors, He need not resent the disgrace, But cry: 'My dear sir, I'm eternally yours, For your kindness in changing my base.'"

McClellan ordered his supply dump burned and his troops to start marching southward for the James. Throughout Saturday, June 28, the two armies lost contact: McClellan was marching, and Lee was sending Stuart's cavalry out to learn where he was going. The only fighting that day occurred less than a mile south of the Chickahominy, when a Confederate commander in the area, Brig. Gen. Robert Toombs, jumped the gun and attacked the Federals in his front. This fight at Garnett's farm cost Southerners close to 500 casualties.

When Lee discerned the enemy's movement on June 29, he directed Jackson to pursue the Federals. He also ordered troops protecting Richmond, under Maj. Gen. John Magruder, to push out eastward and try to catch McClellan's column in flank.[8]

Magruder attacked the enemy early on June 29 near Allen's farm, but then backed off when he thought he was about to be counterattacked. He then waited until that afternoon, in the vicinity of Savage's Station to renew his assault, which quickly sputtered out. The day's toll for the actions at Allen's farm and Savage's Station was 1,038 for Northern forces and 473 for Southern.[9]

The *Intelligencer* was quick to print in its telegraphic news column of July 2 an item issued from the capital the day before.

> RICHMOND, July 1. Yesterday afternoon the enemy was attacked by Gen. Huger in the vicinity of White Oak Swamp. The divisions of Longstreet and Hill were also engaged. The action became general and lasted several hours, with heavy loss on our side. The enemy was driven back about two miles further down. Jackson's force was engaged with a column of the enemy, and captured three batteries. The Enquirer states that a Federal officer brought in yesterday reports McClellan mortally wounded, and the Yankee army entirely demoralized.

Stripped of its blatant exaggerations—McClellan mortally wounded, his army entirely demoralized—this dispatch did its best to capture the basics of the battle of White Oak Swamp, Frayser's Farm or Glendale (as it is variously called), fought a dozen miles southeast of Richmond on June 30. The advance of Huger's division was blocked by trees chopped down by the Northerners, so

Longstreet and A. P. Hill's divisions launched the Confederate attack about four o'clock. The Southerners scored important gains: Maj. Gen. George McCall, a Federal division commander, was captured, along with eighteen pieces of artillery (the three batteries mentioned in the Richmond dispatches, though they were not taken by "Jackson's forces").

Casualties for the battle of White Oak Swamp were almost equal for the two sides: among the Northerners 3,797 (297 killed, 1,696 wounded and 1,804 missing) and 3,673 for the Southerners (638 dead, 2,814 wounded, 221 missing).[10]

"The engagement yesterday is reported to have been the most sanguinary of the series of conflicts before this city," read a dispatch sent from Richmond on July 1, referring to the battle of White Oak Swamp. Actually, it had not: so far, the battle of Gaines' Mill, where Lee's infantry charged Porter's lines on June 27, had caused the heaviest casualties (14,830 killed, wounded and missing, both sides) among the engagements that had begun on June 25. Yet in the "sanguinary" category, the battle of June 30 ranked second up to that time, with killed and wounded among Confederates and Federals totaling 5,445. The dispatch, which the *Intelligencer* printed on July 3, nonetheless capably summarized the action at White Oak Swamp: Longstreet and Hill attacked about 4 p.m.; "the Yankees made a desperate resistance, but were driven from their entrenched positions and pursued two miles. . . . darkness prevented our troops from following and routing the enemy." Six hundred prisoners had arrived in the city, Major General McCall among them. "The valor of our troops is beyond praise," the report concluded.[11]

"Our telegraphic news to-day continues to be of a cheering character," Gaulding wrote in an editorial published on July 3. Indeed, he considered McClellan to have already been decisively defeated. "The defeat of the 'Grand Federal Army' will be esteemed in all the future, as a glorious accomplishment," he beamed. Future historians, he promised, will devote "many a page in recording . . . the valor and heroism of the Southern soldiery—the generalship of the leaders of our army—the game cock pluck of the South, which preferred death to being conquered." But the confirming news of the Northern defeat had yet to arrive. "Near Richmond, McClellan's Army, or portions of it, still, in some of its divisions, appear to have been making a final struggle—the struggle of despair," the editorial asserted. No papers from Richmond had arrived on July 2, so Gaulding asked his readers to be patient "till we can spread before them such accounts as we shall be certain to receive from the vicinity of where battles have been fought."

The break in the news-flow from Virginia gave the editor of the *Intelligencer* opportunity to reflect on the Confederate cause in a patriotic editorial placed in his issue of July 4. "It is most gratifying to look back since the States of the Southern Confederacy resolved that they would not submit to Yankee rule and despotism," Gaulding began, "and contemplate the cheerfulness with which great sacrifices have been made by all classes in the cause of Freedom and Independence." Soldiers were volunteering for "the hardships and sufferings of the tented field." Poor folk had sent forth their sons, the editor recounted, while the rich had used their wealth to outfit batteries, clothe troops and feed needy families back home. Even the banks, "those corporations that are said to have no souls," were forsaking the drive for profits to assist the citizenry amidst wartime difficulties. Women, of course, came in for special praise; they furnished comforts for the soldiers and tended to the weakened ones in the hospitals. "With few exceptions," the editor concluded, "everywhere in the Southern Confederacy, men, women, boys, the free blacks, and even most of the slaves, have worked with cheerful hearts and willing hands to redeem our country from the hated yoke of the hypocritical, cowardly and cruel Yankee."

The timely arrival of a letter mailed by a reader in Campbellton allowed the *Intelligencer* to give an example of the kind of patriotism that Gaulding so extolled. The writer explained that a local resident, "Uncle" Henry Phillips, was always seen at the Campbellton post office about the time the mail arrived. Mr. Phillips, the writer explained, had nine sons in the army, and had two more over thirty-five ready to "go in." He constantly hoped to hear from his sons. "It would have done you good to see the old man read the letters he got from his sons under 'Stonewall,'" the correspondent continued; "his eyes would sparkle with patriotic fire as they recounted to him the scenes they had been in." Uncle Henry also talked to his neighbors about the war; "he says nobody ought ever to be allowed to say 'that the Yankees will whip us.'" The "old patriarch," as he was affectionately called, even said that he was prepared to join the army himself. The writer's conclusion was telling: "he has twelve negroes and fifteen or sixteen hundred acres of land, and is willing to put it all on his country's altar."

The *Intelligencer*'s editorial office always welcomed these kinds of letters, but the writers had to identify themselves. Failure to do so, Gaulding explained, doomed their epistles to non-publication. In late May, the paper had explained this practice in connection with a submission it had received from "SENEX." On the third of July, it reaffirmed its rule. A reader signing his letter "C." had failed to provide his name, so "we must decline publishing it," the editor affirmed.

The *Intelligencer* had a strict policy indeed. "In no case will we publish communications, the author's name being withheld from us," the editor repeated.[12]

Gaulding had correctly described the situation before Richmond in his editorial of July 3 on "War News." McClellan's army remained dangerously close to the capital, while the paper in Atlanta awaited news of further developments. When it arrived, in several dispatches from Richmond dated July 2, it referred to a battle fought the day previous, but only vaguely. One, printed on July 3, was titled "Desperate Fighting":

> RICHMOND, July 2.—All accounts concur in representing the battle on yesterday to have been the most desperate and terrific which has yet taken place. The enemy held a very strong position, and maintained it against repeated assaults of our troops for hours.

"Innumerable and conflicting reports have been afloat to-day relative to the fight yesterday," another began. Bits of information in the brief articles allowed one to infer that the Federals, "upon the summit of a hill fortified and defended by several batteries," had been attacked by Confederate infantry, and with some success ("Jackson's forces . . . succeeded in capturing two batteries"). During the night the Union army had withdrawn southward, toward the James River and the protection of its gunboats. Southern forces occupied the battlefield on the morning of the 2nd, according to these reports.

That was all that could be gleaned about the battle of Malvern Hill, July 1, 1862—one of the darkest days of the war for Robert E. Lee's Army of Northern Virginia. After White Oak Swamp, McClellan's troops had continued their retreat to the James and had taken a strong position on high ground, Malvern Hill, along the north river bank. Lee was determined one last time to inflict as much damage upon the enemy, despite reconnaissance that showed the Federal lines well buttressed with cannon. Lee hoped that an artillery barrage might neutralize those guns before his infantry advanced. As it turned out, the Southerners' cannonade never occurred. Not enough field pieces were brought up, and these soon came under fire from the Northern batteries on Malvern Hill. By mid-afternoon, Lee was forced to conclude that his pre-assault bombardment was a failure. The idea of some flanking maneuver was also soon found to be unfeasible. That left frontal assault by infantry as Lee's only option. At 5:30 p.m. the Confederates began their attack, which was predictably and bloodily repulsed. "It was not war—it was murder," D. H. Hill famously wrote after the war. The Union guns kept firing until nightfall.

Losses for the battle were obviously higher in the Southern ranks: 869 killed, 4,241 wounded and 540 missing (most were probably dead), or 5,650 in total—a figure second only to Confederate casualties at Gaines' Mill. Federals on July 1 incurred losses of 314 killed, 1,875 wounded and 818 missing, for a total of 3,007.[13]

The *Intelligencer* paid particular attention to casualties in regiments to which Atlantans belonged. The 7th Georgia Infantry was a case in point; six of its ten companies had been recruited in Fulton, DeKalb and Cobb Counties. On July 8, the paper printed a listing of the killed and wounded from the recent battles in Virginia, as furnished by a regimental officer. The 7th's lieutenant colonel and adjutant had both been wounded; its major, Eli W. Hoyle, had been "mortally wounded while bearing the colors to the front" after the regiment's color bearer had been killed. Beyond these losses, fifteen officers and men were named as killed, another two mortally wounded, ninety-nine more wounded (from severely to slightly), with nine other soldiers listed as missing.

As usual, when the shooting stopped, the eulogies ensued. The *Intelligencer* published a particularly heartfelt one a month after the Seven Days' Battles had ended. It came from Capt. W. Proctor Hughey, Co. I, 7th Georgia, who submitted a remembrance of Major Hoyle, the adjutant who had been mortally wounded at Malvern Hill. "As one who had the honor of his acquaintance and friendship," Hughey began, "I desire to offer a tribute to the many admirable qualities" possessed by Eli Hoyle: bravery, generosity and kindness chief among them. "But the most remarkable characteristic of the man," Captain Hughey recalled, "was his intense unwavering adherence to the principles of Truth and Honor." As further tribute, Hughey enclosed a poem, "To the Memory of Major Eli W. Hoyle," which was unsigned but probably written by Hughey himself in the conventional style of Victorian verse: "He fell as patriots ever wish to fall— Who fought for liberty—upon his field of fame. To freedom, he had freely consecrated all, Then hallow'd now, forever, be his name!"

Details of Major Hoyle's life were offered in a resolution adopted by his lodge of Free Masons, based in Stone Mountain. Volunteering as a private in G. J. Foreacre's company and accompanying it to Virginia, Hoyle had been wounded in one of the regiment's battles. Upon recovery, he was promoted to adjutant and on May 12 was elected major of the 7th. Again wounded on July 1, he died two days later—"another noble sacrifice in the country's cause," as the Masons sadly acknowledged.[14]

In the immediate aftermath of Malvern Hill, the Southern telegraphic news office in Richmond was not only unaware of the tragic outcome of the battle, but was grossly misinformed about it. Its dispatch of July 4, published in the *Intelligencer* the next day, read thus (referring to McClellan's troops as "fugitives"):

COMPLETE VICTORY.

RICHMOND, July 4.—Owing to the remoteness of the fugitives it is very difficult to obtain information of the situation of affairs. Various rumors are afloat, but none can be traced to a reliable source. It is only *certain* that McClellan's army has been COMPLETELY ROUTED, and whilst portions have escaped on transports, a large number will be captured. OUR VICTORY IS COMPLETE.

The *Intelligencer* built on this report with an editorial from the *Richmond Enquirer* published on July 6. So heady was the news of McClellan's defeat and Lee's successful defense of the capital that the *Enquirer* actually forecast an eventual Confederate victory by the end of the war. "The victory of Richmond . . . will prepare the way for a termination of the struggle," the editorial predicted, even if the war turned into a protracted struggle against a vengeful North. The opinion piece was so sure of Southern independence that it even began making recommendations as to what Confederate negotiators should shoot for in the final armistice talks: "if we secure to our Confederacy all the slave states [meaning Maryland, Delaware, Kentucky and Missouri, in addition to the Confederate eleven] and our share of the Territories with the Keys of the Gulf [the Federals still held forts at Key West and the Dry Tortugas], we shall be independent of the North forever." But failure to do so, the editorial warned, would place the new Confederate nation in a position of weakness relative to the United States—"a secondary and dependent relation," as the article phrased it.[15]

Gradually, though, the realization began to sink in that McClellan's army had not been destroyed or captured, but was resting securely down the James River in a position that General Lee did not wish to attack. The *Intelligencer* addressed this situation in an editorial on July 9, entitled "Sees Through a Glass Darkly." "There seems to us to exist a spirit among some of our people, and in more than one Southern Press, to under-estimate what Southern valor has recently won, and to over-estimate the strategy of the defeated, the disgracefully whipped Yankee leader and his army," the piece began. "Hence because McClellan and his army have not all been captured or driven into the James River," it continued, "what has been done is a small matter, not what was expected, not was proclaimed!"

Gaulding then reviewed what General Lee had achieved in the Seven Days' Battles, beginning with the daunting challenges he had faced. He had had to engage an enemy army larger than his, one that was also better equipped and that stood in strong defensive positions, protected by "the finest artillery in the world." His attacking army had had to advance through marshes and swamps. Nevertheless, against these odds, "in every struggle it has been victorious!," the editor exclaimed (overlooking several bloody setbacks). "Who should not rejoice over these glorious achievements of our troops?," he asked, righteously indignant.

Gaulding's voice was all the louder because of an editorial that the *Intelligencer*'s rival, the *Atlanta Southern Confederacy*, had printed the previous day, under the title of "What Has Been Accomplished." In it the *Confederacy* pointed out that McClellan's drive on Richmond had been checked, that the capital was safe, and that Lee's army had won a string of important victories. On the other hand, the Federal army remained "unbroken," and it did not appear to be "demoralized," despite claims to that effect. Indeed, the *Confederacy* declared, "the results of the great fight are not equal to what the people have been led to hope from the meagre telegraphic reports." The *Confederacy* went so far as to credit McClellan as "a great General—a master commander."

This was clearly too much for Archibald Gaulding, who closed his "Sees Through a Glass Darkly" editorial of July 9 by pointing the *Confederacy*'s editors to President Davis' recent message to the officers and men of Lee's army. In it Davis reviewed their "series of brilliant victories," tendering to them "the thanks of the country." Comparing Davis' message with the *Atlanta Confederacy*'s "What Has Been Accomplished" article, the *Intelligencer*'s editor remarked that either "President Davis must know *nothing* of what has been achieved, or the '*Southern Confederacy*,' to use a mild term, must be greatly in error."[16]

Even more greatly in error, though, were Northern accounts of the Seven Days' Battles, starting with McClellan's address to his army, dated July 4. As it hovered at Harrison's Landing on the James River, "the Young Napoleon" claimed that his troops had contended against superior numbers, and called his retreat to the James a successful "flank movement." With McClellan making these kinds of assertions, the *Intelligencer* opined, "we *would* pity him, but for this perversion of the truth." As for the Northern press, Gaulding inveighed against its accounts of the recent battles. "We could easily, too, fill up our columns with these lying details of Yankee newspapers," the editor declared, which the *Intelligencer* got from its exchanges with Richmond papers. "Who can fail to be disgusted with such lies?," he asked, concluding, "we feel satisfied that our readers will agree with us, it is better to fill our columns with other matter."

And it was not just Northern papers. The *Mobile Tribune* had obtained a copy of the *New Orleans Delta*, which after the Union occupation of the Crescent City had shifted its loyalties to favor the Union war effort. According to the *Tribune*, the reoriented New Orleans paper had proclaimed on July 10 that a great battle had been fought in Virginia, that fifty thousand Southern soldiers had been captured, and that Federal forces had even seized the Confederate capital. The *Intelligencer* simply headlined this short article, "How the Yankees Lie."[17]

The phrase "Richmond victories" was catching on in Confederate newspapers. On July 19, the *Intelligencer* reprinted from the *Charleston Mercury* an article, "The Natural Effect of the Richmond Victories." General Lee's battles against McClellan, according to this editorial, demonstrated that the North could not possibly conquer the South. McClellan's huge, well equipped army had been blunted by "not one third of their numbers actually engaged, and by Southern troops, the greater part of which had never been in battle."

But the victories had obviously come at a cost. In a somber article, "THE KILLED AND WOUNDED AT THE BATTLES BEFORE RICHMOND," the *Intelligencer* reported that the superintendent of the Army Intelligence Office had computed Confederate casualties: 2,500 killed, 12,500 wounded, plus some 3,000 soldiers ill and out of action. The total came to 18,000 or 20,000 men. "We look upon this *havoc* with pain," the editor concluded, "but, unlike the Yankees, have no wish to conceal it. The severer our loss, the more we have to revenge."

The *Intelligencer*'s statement was remarkably frank, and its numbers were remarkably accurate. Historians today place Lee's losses from Oak Grove on June 25 through Malvern Hill, July 1, at 3,494 dead, 15,758 wounded and 952 missing, for a total in the Seven Days at 20,204—very close to the newspaper's statement of "18,000, or 20,000—not exceeding, if it reaches the latter number."

The Seven Days' Battles delivered to the *Intelligencer* a metaphorical pill that was hard to swallow. The contest between Lee and McClellan was the first major campaign since Manassas, fought almost a year before. It involved many more troops (some 200,000) than those who had fought in July '61 (60,000). The week-end fighting also produced many more casualties (5,300 at Manassas; 36,000 in the Seven Days, counting both sides). Yet it offered far less decisive results. Manassas had been a clear-cut Southern victory, with the Federal army fleeing the battlefield at the end of the day. After Malvern Hill, however, McClellan's army still held position near the James River southeast of the Confederate capital. (For that matter, Johnston's attacking battle at Seven Pines had also ended indecisively.) When Archibald Gaulding conceded that "McClellan and his army have not all been captured or driven into the James River," he was in fact reckoning with the prospect that the war would not end quickly with a beaming Confederate triumph, but would likely slog on and on in a sort of huge stalemate . . . which was pretty close to what actually happened during the next three years.

In the meantime, there was a war still to be fought. In an editorial, July 10, entitled "MCCLELLAN'S DEFEAT—WHAT NEXT," editor Gaulding endorsed the recommendation that he had seen in the *Richmond Enquirer* of the 5th. Now that McClellan's Army of the Potomac had been dealt with, it was time to turn to the other enemy forces in Virginia. "An advance movement now will swiftly clear Virginia of the others of her detested invaders," the *Enquirer* had posited. The *Intelligencer* noted that in Jefferson Davis' congratulatory order to Lee's army, the president had urged them "to drive the invader from your soil," and winning still further glory by "carrying your standard beyond the outer boundaries of the Confederacy."

Gaulding could not have agreed more with the president's call for a strategic advance by Confederate forces. Once the "ruthless and barbarous invaders" had been swept from Virginia, he advised a two-pronged offensive: an eastern one "to carry the war into Washington, Maryland, and to Philadelphia," and a western advance to "clear Tennessee of the enemy." It was the eastern offensive that most excited Gaulding, judging from his printed commentary: "it will be a glorious day to us, when it comes, to have the privilege of recording the capture of Washington, and the destruction of every public building in it; to write also that down-trodden Maryland has been rescued from her brutal invaders, and that the hypocritical city of 'brotherly love,' Philadelphia, has been shelled into ruins by our brave troops."[18]

Intruding into this euphoric speculation was some tragic news close to home. On July 8, the *Intelligencer* reported that a terrible train wreck had occurred two days before on the Western & Atlantic, "between the down and up trains near Ringgold." Someone had blundered; the single-track line could not admit two-way traffic, and the north- and southbound trains running on it had to be carefully scheduled and managed. Editor Gaulding appended a tabulation of the lives lost: two railroaders, five Confederate soldiers, seven blacks and six horses, to whom were added, "36 or 37 soldiers scalded and crippled."

Of interest, Gaulding's addition came at the end of the main article, which had been filed by "J. H. S."—John H. Steele, who on April 27 had announced in the *Intelligencer* that he had assumed a "humble position." In such a capacity, he was at Dalton, reporting on the locomotives' crash. "I will be in Atlanta to-night," Steele wrote, suggesting he would write more for the paper about the gruesome accident.[19]

He would do more than that. In its issue of Tuesday morning, July 29, the *Intelligencer* printed an article entitled "VALEDICTORY" in which Archibald Gaulding announced that he was selling his half-interest in the newspaper to his co-proprietor, Jared Whitaker. Judge Whitaker extended to Colonel Gaulding his very best wishes, commending him for his "ability and experience as a political writer and journalist," and for bringing the *Atlanta Daily Intelligencer* to "its present position" as a well-respected paper in Georgia. "The separation that has taken place leaves them as both friends," Whitaker added, speaking of himself and Gaulding.

The important question, though, was who would become the new editor of the *Intelligencer*? Whitaker answered it this way:

> While upon MAJOR STEELE the labors and responsibilities of the Editorial Department of the "INTELLIGENCER" will mainly devolve, still the undersigned may be regarded as exercising a proper supervision of its political course and general conduct.
>
> JARED I. WHITAKER [20]

NOTES

1. "WHAT WILL HALLECK'S ARMY DO?," *ADI*, July 17, 1862.

2. "YANKEE DIPLOMACY," *ADI*, June 20, 1862; "BEAUREGARD," *ADI*, June 23; Williams, *Beauregard*, 155–57.

3. "From Richmond," *ADI*, June 24, 1862; Symonds, *Joseph E. Johnston*, 183; Sears, *Gates of Richmond*, 156–57, 174–77, 379–91; Frank J. Welcher, *The Union Army, 1861–1865: Organization and Operations. Volume I: The Eastern Theater* (Bloomington: Indiana University Press, 1989), 300.

4. Emory Thomas, "The Peninsula Campaign, Part IV," *Civil War Times Illustrated*, vol. 18, no. 3 (June 1979), 11–12; Sears, *Gates of Richmond*, 184–89; "First Louisiana Regiment Engage and Drive Back Sickles's Brigade," *ADI*, June 26, 1862.

5. "BATTLE AT RICHMOND," *ADI,* June 27, 1862; Thomas, "Peninsula Campaign, Part IV," 12–13; "The Battle near Richmond," "GLORIOUS NEWS" and "A GLORIOUS VICTORY!," *ADI,* June 28; Thomas, "Peninsula Campaign, Part III," 18; Sears, *Gates of Richmond,* 198.

6. Sears, *Gates of Richmond,* 212–13, 219, 224–26, 228–29, 236–37, 243, 249, 252.

7. "Dispatch from General Lee," "The Battle near Richmond" (*Dispatch*) and "Further from Richmond," *ADI,* June 29, 1862; Sears, *Gates of Richmond,* 252; "Still Later from Richmond," *ADI,* June 29.

8. Sears, *Gates of Richmond,* 210–11, 217, 231, 257–59; "M'CLELLAN'S STRATEGIC MOVE," *ADI,* July 23, 1862; Emory Thomas, "Peninsula Campaign, Part V," *Civil War Times Illustrated,* vol. 18, no. 4 (July 1979), 14–16.

9. Sears, *Gates of Richmond,* 265–66, 271–74; Thomas, "Peninsula Campaign, Part V," 17.

10. "From Richmond," *ADI,* July 2; Thomas, "Peninsula Campaign, Part V," 20; Sears, *Gates of Richmond,* 307.

11. "The Battle Before Richmond," *ADI,* July 3, 1862; Sears, *Gates of Richmond,* 249, 307.

12. "WAR NEWS," *ADI,* July 3, 1862; "DEVOTION TO COUNTRY," *ADI,* July 4; "For the Intelligencer. CAMPBELLTON, June 30, 1862. Colonel Gaulding . . . ," *ADI,* July 3; "SENEX," *ADI,* May 24; "'C.,'" *ADI,* July 3.

13. "Desperate Fighting," *ADI,* July 3, 1862; "From Richmond" and "SECOND DISPATCH," *ADI,* July 4; Sears, *Gates of Richmond,* 318–21, 324–35; Thomas, "Peninsula Campaign, Part V," 21–23.

14. "CASUALTIES IN THE 7TH GEORGIA REGIMENT," *ADI,* July 8, 1862; "For the Intelligencer. TO THE MEMORY OF MAJOR ELI W. HOYLE," *ADI,* August 7; "TRIBUTE OF RESPECT," *ADI,* August 12; Allen, *7th Georgia Roster,* 2.

15. "COMPLETE VICTORY," *ADI,* July 5, 1862; "THE FUTURE OF WAR," *ADI,* July 6.

16. "'SEES THROUGH A GLASS DIMLY,'" *ADI,* July 9, 1862; "What Has Been Accomplished," *Atlanta Southern Confederacy,* July 8; Jefferson Davis, "To the Army of Eastern Virginia," July 5, *OR,* vol. 11, pt. 2, 690.

17. "GEN. McCLELLAN'S ADDRESS TO HIS GRAND ARMY," *ADI,* July 17, 1862; "NORTHERN ACCOUNTS OF THE BATTLES NEAR RICHMOND," *ADI,* July 15; "How the Yankees Lie," *ADI,* July 19.

18. "THE NATURAL EFFECT OF THE RICHMOND VICTORIES," *ADI,* July 19, 1862; "THE KILLED AND WOUNDED AT THE BATTLES BEFORE RICHMOND," *ADI,* August 7; Sears, *Gates of Richmond,* 343; "McCLELLAN'S DEFEAT—WHAT NEXT," *ADI,* July 10; "The President's Congratulatory Address to the Army of Eastern Virginia," *ADI,* July 9.

19. "Special Dispatch to the Intelligencer. Dreadful Accident on the Western & Atlantic Railroad," *ADI,* July 8, 1862; "PERSONAL," *ADI,* April 27.

20. "VALEDICTORY," *ADI,* July 29, 1862.

16. The War Turns Harder

CHIVALRY WAS NOT YET DEAD in the spring of 1862, as Northern and Southern armies entered their second year of war.

A series of letters printed in the *Intelligencer* indicates the civility that could still exist between gentleman officers of the opposing armies, even as their soldiers sought to kill each other on the battlefield.

During the battle of Seven Pines, May 31, the 35th Georgia was engaged against the 20th Massachusetts, a mile north of Fair Oaks Station. After nightfall a severely wounded officer of the 35th, Lt. Col. Gustavus A. Bull, was brought into the Union lines as prisoner. The colonel of the 20th, W. Raymond Lee, saw that Bull received medical care. After the next morning's combat, Colonel Lee learned that the twenty-year-old Bull had died at 8 a.m. The day after that, Monday, June 2, Lee searched for the Confederate officer's grave, intending to place a headboard upon it. He knew its general location, around a house behind the Federal lines that had been turned into a field hospital, but there were so many graves that Lee could not find the burial site of the slain Georgian.

Two weeks later, Colonel Lee wrote to no less than Gen. Robert E. Lee, whom he had known at West Point (they both graduated in the class of 1829), explaining the fate of Lieutenant Colonel Bull, and suggesting that soldiers of Confederate Brig. Gen. Wade Hampton's command, against whom his men had fought, might know of the house and its graveyard. General Lee in turn had a staff officer, Maj. Charles Marshall, mail Colonel Lee's letter to Lieutenant Colonel Bull's father, Orville Augustus Bull, a prominent attorney and Superior Court judge living in LaGrange, Georgia. Major Marshall offered the grieving father assistance in trying to find his son's grave near Fair Oaks. Mr. Bull then sent the two letters to the local newspaper, the *LaGrange Reporter*, asking that its editor, Charles H. C. Willingham, print them. When the *Reporter* obligingly did so, the *Intelligencer* picked up the correspondence among its exchanges, and accordingly published it in its entirety on July 27.

THE LATE LIEUT-COL. G. A. BULL

LA GRANGE, JULY 23d, 1862.

Mr. Willingham: As numerous friends of my gallant son have expressed an anxious solicitude about his fate, I think it due to them to communicate the following sad intelligence which reached me this morning. Nothing remains for me but to submit to the inexorable doom that has consigned my brave and noble boy to an untimely death and my own gray hairs to sorrow and gloom.

Respectfully, O. A. BULL.

H'D Q'RS., DEP. N.V., 19th July, 1862.

O. H. [sic] BULL, *Esq., LaGrange, Georgia:*

SIR: General Lee directs me to enclose to you the accompanying communication from Col. Lee, U.S.A., and to express to you his sincere sympathy and condolence for the sad loss that it will announce to you. Gen. Lee also requests me to say that any assistance that can be rendered to enable you to recover the remains of Col. Bull, will be readily rendered to you. The ground where he lies is now entirely free from the presence of the enemy, and easily accessible to our citizens. I have the honor to be, with great respect, your obedient servant.

CHARLES MARSHALL,

Major and Aid [sic]-de-Camp.

CAMP NEAR RICHMOND, VA.

July 15, 1862.

GENERAL.—As a consequence of the battle at Fair Oaks, May 31st, last, Lieut. Col. Bull, 35th Georgia Regiment, fell into my hands a prisoner of war. Col. Bull was badly wounded by a musket ball in the side. It was about 9 o'clock in the evening when he was brought in; and occupying an advance position, my means for the care of the wounded were necessarily very limited; but I assure you that all in my power to do was done for Col. Bull. He was made as comfortable as possible under the circumstances—provided with a bed of blankets—and such restoratives as we had were administered to him. Towards morning, it became evident that he was fast sinking.—He was sensible of his extreme condition, and spoke freely to me of his approaching death calmly and resignedly—desiring me to communicate to his family messages of tender love and affection. This painful duty I now perform; and recalling our early and intimate relations, I beg to make you the medium of my communication to Col. Bull's father, O. A. Bull, La Grange, Troup County, Georgia.

I have the sword and watch of Col. B., and it will afford me the greatest pleasure to send them to his family by the first opportunity which offers. I left Col. B. to take position in line of battle at 7, A.M. on June 1st. He was then perfectly calm and entirely free of pain; indeed, he had not suffered in the least degree at any time. He died about 8, A.M., as I am informed. I was not at liberty to leave my command during the day or night of June 1st; but on Monday I made diligent search for his grave—I am sorry to add, without success. My intention was to place a head-board to designate the spot. Generally, I do know that the grave is near a house where the left of our battle [line] rested, about half a mile north of Fair Oaks station. It is one of many graves there. Any of the Hampton Legion—which corps fought opposite our left on May 31st—will be able to point out the house referred to, if desirable.

Very respectfully,

Your obedient servant,

W. RAYMOND LEE,

Colonel, 20th Mass. Regiment.

GEN. ROBT. E. LEE, C.S.A., Richmond, Va.–*LaGrange Reporter*.

Gustavus Adolphus Bull had been elected second lieutenant of Co. B, 4th Georgia Infantry on April 26, 1861. He resigned on October 17, the date he was elected lieutenant colonel of the 35th. His father, Orville A. Bull, was a Superior Court judge in Clayton County, south of Atlanta. He was never able to bring his son's remains home. A memorial in the family plot in LaGrange's Hillview Cemetery reads, "Sacred to the memory of Gustavus Adolphus Bull, whose remains lie among the unknown dead of the battle field of Seven Pines."[1]

Colonel Lee's chivalry was touching, but it was also fleeting, as during the spring and summer of 1862 the war—at least the North's prosecution of it—was changing.

In the first year of the conflict, Northern leaders, both civilian and military, believed that the South's plain folk would turn against the political ruling class that had led the region to secession. Northerners thought that given time these commoners, especially when their homelands fell under Union troops' occupation, would turn against the Confederacy. To encourage them, Federal officers carefully avoided measures that threatened their property. Chief among its practitioners was none other than Union Maj. Gen. George Brinton McClellan. As his troops took over much of western Virginia in the summer and fall of 1861, McClellan had assured the populace that his troops would scrupulously respect their private property, even their slaves. McClellan's leniency seemed to work; sufficient Unionist sentiment arose that by 1863 the Federal government was able to forge Virginia's western counties into a new state with Unionist leaders.

In the spring of 1862, as his army pushed up the Peninsula, McClellan again issued strict orders for the protection of Virginians' property. Indeed, a "soft war" against the Rebels made sense to most Northerners at the time. After Forts Henry and Donelson, Island No. 10, Shiloh, New Orleans and Corinth, and with Richmond likely to be captured, the conflict in mid-May 1862 seemed headed for a quick resolution and Northern victory.

But two sets of events worked toward the end of the Federals' conciliatory policy in the spring of 1862. Despite their recent setbacks, Confederates' morale showed few signs of weakening, as demonstrated by the defiance shown by the ladies of New Orleans to the city's Northern occupiers. Moreover, Southern civilians in occupied areas of Tennessee and northern Alabama exhibited growing hostility to Union troops, including outright guerrilla violence.

The second set of events occurred on the battlefield. By early July 1862, the rebellion that earlier had seemed to be reeling had resurged with impressive triumphs in Virginia, most notably Stonewall Jackson's brilliant Valley Campaign and Lee's Seven Days' Battles, which not only saved Richmond from capture, but left McClellan's army cowering on the banks of the James.[2]

Pressed by "Radicals" in his own party, and tiring of McClellan's timidity, President Lincoln himself began to turn the soft war harder. He brought Maj. Gen. John Pope, hero of Island No. 10 and New Madrid, eastward and on June 26 put him in charge of a new Federal Army of Virginia, comprised of troops from the several commands in the Valley, plus others that he drew from the Washington area and the Army of the Potomac (essentially shelving McClellan for the time being).

After arriving in Virginia and taking command of his newly assembled forces, Pope issued a series of orders that signaled a new policy toward the Rebels. General Order No. 5, put forth on July 18, announced that so far as possible, Pope's army would live off the land—meaning, taking all it needed in foodstuffs from the people in the areas it was occupying. "Secesh," in the common terminology, would not be paid for goods taken; to those citizens professing loyalty to the Union, vouchers would be issued, and only redeemed at the end of the war if the holders could prove their loyalty.

Order No. 6 of that same date reinforced No. 5 by stating that as Pope's forces advanced through central Virginia, the men were to carry only two days' rations. The army's main source of food and forage would be the countryside. "All villages and neighborhoods through which they pass will be laid under contribution"—a fancy way of saying that Pope's troops would take from civilians what they needed.

General Order No. 7, issued a couple of days later, stirred a hornet's nest in the Southern press. Seeking to counter guerrilla activity and sabotage, the edict declared that the people in the immediate area of any such action would be held accountable and punished. If a railroad or telegraph were broken, for example, all the people within five miles of the site would have to come out and fix the damage, or pay for the repair. If someone fired upon a Union soldier, his or her house would be burned. Needless to say, any person caught in any of these acts would be executed summarily.[3]

The *Intelligencer* reported this order on July 27 with a short article taken from the *Richmond Examiner*, which in turn had gotten it from a Baltimore newspaper. The *Intelligencer* offered no immediate comment, but on the 30th reprinted a lively opinion piece from the *Richmond Dispatch* that declared Pope's recent orders "surpass in barbarity anything ever yet proclaimed by the Federals in a Virginia latitude. They sweep away from every citizen who refuses to convert himself into a slave, every vestige of his possessions on the face of the earth." The editorial closed by calling for Confederate leaders to enact "the most summary vengeance for every deed of inhumanity and crime" perpetrated by Pope's men.

Two weeks later, the *Intelligencer* reprinted a piece from the *Petersburg Express* written by one "S.C.," who claimed that he had known "Proclamation Pope," as he had come to be called, for many years. The writer described Pope as "one of the most vulgar, coarse, obscene and licentious poltroons on the face of the earth." He went on: "an admitted coward, the grossest of debauchees, the most reckless spendthrift of borrowed money, the most notorious of liars, the most inflated of braggarts, is now playing the tyrant upon the soil of Virginia."[4]

But Pope was not finished. General Order No. 11, dated July 23, authorized his officers to arrest "all disloyal male citizens" within their lines—meaning those who refused to take the federal oath of allegiance. Then there was this provision, as well: "If any person, having taken the oath of allegiance . . . be found to have violated it, he shall be shot, and his property seized and applied to the public use." Two days after that came General Order No. 13, which prohibited the placing of guards on civilians' houses. "Soldiers were called into the field to do battle against the enemy," it declared, "and it is not expected that their force and energy shall be wasted in protecting private property of those most hostile to the Government."

President Lincoln not only approved of Pope's orders, he built upon them. A confiscation act, passed by Congress on July 17 and signed by Lincoln the same day, called for the seizure of property owned by persons in rebellion against federal authority. Slaves who entered Union lines were declared "forever free"; the president was also authorized to enlist "persons of African descent" into the military service. (The *Intelligencer* paid little attention to "the Confiscation Bill of the Lincoln Congress," assuring readers in an editorial on August 3 that "all this abolition confiscation legislation is just about as interesting to us as would be a confiscation Ukase of the Sultan of Turkey.")

Pope's soldiers took his orders as license to confiscate and destroy property as they advanced farther into Virginia. Culpeper County, south of the Rappahannock River, was particularly hit hard, as related in the Southern press. "The Yankees are treating the inhabitants of Madison and Culpeper outrageously," the *Intelligencer* stated on August 6, reprinting from the *Richmond Dispatch*. "They steal horses, cattle and sheep," the article maintained, "induce the negroes to run away, and commit all sorts of depredations upon private property." So angry was the Southern press at these indignities that when Jeb Stuart's cavalry captured a hundred of Pope's men, the event was announced in a telegraphic news item from Richmond, published in the *Intelligencer* on August 9. In a separate article, the editor—now John H. Steele, following Archibald Gaulding's "Valedictory" of July 29——voiced the opinion, under the headline "CHEERING, CHEERING NEWS," that this capture "will be *agreeable* to our people."[5]

But John Pope was not the only target of Southern editorial invective in the summer of 1862. There was always Ben ("the Beast") Butler in New Orleans, infamous already throughout the South for his "woman order." Cracking down on public displays of disloyalty, Butler ordered a Confederate sympathizer, Mrs. Eugenia Phillips, confined at the Federal-held fort on Ship Island at the mouth of the Mississippi, "there to remain till further orders, for laughing on her balcony while a Yankee funeral was passing." Butler's Special Order No. 150 against Mrs. Phillips drew special ire in an *Intelligencer* editorial printed on July 15. The paper published the order in full, introducing it as "the infamous order issued by the scoundrel and brute Butler to imprison Mrs. Phillips. How slow *vengeance* is!," Steele exclaimed; "will it not *soon* reach the villain?" (As it turned out, Mrs. Phillips' confinement proved short. The *Mobile Register* on

July 24—reprinted in the *Intelligencer* a week later—stated that she had been released.)[6]

As reprehensible as was Butler's treatment of Mrs. Phillips, it was his hanging of William Mumford, reported in the *Intelligencer* on June 22, which continued to enrage Confederates, including those high-up in the Davis administration. On June 29, Secretary of War George W. Randolph had requested General Lee to send through the lines to the U.S. War Department a written inquiry about Union officers' alleged murder of several Southern civilians, including Mumford. Lee did so, but a month later President Davis informed him that no reply had been received. Davis asked Lee to send another letter, asking the Federal general-in-chief (by then, Maj. Gen. Henry Halleck) whether the conduct of Butler and other generals charged with civilian executions "is sanctioned by their Government." Davis added a threat: if the Federals did not respond in fifteen days, his government would conclude that Union officers' hanging of civilians was officially sanctioned. "Retribution or retaliatory measures" could follow, Davis warned, whose intention was "to put an end to the merciless atrocities which now characterize the war against us."

General Lee dutifully mailed Davis' message to General McClellan on August 3. Then, after repeated follow-ups by Lee to Halleck failed to produce any response on the issue of William Mumford's execution, President Davis finally acted with a proclamation dated Dec. 23, 1862, declaring Benjamin F. Butler to be "a felon deserving of capital punishment." If captured, Confederate authorities were instructed to have him hanged. The *Intelligencer* summarized the long proclamation in its issue of December 25, and editorialized about it on the 30th. A half-year had passed since Butler hanged "the gallant Mumford," but the paper's vengefulness had not abated. Even if Butler were not caught and hanged, it declared, the president's proclamation "consigns . . . the notorious villain to worse than ignominious death by the halter—it consigns him to eternal infamy, as *history* will hereafter write."[7]

Several important events, seemingly unrelated, combined to keep John Pope's name in Confederate newspapers. First was Pope's Order No. 11 of July 23, calling for the execution of Virginia citizens if caught in sabotage or espionage; but another was the order of one of Pope's subordinates, Brig. Gen. Adolph von Steinwehr, announcing that five civilian hostages would be taken and held for execution if any of his men were ambushed ("suffer death, unless the perpetrators of the deed are delivered to me"). Then there was President Lincoln's authorization of the confiscation of Rebels' property, announced on July 22 in an executive order issued by Northern Secretary of War Edwin Stanton. It authorized Union officers essentially to take any Southerners' property needed for their commands, although they were to issue vouchers for possible future compensation to the owners.[8]

All of this was mentioned by President Davis in a letter to General Lee, dated July 31. He began by mentioning Lincoln's/Stanton's order on property confiscation, but he concentrated on Pope and his minions. In particular, he outlined General Order No. 11 and the announcement of Steinwehr that he would hold five hostages against possible bushwhacking. (The *Intelligencer* had printed this odious edict on August 2.) The president was stern: the enemy's proclamations suggested that they were prepared to embark upon, as the president wrote in his letter to Lee, "a savage war in which no quarter is to be given." If Virginians continued to be mistreated under Pope's orders, Davis warned that Pope and his officers, if captured, could face retaliatory penalty. Lee was therefore instructed by Davis to send through the lines to Washington his letter as a warning, plus a general order that had just been issued by the Confederate War Department.

Adjutant General Samuel Cooper's General Order No. 54, issued from Richmond on August 1, began by referring to Lincoln's/Stanton's executive order of July 22 directing Union officers to seize and appropriate Southern civilians' property. It also reprinted portions of Pope's General Order No. 11 and made mention of Steinwehr's as well. All of this offensive language, Cooper charged, suggested that some U.S. officers "have now determined to violate all the rules and usages of war and to convert the hostilities . . . into a campaign of robbery and murder against unarmed citizens and peaceful tillers of the soil." Cooper further announced that if Pope, Steinwehr and their officers were captured, they would be held in special confinement. Then, if any Southern civilian were wrongfully killed under the offending new Federal orders, Union officers were to be duly hanged in equal number to the civilian victims.[9]

All of this was dramatic stuff, but better yet, for readers of the *Intelligencer*, Confederate authorities released Davis' letter and Cooper's order to the press. Editor Steele published both documents on August 5. Cooper's directive bore the headline of "LEX TALIONIS"—Latin for "law of punishment in kind," or retaliation. In that same issue, the paper editorialized on General Cooper's orders, which it argued "do not go far enough; "he will have to issue more stringent ones." Considering the enormity of the enemy's proclamations and excesses, the paper became vengeful, calling for retaliation not only upon officers, "but the brute soldiery they command! Let it not stop at imprisonment, to wait future enormities, but let it hang the villains for what they have done in the past!," such as the execution of Mumford in New Orleans. Steele concluded, "if the war is to be a *savage* one—one of *extermination*—let there be a beginning on our side, also, that as many of the *Yankees* may be exterminated as can be through Southern arms on the field, and on the gallows afterwards."[10]

The *Intelligencer* was so agitated over Proclamation Pope and Picayune Butler (as it called them) that it seemingly missed a more serious threat to the Confederacy: Lincoln's gradual adoption of the idea of emancipating Southern slaves.

Lincoln backed into freeing the Southern slaves very slowly. He had signed the first Confiscation Act, August 1861, but it only authorized slaves entering Union lines to be freed if they proved they had aided the rebellion (hence were "contraband of war," to use Ben Butler's term). On the other hand, when later that same month Maj. Gen. John C. Fremont in Missouri had issued a proclamation freeing slaves taken from Rebels, Lincoln asked him to change its language so as to conform to the law. When Fremont declined, Lincoln removed him from command. Similarly, in May 1862, when Maj. Gen. David Hunter had declared slaves free in coastal South Carolina, the president countermanded the order.

But Lincoln was coming to the conclusion that slavery would have to be destroyed if the North were to win the war. Slavery was still protected by the Constitution, so Lincoln moved carefully, especially regarding slavery in the border slave states (Missouri, Kentucky, Maryland and Delaware). For these states Lincoln developed the idea of a soft emancipation. In early March 1862, he asked Congress for money to give to any state that enacted a plan for gradual, compensated abolition. Then Lincoln convened representatives of the border states and pitched his idea to them. They turned him down. They did so again in May, and for a third time on July 12, 1862, when Lincoln gave the border spokesmen one last chance to mitigate the impact of sudden, uncompensated emancipation.[11]

The *Intelligencer* tracked these events as editor Steele learned of them. The paper reported on July 24 the border representatives' reasons for rejecting Lincoln's overture (constitutionality, Radical Republican opposition, &c.). A week later, it was able to relate details of the president's meeting held on July 12, even quoting from the statement that Lincoln had read to the border statesmen.

The *Intelligencer*, in effect, said that it served Lincoln right. "The Abolition Congress would never vote a dollar to pay for a slave," the editor surmised on August 1. A week later John Steele ridiculed "ANOTHER PROCLAMATION FROM 'KING ABE.'" The president had called upon "all persons. . . . participating in, aiding, countenancing, or abetting the existing rebellion . . . to return to their proper allegiance to the United States." Steele found this "most superlatively ridiculous." Southerners harped on Abraham Lincoln's coarse looks, deriding him as "the Illinois Ape," a "Gorilla" and "Baboon." The *Intelligencer*, for instance, called the Northern president "Baboon Lincoln" in an editorial as early as September 1861. The paper continued to play into the caricature in its editorial on "King Abe's" proclamation. "We are often idle enough to laugh at the monkey President," it declared; "with all our indignation, we cannot help sometimes indulging in laughter at the silliness of 'King Abe's' *antics*." Antics aside, the paper made no comment on Lincoln's obvious commitment to eventual abolition.[12]

Indeed, the South's "peculiar institution" seemed pretty safe in the summer of 1862, judging from the pages of the *Atlanta Daily Intelligencer*. The paper announced on August 2 that a "Sheriff's Sale Day" would take place on Tuesday, the 5th, at City Hall; fifty "likely and very valuable men, women, boys and girls" would be auctioned off. After the slave sales, the *Intelligencer* reported on the prices some of the "property" had fetched: "one negro girl about 16 years old brought $1,240"; "a negro man, about 25 years old, a negro woman 26 years old; and a negro 7 years old; were sold together and brought $3,400" [no mention that the group was likely a family]; and "a negro man about 35 years with 4 little boys, sold for $4,000."

Setting pecuniary value on human beings was a brutish business, but it was indeed a business in the antebellum South. This was abundantly evident when the *Intelligencer* published tax returns from Campbell County, southwest of Fulton, in early August 1862. Fully 2,249 slaves had been counted in Campbell, and their aggregated value was placed at $1,185,190—approximately $527 each, on average (in other words, more than a year's salary for a night watchman employed by the city of Atlanta). To place the slaves' aggregate price in context, the tax digest calculated the value of all land in the county as worth $1,224,570—only three tenths of one percent more than the value of the slaves who worked it. Put another way, of the estimated $3.5 million worth in all property in Campbell County (including household possessions, merchandise, *et al.*), slaves accounted for a third of the total sum.[13]

Meanwhile, the American civil war that would decide the preservation or abolition of slavery in the United States was being fiercely waged in Virginia. "The ball is about to be opened between Stonewall Jackson and Pope," the *Intelligencer* reported in its telegraphic news column on August 6. And indeed it was. With McClellan's army inert on the James southeast of Richmond, Robert E. Lee turned his attention to Pope's Army of Virginia, whose southward advance had reached the vicinity of Culpeper, twenty-seven miles from the Virginia Central Railroad, the vital link between Richmond and the Shenandoah Valley. Terming Pope a "miscreant" who needed to be "suppressed," Lee sent Jackson and some 24,000 men to Gordonsville (two dozen miles south of Culpeper) to keep watch on the enemy. When Pope sent more troops to Culpeper in early August, Jackson saw a chance to attack and damage a part of the Federal army before all of it could unite. On August 9, at Cedar Mountain, eight miles south of Culpeper, the Confederates attacked the two Union divisions of Nathaniel Banks—the same "Commissary Banks" Jackson had trounced in the Valley. This time, Banks' 8,000 troops fought with more pluck against Jackson's larger force, and at the end of the day only reluctantly gave up the field. This allowed Jackson, as he had done before, to send Lee his characteristic announcement: "God has blessed our army with victory." Confederate casualties, as counted by the historian of Cedar Mountain, Robert K. Krick, were 314 killed, 1,062 wounded and 42 captured or missing—1,418 in total. (Among the dead was Brig. Gen. Charles S. Winder, mortally wounded by a shell.) Banks suffered 320 dead, 1,466 wounded and 617 missing (including Brig. Gen. Henry Prince, captured), a total of 2,403.

It should be noted, after all the journalistic heat stirred up by Pope's notorious proclamations, that no retaliatory measures were taken against General Prince or the other Union officers captured at Cedar Mountain. Pope had not overseen any execution of Virginia civilians, so no capital punishment was meted out to Prince, who upon arriving in Richmond "affected to be ignorant of Pope's brutal orders" and "vented his execrations upon Pope," according to John Beauchamp Jones, a clerk in the Confederate War Department.[14]

The "miscreant" (Lee's term) and the "knave" (Steele's) was about to get his just desserts. On August 13, four days after Cedar Mountain, Lee began marching 28,000 troops under Maj. Gen. James Longstreet to join Jackson at Gordonsville, leaving 25,000 men to defend Richmond against the still dangerous McClellan. But the Young Napoleon was being defanged, as Washington stripped his Army of the Potomac of more troops to strengthen Pope. The *Intelligencer* followed these events, based on telegraphed news from Richmond:

"the opinion gains ground that McClellan is gradually evacuating Berkley [on the James], and reinforcing Pope" (July 30); "the Federals have quit Malvern Hill" (August 10); "his Government is still stripping him of his forces" (August 19); "McClellan has certainly evacuated James river, and gone to unite with Pope or Burnside, on the Rappahannock" (August 20).[15]

The *Intelligencer*'s focus then shifted from Stonewall Jackson to Jeb Stuart, who led 1,500 horsemen in a raid on August 22–23 to Pope's headquarters at Catlett's Station. A "contraband" volunteered to take the Confederates to the Union general's tent. Pope was absent, but Stuart's men bagged the Northern commander's hat, cloak, a dress uniform and an HQ dispatch book with important intelligence. Riding triumphantly back into Confederate lines, Stuart also brought with him 300 prisoners, hundreds of horses and mules, plus the Union Army of Virginia's money chests. The *Intelligencer* exulted at Stuart's feat, terming it a "brilliant affair."[16]

Based on the dispatch book Stuart brought back, divulging Pope's strength (45,000) and the movement of McClellan's troops to reinforce him, on August 24 Lee devised a bold plan. He would divide his army, sending Jackson's half around Pope's flank, marching northward into his rear. Longstreet would hold the Confederate lines along the Rappahannock River until Jackson's presence forced Pope to retreat and chase after him. Then Longstreet would retrace Jackson's route to unite with him—assuming Pope by then had begun to engage Jackson's force.

Stonewall's infantry set out on the morning of August 25, earning again its name of "foot cavalry," and covering fifty-four miles of road in thirty-six hours. By midnight, August 26–27, the Confederates had captured Pope's supply base at Manassas Junction. All day the famished Southerners plundered the enemy's storehouses for food, clothing and equipment. At midnight of August 27–28, as the historian of Second Manassas, John Hennessy, has written, "with every available cranny of haversack stuffed with meat, hardtack and cigars, and a slab of ham slashed to every pommel," Jackson ordered the rest of the Federals' supplies burned. Pope responded to news of the Rebels' picnic by ordering his army to march northward on the morning of the 28th.[17]

The *Intelligencer*, without its own reporters in the field, struggled to keep up with these events as best as it could. Stonewall Jackson was in no position to send dispatches back to Richmond, and General Lee would not have authorized their publication anyway. A sharp battle was fought at Groveton (maybe six miles northwest of Manassas Junction) on August 28 after Pope's forces fixed Stonewall's position. As it happened, Jackson took a defensive stand on the same battlefield of July '61 where he had earned his nickname, causing the ensuing engagement to bear the name of Second Manassas. Federal assaults on the 29th were repulsed by the Southerners, fighting from an unfinished railroad bed. Pope persisted in his attacks on the 30th, even as Longstreet's force arrived and delivered a crushing flank attack that sent the Northern army retreating from the field.

"Stonewall Victorious—Pope Whipped at Manassas!" was the headline in the *Intelligencer*'s issue of September 3. Beneath it, the paper published General Lee's message to President Davis on the battle, written on the night of August 30. "This army achieved, on the Plains of Manassas, a signal victory over the combined forces of Generals McClellan and Pope on the 28th and 29th," it began. "We mourn the loss of our gallant dead in every conflict," it continued; "yet our gratitude to Almighty God for His mercies rises higher each day. To Him, and to the valor of our troops a nation's gratitude is due."

The *Intelligencer*'s ability to report the details of Lee, Longstreet, and Jackson's victory at Second Manassas depended on the flow of telegraphed messages from Richmond. As usual, they were initially brief. "RICHMOND, Sept. 4.— Passengers report that the official dispatches in Northern papers all indicate a complete victory over the Yankees, and of the pursuit by the Confederates of the routed enemy," read a short article printed on September 5. A longer report was published the next day on the paper's third page, its customary place for telegraphic news. But the editor gave over his entire second page to a long article reprinted from the *Richmond Examiner* of September 3. Such an extensive commitment of space demonstrated the *Intelligencer*'s awareness of just how important Lee's victory had been. "We yield all the space we can to-day to the accounts of the late battles at Manassas," Steele began in an editorial prefacing the *Examiner*'s account. He termed the battle "one of the most glorious victories ever won, in this or any other age, and in this, or any other country." Yet of the glorious victory the editor apparently could not get enough information. A telegraphic dispatch from Richmond, dated September 5, stated that "the Yankees were still flying towards Alexandria," but Steele wanted more confirmation of the position of the two opposing armies, and especially word of any new fight between Lee and Pope. "We give to our readers at the time we write, all that we have. . . . We must be patient," he wrote on September 7. Two days later he again shrugged: "little or nothing has been added to the scant stock of information regarding the recent great battle on the plains of Manassas." A short telegram from Richmond, dated the 7th, reported that there had been an engagement at Chantilly on September 1. (Confederates attacked part of Pope's army nine miles northeast of Manassas, but were repulsed).[18]

But the larger details remained elusive—especially casualties. Historians have numbers that Steele's *Intelligencer* did not: for Pope's army, 1,750 killed, 8,450 wounded and 4,250 captured or missing, for a total of 14,450—a fifth of its 70,000 officers and men engaged. For Lee, the totals ran to 1,550 killed, 7,750 wounded and just a hundred unaccounted for—9,400, or 17 percent of his 55,000. As for Georgia units, the paper could only report from fragmentary information, such as a casualty statement from the First Georgia Regulars, printed on September 10. Dearth of information, however, did not prevent the paper from guessing the enemy's losses, which it placed in an article on the 12th at "50,000 men in killed, wounded and prisoners."

Even without this hyperbole, there was reason enough for the *Intelligencer* to celebrate the news from the Manassas Plains, as it did in its editorial of September 11. In the wake of Pope's defeat, Steele wrote, "*dreadful consternation* . . . pervades through the North." The editor predicted even more good news from the battlefield: "the lion, they see, has at last been aroused from his den, and they tremble at his roar."[19]

Amidst Southerners' euphoria after Second Manassas, it was easy to miss what was happening in the summer of 1862. The war was turning harder, with Union generals such as John Pope taking the war directly to civilians in Virginian and Ben Butler punishing Rebel sympathizers in New Orleans. More alarming still to Confederates was Lincoln's announcement that he would be targeting slavery in the South. When the *Intelligencer* laughed off "King Abe's antics," it was overlooking that in the Lincoln administration and among large parts of the Northern populace, the conflict was morphing from a war to restore the Union into one of abolishing slavery, two and a half centuries after it had begun to be instituted in colonial Virginia.

NOTES

1. Sears, *Gates of Richmond*, 137–39; Derry, *Georgia*, 114; "THE LATE LIEUT-COL. G. A. BULL," *ADI*, July 27, 1862; Thomas Amory Lee, *Colonel William Raymond Lee of the Revolution* (Salem MA: Essex Institute, 1917), 28; Henderson, *Roster Confederate Soldiers*, vol. 1, 562; vol. 3, 843–44; "CHAMBERS, Oct. 22, 1862 . . . ," *ADI*, October 25.

2. Steven V. Ash, *When the Yankees Came: Conflict and Chaos in the Occupied South, 1861–1865* (Chapel Hill: University of North Carolina Press, 1995), 26, 29, 38–50; Mark Grimsley,

The Hard Hand of War: Union Military Policy toward Southern Civilians 1861–1865 (New York: Cambridge University Press, 1995), 33–34, 72–73; McPherson, *Battle Cry,* 454.

3. James M. McPherson, *Ordeal by Fire: The Civil War and Reconstruction,* Second Edition (New York: McGraw-Hill, 1992 [1982]), 268–70; Daniel E. Sutherland, *The Emergence of Total War* (Fort Worth: Ryan Place Publishers, 1996), 15–16; 21–22; Grimsley, *Hard Hand of War,* 85–87; Cozzens, *Pope,* 83–84; General Orders No. 5, July 18, 1862; General Orders No. 6, July 18; General Orders No. 7, July 10 [?], 1862, *OR,* vol. 12, pt. 2, 50–51.

4. "LATEST FROM THE NORTH. GENERAL ORDERS FROM POPE," *ADI,* July 27, 1862; "A MILITARY DESPOT," *ADI,* July 30; "MAJOR GENERAL JOHN POPE," *ADI,* August 13.

5. General Orders No. 11, July 23, *OR,* vol. 12, pt. 2, 52; General Order No. 13, July 25, *OR,* vol. 12, pt. 3, 509; McPherson, *Ordeal,* 266, 269–70; Sutherland, *Total War,* 22–25; Roy P. Basler, ed., *The Collected Works of Abraham Lincoln,* 9 vols. (New Brunswick NJ: Rutgers University Press, 1953), vol. 5, 328; Phillip Shaw Paludan, *The Presidency of Abraham Lincoln* (Lawrence: University Press of Kansas, 1994), 146; "LABOR LOST," *ADI,* Aug. 3, 1862; "From the Richmond Dispatch. AFFAIRS ON THE RAPPAHANNOCK." *ADI,* August 6; "Prisoners from Pope's Army" and "CHEERING, CHEERING NEWS," *ADI,* August 9.

6. Hearn, *Devil Came to Dixie,* 168–69; "BUTLER'S INFAMOUS ORDER TO IMPRISON MRS. PHILLIPS," *ADI,* July 15, 1862; "NEW ORLEANS—Mrs. Phillips and Mr. Andrews . . . ," *ADI,* July 31.

7. "YANKEE DISAPPOINTMENT," *ADI,* June 22, 1862; Davis to Lee, Aug. 1, 1862, *OR,* Ser. 2, vol. 4, 835; Crist, *et al.,* eds., *Papers of Jefferson Davis,* vol. 8, 319–320, 564; James D. Richardson, comp., *A Compilation of the Messages and Papers of the Confederacy including the Diplomatic Correspondence 1861–1865,* 2 vols. (Nashville: United States Publishing Co., 1906), vol. 1, 269–74; "President Davis' Proclamation," *ADI,* Dec. 25, 1862. "BEAST BUTLER," *ADI,* December 30.

8. General Orders No. 11, July 23, 1862, *OR,* vol. 12, pt. 2, 52; "ANOTHER BRUTAL ORDER," *ADI,* Aug. 2, 1862; Frank Moore, ed., *The Rebellion Record: A Diary of American Events,* 12 vols. (New York: Arno Press, 1977 [1861–68]), vol. 5, 559.

9. Davis to Lee, July 31, 1862, Crist *et al.,* eds., *Papers of Jefferson Davis,* vol. 8, 309–312; General Orders No. 54, August 1, *OR,* Ser. 2, vol. 4, 836–37.

10. "Orders from the President to Gen. Lee" and "LEX TALIONIS. Gen. Cooper's Orders," *ADI,* Aug. 5, 1862; "LEX TALIONIS—THE LAW OF RETALIATION," *ADI,* August 5.

11. Paludan, *Presidency of Lincoln,* 87, 126–27, 133, 153; McPherson, *Ordeal,* 161, 266, 270–71; Alfred H. Keely and Winfred A. Harbison, *The American Constitution: Its Origins and Development* (New York: W. W. Norton, 1963 [1948], 429; Allen C. Guelzo, *Lincoln's Emancipation Proclamation: The End of Slavery in America* (New York: Simon & Schuster, 2004), 113, 255.

12. "REPLY OF THE BORDER SLAVE STATE REPRESENTATIVES TO LINCOLN'S EMANCIPATION PROCLAMATION," *ADI,* July 24, 1862; "THE INTERVIEW BETWEEN THE BORDER STATE REPRESENTATIVES AND

LINCOLN—OLD ABE APPEALS UNDER A PRESSURE—THE RESULT," *ADI,* July 31; "BORDER EMANCIPATION AND NEGRO STEALING," *ADI* , August 1; "ANOTHER PROCLAMATION FROM 'KING ABE,'" *ADI,* August 8; Basler, ed., *Papers of Lincoln,* vol. 5, 317–19, 336–37; Michael Davis, *The Image of Lincoln in the South* (Knoxville: University of Tennessee Press, 1971), 67; "THE BLOCKADING FLEET OF OLD LINCOLN," *ADI,* Sept. 8, 1861.

13. "NEGROES AND OTHER PROPERTY FOR SALE," *ADI,* Aug. 2, 1862; "SALE OF NEGROES AND REAL ESTATE," *ADI,* August 7; "For the Atlanta Intelligencer. CAMPBELLTON, Ga., July 28, 1862 . . . ," *ADI,* August 5; "CITY GOVERNMENT OF ATLANTA...SALARIES," *ADI,* September 13.

14. "Skirmish with Pope's Forces," *ADI,* Aug. 6, 1862; Robert K. Krick, *Stonewall Jackson at Cedar Mountain* (Chapel Hill: University of North Carolina Press, 1990), 7, 357, 372, 376; Lee to Randolph, July 28, 1862, *OR,* vol. 11, pt. 2, 936; Dennis Kelly, "The Second Battle of Manassas," *Civil War Times Illustrated,* vol. 22, no. 3 (May 1983), 14–18; "POPE'S CAPTURED OFFICERS," *ADI,* August 17; J. B. Jones, *A Rebel War Clerk's Diary At the Confederate States Capital,* ed. by James I. Robertson Jr., 2 vols. (Lawrence: University Press of Kansas, 2015), vol. 1, 132.

15. Kelly, "Second Manassas," 18, 21 (Longstreet's 28,000); "BY TELEGRAPH. From Richmond," *ADI,* July 30, 1862; "The Enemy Evacuate Malvern Hill, and Fortify Coggin's Point," *ADI,* August 10; "THE LATE GEN. MCCLELLAN," *ADI,* August 19; "The Yankees disappeared from James River," *ADI,* August 20.

16. Kelly, "Second Manassas," 19–21; Longacre, *Lee's Cavalrymen,* 116–19; "BRILLIANT AFFAIR," *ADI,* Aug. 29, 1862.

17. John Hennessy, *Return to Bull Run: The Campaign and Battle of Second Manassas* (New York: Simon & Schuster, 1993), 80, 137–39.

18. Kelly, "Second Manassas," 26–44; "GLORIOUS NEWS!! Stonewall Victorious— Pope Whipped at Manassas!," *ADI,* Sept. 3, 1862; "The Victory at Manassas Complete," *ADI,* September 5; "THE BATTLE AT MANASSAS" and "ACCOUNTS OF THE LATE BATTLES AT MANASSAS," *ADI,* September 6; "Further from Manassas" and "THE LATE VICTORIES," *ADI,* September 7; "FROM THE ARMY OF NORTHERN VIRGINIA" and "From Manassas," *ADI,* September 9; Jeffry D. Wert, "Battle of Chantilly (Ox Hill), Va.," in Patricia L. Faust, ed., *Historical Times Encyclopedia of the Civil War* (New York: Harper & Row, 1986), 129–30.

19. Kelly, "Second Manassas," 43; David G. Martin, *The Second Bull Run Campaign July-August 1862* (Conshohocken PA: Combined Publishing, 1997), 248; "THE FIRST GEORGIA REGULARS," *ADI,* Sept 10, 1862; "THE ENEMY'S LOSSES," *ADI,* September 12; "THE TABLES TURNED," *ADI,* September 11.

17. A "Great Victory in Maryland" Turns Sour

SECOND MANASSAS was not the only gratifying victory for the Confederacy in late August 1862. "GLORIOUS NEWS!" was reported in the *Intelligencer* on September 5, concerning a battle fought at Richmond, Kentucky on August 29 and 30—the same days as Lee's and Jackson's engagement at Manassas. Generals Braxton Bragg and Edmund Kirby Smith were leading a two-pronged offensive into Kentucky. Smith's column of 12,000 men marched north from Knoxville on August 14, heading toward Lexington. On the 29th his troops encountered Federal cavalry near Richmond, Kentucky, 125 miles north of Knoxville. The next morning Union infantry attacked, were repulsed, and eventually broke into retreat. Vigorous Confederate pursuit turned the Federals' retrograde into a rout, in which more than 4,000 Union prisoners and nine cannon were scooped up (5,353 total casualties). Kirby Smith's loss totaled 78 killed, 372 wounded and one man missing out of 6,850 troops engaged. One authority has termed the battle "the most lopsided Confederate victory of the war."

This was the "glorious news" reported by the *Intelligencer* on September 5. The paper published a brief dispatch issued by General Smith, with the editor helpfully adding that Richmond was twenty-five miles south of Lexington. (What Steele did not explain was how Edmund Kirby Smith, "Edmund" growing up, referred to himself as Kirby after the death of his brother Ephraim Kirby Smith in the Mexican War.)[1]

Fittingly, given the victories in Virginia and Kentucky, President Davis set aside Thursday, September 18 as a day of prayer and thanksgiving—the fifth such day he had announced since the start of the war. The *Intelligencer* issued a short announcement in its telegraphic news column of September 6, followed by the printing of the president's complete proclamation three days later. As it had done before (June 13 and November 15, 1861; February 28 and May 16, 1862, the president's previous prayer days), the *Intelligencer* office was closed on September 18, so that "employees may have the opportunity of yielding that respectful observance to the PRESIDENT's Proclamation." There was accordingly no paper issued on Friday, September 19.

Atlantans' observance of the national day of fasting and prayer gratified the *Intelligencer*'s editor, as he commented on September 20. On the fast day, the people had flocked reverently to places of worship, Steele wrote, to thank "the LORD for his bountiful goodness in granting us victory over our foes." Services were held at First Presbyterian at 10:30; congregants of Trinity Methodist, Central Presbyterian and Second Baptist all gathered at the latter church, also at 10:30. Among them was Sam Richards, the downtown bookseller; he heard Dr. William Brantley, the pastor of Second Baptist, speak on the theme of "Now I may boldly say 'the Lord is my helper.'" ("The sermon of course was good and appropriate," Richards recorded in his diary that night.) On the special day, ladies prepared delicacies for the soldiers ailing in the city's hospitals. The paper also mentioned that the Western & Atlantic Railroad had suspended operation all day.[2]

Meanwhile the price of the *Intelligencer* was increasing. The paper announced its new subscription rates on July 27: up a dollar, from six to seven, for twelve months; up 25 cents per month, from 50 to 75 cents. Prices for advertising were also increased. A square of space up to ten lines deep cost $5 a month before the price hike; now it would be $7. Costs for two, three, four and six months of insertions all went up proportionally. A square running for a full year, once $20, now went for $30.

The paper took pains to explain its new price schedule. Just a few months before, in mid-April, the *Intelligencer* had taken pride in reminding readers that it had not raised its subscription prices since its inception. Yet the cost of paper, the very essential for publishing, was rising, and significantly at that. In mid-February 1862, the *Intelligencer* had reported the complaint of a Vicksburg, Mississippi newspaper that it was now paying $440 for a quantity of newsprint that before the war had gone for $200. Nonetheless, the price of paper alone did not necessitate an increase in rates, the editor explained; "every other article used in the publication of paper has increased its cost to us, upon an average, over one hundred per cent."

Then there was the price of labor. Consumers throughout the Confederacy were paying considerably more for goods, on account of both wartime shortages and monetary inflation. The *Intelligencer* gave a few examples in an article printed in mid-September 1862: "oil, that sold previous to the war at 80 cents, is now selling at $1.25 per gallon." Tallow (animal-based candle wax), once 3 ½ cents, now commanded a half dollar per pound. The rates of inflation were not uniform, though: "nails, that sold at 18 cents, are now selling at 25 cents per pound."

Inflation meant that wage earners needed more money to provide for their families. The editor acknowledged that recently its printers had gone on strike for more salary (this explains why there were no issues of the *Intelligencer* on Friday, July 25 and Saturday the 26th). The editor gave no details of the strike, but it is likely that printers for the *Southern Confederacy* and *Commonwealth* all went out together—the 1860 Census showed there were thirty-two printers in the city. The strike succeeded; Steele admitted that "we yielded." The paper's new prices would go into effect on August 1, he explained, but he pointed out that at seven dollars a year, the *Daily Intelligencer* would have the same subscription price as its rival, the *Atlanta Daily Southern Confederacy*.

The editor's overriding message, though, was that the *Intelligencer* would persevere. "Thus far, we have not been forced to resort to a half-sheet issue for our subscribers"—meaning, on a single sheet, back/front, instead of the two big sheets printed for a four-page newspaper. (By this time, for example, all the dailies in the Confederate capital had resorted to half-sheets). Even more important, the *Intelligencer* showed no sign of going under, as had a number of Confederate newspapers. In the first year of the war, for instance, fifty papers in Texas had ceased operation, out of sixty in the state.[3]

With its new rate schedule after August 1, 1862, the *Intelligencer* searched for more advertising revenue. In mid-July, a reader in Sparta, Georgia (eighty miles southeast of Atlanta), wrote the *Intelligencer*, asking why so few commission merchants in the city advertised in its pages (he was looking to buy some grain). The editor answered that he would deliver the writer's letter to a commission house in town, "hoping that the gentle hint contained in his letter will induce those engaged in this business to be more liberal hereafter in patronizing the press."

The gentle hint apparently worked, as within a few weeks "A. C. Wyly & Co., COMMISSION MERCHANTS" began advertising in the *Intelligencer*, with Steele giving them a plug on August 7. "We take pleasure," it read, "in saying no safer or more responsible house, does a commission business in this city. . . . All the business of this house is characterized by promptness, energy, and dispatch. See its advertisement in to-day's paper."[4]

On August 3, the *Intelligencer* informed readers receiving their issues by mail that when they did not arrive, "the fault is not in this office." The Confederate postal service was often to blame; "some of our subscribers receive some day no papers, and then another day two or three." The editor pledged to address these aberrations with the postal service. There were other problems, closer in. When some readers in the city complained that their papers had not been delivered, Steele conceded that the fault might lie with the carriers employed to deliver morning issues, but he chose also to point elsewhere: to thieves sneaking up to door fronts and making off with newspapers. "Our patrons will please keep a lookout for such intruders, as well as the carrier," he advised.[5]

Aside from paper-thieves, the editor dealt with the day-to-day task of getting the news and offering editorial comment upon it. In late August, John Steele frankly apologized to his readers "for the little labor which appears in our editorial columns to-day"; the day before he had had to attend a meeting on various city matters that took up several hours. "Time is most valuable to an Editor . . . who edits a daily paper read by thousands," he explained.

Telegraph operators did not help when they incorrectly transcribed wired dispatches. On September 2, the *Intelligencer* published in its "BY TELEGRAPH" column a dispatch to President Davis dated September 1 from Lee's headquarters: "this army achieved to-day on the plains of Manassas a signal victory." Later the editor noticed that the *Macon Telegraph* carried the same dispatch, but it was dated August 30. An annoyed John Steele on September 3 printed the *Telegraph*'s text and reprinted the *Intelligencer*'s message of the day before, to show the sloppy transcription by the Atlanta telegraphers. "[More care should be taken to avoid these mistakes," he lectured; "it seems now that there was no fight at all on the 1st inst., if the *Macon Telegraph* is right.—ED. INT.]"

A helpful source of news remained the various letters written by soldiers and sent from the war fronts. In an article published July 22, the editor stated that he had a good number of letters mailed home from Virginia to Atlantans, who requested that they be printed in the newspaper. "We have read these letters," he affirmed, "as have their friends at home, and would take pleasure in complying with the several requests of the latter to insert them in our columns, if we could do it." The problem, though, was severalfold: there were so many letters, mostly written in pencil and requiring transcription for the compositor. This was a task "which we have not the time to perform," the editor admitted. Besides, most missives bore dates two or three weeks back, relating events that had ceased to be newsworthy. "For these reasons, we must decline publishing most of them."[6]

John Steele and the *Intelligencer* adhered to their policy of not publishing correspondence of writers who failed to identify themselves. On August 19, the paper made an exception for a letter received from "BETA." The writer, a soldier in Maj. Gen. William J. Hardee's command in east Tennessee, paid tribute to Hardee with such eloquence that the editor relented and printed his epistle. Nonetheless, Steele added pointedly "we publish 'BETA's' communication with pleasure, and shall be pleased to hear often from and *know* him."

Newspaper editors considered themselves something of a fraternity, and were usually inclined to make time in their busy day when a colleague dropped in on them. "We had the pleasure, on yesterday," Steele wrote on August 8, "of seeing in our office, COL. M. C. GALLOWAY, the able editor of the Memphis Avalanche." After Federal capture of Memphis, the *Avalanche* closed down; Galloway, Steele wrote, had lost all of his property. "But his patriotism and honor are untarnished," he declared; "we shall be happy to see him often in our *sanctum*," using the Latin noun by which editors customarily referred to their offices.[7]

Richmond papers were particularly important sources of information about Lee's and Jackson's forces, as the editor acknowledged on August 30. Steele informed readers that he had not seen the *Richmond Examiner* for several days, but then issues dated August 25 and 26 suddenly appeared among his other exchanges. "We missed it much during its absence," he added, referring to the *Examiner*, "and heartily welcome it back." It showed. On that very page of the *Intelligencer* were two articles reprinted from the *Examiner* and one from the *Richmond Enquirer*.[8]

Evaluating the reportorial worth of "gossip" was akin to the editor's task of separating reported rumors from reality. After he had heard that Confederates in Tennessee had attacked Nashville, Steele advised readers of the skepticism he exercised in such cases. "At the corners of our streets, on the highways, and by-paths, and even in our *sanctum*, we hear rumors of movements in Tennessee which are of a most gratifying nature, if true." He was especially careful when reading Northern papers that came to his office, brought by well-wishing travelers. "By a recent arrival from Nashville, we have been favored with a late New York Herald, Cincinnati Commercial, and Cincinnati Enquirer," he wrote on August 1. Drawing "exceedingly interesting extracts" from these papers, Steele was careful to point out obvious enemy propaganda, as when (continuing the practice of his predecessor, Archibald Gaulding) he posted at the end of one article, "[A Yankee *lie*. ED. INT.]"[9]

New exchanges also developed. The *Intelligencer* announced on August 3 that it had just received the first two issues of a new paper being printed in Tennessee, the *Chattanooga Rebel*. Despite the problems and pressures that were killing off newspapers throughout the Confederacy, thirty-year-old Franc M. Paul, a Nashville printer displaced by the Federal occupation, believed he could start a new paper in Chattanooga. With two other workers, Paul cranked out the first issue of the *Rebel* on August 1. "It presents, typographically, a handsome face," Steele observed. "We welcome Mr. Paul into the corps editorial," the *Intelligencer*'s editor commented, adding "we with great pleasure place it upon our exchange list." A month and a half later, Steele had opportunity to relay his well-wishes personally when Franc Paul visited him in his *sanctum*. "We have found the *'Rebel'* profitable to us as an exchange, as well as serviceable to the cause of Southern Independence," the editor declared in a brief article on September 24. In other words, the *Chattanooga Rebel* was dutifully fulfilling its dual roles as news reporter and patriotic champion of the Confederate cause.[10]

The *Atlanta Daily Intelligencer* could genuinely celebrate its own private victory when Confederate Gen. Braxton Bragg declared martial law in Atlanta on August 11, to secure safety of railroads and maintain discipline of soldiers in the city.

Having loudly and repeatedly called in March and April for the imposition of martial law in Atlanta, and having had to defend its position against the *Southern Confederacy* and other critics, the *Intelligencer* got the last laugh when Bragg, commander of the huge "Confederate Department No. 2" (which included Alabama, Mississippi, most of Tennessee and northwest Georgia), issued a brief announcement from Chattanooga:

HEADQUARTERS DEPARTMENT NO. 2,
CHATTANOOGA, August 11, 1862.
SPECIAL ORDER NO.14

III. Martial law is hereby established within the corporate limits and environs of the town of Atlanta, Ga.

By command of GEN. BRAGG.

GEO. G. GARNER,

A. A. General.

The terse proclamation did not offer Bragg's reasons for imposing martial law, but this was not the first instance of his having done so. Bragg had declared martial law in Memphis, Tenn., on March 5, 1862 (General Albert Sidney Johnston had done so two weeks later in Jackson and Grenada, Miss.). Paul

Lack, writing in the *Georgia Historical Quarterly*, has speculated on Bragg's motivation: "he apparently acted because the previous combination of civil and military authority had failed to curb the disorder which demoralized those troops stationed in or passing through Atlanta." Historian Thomas G. Dyer adds that Bragg was also motivated by his contempt for Provost Marshal G. W. Lee, whom he termed "a man without education or character." "You will observe," he later wrote, "he never signs his own name."

The *Intelligencer* published Bragg's order on August 13 and reprinted it the next day, along with a very approving editorial. John Steele chose not to gloat or assume an "I-told-you-so" tone, but rather pointed out that given the privations and sufferings of soldiers in the field, the least civilians back home could do was to comply with sensible regulations that provided for the general safety of the community. The paper even declined to put forth "to our readers many reasons why the restrictions of Martial Law are now placed over this city," as such a narrative might give the enemy some useful intelligence. "Therefore it is that we counsel a cheerful observance of the military regulations which the efficient PROVOST MARSHAL at this point will most surely enforce."

Regulations there indeed were. From his office on August 12, Col. G. W. Lee, military post commander and provost marshal, issued an order stipulating that keepers of hotels and boardinghouses in Atlanta should not register an out-of-towner who had not secured a permit issued by his office.

Then, on August 16, Bragg named Atlanta mayor James Calhoun as "civil governor" in the city. Again, the general did not explain his purpose. But in an editorial accompanying its printing of the Bragg order, the *Intelligencer* surmised that Calhoun's appointment was "to prevent any collision between the Military and Civil Authorities of the city." A bit perplexed, Calhoun wrote Benjamin Hill, senator from Georgia, as to what his duties were. Hill deferred to no less than Vice President Alexander H. Stephens. The mayor/civil governor then received a reply from Stephens, who objected to Bragg's appointment in the first place. "Gen. Bragg had no more authority for appointing you civil governor of Atlanta than I had," Stephens objected, "and I . . . have no more authority than a street walker in your city." The vice president in this and related matters regarding governmental power was unwavering. As his biographer, Thomas E. Schott, puts it, Stephens "was as dedicated as any southerner to achieving independence, but not at the cost of trampling underfoot the Constitution he had revered all his life."[11]

Things got even hotter when the Adjutant and Inspector General's Office in Richmond on September 3 declared that the privilege of *habeas corpus* was suspended in Atlanta and five miles around the city limits (which were a circle of one mile's radius from the downtown train depot, or "car shed"). Again, no reason was given in Gen. Samuel Cooper's order suspending the writ (a basic principle in American jurisprudence protecting citizens from arrest and detention without specific charges). In publishing General Cooper's order on September 10, the *Intelligencer* editorially added that the need for the suspension was known by the Secretary of War; "we are not advised of that necessity." Consistent with its earlier calls for martial law, the newspaper not surprisingly voiced support of the revocation of the writ.

Constitutional strict constructionists from Alexander Stephens on down argued that military authorities had no authority to suspend *habeas corpus*. Gov. Joseph E. Brown of Georgia confided to the Vice President that the Southern people had "much more to apprehend from military despotism than from subjugation by the enemy."

After much discussion in the Confederate Congress, President Davis instructed the War Department to annul all military proclamations concerning suspension of the writ. On September 12, the Adjutant General's Office in Richmond issued the order stating that military commanders had no authority to declare martial law (only the president could). Braxton Bragg's decree of August 11 was thereby annulled. This prompted a bit of gloating by the *Atlanta Southern Confederacy*—martial law had lasted in the city all of one month, from August 11 to September 12. This was noticed by the *Intelligencer* on September 20. Nonetheless, editor Steele reminded readers that Atlanta was still designated as a military post, with Col. G. W. Lee as post commander and provost marshal. Lee's enforcement of law and order, the paper declared, made Atlanta "one of the most orderly cities of the South," protecting it "from the wicked designs of enemies, and the lawless of every description."[12]

Editorial eyes turned to the fighting front when "glorious news" came from Kentucky. On September 10, Steele prefaced his "BY TELEGRAPH" column with a short editorial: "for glorious news, read our telegraphic dispatches. We are in too happy a condition to elaborate upon the present flattering prospects of the Southern Confederacy, and the favorable position of our armies West and North."

The western Confederate forces were those of Gen. Braxton Bragg and Maj.

Gen. Edmund Kirby Smith, which had driven farther into Kentucky. According to telegraphed reporting, Smith had captured Covington and Newport, Ky., towns south of the Ohio River just across from Cincinnati. Word had it that Smith had even demanded the surrender of Cincinnati.[13]

Riverine news came also from the Potomac, as announced in the *Intelligencer* of September 13, albeit in a surprisingly stoic style. "That our army has crossed the Potomac, in large part, is beyond a doubt," the paper editorialized. Richmond exchanges reported Lee's army had reached Frederick, Maryland, forty miles northwest of Washington. The *Intelligencer* pointed out the distance from Frederick to Harrisburg, Pennsylvania, was seventy miles. Steele assumed that Lee would maintain the offensive. "Whether our army will proceed to Washington, Baltimore, or Harrisburg first, we must wait patiently to learn," he counseled.

Patient he would indeed have to be. The *Intelligencer*'s telegraphic news section of September 14 stated that "dispatches giving the whereabouts of the Confederate army are contradictory," although it was said that some of Robert E. Lee's forces had reached Hagerstown, Maryland, two dozen miles northwest of Frederick. That day, too, the paper carried an article taken "from the Charleston Mercury, 12th inst." (*instant*, in the talk of the time, meaning this very month, as opposed to "ulto." or *ultimo*, meaning the previous month). The *Mercury* had reported "the transmission, by telegraph, of news from our army in Maryland, is not allowed as yet by the Government."

Richmond authorities had issued no such ban; reporters Peter Alexander ("P.W.A." for the *Savannah Republican*) and Felix de Fontaine ("Personne" for the *Columbia Daily South Carolinian*) were with Lee's army in Maryland and sent unfettered letters back to their papers. A better explanation for Steele's dearth of information was that it took a lot of time for dispatches from Lee's army to reach the Confederate capital. Regardless, the editor was starved for news, as he acknowledged on September 17. "Of the situation of our army in Maryland, we have but little information," he admitted; even the Richmond exchanges were news-bare. He hoped that the telegraph would soon bring some enlightening reports. Until then, with rumors aswirl, the editor reaffirmed, "we know these are unreliable, and we will not trouble our readers with them."[14]

Within a week, in the *Intelligencer* of September 23, there was printed the first telegraphic dispatch received regarding the titanic battle fought along Antietam Creek on September 17.

> Great Victory in Maryland.
> We have just received the following important intelligence.—Ed. INT.
> RICHMOND, Sept. 21.—The "Enquirer" has a dispatch from Warrenton, announcing a terrific fight at Sharpsburg on Wednesday, with the advantage on our side.
> Great loss on both sides.
> Generals Starke, Manning, and Branch were killed.
> Generals D. R. Jones, R. R. Jones, and Ripley and Lawton were wounded.
> The whole strength of both armies were engaged in the fight.
> Report says the fight was renewed on Thursday and the enemy was routed and driven nine miles.

McClellan's army "routed and driven nine miles" by Lee was scarcely the result of the battle of Antietam (Northerners' preferred name for the battle), fought on Wednesday, Sept. 17, 1862, near the town of Sharpsburg (Southerners' preferred name), just a couple of miles from the banks of the Potomac River. But this did not matter to a newspaper editor conscientiously serving the propagandistic purposes of the Confederate press as much as the informational interests of his readers.

Then came disquieting news, in a dispatch from Richmond. Amid reports on the battle of the 17th that "are meagre and somewhat contradictory," the update disclosed, "the city papers of this morning report, on the authority of passengers who arrived last night, that Gen. Lee recrossed to the Potomac on Friday at Shepherdstown." This caused Steele on September 24 to admit that the report of Lee's withdrawal back to Virginia "has created some disquietude in this community, and in some instances, fears for the success of our arms in Maryland." But in his characteristic manner, the editor advised readers not to despond; a mere withdrawal across the Potomac could be "the best move which our army could make to thwart the enemy, and obtain advantage over them." The paper urged, "let our readers, then, not be discouraged by any movement of General Lee!"[15]

The *Intelligencer* followed its own advice in an article printed on September 27. News received since the battle of Sharpsburg "restores confidence in the invincibility of our arms," it affirmed. Indeed, the editor stated that Lee's army was still in Maryland. At Sharpsburg, "McClellan's army was repulsed with dreadful slaughter, and since then . . . has been cut to pieces." As he encouraged readers to share his confidence, John Steele acknowledged, "we look for more important news every moment."

As one would expect, the first detailed report on the big battle came from a "special," a newspaper correspondent in the field. The reporter was Peter Alexander of the *Savannah Republican*, who dated his account as 9 p.m., September 17: "A bloody battle has been fought to-day.—It commenced at daybreak and lasted until 8 o'clock at night—fourteen hours. The enemy made the attack, and gained some advantage early in the day on the left, and subsequently on the right, but was finally repulsed with great slaughter. Our own losses have been heavy, including many officers of worth and position."

Alexander began to list those officers, but cut short his writing "because an opportunity is offered to forward it to the post office at Winchester." Meaning, Confederate couriers or wagons were starting to head south from Sharpsburg to Winchester in the lower Shenandoah, and he had a chance to get his handwritten article on the railway from Winchester to Savannah. That the *Republican* published Alexander's article on September 27, nine days after its composition, informs us of how long it took for train-borne reports to get from the field to the editor's desk. But the fact that the *Intelligencer* was able to reprint "P.W.A.'s" account on the 28th, just a day after its publication in Savannah, shows also how quickly the newspaper exchange system worked within Georgia. The *Savannah Republican* was a morning daily; after release it was put on the train through Macon to Atlanta, reaching the *Intelligencer* office in time to be laid into print for the paper's issue the next morning. The process further shows the eagerness of editor John Steele to get into his newspaper a correspondent's boots-on-the-ground report as soon as he could.[16]

In its accounting of the big battle in Maryland, the *Intelligencer* got it both right and wrong. True, Lee's troops had repulsed McClellan's attacks all along the line, and thus had won a tactical victory in the narrowest sense of the term. But after a day of holding that line against attacks that never came, Lee's army withdrew back across the Potomac River, giving the North a strategic victory. And as "P.W.A." reported, "our losses have been heavy": Confederate casualties, according to Stephen W. Sears, were 1,546 killed, 7,752 wounded and 1,108 missing, for a total of 10,318—31 percent of Lee's effectives. McClellan's losses toted to 2,108 KIA, 9,540 W, 753 MIA, or a number amounting to 25 percent of soldiers committed into the fight.[17]

Given such magnitude of bloodletting—which, in truth, Southerners would not learn about until well after the war, and then certainly not through their newspapers—it was well that the *Intelligencer* should publish from time to time graphic descriptions of a battlefield after the fighting had ceased. Such it did in an article entitled, "War and Its Horrors." The witness was a Confederate soldier in Lee's army writing to his father in Charleston after a recent battle. "Men, mangled in every conceivable manner, to the number of 10,000, were strewn out before me," he attested.

> The painful details of our wounded I will spare you; but will pass to the enemy's side of the field, where one-half of the number laid; there were men with their arms, legs, and hands shot off, bodies torn up, features distorted and blackened. All this I could see with indifference, but I could not but pity the wounded; there one poor devil, with his back broken, was trying to pull himself along by his hands dragging his legs after him, to get out of the corn rows, which the last night's rain had filled with water; here another, with both legs shot off, was trying to steady the mangled trunk against a gun stuck in the ground; there, a fair haired Yankee boy of sixteen was trying with both legs broken, half of his body submerged in water, with his teeth clinched, his finger nails buried in the flesh, and his whole body quivering with agony and benumbed with cold. In this case my pity got the better of my resentment, and I dismounted, pulled him out of the water, and wrapped him in a blanket—for which he seemed very grateful. One of the most touching I saw, were a couple of brothers (boys), both wounded, who had crawled together, and one of them in the act of arranging a heading for the other, with a blanket, had fallen, and they had died with their arms around one another and their cheeks together. But your heart sickens at these details, as mine did at seeing them, and I will cease.[18]

In downplaying Lee's retreat from Maryland, the *Intelligencer* was in abundant company among Confederate newspapers, including those in Georgia, as journalism historian Ford Risley has observed.[19] In his exhortation that readers "not be discouraged by any movement of General Lee," John Steele was demonstrating the kind of prejudicial resilience that would characterize the *Intelligencer*'s editor throughout the rest of the war.

NOTES

1. "GLORIOUS NEWS!," *ADI*, Sept. 5, 1862; Earl J. Hess, *Braxton Bragg: The Most Hated Man in the Confederacy* (Chapel Hill: University of North Carolina Press, 2016), 56–57; Joseph H. Parks, *General Edmund Kirby Smith C.S.A.* (Baton Rouge: Louisiana State

University Press, 1954), 118–19, 211–16; Kenneth W. Noe, *Perryville: This Grand Havoc of Battle* (Lexington: University Press of Kentucky, 2001), 39; Earl J. Hess, *Banners to the Breeze: The Kentucky Campaign, Corinth, and Stones River* (Lincoln: University of Nebraska Press, 2000), 42; J. H. DeBerry, "Kirby Smith's Bluegrass Invasion," *America's Civil War*, vol. 10, no. 3 (March 1997), 58.

2. "THANKSGIVING DAY," *ADI*, Sept. 6, 1862; "THANKSGIVING," *ADI*, September 9; "DAY OF THANKSGIVING AND PRAYER," *ADI*, September 18; "THANKSGIVING" and "THANKSGIVING DAY SERVICE," *ADI*, September 18; 'THANKSGIVING DAY," *ADI*, September 20.

3. "REVISED TERMS OF THE DAILY INTELLIGENCER," *ADI*, July 27, 1862; "THE DAILY INTELLIGENCER," *ADI*, April 17; "QUITE A DIFFERENCE," *ADI*, February 14; "THE WESTERN AND ATLANTIC RAILROAD," *ADI*, September 14; Garrett, *A & E*, vol. 1, 491; Andrews, *South Reports*, 42, 44; "DEMISE OF NEWSPAPERS," *ADI*, March 20, 1862; van Tuyll, *Confederate Press*, 17.

4. "SPARTA, GEO., 14th July, 1862 . . . ," *ADI*, July 19, 1862; "A. C. Wyly & Co." (advertisement) and "A. C. WYLY & CO.," *ADI*, August 7.

5. 'THE MAILING OF THE INTELLIGENCER," *ADI*, Aug. 3, 1862; "CITY SUBSCRIBERS," *ADI*, September 27 (repeated September 28 and 30).

6. "AN EDITOR'S TIME," *ADI*, Aug. 30, 1862; "Stonewall Victorious—Pope Whipped at Manassas!," and *"From our yesterday Morning's Edition," ADI*, September 3; "ARMY LETTERS," *ADI*, July 22.

7. "We publish BETA's communication"" and "Beta," "FROM EAST TENENESSEE. General Hardee and his Brigade," *ADI*, Aug. 19, 1862; "PERSONAL," *ADI*, August 8.

8. "THE RICHMOND EXAMINER," "DESPERATE AFFAIR," "FROM THE RAPPAHANNOCK," and "FROM GORDONSVILLE," *ADI*, Aug. 30, 1862.

9. "RUMORS," *ADI*, July 19, 1862; "LATEST YANKEE NEWS," *ADI*, August 1; "AN AFFAIR OF HONOR IN WASHINGTON," *ADI*, July 31.

10. "'THE DAILY REBEL,'" *ADI*, Aug. 3, 1862; Roy Morris, "The *Chattanooga Daily Rebel*," *Civil War Times Illustrated*, vol. 23, no. 7 (November 1984), 16; James W. Livingood, "The Chattanooga Rebel," *East Tennessee Historical Society's Publications*, No. 39 (1967), 42; "PERSONAL," *ADI*, September 24.

11. Rudolph von Abele, *Alexander H. Stephens: A Biography* (New York: Alfred A. Knopf, 1946), 215; Thomas Lawrence Connelly and Archer Jones, *The Politics of Command: Factions and Ideas in Confederate Strategy* (Baton Rouge: Louisiana State University Press, 1973), 100; "General Orders, No.2," Mar. 5, 1862, *OR*, vol. 10, no. 2, 297–98; "Special Orders, No.1," March 30; Lack, "Law and Disorder," 182–83; Dyer, *Secret Yankees*, 98–100; "HEADQUARTERS DEPARTMENT NO. 2 . . . ," *ADI*, Aug. 13 and 14, 1862; "MARTIAL LAW," *ADI*, August 14; "HEADQUARTERS, ATLANTA, August 12," *ADI*, August 13; "MARTIAL LAW—A CIVIL GOVERNOR AND AIDS [*sic*] APPPOINTED FOR ATLANTA," *ADI*, August 22; William E. Richards, "'We Live Under a Constitution': Confederate Martial Law in Atlanta," *Atlanta History*, vol. 33, no. 2 (Summer 1989), 31–32; Thomas E. Schott, *Alexander H. Stephens of Georgia: A Biography* (Baton Rouge: Louisiana State University Press, 1988), 360.

12. "EXTRACT. ADJUTANT AND INSPECTOR GENERAL'S OFFICE . . . ," *ADI,* Sept. 10, 1862; Davis, *What the Yankees Did to Us,* 3, 8–9; "SUSPENSION OF THE WRIT OF HABEAS CORPUS IN ATLANTA AND ITS VICINITY," *ADI,* September 10; Davidson and Lytle, *United States,* 166; Lack, "Law and Disorder," 183; Richards, "Martial Law in Atlanta," 34; General Orders No. 66, September 12, *OR,* ser. 4, vol. 2, 83; Frank Lawrence Owsley, *State Rights in the Confederacy* (Gloucester MA: Peter Smith, 1961 [1925]), 163–72; Thomas B. Alexander and Richard E. Beringer, *The Anatomy of the Confederate Congress* (Nashville: Vanderbilt University Press, 1972), 170; "MARTIAL LAW—HABEAS CORPUS," *ADI,* September 20.

13. "GLORIOUS NEWS," (editorial) and "GLORIOUS NEWS. The Capture of Covington and Newport, Ky.," *ADI,* Sept. 10, 1862; Parks, *Edmund Kirby Smith,* 221; James Lee McDonough, *War in Kentucky: From Shiloh to Perryville* (Knoxville: University of Tennessee Press, 1994), 154.

14. "INTELLIGENCE FROM THE ARMY, AND ARMY INCIDENTS," and "From the Richmond, Examiner, 10th inst. FROM MARYLAND," *ADI,* Sept. 13, 1862; "From Maryland," *ADI,* September 14; "Important, if true, from Maryland, *ADI,* September 14; Andrews, *South Reports,* 209; "THE NEWS," *ADI,* September 17.

15. "NOTES ON THE RECENT BATTLES," "Great Victory in Maryland" and "WHERE THE FIGHT TOOK PLACE," *ADI,* Sept. 23, 1862; "From Our Yesterday Morning's Edition." "From the Battle of Sharpsburg" and "THE SEAT OF WAR IN MARYLAND AND VIRGINIA," *ADI,* September 24.

16. "NEWS OF THE WAR IN MARYLAND AND VIRGINIA," *ADI,* Sept. 27, 1862; "P.W.A.," "From the Savannah Republican. BATTLE OF SHARPSBURG—TERRIBLE CONFLICT—THE ENEMY REPULSED," *ADI,* September 28; William B. Styple, ed., *Writing & Fighting the Confederate War: The Letters of Peter Wellington Alexander Confederate War Correspondent* (Kearny NJ: Belle Grove Publishing Co., 2002), 105.

17. Perry D. Jamieson, *Death in September: The Antietam Campaign* (Fort Worth TX: Ryan Place Publishers, 1995), 104; Stephen W. Sears, *Landscape Turned Red: The Battle of Antietam* (New Haven: Ticknor & Fields, 1983), 295–96.

18. "WAR AND ITS HORRORS," *ADI,* Aug. 2, 1862.

19. Risley, "Georgia's Civil War Newspapers," 126.

18. "Our Prospects Bright"

ON JULY 31, 1862, even before General Lee's triumph over Pope at Second Manassas, the *Atlanta Daily Intelligencer* had perorated on the sunny outlook for the Confederacy. In an editorial entitled, "Our Prospects Bright," the paper declared, "a distinguished military chief said in our hearing on a recent occasion, that the prospects of the Confederacy were never brighter since the opening of the war than they are at present."

The paper, however, cautioned its readers not to hope that Northern political dissensions would weaken Lincoln's prosecution of the war, nor to hope that European powers would diplomatically intervene in support of the South. "Upon hard blows only," editor John Steele advised, "bestowed upon the enemy, ought we to depend, to make the revolution a successful one, and to free ourselves of Yankee despotism."[1]

The exploits of Confederate cavalry in the west brought in more good news. A dispatch from Chattanooga, dated July 23, stated that Col. John H. Morgan's horsemen had captured Frankfort, Kentucky, and that Brig. Gen. Nathan B. Forrest's command had captured Lebanon, Tennessee, headed for Nashville. Steele added at the end of his column, "[*Yankee Doodle* is getting scared.—ED. INT.]" That was good for propagandistic punch, but not entirely founded in fact. In their first Kentucky raid of July 1862, Morgan's horsemen rode north between Frankfort and Lexington, but occupying neither city, sending only feints in the direction of each. As for Forrest, his cavalrymen indeed occupied Lebanon on July 20 and headed toward Nashville, thirty miles to the west, but rode back south before reaching the Tennessee capital.

A month later, Steele could celebrate further exploits of Confederate cavalrymen. In a commentary printed on August 29 entitled "WATCHMAN, WHAT OF THE NIGHT? ALL'S WELL!," the *Intelligencer* reported Stuart's sudden swoop upon Union Maj. Gen. John Pope's headquarters near Catlett's Station, Va., on August 22. The paper gleefully related "the capture of that vain gasconade's horses, servant, coat and money, with hundreds of his soldiers, and the precipitate flight of the remainder to Alexandria on the Potomac." Actually, most of the Northern prisoners escaped during Stuart's nighttime withdrawal from Catlett's. But the Confederates made off with a half-million greenback dollars and $20,000 in gold. Furthermore, General Lee found useful information by gleaning Pope's dispatch book.

Alongside Stuart's raid, in the same column John Steele related a fight near Gallatin, Tennessee on August 21 in which General Morgan's horsemen "cut to pieces" a Union cavalry force under Gen. Richard Johnson. "All this is indeed cheering news!," the editor exclaimed. "Not once has a *doubt* ever entered our minds of ultimate success in the achievement of our Independence, but now we look upon it as a certain, and an *early* event," he added, closing with "throughout the whole South, the people are resolute, and our Army confident of its *invincibility*!"[2]

A measure of Southerners' resolution was on display when the *Intelligencer* published a mid-August report on the extent to which Georgia's men were signing up for service to the cause. From the *Milledgeville Recorder*, the *Intelligencer* picked up an item that showed, according to the state's Inspector General, that Georgia had contributed so far 59 infantry regiments, four of cavalry, two legions (comprising infantry, cavalry and artillery), fourteen independent battalions of infantry and artillery, plus five independent companies. Authorities did not offer the numerical strength of all these units, but they definitely approached the eighty regiments and twenty-two battalions that the state would eventually contribute to the Confederate cause—some 100,000 to 125,000 men.[3]

There were clearly plenty out there doing their duty. The *Intelligencer* reported on August 1 that a Yankee prisoner, escaped from Macon, had been caught with the help of Jim, a slave. Several days later a reader, signing himself "Q.," praised Jim as a hero and even offered to raise money as a means of thanking him. "I think that such faithfulness in a negro should be rewarded substantially," wrote "Q.," suggesting that fifty dollars might be the right amount. A Cobb County reader, D. R. Turner, wrote the paper the next day, recommending that only voluntary contributions should go to Jim. There is no further report in the *Intelligencer*, however, of any such reward going to the faithful servant.[4]

Advertisers came and went in the pages of the wartime *Intelligencer*, but one constant in Atlanta commerce was the sale of enslaved African Americans. In addition to downtown commission merchants, who would buy or sell just about anything (*e.g.*, S. H. Griffin, dealer in "Merchandize, Produce, Real Estate, and Negroes"), several specialized slave dealers competed in the city, making Whitehall Street south of the downtown railroad something of a mart for commoditized human flesh. In the paper's issue of October 11, juxtaposed on page three were ads by R. M. Clarke, "NEGROES FOR SALE!" and Solomon Cohen, "Dealer in NEGROES." The latter informed the public that he was in the business of "buying and selling SLAVES" and that he was always "supplied with the choicest stock." Clarke announced that he had "150 likely young negroes for sale," including field hands, cooks, house servants, seamstresses and blacksmiths; "also, some nice young families, with their husbands." An unusual advertisement proposed a reverse of the usual transaction. R. L. Crawley, the commission merchant in the Franklin Building on Alabama Street, placed a notice in mid-October calling attention to "a No. 1 likely young negro man . . . [who] wishes to be sold to a citizen of Atlanta." The ad did not explain why the young man sought servitude in Atlanta, only that he "will try to be a faithful and obedient servant."[5] [The reader should note how we report on the *Intelligencer*'s ads for slave dealers. When we quote them, we are referring to what readers of the paper saw—and probably expected to see in their newspaper. In this we are relating history (even if it is uncomfortable by today's standards), not running from or trying to hide it.]

From time to time Southerners, as reflected by editorials in the *Atlanta Daily Intelligencer*, were compelled to realize that the war had evolved into one waged by the federal government to eradicate slavery. Even if slavery had not "caused" the sectional conflict, by late 1862 the American civil war had become a struggle to determine whether the institution would survive in what was once part of the United States. Lincoln, who had hinted during the summer of 1862 that he was on the verge of a wholesale emancipation of slaves in Southerners' hands, issued a preliminary Emancipation Proclamation on September 22, just days after the battle of Antietam. Slavery was still sanctioned by the Constitution, but as commander in chief the president possessed unique war powers. Deeming the weakening of Southern slavery essential to the federal government's war effort, Lincoln declared that slaves in Confederate-held territory were to be free as of the start of 1863. (Enslaved blacks in Union-held areas such as Tennessee and the border states were thereby exempted from the emancipating decree.)

The *Intelligencer* railed against Lincoln's Emancipation Proclamation. In an editorial appearing on October 3, the paper termed the edict "the last resort of that bloody-minded and wicked despot"—meaning the president of the once-United States. By promising freedom for slaves in Confederate-held territory, Lincoln was, in the *Intelligencer*'s opinion, trying to stir up a violent slave rebellion and race war. This immense issue was laboriously laid out in a long editorial carried by the paper on Oct. 14, 1862. Under the title, "THE SIGNS OF THE TIMES," John Steele predicted that in the coming months, Union gunboats would ply up Southern rivers and Federal troops would land on the Confederate coast. At every such point, the enemy would implement Lincoln's Emancipation Proclamation. Such a strategy, in the opinion of the editor, demonstrated "the *determined resolve* of the North, in its *power,* which is now an *abolition power,* to wage war against the South, not only a war of subjugation, but a war against the existence of negro slavery." With these enormous stakes before them, the *Intelligencer* exhorted the Southern people and their government to prepare for a long and deadly contest. Yet it did not despond. "God will be with the right," Steele concluded, "and the right is with the South."

As for Lincoln himself, the editor composed the most colorful characterizations. "The inhuman monster who now rules the North with more despotic sway than any autocrat ever ruled of whom history writes," Steele wrote in a piece printed on October 5, had nonetheless ascended to what once had been an exalted and dignified political office: "Sprung himself from a polluted source; accustomed in his youth to the teachings of the low and depraved; practising in his early manhood the vices his youth was schooled in; fortune yet favored him, and notwithstanding his innate brutality and vicious nature, artfully concealed by a natural buffoonery, this *thing,* Lincoln by name, has risen to a position, once esteemed the proudest in the civilized world."

Thus nakedly exposed, the Northern president and his forces were sure to be confronted and defeated by the sturdy sons of the South. Of this John Steele had no doubt. "When the alternative is presented," the editor concluded, "that *equality* shall exist between the white and negro race, or that we must perish. . . . the South . . . will *strike* as never blows were struck before."⁶

In late August the Confederate War Department assigned Gen. P. G. T. Beauregard, the hero of Sumter and Manassas, to command the Department of South Carolina and Georgia, with headquarters at Charleston. President Davis had relieved him from command of Southern forces in Mississippi in June 1862; Beauregard returned to the service with this new assignment. The *Intelligencer* called attention to Beauregard's arrival at Charleston in a flattering article, "THE GALLANT BEAUREGARD AT CHARLESTON." Editor Steele took pains to inform readers that Beauregard's new position should not be viewed as "too unimportant a command for him," following his roles in Virginia and out west. Rather, given "the *fiendish hate* which the North entertains to South Carolina, and especially to that city"—meaning Charleston, where South Carolina's ordinance of secession had been adopted in December 1860—the *Intelligencer* instructed readers that the defense of Charleston was an important military goal, one fully recognized by "the chivalrous leader that is now in command there."[7]

Even Confederate setbacks had to be reported, though, as one sees in the *Intelligencer*'s handling of reverses in Kentucky and Mississippi in early October 1862.

The news from Corinth, Mississippi came through in a telegram sent late October 3 from the headquarters of Confederate Maj. Gen. Earl Van Dorn about an engagement fought that day. "We have driven the enemy from every position," he declared; "so far, all is glorious, and our men behaved nobly. Our loss, I am afraid, is heavy. It is nearly night. Lovell's and Price's troops have our thanks." This last reference was to Maj. Gens. Mansfield Lovell and Sterling Price, two of Van Dorn's commanders. On October 3, the Confederate forces, numbering about 22,000, attacked an equal number of Federals under Maj. Gen. William S. Rosecrans, fortified at Corinth. The Southerners pushed their way to the enemy's inner works, but could not take them. Renewed attacks on the next day also brought Confederates initial success. But the Northerners held their key positions and Van Dorn eventually ordered a retreat.

As was too often the case following initial accounts of Confederates' victory ("all is glorious"), more somber news began to arrive at the *Intelligencer* office. After the triumph that Van Dorn announced on the evening of Friday, October 3, a further report stated that on the 4th the Southern force at Corinth "drove the enemy from and occupied their entrenchments, but was afterwards forced to fall back from the town." Steele tried to put the best face he could on Van Dorn's reverse at Corinth, as in this headline, posted at the top of the *Intelligencer*'s "BY TELEGRAPH" column on October 10, "Confederates not so badly whipped after all,"[8] . . . which was not true. Historian Peter Cozzens, recent chronicler of Corinth, counts 7,707 Confederate casualties, including 2,257 captured or missing. Of Rosecrans' 22,000 officers and men, 355 were killed, 1,841 wounded and 324 missing. Another 570 fell on October 5 as the Federals pursued Van Dorn's retreating army, bringing Union casualties to 2,090.[9]

Then, even as Steele struggled to make sense of the "news" from Mississippi, in came a bunch of it from Kentucky.

Braxton Bragg's and Edmund Kirby Smith's columns had entered Kentucky separately, but in its telegraphic news section on September 30, the *Intelligencer* incorrectly reported their junction twenty miles from Louisville. Facing them there was Union Maj. Gen. Don Carlos Buell, commander of the Army of the Ohio. Then the wires brought little news from that quarter. A dispatch dated Chattanooga, October 2, stated, "the impression in Nashville is that Bragg has taken Louisville." A telegraphic message, October 5, declared that Buell's army was drawn up for battle twenty-one miles southeast of Louisville and that a battle was anticipated.

Steele printed it on Wednesday, the 8th, although adding his complaint, "we should have received the foregoing telegrams on Sunday or Monday last—why the PRESS here [presumably all Atlanta newspapers] did not, we should like to know.—ED. INT." Subsequent reports were only sketchy and dated, such as a dispatch of October 5 (printed on the 12th), relating that "heavy firing was heard in the direction of Louisville."

The first news of an actual battle was published in the *Intelligencer* on October 14: reports of 5,000 Federals captured at Perryville, Kentucky, by General Hardee's troops. Steele penned an editorial on this "CHEERING NEWS," informing readers that "Perryville is South of Frankfort some forty-five miles, and about thirty five miles a little Southwest of Lexington according to the map of that State." But then, the very next day, the *Intelligencer* had to publish contradictory reports. Dispatches dated October 10, received by the *New York Herald*, reported "a signal and decisive Union victory at Perryville." Coming through Richmond, to this telegram a note was added that none of these dispatches "can be traced to authentic sources."

Complicating the editor's task of trying to learn what indeed had transpired was the uncertainty of the very arrival of telegraphed news. The *Intelligencer* of October 16 carried no telegraphic column at all, as it had on previous days when no wired dispatches had been received.[10]

Then the pendulum swung back. The *Intelligencer* on the 17th reprinted an article from the *Knoxville Register* bearing the date of October 14. The headline blared,

BATTLE AT PERRYVILLE, KY.!
Reported Confederate Victory!!
5,500 PRISONERS TAKEN!!!

The article related that a battle had begun at Perryville on October 7, "when the Confederates drove back the Federals, capturing 1,500 prisoners." On the next morning, the piece continued, "the fighting was renewed, when the Federal forces were routed, and 4,000 prisoners and ten pieces of cannon captured."[11]

The dimensions of the Confederate victory magnified with succeeding dispatches. One wired from Mobile, October 16, stated, "Bragg whipped Buell, drove him across the Kentucky river, and is in hot pursuit." An article in the *Richmond Examiner* declared, "the Yankees try to disguise their defeat by vague wording of their dispatches, but it is plain to us that our army in Kentucky has gained a great victory." In its telegraphic news column of October 19, the *Intelligencer* printed a dispatch to the *Augusta Constitutionalist* and several other papers that asserted the enemy had been driven three or four miles and that Bragg's troops had captured twenty-one field pieces (but only eight were carried off, for want of horses). "We have prisoners from five divisions—at least 30,000 men," this report alleged; "with one more division, the enemy would have been utterly destroyed."[12]

Then came the counterpoint: it was all untrue, or at least much of it was. A message from Chattanooga, October 20, printed in the *Intelligencer* the very next day, announced simply, "the last we heard from Bragg's army, he was at Loudon, Kentucky, falling back in order towards Cumberland Gap." Buell was pursuing, attempting to outflank Bragg's forces. Needless to say, as this account concluded, "the report of the capture of a large number of prisoners at Perryville by our army proves untrue."

What *has* been proven true is historians' review of Bragg's Kentucky expedition and its culmination at the battle of Perryville. Bragg had hoped to unite with Kirby Smith to defeat Buell's army, but the two Confederate forces failed to connect. Bragg himself vacillated as to his goals. He spent October 4 in Frankfort, the state capital, staging the inauguration of a pro-Confederate governor, Richard Hawes, unaware that Buell and his army had marched out of Louisville, looking for battle. Indeed, Bragg's uncertainty as to Buell's movements prevented him from concentrating his two corps, led by Maj. Gens. Leonidas Polk and William J. Hardee. On October 7, Hardee's troops encountered Buell's advance near the village of Perryville, some seventy miles southeast of Louisville. Hardee called for reinforcements as Buell brought up his army. Polk arrived with his troops and by seniority took over from Hardee. Yet Polk wavered on the morning of October 8 until Bragg arrived around 10 a.m. Three hours later the Confederates launched an attack that by darkness had driven the left of the Federal line back a mile. Casualties for the day favored Bragg: 3,396 Confederate (510 killed, 2635 wounded, 251 missing) *versus* 4,211 Federal (845 killed, 2851 wounded, 515 missing).

Bragg's battle ardor, however, left him that night when information came in that Buell's army badly outnumbered his own. At 9 p.m. he issued orders for a retreat. By the next morning Confederates had abandoned Perryville, marching to join up with Smith. Buell did not pursue (and was relieved of command on October 30). On October 12, Bragg and Smith decided that that their position was untenable, so the Southerners began their withdrawal back to Tennessee, through Cumberland Gap.[13]

As a stalwart Confederate newspaper, the *Atlanta Daily Intelligencer* sought to put the best face possible on these developments. In "AFFAIRS IN KENTUCKY," Steele on October 22 editorialized, beginning with an honest statement of his disappointment: "the report which reached us on yesterday, that General Bragg had fallen back to Cumberland Gap, created quite a disagreeable sensation here." Nonetheless, the editor tried to make sense of it all. Buell must have been reinforced. The Confederates were outnumbered. With the enemy threatening his rear, Bragg had to retreat. There was still a silver lining: the Confederates had acquired immense stores, and in their organized withdrawal were able to carry them off. And drawing Buell farther south, away from his base, Bragg could select the ground for his next battle, in which he, as Steele continued, "will obtain a great victory."

In the meantime, as it had done so many times before, *the Intelligencer* counseled patience among its readers. "We must therefore," Steele advised, "bide forthcoming events, trusting that when the two armies do begin their conflict, Providence will bless us with another victory over the invading vandals."[14]

All the while, John H. Steele had a newspaper to run. On Friday, October 10, the editor complained in a short piece about the indifferent service of telegraph operators responsible for transmitting news items over the wires. Telegraphed dispatches published that day "should have been received here on Wednesday night, in time for our yesterday's edition," he groused. All the more galling, Augusta papers had gotten their "Telegraphic News" when the Atlanta ones had not. "Why it did not reach Atlanta, when it did Augusta, we are at a loss to conjecture," the editor shrugged; "this is the second time within a week that such an occurrence has transpired." Steele closed with the admonition that "the telegraphic operators somewhere must '*wake up.*'"[15]

Then there were the usual vexations complicating an editor's day-to-day work. A typesetter's mistake had to be corrected with an "ERRATA" item; a sentence intended to state that the enemy took no *prisoners* came out as *provisions*. Persons submitting communications to the *Intelligencer* office for printing in the paper had to be reminded —"for the hundredth time," Steele wrote exasperatedly—that pieces would not be published unless accompanied by the writer's name. Sometimes the volume of news, all of which had to be sifted through, was so heavy that Steele ran out of space for his usual editorializing on the second page. Then, on October 31, the editor apologized for no editorial matter in that morning's issue; he had been too sick ("indisposed") to write.[16]

There were, to be sure, offsetting pleasures for an enterprising editor. Steele informed readers in late October that he had just been visited in his *sanctum* by Durant Da Ponte, former editor the *New Orleans Delta*, who was now attached to Maj. Gen. John B. Magruder's staff in Texas and was passing through Atlanta on his way to that new post. And it was always enjoyable to welcome new members of Atlanta's literary fraternity, as Steele did in recognizing the new editors and publishers of the *Banner and Baptist*, James N. Ells and the Rev. Henry C. Hornady, minister of Atlanta's First Baptist Church.[17]

It was obviously a good thing when an editor could announce improvements in service and also additional advertisers. A list of the latter appeared in the paper's issue of October 15 (including J. B. Smith & Co., which would auction "an extensive assortment of FRENCH TOYS"). In late October Steele related that by arrangement with the local express company, the *Intelligencer* would now be delivered by train to subscribers north of Dalton along the East Tennessee & Georgia Railroad toward Knoxville. This allowed him to beckon new business. "Those now who desire to subscribe for this journal, but were restrained because of the snail-like progress of the *mail*, or its detention at Dalton, can do so with the assurance that it will reach them with the *latest news*, twenty-four hours earlier than heretofore," Steele affirmed. He added, "we have heard of many friends on that route, who only waited for his change to become subscribers. . . . We shall be happy to hear from them."[18]

It was always a happy task to report instances of patriotic expression. The Atlanta post commander, Col. George W. Lee, wrote the editor in mid-October that he had received fifty-six dollars for the Atlanta soldiers' hospitals, "proceeds arising from an entertainment for persons of color, gotten up by Albert Scott, a barber of this city." Indeed, it had become a function of the *Intelligencer* to remind Atlantans—if they needed reminding—that their city had become a major military medical center. On October 29, the paper published the call by Post Surgeon J. P. Logan for slave laborers to help construct a new hospital "in consequence of a sudden and large influx of sick soldiers."[19]

From time to time, matters also needed to be editorially addressed with a public scolding. In a long piece titled "CAN IT BE SO?," Steele told of how he had been visited by a woman, "modestly attired, pale and dejected, with grief stamped upon her face," who lived in the suburbs of the city. She explained how she was tending to her husband, a soldier who had lost his arm in battle and been sent home from Virginia. Her sole livelihood for her family was as a seamstress, but she was having trouble finding work. Even worse, as she tearfully told the editor, she was being turned down as she applied for work at government offices, "while others," Steele emphatically wrote, "more favored by fortune and influence, get as much of the government work as they can do."

Angered, the editor called for some justly administered punishment for anyone "who would insult by snubbing and impolite treatment this woman of toil and of poverty. . . . Shame upon the creature calling himself a man, who would thus act! In the exercise of 'a little brief authority,' the creature who would thus act, and deprive work a defenseless woman, striving to feed her helpless one-armed husband, as he lays at his humble home unable to toil for the support of his family—the creature we proclaim it to who would thus act, merits the scorn of the community in which he dwells."

The desperate lady gave John Steele a written communication for printing in the paper; we may assume that it was an appeal for work. But the editor chose not to publish it, out of respect for the lady's dignity. Instead, Steele appealed to the good citizens of the city to come to his office as "we are prepared to give the name of the wounded Soldier's wife" to those who would come to her aid. Explaining his preference for "this mode of calling attention to her case," the editor expressed his fear that this "is not a solitary one."[20]

Sadly, John Steele was probably right.

NOTES

1. "OUR PROSPECTS BRIGHT," *ADI*, July 31, 1862.

2. "More Good News from Morgan and Forrest," *ADI*, July 24, 1862; James A. Ramage, *Rebel Raider: The Life of General John Hunt Morgan* (Lexington: University Press of Kentucky, 1986), 94–96; John R. Scales, *The Battles and Campaigns of General Nathan Bedford Forrest 1861–1865* (El Dorado Hills CA: Savas Beatie, 2017), 53–56; "WATCHMAN, WHAT OF THE NIGHT? ALL'S WELL!" and "BATTLE NEAR GALLATIN. Morgan Engages the Enemy. Complete Victory," *ADI*, Aug. 29, 1862; John W. Thomason, Jr., *Jeb Stuart* (New York: Charles Scribner's Sons, 1930), 233; Emory M. Thomas, *Bold Dragoon: The Life of J. E. B. Stuart* (New York: Harper & Row, 1986), 148–49; Dee Alexander

Brown, *The Bold Cavaliers: Morgan's 2nd Kentucky Cavalry Raiders* (Philadelphia: Lippincott, 1959), 114–14.

3. "GEORGIA IN THE FIELD," *ADI*, Aug. 17, 1862; Bell Irvin Wiley, *Why Georgia Should Commemorate the Civil War* (Atlanta: Department of State, 1960), 10.

4. "Q.," "'Jim,'" *ADI*, Aug. 6, 1862; "Mr. D. R. Turner, of Cobb county . . . ," *ADI*, August 7.

5. S. H. Griffin advertisement, *ADI*, Oct. 15, 1862; "SOLOMON COHEN, Dealer in NEGROES" and R. M. Clark ad, "NEGROES FOR SALE!," *ADI*, October 11; "A No. 1 likely young negro man . . . ," *ADI*, October 12.

6. James M. McPherson, *Abraham Lincoln and the Second American Revolution* (New York: Oxford University Press, 1990), 34, 83–86; Arthur M. Schlesinger, Jr., "War and the Constitution: Abraham Lincoln and Franklin D. Roosevelt" in Gabor S. Boritt, ed., *Lincoln the War President: The Gettysburg Lectures* (New York: Oxford University Press, 1992), 157; "LINCOLN'S PROCLAMATION. THE LAST RESORT OF THE BLOODY DESPOT," *ADI*, Oct. 3, 1862; "THE SIGNS OF THE TIMES, *ADI*, October 14; "THE IRREPRESSIBLE CONFLICT," *ADI*, October 5.

7. Williams, *Beauregard*, 164–66; "THE GALLANT BEAUREGARD AT CHARLESTON," *ADI*, Oct. 15, 1862.

8. "Lovell and Price Engaged" and "News from the West," *ADI*, Oct. 8, 1862; Albert Castel, "Victory at Corinth," *Civil War Times Illustrated*, vol. 17, no. 6 (October 1978), 12–22; Richard Collins Suhr, "Attack Written Deep and Crimson," *America's Civil War*, vol. 4, no. 1 (September 1991), 48; "Later from the Battle of Corinth," *ADI*, October 10.

9. Peter Cozzens, *The Darkest Days of the War: The Battles of Iuka & Corinth* (Chapel Hill: University of North Carolina, 1997), 305–306.

10. "LATEST FROM KENTUCKY," Sept. 30, 1862; "From New York and Kentucky," *ADI*, October 3; "From Nashville and Louisville," *ADI*, October 4; "Later from the North," *ADI*, October 8; "DIRECT FROM KENTUCKY. FIGHTING IN THE DIRECTION OF LOUISVILLE," *ADI*, October 12; "Capture of Five Thousand Federals at Perryville, Ky." and "CHEERING NEWS," *ADI*, October 14; "Northern News," *ADI*, October 15.

11. "From the Knoxville Register, 14th inst. BATTLE AT PERRYVILLE, KY.!," *ADI*, Oct. 17, 1862.

12. "GREAT BATTLE IN KENTUCKY!" and "From the Richmond Examiner. VERY LATEST FROM THE NORTH," *ADI*, Oct. 18, 1862; "BY TELEGRAPH. From the Battle," *ADI*, October 19.

13. "FROM BRAGG'S ARMY," *ADI*, Oct. 21, 1862; Stanley F. Horn, "The Battle of Perryville," *Civil War Times Illustrated*, vol. 4, no. 10 (February 1966), 7–11, 42–47; Parks, *Edmund Kirby Smith*, 235; Noe, *Perryville*, 128–29, 313; Hess, *Bragg*, 67–70; Lowell Harrison, "Perryville: Death on a Dry River," *Civil War Times Illustrated*, vol. 18, no. 2 (May 1979), 47.

14. "AFFAIRS IN KENTUCKY," *ADI*, Oct. 22, 1862.

15. "TELEGRAPHIC NEWS," *ADI*, Oct. 10, 1862.

16. "ERRATA," *ADI*, Oct. 21, 1862; "COMMUNICATIONS," *ADI*, October 25; "We have yielded so much space . . . ," *ADI*, October 21; "The readers of the 'INTELLIGENCER,'" *ADI*, October 31.

17. "PERSONAL," *ADI*, Oct. 25, 1862; "THE BANNER AND BAPTIST," *ADI*, October 23; Venet, *Changing Wind*, 22.

18. "NEW ADVERTISEMENTS," *ADI*, Oct. 15, 1862; "THE 'INTELLIGENCER' NORTH OF DALTON," *ADI*, October 31.

19. G. W. Lee, "MILTIARY [*sic*] POST, ATLANTA, GA., Oct. 11, 1862," *ADI*, Oct. 12, 1862; "In consequence of a sudden and large influx . . . ," *ADI*, October 29.

20. "CAN IT BE SO?," *ADI*, Oct. 4, 1862.

19. "Clio" Writes of Fredericksburg

GROWTH WAS A NICE PROBLEM TO HAVE for an enterprising newspaper. On Nov. 1, 1862, editor John Steele announced that "owing to the large increase of the circulation of the 'INTELLIGENCER,'" the paper was hiring a manager for its mail department. The new employee, John T. Smith, would be responsible for getting subscribers' papers in the mail as quickly as possible.

That was not all. In the same issue the paper announced that proprietor Jared Whitaker had engaged the services of "MR. A. E. MARSHALL, the well-known and accomplished Stenographer" as its reporter covering the state legislature's session in Milledgeville, then Georgia's capital. Alexis Marshall—"M.," as he sometimes signed himself—mailed regular reports to Atlanta on the General Assembly's doings, as well as transcripts of important speeches delivered on the House or Senate floor. When the session was over, Marshall returned to Atlanta. On December 20, the *Intelligencer* informed readers that Marshall would continue working for the paper, though it did not disclose how. "His time will be devoted to the Intelligencer," the announcement read, "which he hopes by his humble efforts to render more worthy of public patronage."[1]

There was one more important change. "We introduce to-day to our readers, our Richmond Correspondent 'CLIO,'" began this announcement in the *Intelligencer* of Tuesday morning, Nov. 18, 1862. Editor John H. Steele informed readers that the paper's proprietor, Jared I. Whitaker, was "determined to make it as interesting and valuable to its readers as any paper in the Southern Confederacy," and that he "will spare no expense in the employment of contributors to it as will carry out his views to that end." Accordingly, Commissary General Whitaker—he was still serving in that position under the administration of Georgia Governor Joseph E. Brown—"has engaged as a regular Richmond Correspondent, 'Clio,' one of the most distinguished Southern writers." Respecting the anonymity of pen-names, the *Intelligencer* declined to provide the identity of its new correspondent, but added that his "facilities at Richmond for obtaining the most reliable information are surpassed by no contributor to any Southern journal, and equaled by but very few."

[In contrast to some hoarier historical genres, the study of Confederate newspapers is juvenescent. For example, fifty years ago J. Cutler Andrews could only *guess* that "Shadow" of the *Mobile Advertiser & Register* was Henry Watterson. In the last quarter-century, Barbara G. Ellis and Stephen J. Dick confirmed Watterson by using a computerized word content analysis based on Watterson's postwar writing in the *Louisville Courier-Journal*.[2] So here it is, 150 years after the war, and we still don't know the identity of "Clio," who wrote more than 160 articles for the *Intelligencer* between November 1862 and June 1864. Obviously, John Steele kept his secret very well.]

Like Peter Alexander ("P. W. A.") for the *Savannah Republican* and other "specials" in the field, "Clio" would send his long, handwritten articles to Atlanta by mail. Steele informed readers that three of the correspondent's letters had recently arrived, and "to the exclusion even of much editorial matter, which we had prepared," he had decided to print all three in this issue.

The editor commended them to his readers, as "the writer is *reliable, and true* to the South now, as he has been for more than thirty years during which period his pen has done valuable service to it."[3]

"Clio's" first letter opened with a slyly comic understatement: "We are likely soon to have stirring times." Lee's and McClellan's armies kept wary watch on one another across the waters of the Rappahannock; inevitably they must engage in "a terrific, if not final struggle."

"Clio"—the name, by the way, of the Greek muse of history—also traded in rumor and prognostication. In his letter dated November 12, he offered the prediction that next spring the enemy would make a more determined effort to capture Richmond. "The whole Northern heart throbs with the fond expectation of the capture especially of President Davis," he wrote, "whom it desires to see hung on a gibbet."[4]

"Clio" delved also into matters political. "What, it is asked," he pondered in his letter penned on November 14 (in the *Intelligencer* of the 20th), "has Lincoln under the Northern Government to do with the slaves of the South? Slavery is peculiarly a Southern institution. What constitutional right has he to emancipate our slaves?" Clio answered himself crisply: "None, whatsoever."

And there was Northern news to digest, such as the removal by President Lincoln of General McClellan from command of the Army of the Potomac. On November 5, Lincoln had signed an order relieving "the Young Napoleon," ostensibly because of his dilatory "pursuit" of Lee after Antietam, and his inactivity in the subsequent month and a half. "Whatever may be said of his incompetency as a General," "Clio" declared, McClellan had been much revered by his soldiers.[5]

And there was diplomacy afoot. Ever since the *Trent* affair of December 1861, the *Intelligencer* had occasionally raised the question of whether England would bestow diplomatic recognition on the Confederate States of America. On June 24, 1862, for example, the *Intelligencer* reprinted an article from the *Richmond Enquirer* cautioning against all the unfounded rumors about French recognition. England, however, was viewed as the more important country. In the summer of 1862, after Lee's and Jackson's victories in Virginia, Lord H. J. T. Palmerston, the British prime minister, and Lord John Russell, the foreign minister, began speculating on whether the time had come to mediate the Americans' civil war, with a view to recognize the Southern Confederacy. After James Mason, Richmond's representative in Britain, reportedly received a cordial welcome in Glasgow, Scotland, the *Intelligencer* wondered whether this was an augur of English recognition.[6]

"Clio" voiced such optimism. "From the Northern papers I learn that dispatches of a grave character have been handed to the Federal government by the French minister.... In all probability they have reference to the recognition of the French Emperor," he wrote from Richmond on November 11, adding "all our late advices from Europe unequivocally indicate that recognition by the great powers of Europe is an event near at hand." In a letter dated November 14, "Clio" reiterated that "the conclusion, in most political circles, is that the recognition of our independence by European powers will take place at an early day."

"Clio" was misinformed. Two weeks after Antietam, news of the battle reached England. British leaders recognized that the Americans were locked in a long and bloody civil war that, some argued, required European mediation. While Lord Russell favored some intervention to bring peace, he was opposed by the English secretary of war, George C. Lewis. Prime Minister Palmerston came to oppose intervention, writing to Russell on October 22 that the British should remain "onlookers on till the war shall have taken a more decided turn." The next day cabinet members voiced support for Lewis' hands-off policy. For his part, French emperor Louis Napoleon favored some form of mediation in the American conflict, but he was not willing to act without British support.[7]

"Clio's" commentary, as published in the *Intelligencer*, was quite varied indeed. Writing on Monday, November 17, he described Richmonders' Sunday religious practices. "The most fashionable church of the city is St. Paul's (Episcopal) where his Excellency the President worships," he observed. The *Intelligencer* printed this letter, and another two (dated November 18 and 19) in its issue of November 26, with a grousing editorial. John Steele, who regularly received Richmond newspapers by train, complained that he was receiving news from the Confederate capital faster from his rail-borne exchanges than from his paid correspondent using the mail. Exasperated, he asked, "why it is that the letters of our Richmond Correspondent are often behind the Richmond papers in their reception here?"[8]

Two days later, on November 28, Steele again complained about the Richmond mail. The day before, three of "Clio's" letters arrived all at one time, though bearing the dates of November 20, 21 and 22. This erratic postal delivery not only diminished the timeliness of the *Intelligencer* correspondent's news and commentary, but also it forced the editor to find space for all three epistles in the next available issue. As it turned out, the paper of November 28 carried only two of the three.

"The triumph of the Democratic party in the recent elections is thought here to be indicative of a radical change in the public sentiment and opinion of the North on the subject of the war," began "Clio's" epistle of the 20th. He was referring to Northern elections for the U. S. Congress, governorships and state legislatures, in which Democratic candidates racked up victories. Union military reverses during the summer plus the onset of war weariness were major factors. Historians have also discerned that the midterms in the North offered not so much a plebiscite on the federal government's prosecution of the war, as on Lincoln's preliminary Emancipation Proclamation. Democratic speakers in the Midwest were unashamedly racist in their appeal for votes. Horatio Seymour, running for governor in New York, was promoted by Democratic-leaning newspapers such as the *New York World*: "a vote for Seymour is a vote to protect our white laborers against the association and competition of Southern negroes."

The approach worked. Democrats won thirty-two net seats in the U. S. House of Representatives. Seymour won in New York, as did a Democrat in New Jersey's gubernatorial race. They also gained a majority in the legislatures of Illinois and Indiana.[9]

The Southern press quickly began reporting the results of the Northern voting, which took place on Tuesday, November 4. For Confederates, any word of Democratic electoral wins in the North was cheering news. John Steele offered his reflections on these events on November 13. "The elections in the North and West," he opined, meant that "the administration of Abraham Lincoln and his emancipation policy, have been severely denounced, and that the *programme* of the abolitionists has received a check from which it can hardly recover, portentous of their future downfall." The inference to be drawn, in the editor's words, was that "the *barbarous* conduct of the war does not meet with the approval of the majority of the Northern people."

Regardless of the recent elections, the *Intelligencer* warned that the Lincoln government would prosecute the war even more harshly in the coming months. With his usual bellicosity, Steele promised, "the South is ready for the Abolition onset, let it come where and whenever it may. Mobile, and Savannah, and Charleston, may become a pile of ruins, but the States of the South will still remain as free as when they first united and became the CONFEDERATE STATES OF AMERICA."[10]

As if in fulfillment of the editor's prediction of more quick, hard strokes by the enemy, "CLIO" wrote from Richmond on November 22 that on the previous day Federals had demanded the surrender of Fredericksburg, on the south side of the Rappahannock River, fifty miles north of the Confederate capital. General Lee refused, and in anticipation of a Northern bombardment of the city he directed that women, children, and other non-combatants should evacuate. "Clio" wrote that the citizenry readily complied, "cheerfully and with one accord." Federals could see the exodus; a moved Maj. Gen. Edwin V. Sumner, in charge on the north bank, sent word to General Longstreet, on the south side, that his guns would not bombard the city so long is it remained militarily inactive.

The *Intelligencer* reported the drama on the Rappahannock. A dispatch from Richmond, November 23, stated that the Federals had not yet begun to bombard Fredericksburg. The message offered the suggestion that perhaps "they have changed their programme."

"Clio" pondered this possibility, offering the opinion in his letter of November 22 that "the threat against Fredericksburg was a feint to conceal the ulterior designs of the enemy, who, it is supposed, do not intend to approach Richmond by the way of Fredericksburg, but more probably Petersburg." Two days later he had changed his mind: "the idea is quite prevalent here to-day that the movement on Fredericksburg is indicative of a purpose, on the part of the enemy, to make that place and Acquia creek the base line of its operations against the capital of the Southern Confederacy." Indeed, as the *Intelligencer* reported on November 30, from the *Richmond Examiner*'s reading of Northern newspapers, "On to Richmond" had become the rallying cry for Burnside's Army of the Potomac.[11]

Union general Ambrose Burnside was about to begin his march "on to Richmond." He had reorganized the Army of the Potomac into three "grand divisions" that numbered 120,000 troops. On November 15, they started marching toward Fredericksburg. In two days the troops of General Sumner, in the advance, reached Falmouth, across the Rappahannock from Fredericksburg. Lee saw them coming and arrayed his army—80,000 troops in two corps under Lt. Gens. James Longstreet and "Stonewall" Jackson—along the south bank. The Federals did not immediately force a crossing because the three dozen pontoon boats needed to bridge the river were slow in reaching the Union forces. The resulting stalemate—Burnside and Lee eyeing each other across the Rappahannock—led "Clio" to speculate that Burnside's "on to Richmond" campaign had fizzled out. "It is believed here by many that the winter campaign of the Northern army is over," he wrote on November 27, adding, "the disappointment which Burnside experienced on finding General Lee and his army at Fredericksburg . . . has so disheartened him that he will make no further attempt."[12]

Then came rumors that Northern public opinion had begun calling for Burnside to get moving. "There is said to be an irresistable pressure on Burnside from the north to advance his forces at once for the capture of Richmond," "Clio" wrote on November 29. In truth, President Lincoln and General Halleck visited Burnside on November 27. While they assured the general that they were not recommending him to attack Lee before he was ready, Burnside nonetheless began to feel pressure from Northern public opinion. Three days later, "Clio" reported from Richmond, "it is the general impression that the Federals will attempt to throw a column of their army across the Rappahannock at Port Royal [thirty miles downstream from Fredericksburg] under cover of their gunboats."[13]

The stalemate on the Rappahannock put punsters to work. Amid speculation that Lee could send Jackson upriver in another of his famous flank marches, "Clio" wrote on December 5 that Burnside "has taken to ditching on the other side of the Rappahannock in the mud, and does not venture across for fear of falling on a Lee shore with a Stonewall in the rear."

From his desk, editor Steele took note that "the Northern press have been down upon Burnside, condemning his tardy movements, and calling for his removal." The *Intelligencer* predicted that Burnside would eventually be removed. So long as Lee, Jackson, Longstreet and "the two Hills" (Ambrose P.

and Daniel H.) stood in his way, Burnside would fail in his campaign, "for he is incompetent to the task assigned him, and must fall by the way."[14]

Meanwhile, as "Clio" wrote on December 3, Burnside held a strong position north of the river. "The banks on the other side of the Rappahannock," he commented, "are every where bristling with cannon of the most formidable character." Those guns started to bark. The *Intelligencer*'s telegraphic news from Richmond, dated December 11, stated that several Northern shells had been thrown into Fredericksburg, resulting in the death of "an old citizen," Jacob Grates, one of four civilians to lose their lives. Another telegraphic dispatch reported that "a considerable portion of Fredericksburg was destroyed . . . by the enemy's shells."[15]

Finally, there came word of the long-expected battle. On December 16, the *Intelligencer* published the brief message that General Lee had sent to Adjutant General Samuel Cooper in Richmond: on the morning of December 13, the enemy had attacked his defensive positions; the battle had lasted six hours; the enemy had been "repulsed at all points thanks to God." Casualty reports had not yet begun to come in, but the paper's telegraphic column that day brought word that Confederate Gen. T. R. R. Cobb of Georgia had been killed in the engagement. (Cobb was mortally wounded by a shell fragment.) A longer report, issued from Richmond on the 15th, added particulars. Federals had crossed the river, resisted by Brig. Gen. William Barksdale's brigade. During the Federals' shelling of the town, some residents had remained, among whom there had been "many hair-breadth escapes." Union troops launched their attack on the morning of Saturday, the 13th—but then the message was cut short. Editor Steele explained, "here the operator informs us the line went down," so no further news could be received by telegraph.[16]

Because "Clio's" handwritten articles reached the *Intelligencer* office by mail, they were all several days behind the paper's telegraphic reporting on the recent battle in Virginia. Enough information had arrived by December 18 for Steele to begin editorializing on Fredericksburg. "We have but few of the details," he began his piece, and "our telegraphic columns are meagre indeed." Because of this, he could not even have known the basic outlines of the battle. Burnside's infantry attacked midmorning on December 13, after fog had lifted. Federals achieved a temporary breakthrough on the Confederate right (Stonewall Jackson's sector), but were pushed back. On the Confederate left, many of Longstreet's troops fought behind a stone wall and mowed down repeated assaults. December darkness, beginning around 5 p.m., brought the slaughter to an end.

Yet there was no news of Burnside's retreat. Steele contemplated that Burnside's army might hover in the vicinity of Fredericksburg throughout the winter, resuming its campaign against the Confederate capital in the spring. If so, the editor placed high confidence in Lee and his "brave troops . . . that Richmond will never be occupied by the demon horde of Northmen who seek to subdue the South."[17]

Then the casualty reports started coming in. Atlantan James Ormond had received a personal telegram from F. M. Johnston, captain of Company A, 19th Georgia Infantry Regiment. In publishing it, Steele prefaced by reminding readers, "this company went from this city." One man had been killed, eight wounded, and seven had been captured; the 19th had fought in Jackson's line and had been pushed back by the assault of Union Maj. Gen. George Meade's division. Captain Johnston closed his report by adding, "Maj. Neal is safe," referring to James H. Neal, who had contributed letters to the *Intelligencer* from the front.[18]

John Steele also relied on his Richmond exchanges, which were usually the first to relate reliable news from the Virginia front. The *Enquirer* of December 16 allowed the *Intelligencer* on the 20th to update its readers on the reports that the Richmond paper had received. "The estimate of our killed and wounded in the several days' encounters amounts to about 2,000," it declared; "the loss of the enemy is believed to be fully 6,000." As we know today, both figures were way too low. Union casualties totaled 12,653: 1,284 dead, 9,600 wounded and 1,769 missing. In their defensive victory Confederates lost 595 killed, 4,061 wounded and 653 missing—5,309 in all.[19]

Steele explained his reliance upon the *Enquirer* in an editorial of December 20: it had been the only Richmond paper he had received in the past two days, providing him the only news of Fredericksburg he had seen beyond short telegrams. Moreover, it was still too early for letters to arrive from Atlantans serving in Lee's army.

It was not too early, though, for the *Intelligencer* editor to rail against the enemy. In their occupation of Fredericksburg, Northern troops had been found to have committed "all the outrages upon that defenceless town and its people, which Yankee and Abolition malignity could conceive and perpetrate." These outrages provoked Steele to express his hope that "the time . . . will soon come when we trust, in God, they will reap their reward."[20]

NOTES

1. "THE MAILING DEPARTMENT OF THE 'INTELLIGENCER'" and "THE INTELLIGENCER—THE LEGISLATURE," *ADI*, Nov. 1, 1862; "MILLEDGEVILLE CORRESPONDENCE OF THE INTELLIGENCER," *ADI*, November 27; "AT HOME," *ADI*, December 20; "THE REPORTER'S DICTIONARY," *ADI*, March 4, 1865.

2. Barbara G. Ellis and Steven J. Dick, "Who Was 'Shadow'? The Computer Knows: Applying Grammar-Program Statistics in Content Analyses to Solve Mysteries about Authorship," *Journalism & Mass Communication Quarterly*, vol. 73, no. 4 (Winter 1996), 947–62.

3. "OUR RICHMOND CORRESPONDENT, 'CLIO,'" *ADI*, Nov. 18, 1862.

4. "CLIO," "Special correspondence of the Atlanta Intelligencer. FROM RICHMOND," (November 10) and "CLIO," "FROM RICHMOND" (November 12), *ADI*, Nov. 18, 1862.

5. "CLIO," FROM RICHMOND" (November 14), *ADI*, Nov. 20, 1862; T. Harry Williams, *Lincoln and His Generals* (New York: Alfred A. Knopf, 1952), 174–77.

6. "RECOGNITION," *ADI*, June 24, 1862; Robert W. Young, *Senator James Murray Mason: Defender of the Old South* (Knoxville: University of Tennessee Press, 1998), 132; "EUROPEAN SENTIMENT—SCOTLAND," *ADI*, October 9.

7. "CLIO," "FROM RICHMOND" (November 11), *ADI*, Nov. 18, 1862; "FROM RICHMOND" (November 14) *ADI*, November 20; Howard Jones, *Union in Peril: The Crisis over British Intervention in the Civil War* (Chapel Hill: University of North Carolina Press, 1992), 168, 171, 189, 191; Dean B. Mahin, *One War at a Time: The International Dimensions of the American Civil War* (Washington: Brassey's, 1999), 135–36; Crook, *Diplomacy*, 105.

8. "CLIO," "FROM RICHMOND" (November 17), *ADI*, Nov. 26, 1862; "OUR RICHMOND CORRESPONDENT," *ADI*, November 26.

9. "THE RICHMOND MAIL" (editorial), *ADI*, Nov. 28, 1862: "CLIO," "THE RICHMOND MAIL," November 28; Nevins, *War Becomes Revolution*, 320; McPherson, *Ordeal*, 294–95; V. Jacque Voegeli, *Free but Not Equal: The Midwest and the Negro During the Civil War* (Chicago: University of Chicago Press, 1967), 55.

10. "THE ELECTIONS IN THE NORTH AND WEST," *ADI*, Nov. 13, 1862.

11. "CLIO," "FROM RICHMOND" (November 22), *ADI*, Nov. 28, 1862; Edward J. Stackpole, *Drama on the Rappahannock: The Fredericksburg Campaign* (Harrisburg: Stackpole Company, 1957), 93–94; "BY TELEGRAPH. From Fredericksburg" (Richmond, November 23), *ADI*, November 25; "CLIO," "FROM RICHMOND" (November 24), *ADI*, November 30; "LATE NORTHERN NEWS. 'ON TO RICHMOND' ONCE MORE," *ADI*, November 30.

12. George C. Rable, *Fredericksburg! Fredericksburg!* (Chapel Hill: University of North Carolina Press, 2002), 59, 66, 87–88, 144, 148; "Northern News," *ADI*, Dec. 5,1862; "CLIO," "FROM RICHMOND" (November 27), *ADI*, December 3.

13. "CLIO," "FROM RICHMOND" (November 29), *ADI*, Dec. 6, 1862; Vorin E. Whan, Jr., *Fiasco at Fredericksburg* (Gaithersburg MD: Butternut Press, 1986 [1961]), 30; "CLIO,"

"FROM RICHMOND" (December 2), *ADI*, December 6; Bradley M. Gottfried, *The Maps of Fredericksburg* (El Dorado Hills CA: Savas Beatie, 2018), 41.

14. "CLIO," "FROM RICHMOND" (December 5), Dec. 9, 1862; "BURNSIDE CONDEMNED," *ADI*, December 10.

15. "CLIO," "FROM RICHMOND" (December 3), *ADI*, Dec. 11, 1862; "SECOND DISPATCH," *ADI*, December 13; "From Fredericksburg" (Richmond, December 13), *ADI*, December 14; William A. Blair, "Barbarians at Fredericksburg's Gate: The Impact of the Union Army on Civilians," in Gary W. Gallagher, ed., *The Fredericksburg Campaign: Decision on the Rappahannock* (Chapel Hill: University of North Carolina Press, 1995), 153–54.

16. "Battle at Fredericksburg," "Private Dispatch from Capt. L. J. Glenn to his Son" and "Particulars of the Battle in Virginia," *ADI*, Dec. 16, 1862; William B. McCash, *Thomas R. R. Cobb: The Making of a Southern Nationalist* (Macon: Mercer University Press, 1983), 317.

17. "THE BATTLE OF THE RAPPAHANNOCK," *ADI*, Dec. 18, 1862; Daniel E. Sutherland, *Fredericksburg and Chancellorsville: The Dare Mark Campaign* (Lincoln: University of Nebraska Press, 1998), 45–57, 64–66.

18. "PRIVATE DISPATCH," *ADI*, Dec. 18, 1862; Rable, *Fredericksburg! Fredericksburg!*, 206–207.

19. "From the Richmond Enquirer, 16th. THE NEWS. FREDERICKSBURG," *ADI*, Dec. 20, 1862; Rable, *Fredericksburg! Fredericksburg!*, 288.

20. "THE 'SITUATION' AT FREDERICKSBURG," *ADI*, Dec. 20, 1862; Gary W. Gallagher, "The Yankees Have Had a Terrible Whipping: Confederates Evaluate the Battle of Fredericksburg," in Gallagher, ed., *Fredericksburg Campaign*, 119.

20. "Glorious Victory at Murfreesboro"

FOLLOWING HIS WITHDRAWAL FROM KENTUCKY, Gen. Braxton Bragg and his forces were encamped at Murfreesboro, in middle Tennessee. Some 40,000 strong, the Army of Tennessee was the largest Confederate force west of the Appalachians; Lt. Gen. John C. Pemberton's forces in Mississippi were second in size.[1]

Union Major General Rosecrans, with 47,000 officers and men in the Army of the Cumberland, was at Nashville, thirty miles to the northwest. On Christmas Day 1862, even though winter had arrived, Rosecrans ordered an advance against Bragg. Rain, fog and Rebel cavalry slowed the Federals' march, so that they did not approach Murfreesboro until the evening of December 30. Both commanders planned to launch attacks the next morning, but Bragg moved first.

The Confederates charged the Union left and by 10 a.m. on the 31st had sent two divisions retreating back some four or five miles. With his right flank bent back, Rosecrans reformed his line into a V, its left resting on Stones River. Southerners kept up their assault, but the Federals stood firm till darkness ended the fighting.[2]

With his troops occupying much of the battlefield, Bragg wired Richmond that night, declaring that he had won a big victory: "God has granted us a Happy New Year." In another dispatch, Bragg stated (exaggeratingly) that in ten hours of fighting his troops captured 4,000 prisoners, including two brigadier generals, thirty-one field pieces and 200 wagons with teams.

This was the kind of premature announcement that led the *Intelligencer* to jump the gun. "Glorious Victory at Murfreesboro," the paper headlined on January 3. The editor that day praised Bragg, though he reminded readers that he had been critical of the general for his Kentucky campaign. "All honor to this intrepid leader and the brave army which he led," editor John Steele asserted. "It gives the South *'assurance'* that in General Bragg it has a leader upon whom, in any emergency, it can safely depend to vindicate its rights, and whip its dastardly invaders."³

Bragg expected Rosecrans to retreat, but the Union army stayed put. The first day of the new year passed without any major fighting. Bragg renewed his assaults on January 2, but the Southerners failed to budge the Federal line. Some of his generals that night recommended the army, weakened by heavy losses, should retreat. Believing that the enemy had been reinforced, Bragg reluctantly agreed. His troops began falling back that night.⁴

How the *Intelligencer* handled this turn of events—from a "glorious victory" to a depressing retreat—shows the difficulties of reporting war news far from the battlefront. On January 7 it published, without comment, General Bragg's dispatch sent on the 5th from Tullahoma, south of Murfreesboro: "Being unable to dislodge the enemy from his entrenched position and hearing of reinforcements sent to him, I withdrew from his front night before last—he has not followed. My cavalry are still close in his front." Another message sent that day added, "we retired from Murfreesboro' in perfect order."⁵

We've seen it before, notably when the *Intelligencer* hailed the Confederate army's "complete victory" at Shiloh, based on General Bragg's message sent at the end of the battle's first day. Here again the paper struggled to explain why, after trumpeting a "Glorious Victory at Murfreesboro," it had to report the glum news of the Army of Tennessee's retreat. This emotional animadversion was not bad journalism, so much as ardent Confederates' eagerness to snatch any good news in a war that was beginning to go against them.

John Steele was compelled to address the reverse on January 9, albeit with a long preamble: "After one of the severest battles on record, with an inferior over a vastly superior force, in which the most daring valor was displayed by our gallant army before Murfreesboro', as well as superior military skill on the part of Gen. Bragg and his Generals of Divisions and Brigades, and in which the enemy suffered defeat and terrible slaughter, Gen. Bragg was forced to retire."

Yet the editor saw in the Murfreesboro news something of a victory after all, based on news from the *Chattanooga Rebel*: "5,000 prisoner taken, 61 pieces of artillery, 7,500 small arms, 950 wagons destroyed, 9000 of the enemy killed and wounded," with the Confederates' loss of "only four thousand."

To be sure, most of this was not accurate. True, Rosecrans had the larger army: 46,953 troops engaged against Bragg's 37,719. Otherwise, the *Rebel*'s numbers were way off. Although Bragg later reported thirty cannon captured, Rosecrans' chief of artillery admitted after the battle to having lost only a dozen field pieces (but adding that six Rebel guns had been taken). As for wagons, Bragg's cavalry commander, Brig. Gen. Joseph Wheeler, had raided behind Federal lines and had destroyed or wrecked a number of Northern wagons, but he offered no count of them.

The most important statistics, of course, were the casualties. The Army of Cumberland suffered the loss of 1,730 killed, 7,802 wounded and 3,717 captured. The Army of Tennessee lost 1,294 dead, 7,945 wounded and 1,027 missing. Totals thus were 13,249 Federal to 10,266 Confederate—a proportional disparity of 1.29, rather than the 14,000–4,000 claimed by the *Intelligencer* (3.5).[6]

In a short piece titled "THE YANKEES! THE YANKEES!," the *Intelligencer* reported the arrival in the city of some 3,000 prisoners from the battle of Murfreesboro, in transit to imprisonment elsewhere. Before this influx, the paper reported that the City Barracks (on Peachtree Street, four or five blocks north of the Car Shed) had been converted into a jail for those being held for "crimes of various grades," including counterfeiting. The building also served as a military prison. Steele had chosen to visit the place, and from its commandant, a Captain Conway, got a list of the enemy occupants, which it published on January 1: seventeen Yankee officers, as well as a woman, Mrs. E. F. Carter, charged with being a spy. Steele took a tour of the place, and observed that the Yankee officers were being kept in two comfortable rooms. In one they had just had lunch ("as good as that of our own officers"); in the other there was a fire emitting "genial warmth." The editor could not help commenting on the difference between "the kind treatment as captives confined in our city enjoy" and the harsh Northern prisons in which Confederate POWs were said to be languishing.[7]

In addition to Northern prisoners from Murfreesboro, there were arriving wounded Confederate soldiers—so many that they filled Atlanta's hospital beds to capacity. Of these there were many, at least 800. In June 1862 authorities had called for the construction of forty buildings on the large acreage of the city's Fair Grounds, the site southeast of downtown that had hosted regional farm shows before the war. The hospital complex eventually provided for 400 beds in each of two facilities, called Fair Ground Hospitals Nos. 1 and 2. They were in operation by the advent of autumn; the first unfortunate Fair Ground patient was buried in the City Cemetery on October 1.

With the Fair Grounds facilities apparently filled, Dr. J. P. Logan, post surgeon, appealed to citizens to open up their homes, especially as more ailing soldiers were surely on their way. Publishing his call on January 4, Steele added his own encouragement, with subtle warning that Logan had the authority to commandeer private quarters for the needed space. On the 6th, the *Intelligencer* reported that Col. G. W. Lee, the post commander in Atlanta, was helping to find accommodation for the wounded, "who are arriving on every train."

So many were arriving, in fact, that a "wayside hospital" had to be set up near the passenger depot. Steele visited the place and wrote about it on January 11. He saw "a thousand Yankee prisoners" under guard, awaiting transport elsewhere. The editor observed several hundred sick and wounded Confederate soldiers crowding the medical facilities, tended to by four physicians and staff. The worst cases were placed in trackside bunks; those who could be moved to other city hospitals walked or were borne in ambulances—hence the name "Distributing Hospital" that soon began to be used. Citizens' committees provided "such refreshments as they may need." Contributions were coming in from across the state. The paper printed on January 13 correspondence showing that citizens of Upson County (forty miles south of Fulton) had sent pillows and pillow cases, clothing (pants, shirts, socks, drawers), linen cloth for bandages, plus food items (butter, pepper, potatoes, fruit and eggs.)[8]

Arriving by train into Atlanta during January was a distinguished visitor, the president of the Confederate States. In the second week of December 1862, Davis set out on an extended tour that took him through Tennessee, where he met with General Bragg, through Alabama to Mississippi; the *Intelligencer* on January 3 published the president's address to the Mississippi legislature in Jackson. His return trip through Mobile brought him to Atlanta around 7 p.m. on New Year's Day. The train to Augusta allowed only a half-hour's stopover, during which time an awaiting carriage bore him to "a sumptuous supper," as the *Intelligencer* reported on the 3rd. Before departing he was called upon by a crowd at the Car Shed for a few remarks.

John Steele, or one of his employees, was there to hear him. "He spoke with deep feeling of admiration of the conspicuous part Georgia had borne in the contest now waging for the subjugation of our country," the writer reported. Davis mentioned that his father had been born in Georgia (1758, Wilkes County). Just as he was finishing, the train started to move. "He then closed with an earnest appeal to all in Georgia," the writer concluded, "to stand by the Conscription acts of Congress, whose prompt and rigid enforcement were now all that could save the country."[9]

On New Year's Day 1863, Steele and his staff had the day off, so there would be no issue for Friday, January 2. "Should the telegraph bring to us any news of importance," he added, "we shall issue an 'extra Intelligencer,' and place the same on our bulletin board," which hung on the sidewalk wall of the newspaper office at Whitehall and the railroad at the center of the city.¹⁰

On January 1 Atlantans also learned that they would soon have a new weekly paper, *The Soldiers' Friend*. An ad in the *Intelligencer* announced that the publication, whose first number was scheduled for January 10, would be "devoted to the intellectual, moral and religious interests of the soldier."

Owner and editor was the Rev. A. S. Worrell, who would offer a blend of war news, Christian inspirational messages and Confederate patriotism. Offices of the new weekly were located above the bookstore on Whitehall Street owned by Samuel and Jabez Richards, but the printing was being done by the *Intelligencer*'s job press. *The Soldier's Friend* was not inexpensive, though. Worrell stated that a single copy would cost $1.10. Fifty copies, or four months of issues, were pegged at $40.¹¹

In contrast were the *Intelligencer*'s subscription rates, which at the start of 1863 were still $8 per year—and it was a six-days-a-week publication, at that. This would change, however. On January 1 Steele reminded readers that the rising cost of paper and ink—indeed, "every article used in publishing a newspaper," including labor—necessitated an increase in subscription rates. The owner, Jared Whitaker, had decided not to post the new pricing until after a meeting in Macon, an "Editorial Convention" slated for the fifth of January. At that time, assembled editors would discuss subscription and advertising prices and possibly, as Steele explained, "enter into some arrangement as to uniformity of rates."

So few papers, however, sent representatives to the Macon meeting that it adjourned after only informal discussions. It was decided to try to hold another convention, this time in Augusta on February 4. Informing readers of the planned meeting on January 8, editor Steele voiced his hope that "delegates from the press in every city in the South" would attend.

With the failure of the editorial meeting on January 5, the *Intelligencer* went ahead and announced its price increases on the 8th. Annual subscription rates rose 25 percent, from $8 a year to $10. Rates for shorter terms went up proportionally. The new pricing, Steele explained, would take effect on the 15th. "Our old patrons, who desire to renew their subscriptions," he added, "have now a week offered to them to renew at present rates."¹²

NOTES

1. Horn, *Army of Tennessee*, 190–92; Michael B. Ballard, *Pemberton: A Biography* (Jackson: University Press of Mississippi, 1991), 116, 120.
2. Stanley F. Horn, *The Battle of Stones River* (Gettysburg: Historical Times, 1972), 3–7.
3. James Lee McDonough, *Stones River—Bloody Winter in Tennessee* (Knoxville: University of Tennessee Press, 1980), 159; "Bragg's Official Dispatch," "Glorious Victory at Murfreesboro" and "GENERAL BRAXTON BRAGG," *ADI*, Jan. 3, 1863.
4. Horn, "Stones River," 7–10.
5. "SECOND DISPATCH," *ADI*, Jan. 7, 1863; "From Tennessee," *ADI*, January 8.
6. "THE SITUATION OF BRAGG'S ARMY" *ADI*, Jan. 9, 1863; Alexander F. Stevenson, *The Battle of Stone's River near Murfreesboro', Tenn. December 30, 1862 to January 3, 1863* (Dayton OH: Press of Morningside Bookshop, 1983 [1884]), 191, 197; Bragg report, Feb. 23, 1863, *OR*, vol. 20, pt. 1, 669; James Barnett report, Feb. 8, 1863, *OR*, vol. 20, pt. 1, 235–41; Edward G. Longacre, *A Soldier to the Last: Maj. Gen. Joseph Wheeler in Blue and Gray* (Washington: Potomac Books, 2007), 82; Larry J. Daniel, *Battle of Stones River: The Forgotten Conflict between the Confederate Army of Tennessee and the Union Army of the Cumberland* (Baton Rouge: Louisiana State University Press, 2012), 198, 201.
7. "THE YANKEES! THE YANKEES!," *ADI*, Jan. 6, 1863; "THE MILITARY PRISON," January 1; Davis, *What the Yankees Did to Us*, 54.
8. Steve Davis, "Another Look at Civil War Medical Care: Atlanta's Confederate Hospitals," *Journal of the Medical Association of Georgia*, vol. 88, no. 2 (April 1999), 10–11; "A CALL THAT SHOULD BE RESPONDED TO," *ADI*, Jan. 4, 1863; "OUR WOUNDED," *ADI*, January 6; "THE LADIES' WAYSIDE HOSPITAL," *ADI*, January 11; "DISTRIBUTING HOSPITAL," *ADI*, January 13.
9. Hudson Strode, *Jefferson Davis Confederate President* (New York: Harcourt, Brace, 1959), 343–51, 356; "From the Jackson Mississippian, Dec, 27, "SPEECH OF PRESIDENT DAVIS TO THE LEGISLATURE OF MISSISSIPPI, *ADI*, Jan. 3, 1863; Crist *et al.*, eds., *Papers of Jefferson Davis*, vol. 9, 3; "ARRIVAL OF THE PRESIDENT," *ADI*, January 3; Cooper, *Jefferson Davis*, 11.
10. "NEW YEAR'S DAY being considered . . . ," *ADI*, Jan. 1, 1863.
11. "THE SOLDIERS FRIEND," *ADI*, Jan. 1, 1863; Venet, ed., *Sam Richards's Civil War Diary*, 76, 185; "THE SOLDIERS' FRIEND," *ADI*, January 11.
12. "Subscription and Advertising Schedule," *ADI*, Jan. 1, 1863; "ADVANCE IN NEWSPAPER RATES A NECESSITY," *ADI*, January 4; "EDITORIAL CONVENTION" and "SUBSCRIPTION RATES OF THE 'DAILY INTELLIGENCER," *ADI*, January 8.

The Car Shed, looking east. Atlanta's train depot was at the city's very center. The huge brick structure had three twenty-five foot-wide entrances, able to accommodate three trains loading or unloading at the same time. Indeed, three separate rail lines converged on Atlanta from the northwest, east and south. (Library of Congress.)

Federal wagon train going up Peachtree Street. George N. Barnard was a Northern photographer hired by General Sherman's chief engineer to take pictures in Atlanta during the Federal occupation. Sometime between mid-September and mid-November Barnard took this view. (Library of Congress.)

LEFT Gustavus Bull. In the battle of Seven Pines, Va., May 1862, Lt. Col. Gustavus Bull, of the 35th Georgia, was mortally wounded and died in a Federal hospital. Union Col. Raymond Lee, drawing upon his West Point days with Robert E. Lee, wrote General Lee, offering his help if family members sought to locate his grave. Bull's burial site remains unknown. (www.waroftherebellion.com.)

BELOW Alfred Waud, "The Battle of Resaca." Waud illustrated the battle of May 14-15, 1864, for *Mountain Campaigns in Georgia* (1886) by Joseph M. Brown, son of Georgia's wartime governor. The *Intelligencer*'s statement about the engagement, "severe loss on their side and few casualties on our part" typifies the paper's Confederate partisanship. (Library of Congress.)

Joseph Emerson Brown. Twenty-three-year-old Brown was admitted to the Georgia bar in 1845. Twelve years later he was elected governor, the first of four terms. In each election the *Intelligencer* loudly voiced support for Brown, even when he opposed Confederate policies such as conscription. (Library of Congress.)

Fighting at Shiloh. "COMPLETE VICTORY" was the *Intelligencer*'s headline on April 8, 1862, based on General Beauregard's telegram at the end of April 6. The next day's fighting did not go as well for the Confederates, so the *Intelligencer* had to backtrack. It would not be the last time. (Library of Congress.)

The *Intelligencer* Office in the Autumn of 1864. During the Federal occupation of Atlanta, George Barnard took many photographs of the city, including this view of Whitehall at the downtown railroad. The *Intelligencer* did not own its own building—few Southern newspapers did—but rented the upper floor in which M. Wittgenstein sold wine, liquor, and cigars. (Library of Congress.)

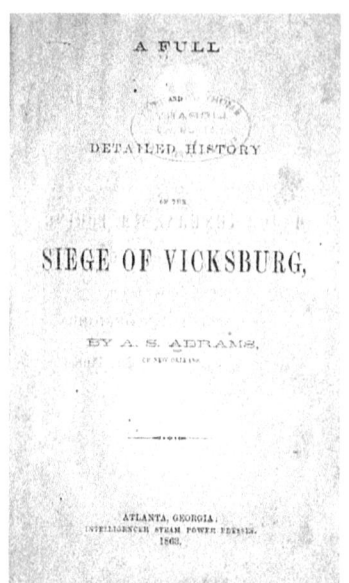

Alexander St. Clair Abrams' booklet title page. (Emory University.)

Rallying the troops of Bee, Bartow, and Evans at Manassas. In January 1861 Atlanta attorney Lucius Gartrell organized the 7th Georgia Infantry, which became part of Col. Francis Bartow's brigade and fought at Manassas, July 21, 1861. During the battle Gartrell was wounded and his sixteen-year-old son, Henry Clay, was killed. The *Intelligencer* listed the regimental casualties four days later. (New York Public Library.)

When the *Intelligencer* returned to Atlanta. After five months' sojourn in Macon, the *Atlanta Daily Intelligencer* returned home. Its first issue in the city was this "Extra" issued on Dec. 10, 1864—one page, printed on front only. A highlight of the sheet was a street-by-street account of buildings left standing after "the ruin detailed upon us by the God-forsaken, miserable and deluded Yankee crew." (Newseum.)

Jared Irwin Whitaker. Son of a Georgia governor, Jared Whitaker rose in Atlanta politics: city councilman, state senator and mayor, elected in January 1861. At first a co-owner of the *Intelligencer*, Whitaker became sole proprietor in July 1862 when Archibald Gaulding sold his half-share. He remained the paper's owner until its demise in 1871. Whitaker is buried in Atlanta's Oakland Cemetery beside his wife Nannie. (Stuart Thurston Hendrick.)

RIGHT Front page of the *Intelligencer*, April 20, 1861, shortly after the attack on Fort Sumter and the beginning of the American Civil War.

BELOW Second page of the *Intelligencer*, May 19, 1864. The Atlanta Campaign was just two weeks old, and already Confederate General Johnston had retreated twice, and had abandoned nearly forty miles of north Georgia territory. Atlantans were becoming alarmed. So John Steele addressed the "long faces" with this editorial. The *Intelligencer* editor sought to buck up the people's morale to the very end of the war.

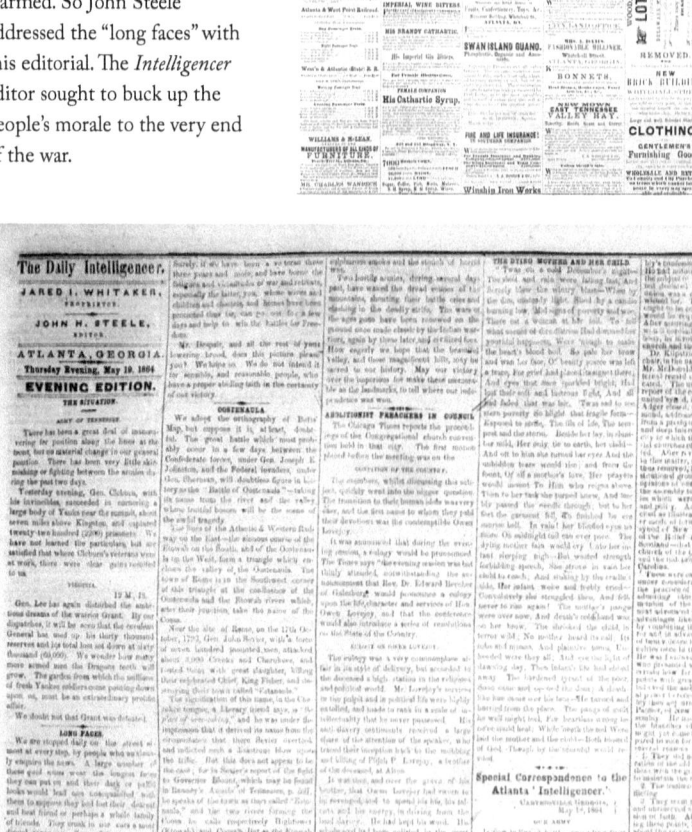

21. The Press Association of the Confederate States of America

THE *ATLANTA DAILY INTELLIGENCER* and the *Atlanta Southern Confederacy* were the city's two largest newspapers during the war, but there was a third too, the *Commonwealth*. The *Intelligencer* and *Confederacy* had sparred editorially on more than one topic, and Steele on occasion had let loose forceful criticism of his competitors, George Adair and Henly Smith, as when he charged that the *Southern Confederacy* was to be faulted for "publishing news items, baseless of truth, calculated to excite needless alarm and panic among our people." The *Intelligencer* editor was much nicer to the *Commonwealth*. On Feb. 4, 1863, Steele noted that the *Commonwealth* had suspended operations for over a month, but had reappeared on Monday afternoon, March 2. Steele observed that it was "improved in appearance, with additional editors and proprietors." Joining its "old editor," J. S. Peterson, was H. S. Hill, who had worked for the *Chattanooga Advertiser*. The *Intelligencer* noted that serving as corresponding editors for the *Commonwealth* were "Gen. Duff Green" and his son, Benjamin.

In 1836 Green, a Kentuckian, bought the *United States Telegraph*, a Washington newspaper that became the organ of the Andrew Jackson administration. After stints with other papers, Green settled in Dalton, Georgia before the war and with his son Ben started an arms company that manufactured for the Confederacy. "With such an array of editorial experience and ability," Steele commented, "we doubt not the future success of the 'Commonwealth,' even in these hard times." The *Intelligencer*'s prediction was proven wrong; the *Commonwealth* perished in August 1863 when owner J. S. Peterson sold the paper to an owner who changed its name, but never resumed publication.[1]

Pluck and hopefulness continued to be demonstrated in Confederate journalism. The *Intelligencer* announced on February 5 that a new paper had appeared in Macon: the *Daily Confederate*, under the editorship of L. F. W. Andrews. Dr. Andrews had been the prewar proprietor of a weekly and semi-weekly, the

Georgia Citizen. "These are hard times in which to start a daily," Steele acknowledged, but he wished the *Confederate* well: "we shall welcome to our sanctum the newspaper, and heartily wish success." After another paper, the *Richmond* (Va.) *Sentinel,* appeared on March 1, Steele also extended his wish for its "unbounded success." The *Sentinel* thus became the fifth daily in the Confederate capital, soon replacing the *Enquirer* as the organ of the Davis administration.[2]

In January 1863 the hard times for Southern editors got even harder. The Southern Telegraph Company, which conveyed news items circulated by the Southern Associated Press, announced in mid-January that it would levy extra charges on articles of over five hundred words. It was evident that editors would have to do something, as Steele made clear in an editorial in late January: "under the present telegraphic news agency system, great injustice has been done, and continues to be done to us."

The editorial convention that had been rescheduled for Augusta on February 4 (after the fizzled Macon meeting the month before), was publicized by a circular issued by Joseph Clisby, editor of the *Macon Telegraph.* In it Clisby called upon his colleagues to "rest from daily duty long enough to meet for consultation" on such matters as the telegraphic news service, shortages of paper and its rising costs. Editor Steele strongly supported the meeting, urging "every paper in the Confederacy" to be represented at the Augusta convention.[3]

That was a tall order, as it turned out on the appointed day. Steele was present for the *Intelligencer,* but only eleven other papers sent delegates. George Adair represented the *Atlanta Southern Confederacy;* the *Commonwealth* sent its proxy to Nathan G. Morse, owner of the *Augusta Chronicle & Sentinel.* Two other papers also sent proxies, bringing the number represented to fifteen. Clisby of the *Telegraph* was named chairman and Samuel G. Reid of the *Montgomery Daily Advertiser,* secretary.[4]

The meeting began with acknowledgment of receipt of correspondence from Richmond. The previous autumn, editors of the then-four dailies in the Confederate capital had formed the Richmond Associated Press to improve their telegraphic news reporting. The Richmonders' letter explained why they had formed their association and described its goals, as well as the difficulties they were facing. It was apparently doing all right, though: thirty-one newspapers subscribed to the news service it provided from the capital.

Perhaps the Augusta attendees needed no such roadmap, for they quickly set to work. On the morning of February 5, they adopted a constitution that set forth an organizational plan for a new entity, "the Press Association of the

Confederate States of America." The association's constitution described its primary purpose: establishing a new system for obtaining the telegraphic news reporting upon which all depended. Membership in the Press Association (called the P. A.) would be open to papers deemed eligible (and able to pay membership and service fees). Officers were then elected: a president, Robert W. Gibbes of the *Columbia South Carolinian,* and five directors (including Adair of the *Atlanta Confederacy,* John Steele's rival). The directors would have authority to determine the association's policies and to hire a superintendent. The conventioneers then adjourned *sine die.*[5]

The board chose John S. Thrasher, a former newspaperman living in Macon, to manage the association as superintendent. Thrasher assumed the position on March 9. The *Intelligencer* announced to its readers on the 12th that the new general manager of the P.A. was not a citizen of Atlanta, but of Macon. It also took pains to inform readers that this was John S. Thrasher, not the longtime Atlantan John J. Thrasher, known around town as "Cousin John."

Thrasher set to work quickly. He took a six-week tour of the Confederacy's major cities, hiring reporters in key areas, offering a salary of $25 a week (Thrasher's pay with the association was $3,000 per year). He worked a deal with the Southwestern Telegraph Company, which served the Confederacy's western areas. He also visited newspaper offices, seeking subscribers to the association. In Tennessee and Mississippi he met with Generals Bragg, Johnston and John C. Pemberton, assuring them that his press reports would not divulge sensitive information.

Thrasher needed a headquarters, and he chose Atlanta. At its first meeting, May 15, 1863, the P. A. board was presented with his reasons: geographic centrality, wire and rail communication, and healthful climate (pluses for himself and family). The Thrashers took up residence in the city in "a pretty gothic cottage," as one writer described it, on Whitehall Street so well south of the downtown railroad and business area as to be considered the suburbs.[6]

Concision and clarity would be important elements in the dispatches that Thrasher wired to his subscribers. Telegraph companies charged by the word, so brevity was at a premium. Besides, the superintendent knew that editors paying for product could be picky. Thrasher therefore drafted and circulated "General Rules for Telegraphic Press Reports," a baker's dozen of maxims for his hired writers, such as "Keep within the maximum of words assigned to you," and "Write in a clear, plain hand." Then, too, was this advice: "See that you are not beaten by special reporters for particular journals."[7]

With such exacting requirements, John S. Thrasher quickly proved himself to be an efficient administrator. In his first report to the P. A. Board of Directors, submitted nine weeks after his assumption of the superintendent's duties, he could name forty-four Confederate newspapers as members of the Press Association. They ranged from Richmond and Petersburg, Va. to Vicksburg, Miss. and Port Hudson, La. In the list were all three Atlanta dailies, the *Intelligencer*, the *Southern Confederacy* and the *Commonwealth*.[8]

The organization of the P. A. was a significant event in the history of Confederate journalism. With their cut-off from the American Telegraph Company in April 1861, and amidst their frustration with William Pritchard's telegraphic news service in early 1862, Southern editors—though they were sometimes business competitors—came together and formed an organization to help them offer better war-news for their readers. Their judicious selection of an industrious superintendent, and energetic solicitation of Confederate newspapers as members altogether was no small feat. Moreover, it is not too much to regard it as another instance of what historian Mary Elizabeth Massey calls "ersatz in the Confederacy"—Southerners' frequently ingenious procurement of substitutes for essential goods.

A measure of a newspaper's popularity is the volume of mail it receives. So many soldiers and other would-be contributors to the *Intelligencer* had sent in letters for publication that John Steele in late January advised submitters that they may have to wait. "In our desk we have now original matter enough to fill up three or four issues of our daily," he acknowledged. The editor implored those who had sent letters to him to be patient; "all will be attended to in due time."[9]

Another welcome source of materials was the paper's exchanges, which Steele received from near and far. The editor introduced a clipping from the *Vicksburg Citizen* by stating, "if there be one man in the range of this paper's circulation, who entertains the idea of a reconstruction of the old Union, we ask him to read the following truths." Editor of the *Vicksburg Daily Citizen* was James M. Swords, an ardent Confederate propagandist. It was probably he who wrote the article featured in the *Intelligencer* in early February entitled "National Hatred." The author reviewed the Yankees' blame for the war, and the ruthless deeds of invading Northern soldiers. "Robbers, murderers, and outlaws, as they are, how can we otherwise than detest them?" he asked.

To the *Citizen* piece Steele appended another article, this one taken from the *Richmond Examiner*. The writer, either editor John M. Daniel or associate editor Edward A. Pollard, presented some of the terms being used to denounce the

Yankees. Jefferson Davis called them hyenas; Virginia governor John Letcher characterized them as "a heaven-defying, hell-deserving race." "The practice of vilifying the Yankees has gotten into the newspapers," the *Examiner* affirmed with understatement, as it launched its own vilification ("a contemptible race, whose only defect is a proneness to all that is foul and everything that is evil"). Then the *Examiner* checked itself when it considered other orders of the animal kingdom. "To the well regulated mind, the beastly practices of beasts excite no disagreeable emotion," the paper reasoned. A vulture feeding on carrion was not reprehensible; instead such a sight "occasions in the beholder no special wonder, and never any animosity against the bird for gratifying his somewhat peculiar tastes." If, as the Richmond writer suggested, "the tiger that laps blood, and the beetle that gorges excrement, are but Yankees of the animal kingdom," so Southerners should understand their enemy in the same somewhat detached manner. "The scaraboei and vipers of humanity should be characterized neither by rage nor by nausea," he explained; in essence, Yankees could not help themselves. Still, they had to be exterminated as one would do other pests: "as a general thing, to kill them wherever we find them, without idle questions as to whether they are reptiles or vermin."[10]

Editor Steele got more instruction in nomenclature from the *Lynchburg* (Va.) *Republican* of February 17, which he reprinted in the *Intelligencer* on the 22nd. Entitled "What Shall We Call Them?"—"them" being the enemies of the South—the article related that it was the Lynchburg paper's practice to use *Yankee* as "the synonym of everything mean that the mind of man can conceive." The *Republican* regularly employed *Yankee*, and now noted that a new book further justified the term. "We are gratified to find that the reverend author of 'the campaign from Texas to Maryland,'" the article explained, "concurs with us."

The "reverend author" was Nicholas A. Davis, chaplain of the 4th Texas Infantry, in Hood's division. Davis' book, *The Campaign from Texas to Maryland, with the Battle of Fredericksburg*, had just been published by a Richmond printer, and as the Lynchburg article showed, the book was getting around. (After receiving a copy, Steele in the *Intelligencer* gave it a flattering review: "it will be read with interest by all who can appreciate exalted patriotism and unflinching courage in the day of battle. It ought to be in the library of every Southern patriot.")

The *Republican* excerpted a passage in which Chaplain Davis explains his use of the word *Yankee*.

It is the only name or word in the English or any other language, living or dead, that can be applied with full scope and force. It extends to all their ten thousand schemes of deception and fraud, and comprehends their every act of lying and stealing from the days of Washington till the present hour, in all their political, legislative, executive, commercial, civil, moral, literary, sacred, profane, theological, and diabolical history. . . . And thus applied, it means meddlesome, impudent, insolent, pompous, boastful, unkind, ungrateful, unjust, knavish, false, deceitful, cowardly, swindling, thieving, robbing, brutal, and murderous.

Thus, and for all of these reasons, the Reverend Davis concluded, "I prefer to use that word, and thereby say all that can be said on this subject—the term is Yankeeism."[11]

NOTES

1. Garrett, *A & E*, vol. 1, 360 n.7; Rabun Lee Brantley, *Georgia Journalism of the Civil War Period* (Nashville: George Peabody College for Teachers, 1929), 63; "THE COMMONWEALTH," *ADI*, Feb. 4, 1863; Charles H. Sydnor, *The Development of Southern Sectionalism 1819–1848* (Baton Rouge: Louisiana State University Press, 1948), 195; Harwell, "Atlanta Publications," 194; "City Newspaper Changes," *ADI*, Aug. 12, 1863.

2. "A NEW DAILY IN MACON," *ADI*, Feb. 5, 1863; Iobst, *Civil War Macon*, 17; "THE SENTINEL," *ADI*, April 4; Andrews, *South Reports*, 33.

3. Risley, "Confederate Press Association," 224–25; Ruby Florence Tucker, "The Press Association of the Confederate States of America in Georgia," master's thesis, University of Georgia, 1950, 26; "THE EDITORIAL CONVENTION AT AUGUSTA," *ADI*, Jan. 27, 1863; "THE TELEGRAPH—EDITORIAL CONVENTION," *ADI*, January 28.

4. Press Association, 6; Van Tuyll, "Essential Labor," 77; Mark K. Dolan, "Samuel Chester Reid, Jr.: A Professional Goes to War" in Patricia G. McNeely, Debra Reddin van Tuyll and Henry H. Schulte, eds., *Knights of the Quill: Confederate Correspondents and their Civil War Reporting* (West Lafayette IN: Purdue University Press, 2010), 261.

5. Press Association, 6–10; Tucker, "Press Association," 27–29; Risley, "Confederate Press Association," 226–27; Wood, "John S. Thrasher," 366; Debra Reddin van Tuyll and Patricia G. McNeely, "Robert W. Gibbes: The 'Mind' of the Confederacy," in *Knights of the Quill*, 95, 99.

6. Wood, "John S. Thrasher," 363–66; "THE PRESS ASSOCIATION," *ADI*, Mar. 12, 1863; Risley, "Confederate Press Association," 227; "Report of the Superintendent of the Press Association. Presented to the Board at Atlanta, May 15, 1863" in *Press Association*, 19, 29, 37–38; Wilson, "Confederate Press Association," 161–62; Tucker, "Press Association," 34; Davis, *What the Yankees Did to Us*, 175 and n.

7. Press Association, 29.

8. Press Association, 53.

9. "TO CORRESPONDENTS AND CONTRIBUTORS," *ADI*, Jan. 27, 1863.

10. "SOMETHING FOR RECONSTRUCTIONISTS" and "From the Richmond Examiner," *ADI*, Feb.1, 1863; A. A. Hoehling, *Vicksburg: 47 Days of Siege* (Englewood Cliffs NJ: Prentice-Hall, 1969), 8; Andrews, *South Reports*, 30–31.

11. "WHAT SHALL WE CALL THEM?" *ADI*, Feb. 22, 1863; "THE CAMPAIGN FROM TEXAS TO MARYLAND," *ADI*, March 13; Donald E. Everett, ed., *Chaplain Davis and Hood's Texas Brigade* (Baton Rouge: Louisiana State University Press, 1999 [1863]), xv, 147–48.

22. Plant Corn, Not Cotton

ON MARCH 11, 1863, Governor Joseph E. Brown called for a special session of the Georgia legislature to convene in the state capital, Milledgeville, on the 25th. His main purpose was to obtain legislation to induce or compel Georgia farmers to plant less cotton and more grain. Another priority was to bar the distillation of food crops into alcoholic beverages.

The *Intelligencer* had already issued its own call to increase corn production in the state. "The planting season is rapidly approaching, and to the farmers of our State we would say a few words," the paper editorialized in late January: "PLANT CORN." Farmers of the cotton states, it declared, "hold the destinies of the Confederacy in their hands." The war could drag on indefinitely, and planters needed to provide the Southern people and their armies with sufficient sustenance. Besides, corn prices were up, and farmers could make more money with the crop than even with cotton. "We cannot eat cotton," editor Steele reasoned, "nor can it be disposed of to advantage"—meaning by export through the blockade. Thus, he concluded, "both interest and patriotism alike demand that corn shall be planted to the extent of the ability of our farmers."

On March 12, the *Intelligencer,* which usually supported the governor's legislative initiatives, voiced approval of this one as well. "The armies of the Northern Dictator, we can meet with powder and ball, but when *Famine* comes, neither powder, nor ball, nor the bayonet, nor the sword, nor stout hearts and strong arms, can resist her desolating march," Steele pleaded. "Plant Corn! Plant Corn!"

The legislature in its previous session in December 1862 had set the date for reconvening on April 22. The governor was jumping it up five weeks, before corn planting season began. In the preceding session, lawmakers had passed a measure setting three acres of cotton per hand as the maximum limit, but the *Intelligencer* considered this too much, as it explained in another editorial on March 13.

The General Assembly duly convened on March 25, but during the session did not pass any bill regulating cotton agriculture. Instead, it enacted a prohibition against grain crops being distilled into alcohol. Yet even without legislative prodding, Georgia planters complied with the calls for food over lint. The *Intelligencer* of April 5 related the cheering news coming from Milledgeville of a bountiful wheat crop.[1]

In early March President Davis called for another national day of prayer, set for Friday, the 27th of the month. This would be his sixth such day so designated since the start of the war. As it had done before, the *Intelligencer* published the president's proclamation on March 5 and again on the 27th. Two days before, Steele urged Atlantans to spend time in activities of worship. On the appointed day itself, he published notices of services to be held at several of the city's churches. As he had also done before, the editor announced that on March 27 his staff had the day off, so they could go to church. There would accordingly be no paper circulated on Saturday, the 28th.[2]

The soldiers for whom the supplicants were to pray were establishing a reputation (at least to Confederate onlookers) as true American soldiers—brave, dedicated to ideal, and at once individualistic: not professional soldiers, but citizens who accepted their country's call to arms.

That meant that even in an organized army, "Johnny Reb," as he came to be called, maintained his proud individuality, even when faced with the constrictions of military hierarchy and rank.

The *Intelligencer* on March 7 related the anecdote of an Alabama Confederate soldier's encounter with "Gen. Rhodes" (Brig. Gen. Robert E. Rodes, commanding a brigade of Alabamans in Lee's army in Virginia). The story was told in the *Eutaw* (Ala.) *Whig and Observer,* and clipped by editor Steele. The soldier in question was a "conscript"—he had not volunteered in the first year of war, but had been drawn into the army by the Confederate conscription law. As the Eutaw paper told the story,

> The General was riding around his Brigade, and came up with the Conscript, who had taken his gun to pieces for the purpose of cleaning and scrubbing it up.
>
> Gen. Rhodes,—"What are you doing, Sir? What are you, anyhow?
>
> Conscript,—"I am a sort of a sentinel.—What are you, anyhow?"
>
> Gen. Rhodes.—"I am a sort of a General."
>
> Conscript.—"Well, General, if you will hold on, I will show, or give you, a sort of salute."
>
> Gen. Rhodes.—"Well, sir, you hold on a little while, and I will show you a sort of guard-house."

> The last we heard of the conscript, Gen. Rhodes had him in the guard house at his headquarters, bucked and gagged.

The conscript's sauciness proved painful, if the press account is accurate. "Bucking and gagging" involved the delinquent soldier being seated on the ground with his knees pulled up. A thick stick was slid under his knees, his arms were drawn up on the side of each knee, and his hands were tied. The punishment, maintained for several hours, was excruciatingly painful. Passing soldiers jeered, adding insult. The bucked soldier could not taunt back; he was gagged by a bayonet tied in his mouth.[3]

Exchanges such as that of the *Eutaw Whig and Observer* demonstrate that John Steele read far and wide. He occasionally observed his own articles being reprinted in other newspapers—sometimes, though, incorrectly or without attribution. Steele complained about these abuses in a piece printed on March 24. "On the reproduction of some of our articles, by our brethren of the press," the editor declared, "we have seen not only errors of thought, but, to our mortification, sometimes badly constructed sentences"—apparently editors were taking *Intelligencer* articles and rewording them amateurishly.

Just as bad—or maybe worse—was the editor who clipped an article from the *Intelligencer* and attributed it to the *Atlanta Southern Confederacy*. "This is all wrong," Steele groused, understandably; "we pray you, brethren, as *Hamlet* did the players, to 'avoid it.'"

Then, too, was the lesson of what goes around, comes around. On May 14, the *Intelligencer* editor pointed out that the *Atlanta Southern Confederacy* had on the day before published an article, "'Old Pap' and Kirby Smith," which it credited to the *Selma* (Ala.) *Reporter*. Steele noticed that the piece, though, was actually his, published in the *Intelligencer* some ten days before. The editor pronounced sly satisfaction that his article "has 'gone the rounds' and come back again to the starting point."[4]

John Moncure Daniel and Edward Pollard of the *Richmond Examiner*, John Forsyth of the *Mobile Register* and John Linebaugh of the *Memphis Appeal* are usually considered among the best newspaper editors in the wartime South. Because of his ardent Confederate patriotism, skillful editing, and facile writing we would argue that John H. Steele should be placed in at least a second echelon of Southern newspapermen.

Conscientious editors such as Steele could count on the professional reporters who were writing for numerous newspapers throughout the South. In an article printed in mid-March, the *Intelligencer* editor paid compliments to several noted field correspondents, including "Personne" of the *Charleston Courier*, Felix de Fontaine. In another article, appearing on March 8, Steele singled out Samuel Chester Reid as a particularly talented reporter. Reid wrote as "Ora" for the *Mobile Advertiser & Register* as well as other papers. Steele reprinted one of his letters, sent from Charleston in late February, as evidence of the "force and truth" of his writing.[5]

What the editor could not divulge to his readers was that he would soon strike a deal with Reid to write articles for the *Intelligencer*. When he announced the hiring of "a special telegraphic and army correspondent for the Intelligencer" on April 26, Steele could only refer to him by a pen-name, "290." He could not even explain that "290" was "Ora" for the Mobile and Montgomery press, because he had identified Reid as "Ora" in his article of March 8. "We now only introduce him to the reader as a gentleman of high character and attainments," Steele affirmed, and one "upon whose statement of army movements and occurrences the public may be confident."

Actually, the first letter of "290" had already appeared in the *Intelligencer* on April 21. Writing from Chattanooga on the 18th, Reid speculated that after Rosecrans' army at Murfreesboro had been reinforced, it would move against Bragg's Army of Tennessee at Tullahoma, some thirty miles to the southeast.[6]

"290" would be Steele's eyes and ears close to Bragg's army. For news from the eastern theater, the *Intelligencer* continued to rely upon "Clio." The energetic reporter in Richmond sent more than thirty long articles to the Atlanta paper in the first three months of 1863. As a conscientious Confederate journalist, "Clio" emphasized events that favored the cause, and understated those that did not. An example of the latter was the Richmond "Bread Riot" of April 2, 1863.

Inflation, government impressment, mercantile greed and urban overpopulation contributed to food shortages in the Confederate capital. Foodstuffs that got into the city fell into the hands of speculators and extortioners who jacked up prices to double or triple their own purchase costs. Women in the capital—especially those with husbands in the army and with children to feed—had had enough. On the morning of April 2 Richmond women thronged together at a church, then proceeded to the governor's mansion. Governor John Letcher listened sympathetically to the ladies' grievances, but that was not enough; the peaceable assembly quickly morphed into an unruly mob. Storming down Main Street, crying "Bread!," the mob (with some men and boys now joined in) smashed store windows and seized food, clothing and shoes. The governor and Mayor Joseph Mayo pleaded for order, but in vain.

Finally, with local troops lined up and brandishing rifles before the mob, President Davis arrived. Standing on a buggy, he got the crowd's attention, announced they had five minutes to disperse or be fired upon, and started looking at his watch.

The mob melted away.

War Department officials urged newspapers in the capital to say nothing about the unseemly incident, and ordered the telegraph service not to spread word of it.[7]

"Clio" was thus doing his civic duty when he made no mention of the bread riot. His letter to the *Intelligencer*, written on April 2, the day of the fracas, focused on discussions in the Confederate Congress. His missive of April 4 dealt with Lincoln and England. That of the 8th reflected upon a recent naval battle at Charleston, as did his article written from Richmond on April 11. His piece of the 13th was about the president's recent fast day proclamation. Only on April 16, two weeks after the riot, did "Clio" refer to "the miserable abortion of a riot which occurred here ten days ago"—and promptly dropped the subject. The *Intelligencer*, however, eventually picked up the story when Richmond newspapers, despite the War Department's urging, published details of the riot. In its article on April 9, the *Intelligencer* described Mary Jackson, a leader of the mob, as "a good specimen of a forty year Amazon, with the eye of the Devil."[8]

The Richmond "bread riot" was the most famous of a series of similar disturbances across the Confederacy in the spring of 1863, when women took the law into their own hands to obtain food for their families. In Georgia, bread riots took place in Augusta, Columbus and Macon. Atlanta had its own bread riot, too, as reported by the *Intelligencer* on March 19. The day before, a dozen women, soldiers' wives, had taken action. At least some of them were not poor; well-dressed, they displayed gold earrings and breast pins. Their chief complaint was directed against greedy merchants who were charging high prices for food. The group strode into a grocery store on Whitehall Street. Their leader, recognized as the wife of a shoemaker, asked the price for bacon. The merchant answered $1.10 a pound—when that very day in its weekly "ATLANTA PRICES CURRENT" column, the *Intelligencer* announced that bacon was going for seventy-five cents per pound. The group's leader declared that women could not afford such prices. The store owner refused to give in, whereupon the mob leader drew from her blouse a long Navy revolver, telling the other women to take what they wanted—which they did, grabbing up some $200 worth of meat. The city's marshal, Benjamin Williford, quickly arrived and sent the women home, promising to give them money for food if they returned the next day.

Some men watched as the women dispersed outside. They conversed, and learned of the ladies' complaints. The gentlemen were so moved, as the *Intelligencer* reported in its article on the "riot," that they pooled a sum of money and gave it to John Steele to disburse to the needy. In his article the editor invited "any wives or daughters of soldiers' families, who are in extreme want, to apply at the office of the Intelligencer, and they will receive a small amount for pressing necessities."[9]

After that, the paper's editor moved on to other news, including the addition of a new associate editor, Alexis E. Marshall. Steele had complimented Marshall as "the well-known and accomplished Stenographer" in November 1862, when he announced that Marshall would be reporting on the legislative session in Milledgeville. Then, suddenly, in the *Intelligencer*'s issue of March 20, 1863, there appeared in the paper's masthead on page two (under Jared I. Whitaker, proprietor, and John H. Steele, editor) "A. E. MARSHALL, ASSOCIATE EDITOR AND REPORTER." No article explained the new staff assignment. Maybe Marshall wanted a larger salary, and giving him a new title allowed such a raise. But his main job, at least during the session of the Georgia General Assembly, was to continue to send reports from Milledgeville (as he did about the legislature's first day, March 25).[10]

In early January 1863, the *Intelligencer* had informed readers that a subscription rate increase was on its way, due to "the *increased* prices of our paper manufactories, as well as the manufacturers and vendors of every article used in publishing a newspaper." The price hike, effective on January 15, raised a year's subscription to the *Daily Intelligencer* from $8 a year to $10—twenty-five percent more.

Without even an announcement or explanation, however, the front page of the *Intelligencer* on February 11 simply posted "OUR NEW RATES." Taking the daily for a year now cost $12 (another twenty percent more.) The *Intelligencer* had thus doubled its price from the annual subscription rate advertised at the start of the war ($6).

Even this was not enough. A paper mill in Bath, South Carolina (across the Savannah River from Augusta) was destroyed by fire in early April. The calamity—the mill was the largest in the Confederacy at the time—compelled the *Augusta Constitutionalist* to announce its possible suspension, or at least its reduction to a half sheet.

The *Intelligencer* cited the burning of the Bath paper plant as the chief reason, together with "increasing *demands* for paper," that it had to raise its subscription rates yet again on April 12—the third time in three months. More ominously as a predicter of still more rate increases, the *Intelligencer* announced that it would no longer take year-long subscriptions, but would sell the paper on three-month terms (as other Southern newspapers were also doing). The new pricing posted a three-month subscription at $5. Annualized, this would work out to be $20. In other words, the newspaper that started 1863 selling at $8 per year was now selling subscriptions at 250 percent of its start-of-the-year pricing.

And it was only April.

John Steele, the ever-sanguine newspaperman, tried to sugar-coat the bad news to readers. Directing them to the new price tables, he added that he was "trusting the time will soon come when we may be able to fall again to previous rates."[11]

We shall see.

NOTES

1. "The Legislature of Georgia Convened by Governor Brown," *ADI,* Mar. 12, 1863; Parks, *Joseph E. Brown,* 233, 236; "PLANT CORN," *ADI,* January 25; "THE WHEAT CROP—PLANT CORN," *ADI,* March 12; "THE LEGISLATURE TO BE CONVENED," *ADI,* March 13; "From Milledgeville" (March 25), *ADI,* March 27; "WHEAT CROP" and "THE CROPS," *ADI,* April 5.

2. "PROCLAMATION BY THE PRESIDENT," *ADI,* Mar. 5, 1863; "FRIDAY THE TWENTY-SEVENTH," *ADI,* March 25; "FAST DAY," "PROCLAMATION BY THE PRESIDENT," and "We republish the Proclamation ," *ADI,* March 27.

3. "CAMP ANECDOTES," *ADI,* Mar. 7, 1863; Jay Luvaas and Harold W. Nelson, eds., *The U.S. Army War College Guide to the Battles of Chancellorsville & Fredericksburg* (Carlisle PA: South Mountain Press, 1988), 327; James I. Robertson, *Soldiers Blue and Gray* (Columbia: University of South Carolina Press, 1988), 133.

4. "ASSUMING AND NEGLECTFUL," *ADI,* Mar. 24, 1863; "'OLD PAP' AND KIRBY SMITH," *ADI,* May 14.

5. "REPORTERS OF THE CONFEDERACY," *ADI,* Mar. 19, 1863; Andrews, *South Reports,* 548; "WAR CORRESPONDENTS," *ADI,* March 8; Dolan, "Samuel Chester Reid," 249, 256, 259; "From the Mobile Advertiser & Register. OUR ARMY CORRESPONDENCE—LETTER FROM CHARLESTON," *ADI,* March 8.

6. "OUR ARMY CORRESPONDENT, '290,'" *ADI,* Apr. 26, 1863; "290," "ARMY CORRESPONDENCE," *ADI,* April 21.

7. Douglas O. Tice, "'Bread or Blood!': The Richmond Bread Riot," *Civil War Times Illustrated*, vol. 12, no. 10 (February 1974), 12, 14; Emory M. Thomas, *The Confederate State of Richmond: A Biography of the Capital* (Baton Rouge: Louisiana State University Press, 1988 [1971]), 119–21; Ernest B. Furgurson, *Ashes of Glory: Richmond at War* (New York: Alfred A. Knopf, 1996), 193–94.

8. "CLIO," "Special Correspondence of the Atlanta Intelligencer. FROM RICHMOND" (April 2), *ADI*, Apr. 8, 1863; "FROM RICHMOND" (April 4), *ADI*, April 10; "FROM RICHMOND," (April 8), *ADI*, April 14; "FROM RICHMOND" (April 11), *ADI*, April 16; "FROM RICHMOND" (April 13), *ADI*, April 18; "FROM RICHMOND" (April 16), *ADI*, April 22; "THE RICHMOND RIOT," *ADI*, April 9.

9. Francis Butler Simkins and James Welch Patton, *The Women of the Confederacy* (Richmond: Garrett & Massie, 1936), 127; James Dabney McCabe, *The Grayjackets; and How They Lived, Fought and Died, for Dixie* (Dahlonega GA: Confederate Reprint Co., 2009 [1867]), 547–49; Emory M. Thomas, *The Confederate Nation 1861–1865* (New York: Harper & Row, 1979), 204–205; "THE WOMEN RISING," *ADI*, Apr. 5, 1863; "RELIEVE THE DISTRESSED" and "ATLANTA PRICES CURRENT," *ADI*, March 19; Venet, *Changing Wind*, 102–103; Coulter, *Confederate States of America*, 423.

10. "THE INTELLIGENCER—THE LEGISLATURE," *ADI*, Nov. 1, 1862; "Special Correspondence of the Atlanta Intelligencer. LEGISLATIVE PROCEEDINGS," March 29.

11. "ADVANCE IN NEWSPAPER RATES A NECESSITY" *ADI*, Jan. 4, 1863; "SUBSCRIPTION RATES OF THE 'DAILY INTELLIGENCER,'" *ADI*, January 8; "OUR NEW RATES," *ADI*, February 11; van Tuyll, *Confederate Press*, 185, 205; Risley, "Georgia's Confederate Newspapers," 145–46; "THE WANT OF PRINTING PAPER," *ADI*, April 9; "OUR NEW RATES FOR SUBSCRIPTION AND ADVERTISING" and "RATES OF SUBSCRIPTION," *ADI*, April 12; Risley, *Civil War Journalism*, 111.

23. Chancellorsville

PIECING TOGETHER A BATTLE NARRATIVE

IN LATE APRIL 1863, Maj. Gen. Joseph Hooker, who had succeeded Ambrose E. Burnside as commander of the Army of the Potomac, outmaneuvered Robert E. Lee by marching 75,000 men around the left flank of the Confederate army, which was quartered at Fredericksburg.

Lee left 10,000 men at Fredericksburg and with the rest, some 50,000, marched west to engage Hooker, who had crossed the Rappahannock River well upriver of Fredericksburg. On May 1 the Confederates encountered Hooker's forces east of a huge woodland called the Wilderness. Hooker lost his nerve and retired into the woods, pitching his headquarters in the village of Chancellorsville.

Possessing the initiative, Lee decided to attack after Confederate cavalry reported that the Federal right flank was "in the air," unprotected by cavalry and apparently unsuspecting of being attacked.

On the evening of May 1, Lee and Jackson planned a bold attack on the Federal right flank. Stonewall would lead more than half of Lee's troops, about 26,000 men, march a dozen miles through the Wilderness, deploy on the enemy flank and rear, then attack.

Jackson's assault was brilliantly successful. Commander of the Union XI Corps, Maj. Gen. Oliver O. Howard, dismissed intelligence that the Rebels were marching toward him. Around 5 p.m. on May 2, the Confederates overwhelmed Howard's troops, sending them running to the rear.

After sunset Jackson, determined to press his attack, reconnoitered ahead of his line. Returning, the general and his staff were mistaken by a regiment of North Carolinians, who fired a volley into them. Jackson was wounded three times, most seriously in his left arm. He was taken to a Confederate hospital where surgeons amputated the limb.

The next day Lee renewed his advance against Hooker's force, which retreated across the river on the night of May 5–6. Meanwhile his contingent at Fredericksburg had been pushed back by Maj Gen. John Sedgwick's VI Corps (some 40,000 men). Lee sent troops marching eastward and after an engagement at Salem Church, west of Fredericksburg on May 4, forced Sedgwick back across the Rappahannock.

Lee, according to military historians, had won his greatest victory. Outnumbered almost two-to-one, he had *twice* daringly divided his army, boldly showed fight before Hooker, cowed him into defensive position, then launched the most successful flank attack of the entire American civil war.

The cost had been high, though. Confederates lost 1,665 killed, 9,081 wounded and 2,108 missing: 12,764 all told. Federal casualties numbered 17,287 (1,606 killed, 9,762 wounded and 5,919 missing—mostly captured).

For the South, the worst blow was the loss of Stonewall Jackson. Eight days after his wounding, the general, beset by pneumonia, died on the afternoon of May 10.[1]

Historians have echoed these outlines, terming Chancellorsville Lee's greatest battle.[2] Lee, with 48,080 officers and men at Chancellorsville, had defeated an enemy twice his size (Hooker's 104,891).[3] Jackson had brilliantly crushed the Union XI Corps, attacking it in flank and rear, overwhelming it in detail.[4]

Scholars have similarly spoken in unison as to the calamitous impact of Thomas Jonathan Jackson's death upon the Confederacy. Longtime National Park Service historian Robert K. Krick has termed the North Carolinians' firing on Jackson's reconnaissance party "the smoothbore volley that doomed the Confederacy."[5]

Upon word of the general's death, Lee's soldiers were stunned. The tragic news cut short the celebration of their victory at Chancellorsville. "The sounds of merriment died away as if the Angel of Death himself had flapped his muffled wings over the troops," recalled one officer. Across the South, people grieved for a dead hero that almost all had only read about. Church bells tolled; newspapers published eulogies and reverential poetry in his honor. A hymn was even written about his last words.[6]

Stonewall's early biographers also reflected eulogistically on the man and his legend.[7] Those abroad joined in the praise, such as Englishman G. F. R. Henderson. The eulogistic tradition continues to modern biographies, which praise Jackson's military genius.[8]

Some have speculated on what might have been had that genius survived.

Others have even posited that if Jackson had not been struck down at Chancellorsville, Lee could even have destroyed the Army of the Potomac before the battle ended.[9] But Jackson had been struck down. Some of his biographers conclude their narratives of the hero's life and death by simply quoting his last words: "Let us cross over the river, and rest under the shade of the trees."[10]

Such is the story of the battle of Chancellorsville, May 1–4, 1863.

John Steele, in his *sanctum* at the *Intelligencer* offices, located at Whitehall Street and the downtown railroad, had neither the advantage nor luxury of such knowledge by hindsight.

Taking a look at daily issues of the newspaper, for the first two weeks of May, demonstrates the challenges faced by a Civil War newspaper editor as he labored to deliver important news to his readers.

FRIDAY, MAY 1 : "Clio," the *Intelligencer*'s special correspondent based in Richmond, did not see it coming. The newspaper this day printed his letter, written from the Confederate capital on April 17, which for the most part discussed the design for a Confederate Seal being discussed by a Senate committee (a motto, "Deo Vindice Vigent" seemed to have won out over another idea, "Deo Duce Vincemus"; a mounted George Washington would be the central image).

In the "BY TELEGRAPH" column on page three, the top dispatch related that a Northern tug boat, towing two barges, had run past the Confederate batteries at Vicksburg during the night.[11]

SATURDAY, MAY 2: Two items in the telegraphic news section offered portents of events to come.

From Richmond came a message, dated April 29, that "the Yankees have crossed the Rappahannock near Fredericksburg." Below it, in much larger type, ran the headline, "News from Fredericksburg. A Battle Imminent." The short article repeated that "the Yankees have crossed in force at points above and below Fredericksburg."

As for the imminent battle, the report concluded, "The troops are in fine spirits and ready for action."[12]

SUNDAY, MAY 3: The *Intelligencer*'s third page featured eight reports sent in by telegraph. Six had to do with events in Tennessee and Mississippi; one related to C.S. Congressional doings. Fourth in line, "STIRRING NEWS FROM THE RAPPAHANNOCK" (datelined Richmond, May 1) stated that enemy forces had crossed the river fifteen or twenty miles above Fredericksburg and were advancing on Chancellorsville. Brig. Gen. William Mahone's brigade attacked and repulsed them, the report claimed, without adding any detail other than "our loss slight."

Yankees who had crossed near Fredericksburg were digging in. "Both sides are preparing for a great battle."[13]

TUESDAY, MAY 5: The *Intelligencer*'s "BY TELEGRAPH" began with bold headlines celebrating an exploit of Confederate cavalryman Nathan Bedford Forrest in northern Alabama. News of a battle at Chancellorsville had yet to arrive.[14]

WEDNESDAY, MAY 6: This issue included another letter from "Clio," but because he had written on April 29, he had nothing to offer about the battle that was fought May 1–3 at Chancellorsville.

Train service from Richmond, however, brought to Steele's office the *Enquirer* of the 2nd, with the longest article yet (thirty-one lines) printed by the *Intelligencer* offering news "from the Rappahannock." The article mentioned fighting around Fredericksburg, but "Chancellorsville" was not mentioned.

In the *Intelligencer* of this day, also from the *Richmond Enquirer*, was a letter from "X.," dated May 1, written eight miles downriver from Fredericksburg. The correspondent, evidently one of the many Confederate soldiers who wrote to their local papers, sagely remarked, "the belief here, now, is that the battle will be fought above Fredericksburg, and in the vicinity of Chancellorsville. The crossing below town is in all probability a mere feint."

A telegraphed dispatch on page three, sent from Richmond on May 4, stated that "Gen. Jackson occupies all the fords except Ellis' ford and has taken 5,000 prisoners—more were coming in."

This brief report did not convey the key elements of information contained in General Lee's message to President Davis, which was also printed in the paper's telegraphic news space. Sent from his headquarters on May 4, Lee reported that Jackson's troops had gotten into the rear of the enemy's position, attacked and "drove him from all his positions from the Wilderness to within one mile of Chancellorsville." Then, the next morning, Lee's troops drove the enemy farther back toward the Rappahannock, "over which he is now retiring."

"I regret to state that General Paxton was killed," Lee concluded; "General Jackson was seriously, and Generals Heth and A. P. Hill slightly wounded."[15]

THURSDAY, MAY 7: "No further official dispatch was received from Gen. Lee's headquarters last night or this morning," began an undated item in the

Intelligencer's "BY TELEGRAPH" section, "but private telegrams announce that the victory is complete."

The same report disclosed that Gen. Jackson's arm had been amputated below the shoulder, and that the general was "doing well."

Also on page three was the dispatch that General Lee had sent the president. "At the close of the battle of Chancellorsville on Sunday," he had sent some of his troops to Fredericksburg "and succeeded, by the blessing of Heaven in driving Gen. Sedgmake [*sic:* Sedgwick] across the Rappahannock."[16]

FRIDAY, MAY 8: Under "Press Dispatches" was the headline, "Battle of Chancellorsville"—the first one giving the engagement that name (as opposed to "Fredericksburg").

The news was of such importance that on May 6 the *Richmond Dispatch* had issued an afternoon "extra" edition. From it came these particulars, as reported by the *Intelligencer* on the 8th: "may be regarded one of the bloodiest of the war"; heavy loss in officers and men; enemy entrenchments "carried by our troops"; many prisoners taken; Generals A. P. Hill, Heth and McGowan slightly wounded.[17]

SATURDAY, MAY 9: "CLIO"'s letter, written from Richmond on May 4, related that in its advance southward, General Hooker and his army had crossed the Rappahannock and marched to Chancellorsville. With his statement, "General Jackson, by ascending the Rappahannock, succeeded in getting into the rear of the enemy," "Clio" gave readers of the *Intelligencer* their first information about Stonewall Jackson's legendary flank attack, launched on the afternoon of May 2.

"Clio" mentioned that, according to reports, Jackson had captured 5,000 prisoners. From all of these sources he concluded, "there can be no doubt that our victory of yesterday was most complete and decisive."

The *Intelligencer* on the 9th also printed General Lee's message of May 7 to President Davis, relating that Hooker's army had taken a position on the north side of the Rappahannock that could not be successfully assailed.[18]

SUNDAY, MAY 10: Of nine articles in the paper's telegraphed news section, three related concerned Chancellorsville. "More Glorious News of the Late Battle" stated that "we have captured about ten thousand prisoners, many valuable horses, wagons, and a large quantity of ammunition and small arms"; also, "Sickles is reported killed." In "From Richmond" was the repeated conclusion, "our victory is a very decided one."

Longest of the three pieces printed in the *Intelligencer* on May 10 was the text of General Lee's order to his army, dated May 7, in which he declared, "a glorious victory entitles you to the praise and gratitude of the nation." Because by then everyone in the Army of Northern Virginia knew what had befallen Stonewall Jackson, Lee did not even have to refer to him by name when he wrote, "the army and the country alike lament the absence, for a time, of one to whose bravery, energy and skill so much is indebted for success."

Arrival by train of the *Richmond Examiner*'s issue of May 6 allowed the *Intelligencer* to present readers with details about the wounding of Stonewall Jackson. In the evening darkness on May 2, Jackson and his staff were scouting the enemy's position. "Whilst he was engaged in reconnoitering," the article stated, "his men being unaware of his movement, mistook himself and staff for enemies and fired a volley into them, instantly killing one of his staff and severely wounding General Jackson and Major Crutchfield."[19]

TUESDAY, MAY 12
THE DEATH OF GENERAL T. J. JACKSON

The telegraph on yesterday brought to us sad tidings. It tells us that the great and good JACKSON, the Christian soldier and patriot, is gone from Time to Eternity. The news of his death has cast a gloom over this community, as indeed it will over the whole land. The idol of the people and army, his memory will ever be cherished. Truly a great man has fallen. We are in no mood for eulogy now. Our sorrow is too deep to write of the virtues of the gallant hero who has fallen in his career of glory.

"He was man, take him for all in all,
We ne'er shall see his like again."
Peace to his ashes!

The *Intelligencer* did not publish on Mondays, so John Steele had to wait till Tuesday morning's issue to announce the news that the telegraph had brought of Stonewall Jackson's death. The wires brought few details. "Gov. Letcher received a dispatch this p.m.," began a short item in the paper's telegraphic column (datelined, Richmond, May 10), "announcing the death of Gen. Jackson, at Guinea's, at 3.50 p.m. He died from the combined effects of his wound and an attack of pneumonia. His body will be brought to this city to-morrow by special train."[20]

Other articles in the *Intelligencer*'s issue of May 12 rounded out the story of the battle of Chancellorsville. Editor Steele reprinted a long piece from the *Richmond Examiner* of the 7th. "Our loss in killed, wounded and missing is roughly estimated at ten thousand," the *Examiner* reported. "Clio," drawing on the talk in Richmond for his letter printed in the *Intelligencer* on the 12th (written on May 7), echoed, "our losses have been very heavy. From eight to ten thousand of our brave countrymen are reckoned among the killed, wounded and missing."

Among those casualties was Samuel H. Whitaker of the 10th Georgia—brother of Jared Whitaker, the *Intelligencer*'s owner. A chilling telegram had arrived from Richmond, "To Col. J. I. Whitaker: Your brother is here mortally wounded. J. T. CRAWFORD." Indeed, twenty-two-year-old Samuel Whitaker of Co. I, 10th Georgia, had been wounded on May 3. After amputation of his left arm he had been taken to the general hospital located in Seabrook's Warehouse on Grace Street in the capital. There he died.

More chilling still was the fact that the owner of the *Intelligencer* had already lost two other brothers in the war. Richard Whitaker, who had enlisted as a private in Co. E, 13th Georgia in July 1861, died of illness in Virginia three months later. Another brother, Edwin, had joined up with the 10th Texas; he died at Grenada, Miss. in 1862.[21]

WEDNESDAY, MAY 13: With the people of the Confederacy mourning the death of their national hero, details of the battle of Chancellorsville seemed of secondary importance. But they kept coming in, and the *Intelligencer* on May 13 printed a good number of them.

Steele had gotten his Richmond exchanges, and from them gleaned more estimates of casualties in Lee's forces. The *Examiner* reported that army surgeons counted 800 killed, 7,000 wounded and 1,200 missing, for a "total of 9,000." "The estimate is said to be liberal," though, the editor added, "and it is believed the actual loss will fall below, rather than exceed that sum."

The *Richmond Enquirer* was similarly hopeful, judging that Confederate losses would reach 8,000. The *Enquirer*'s correspondent noted that many soldiers had been only slightly wounded "and will soon be fit for duty."

A long article about the battle, written by "X," a correspondent for the *Richmond Enquirer*, took up two of the five long columns on page three. The *Intelligencer* had its own correspondents, to be sure. "290" (Samuel Chester Reid), writing on May 6, described the excitement among Richmond residents caused by a Yankee cavalry raid nearby. Another writer, having arrived in the capital from Atlanta, related the people's rejoicing over General Lee's victory.

These accounts, though, were over a week old. More immediate were the telegraphed items arriving from Richmond. A dispatch of May 11 mentioned that the special train bearing Jackson's body from Guiney Station had arrived, met by solemn military escort and a crowd of mourners. The general's remains were to lie in state at the capitol for a day before being transported to his home town of Lexington in the Shenandoah Valley. In the same column appeared the text of General Lee's announcement to his army of the great Stonewall's death. "The daring skill and energy of this great and good man, by the decree of Almighty Providence, is now lost to us," he lamented.

Amidst these doleful dispatches, the *Intelligencer* tried to inject something positive. "Let us, then, not so much mourn his loss," the paper enjoined its readers, "as return thanks to God for his presence so long among us."[22]

The *Intelligencer* would continue to report on the battle of Chancellorsville throughout the remainder of May, 1863, and beyond. But its sources would remain the same.

Exchanges were vital, especially the Richmond papers. On May 14 Steele announced that on the morrow he would publish a long and detailed account of Chancellorsville. "Thus far the accounts of that great battle received through the Richmond papers have been rather meagre," he observed. The *Enquirer* of May 11, however, promised to change that; Steele devoted nearly three-fourths of a page to the long article.

Other papers could be helpful as well. From the *Augusta Chronicle & Sentinel* the *Intelligencer* reprinted an account of Georgia regiments in the big battle—and on the front page, no less. The distant *Lynchburg Republican* allowed John Steele to educate his readers on the location of the battlefield in central Virginia. Even Northern papers making their way to Steele's *sanctum* offered at least filler, if not reliable news. The *New York Tribune*'s account of Chancellorsville occupied nearly two columns in the *Intelligencer* of May 23.[23]

Field correspondents had the advantage of being able to write at length in their letters, which balanced the disadvantage of the time it took (a week or so) for their mailed missives to reach their destination and be set into print. Between May 9 and May 25, "Clio" wrote the *Intelligencer* fully seven letters. "290," less prolific, sent a long one as "army correspondence" under the date of May 20; Steele editorialized on its delayed arrival. Occasional correspondents also contributed pieces, such as Lieutenant Colonel Neal of the 19th Georgia.[24]

Even with exchanges, reporters in the field, soldier correspondents at the front and official dispatches from both the government and the army, the *Intelligencer*'s accounting of the battle of Chancellorsville was, to say the least, spotty and uneven. With good reason, then, does Prof. Ford Risley judge that

"Chancellorsville was one of the most poorly reported battles of the entire war from the Confederate perspective."[25]

"Old Stonewall," however, was the story that would not quit. The *Intelligencer* of May 14 reported on the funeral procession in Richmond, where on the 12th President Davis, his cabinet members and other dignitaries "marched to solemn music" as the general's body was conveyed to the Hall of Congress. Jackson's last words, according to an early report—"TELL MAJOR HAWKES TO SEND FORWARD PROVISIONS FOR THE MEN!"—became the topic for a long, reverent editorial (Wells J. Hawks was Jackson's commissary officer). When the general's remains arrived at Lexington for burial in the town cemetery, that made the news as well. The *Intelligencer* of May 23 reported on Jackson's body lying in state and on the funeral procession. "Guns were fired every half hour during the day in honor of the departed chieftain," the article stated, "and an air of gloom was visible on every face." As late as May 29, the *Intelligencer* was still quoting Jackson's last words: "Let us cross the river, and rest under the shade of the trees."[26]

This did not end the story, however, as the *Intelligencer* would continue to print articles about Stonewall for months to come.

NOTES

1. Jeffry D. Wert, "Chancellorsville Campaign" and "Battle of Chancellorsville" in Patricia L. Faust, ed., *The Historical Times Illustrated Encyclopedia of the Civil War* (New York: Harper & Row, 1986), 126–29.

2. Edward J. Stackpole, *Chancellorsville: Lee's Greatest Battle* (Harrisburg PA: Stackpole Co., 1958), 361.

3. Jay Luvaas and Harold W. Nelson, eds., *The U.S. Army War College Guide to the Battles of Chancellorsville & Fredericksburg* (Carlisle PA: South Mountain Press, 1988), 349; Samuel P. Bates, *The Battle of Chancellorsville* (Gaithersburg MD: Ron R. Van Sickle Military Books, 1987 [1882]), 199.

4. Augustus C. Hamlin, *The Attack of Stonewall Jackson at Chancellorsville* (Fredericksburg VA: Sergeant Kirkland's 1997 [1896]), 127.

5. Robert K. Krick, "The Smoothbore Volley That Doomed the Confederacy" in Gary W. Gallagher, ed., *Chancellorsville: The Battle and Its Aftermath* (Chapel Hill: University of North Carolina Press, 1996), 134.

6. S. C. Gwynne, *Rebel Yell: The Violence, Passion, and Redemption of Stonewall Jackson* (New York: Scribner, 2014), 552; Ernest B. Furgurson, *Chancellorsville 1863: The Souls of the Brave* (New York: Alfred A. Knopf, 1992), 343; Byron Falwell: *Stonewall: A Biography of General Thomas J. Jackson* (New York: W. W. Norton, 1992), 530; Davis, *Maryland, My Maryland*, 185.

7. [John Esten Cooke], *The Life of Stonewall Jackson* (New York: Charles B. Richardson,

1864 [1863]), 271; R. L. Dabney, *Life and Campaigns of Lieut.-Gen. Thomas J. Jackson, (Stonewall)* (New York: Blelock & Co., 1866), 735.

8. G. F. R. Henderson, *Stonewall Jackson and the American Civil War* (New York: David McKay, 1961 [1898]), 701; Lenoir Chambers, *Stonewall Jackson*, 2 vols. (New York: William Morrow, 1959), vol. 2, 460.

9. Bevin Alexander, *Lost Victories: The Military Genius of Stonewall Jackson* (New York: Henry Holt, 1992), 334.

10. Frank Vandiver, *Mighty Stonewall* (New York: McGraw-Hill, 1957), 494; Allen Tate, *Stonewall Jackson, the Good Soldier: A Narrative* (New York: Minton, Balch, 1928), 316; Jack I. Brown, *The Shade of the Trees: A Narrative Based on the Life and Career of Lieutenant General Thomas Jonathan "Stonewall" Jackson* (Great Neck NY: Todd & Honeywell, 1988), 195; John Bowers, *Stonewall Jackson: Portrait of a Soldier* (New York: William Morrow, 1989), 355.

11. "CLIO," "FROM RICHMOND" (April 27) and "From Vicksburg" (April 27), *ADI*, May 1, 1863.

12. "Yankees Crossed Rappahannock" and "News from Fredericksburg. A Battle Imminent," *ADI*, May 2, 1863.

13. "Stirring News from the Rappahannock," *ADI*, May 3, 1863.

14. "GLORIOUS NEWS," *ADI*, May 5, 1863.

15. "CLIO," "FROM RICHMOND" (April 29); "From the Richmond Enquirer, 2d inst. FROM THE RAPPAHANNOCK"; "X," CORRESPONDENCE OF THE ENQUIRER"; "Battle at Fredericksburg—5,000 Prisoners Taken"; "Press Dispatches. Further from Fredericksburg . . . . GEN. LEE'S OFFICIAL REPORT" and "FIGHTING AT FREDERICKSBURG," all in *ADI*, May 6, 1863.

16. "Further from Fredericksburg" and "Official Dispatch of Gen. Lee," *ADI*, May 7, 1863.

17. "Press Dispatches. Battle of Chancellorsville," *ADI*, May 8, 1863.

18. "CLIO," "FROM RICHMOND" (May 4) and "Later from Fredericksburg," *ADI*, May 9, 1863.

19. "More Glorious News of the Late Battle"; "From Richmond"; Address of Gen. Lee to the Army"; "OLD STONEWALL" and "THE BATTLE ON THE RAPPAHANNOCK," *ADI*, May 10, 1863.

20. "THE DEATH OF GENERAL T. J. JACKSON" and "Press Dispatches. . . . STONEWALL JACKSON DEAD," *ADI*, May 12, 1863.

21. "From the Richmond Examiner, May 7. FROM FREDERICKSBURG," "CLIO," "FROM RICHMOND" (May 7) and "Private Dispatch," *ADI*, May 12, 1863; "FIFTY-SIXTH GEORGIA," *ADI*, June 9, 1863.

22. "OUR LOSSES IN THE LATE BATTLES"; "Casualties in the Second Georgia Battalion"; "The Fourth Georgia"; "We regret to learn. . . ."; "X," "From the Richmond Enquirer. THE BATTLES OF CHANCELLORSVILLE AND FREDERICKSBURG"; "FROM '290' AT RICHMOND" (May 6); "LETTER FROM RICHMOND" (May 5); "Jackson's Remains" (Richmond, May 11) and "STONEWALL JACKSON," *ADI*, May 13, 1863.

23. "DETAILED ACCOUNTS OF THE BATTLE OF CHANCELLORSVILLE," *ADI*, May 15, 1863; "From the Richmond Enquirer. THE BATTLES AROUND FREDERICKSBURG," *ADI*, May 16; "GEORGIA REGIMENTS IN THE LATER BATTLES"

and "THE LOCATION OF THE LATE BATTLE FIELD," *ADI*, May 14; "THE NEW YORK TRIBUNE ON HOOKER'S DEFEAT," *ADI*, May 23.

24. "CLIO" letters in *ADI*, May 14, May 17, May 20, May 22, May 24, May 27 and May 31, 1863; "290" and "ARMY CORRESPONDENCE," *ADI*, May 30; "THE BATTLE ON THE RAPPAHANNOCK," *ADI*, May 14.

25. Risley, "Georgia's Confederate Newspapers," 152.

26. "Funeral of Gen. Jackson," *ADI*, May 14, 1863; "'SEND FORWARD PROVISIONS FOR THE MEN,'" *ADI*, May 21; "GENERAL JACKSON'S REMAINS AT LEXINGTON," *ADI*, May 23; "FURTHER PARTICULARS OF THE LAST MOMENTS OF GEN. JACKSON—HIS RELIGIOUS CHARACTER," *ADI*, May 29.

24. The Running Down of Streight

GLORIOUS NEWS!
THE WHOLE YANKEE FORCE
CAPTURED.
Rome Out of Danger.
Three Cheers for Forrest.
The Enemy 2,000 Strong.
&c. &c. &c. &c.

MARIETTA, May 4. The latest news from Rome states that the citizens met, fought, and checked the enemy near Rome. Forrest is in their rear, and, it is thought, will capture the whole party.

ETOWAH, May 4—Gen. Forrest has captured the whole force, near two thousand strong.[1]

THIS WAS THE FIRST INKLING of information that readers of the *Atlanta Daily Intelligencer* received about a major military event to their northwest. Confederate Brig. Gen. Nathan Bedford Forrest had run down and captured a Union mounted force.

The operation was called Streight's Raid.

On March 5, 1863, Col. Abel Streight, an officer in Union Maj. Gen. William S. Rosecrans' Army of the Cumberland, volunteered to lead a mounted force on a raid into Confederate territory. Streight himself was not a cavalryman; he was serving at the time as commander of the 51st Indiana Infantry. After Rosecrans approved the proposed raid, Streight was put in charge of four midwestern infantry regiments, some 1,700 men, and was provided with mules, not horses (which were in short supply). His orders were to ride through north Alabama into northwest Georgia, head for the Western & Atlantic Railroad between Chattanooga and Atlanta, cut the railway, then get back as best as he could. Even his superiors, however, were not sanguine as to the latter part of the plan. "Should you be surrounded by rebel forces and your retreat cut off," his orders read, "defend yourself as long as possible and make the surrender of your command cost the enemy as many of their number as possible."[2]

On April 26, Streight and his command left Tuscumbia in northwest Alabama, riding southeast. Within a few days Forrest was in pursuit, albeit with a force much smaller than Streight's. On April 30, the Confederates began skirmishing with the Federals twenty miles south of Decatur, Alabama. Streight disengaged and continued riding eastward. Forrest pursued, telling his men, "shoot at everything blue and keep up the scare."[3]

They did, in essentially a running fight for the next four days. With some 600 troops dogging Streight's rearguard, Forrest sent a warning ahead to Rome in northwest Georgia: "a Federal Force of Fifteen Hundred cavalry [is] Marching on your place I am pressing them they air running for their lives."

Forrest was correct: Streight and his men *were* running for their lives. They were exhausted from all-night marches and depleted in number by the constant fighting. Most of their ammunition had been ruined in botched stream crossings, and Forrest showed no sign of relenting on "the scare." Streight had no choice, though, but to keep on riding. He sent forward some 200 of his men to take and hold the bridge across the Coosa River near Rome.

Yet about twenty miles west of Rome, when Forrest sent an officer under a truce flag to propose that the Federals surrender, Streight agreed. He believed that Forrest had a larger force than his (when in fact it was less than half in size). When counted, 1,466 Union prisoners fell into Confederate hands, to whom were soon added another 200, the detachment Streight had sent ahead toward Rome.[4]

This was the "brilliant exploit" that the *Intelligencer* related to its readers on May 6. Editor John Steele called it "absolutely marvelous" and "a brilliant and dashing affair." Forrest had bagged a bunch of "Yankee scoundrels," Steele averred. "These marauding rascals," the editor charged, "these devils in human shape" had ridden toward Georgia "to devastate the country, to capture and destroy Rome, Atlanta, and such bridges on the State Road, as would interfere with transportation, if not effectually to prevent it."[5]

With these as the enemy's objectives, Atlantans joined the citizenry of Rome in thanking Forrest. Steele announced on May 10 that there had begun a fundraising effort in the city for money enough to buy and present the general with a fine steed. In "A HORSE FOR GEN. FORREST," the editor informed readers that they could come by the *Intelligencer* office and sign up as contributors. Two months later, Steele announced that Atlantans had raised $2,000 to buy a horse for Forrest, and another $1,200 for an elaborate saddle, bridle and halter. The editor expressed his hope that the general would soon be riding "Highlander," the "splendid charger."

(Steele would get his wish. Forrest was riding Highlander at the time, September 1863, of the north Georgia battle of Chickamauga, which resulted in the Confederate army driving the Federals from the field. On September 21, the day after the battle, Forrest's cavalry was pursuing the retreating enemy. The Confederates encountered Union horsemen, and in the fight Highlander was shot in the neck. In one of the most famous exploits of the war, Forrest reached forward and stuck his finger in his horse's wound till he could remove his finger and dismount. Highlander then dropped dead.)

For its part, the City Council passed a resolution of thanks to Forrest and extended a warm welcome to him whenever he should visit the city. At the same council meeting, held on May 8, the city fathers issued another call for Atlantans to organize more companies for local defense in case the Yankees staged another threatening raid.[6]

Southerners could celebrate the triumph of Confederate cavalry over Col. Abel Streight, but they had nothing to celebrate about the Confederate cavalry's response to another Union raid in the spring of 1863—that of Col. Benjamin Grierson.

In late March, Federal leaders planned a cavalry raid out of southwest Tennessee through Mississippi to strike the Southern rail line running west-east from Vicksburg to Meridian. When the Northern commander in Memphis planning the operation, Maj. Gen. Stephen A. Hurlbut, learned that General Rosecrans was planning to do the same thing (Streight's raid against the W. & A. in Georgia,), the two generals coordinated their operations for about the same launch date in order to distract and disperse the Confederate cavalry.

Colonel Grierson rode out of LaGrange, Tenn. with 1,700 troopers on April 17. Confederates went after a diversionary force sent out by Grierson, allowing him to proceed on much of his raid without opposition. He cut the railroad at Newton Station, seventy-five miles east of Jackson, and continued south. Confederate cavalry had started after him, but Grierson eluded them. He arrived at Baton Rouge, La., after a 600 mile-long ride on May 2.[7]

In the pages of the *Intelligencer* during May 1863, Grierson's cavalry raid was overshadowed by news of the murder of Confederate Maj. Gen. Earl Van Dorn.

Van Dorn, a Confederate cavalry commander in Braxton Bragg's army, was a ladies' man. He was also a husband and father, which does not explain why in the spring of 1863 he enjoyed the company of Jessie Peters, wife of George B. Peters, a physician in Bolivar, Tenn. Dr. Peters heard tales of a more than casual relationship between his wife and the general. On May 7, 1863, he walked into Van Dorn's headquarters and shot and killed the general as he was sitting at his desk.[8]

"General Van Dorn Killed," read the headline of the lead article in the *Intelligencer*'s "BY TELEGRAPH" section on May 9. But the news of the general's death came from an unusual source. Van Dorn's aide-de-camp had wired Colonel Lee, post commandant at Atlanta, "Can you send quickly a metallic coffin for the remains of General Van Dorn. Length five feet ten inches. Answer." Editor Steele added that he was able to announce Van Dorn's death because Lee had shared the telegraphic coffin request. Further down the column was another wired item declaring "General Van Dorn was murdered by Dr. Peters."[9]

Sensational murders provided variety for readers of the *Intelligencer*, while providing editor Steele with filler for his paper. Advertising, to be sure, was the largest consumer of column space in the newspaper. Pages 1 and 4 continued to be the usual placement for ads. On the back page of the issue for May 7, 1863, was to be seen the announcement that J. W. Birth had reopened the ambrotype and photograph gallery that before the war had been operated by C. W. Dill. On the front page for May 16, the Confederate Shoe Blacking Company on Whitehall Street promoted "a very superior article"; Singer sewing machines, as announced by another notice, could be purchased in a store "at No. 7, Cherokee Block, over McLendon's store" northeast of Marietta and Peachtree streets.[10]

One of the largest advertisers in the *Intelligencer* was "CRAWFORD, FRAZER & CO., GENERAL COMMISSION MERCHANTS, AUCTIONEERS AND DEALERS IN NEGROES, No. '8,' Whitehall Street, OPPOSITE INTELLIGENCER OFFICE," as it announced in its ad of May 15. "Our NEGRO YARD AND LOCK-UP, at No. 8, are SAFE AND COMFORTABLE. DEALERS and other parties will find us prepared to FEED and LODGE WELL (and FROM EXPERIENCE IN THE BUSINESS SINCE OUR BOYHOOD,) To Handle the Negro Properly." Evidently, being in the slave-selling business since boyhood did not disqualify one for public office; Robert Crawford was elected to the Atlanta City Council and other offices throughout the 1850s and '60s.

In the *Intelligencer* of May 2, 1863, big ads for Crawford, Frazer appeared on pages one and three. In the latter, the firm further explained its business. "Our stock of negroes is replenished every day," it announced, "and no assortment south of Richmond is kept more complete." The merchants made clear that they took good care of their merchandise: "sleeping apartments and cook house" were "closely looked after" so that "our stock is thereby kept in health."

There was plenty of it, as the ad listed by name (first only) and principal proficiency fully seventy-one African Americans. Fifty of them were field hands or "plough boys," which meant that buyers would be taking them to country plantations or farms. Five were house servants; another four were listed as "house girl & nurse." A few males had special skills as blacksmith, carpenter or wagoner. Among the women, eight had experience as seamstresses, two as cooks and one as dress maker. The listing mentioned that eight women had altogether fourteen children, ages not mentioned.[11]

The high prices that people were willing to pay for slaves attested as much to their confidence in the future of the South's "peculiar institution"—in the midst of war and the Emancipation Proclamation—as to their need for labor. On April 15, the *Intelligencer* stated that on the day before, Crawford, Frazer had auctioned away "a likely waiter" for $3,500 and "a likely maid servant" for $3,000. Even a nine-year-old boy fetched $2,150. The editor commented that "this working and enterprising house has accomplished its full share in bringing Atlanta almost up to Richmond as a negro mart." He added a plug for his generous advertiser ("liberal to the press," he wrote elsewhere): "Call, if you want to buy or sell negroes, and, our word for it, you will find 'all right.'"[12]

The numerous advertisements that completely filled the front pages at the start of the war began to give way to news reports and other articles halfway through the conflict. A letter from Samuel Reid/"290," a citizen's letter urging the election of a congressional candidate, an opinion piece on Confederate bonds, a column from the *Augusta Chronicle & Sentinel* about the forthcoming Georgia governor's election, news of the fall of Jackson, Miss. and of a Confederate cavalry raid, plus an update on the Cotton Spinners' convention held recently in Atlanta: all of this was crowded into three of the five columns on the front page of the paper on Thursday, May 21.[13]

The front page also occasionally carried a poignant story; such was that of the execution of Pvt. Jacob Adams, a deserter from the 46th Georgia. As reported by the *Charleston Courier,* and picked up by John Steele, on May 18 Private Adams was executed at the race course outside of Charleston. Confederate troops and the city garrison were formed under arms to witness the event; a crowd of citizens also gathered to watch.

The scene was very solemn and imposing. The unfortunate man was marched into the hollow square, the band playing the dead march. As he entered the square the music of his escort ceased, and the several bands of the various commands, as the prisoner approached the sides of the square, took up the funeral strain successively.

Adams bore himself with great intrepidity, and arriving at the fatal spot he received the last consolations of religion from the Rev. Father Leon Fillion. Then left to himself he knelt upon his coffin, crossed his arms, and suddenly looking up, took off his hat and threw it composedly to the right. He refused to have his eyes bandaged, and looking at the execution party full in the face, awaited the order to fire with apparent perfect calmness. The order was given—there was a flash, a report, and Adams lay prostrate upon the ground dead. The Surgeon examined the body and pronounced it lifeless.

"The execution was an awful but necessary infliction of military justice," the *Courier* story concluded. The writer added that all the soldiers who had been brought out to witness the execution, especially anyone secretly pondering slipping from the ranks, "will be returned to their regiments wiser men."[14]

Newspaper articles about the Charleston execution—printed as far away as in London, Liverpool and Glasgow—plus Adams' compiled service record in Washington fill in his background. An Englishman, he had deserted from the British army, was caught and branded with a "D." After emigration to America he had enlisted for a year's service in the 1st South Carolina Infantry. Adams was arrested, according to the Confederate assistant adjutant general in Charleston, "for attempting to murder a comrade and for other breaches of discipline." Sentenced to death, Adams was spared by President Davis, who commuted his penalty to imprisonment with ball and chain for the rest of his term of service.

Jacob Adams was a rough fellow. During his imprisonment "he several times attempted to murder people though heavily ironed," the A. A. G. stated. He was also a bounty jumper—one who enlisted, collected his bounty (financial reward for volunteering), then deserted. When he was released from jail, on Sept. 6, 1862 he joined the 46th Georgia, which was stationed at Charleston. In October he deserted, was caught, tried and sentenced to execution. This time the punishment was carried out, though not before Adams spent seven months in a Charleston jail.

Adams was one of 103,400 Confederate deserters during the war. Through the efforts of Robert E. Lee and others, most men caught absent without leave were given lenient sentences. Indeed, only 229 Confederate deserters were executed between December 1861 and the end of the war. Like Jacob Adams, 204 were killed by firing squad (25 by hanging).[15]

Private Adams was executed on May 18, 1863, the time when war news in the *Intelligencer* was dominated by the battle of Chancellorsville. About the same time a steady stream of news came to John Steele's *sanctum* from a different theater of war: Mississippi.

After the fall of Baton Rouge and Natchez in May 1862, Federal naval vessels had steamed upriver and shelled the town of Vicksburg. The *Intelligencer* reported the incident, in which Confederate batteries on the 200 hundred-foot cliffs had fired back. The Southern guns were so high that Union cannon could not reach them. Instead, the Confederates' plunging fire forced the Northern ships to retire downriver.

The Union drive against Vicksburg resumed six months later, this time from the fortress' land side. Maj. Gen. Ulysses S. Grant, commanding the Union Army of the Tennessee, then deployed in southwestern Tennessee, devised a two-pronged advance against Vicksburg in December 1862. He sent Maj. Gen. William T. Sherman with 32,000 troops down the Mississippi by boat to land near Vicksburg and attack it. With the rest of his forces, Grant marched from Grand Junction, Tenn. (fifty miles east of Memphis) southward into Mississippi as a diversion in favor of Sherman.

Confederate cavalry, however, proved to be Grant's undoing. In western Tennessee, Dec. 20–21, Brig. Gen. Nathan Bedford Forrest led his troopers upon the Mobile & Ohio Railroad, which served as Grant's rail supply line, tearing up track and burning bridges between Humboldt and Union City.

Then, on December 20, Maj. Gen. Earl Van Dorn's horsemen rode into Holly Springs, Miss., Grant's supply depot, and set fire to $1.5 million worth of Northern army supplies. The combined effect of the two raids compelled Grant to retreat back into southwest Tennessee.

Sherman also suffered reverse. On December 29, his troops attacked Confederate forces northwest of Vicksburg at Chickasaw Bluffs and were soundly repulsed by Lt. Gen. John C. Pemberton's 15,000.[16]

The *Intelligencer* did its best to follow these events, based upon the telegraphic news it received. On December 25, the paper ran the headline "Grant's Army Falling Back," the first inkling that Southern forces had secured some kind of success. The *Intelligencer* shared Mississippians' initial exultation. "Van Dorn's attack upon Holly Springs . . . was a complete success," the paper declared on

December 27. It correctly reported $1.5 million worth of supplies destroyed, but inaccurately stated, "Gen. Grant barely escaped capture"; Grant was not at Holly Springs, whose garrison had been surrendered by a subordinate officer. Another dispatch correctly reported that Van Dorn had captured 1,500 prisoners. Yet with its assertion that "at last accounts Grant was skedaddling as fast as possible," the dispatch, sent from Mobile on December 21, was exaggerating in the usual manner of the Confederate press.[17]

Forrest's contribution to Grant's supply problems did not go unreported. "On the 19th Forrest destroyed the Rail Road communications near Hemholt [sic: Humboldt, Tenn.] cutting off the Yankee supplies," the *Intelligencer* announced on December 30. The next day it added that "Forrest . . . has been tearing up Railroad tracks and doing good service generally."[18]

When the 1863 spring campaign season arrived, Grant resumed his plans to capture Vicksburg. The previous December he had tried the overland route through Mississippi; Sherman had attempted a direct attack from across the river. Both had failed. Grant therefore adopted a new approach: he would march down the west side of the Mississippi, cross over with help from Adm. David Porter's river fleet, march into the interior of Mississippi, then head west so as to advance on Vicksburg from the east. This he did starting on April 30, crossing the river with 22,000 men of Maj Gen. John A. McClernand's XIII Corps and Maj. Gen. James B. McPherson's XVII Corps (Maj. Gen. William T. Sherman's XV Corps would later join them). On the morning of May 1 at Port Gibson, some ten miles east of their river crossing point, the Federals encountered fewer than 7,000 Confederates under Brig. Gen. John S. Bowen. The Northerners launched a series of attacks that by the end of the day forced the Confederates to retreat. Casualties in this small battle totaled 875 for the Federals (131 killed, 719 wounded, 25 missing) and 832 for the Confederates (68 killed, 380 wounded, 384 missing/presumed captured). Among the dead was Brig. Gen. Edward D. Tracy—the first of three Confederate generals to die in the Vicksburg Campaign.[19]

Yet actual reporting of Port Gibson and ensuing events in Mississippi was scanty. "An extra, from the [Jackson] Mississippian office, says General Bowen fell back from his position," the *Intelligencer* stated on May 6, "having been attacked by overwhelming numbers and out-flanked."[20]

After the Federal victory on May 1, General Pemberton, the Confederate commander in Mississippi, expected Grant to march north along the river, directly toward Vicksburg. He was surprised and confused when the Union army marched northeast toward Jackson. It was more than a week before the Atlanta newspaper could offer any information on Grant's advance. From Jackson, dated May 13, a report came of another small battle at Raymond, fought the day before. Once again, the Federals attacked and again the outnumbered Confederates retreated. The *Intelligencer* of May 19 declared that Federal forces had captured Jackson, the capital of Mississippi on May 14. "Our forces, under General Johnston, fell back before them towards Canton," it announced, which was true. Joseph E. Johnston, having recovered from his wound incurred in May 1862, had been placed by President Davis in command of a "Department of the West" six months later. As Grant marched through Mississippi, the Confederate government assembled about 6,000 troops at the capital, but as Grant's army advanced, Johnston evacuated the city and marched northward.[21]

Grant had now gotten his army of 32,000 between Pemberton's and Johnston's forces. After torching railroad facilities and factories in Jackson, he headed west toward Vicksburg. Pemberton marched east with some 23,000 troops to meet him. In battle at Champion's Hill on May 16, the two clashed amid Federal attacks and Confederate counterattacks. At the end of the day, Pemberton retreated to his Vicksburg defenses, having lost 3,840 men (381 killed, 1,018 wounded and 2,441 missing) to Grant's 2,441 (410K; 1,844W; 187M). Adding to the sting of their defeat, the Southerners left twenty-seven pieces of artillery on the field. Grant pursued the next day as Confederates attempted a stalling action at Big Black River. There, too, they were mauled, losing 1,752 men captured and eighteen more cannon. On May 18, Grant's troops made their first contact with Pemberton's Vicksburg garrison.[22]

"Rumors, good and bad, are plentiful," declared a telegram from Mobile dated May 18 and printed in the *Intelligencer* on the 21st. The dispatch related that "in Saturday's fight [May 16 at Champion's Hill] their loss was six thousand, and that they took sixteen of our guns." The article also stated, "our forces fell back across the Big Black destroying the bridge. . . . our advices say no artillery was lost," and that the Confederates engaged "sustained themselves, and fell back at night to our entrenchments." Another wire, this one from Jackson, sent on May 18 and printed in the *Intelligencer* on May 23, reported that at Champion's Hill General Lloyd Tilghman had been killed, and that Pemberton's army was falling back across the Big Black River.

In that same issue of the 23rd came this ominous news: "Vicksburg is closely besieged. The enemy is closing in on every side."[23] Yet the *Intelligencer*, and the Confederate press as a whole, evinced no awareness or foreboding that in less than a month Grant had beaten and cowed Confederate forces in Mississippi and was closing in on Vicksburg with a rapidity that portended the fall of the river fortress.

NOTES

1. "GLORIOUS NEWS," *ADI,* May 5, 1863.
2. Brandon H. Beck, *Streight's Foiled Raid on the Western & Atlantic Railroad: Emma Sansom's Courage and Nathan Bedford Forrest's Pursuit* (Charleston SC: History Press, 2016), 29, 39, 42–43; Edward G. Longacre, *Mounted Raids of the Civil War* (Lincoln: University of Nebraska Press, 1994 [1975]), 67.
3. Beck, *Streight's Raid,* 46, 50, 53, 56–57; Robert Selph Henry, *"First With the Most" Forrest* (Jackson TN: McCowat-Mercer Press, 1969 [1944]), 146–48.
4. Beck, *Streight's Raid,* 59, 73–76; Jack Hurst, *Nathan Bedford Forrest: A Biography* (New York: Alfred A. Knopf, 1993), 122–24.
5. "Official Account of General Forrest's Brilliant Exploit," "MORE GLORIOUS NEWS!" and "FORREST AND HIS MEN," *ADI,* May 6, 1863; "THE LATE RAID OF THE ENEMY INTO GEORGIA—ITS OBJECT," *ADI,* May 8.
6. "A HORSE FOR GEN. FORREST" and "COUNCIL PROCEEDINGS," *ADI,* May 10, 1863; "MAGNIFICENT PRESENT TO GEN. FORREST," *ADI,* July 14; J. D. R. Hawkins, *Horses in Gray: Famous Confederate Warhorses* (Gretna LA: Pelican Publishing Co., 2017), 77.
7. Edwin C. Bearss, "Grierson's Raid" in Patricia L. Faust, ed., *The Historical Times Illustrated Encyclopedia of the Civil War* (New York: Harper & Row, 1986), 326; D. Alexander Brown, *Grierson's Raid* (Dayton OH: Press of Morningside Bookshop, 1981 [1954]), 218–19; Timothy B. Smith, *The Real Horse Soldiers: Benjamin Grierson's Epic 1863 Civil War Raid Through Mississippi* (El Dorado Hills CA: Savas Beatie, 2018), vi.
8. Edwin C. Bearss, "Earl Van Dorn" in William C. Davis, ed., *The Confederate General,* 6 vols. (Harrisburg PA: National Historical Society, 1991), vol. 6, 75; Robert G. Hartje, *Van Dorn: The Life and Times of a Confederate General* (Nashville: Vanderbilt University Press, 1967), 308–12.
9. "General Van Dorn Killed" and "Van Dorn's Murder Confirmed," *ADI,* May 9, 1863.
10. Risley, "Georgia's Confederate Newspapers," 142; Williams, *Directory,* 75; "CONFEDERATE SHOE BLACKING CO.," *ADI,* May 16; "I. W. SINGER'S SEWING MACHINES," *ADI,* May 2; Davis, *What the Yankees Did to Us,* 162.
11. "No. 8. CRAWFORD, FRAZER & CO.," *ADI,* May 2 and 15, 1863; "No. 8," *ADI,* May 2; Garrett, *A & E,* vol. 1, 387–88, 563, 669, 702, 733, 586.
12. Venet, *Changing Wind,* 98; "CRAWFORD, FRAZER & CO. sold . . . ," *ADI,* Apr. 15, 1863; "CRAWFORD, FRAZER & CO.," *ADI,* March 19.
13. Van Tuyll, *Confederate Press,* 191; "290," "THE DEFENSE OF ATLANTA"; "DAWSON," "NINTH CONGRESSIONAL DISTRICT"; "ENDORSEMENT OF CONFEDERATE BONDS"; "From the Chronicle & Sentinel. THE NEXT GOVERNOR

OF GEORGIA"; "From the Montgomery Advertiser. FROM JACKSON"; "[From the Lynchburg Virginian of the 12th.] THE RAID INTO PENNSYLVANIA"; and "COTTON SPINNERS' CONVENTION," all in *ADI*, May 21, front page.

14. "EXECUTION OF JACOB ADAMS," *ADI*, May 22, 1863; Speer, *Portals to Hell*, 28.

15. Henderson, *Roster Confederate Soldiers*, vol. 4, 939; Jack A. Bunch, *Roster of the Courts-Martial in the Confederate States Armies* (Shippensburg PA: White Mane Books, 2001), 2; "A MILITARY EXECUTION AT CHARLESTON," *London Guardian*, June 29, 1863; Jacob Adams Compiled Service Record, National Archives; Robertson, *Soldiers Blue and Gray*, 37; Derry, *Georgia*, 121; Mark A. Weitz, *More Damning than Slaughter: Desertion in the Confederate Army* (Lincoln: University of Nebraska Press, 2005), ix, 287–88

16. "Important from the West," *ADI*, June 6, 1862; Terrence J. Winschel, *Triumph and Defeat: The Vicksburg Campaign* (El Dorado Hills CA: Savas Beatie, 1999), 5–6; Ron Chernow, *Grant* (New York: Penguin Press, 2017), 240–41; Virgil Carrington Jones, "Vicksburg" in Patricia L. Faust, ed., *Historical Times Illustrated Encyclopedia of the Civil War* (New York: Harper & Row, 1986), 784; Leonard Fullenkamp, Stephen Bowman and Jay Luvaas, eds., *Guide to the Vicksburg Campaign* (Lawrence: University Press of Kansas, 1998), 51; Brian Steel Wills, *A Battle from the Start: the Start: The Life of Nathan Bedford Forrest* (New York: Harper Collins, 1992), 86, 89–90, 96; James D. Brewer, *The Raiders of 1862* (Westport CT: Praeger, 1997), 95–97; Hartje, *Van Dorn*, 264.

17. "Grant's Army Falling Back," *ADI*, Dec. 25, 1862; "Van Dorn's Attack on Holly Springs" and "Interesting from the North-West" (Mobile, December 21), *ADI*, December 27; Longacre, *Mounted Raids*, 54.

18. "From the South-West," *ADI*, Dec. 30, 1862; "Van Dorn at Work," *ADI*, December 31.

19. Winschel, *Vicksburg*, 6–9; Arnold, *Grant Wins the War*, 98, 105–16; John E. Stanchak, "The Battle of Port Gibson" in Patricia L. Faust, ed., *Historical Times Illustrated Encyclopedia of the Civil War* (New York: Harper & Row, 1986), 595–96.

20. "From the Southwest," *ADI*, May 6, 1863.

21. John E. Stanchak, "Second Vicksburg Campaign" and "Engagement at Jackson" in Faust, ed., *Historical Times Illustrated Encyclopedia*, 783; "Fighting at Raymond, Miss.," *ADI*, May 15, 1863; Edwin C. Bearss, "Engagement at Raymond," in Faust, ed., *Historical Times Illustrated Encyclopedia*, 617; "Jackson in Enemy's Possession," *ADI*, May 19; Esposito ed., *West Point Atlas*, 104; Symonds, *Joseph E. Johnston*, 187, 205–208.

22. Stephen E. Ambrose, "The Struggle for Vicksburg," *Civil War Times Illustrated*, vol. 6, no.4 (July 1967), 26, 44, 46; Edwin Cole Bearss, *The Campaign for Vicksburg*, 3 vols. (Dayton OH: Morningside, 1985–86), vol. 2, 642; Winschel, *Vicksburg*, 111–12.

23. "The Battles in Mississippi," *ADI*, May 21, 1863; "From Mississippi" and "Vicksburg Besieged," *ADI*, May 23; Arnold, *Grant Wins the War*, 192.

25. Vicksburg

FROM HIS *SANCTUM*, John Steele occasionally informed readers of visits by other members of the "fraternity," colleagues of other papers who happened to visit Atlanta and drop into the *Intelligencer* office. One such was Franc M. Paul of the *Chattanooga Rebel* on May 9; the *Intelligencer* editor observed the next day that "we were pleased to see our esteemed contemporary looking so well, and appearing so cheerful."

Atlanta's editorial fraternity got a new member in May of 1863, when the *Memphis Daily Appeal* relocated in the city. The "moving Appeal" had fled its home before the Federal occupation in June of 1862, and had migrated to Grenada, then to Jackson, Mississippi. Just before the fall of the capital city (its last issue in Jackson was dated May 14), the *Appeal*'s owner and chief editor, John R. McClanahan, decided upon moving to Atlanta. The *Intelligencer* announced the *Appeal*'s arrival on May 27. Soon McClanahan would be introducing himself to John Steele; the *Intelligencer* announced on June 5 that the relocated *Appeal* "will be issued in this city to-day or to-morrow." The first issue of the *Atlanta Appeal* was published on June 6; in his paper on the 9th, Steele welcomed "again to our *sanctum* the appearance of this interesting journal."

The *Intelligencer*'s editor got a lot of other social calls when the Board of the Press Association met in Atlanta in mid-May 1863. Steele was visited by Dr. Robert Gibbes of the *Columbia Daily South Carolinian* (who was president of the association), as well as board member Joseph Clisby of the *Macon Telegraph*. Steele wrote a short piece about both visitors, whom he commended for their "fine health and spirits."[1]

On May 14, the day set for the P. A. board meeting, Gibbes and Clisby were joined only by George Adair of the *Atlanta Daily Southern Confederacy*. Without a quorum, the "board" still met, receiving and discussing the report of its superintendent, John Thrasher. The *Intelligencer*, a P. A. member, offered its occasional assistance to the superintendent, as when it printed on May 6 his open letter asking "gentlemen having experience as reporters or correspondents of newspapers" to send him their credentials for possible employment.

At the board meeting Thrasher explained his efforts to improve the telegraph companies' transmission of news articles and to make efficient use of the association's funds. One of his approaches was to enforce among his field correspondents a strict discipline in the number of words for their articles—words cost money when sent over the wires. He therefore enjoined his writers in their articles to stick to the most necessary words. Then, when he received a correspondent's article in Atlanta, he added in prepositions, article adjectives and auxiliary verbs to make the piece readable and more informative.[2]

In addition to getting out the news to members of the Press Association, Thrasher dealt with the issue of authorities who interfered with his field correspondents' telegraphing of reports. The *Intelligencer* on April 29 printed the superintendent's letter, "To Press Reporters," instructing them to send him "the name and rank of the person refusing to give them course"—meaning, military officers exercising censorship.

John Steele had his own problems in getting the news, and was not shy about writing about them. In an article titled "Provoking" on May 19, the editor complained about the delayed arrival by mail of the *Mobile Tribune*, especially because it allowed the *Atlanta Southern Confederacy* to scoop his paper on the fall of Jackson, the Mississippi capital. Evidently the city's postmaster, Thomas C. Howard, felt a personal affront, and got in touch with Steele's office. The editor on the 20th accordingly backtracked in a follow-up article. He had only wished to explain why, he wrote, "a contemporary in this city" had been able to publish "important news" before the *Intelligencer* could. As for the postmaster and his clerks, Steele declared, "we. . . . take pleasure in bearing testimony to their ever prompt and efficient management of the Post Office here."[3]

To erratic mail service were the occasional mechanical difficulties of sheer production. In late March 1863 Steele informed readers that the *Intelligencer* would be issued as a half sheet for a few days while its steam power press was being moved. On May 7, the paper announced that it would temporarily shrink its size again due to the "the decree of the Paper Mills." The editor hoped to resume the *Intelligencer*'s regular size "early next week." It would prove, however, much longer than that—a full three weeks, in fact. Not until May 29 could Steele inform readers that the paper was resuming its "old dimensions." The editor used the announcement to affirm his intention to maintain those dimensions; "this will give us more space for advertisers, as well as for reading matter." He frankly solicited the patronage of both subscribers and advertisers. As the latter sometimes inquired as to the *Intelligencer*'s circulation, Steele wrote that it "is equal to any paper in the State, and much larger than most of the Dailies and Weeklies." He did not mean to be evasive with this statement. "Any one," he explained, "who desires to know the extent of our circulation, will be made acquainted with it." He preferred to impart the numerical data personally rather than by, as some papers did, "claiming through their columns . . . having the 'largest circulation in the State.'"

As a further occasional complication, news blackouts were occasionally caused by *gas* blackouts. On Wednesday, April 15, the *Intelligencer* informed readers that several telegraphic items did not appear in its issue of the 14th because around 9 p.m. Tuesday, the gas lights went out at the newspaper's headquarters. Steele had no candles, so he sent his typesetters home. The same thing happened the following Thursday around 11 p.m. At least when the lights failed again Friday night, the *Intelligencer* staff was equipped with candles to continue working on Saturday morning's paper. After reporting on the 19th that the blackouts had occurred because the city's gas company had been running low on coal, Steele turned rather jolly in declaring, "we must return, therefore, to the good old days of working by candle light."

At the same time, he reminded readers that candles were scarce and expensive; "this entails upon us a heavy expense." As he had done before, Steele used the occasion to remind Atlantans that the *Intelligencer* needed subscribers, not merely readers of "*borrowed* papers." The editor even offered that "when a man reads his own paper at home . . . it does him more good than to . . . hear them read by others." To reinforce the point, Steele published excerpts from a letter recently received by a subscriber (who was sending in his renewal). "Had I known my time was out, I would have sent the money to renew my subscription," he wrote, "and would have been up with the news." The editor underscored his responsibility to provide that very news. "Our readers must have the telegraphic news that nightly comes to us," he declared, so he and his staff would work to provide it, even by candle light.[4]

The news from a particular war front—Vicksburg, Mississippi—became a regular feature of the *Intelligencer*'s third-page telegraphic column late in the spring of 1863. Steele commented on it in an article appearing on May 23. "The enemy are besieging Vicksburg on every side," he began. "The whereabouts of [Gen. Joseph E.] Johnston," who was known to be gathering a relief force in the vicinity of Jackson, "is left to conjecture." Grant was thought to have 40,000 or 50,000 troops, but if Johnston could fall on his rear, Vicksburg could be saved. "Much, however, depends upon Pemberton's generalship, and his ability to keep Grant at bay."

Mobile, Alabama, was the point from which telegraphic news about Vicksburg usually came to the *Intelligencer*, and the dispatches remained upbeat. "The garrison is well supplied and confident of holding the place," read the message of May 23. From Jackson came word that "troops are continually arriving, and we will have a fine army." On May 19 and again on the 22nd Grant launched repeated assaults on the Vicksburg fortifications and had been bloodily repulsed. "There was great slaughter each time," another report stated; "our loss was only eighty-seven." After his bloody repulse on May 22, Grant did not call for a truce so his men could bury their dead comrades. A wired message to the *Intelligencer* related that Pemberton's soldiers were burning tar and other disinfectants to ameliorate the stench of "the Federal dead rotting in front of their works."

After his failed attacks Grant settled in for a siege. The Federals were "ditching," as the Mobile wire news of May 26 put it. Commenting on the report, Steele counseled, "our people need not be alarmed at this." In the inactivity of their siege lines, the editor predicted that the enemy soldiers would "become weaker every day, both in numbers and morale," especially as summer pestilence worked its way among the Northerners. "We hope to see them dislodged before they get a firm holding," he declared.

John Steele seized on anything that could sustain this hope. A letter from a correspondent writing to the *Mobile Advertiser & Register*, one of his exchanges, led to an editorial on May 29. General Pemberton had issued an address to his troops that Steele believed "will inspire confidence in that General's army." General Johnston was reported to have 40,000 men to lead to Vicksburg's aid. Grant's losses in the battles at Raymond and the Big Black River, as well as his assaults on Pemberton's works, were said to be "enormous." Steele even dared to prophesy that "we shall soon hear that Grant is taking to his boats, and has abandoned the siege of the heroic city."[5]

No such thing happened. The most elemental knowledge of the American civil war has as one of its staples Ulysses S. Grant's capture of Vicksburg on July 4, 1863 and John C. Pemberton's surrender of thousands of Southern soldiers. So it is not giving away the story to simply summarize it: throughout June Federals strengthened their entrenchments, while Confederates ran low on food and neared starvation until Pemberton was forced to surrender.

The real story is how Confederate newspapers, including the *Intelligencer*, not just got the reportorial narrative wrong from the limited telegraphic news reaching them, but in effect misled the people by printing reports that would be proven false.

Sanguine dispatches were the stuff of Confederate newspapers. The *Mobile Advertiser & Register* published the message that Grant's forces were retreating from Vicksburg for want of drinking water. "CLINT," a correspondent stationed in Jackson for the *Advertiser & Register*, wrote on May 27, "the news from Vicksburg is cheering." Publishing "Clint's" letter on June 2, the *Intelligencer*'s editor explained that telegraphic news from the west had been skimpy, due to "some derangement caused by the thunder storms that have been prevailing . . . in that direction." Steele urged his readers to be patient and, tellingly, not to give credence to "the rumors at the car-shed, and on the streets . . . especially the one we hear every morning, that 'Vicksburg has fallen.'"[6]

As if to buck up the people's morale, the next day the *Intelligencer*'s telegraphic news column blared a headline, "Latest from Vicksburg! Another Attack! Greatest Slaughter Ever Known."

Of course, nothing of the kind had occurred. The wired report, dated June 1, was a total fabrication: in the last days of May Grant's troops were busy digging zig-zags and parallels closer to the Rebel works to allow Federals better jump-off positions if an assault were ordered. Because the headline declared that thirty thousand Yankees (including five generals) had been killed, this allowed the paper to assert the "greatest slaughter every known" in the Civil War— except that it did not happen.[7]

John Steele was too savvy an editor to place much stock in such hyperbole. Instead, on June 4, he candidly declared, "the question is often asked . . . what will become of us if Vicksburg falls." He answered soberly that in such an eventuality, "we have only to fight on."

Every now and then, authenticity would break through. "Grant is being heavily reinforced," the paper's "BY TELEGRAPH" section announced on June 4. Indeed he was; by June 18 Grant had 77,000 men under his command, against Pemberton's 30,000. They "had quit the storming process," as a report from Jackson stated, and were "going to try the starving."[8]

Meanwhile, news from Port Hudson, La., was coming in as well. While Grant was besieging Vicksburg, Maj. Gen. Nathaniel Banks' Army of the Gulf moved against the Confederate garrison at Port Hudson, a river fortress twenty-five miles above Baton Rouge. The *Jackson Mississippian* stated that Port

Hudson "is completely invested by a very strong force under General Banks"; the *Intelligencer* carried the report on June 5. Yet that same piece, ten lines long, was thoroughly overshadowed by the bold and big headline right next to it: "LATEST FROM VICKSBURG./Enemy Repulsed in every attempt to storm our works with immense loss./ The Yankees Discouraged."

Even this was eclipsed by the headlines in the *Intelligencer* of the next day, June 6: "Grant Preparing to Fall Back./Brilliant Victory at Port Hudson./Banks Lost an Arm./Johnston on the March./Gen. Sherman Killed./Yankee News and Lies./Grierson's Command Captured./ Kirby Smith at Port Hudson." Short articles beneath these lines filled in a few details. The headline that blared "Grant Preparing to Fall Back" was supported by an item that declared only that "Grant is evidently preparing to move in some direction." The claims of "brilliant victory at Port Hudson" and that Banks had lost an arm were merely based on hearsay from "refugees at Pascagoula." To be sure, Banks had ordered an assault against the Confederate works on May 27 and had been repulsed, but the general had certainly not "lost an arm."

As for "Johnston on the march" (presumably toward Vicksburg), not only had Johnston and his small army not left Jackson, but he was sending despondent messages to Richmond declaring, "I consider saving Vicksburg hopeless." It goes without saying that William T. Sherman had not been killed (a later report adjusted the story to state that his left arm had been amputated). Similarly, Col. Benjamin Grierson's cavalry command had not been captured, just as Confederate Lt. Gen. Edmund K. Smith was not at Port Hudson (in early June 1863, he was issuing orders from Shreveport, La.).[9]

This overly sanguine pattern of "reporting" news about Vicksburg continued for a month, until the Confederate garrison's surrender. There were occasional exceptions, as when the *Intelligencer* quoted Northern sources, such as the *New York Herald* or other papers. Under "Yankee Reports," the *Intelligencer* on June 7 stated that "Johnston was at Jackson with a force of 15,000 and was unable to get more" (Johnston actually had 23,000, but he was asking for 7,000 more). "Johnston has not crossed the Big Black" (his small army started for the Big Black only on June 29). "The inhabitants and soldiers in Vicksburg are suffering from want of water" (the city's water system, designed to serve 5,000 people, now had to provide for 30,000). "Grant is building works within one hundred yards of the rebel lines" (the Federals had actually dug to within seventy-five yards by June 8).[10]

But such facts succumbed to buoyant, if strained, expressions of optimism in the pages of the *Intelligencer*. "Clio" wrote from Richmond on June 4, "we have every reason, now, [to] hope and believe" that Grant's troops will be "completely whipped in their present advance upon the Queen City of the Southwest." From Mobile came another "Vicksburg Safe" dispatch, printed in the *Intelligencer* on June 10. A correspondent signing himself as "A." reported to the *Mobile Tribune* from Jackson that he had learned from a courier out of Vicksburg that "affairs at that place are in so good a condition that there is no need for Johnston to come immediately to its relief." On June 12, the *Intelligencer*'s "BY TELEGRAPH" column included a dispatch that declared, "our troops are in fine spirits and very confident" and that "Gen. Pemberton has plenty of provisions and munitions."[11]

John Steele reinforced these sunny reports with his own commentary, as he did in an editorial printed on June 16. The enemy losses had amounted to 40,000–50,000 men since April 27, the start of Grant's campaign, he wrote, "while ours have only been 6,000." Pemberton's men, though completely hemmed in, had plenty to eat; "the rations being issued there are abundant." On the other side of the lines, Grant's men wanted water, were wilting in the heat, were grousing and deserting, and had no steady supply line. Moreover, Johnston and his army of relief were expected to be in Grant's rear before the Vicksburg garrison ran low on supplies. Because of all of this, Steele concluded, "the news before us is cheering in the extreme."

Falsehoods floated also from Port Hudson. "Siege of Port Hudson said to be Raised," trumpeted a telegraphic headline in the *Intelligencer* of June 23. *Said* was the operative word, which could excuse any misinterpretation of the facts. The next day's paper demonstrated the confusing nature of the telegraphed dispatches being received; the same column included one item that announced "Banks Leaving Port Hudson" while another disclosed that he had received eleven transports of reinforcements. (Confederate Maj. Gen. Franklin Gardner would surrender Port Hudson on July 9, five days after Pemberton capitulated.)[12]

On July 11, the *Intelligencer* offered an update on the Federal bombardment of Vicksburg, which had begun in late May. Thousands of Northern shells had been thrown into the city, but only three casualties had been counted. The paper's issue of July 3 carried a message from Jackson: a courier arriving from Vicksburg reported "our army is in fine health."[13]

The stage was thus set for the bombshell telegram, and John Steele's reaction to it.

Vicksburg Reported Fallen.

JACKSON, July 6.—The mail carrier has just arrived, and states positively that Vicksburg has fallen.

This same news has been received this morning from different sources, but not by any one here officially. [We do not credit this news.— ED. INT.]

Printing this on July 8, the editor added a side item in the same issue: "We have no time for comment on the telegraphic news received to-day, save to say, we do not believe Vicksburg has fallen."

The next day, the 9th, Steele repeated himself. "Notwithstanding the telegraphic item published yesterday that Vicksburg had fallen into the hands of the enemy, not a word of which we believe to be true, what we learn of the *situation* there, is highly encouraging." To support his contention the editor added, "a gentleman was in this city on yesterday, who left the vicinity of Vicksburg on Monday [July 6], who states on that day all was right at Vicksburg."

Steele held out hope as long as he could. The *Intelligencer*'s telegraphic column on July 10 included a short piece, "Vicksburg not Fallen," in which a Confederate officer at Jackson stated that the unfounded rumor had arisen "among civilians and couriers." But just above it was Gen. J. E. Johnston's telegram, sent to Richmond on the 7th: "Vicksburg capitulated on the 4th inst."

This compelled Steele to pen a painful editorial, "VICKSBURG HAS FALLEN." "These words are to-day upon the tongues and in the hearts of all our people, throughout the length and breadth of the Confederacy," he wrote. Despite all the messaging about Pemberton's troops having plenty of provisions and being in fine spirits, it turned out that the troops were "in a starving condition, and completely worn out with excessive fatigue." There were other causes as well. The Federals, for instance, had destroyed the fifty miles of railroad between Jackson and Vicksburg; this hindered Johnston's attempt to come to Pemberton's aid (there was no mention of whether Johnston had waited too long before starting his troops moving).

The *Intelligencer*'s coverage of the Vicksburg Campaign demonstrates the lengths to which Confederate newspapers would go to project optimism and confidence in the face of mounting adversity. In late May John Steele focused on the possibility of Gen. Joseph E. Johnston leading an army of relief and assailing Grant's forces after they had laid siege lines around Pemberton's trapped army. Then there was the (mistaken) belief that the Confederates and townspeople had enough food to hold out indefinitely. After the Federals launched attacks on May 22, the paper reveled in their high casualties. When Grant's troops dug in for a sustained siege, the *Intelligencer* predicted that a hot Mississippi summer would bring sickness and depressed morale among them. It even foresaw Grant giving the whole thing up and "taking to his boats." Headlines that read "Greatest Slaughter Ever Known," while comic in their exaggeration, on a more serious level misled Steele's readers (or perhaps just the more gullible ones).

In other words, the *Intelligencer* had tried to assure readers as long as it could: "Vicksburg safe" (June 10); "rations are abundant" (June 16); "our army is in fine health" (July 3—the very day before Pemberton surrendered).

But as he had done with other Confederate defeats and disasters, John Steele put the best face on this one that he could. Yes, "Vicksburg has fallen," he conceded, but the enemy had lost thousands of lives and expended millions in treasure in taking it. Its defenders succumbed not to defeat but to starvation. And even in surrendering, the troops had marched out proudly and with colors flying.

A month earlier, Steele had asked what the South would do if Vicksburg fell ("we have only to fight on, trusting in the justice of our cause and the favor of heaven"). This was the spirit he voiced as he concluded his editorial: "Let us never forget that our cause is in the hands of a just God, who will defend the right. Let us think of the terrible fate that awaits a subjugated people, and nerve our hearts and our hands to do all and suffer all for the achievement of our liberty and independence."[14]

NOTES

1. "PERSONAL," *ADI*, May 10, 1863; "A WELCOME VISITOR," *ADI*, May 14; "On yesterday . . . ," *ADI*, May 15; Andrews, *South Reports*, 40; Ellis, *Moving Appeal*, 221; "THE MEMPHIS APPEAL," *ADI*, May 27; "We understand that the Memphis (late Jackson) Appeal . . . ," *ADI*, June 5; "THE MEMPHIS APPEAL," *ADI*, June 9.

2. "MINUTES OF THE SECOND SESSION OF THE BOARD OF DIRECTORS OF THE PRESS ASSOCIATION," 14–16; "REPORT OF THE SUPERINTENDENT OF THE PRESS ASSOCIATION OF THE CONFEDERATE STATES OF AMERICA. ATLANTA MAY 13, 1863," 39, 46–49; Andrews, *South Reports*, 57; Risley, "Confederate Press Association," 230–31; "Later from Mississippi," *ADI*, Apr. 28, 1863; "What are we Fighting For?' . . . ," *ADI*, May 17, 1863; "PRESS AGENT AT ATLANTA," *ADI*, July 7.

3. "To Press Reporters," *ADI*, April 29, 1863; "PROVOKING," *ADI*, May 19; "In our

notice on yesterday . . . ," *ADI*, May 20; "ARRIVAL AND CLOSING OF THE MAILS," *ADI*, February 25.

4. "TO OUR READERS," *ADI*, March 26, 1863; "REDUCED IN SIZE," *ADI*, May 7; "THE DAILY INTELLIGNECER,'" *ADI*, May 29; "LEFT IN THE DARK," *ADI*, April 15; "Again the gas failed us . . . ," *ADI*, April 18; "GOOD OLD TIMES," *ADI*, April 19; "A SENSIBLE CONCLUSION," *ADI*, April 16.

5. "THE SITUATION AT VICKSBURG," *ADI*, May 23, 1863; "Latest from Vicksburg" (Mobile, May 23), *ADI*, May 26; "Latest from Vicksburg" (Mobile, May 25), *ADI*, May 27; "Later from Vicksburg" (Mobile, May 26) and "THE ENEMY DITCHING AT VICKSBURG," *ADI*, May 28; "Latest from Vicksburg . . . Confederates Burning Tar to ameliorate the stench of the Dead Yankees," *ADI*, May 29.

6. "Important from Vicksburg" *ADI*, May 31, 1863; "CLINT," "LETTER FROM JACKSON" (May 27) and "THE SITUATION AT VICKSBURG," *ADI*, June 2.

7. "BY TELEGRAPH," *ADI*, June 3, 1863; Winschel, *Vicksburg*, 14, 130–31.

8. "VICKSBURG" and "Important from Vicksburg," *ADI*, June 4, 1863; Ambrose, "Vicksburg," 54; "Yankees Intrenching," *ADI*, June 4.

9. Emory M. Thomas, "Port Hudson, La." in Patricia L. Faust, ed., *The Historical Times Illustrated Encyclopedia of the Civil War* (New York: Harper & Row, 1986), 596; "FROM PORT HUDSON" and "LATEST FROM VICKSBURG," *ADI*, June 5, 1863; "LATEST FROM VICKSBURG," "From Vicksburg" and "From Port Hudson, *ADI*, June 6; Fred Harvey Harrington, *Fighting Politician: Major General N. P. Banks* (Westport CT: Greenwood Press, 1970 [1948]), 121–22; Symonds, *Joseph E. Johnston*, 214; Johnston to Seddon, June 14, 1863, *OR*, vol. 24, pt. 1, 227; "Banks Fortifying," *ADI*, June 16; Edwin C. Bearss, "Benjamin Henry Grierson" in John T. Hubbell and James W. Geary, eds., *Biographical Dictionary of the Union: Northern Leaders of the Civil War* (Westport CT: Greenwood Press, 1995), 214; Parks, *Edmund Kirby Smith*, 270; E. Kirby Smith to Thomas C. Reynolds, June 4, 1863, *OR*, vol. 22, pt. 2, 855.

10. "Yankee Reports," *ADI*, June 7, 1863; Gilbert E. Govan and James W. Livingood, *A Different Valor: The Story of General Joseph E. Johnston, C.S.A.* (Westport CT: Greenwood Press, 1973 [1956]), 208, 219; Symonds, *Joseph E. Johnston*, 212; Peter F. Walker, *Vicksburg: A People at War, 1860–65* (Chapel Hill: University of North Carolina Press, 1960), 181; Winschel, *Vicksburg*, 133.

11. "CLIO," "FROM RICHMOND" (June 4), "Vicksburg Safe" and "A.," "First Dispatch," *ADI*, June 10, 1863; "BY TELEGRAPH," *ADI*, June 12.

12. "GRANT'S OPERATIONS UPON VICKSBURG," *ADI*, June 16, 1863; "Siege of Port Hudson said to be Raised," *ADI*, June 23; "Banks Leaving Port Hudson" and "From Port Hudson" *ADI*, June 24; Lawrence Lee Hewitt, *Port Hudson: Confederate Bastion on the Mississippi* (Baton Rouge. Louisiana State University Press, 1987), 173.

13. "From Vicksburg," *ADI*, July 1, 1863; "From the Mobile Advertiser & Register," *ADI*, July 3.

14. "Vicksburg Reported Fallen" and "We have no time for comment . . . ," *ADI*, July 8, 1863; "OUR SUCCESSES," *ADI*, July 9; "Vicksburg not Fallen," "Official from Jackson" and "VICKSBURG HAS FALLEN," *ADI*, July 10; "VICKSBURG," *ADI*, June 4.

26. Gettysburg

"CLIO," the *Atlanta Daily Intelligencer*'s correspondent in Richmond, had had more than fifty of his letters published in the paper during the first part of 1863 when he turned his attention on June 2 to the movements of General Lee's army. "It is currently reported and generally believed in this city, that General Lee is about to assume the offensive, and march his army into Maryland and Pennsylvania," "Clio" declared.[1]

Following his army's victory at Chancellorsville, on May 15 Robert E. Lee won approval for a northern advance. An initially skeptical Jefferson Davis was eventually won over, to the point of committing reinforcements for the Army of Northern Virginia. Lee's army numbered 64,799 officers and men on April 30, 1863—and that was before Chancellorsville—but could boast 74,459 present for duty on May 31.[2]

On June 3, Lee started his army moving westward along the Rappahannock toward Culpeper, thirty miles west of Fredericksburg. As he had done the previous September, the army would use the Blue Ridge Mountains and Shenandoah Valley as its march route. Before he could win Jefferson Davis' approval of the forthcoming campaign, however, Lee had had to assure the president that Richmond would be safe as he marched north. "Clio" reflected on all this in his article of June 6. "Gen. Lee has advanced with the bulk of his army to Culpeper Court House or its neighborhood," he wrote, "leaving behind him about twenty thousand troops for the protection of Richmond."[3]

One subject that the *Intelligencer*'s reporter in Richmond did not touch upon was Robert E. Lee's reorganization of his army. The loss of Stonewall Jackson led the commanding general to decide upon a structure based on three infantry corps, rather than the two that had been led by Jackson and James Longstreet. On May 20 Lee wrote President Davis about his idea and won quick approval. He chose to promote Ambrose Powell Hill and Richard S. Ewell as lieutenant generals and commanders of the new Second and Third Corps. Brigades were moved around to constitute the army's nine infantry divisions (three to a corps). The new organization was announced on May 30.[4]

Despite his drubbing at Chancellorsville, General "Fighting Joe" Hooker still had some fight left in him. On June 7 he ordered his cavalry chief, Maj. Gen. Alfred Pleasonton (who had taken over from George Stoneman on May 22) to advance on Culpeper, seventy miles north of Richmond, where Jeb Stuart's cavalry was known to be concentrated, and "disperse and destroy the rebel force." Pleasonton attacked on the morning of June 9 near Brandy Station. Stuart, not expecting it, was surprised, but he recovered enough to fight off the Federal horsemen. Federal casualties totaled 866; Confederates counted 523 men lost as killed, wounded, missing or captured. Brandy Station, the largest cavalry battle fought on the North American continent, was technically a Southern victory, as Confederates held the field. Yet Stuart's pride had been wounded by Pleasonton's attack, which demonstrated that in the field Union cavalrymen were at last a match for Confederate mounted troops.[5]

"Clio" addressed Brandy Station the day after the battle. "Yesterday morning," he wrote from Richmond on June 10, a large Federal force had crossed the Rappahannock fords, "and made an assault upon our lines, which was continued till 5 o'clock in the afternoon, when Gen. Stuart drove the enemy across the river." More than this information, however, the *Intelligencer* correspondent could not offer, but he knew that Stuart had been surprised. In his letter dated June 13, "Clio" expressed his belief that Hooker had ordered Pleasonton's advance "for the purpose of surprising our army and checking the operations of Gen. Lee, which we supposed to embrace an invasion of the North." "Clio" joined the other journalists who had criticized Stuart: "it was certainly a great mistake on his part."[6]

Within a week of Brandy Station, there came news of a "glorious" Confederate victory that swung Southerners' moods right around. Ewell's corps led the army's march into the Shenandoah, followed by Longstreet's, then Hill's. On June 15, Ewell's troops approached Winchester, thirty miles southwest of Harpers Ferry, and forced the surrender of 4,400 officers and men there. The capture of Winchester brought forth an editorial, "GLORIOUS NEWS," that once more demonstrated Steele's perspective as to Confederate military fortunes. Besides, there was still the sting of Stuart's surprise. "For a few days past," the editor confessed on June 20, "we have felt chagrined at the late affair of Stuart's cavalry, and we wanted something cheering to dispel our chagrin."[7]

Steele found something even more cheering the farther Confederate soldiers marched northward. Maj. Gen. Robert Rodes' division, as the advance of Ewell's corps, reached the Potomac on June 15, crossing the river into Maryland during the next two days. Farther in front, Southern cavalrymen actually rode through Greencastle, Pa. to Chambersburg, a town nearly twenty miles north of the Maryland line. The rest of Lee's army was well behind, though; by June 18, Longstreet's corps was about to march through the Blue Ridge gaps into the Shenandoah. Hill's corps was at Culpeper, forty miles to the south, preparing to follow Longstreet. On June 21, General Lee gave Jeb Stuart discretion to set his northbound route, notwithstanding the cavalry's main task of screening Ewell's flank from probing U.S. cavalry.

By June 23 Ewell had entered Pennsylvania and Longstreet's and Hill's corps had forded the Potomac.[8]

In Richmond, "Clio" wrote a letter on June 20 that began with "Lincoln is said to be terribly frightened at the advance of the Confederate forces towards the capital of the old, but now tottering Union." He mentioned that a bulletin had just been posted at one of the Richmond dailies that "represents in lively colors the consternation produced in the leading Northern cities by the advance of our forces." The citizens of Harpers Ferry "are flying for safety." Gov. Andrew Curtin of Pennsylvania was calling for Philadelphians to rally in defense of the city. On June 16 the mayor of Philadelphia ordered all stores closed so the men could fall in. Headlines of the short items printed in the *Intelligencer*'s "BY TELEGRAPH" column of June 21 said it all: "Panic in Philadelphia," "Lee Advancing," "Confederate Cavalry Advancing" and "Carrying the War into Africa"—the latter a reference to the war between Rome and Carthage that led to the Romans' destruction of the Carthaginian capital.[9]

In its search for news of Lee's army, the Confederate press turned to Northern newspapers, as the *Intelligencer* did on June 26. That day John Steele reprinted an article from the *Richmond Examiner* that commented, "we have been able to learn little more of the movements of our armies under Gen. Lee than is contained in the extracts from Yankee papers."

There was enough to go on, however, for the *Intelligencer*'s editor to opine on an incontrovertible fact: General Lee's Army of Northern Virginia had carried the war into Maryland and Pennsylvania, and Yankee noncombatants were about to experience the property loss and destruction that the Southern people had been enduring for the past two years. Indeed, Steele rather enjoyed the prospect of a "*big scare* or panic" among "a race of people . . . who regard the almighty dollar and the promotion of their selfish interests, as the chief end of their being." Indeed, Steele quoted the *Richmond Enquirer* as declaring that "we do know that the heart of his country is burning for vengeance," referring to General Lee. Steele added his voice in agreement by citing the golden rule: "we trust that according as they have done unto others, so shall General Lee do unto them." The editor concluded, "we would make them pay dear for the perpetration of all their crimes. Retaliation in kind we would avoid, and yet, we would *retaliate* so as to make them feel that *retribution* has overtaken them at last."[10]

On June 28, President Lincoln, exasperated at Hooker's cautious response to the Rebels' incursion, relieved him of command and to succeed him appointed Maj. Gen. George G. Meade, commander of the Army of the Potomac's V Corps. Meade swung into action swiftly, sending his infantry marching north. Stuart's cavalry failed to pick up the enemy's sudden activity, though; Jeb had decided to ride around the Union army (and would not rejoin Lee until July 2). Instead, it was a Southern spy, Henry Harrison (formerly an actor from Mississippi), who on the night of June 28 brought word to Lee that the Federal army was heading toward him. At that time the Army of Northern Virginia was spread out over central Pennsylvania. Ewell's advance was near Carlisle, twenty miles west of Harrisburg; forty miles to the southwest were Longstreet's and Hill's corps. In view of the changing situation, Lee ordered Ewell to halt his advance on Harrisburg and march west toward Chambersburg.[11]

When the long-expected battle came—Confederate infantry ran into Federal cavalry west of Gettysburg on the morning of July 1—the *Atlanta Intelligencer,* and the Southern press in general, spent days trying to catch up with events. On July 1 the paper carried "Clio's" letter of June 25 that began "we have received at the war department no dispatches from General Lee or any of his officers as to the present whereabouts of his army." On July 2 the only pertinent dispatch in the *Intelligencer* was dated June 26; taken from the *Richmond Whig*, it related that Ewell had taken Harrisburg (he had not). The paper's telegraphic column on July 3 only provided particulars taken from Northern papers. On the 4th, the *Intelligencer*'s "BY TELEGRAPH" section carried no news at all from Pennsylvania.

The Atlanta paper was indeed well behind events. The titanic battle of Gettysburg was fought July 1–3, ending in Confederates' failure to break Meade's line in three days of infantry attacks. Early on July 4 Lee's army began its retreat back to Virginia.[12]

The news drought continued. The *Intelligencer* staff did not work on July 4, so there was no paper put out on the 5th—"the employees of this office having as much right to observe the day as a holiday as the Yankees," as the editor announced. Monday, July 6, was the staff's weekly day off, so it was not until July 7 that another telegraphic news column appeared in the *Intelligencer*. Still there was no news about a battle in Pennsylvania.

First inklings appeared on July 8. "The Yankee Army Routed, and 10,000 Prisoners Taken," blared one headline. "All the reports concur that the enemy was defeated yesterday and driven back three miles," declared a short article. "This was the bloodiest battle of the war," another attested; "our loss very great, the enemy's immense." The first telegraphed item to actually mention the town of Gettysburg summarized the battle: "Yankee accounts represent the battle as indecisive—both sides suffering severely."[13]

As to be expected, John Steele chose to overlook the grimmer dispatches and focused on those that proclaimed a Confederate victory. "In Pennsylvania, the success of General Lee's army, according to the admission of the Northern press, is unprecedented," the editor declared on July 9; "Hooker's old army, commanded by his successor, Meade, has been completely demolished, 40,000 of them having surrendered as prisoners of war, while, doubtless, many thousands of them have been wounded and slain." Yet Steele admitted that he was waiting for further news of the big battle "with great anxiety."[14]

Then word began to arrive that perhaps Lee had not won a victory after all. Telegraphed items printed on July 11 in the *Intelligencer* reported that "Gen. Lee's army is at Hagerstown," Maryland—a hint of retreat. An article misleadingly titled "Cheering from Pennsylvania" told of heavy fighting on July 1 and 2 ("our loss the first two days was not very great"), but on Friday, July 3, "it was heavy, especially Pickett's division." Then, in the next-to-last paragraph came this: "our army fell back with the greatest deliberation. No demoralization." Following was an attempt at explanation: "It was generally understood that the falling back was caused by the difficulty in obtaining supplies through so long a line of communications. The men are in fine spirits, and ready for another fight."

One had to read very closely another item, "Further from Pennsylvania" (dated July 8 from Richmond) to understand what had transpired. "We gained a decided and telling advantage over the enemy at Gettysburg, on Wednesday and Thursday" (July 1–2), the article stated; "on Friday we charged and took his works but were unable to hold them." The report continued with mixed messages: "we fell back towards Hagerstown"; "so far the victory has been on our side"; "everything is indefinite"; "40,000 prisoners are now at Williamport [*sic*] on their way to Richmond."[15]

Thus, a week after the battle of Gettysburg, a thoughtful reader of the *Intelligencer* would have deduced that a climactic battle had occurred in Pennsylvania, with many casualties on each side, and that Lee's army had retreated back to Virginia. Newspaper ink in the next several weeks would not alter that conclusion.

"Clio," writing in Richmond on July 6, wrestled with Northern newspapers' claims of Union victory at Gettysburg. "Notwithstanding the efforts of the enemy to mistify [*sic*] and misrepresent facts, our cause is triumphant," he concluded. Indeed, "up to this time, our invasion of the enemy's territory has been attended with signal success."

Editor Steele observed that Northern accounts of the battle in Pennsylvania "are denounced by the Richmond presses as false." He quoted the *Examiner*'s statement that President Davis had received a dispatch asserting that "General Lee had been victorious in every engagement with the enemy and had fallen back to Hagerstown simply that he might put across the Potomac his wounded and prisoners."[16]

Peter W. Alexander of the *Savannah Republican* had accompanied Lee's army on the campaign and wrote arguably the best account of the battle to date for his paper; the *Intelligencer* printed it on July 17. The battle at Gettysburg, he wrote, had begun on July 1 when Ewell's and Hill's troops had engaged Federals under Maj. Gen. John F. Reynolds, commander of the Union I Corps. "We drove the enemy back the first day, and killed Gens. Reynolds and Paul [Reynolds had indeed been killed; Brig. Gen. Gabriel R. Paul was shot in the temple and permanently blinded, but he survived his wound and the war] and captured three thousand prisoners" [Confederates succeeded in routing both the Union I and XI Corps on July 1; Federal army returns put the number of captured and missing for the two infantry corps at 3,090].[17]

"On the 2d of July both armies concentrated at 4 o'clock. McLaws and Hood, of Longstreet's corps, held the right, attacked and drove the enemy a mile and a half. Hill attacked the centre, and Ewell the left. Our success on the left and centre was not equal to that on the right wing. McLaws' and Hood's divisions took 1,500 prisoners and several guns and flags, inflicted a terrible loss on the foe, and suffered heavily themselves."

Here "P. W. A." got more right than wrong. On July 2, the opposing armies faced each other in lines running north-south; the Federals held Cemetery

Ridge, the Confederates Seminary Ridge a mile to the west. Lee had decided to retain the initiative by attacking Meade, who was content to stand on the defensive. Two of Longstreet's divisions, led by Maj. Gens. John B. Hood and Lafayette McLaws, held the right of Lee's line (Maj. Gen. George E. Pickett's division had not yet arrived). Longstreet was to lead the attack, which would be taken up by Hill's infantry. Ewell was to advance upon Cemetery and Culp's Hills, on the right of the Union line, when he heard Longstreet's guns.

Hood's and McLaws' infantry pushed back the Federals, but not to the extent of 1 ½ miles (here Alexander erred). He also exaggerated the number of prisoners taken (in Union Maj. Gen. Daniel E. Sickles' III Corps, which took the brunt of the Rebels' assaults, 589 men were counted missing). But the reporter accurately assessed the bloody toll of the fighting in Hood's and McLaws' sector (Little Round Top, Devil's Den, the Peach Orchard and Wheatfield); the two Confederate divisions each lost about 2,200 men, thirty percent of their strength.[18]

"On the 3d the battle was resumed," "P. W. A." continued, "on the afternoon the enemy was driven from several strong positions, but not dislodged entirely from his main position when night came." This was not only a rather slippery characterization of one of the most famous (tragic, really) charges in the Civil War, that of Pickett's division and brigades from two others. The heroic Southerners neither drove nor dislodged the Federals from their positions, even though the Confederates suffered more than fifty percent casualties.[19]

Such was the battle of Gettysburg. When "Clio" wrote his letter of July 16, he sagely observed, "it will have been noticed, I think, that Gen. Lee never sends a telegraphic dispatch regarding a battle, until he had achieved decided success." This was the correspondent's veiled way of admitting that such success had eluded Lee in Pennsylvania. Still, "Clio" expressed hope that Confederate forces in Virginia could yet rebound to the point of threatening Baltimore and Washington, even forcing "the overthrow of the Lincoln Government."

John Steele interjected, "[This opinion does not prevail, the 21st inst.—ED. INT.]"[20] For once, the *Intelligencer* editor was reining in his impulse to jump on the brightest possible news items, accept them readily, and present them to readers as fact. The editor in Atlanta was also pointedly contradicting his correspondent in Richmond. Perhaps Peter Alexander's long article, printed in the *Intelligencer* on July 17, and the long stream of telegrams out of Richmond following the battle had accumulated a body of evidence so weighty as not to be denied.

One telegram was particularly poignant, and quite personal: "RICHMOND, July 14.—To Mr. J. W. Neisbet, care of the Intelligencer: Dear Father—I am at Jordan Springs Hospital near Winchester. I lost my left arm at Gettysburg, Pennsylvania. Come to me. Answer by telegraph. W. H. NEISBET."[21]

Unfortunately, John Steele added that he knew no such Neisbit (it didn't help that the telegrapher misspelled Nesbit), so all he could do to help the crippled soldier was to print his message and hope that someone would come forth.

No one did, yet the story of twenty-two year-old Lt. William Hoyle Nesbit, 22nd Georgia Infantry, ended well: he resigned on account of wounds in November 1863. He lived to be 83.

NOTES

1. "CLIO," "LETTER FROM RICHMOND" (June 2), *ADI*, June 7, 1863.

2. Douglas Southall Freeman, *Lee's Lieutenants: A Study in Command*, 3 vols. (New York: Charles Scribner's Sons, 1942–44), vol. 2, 710; "Consolidated abstract," *OR*, Ser. 4, vol. 2, 615.

3. Steven E. Woodworth, *Davis and Lee at War* (Lawrence: University Press of Kansas, 1995), 237; Noah Andre Trudeau, *Gettysburg: A Testing of Courage* (New York: HarperCollins, 2002), 5; "CLIO," "FROM RICHMOND," (June 6), *ADI*, June 11, 1863.

4. Freeman, *R.E. Lee*, vol. 2, 8–12; Lee to Davis, May 20, 1863, *OR*, vol. 25, pt. 2, 810–12; Special Orders No. 146, May 30, *OR*, vol. 25, pt. 2, 840.

5. Trudeau, *Gettysburg*, 28–32; Joseph W. McKinney, *Brandy Station, Virginia, June 9, 1863: The Largest Cavalry Battle of the Civil War* (Jefferson NC: McFarland, 2006), 57.

6. "CLIO," "FROM RICHMOND" (June 10), *ADI*, June 16, 1863; "CLIO," "FROM RICHMOND" (June 13), *ADI*, June 18.

7. Trudeau, *Gettysburg*, 35; Glenn Tucker, *High Tide at Gettysburg: The Campaign in Pennsylvania* (Indianapolis: Bobbs-Merrill, 1958), 22; Eric L. Wittenberg and Scott L. Mingus, *The Second Battle of Winchester: The Confederate Victory that Opened the Door to Gettysburg* (El Dorado Hills CA: Savas Beatie, 2016), 335–36; Larry B. Maier, *Gateway to Gettysburg: The Second Battle of Winchester* (Shippensburg PA: White Mane, 2002), 304; "BATTLE OF WINCHESTER!" and "GLORIOUS NEWS," *ADI*, June 18, 1863.

8. Trudeau, *Gettysburg*, 46–48, 51, 55, 58, 65–66, 68.

9. "CLIO," "FROM RICHMOND" (June 20), *ADI*, June 25, 1863; "BY TELEGRAPH," *ADI*, June 21.

10. "LATEST NEWS FROM THE NORTH" and "From the Richmond Examiner, 22d inst. FROM THE ARMY OF NORTHERN VIRGINIA," *ADI*, June 26, 1863; "BEYOND THE POTOMAC," *ADI*, June 27.

11. Trudeau, *Gettysburg*, 73–74, 88, 103, 114–15, 316; James O. Hall, "The Spy Harrison," *Civil War Times Illustrated*, vol. 24, no. 10 (February 1986), 22.

12. "CLIO," "FROM RICHMOND" (June 25), *ADI*, July 1, 1863; "Another Raid—Reported Capture of Harrisburg," *ADI*, July 2; "Our Troops in Pennsylvania" and "Later from

the North," *ADI*, July 3;"BY TELEGRAPH," *ADI*, July 4; Kent Masterson Brown, *Retreat from Gettysburg: Lee, Logistics, and the Pennsylvania Campaign* (Chapel Hill: University of North Carolina Press, 2005), 76–77.

13. "THE FOURTH OF JULY," *ADI*, July 4, 1863; "BY TELEGRAPH," *ADI*, July 7; "The Yankee Army Routed," "Further Details of the Late Battle" and "Great Battle in Pennsylvania," *ADI*, July 8.

14. "OUR SUCCESSES," *ADI*, July 9, 1863.

15. "RICHMOND, July 10," "Cheering from Pennsylvania" and "Further from Pennsylvania," *ADI*, July 11, 1863.

16. "CLIO," "FROM RICHMOND" (July 6), *ADI*, July 12, 1863; "FROM GENERAL LEE'S ARMY," *ADI*, July 14.

17. "From the Savannah Republican. FROM PENNSYLVANIA AND MARYLAND. THE GETTYSBURG FIGHT IN RELIABLE SHAPE," *ADI*, July 17, 1863; Harry W. Pfanz, *Gettysburg—The First Day* (Chapel Hill: University of North Carolina Press, 2001), 184, 350.

18. "From the Savannah Republican," *ADI*, July 17, 1863; Stephen W. Sears, *Gettysburg* (Boston: Houghton Mifflin, 2003), 239, 249, 257, 261; Harry W. Pfanz, *Gettysburg: The Second Day* (Chapel Hill: University of North Carolina Press, 1987), 292, 405, 429; Harry W. Pfanz, *Gettysburg: Culp's Hill and Cemetery Hill* (Chapel Hill: University of North Carolina Press, 1993), 266, 327.

19. "From the Savannah Republican," *ADI*, July 17, 1863; George R. Stewart, *Pickett's Charge: A Microhistory of the Final Attack at Gettysburg, July 3, 1863* (Dayton OH: Press of Morningside Bookshop, 1980 [1959]), 263; Earl J. Hess, *Pickett's Charge—The Last Attack at Gettysburg* (Chapel Hill: University of North Carolina Press, 2001), 333.

20. "CLIO," "FROM RICHMOND" (July 16), *ADI*, July 21, 1863.

21. W. H. Neisbet to "Dear Father," *ADI*, July 26, 1863.

27. Charleston Is Shelled

We call attention of our readers to the letter from Charleston of our able correspondent, "290," which appears in our paper to-day. No one will rise from its perusal, who will not feel gratified at the clear and comprehensive accounts it embraces. It is like a chapter in *history,* and will, doubtless, add to the popularity of the writer with the readers of this journal.

WITH THIS PIECE John Steele was doing more than calling readers' attention to a long letter printed in the *Intelligencer* on Aug. 1, 1863. The editor was celebrating that he had a skilled reporter sending solid news accounts from the war-front. While "Clio" reported Richmond rumors and offered opinion on the latest stories, "290," Samuel Chester Reid, was serving up first-rate journalism direct from the scene of events. Steele virtually beamed when he termed Reid's writing "like a chapter in *history.*"[1]

In 1863 Reid was writing for the *Mobile Daily Advertiser & Register* and the *Mobile Daily Tribune* as "Ora"; the *Memphis Daily Appeal* and the *Chattanooga Daily Rebel* (both as "Sparta"); and the *Atlanta Daily Intelligencer* as "290." The conscientious correspondent wrote different variants of the same story for his several papers, with an eye to which elements would be of interest to readers in each locale. And he did pretty well by it. In his diary he tallied his wages for the first two and half years of the war as $12,000, plus money for lodging and horse fodder.[2]

Earlier in the spring, Reid was at Chattanooga, reporting on events in Middle Tennessee, leading Steele in the *Intelligencer* to predict on April 17 that "the great battle of the war, we feel more assured, will come off in less than sixty days." It did not, however. Following the battle of Stones River in December 1862, Union Maj. Gen. William S. Rosecrans' Army of the Cumberland held position around Murfreesboro, thirty miles southeast of Nashville. Gen. Braxton Bragg's Army of Tennessee was thirty miles farther southeast. For six months, January–June 1863, the Tennessee front remained stationary.[3]

Reporting *sitzkrieg* can be dull, and it certainly offered no challenge for a correspondent of Samuel Reid's acumen. Thus after things started heating up at Charleston—a Union naval attack on Fort Sumter in Charleston Harbor in April, and an amphibious landing on Morris Island, five miles southeast of the city in early July—"290" went there. John Steele announced that the *Intelligencer* correspondent had passed through Atlanta on July 14, heading for Charleston. Still cloaking Reid's identity, Steele simply referred to "the Army Correspondent of the Mobile Tribune, the well-known and accomplished 'ORA,' and '290,' of this paper."

Reid/ "290" arrived at Charleston in time to report the Union attack on Battery Wagner, July 18, in which participated the 54th Massachusetts, a regiment of African Americans.

All the Federals' attacks were repulsed with heavy loss. "The negroes of the 54th Mass., who were forced in the front ranks"— Col. Robert Shaw had actually requested the lead position—"were nearly all killed, with their officers, including the colonel." And while he overstated Union casualties ("estimated to exceed 2,000," when the actual count was 1,515, including 272 killed, wounded and missing in the 54th), "290" delivered a rarity in Southern wartime reporting: the exact number, 174, of Confederates killed, wounded and missing in the battle. It was innately for this and other reasons that the *Intelligencer*'s editor hailed his correspondent's writing as "like a chapter in *history*."[4]

As the events in Charleston played out, the *Intelligencer* reported local news as well. An occasional feature in the *Intelligencer*'s pages was a rundown of proceedings in the city court presided over by Atlanta mayor James M. Calhoun. One such installment, published on August 1, described disorderly conduct charges brought against one L. Moran and his wife, Hannah. It seems that on the 24th of July, Mr. Moran "was chastising a negro with a cowhide when his wife came up and interfered." Moran then turned the cowhide on his wife, who threw a glass tumbler at him. The mayor issued his judgment: "notwithstanding some men seem to think they have a right to whip their wives," Calhoun did not. In fact, His Honor judged that Hannah had a right to throw that glass after she had been struck, and that he would not have punished her at all had she not pleaded guilty to disturbing the peace. As it was, Mr. Moran received a fine of $40, and Mrs. Moran that of a single dollar.[5]

Intelligencer owner Jared Whitaker had employees to pay in an inflationary war economy. In announcing yet another subscription price increase on July 29—the paper's fourth of the year—editor Steele cited "the increased rates demanded by our own workmen" as just one of the causes. Costs of everything needed to publish were going up 25 to 30 percent, he declared.

Paper mills in particular were charging more, as he had explained in the *Intelligencer*'s previous price hike of April. Shortly after that, readers of the *Intelligencer* would have held in their very hands the physical evidence of a wartime newspaper's financial stresses. On July 1, 1863, Jared Whitaker's and John Steele's journal ceased to be printed on its familiar lightly brown-tinged pages, but on newsprint of a darker, blue-gray hue. As rags, the usual paper-making product, became scarcer and dearer in the Confederacy, manufacturers turned to straw and other substances (cotton, corn husks, sunflower stalks). The resulting sheets when unbleached came out in different colors, some rather festive. The *Charleston Mercury* in January 1862 assumed a lovely fuschia look; a few months later, the editor of the *Savannah Republican* claimed that one of his Mississippi exchanges had arrived in fully five colors. In its new tint, then, the *Intelligencer* was joining other Confederate newspapers in at least two trends: more colorful pages and higher prices. The increase of April 12, 1863 had taken subscription rates to $5 per month. The new increase of late July raised that price another dollar.[6]

The day after announcing its rate hike, the *Intelligencer* followed its practice of endorsing President Davis' fast days. On July 30, John Steele announced that "the 21st proximo"—from the Latin *next* [as in month, or August] as set aside for "fasting, humiliation and prayer throughout the Confederate States." And as it had done previously, the paper also printed the proclamation. Davis did not mention Vicksburg or Gettysburg, only "our recent reverses" as further reason that the people should engage in prayer and supplication unto "that God who has hitherto conducted us safely through all the dangers that environ us." Steele chimed in. "Let importunate prayer ascend from every tongue, and soon songs of praises will take the place of dolorous compaints."[7]

John Steele was proud of "290's" reporting, and he evidently looked for it in the other papers for which Samuel Reid wrote. On August 2, he excerpted a long passage from "Ora's" article in a recent issue of the *Mobile Tribune*, declaring that it set the bar for "correspondents and editors in what they write for the newspapers of the country in these stirring times." "The highest standard of excellence for the reputation of a journal, or public writer, is TRUTH," "Ora" declared, as he affirmed his determination to pursue that standard in his own work. Steele cited "290's" letter that he had published the day before as evidence that the *Intelligencer*'s correspondent in Charleston was, like the *Tribune*'s "Ora," dedicated to the pursuit of truth in journalistic writing. Modern scholars of Confederate journalism agree. Mark K. Dolan has recently commented that "his dedication to truth-telling under adverse conditions showed Reid's devotion to accuracy and fact-finding."[8]

"290" sent short telegraphic dispatches to the *Intelligencer* from Charleston, but he was not the Press Association's man on the scene; Bartholomew R. Riordan also sent to John S. Thrasher, the P. A. superintendent in Atlanta, updates on the shelling of Sumter and Wagner. On August 5, the *Intelligencer* published Thrasher's announcement that the P. A. Board of Directors had voted to take out a copyright on all telegraphic dispatches that it sent to its members. Thrasher explained that after the Press Association's "BY TELEGRAPH'" columns appeared in member papers, copies of them were taken to telegraph offices, where the P. A. texts were wired to "numerous clubs along the line of the telegraph and published by bulletins" that were not P. A. members and that therefore had not paid for the news thus received. Not only was this unfair to P. A. members, but it diminished the value of their telegraphic columns, when the news was disseminated before the members' papers could be mailed to subscribing readers. Thrasher complained that "one of the great telegraph companies has lent itself to this practice," although he did not name it (the culprit was the Southwestern Telegraph Company in Mobile).

For all of these reasons, Thrasher announced that henceforth the "Telegraphic Reports of the Press Association" would be copyrighted, and thus protected by law against unauthorized use. As a result, starting in early August, at the top of the *Daily Intelligencer*'s "BY TELEGRAPH" column, instead of "Expressly for the Intelligencer," this notice began to be printed: "REPORTS OF THE PRESS ASSOCIATION. Entered according to act of Congress in the year 1863, by J. S. THRASHER, in the Clerk's office of the District Court of the Confederate States for the Northern District of Ga."

The Southwestern Telegraph Company resisted the Press Association's copyright to the point of persuading an Alabama congressman to introduce a resolution in the C.S. House of Representatives, challenging the legitimacy of copyrighting news dispatches. Timely intervention by one of Thrasher's Richmond agents succeeded in getting the congressman's resolution killed in the House Judiciary Committee. It is worth nothing that the Confederacy was first to grant copyright protection of newspaper dispatches; the United States did not do so until the twentieth century.[9]

At the time, all four daily newspapers in Atlanta were members of the Press

Association: the *Intelligencer,* the *Southern Confederacy,* the *Commonwealth,* and the newly arrived *Memphis Appeal.* Jared Whitaker had been sole proprietor of the *Intelligencer* since July 1862 (when Archibald Gaulding sold his half-share), just as John McClanahan was sole owner of the *Appeal.* But the two other papers were going through changes at the top, as the *Intelligencer* announced on August 12. George Adair and Henly Smith, longtime owners of the *Southern Confederacy,* had sold out to "Messrs James & Daniels." J. S. Peterson of the *Commonwealth* had also sold his paper to one M. W. Hutcheson, who was renaming it the *Gazette.* While the *Intelligencer* had occasionally sparred with the *Confederacy* over political positions and the issue of martial law, John Steele nonetheless offered all of his competitors the best. "There is in Atlanta room enough, and business enough for us all," he charitably noted.

Similarly, when two other papers shifted operation from Chattanooga to Marietta, not twenty miles northwest of Atlanta, the *Intelligencer* editor welcomed them to north Georgia. Huntsville, Ala., had fallen in April 1862; its paper, the *Confederate,* sought refuge in Chattanooga. After the advance of Rosecrans' Union army fired artillery shells into that city on August 22, 1863, both the *Confederate* and the *Chattanooga Rebel* fled southward (earning Franc Paul's paper a nickname, "*Chattanooga Rebel* on Wheels"). Steele wished them well, and expressed hope that they would be able to return to their respective homes.[10]

In August the *Intelligencer* began to run an occasional series, "Our City," first presented on August 16. "Our streets are filled with strangers, and it will do no harm for our people to keep a good watch on all of them," Steele warned. All about were signs of war. The government had seized all the fine carriage horses; ladies would simply have to do more walking, the editor remarked.

> Speaking of ladies—sister Jemima! Did you ever see so many of your sex in Atlanta before? Every street, house, garret and cellar appears full of them, there they go in one ceaseless string all day long; some pretty (those *we* like to spend a few minutes looking at), some ugly and some neither one thing or the other, but all dressed up in blockade runners' toggery, that cost a small fortune to purchase. We have seen but one young lady this week in our streets dressed in homespun, she was very pretty and looked so neat that we almost felt like—never mind what. As a "little of a good thing is as good as a feast" we will dispense with the ladies for the present. . . .[11]

Ladies in Atlanta would have been more aware than anyone else of the rise in the cost of living, which the *Intelligencer* addressed on August 12. A night's stay in a local hotel was now going for $8 (meals included). Private boarding houses offered room and board for $3 a night (a price that had led "Clio" in Richmond the previous December to characterize boarding house matrons as "female blood-suckers"). With food prices soaring—corn meal $4 a bushel, bacon $2 a pound—working families were having to go without such "luxuries" as sugar, coffee and tea. Editor John Steele laid much of the blame on farmers; "the lust of avarice has taken hold of the hearts of too many of them." He urged food-producers in the Confederacy "to let conscience govern in their prices, and not the heartless law of trade."

The *Intelligencer*'s editorial evidently struck a nerve, as it was reprinted elsewhere. After it appeared in the *Lynchburg* (Va.) *Republican,* one of Steele's exchanges, the editor groused that he had not been credited as author. Worse, the *Republican* had attributed the article to the *Intelligencer*'s rival, the *Atlanta Daily Southern Confederacy*.[12]

In half a dozen letters and telegrams sent during August, "290" kept readers of the *Intelligencer* informed of events in Charleston harbor, as when on August 19 he wired back that "the casualties in Sumter to-day is one killed and four wounded in all during the bombardment." Then came the bombshell (literally), when "290" reported that the Yankees had actually begun to fire not just at Fort Sumter, but into the city of Charleston itself, which was still occupied by many civilians. "The enemy commenced shelling the city at half past one o'clock this morning with 100 pound shell, from their advance battery on Morris Island, throwing thirteen shells," he stated.[13]

There were no reports of casualties from the bombardment of August 22. One observer wrote an *Intelligencer* employee about the event, from which the editor printed some passages: a shell-started fire in Williams' Drug Store on Hayne Street was extinguished by firemen; projectiles striking street pavement sent rocks flying in all directions.

John Steele's response to the Yankees' "gross outrage" was predictable, yet relatively restrained: "one of the many cowardly acts they have been guilty of since the war commenced."[14]

NOTES

1. "We call the attention . . . ," *ADI*, Aug. 1, 1863.
2. Dolan, "Samuel Chester Reid," 261.
3. "MOVEMENTS OF THE ENEMY," *ADI*, Apr. 17, 1863; Edwin C. Bearss,

"Tullahoma Campaign" in Patricia L. Faust, ed., *Historical Times Illustrated Encyclopedia of the Civil War* (New York: Harper & Row, 1986), 764–65.

4. "The Army Correspondents . . . ," *ADI*, July 15, 1863; E. Milby Burton, *The Siege of Charleston 1861–1865* (Columbia: University of South Carolina Press, 1970), 162–71; Edward G. Longacre, "Siege and Evacuation of Battery Wagner, S.C." in Patricia L. Faust, ed., *Historical Times Illustrated Encyclopedia of the Civil War* (New York: Harper & Row, 1986), 46; Russell Duncan, *Where Death and Glory Meet: Colonel Robert Gould Shaw and the 54th Massachusetts Infantry* (Athens: University of Georgia Press, 1999), 110–13.

5. "MAYOR'S COURT," *ADI*, Aug. 1, 1863.

6. "OUR NEW RATES FOR SUBSCRIPTION AND ADVERTISING," *ADI*, Apr. 12, 1863; "NEW RATES OF SUBSCRIPTION AND ADVERTISING," *ADI*, July 29; Massey, *Ersatz in the Confederacy*, 140–41.

7. "THE PRESIDENT'S FAST DAY," *ADI*, July 30, 1863; "PROCLAMATION BY THE PRESIDENT OF THE CONFEDERATE STATES," *ADI*, July 31.

8. "TRUTH," *ADI*, Aug. 2, 1863; Dolan, "Samuel Chester Reid," 255.

9. Risley, "Confederate Press Association," 132; Patricia G. McNeely, "Bartholomew Riordan: Spying on Washington, D.C." in Patricia G. McNeely, Debra Reddin van Tuyll and Henry H. Schulte, eds., *Knights of the Quill: Confederate Correspondents and their Civil War Reporting* (West LaFayette IN: Purdue University Press, 2010), 127; J. S. Thrasher, "PRESS DISPATCHES COPYRIGHTED," *ADI*, Aug. 5, 1863; van Tuyll, *Confederate Journalism*, 135–36.

10. "THE MEMPHIS APPEAL," *ADI*, May 27, 1863; "VALEDICTORY," *ADI*, July 29, 1862; Ellis, *Moving Appeal*, lxvi; "CITY NEWSPAPER CHANGES," *ADI*, Aug. 12, 1863; McMillan, ed., *Alabama Confederate Reader*, 127; Morris, "*Chattanooga Rebel*," 22; Diane Bragg, "An Affair of Words: Tennessee's Civil War Press and the Confederate Nation" in David B. Sachsman, ed, *A Press Divided: Newspaper Coverage of the Civil War* (New Brunswick NJ: Transaction Publishers, 2014), 115.

11. "OUR CITY," *ADI*, Aug. 16, 1863.

12. "COST OF LIVING," *ADI*, Aug. 12, 1863; "CLIO," "FROM RICHMOND," *ADI*, Dec. 3, 1862; "WRONG CREDIT," *ADI*, Aug. 26, 1863.

13. "290," "BY TELEGRAPH. FROM CHARLESTON" (August 19), *ADI*, Aug. 21, 1863; "290," "Special to the Intelligencer from '290.' Shelling of Charleston. The British Consul Protests," *ADI*, Aug. 25, 1863.

14. "A. K.," "THE SHELLING OF CHARLESTON" and "CHARLESTON," *ADI*, Aug. 25, 1863.

28. Chickamauga

WHEN CHICKAMAUGA—the biggest battle ever fought in Georgia, and sixth largest in the entire American civil war—erupted on Sept. 19, 1863, ten miles south of Chattanooga, editor John Steele had a man on the scene—or close to it. And well he should have, as readers of the *Intelligencer* had known for some time that a battle was brewing in northwest Georgia between the armies of Union Maj. Gen. William S. Rosecrans and Confederate Gen. Braxton Bragg. "The armies are in . . . close proximity," the paper declared on September 6; Bragg's army was ready "to meet the enemy and to give them battle" (September 11).[1]

Just as Steele had shifted his ace reporter Reid from middle Tennessee to Charleston when things heated up on the coast in the spring of 1863, so too did he send him back to the Bragg-Rosecrans theater when battle loomed a few months later. On September 3, the *Intelligencer* informed readers that "290" was *en route* to Chattanooga, "where he is called by the pending battle in Tennessee, and which will prove one of the greatest events of this war."[2]

But the front in Tennessee was changing. On September 1, Knoxville in east Tennessee had been abandoned by Confederate forces. Two weeks later, the refugeeing *Knoxville Register* reappeared in Atlanta and released its first relocated issue. Steele printed an announcement from the *Register*'s publisher, who informed Tennesseans living in the city that they would be welcome to visit the paper's new "Tennessee Headquarters" on Whitehall Street downtown. A few days later Steele extended the "right hand of fellowship" to the *Register* and wished it "a prosperous career."[3]

News of the fall of Knoxville—Union troops entered on September 2—was upstaged by direr reports still. On September 9, "290" delivered the bad news that Bragg's forces had abandoned Chattanooga; Rosecrans had gotten troops across the Tennessee River downstream from the city that were threatening the Confederate rear. John Steele responded predictably. "Let our people cheer up," he exhorted on the 11th. "The grand battle of the revolution may begin at any moment," he added on September 13. "ALL WILL BE WELL" was the headline of another article appearing in the *Intelligencer* that day.⁴

The *Intelligencer* on September 20 published the "Battle Order of General Bragg." Dated September 16 from Lafayette, Ga., the hortatory address delivered encouragement to his troops. They had been recently reinforced (by two infantry divisions, under Lt. Gen. James Longstreet from Lee's army). "Trusting in God and the justice of our cause," Bragg concluded, "and nerved by the love of the dear ones at home, failure is impossible, and victory must be yours."⁵

As it turned out, in one of those rare occasions in the Civil War when a commanding general's hot oratory actually coincided with events, victory did indeed belong to Confederate soldiers in the battle fought at Chickamauga.

With Longstreet's reinforcements, Bragg's army outnumbered Rosecrans' forces, 68,000 to 58,000. The Confederates attacked on September 19 throughout the day and were repulsed at all points. Bragg renewed his offensive on the 20th, but midmorning Rosecrans blundered. He ordered an infantry division out of the center of his line at the very point where Longstreet and 11,000 troops were going to attack. Shortly after 11 a.m. the Southerners broke through the gap, forcing the right wing of the Union line to flee in confusion. In the afternoon Maj. Gen. George Thomas stood firm on the left (north) end of Rosecrans' line, as the commanding general himself galloped back to Chattanooga, leading his routed troops.

At Chickamauga Confederates won a decisive victory, but at a steep cost: 2,312 killed, 14,674 wounded, 1,468 missing (18,454). Union losses totaled 1,656 dead, 9,749 injured and 4,774 absent (16,179).⁶

Headline for the *Intelligencer*'s 'TELEGRAPHIC" column for Tuesday, September 22 screamed "Great Battle near Ringgold!" The Press Association released from Atlanta a dispatch dated September 21 that generalized about the fighting on Saturday (September 19) and Sunday (the 20th). The Confederates had attacked both days, the report declared; on the latter, the Federals were driven back eight miles toward Chattanooga. "The slaughter of the Yankees is represented . . . to have been unprecedented," the dispatch stated; Confederates killed, wounded and missing were said to be about 5,000, including several general officers. This was about all the *Intelligencer* could report on September 22. John Thrasher, the Press Association superintendent, posted an announcement at the end of his telegraphic column. Addressed "TO THE PRESS," it stated that he had on the 21st prepared a press dispatch carrying the latest news of the battle of Ringgold, but when he took it to the office of the Atlanta post commander, he found that Col. Marcus Wright was not there to approve the text. "Consequently no report of the battle can be sent," Thrasher explained.[7]

Thus even before wounded men from Bragg's army began arriving in the city—"but few of the wounded from Saturday's fight have yet reached here," the paper announced on the 23rd—Atlantans could anticipate a virtual avalanche of ailing soldiers. Several dozen prominent citizens had met downtown to raise money to help care for them. The *Intelligencer* also announced that women willing to roll bandages and make lint for wound dressing were to meet Wednesday morning at the government storeroom on Peachtree Street.[8]

The previous major battle on the Tennessee-Georgia front, Murfreesboro, had filled Atlanta's army hospitals. Nine months later, in the late summer of 1863, there were five large medical facilities, housing altogether 1,550 beds: the two on the old fairground acreage southeast of downtown (four hundred beds each); the Gate City and Empire Hospitals in the two hotels (300 and 250 beds, respectively); and the Medical College Hospital (200). In addition to these five big hospitals there were smaller ones, such as the Winship and Blackie Hospital on Peachtree Street.

As prospects for a big battle loomed in late August, Dr. Samuel H. Stout, Medical Director of Hospitals for Bragg's army, had warned Dr. Joseph P. Logan, Atlanta's hospital director, to clear as many sick from his wards as he could—all available beds in Atlanta would be needed for the wounded. In the next two weeks Logan was able to transfer about 500 patients to Newnan, LaGrange and other places south of the city. Dr. Logan took the additional step of looking for another hospital site. On September 15, he reported to Stout, "I think that I shall endeavor to get possession of the Female Institute Building," a three-story structure on Ellis Street. This he did on September 21, the day after the battle, but just before the avalanche of wounded from Chickamauga began pouring into the city. On the 26th, the *Intelligencer* published the school's announcement that it had been appropriated for the medical work ahead.

Complicating the work of Confederate surgeons in Atlanta was that the city had no formal receiving and distributing hospital. A facility so designated would take in patients from the trains, to be registered and sent on to the Fair Grounds or other general hospitals in town. Obviously an "R & D" hospital had to be near the Car Shed downtown, but in the summer of 1863 no suitable structure was available. So Dr. Logan had erected a "rough shed," as he put it, "to which soldiers could be removed from the railroad depot, until the ambulances could remove them to the hospitals." In late August Dr. Logan was eyeing the Gate City Hotel Hospital as site for a permanent R & D facility. But before he could act, there came the big battle of September 19–20.[9]

The *Intelligencer* carried news of the engagement as it trickled in from Chickamauga. During the battle nine Confederate general officers had been taken from the field. Brigadiers Preston Smith and Ben Hardin Helm were killed. Among those wounded, Hood had been so seriously injured that his right leg had to be amputated at the thigh. Two days after the battle a rumor circulated that Hood would not survive his surgery. From its headquarters in Atlanta, the Press Association on the 22nd sent out a telegraphic report, "Further from the battlefield," which stated, "Our loss in general officers is very great. Brig. Gen. Helm, of Ky., was killed while leading a charge. Gen. Hood's wound is reported to be a mortal one." The *Intelligencer* ran this anew. "Gen. Hood's leg was amputated some distance from the knee, and it is our painful duty to state that he died after the operation." Papers as far away as Richmond carried this incorrect news on the 23rd. "We understand that Major General Hood is dead," lamented the *Richmond Enquirer*, "if true the victory, however great and decisive, has been most dearly purchased." Col. Josiah Gorgas of the Ordnance Bureau noted in his diary, "our job is damped by the loss of General Hood, who died under the operation of amputating his leg. . . . His loss is a severe one, second only to that of Jackson." General Lee took the news hard. "I grieve for the gallant dead," he wrote General Longstreet, "and mourn for our brave Hood."

Then came word that Hood was not dead, after all. The Press Association sent out a corrective note: "Gen. Hood is not dead. His right leg was amputated. He says he will live to fight the Yankees at least another battle." "We learn to-day," wrote War Department clerk John B. Jones on the 24th, "that Gen. Hood is not dead, and will recover." John Thrasher, superintendent of the Press Association in Atlanta, later felt compelled to explain to his board how he had gotten the story wrong. Several days before the battle, General Bragg had sent the Press Association reporter attached to his army, Will Woodson, back to Atlanta. As a result, John Thrasher complained, "I was compelled to make up in Atlanta the Press reports of the interesting events on the Chickamauga from intelligence obtained from wounded brought from the field, and information received from persons coming from that vicinity." Someone from the battlefield had evidently said that Hood had died there, and the P. A. printed it. In the *Intelligencer* Thrasher publicly criticized "the unwise course of Gen. Bragg in not permitting the Press Association to remain in the front." Bragg later relented and Thrasher's news service could circulate more reliable telegraphic dispatches from the Army of Tennessee.

In addition to sending back Woodson, Bragg had also taken even harsher measures against John Linebaugh, reporter for the *Memphis Appeal*. On September 17 (two days before the battle of Chickamauga), the general had had Linebaugh arrested on a charge of treason, arising from his writing about the army's movements. A few weeks later Linebaugh was released after the *Appeal* had lodged a *habeas corpus* complaint. This meant that Atlanta newspapers were without field correspondents with Bragg's army. Fortunately, *Intelligencer* editor Steele had "290," who by the 21st had moved to near the combat zone; he headed his dispatch of that day, "BATTLE-FIELD." He could only offer a few generalities, but suggested the scope of the Confederate victory by stating that thirty pieces of Union artillery had been captured (actually, the final count was a stunning sixty-six guns). "290's" statement that the enemy was being pursued led Steele to forecast, "we have no doubt that our forces will be in possession of Chattanooga." In an accompanying editorial he expressed further hope that "a large portion of Tennessee will soon be delivered from the presence of the vandal foe that has so long devastated her fields, insulted, outraged, and plundered her gallant people."[10]

On September 25, the *Intelligencer* was able to print two telegrams from "290," who was still situated at the battlefield and thus able to relate what he was hearing. Casualties in Bragg's army were said to run as high as 8,000–10,000, while the enemy's were guessed to be from 25,000 to 30,000. Also on the 25th Steele ran a long letter from Reid at "Chicamauga," dated September 22 that filled in further particulars of the "great and complete victory." Reid included the text of a congratulatory address distributed by General Bragg to his troops. In his issue of that day Steele commended this article "from the graphic pen of our talented correspondent '290,'" whose identity the editor still conscientiously concealed.[11]

The wounded Southern soldiers from whom the P. A.'s John Thrasher strained to glean information about the battle had begun to arrive in Atlanta by rail on September 21. "Two heavy trains with the wounded arrived here yesterday afternoon," announced the Press Association's article of the 22nd (printed in the *Intelligencer* on the 24th), "and our reporters have sedulously endeavored to obtain from the officers among them the particulars and incidents of the most important battle which has been fought during the present year" (to those in Atlanta, apparently Chickamauga was more important than the distant Gettysburg).[12]

Sedulous endeavor was also required to care for the wounded once they had begun to be unloaded from the cars and carried to the Fair Ground, Gate City and Medical College hospitals. A quartermaster officer, Maj. G. R. Fairbanks, issued an appeal for donated straw to use in the men's bedding. An Executive Aid Committee of thirty-one of the city's citizens was organized to raise money to help the ladies' relief and hospital societies. On September 26, the *Intelligencer* publicized a very generous response: the Roswell Manufacturing Company, the cotton mill north of Atlanta, had appropriated $5,000 for the Committee's work.[13]

Then there was the work itself. Medical officers, nurses, litter-bearers and citizen volunteers gathered at the railway depot to intercept the casualty-laden trains. The women helping out came in for special mention from editor Steele in his "OUR CITY" column for September 26. "The ladies in town are all engaged in the noble work of alleviating the suffering of our wounded," he wrote. "Heaven speed them in their patriotic task!" The men did their part, too. A list published in the *Intelligencer* on September 24 reminded volunteers of their around-the-clock duty. A "Car Shed Committee" was to help unload the stricken from the trains; a "Wayside Hospital Committee" was to help at the Receiving & Distributing facility downtown.[14]

Registry at the R & D, then transfer to the various city hospitals, allowed the *Intelligencer* as a public service to print the soldiers' names and hospital assignments. The paper's first such listing appeared on September 26, showing 63 patients at the Gate City, 119 at Fair Ground No. 2, and 172 at the Medical College.[15]

With more patients coming in every day, beds had to be emptied and room had to be found. At the Winship & Blackie Hospital on Peachtree, 208 men had been admitted up to September 24. Medical officers sorted through them and identified the slightly wounded and other cases that could be removed to the army hospitals that Bragg's hospital director, Dr. Samuel Stout, had established at Griffin, LaGrange and other points. So many were sent farther south that the Winship & Blackie on the morning of the 25th had only 45 patients. But every facility was busy if not at full bed capacity. The Institute Hospital listed 150 patients as of September 27. At the end of the month, the Fair Ground #1 had 433 names.[16]

At the other end of the line, however, things were not going so smoothly. Distressing reports filtered out about care—and lack of it—for those soldiers still at the field hospitals in north Georgia. After a group of Atlanta's civilian volunteers arrived at Ringgold on the morning of September 23, looking for ways to help, they traveled to the battlefield. They were gratified to see that all wounded men had been removed from the field and taken to care stations. But at a large number of those field hospitals, as reported by one of the group, O. H. Jones (in the *Intelligencer* on September 26), the Atlantans found the wounded "suffering from want of nurses, provisions, and medicines." There was even a shortage of surgeons; in expectation of another engagement near Chattanooga, many doctors had gone forward to be with Bragg's army.[17]

These hurts could only be wanded away by the suave hand of a patriotic editor, such as John Steele. On September 26 he reflected on Braxton Bragg. True, the general had achieved a checkered career thus far as commander of the Army of Tennessee at Perryville, Murfreesboro and Tullahoma. But at Chickamauga the Confederate leader had proven his mettle. Against Rosecrans' forces, Steele hailed Bragg for having "inflicted on the vaunted flower of their army the most complete and total defeat of the war."[18]

NOTES

1. Livermore, *Numbers and Losses*, 140–41; "From Bragg's Army," *ADI*, Sept. 6, 1863; "THE SITUATION IN FRONT," *ADI*, September 11.

2. "SIEGE AND BOMBARDMENT OF CHARLESTON," *ADI*, Sept. 3, 1863.

3. "KNOXVILLE EVACUATED," *ADI*, Sept. 1, 1863; Thomas L. Connelly, *Civil War Tennessee: Battles and Leaders* (Knoxville: University of Tennessee Press, 1979), 70; "KNOXVILLE REGISTER," *ADI*, September 15; "KNOXVILLE DAILY REGISTER," *ADI*, September 17.

4. Steve Cottrell, *Civil War in Tennessee* (Gretna LA: Pelican Publishing, 2001), 89–90; "190," "Chattanooga and Cleveland Evacuated," *ADI*, Sept. 10, 1863; "THE SITUATION IN FRONT," *ADI*, September 11; "THE SITUATION IN FRONT" and "ALL WILL BE WELL," *ADI*, September 13.

5. "BATTLE ORDER OF GENERAL BRAGG," *ADI*, Sept. 20, 1863.

6. Peter Cozzens, *This Terrible Sound: The Battle of Chickamauga* (Urbana: University of Illinois Press, 1992), 59–60, 368, 532; John E. Stanchak, "Battle of Chickamauga" in Patricia L. Faust, ed., *Historical Times Illustrated Encyclopedia of the Civil War* (New York: Harper & Row, 1986), 136–37.

7. "TELEGRAPHIC. Great Battle near Ringgold!," *ADI*, Sept 22, 1863; J. S. Thrasher, "TO THE PRESS," *ADI*, September 22.

8. "MEETING FOR THE RELIEF OF WOUNDED SOLDIERS" and "LADIES! LADIES!," *ADI*, Sept. 23, 1863.

9. "OUR WOUNDED," *ADI*, Jan. 6, 1863; Stephen Davis, "An Avalanche of Wounded:

Atlanta's Confederate Hospitals and the Challenge of Chickamauga, Fall 1863," *Atlanta Medicine*, vol. 78, issue 3, (2005), 6–7; Mohr, *Threshold of Freedom*, 130–31; "A CARD," *ADI*, Sept. 26, 1863.

10. "The Victory of Chickamauga. Incidents from the Battle-Field" (Atlanta, September 22), *ADI*, Sept. 24, 1863; "TELEGRAPHIC. Further from the battlefield" (Atlanta, September 22), *ADI*, September 23; "TELEGRAPHIC. The Victory of Chickamauga," *ADI*, September 24; John P. Dyer, *The Gallant Hood* (Indianapolis: Bobbs-Merrill, 1950), 211; Richard M. McMurry, *John Bell Hood and the War for Southern Independence* (Lexington: University Press of Kentucky, 1982), 79; Lee to Longstreet, September 25, *OR*, vol. 29, pt. 2 749; "Report of Mr. Woodson," Sept. 9, 1863, in *Minutes of the Board of Directors of the Press Association, Oct. 14, 1863*, 10, 23–24; Ford Risley, "Wartime News over Southern Wires: The Confederate Press Association" in David B. Sachsman, S. Kittrell Rushing and Roy Morris Jr., eds., *Words at War: The Civil War and American Journalism* (West Lafayette IN: Purdue University Press, 2008), 157; Andrews, *South Reports*, 348–49; James M. Perry, *The Civil War Correspondents—Mostly Rough, Sometimes Ready* (New York: John Wiley & Sons, 2000), 161; "Special to the Intelligencer from '290.' Further from the Great Battle" (September 21), *ADI*, Sept. 24, 1863; report of Capt. O. T. Gibbes, C.S. Artillery, *OR*, vol. 30, pt. 2, 40–42; "ED. INT.," "The Latest from the Front" and "THE SITUATION IN FRONT. THE BATTLE OF CHICAMAUGA [sic]," *ADI*, September 24.

11. "290," "The Battle of Chicamauga! GREAT AND COMPLETE VICTORY! [*By Private Express from the Battle-Field.*]" (September 22) and "THE SITUATION IN FRONT," *ADI*, Sept. 25, 1863.

12. "The Victory of Chickamauga. Incidents from the Battle-Field" (Atlanta, September 22), *ADI*, Sept. 24, 1863.

13. "WANTED FOR THE WOUNDED," *ADI*, Sept. 25, 1863; "MEETING FOR THE RELIEF OF WOUNDED SOLDIERS," *ADI*, September 23; "GENEROUS CONTRIBUTION," *ADI*, September 26; Galloway, ed., *Dear Old Roswell*, 3.

14. "OUR CITY," *ADI*, Sept. 26, 1863; "CAR SHED COMMITTEE" and "WAYSIDE HOSPITAL COMMITTEE," *ADI*, September 24.

15. "FROM TENNESSEE. Wounded received at the Gate City Hospital. Dr. Paul F. Eve, of Nashville, Surgeon in Charge"; "LIST OF WOUNDED ADMITTED TO THE FAIR GROUND HOSPITAL, NO. 2, ATLANTA, GA., ON THE 22D"; and "LIST OF WOUNDED RECEIVED AT THE MEDICAL COLLEGE HOSPITAL UP TO THE NIGHT OF THE 22D. INST.," all in *ADI*, Sept. 26, 1863.

16. Davis, "Avalanche of Wounded," 8; Schroeder-Lein, *Confederate Hospitals*, 98.

17. O. H. Jones, "REPORT TO THE ATLANTA EXECUTIVE COMMITTEE FROM THE BATTLEFIELD," *ADI*, Sept. 26, 1863.

18. "REFLECTIONS ON GEN. BRAGG," *ADI*, Sept. 26, 1863.

29. President Davis Visits Atlanta

"COUSIN NOURMA" WAS A REPORTER for the *Mobile Advertiser & Register* who also occasionally submitted pieces to the *Intelligencer* during 1863. On October 6, the paper published his article about how the battlefield of Chickamauga looked ten days after the engagement. His overriding impression from the experience involved the smell of death. Dead horses and unburied and decaying soldiers produced "a most foul stench." Commenting on the body of one dead Yankee, "Nourma" wrote that "a most offensive stink exhales from the carcass." Burial parties were still at work; slain Federal soldiers had been gathered "in piles of four, five and a dozen" amidst a huge battlefield over which were strewn "dead horses, broken caissons . . . torn clothes . . . empty haversacks . . . hundreds of torn shoes and hats."

Apparently the bodies of Southern soldiers, their identities unknown, had been buried under state designations (presumably from uniform buttons). "In one little dell," "Nourma" observed "a large number of our dead.—South Carolina here has representatives from several of her noble regiments. A number of graves of Mississippians," he continued, "are marked at various points in this vicinity."

Roaming from the Snodgrass house to the Kelly farm, "Nourma" found Mr. Kelly packing up his household goods, he evidently could not take it any longer, as "numerous dead Yankees and horses are scattered about his house."

One dead Northerner was found actually sitting up. "The worms were feasting on him. His jaw was hanging down; his black and glistening body, which had swollen until it burst off his clothing, was one of the most horrible and disagreeable sights we ever witnessed." Everywhere, scarred trees showed the marks of bullets, cannonballs and shells; "we are certain that not a single tree has escaped" in an area that "Nourma" judged to be eight miles long and from three to five miles wide.[1]

Some 19,000 Confederates had been killed, wounded or reported missing at Chickamauga. From the site where Longstreet broke through Rosecrans' line in the center of the battlefield, to where the Union army stopped running to entrench south of Chattanooga, was just shy of ten miles. For this modest gain of ground, Bragg at Chickamauga gave up about 2,000 of his men for each mile. He had "pursued" Rosecrans' beaten army in a most dilatory manner before ordering his troops to dig in south and east of the Federals' lines, settling into a sort of siege.[2]

In the aftermath of Chickamauga, the *Intelligencer* carried articles questioning whether all of this was worth the blood expended. On October 6, the paper offered the letter of "Alabama," a soldier in Bragg's army who from Chattanooga on the 1st had written, "after the fight Sunday night [September 20], as fatigued and hungry as our men were, they all say they would rather have pushed forward and beat the enemy to Chattanooga, than have remained behind to wait for our supplies to come up." "290" (Samuel Chester Reid) weighed in with his letter of October 3, also printed in the *Intelligencer* on the 6th. "If we had only a battery of 100-pound Parrott guns," he wrote, referring to long-range heavy artillery, "we could easily shell them from the town." Reid was evidently able to view the enemy's position from heights around Chattanooga. "From the increased number of tents, and fires at night, there is no doubt that they have been largely reinforced within the past two days," he observed, either from Burnside's force at Knoxville or from Grant's in Mississippi. "290" offered his own opinion: "What is to be done, should be done quickly, as every day gives the enemy superior advantages over us."

John Steele joined the conversation with an editorial published on October 3. "There appears to be a desire among some of our people to censure Gen. Bragg for not throwing his army on the enemy's works at Chattanooga, and several of our exchanges are calling for a move on and capture of that place at every hazard," Steele acknowledged. But he defended Bragg against these "bar room generals." After Chickamauga, he reasoned, Rosecrans' army remained strong and dangerous; the Federals at Chattanooga had retired into formidable defenses; and attacking them would cost perhaps 25,000 men, half of Bragg's army. For these reasons, the editor judged that the critics and carpers were demanding the impossible from the Confederate commander.

It further irked Steele that these "stay-at-home patriots" were criticizing General Bragg from the comfort of their homes, having found some way of avoiding military service. "For heaven's sake have done with all such folly!" the editor exclaimed. "If they cannot manfully aid our brave boys in gaining *their* independence, let them at least keep still, and not cast blame and censure on movements and actions on the part of military men, that they are profoundly ignorant of."[3]

Unfortunately, it was not only the "bar room generals" who were criticizing Braxton Bragg, but it was *Bragg's own generals.* In truth, the commanding general of the Army of Tennessee started the trouble after Chickamauga when on September 29 he suspended Lt. Gens. Leonidas Polk and Daniel Harvey Hill from their commands and sent them back to Atlanta, accusing them of dereliction during the campaign, and writing President Davis laying out his grounds. Davis and his War Department tried to get Bragg to stand down; instead Bragg charged Polk with disobedience and neglect of duty. Lt. Gen. James Longstreet, who had brought troops from Lee's army to reinforce Bragg's, on September 26 wrote Secretary of War James A. Seddon, suggesting that Bragg be relieved and that General Lee be sent west to succeed him. Polk wrote the president, his old friend from before the war, blaming Bragg for not chasing Rosecrans to Chattanooga after the recent battle.

There was obviously a lot for Jefferson Davis to be worried about. He sent his aide, James Chesnut, to Bragg's army and to report back. On October 5, Chesnut telegraphed that things were so bad that the president himself had better travel to the army to deal with Bragg's rebellious generals. [4]

The president lost no time; he was on the train heading south from Richmond on October 6. Federal capture of Knoxville prevented him from taking the most direct rail route, so he traveled through the Carolinas before arriving in Atlanta on the evening of October 8. The *Intelligencer* of the 10th made brief mention of Davis' arrival. The president headed out the next morning on the northbound Western & Atlantic train. Editor Steele speculated that Davis' visit to the army was to allow him "to investigate the causes of disagreement between Bragg and Polk, and to arrange the difficulty in an amicable manner." The *Intelligencer* editor was remarkably well informed, for one or both of two reasons. Arriving in Atlanta on October 1, General Polk was offered a room at the Whitehall Street home of John Thrasher, the Press Association superintendent. Receiving visitors there, Polk made no secret of his ill feelings toward and critical opinions of Bragg. John Steele may have been one of those visitors, thanks to Thrasher; the P. A. superintendent may also have told the editor what he had heard the general talking about at his house.[5]

Arriving near Chattanooga that evening, Davis spent the night at Bragg's headquarters in a house on Missionary Ridge. The president spent the next four days, October 10–13, doing the expected, reviewing and addressing the troops. But the president's main mission was to talk to the generals. He had already met with Polk awhile in Atlanta on the evening of the 8th, and had disclosed that he was not inclined to relieve Bragg.

Nonetheless, Davis spent most of October 10 at the commanding general's headquarters, meeting with Bragg and his senior officers. Davis asked Generals Longstreet, Simon B. Buckner, D. H. Hill and Benjamin Franklin Cheatham, the army's infantry corps leaders, what they thought of their commanding general—*with Braxton Bragg sitting there.* Unabashed, Longstreet spoke up and called for Bragg's removal. The others agreed. But by nightfall word spread that Davis had assured Bragg that he would sustain him in army command. More, the president and the general had decided that Bragg's critics would have to be dealt with. Leonidas Polk never returned to the army while Bragg commanded it. Longstreet was sent off to Knoxville, eventually to return to Virginia. Harvey Hill was relieved on October 15, blamed for mistakes at Chickamauga. Buckner was demoted to division command. Frank Cheatham asked to be relieved on October 31.[6]

In Atlanta, the *Intelligencer* editor was unaware and uninformed of this chicanery. All that John Steele could do was to publish the reports issued by the Press Association and received from his man-on-the-scene, Sam Reid. The P. A. dispatch of October 11 mentioned that the president and staff had ridden along the lines that day, receiving "cheer after cheer by our enthusiastic and confident veterans." On the 14th, "290" wired from Dalton that Davis had left Bragg's army and that before he departed people called him from his train car for remarks; "he said that we had been looking in the face of the enemy, but would soon see their backs."

On Friday, October 16, Davis was again in Atlanta. The *Intelligencer* assured readers, "the conference between the President and the military leaders who have the care of the interests of Georgia, will give our people greater assurance than ever, that our houses are destined to be free for at least another six months, and we hope for all time, from the foul foot of the invader."[7]

Reporting war news, publishing graphic descriptions of battlefield carnage, rebuking "stay-at-home patriots," following presidential itineraries, voicing upbeat opinions, supporting authorities' public appeals—all of these aspects of John Steele's editorial work were to be seen in the pages of the *Atlanta Intelligencer* throughout October of 1863. Notably evident as well was the paper's forceful defense of General Bragg after Chickamauga, and of President Davis' handling of Bragg's unhappy generals. John Steele, as we would say today, was a company man.

Also to be seen was his covering of Georgia's fall elections. Wednesday, October 7 was election day in the state: for governor, state legislators and Confederate congressmen. Steele urged a robust turnout by the "Freemen of Georgia"—the Confederate States Constitution, following that of the United States, did not offer women the right to vote. Interestingly, officials did provide Georgia's Confederate soldiers in the field the opportunity to cast their votes. In December 1861, the state legislature had passed an act to allow Georgia volunteers and troops to cast ballots; this would be the first state election with such a feature.[8]

In 1863 Governor Joseph E. Brown was up for re-election to a fourth term. Though he had opposed conscription on constitutional grounds, Brown emphasized his support for the Davis administration and the Confederate war effort in general. He was opposed by two candidates: Joshua Hill of Madison, a former U.S. congressman, and Timothy M. Furlough, former state senator and wealthy planter from Americus in south Georgia.

As it had in 1861, the *Intelligencer* again supported the governor. After election day, returns were slow to arrive, in part because of mailed vote counts from Georgia regiments in Lee's army. But within a week, editor Steele felt confident to write that he had "received intelligence sufficient to warrant the belief that Governor Brown is elected over both his opponents."

On October 21, the *Intelligencer* published the numbers counts from 110 counties in the state: BROWN FURLOW HILL, 19,337 6,310 11,440.

The state constitution prescribed a popular vote majority for the gubernatorial victor, otherwise a run-off would be thrown to the legislature. The *Intelligencer* noted that Brown's majority over his two opponents was 1,579.

Just as interesting was that more than 9,000 Georgia soldiers had voted in the gubernatorial contest, according to a listing published in the *Intelligencer*. Altogether the soldiers gave Brown 6,906 votes, Furlow 1,203 and Hill 986.

[Historians have ballyhooed Union soldiers' being allowed to vote in the 1864 U.S. presidential election, but the Confederate States did much more than the Federal government to allow its soldiers in the field to vote, and much earlier than that. In November 1861, five Confederate states had provisions for soldiers' absentee voting for home district congressmen; camp commanders were to send returns to the appropriate state officials. Another two passed similar laws soon afterward (South Carolina and Georgia; the latter was passed Dec. 14, 1861). Two more states followed after the congressional election of 1863. Finally, the Confederate Congress handled the matter for Louisiana and Missouri. Governors of Texas and Kentucky had provided for the soldier vote on their own initiative. Thus all thirteen states of the Confederacy (as recognized by the government in Richmond) had provided for soldier suffrage.]⁹

The *Intelligencer* also published voting returns for Georgia's ten Congressional districts and for the state House and Senate. But the news continued to swirl around the president's handling of Braxton Bragg and his critics. After the *Atlanta Southern Confederacy* on October 30 criticized Jefferson Davis for not having removed Bragg from command of the Army of Tennessee, John Steele defended both the president and the general in a reply the next day. The editor explained that while with the army, Davis had listened to the criticisms against Bragg, "and after due deliberation, decided that they were not sufficiently strong to warrant his removal." Steele further scolded the *Confederacy* for, in its own words, "rousing the spirit of opposition to the administration" over the matter. He argued that "raising the 'spirit of opposition' can do no good, while it may be followed by evils of the most disastrous character." Steele went so far as to charge that "one false step in the direction proposed by the Confederacy may sound the death knell of Southern Liberty." The editor pledged that his paper would continue to support both President Davis and General Bragg. He also assured readers that "that gallant officer, aided by the heroic Longstreet, is making all the necessary preparations to meet the enemy."¹⁰

"The situation in Tennessee" was on everyone's mind, and the conscientious editor had to mull over what military news he could safely publish. On October 31 Steele explained, "as the Confederacy of yesterday made mention of it, we see no harm in informing our readers that for some days Buckner with a large body of men has been steadily moving towards Knoxville." Indeed, three weeks earlier under the headline, "Reticence," the *Intelligencer* had printed the letter received from a Confederate officer, "In for the War," who urged the Southern press to be guarded in what it published as war news. Steele commended the suggestion; in an accompanying editorial, he urged "our contemporaries"—other newspaper editors—to heed "In for the War's" advice.¹¹

"Reticence" sparked a reply from John Thrasher of the Press Association, published in the *Intelligencer* of October 13. The superintendent voiced full support of prudent journalism and cited the P. A.'s instructions to reporters showing how whole categories of subjects were to be avoided—"in short, whatever would interest . . . the Yankees." He suggested that a respectful, cooperative relationship between army officers and press reporters—not more censorship by the former—was the best way to prevent journalistic indiscretion.¹²

From such concerns, hard-working editors sometimes needed a break. It was in a spirit of levity that the *Intelligencer* on October 28 printed a column, titled "WIT AND HUMOR," containing a dozen or so little yarns. One had to do with the "tender-hearted widower" who was seen to faint at the funeral of his third beloved.

"What shall we do with him?" asked a friend of his.

"Let him alone," said a waggish bystander. "He'll soon revive."

A chuckle could even come from the war front. The *Intelligencer* carried "an anecdote of Gen. Ewell" that had reportedly occurred during Lee's late campaign.

> When Gen. Ewell entered Carlisle, Pa., the clergymen of the city called on him in a body and asked him if they might open their churches on the ensuing Sunday.
>
> "Certainly," said Gen. Ewell; "I wish to attend church myself."
>
> They retired, but soon re-appeared, and in the most deferential tone inquired whether he objected to their praying for the President of the United States.
>
> "Not at all," replied Gen. Ewell; "I know of no man who is more in need of your prayers."
>
> The Yankee preachers silently withdrew.¹³

NOTES

1. Andrews, *South Reports*, 490; "COUSIN NOURMA," "THE BATTLEFIELD OF CHICAMAUGA," *ADI*, Oct. 6, 1863

2. Livermore, *Numbers and Losses*, 105–106; Peter Cozzens, *The Shipwreck of Their Hopes: The Battles for Chattanooga* (Urbana: University of Illinois Press, 1994), 54.

3. "ALABAMA," "ARMY CORRESPONDENCE. FROM GENERAL BRAGG'S ARMY" (Chattanooga, October 3) and "290," "ARMY CORRESPONDENCE" (Chattanooga, October 3), *ADI*, Oct. 6, 1863; "DEMANDING IMPOSSIBILITIES," *ADI*, October 3.

4. Thomas Lawrence Connelly, *Autumn of Glory: The Army of Tennessee, 1862–1865* (Baton Rouge: Louisiana State University Press, 1971), 235–37; "His Excellency Jefferson Davis," Oct. 4, 1863, *OR*, vol. 30, pt. 2, 66.

5. William J. Cooper, *Jefferson Davis, American* (New York: Alfred A. Knopf, 2000), 455; "PRESIDENT DAVIS," *ADI*, Oct. 10, 1863; "OUR CITY," "*ADI*, October 11; Huston

Horn, *Leonidas Polk: Warrior Bishop of the Confederacy* (Lawrence: University Press of Kansas, 2019), 348–49.

6. Cooper, *Jefferson Davis*, 456; Hess, *Braxton Bragg*, 179–80; Stanley F. Horn, *The Army of Tennessee: A Military History* (Indianapolis: Bobbs-Merrill, 1941), 287; Connelly, *Autumn of Glory*, 245–47, 252, 261–62; Christopher Losson, *Tennessee's Forgotten Warriors: Frank Cheatham and His Confederate Division* (Knoxville: University of Tennessee Press, 1989), 115–16.

7. "The President Before Chattanooga" (October 11), *ADI*, Oct. 13, 1863; "290," "Departure of President Davis" (Dalton, October 14), and "THE PRESIDENT," *ADI*, October 16.

8. "THE ELECTIONS TO-DAY" and "ELECTIONS—MANNER OF CONDUCTING THEM," *ADI*, Oct. 7, 1863.

9. Bryan, *Confederate Georgia*, 41–45; Hill, *Joseph E. Brown*, 132–37; "THE ELECTION FOR GOVERNOR," *ADI*, Oct. 13, 1861; "ELECTION FOR GOVERNOR," *ADI*, October 21; Yearns, *Confederate Congress*, 42–43, 250 n.3.

10. "ELECTION RETURNS," *ADI*, Oct. 30, 1863; "THE EVENT, THE DANGER AND THE REMEDY" and "THE SITUATION IN TENNESSEE," *ADI*, October 31.

11. "THE SITUATION IN TENNESSEE," *ADI*, Oct. 31, 1863; "IN FOR THE WAR," "RETICENCE" and "RETICENCE" (editorial), *ADI*, October 10.

12. J. S. Thrasher, "RETICENCE—ARMY MATTERS AND THE PRESS," *ADI*, Oct. 13, 1863.

13. "WIT AND HUMOR," *ADI*, Oct. 28, 1863; "ANECDOTE OF GEN. EWELL," *ADI*, October 29.

30. "290" Is Joined by "A.S.A."

SAMUEL CHESTER REID was "290," a "special" for the *Atlanta Intelligencer.* John Steele had kept his field correspondent's identity hidden from readers, although along the way he had played a few tricks on them. In April 1863, for instance, the editor had complimented "Ora," the correspondent for the Mobile papers, without disclosing that "Ora" was Sam Reid, the same reporter as employed by the *Intelligencer.* Six months later, Steele slyly reprinted a short article from the *Register,* originally of Knoxville, but now relocated to Atlanta, which announced that "SAM C. REID, the indefatigable correspondent of the Intelligencer, goes to the front to-day."[1]

Reid had been at the front earlier than that. From "camp before Chattanooga," on September 28, "290" had laid out the military situation before him. "Our army lies in a valley forming a semi-circle, extending on the left from the base of Lookout Mountain to that of Missionary Ridge on the right"; Maj. Gen. William S. Rosecrans' Federal army, holding Chattanooga, was "very strong and well fortified"; and "there is no probability of a speedy encounter with Rosy's army for some days." A week later, on October 5, Reid stated he had heard that reinforcements were on their way for "Rosy." (He was right; from the Army of the Potomac two infantry corps, some 12,600 men, were on their way west.) From these events, Reid/"290" predicted, "the final contest for the possession of Tennessee is fast approaching."[2]

Yet it was not. Three weeks later, all "290" could report was that Rosecrans had been relieved and Maj. Gen. George Thomas, "the Rock of Chickamauga," had been named to command the Federal Army of the Cumberland.[3]

Things were static on the other front also, as "Clio" reported from the Confederate capital. "General Meade is no nearer Richmond now than McClellan was a year ago," the correspondent wrote on November 1, forecasting that unless "something decisive" took place in the next month and a half, the Union army and Lincoln's government "may give up all expectations of striking an effective blow before next spring." ("Clio" would be proven correct.)[4]

During the first half of November the Richmond correspondent sent at least four letters to the paper, but exchanges were also crucial. The *Intelligencer*'s issue for November 5 carried a long article clipped from the *Charleston Mercury* about the president's reception in the city on his return trip to the capital from having visited Bragg's army in Tennessee. The *Mercury* also kept Atlanta readers informed of the Federals' ongoing bombardment of Fort Sumter, thanks to the *Intelligencer*'s reprinting of its daily columns (example: "THE SIEGE—ONE HUNDREDTH AND THIRTY FOURTH-DAY," November 27).

Someone in Charleston was doing a lot of counting, as the *Intelligencer* on November 11 reprinted a *Mercury* article that gave details of "the second grand bombardment of Sumter," which had begun on October 26 (the first one had lasted from August 17 to September 2). In it was a recapitulation of shots fired by Northern cannon (15,583), number of times Sumter had been struck (12,302), casualties in the fort garrison (96 killed and wounded), and even the number of times the flagstaff had been knocked down (34).[5]

In addition to the Press Association telegraph service, John Steele was fortunate to have Reid/"290" stationed at Missionary Ridge reporting on events. On November 6, Reid wired a short note about Confederate artillery on Lookout Mountain, west of Missionary Ridge, shelling the Federals below. "290" could see the enemy activity and observed on the 10th that "the enemy is making every preparation for the storming of Lookout Mountain." He referred to the reinforcement of Thomas' army by Sherman's troops from Mississippi, but failed to mention that General Ulysses S. Grant had arrived in Chattanooga to take charge of matters there.

Bragg's main forces were deployed along the crest of Missionary Ridge, and "290" predicted that the Federals would attack them there too. General Bragg had made the questionable decision to send Longstreet with part of his army off toward Knoxville to attempt to recapture that place; "290" reported what he heard about this movement as well.[6]

Reid could sense that the Federal offensive he had predicted was about to finally occur. "The struggle of Lookout," he wrote on November 22, "bids fair to become desperate if the enemy attempts to storm it in force." This letter was published in the *Intelligencer* on Wednesday, November 25—the day that the first telegraphed news about fighting at Chattanooga appeared in the paper. "290's" dispatch related the bare details. "Missionary Ridge, Nov. 23.—The enemy formed in three lines of battle in our front this morning, drove in our pickets, and attempted to storm our works. At 2 P.M. they opened on our lines, their batteries playing also. Musketry firing was very heavy but ceased at 3 P.M.—artillery firing only at the present time."

Editor Steele expressed his hopefulness on the 25th as this early news was coming in. Writing of Grant, Steele declared, "the indications, as we write, are that he was repulsed on his first advance, and whether he renewed his attack on yesterday or not, we are not now advised." Further dispatches were opaque, such as Bragg's wire to Adjutant General Samuel Cooper in Richmond, printed in the *Intelligencer* on November 26: "We have had a prolonged struggle for Lookout Mountain to-day."[7]

"290" was able to write a long account on the afternoon of November 24 and put it on the train at Chickamauga station; it appeared in the *Intelligencer* on the morning of Thursday, the 26th. Building on his telegram of November 23 ("at 2 P.M. they opened on our lines"), "290" described the fighting that afternoon as a skirmish involving some twenty Confederate casualties. On the 24th, he wrote, Union infantry attacked Bragg's forces on Lookout Mountain, but at the time of his writing "290" did not know the outcome.[8]

On November 23 Union troops captured Orchard Knob, a low hill in front of Missionary Ridge. On the 24th, Confederates were driven from Lookout Mountain. On the next day Sherman's troops attacked the Confederate right on Missionary Ridge, but were repulsed. Then a massive Union attack broke the center of Bragg's line and sent his troops fleeing to the rear. Samuel Chester Reid did not attempt to sugar-coat the bad news in his telegram sent from Chickamauga the night of the 25th: "after several assaults our lines gave way and our men fell back in some confusion."[9]

Then Reid tried to be a bit cheerier. In a mailed dispatch appearing in the *Intelligencer* on November 28, he emphasized the heavy casualties that the Union troops had suffered in their assaults. They carried Lookout Mountain "at a terrible sacrifice." Sherman's attack against General Patrick Cleburne's troops on the Confederate right "was four times repulsed with frightful loss." Elsewhere, though, Bragg's line had been broken: "Stevenson gradually gave way, as well as Stewart's division, Stevenson's division becoming panic-stricken." The Confederate army's retreat ended at Ringgold, Georgia, "290" related, well south of the battlefield.[10]

John Steele did his part as well to manage news of the rout of Bragg's army at Missionary Ridge. "That we have suffered a partial defeat is not to be denied," the editor admitted on November 28 (without elaborating on what a "partial" defeat actually was), but he added that he had "full assurance for saying that it is not half as bad as many imagine." True, the left of Bragg's line had fallen back "in considerable disorder," yet the Federals had not vigorously pursued due to their high losses, and Bragg's army was standing firm in north Georgia. For "290's" letter published in the same issue, the editor gave the headline, "No Cause for Despondency."[11]

On November 30, "290" sent a telegram that provided perhaps the only good news after the disaster at Missionary Ridge: "DALTON, Nov. 30.—Cleburne's division engaged Osterhaus' division Friday morning one mile this side of Ringgold, driving him back with the loss of 1500, we capturing 320 prisoners, their wounded, and four stands of colors."

Sam Reid was reporting on the battle of Ringgold Gap, a dozen miles southeast of Chattanooga, fought on Nov. 27, 1863. Bragg's army was retreating after the collapse on Missionary Ridge. Federal forces of "Fighting Joe" Hooker's XX Corps were pursuing so vigorously that in the early morning of November 27 one of Bragg's staff officers ordered Maj. Gen. Patrick Cleburne—whose division withdrawing from Missionary Ridge was the only one still in marching order—to take position at Ringgold Gap and hold off the enemy till the army's wagon trains could move southward to safety. With about 4,000 troops deployed in the gap, Cleburne repulsed the attacks of Brig. Gen. Peter Osterhaus' Federals. The five-hour fight left casualties of 65 killed, 424 wounded and 20 missing for the North; 20 killed, 190 wounded and 11 missing for the South. But Cleburne's men had held their ground till all the wagons had passed to safety. For his successful rearguard action, Cleburne earned a formal resolution of thanks from the Confederate Congress.

Reid learned enough particulars of the engagement of November 27 to write a long account, "The Battle of Ringgold," that appeared in the *Intelligencer* of December 25. The reporter likened Cleburne's stand at Ringgold to the legendary stand of Leonidas at Thermopylae. More, he invoked the name of a Confederate hero as well in laying out the stakes of the battle: "the safety of the whole army now depended on the action of the Stonewall of our army, Gen. Cleburne."[12]

A measure of a military disaster is the speed afterward with which the beaten army commander offers his resignation. The *Intelligencer*'s "special" at Dalton, Sam Reid, reported on December 2, a week after Missionary Ridge, that General Bragg had been relieved of command at his own request by President

Davis. This led John Steele to comment, "the enemies of General Bragg are gratified at last." Lt. Gen. William J. Hardee, senior infantry corps commander, was named as his temporary successor.¹³

By December 9, rumors began to swirl that Gen. Joseph E. Johnston had been appointed as commander of the Army of Tennessee. From Dalton "290" wrote on the 10th that he could not confirm Johnston's appointment. Indeed, he believed that the men in the ranks preferred that General Hardee be retained as their commander. "His troops have never forgotten his deeds at Shiloh, Perryville, and Murfreesboro," he added.¹⁴

Then there came a rumor that none other than Robert E. Lee could be coming to lead the army in Georgia. For his part, though, editor Steele expressed satisfaction with General Hardee, "the gallant Georgian."¹⁵

On December 18, "290" sent another telegram: "a dispatch from the president announces that Gen. Johnston has been appointed to command the Army of Tennessee." Reid was well informed; Davis had given Johnston the order just two days before. "290," though, was not John Steele's only source for army news at Dalton. Also, on December 18, one "A. S. A." sent a wire with the same information on Johnston's assumption of command. He was Alexander St. Clair Abrams, a Louisianan who had served in the army until medically discharged in September 1862. He then turned to newspaper work, obtaining a position on the staff of the *Vicksburg Whig*. When that paper folded, Abrams took up a musket and helped defend Vicksburg. He surrendered with Pemberton's army and was soon paroled. Making his way to Atlanta, Abrams came into the acquaintance of John Steele when he had the Intelligencer Steam Press print his booklet, *A Full and Detailed History of the Siege of Vicksburg* (1863).

In early December 1863, the *Intelligencer* also began to print an advertisement, headlining a "Highly Interesting Work," by "A. S. Abrams of New Orleans," that had just been published. The booklet's price: a dollar a copy, or in bulk $18 for a dozen. Purchasers were advised that orders had to be accompanied by cash, sent to the *Intelligencer* office, addressed either to Abrams or J. F. Buchanan, the newspaper's treasurer. The work, just eighty pages long, covered the siege of Vicksburg from Grant's investment to Pemberton's surrender. Abrams had also kept his ears open for how many people had been slain by Grant's shelling of the city during his month-and-a-half siege; the newspaperman counted "one female and a negro."

The soldier-journalist-historian was also something of a poet; the *Intelligencer* on Oct. 27, 1863 carried Abrams' verses titled "Battle-Eve Dreams," which concluded thus:

> The battle is fought,
> And the list of the dead is sought—
> A youthful son falls in the strife,
> And a husband hath yielded his life.
> A father's soul is far away;
> He was killed on that blood day.
> Their battle-eve dream was their last,
> 'Twas a gleam from the light of the past.

Steele had made Abrams an assistant editor of the *Intelligencer* and had sent him to Dalton to report on morale in the army there. In a letter dated December 16, "A. S. A." observed that "the gloom of defeat wears off quickly" and that he had found the men in better spirits than he had expected. They would be satisfied with either General Hardee or Johnston as their new commander, he related, but that "all state that nothing would please them so much as sending Gen. Beauregard to command the Army of Tennessee."[16] General Johnston and staff arrived at Dalton on December 26, as the Press Association reported in the *Intelligencer*; Johnston issued an order the next day announcing his assumption of the army's command.[17]

The end of the year afforded John Steele the opportunity to reflect on how the war had progressed thus far, in an editorial printed on December 24. "The soil of Georgia is no longer pressed by hostile feet"—the Union army was still at Chattanooga. Yet with spring of the new year, Federal forces could be expected to surge into the Empire State. "How will the people meet it?" he asked his fellow Georgians. "Let every man, therefore, nerve his heart for the impending struggle." The volunteers had all gone off; the conscripts had been scraped up; but the editor figured that manpower was still to be had in the state. "Men must fight who never dreamed of fighting when the war began," Steele reasoned. He urged the "strong arms and the stout hearts" to come forth, "that we may resist tyranny to the bitter end."[18]

In the spring of 1864 Peter W. Alexander of the *Savannah Republican* paid a compliment to Atlanta's press fraternity, writing, "next to Richmond, Atlanta may boast of the ablest conducted Press in the country, the most unflagging enterprise, and some of the most accomplished of gentlemen among its editors."[19] "P. W. A." could make this claim because of such editors as John Steele, but also for the talented writers and experienced reporters with whom he surrounded himself. Alexander St. Clair Abrams was certainly one of them.

NOTES

1. "AN ARMY CORRESPONDENT," *ADI,* Apr. 28, 1863; "SAM C. REID" (*Knoxville Register*), *ADI,* October 24.

2. "290," "ARMY CORRESPONDENCE" (September 28), *ADI,* Oct. 1, 1863; "290," ARMY CORRESPONDENCE" (October 5), *ADI,* October 7; Roger Pickenpaugh, *Rescue by Rail: Troop Transfer and the Civil War in the West 1863* (Lincoln: University of Nebraska Press, 1998), 89.

3. "290," "ARMY CORRESPONDENCE" (October 26), *ADI,* Oct. 31, 1863.

4. "CLIO," "FROM RICHMOND," *ADI,* Nov. 8, 1863.

5. "CLIO," "FROM RICHMOND," *ADI,* Nov. 8, 11, 19, 1863; "ARRIVAL AND RECEPTION OF PRESIDENT DAVIS AT CHARLESTON," *ADI,* November 5; "THE SIEGE—ONE HUNDREDTH AND THIRTY-FOURTH DAY," *ADI,* November 27; "THE ENEMY'S BOMBARDMENT OF SUMTER," *ADI,* November 11.

6. "Special to the Intelligencer from 290" (November 6), *ADI,* Nov. 10, 1863; "ARMY CORRESPONDENCE" (November 10), *ADI,* November 13; Steven E. Woodworth, *Six Armies in Tennessee: The Chickamauga and Chattanooga Campaigns* (Lincoln: University of Nebraska Press, 1998), 153; "TELEGRAPHIC" (November 17), *ADI,* November 19.

7. "290," "ARMY CORRESPONDENCE" (November 22), "SECOND DISPATCH" (November 23) and "FROM THE FRONT," *ADI,* Nov. 25, 1863; "TELEGRAPHIC," *ADI,* November 26.

8. "290," "THE VERY LATEST FROM THE FRONT" (November 24), *ADI,* Nov. 26, 1863.

9. James R. Sullivan, *Chickamauga and Chattanooga Battlefields* (Washington: Government Printing Office, 1956), 34–41; "290," "Latest from the Front," *ADI,* Nov. 27, 1863

10. "290," "Latest from the Front," *ADI,* Nov. 28, 1863.

11. "THE SITUATION IN TENNESSEE" and "290," "Latest from the Front. . . . No Cause for Despondency," *ADI,* Nov. 28, 1863.

12. "290," "TELEGRAPHIC. Latest from the Front," (November 30), *ADI,* Dec. 1, 1863; Thomas Robson Hay, ed., *Cleburne And His Command by Capt. Irving A. Buck and Pat Cleburne Stonewall Jackson of the West by Thomas Robson Hay* (Jackson TN: McCowat-Mercer Press, 1959), 346; Mauriel Phillips Joslyn, "An Open, Stand Up Affair: Cleburne's Defense at Ringgold Gap" in Joslyn, ed., *A Meteor Shining Brightly: Essays on Maj. Gen. Patrick R. Cleburne* (Milledgeville GA: Terrell House, 1997), 115, 117, 125, 133, 137, 139; "290," "BATTLE OF RINGGOLD," *ADI,* December 25.

13. "290," "TELEGRAPHIC. Latest from the Front" and "GENERAL BRAGG RELIEVED," *ADI,* Dec. 3, 1863.

14. "RE-ORGANIZATION OF THE ARMY OF TENNESSEE," *ADI*, Dec. 9, 1863; "290," "ARMY CORRESPONDENCE," *ADI*, December 12.

15. "WHO IS TO COMMAND THE ARMY OF TENNESSEE," *ADI*, Dec. 7, 1863.

16. "290," "Special to the Intelligencer From 290" (December 18), *ADI*, Dec. 20, 1863; Symonds, *Joseph E. Johnston*, 248; "A. S. A.," "Dalton, Dec. 18—Gen. Johnston. . . ." (December 18), *ADI*, December 20; Bill Bond, "Abrams Made Mark on County, State," *Orlando Sentinel*, Jan. 28, 1987; Richard B. Harwell, ed., *The Confederate Reader* (New York: David McKay Company, 1976 [1957]), 195, 205–206; Walker, *Vicksburg*, 117, 175; Harwell, "Atlanta Publications," 169, 188; Hoehling, *Vicksburg*, ix, 248, 376; "Battle-Eve Dreams," *ADI*, October 27; "REVIEW OF THE WAR," *ADI*, Jan. 9, 1864; Andrews, *South Reports*, 431; "A. S. A.," "ARMY CORRESPONDENCE" (December 16), *ADI*, December 18.

17. "TELEGRAPHIC. REPORTS OF THE PRESS ASSOCIATION. SECOND DISPATCH," *ADI*, Dec. 30, 1863.

18. "The Pause," *ADI*, Dec. 24, 1863.

19. Andrews, *South Reports*, 38.

31. The Editors Speak

AT THE START OF 1864 the *Atlanta Daily Intelligencer* was going strong. By this time in the war, there were reportedly only three dozen daily newspapers being published in the Confederacy. The *Intelligencer*, however, boasted a circulation that stretched into the thousands (though it was reluctant to publish those figures). Jared I. Whitaker, *Intelligencer* proprietor, colonel and Commissary General for Georgia, was attending to his official duties while leaving the daily operation of his newspaper to editor John H. Steele.[1]

Principal responsibility of a newspaper's editor was to fill his pages with material. As his colleagues in the editorial fraternity did, Steele relied on exchanges with other Confederate newspapers for news on their "beat," and colorful editorial commentary about the same. Steele also benefited from the fact that the *Intelligencer* was publishing in one of the larger cities of the South. Its wide circulation led to readers mailing letters to the editor in hopes of publication. An example is a missive sent by "Georgian" (printed in the paper on October 1), complaining about the prices being charged for leather that reduced the supply of shoes for the men at the front.[2]

The *Intelligencer* enjoyed a good relationship with the Press Association, whose superintendent, John S. Thrasher, worked out of Atlanta. Thrasher in turn from time to time provided exchanges to the *Intelligencer*, as when he delivered to Steele several issues of the *New Orleans Picayune*. "The sight of the 'Pic' reminded us of old times," Steele mused, except for the fact that the *Picayune* in January 1864 was publishing in a city occupied by Federal troops.

Advertisements, of course, offered the dual benefits of page fillers and revenue sources for the newspaper. From time to time the editor called attention to a particular ad, as when he noticed one for Bohnefield's Coffin Shop. Steele laconically referred to this merchandise as an "article of furniture which sooner or later becomes indispensable to all."[3]

As for news from the Confederate capital, the editor depended on his paid correspondent in Richmond, "Clio"—whose identity at the time of this writing the authors have not learned. And from the Confederate Army of Tennessee, Steele relied upon "290," the pen-name of veteran journalist Samuel Chester Reid. Not to be overlooked was that John Steele had surrounded himself with a competent senior staff. A. E. Marshall served as associate editor and legislative reporter; Isaac Pilgrim worked as foreman of the press room. Marshall sent articles from Milledgeville during the legislative session and Pilgrim subbed for John Steele when the latter was out of town. Marshall's name was dropped from the page two masthead in January 1864, having apparently left the *Intelligencer*. Alexander St. Clair Abrams continued, though, as assistant editor.

The editor had a bit of fun on January 6 when he laid out his office staff's respective duties in the manner of an army's chain of command. "Many people are apt to consider that newspaper offices have nothing of the military about them, but are purely a civil affair. They are very much mistaken, as we will show." Steele then characterized his staff's organization as if it were an infantry corps in the Confederate army.

> A newspaper office is an entire corps, of which the proprietor is "Lieut. General Commanding." [owner Jared I. Whitaker]
> It is also divided into five divisions, classed as follows:
> 1st Division. Editorial room. Editor in Chief, Maj. Gen. Comdg. [editor John H. Steele]
> 2d Division. Composing room. Foreman, Maj. Gen. Comdg. [foreman Isaac B. Pilgrim]
> 3d Division. Business room. Maj. Gen. Comdg. [treasurer John E. Buchanan]
> 4th Division. Bindery. Foreman, Maj. Gen. Comdg.
> 5th Division. Job room. Foreman, Maj. Gen. Comdg.
> It will be seen that a newspaper office is really a military affair.
> The Editor in Chief [Steele] is the Senior Major General, and commands the Corps in the absence of the Lieut. General [Whitaker].

John Steele's writing style was evident in the *Intelligencer*'s editorial columns, such as his opinion piece appearing on January 5. "The present is a momentous year to the State of Georgia," he began. "With Tennessee overrun, it is the next State in the Yankee programme for invasion," Steele declared, as he urged Georgians to "meet the issue . . . like brave men." If "her own citizens are true," the editor predicted, "the genius of history, of song, painting and of sculpture stand ready to record their mighty deeds by which Georgia is to be disenthralled." For this sublime prospect the editor offered a ray of hope. "The whole Yankee army, in May, will have to undergo a re-organization on the expiration of the term of enlistment of their three years' volunteers," he declared; this offered the possibility that Union forces' strength could be diminished if Northern volunteers failed to re-enlist. There was another event in 1864 that would have much bearing on the South's prospects for political independence: the U.S. presidential election in the fall, in which Abraham Lincoln would seek another four years' mandate from Northern voters in which to prosecute the war to successful conclusion. As for this portentous event, "what we are to hope and what to fear from this campaign, every man must judge for himself," Steele shrugged; "we are not prophets and cannot foretell."[4]

John Steele took his editorial responsibilities very seriously, as he made clear on January 6 when he enumerated the properties of a good Confederate newspaperman: "encourage the timid, rally the wavering, convince the doubtful, lash the traitor, expose error, and present the truth with boldness and with convincing force."[5]

Steele and the *Intelligencer* continued to promote the published work of Assistant Editor Abrams. It helped that the Intelligencer Steam Press did the printing of *The Siege of Vicksburg*, Abrams' eighty-page booklet. "The book has already had a large sale," a plug appearing on Jan. 7, 1864 declared. "It has been pronounced by the Press a brilliant and graphic account of that memorable siege," the paper affirmed, pointing out that only "a few copies remain unsold." For this remaining inventory the price had gone up (to $2 each), while the marketing for their sale remained aggressive. The *Intelligencer* ran ads for the book ("THE SIEGE OF VICKSBURG. GREAT SUCCESS!!") that directed "Richmond Dispatch, Mobile Advertiser, and Meridian Clarion, copy three times and bill to this office for collection." Not only that, but Abrams had appointed an officer, Col. T. M. Acton, as sales agent for the army at Dalton. Thousands of Vicksburg veterans, paroled and now in the Army of Tennessee, would want to read about their fight.[6]

Alex Abrams proved to be a prolific writer. The *Intelligencer* had announced publication of his *Siege of Vicksburg* in December 1863. Just a month later, the paper declared, "We shall shortly commence the publication of a small work entitled, 'A Review of the War,' by our Assistant, A. S. Abrams, Esq., Author of 'A Full and Detailed History of the Siege of Vicksburg.'" The *Intelligencer* promised that as soon as it had printed Abrams' "Review," it would be offered for sale "in book form."[7]

Abrams' "Review of the War" premiered on the first page of the *Atlanta Daily*

Intelligencer on Thursday, Jan. 21, 1864. The author pledged in his introduction to "present the different phases of this war, with their generalship, statesmanship, errors and shortcomings in an impartial light." Abrams' goals were commendable, and how he strived to achieve them became evident when the *Intelligencer* began to print chapters of his booklet in almost every issue from January 21 to February 7; the final two chapters, XVII and XVIII, appeared on February 20–21. Manassas, Shiloh and other battles are of course covered, but also less dramatic topics such as how the Confederacy lacked inducements to win foreign powers' diplomatic recognition.[8]

Abrams echoes the *Intelligencer*'s assessment of the battle of Murfreesboro, fought on Dec. 31, 1862-Jan. 2, 1863, when he declares, "the battle resulted in a partial victory to the Confederate forces." After Lee's "glorious victory" at Chancellorsville, Abrams contends that Robert E. Lee should never have marched his army into Pennsylvania. More, "the invasion of Pennsylvania caused the fall of Vicksburg," he argues, positing that troops from Lee's army should have been sent to relieve Pemberton's besieged army."[9]

Abrams' "Review" traces the war all the way through Chickamauga and Missionary Ridge, events that had transpired just a month or so prior to the time of his writing. He terms the Confederate victory of Chickamauga "utterly fruitless," pointing out that "no pursuit was kept up with vigor." Then came "the ignominious rout of the Confederate army from Missionary Ridge." The final installment of Abrams' "Review" appeared in the *Intelligencer* on February 21. In his "concluding remarks," the author declares, "all compromises are unfeasible, and nothing is left but to continue fighting until reason resumes her sway." Abrams apparently intended to continue his narrative later, as his last sentence states, "we close our Review, to be resumed at some future period."[10]

As a resource for his "Review," Abrams had access to Edward A. Pollard's *The First Year of the War*, which had been published in Richmond in 1862. Pollard was as opinionated as he was prolific. On January 28, editor John Steele announced that he had received a pamphlet written by Pollard entitled "The Rival Administrations." As associate editor of the *Richmond Examiner*, Pollard was a frequent critic of Jefferson Davis, and he poured these criticisms into his "Rival Administrations." John Steele and the *Intelligencer* were full-throated defenders of the Davis administration, and either at Steele's suggestion or on his own initiative, Alex Abrams soon had written a rejoinder to Pollard's pamphlet. On February 9, Steele announced publication of Abrams' "President Davis and His Administration." "This is a fair and impartial review of an attack lately made on the administration by Mr. E. A. Pollard," the announcement declared, "and as a defence of President Davis and his administration, is equal to anything written in the war." A week later, Steele commended it to purchasers (a dollar apiece, or a dozen copies for six dollars). Then, on February 25, Steele announced that "President Davis and His Administration" "has already had a large sale, and we would advise our readers to secure a copy at once."[11]

Abrams' literary accomplishments—a history of the siege of Vicksburg, a narrative of the war from April 1861 to the present, a polemic on behalf of President Davis, plus a 188-page novel, *The Trials of a Soldier's Wife: A Tale of the Second American Revolution,* also published during 1864 by the Intelligencer Steam Power Presses (and using one of Confederates' favorites terms for their war for independence), mark the man as a prolific writer in the wartime South. Moreover, they were all composed on top of Abrams' work for the *Intelligencer.* On February 26, "the Assistant" reported to readers about his recent short trip to Dalton. He found General Johnston's army in a strong defensive position, with the troops exhibiting "enthusiasm and determination . . . never surpassed, and from these facts we have strong hopes of success."[12]

Also reporting from Dalton was the *Intelligencer*'s field correspondent with the Army of Tennessee, Samuel Chester Reid. On Jan. 1, 1864, the paper published two letters from "290," in which Reid referred to the Federals' obvious plans "to move forward early in Spring, or before if possible, to crush us." His missive of January 2 included the terse order by which Gen. Joseph E. Johnston assumed command of the army at Dalton from Bragg. But generally there was little activity to write about. The weather was very cold and the opposing armies were huddled up for warmth. "I have nothing of interest," Reid acknowledged in his letter from Dalton, dated the 3rd.[13]

More dramatic material came from Reid's interview at Dalton with Capt. T. Henry Hines, who had ridden with Brig. Gen. John H. Morgan in his daring raid into Indiana and Ohio in July 1863. Morgan and his command had been run down and captured; then the officers were imprisoned in the Ohio State Penitentiary at Columbus. Hines figured out a way for them to tunnel their way out, and after several weeks of digging, on the night of November 27, Morgan, Hines and a few others escaped. All of this was related by "290" in a long article that took up five of the six columns in the *Intelligencer*'s second page on Jan. 8, 1864. Reid included an account of Morgan's raid, the Confederates' surrender on July 26, 1863, and the escape four months later. By December 29 Hines had made his way to Dalton, where the reporter interviewed him.[14]

As John Steele had done for the booklets written by Alex Abrams, the *Intelligencer* editor promoted Sam Reid's monograph, "Morgan's Capture and Escape," when it was printed as a sixteen-page pamphlet by the Intelligencer Steam Press. Steele announced its publication on January 8. "It will be found full of interest," the editor trilled, "and as entertaining as a tale of the Arabian Nights."[15]

But then, just like that, "290" disappeared from the pages of Jared Whitaker's and John Steele's newspaper.

A harbinger appeared in the *Intelligencer* on January 28 when a short item announced that M. W. Hutcheson, the Atlanta businessman who had bought a part interest in the *Knoxville Register* when it had reopened in Atlanta the previous September, was leaving and that one M. R. Hurt had succeeded as one of the proprietors. That same day in the *Atlanta Daily Register*, as it was now calling itself, appeared this announcement: "In the reorganization of the REGISTER establishment recently from the withdrawal of Mr. Hutcheson whose tastes lead him to another field of duty, we have secured the services of Mr. Sam Reid, the best news correspondent of Southern newspapers. He is known to the reading public as '290' of the *Intelligencer* and as 'Ora' of the Mobile press. He will furnish us with the latest news from the front by telegraph, and give to our readers minute accounts of every event of general interest transpiring in the Army of Tennessee."

John Steele was silent on why Sam Reid had left the *Intelligencer* and had jumped to a competitor in town. Perhaps the *Register* had offered Reid better terms; Atlanta now had four dailies— the *Intelligencer* and the *Southern Confederacy*, but also the *Memphis Appeal* (as of June 1863) and the *Knoxville Register* (November)—and we may surmise that competition for talented correspondents such as Reid may have been stiff.[16]

One of a wartime editor's responsibilities lay in reminding the people what they were fighting for. John Steele penned a piece under that very title for his issue of February 11. Part of the answer involved the goal of Southern independence—"free and untrammeled and without a single reservation," as Steele put it. Another part involved Southerners' memory of "wrongs committed and hardships endured" before the war, when the South lay in the political thrall of the North. Therefore, he wrote, "the hand of friendship can never be extended to the North." Indeed, the editor concluded, "it is an absurdity to say that the feeling of hatred for the Yankees which now fills the Southern heart, will be obliterated by time."[17]

NOTES

1. Andrews, *South Reports*, 504.
2. "SHOES FOR THE ARMY," *ADI*, Oct. 1, 1863.
3. "THANKS," *ADI*, Feb. 10, 1864; "COFFIN SHOP," *ADI*, February 25.
4. "THE MILITARY STATUS OF A PRITING OFFICE," *ADI*, Jan. 6, 1864; "1864—ITS PROSPECTS AND OR DUTIES," *ADI*, January 5.
5. "A VALUABLE ACQUISITION TO THE PRESS OF THE SOUTH," *ADI*, Jan. 6, 1864.
6. "THE SIEGE OF VICKSBURG," *ADI*, Jan. 7, 1864; "THE SIEGE OF VICKSBURG" (advertisement), *ADI*, January 7, 8, 9 and 10.
7. "Highly Interesting Work" (ad for *Siege of Vicksburg*), *ADI*, Dec. 4, 1863; "REVIEW OF THE WAR," *ADI*, Jan. 9, 1864.
8. "Review of the War, BY ALEXANDER ST. CLAIR ABRAMS," *ADI*, Jan. 21, 1864 (Chapters I-II); January 22 (II-III), January 24 (IV-V); January 26 (VI), January 27 (VII).
9. "Review of the War, BY ALEXANDER ST. CLAIR ABRAMS," *ADI*, Feb. 2, 1864 (Chapter XII); *ADI*, February 5 (Chapter XIV).
10. "Review of the War, BY ALEXANDER ST. CLAIR ABRAMS," *ADI*, Feb. 7, 1864 (Chapter XVI); *ADI*, February 20 (Chapter XVII); *ADI*, February 21 (Chapter XVIII, "concluding remarks").
11. "Review of the War, BY ALEXANDER ST. CLAIR ABRAMS," *ADI*, Jan. 28, 1864 (Chapter VII); Edward A. Pollard, *The First Year of the War* (Richmond: West & Johnston, 1862), 236; Virginius Dabney, *Pistols and Pointed Pens: The Dueling Editors of Old Virginia* (Chapel Hill: Algonquin Books, 1987), 56; "'PRESIDENT DAVIS AND HIS ADMINISTRATION,' BY A. S. ABRAMS," *ADI*, February 9, 18 and 25.
12. Alexander St. Clair Abrams, *A Full and Detailed History of the Siege of Vicksburg* (Atlanta: Intelligence Steam Power Press, 1863); *Review of the War* (Atlanta: Intelligencer Stream Power Press, 1864); *President Davis and his administration. Being a review of the "Rival Administration," published in Richmond and written by E. A. Pollard* (Atlanta: for the author, 1864); *The Trials of a Soldier's Wife: A Tale of the Second American Revolution* (Atlanta: Intelligencer Steam Power Presses, 1864); "FROM THE FRONT," *ADI*, Feb. 26, 1864.
13. "290," "ARMY CORRESPONDENCE," *ADI*, Jan. 1, 2, 7, 1864.
14. "290," "Gen. Morgan's Expedition Across THE OHIO," *ADI*, Jan. 8, 1864; Allan Keller, *Morgan's Raid* (New York: Collier Books, 1962 [1961]), 266, 283–91.
15. "We publish this morning . . . ," *ADI*, Jan. 8, 1864; Harwell, "Atlanta Publications," 187.
16. "KNOXVILLE REGISTER," *ADI*, Sept. 15, 1863; "M. W. Hutcheson & Co.," *ADI*, November 20; "CHANGE OF NEWSPAPER PROPRIETORS," *ADI*, Jan. 28, 1864; "THE REGISTER," *Atlanta Daily Register*, January 28.
17. "WHAT THE SOUTH IS FIGHTING FOR," *ADI*, Feb. 11, 1864.

32. The Dahlgren Raid

ON MARCH 6, 1864, the *Intelligencer*'s telegraphic column led with the report of a cavalry clash east of Richmond, "resulting in the death of Acting Brigadier General Dahlgreen" [*sic*]. "Several papers were found upon Dahlgreen's person stating that the object of the undertaking was to release the prisoners on Bell Island, the destruction of the hateful city, murder of Jeff Davis and traitorous crew, and that everything of service to the rebels must be destroyed. The documents disclose the most vindictive hostility against the Confederacy, and have produced a profound sensation in this community."[1]

Release Richmond prisoners? Burn the capital?! Murder Jefferson Davis?!! These were astounding allegations. They are made more astounding by the story of the Northern raid itself.

During the winter of 1863–64, twenty-eight-year-old Union Brig. Gen. Judson Kilpatrick, commander of a cavalry division in Maj. Gen. George Meade's Army of the Potomac, began bragging how he could lead a mounted raid on the Rebel capital. President Lincoln got word of it, and summoned Kilpatrick to the White House. Lincoln was interested in any foray that might liberate Union POWs confined at Richmond's two big prisons: Libby, a converted warehouse for officers, and Belle Isle, an islet in the James River for enlisted men. Northerners had become distressed by tales of mistreatment in Southern prison camps. After 106 officers escaped from Libby through a 65-foot tunnel on the night of February 9–10 (Col. Abel Streight was among them), they brought eyewitness confirmation of overcrowding and disgusting food. Besides, a Union spy in Richmond, Elizabeth Van Lew, slipped out word that the Confederate capital was lightly garrisoned, and could succumb to a sudden Federal cavalry strike. The president thus approved of Kilpatrick's raid.[2]

Enter Ulric Dahlgren. At first a staff officer for Maj. Gen. Franz Sigel in the Army of the Potomac, Dahlgren—son of the rear admiral whose monitors were battering Fort Sumter at the time—had lost a leg in the Gettysburg campaign. Undaunted, Dahlgren returned to the service and after hearing about

Kilpatrick's planned raid, looked him up. The general liked Dahlgren's grit and appointed him second-in-command.

Kilpatrick himself was not timid—in fact so rash that his men had started calling him "Kilcavalry." Boldly he began to think that after releasing the prisoners, he would have them set fires and burn Richmond down.

First objective, of course, was to get there. Kilpatrick and Dahlgren planned to take two columns and approach the city simultaneously from north and south. Kilpatrick's was by far the larger force, 3,500 men; Dahlgren would lead 500 troopers. They headed out from the area of Culpeper, Va. on the evening of February 28, aiming to approach the capital city on the morning of March 1. Kilpatrick's column was indeed five miles outside Richmond at that time, but unexpectedly stiff Confederate resistance caused him to lose his nerve. He ordered his men to withdraw and ride southeast. They would eventually make their way to Maj. Gen. Benjamin Butler's forces near Williamsburg.

Meanwhile, approaching Richmond, Dahlgren's column encountered a swollen James River. The Federals had with them a free black bricklayer who knew the area and promised to lead them to a ford. They found, however, that recent rains had erased the crossing. Dahlgren was in no mood to blame the weather, so he blamed the guide. Soon the body of Martin Robinson was hanging from a roadside tree.

The Union raiders rode through a lot of rain and muddy roads. On the evening of Monday, February 29, like Kilpatrick, Dahlgren in the Richmond suburbs also came in for more enemy fire than he expected. And like Kilpatrick, he also lost his mettle and ordered a retreat, heading northeast—the direction he mistakenly believed Kilpatrick was heading.

On Wednesday, March 2, home guards, local militia and Confederate soldiers on leave became aware of Dahlgren's route. About 11:30 p.m. they ambushed the Federals some thirty miles from the capital. In the firefight, Ulric Dahlgren fell dead, struck by five bullets. The Southerners were also able to capture most of the raiders.[3]

Here is where the *Intelligencer*'s reporting of the Kilpatrick-Dahlgren raid picked up the story on March 6, just four days after Dahlgren's death. This was fast reporting, due both to the telegraphic transmission of news from Richmond, and to the electric nature of the very news itself.

The ragtag force of Confederates that killed Dahlgren included a thirteen-year-old, one William Littlepage. After the fight and in the darkness, the youngster ranged about the field, feeling bodies for souvenirs. He came upon a notebook and some folded papers. At morning's light Littlepage handed them over to an adult, Edward W. Halbach (who happened to be headmaster of his school and who, like Littlepage, was serving as a civilian volunteer in the local defense force). Halbach read the papers and deduced that they had been retrieved from Colonel Dahlgren's body. Among the handwritten texts in Dahlgren's papers and notebook was this: "We will cross the James River into Richmond, destroying the bridge after us . . . the city must be destroyed . . . made one vast flame . . . Jeff Davis and Cabinet must be killed on the spot."

Sensing their gravity, Halbach dutifully forwarded the documents to Richmond. Soon they reached Jefferson Davis, Judah P. Benjamin, the Secretary of State, and Gen. Braxton Bragg, Jefferson Davis' military adviser. Grave discussions were held as to what the government should do, with talk of executing the raiders who had been captured (General Lee counseled against). The administration then, on March 4, put the papers out for print by the Southern press, which led to a public furor. Lee sent a copy of the shocking text to General Meade, asking for an explanation. Meade in turn questioned General Kilpatrick, who denied knowledge of the Dahlgren papers and notebook.

When the story came out, Northerners contended that the purported documents were Rebel forgeries. The original Dahlgren papers, part of the Confederate War Department archives, made their way safely out of Richmond before it fell, and eventually came into Federal hands. Then they disappeared. But the copy of at least one document in Dahlgren's handwriting—probably the one that had been sent to Meade—circulated and eventually made its way to the National Archives in Washington. The slain colonel's name had apparently been spelled "Dalhgren," not "Dahlgren." Northern apologists, notably Admiral Dahlgren, the father, held this up as proof: surely Ulric would have known how to spell his last name.[4]

The battle lines of the sectional argument were thus drawn. Forgeries? Evidence of intended arson and murder? The *Intelligencer*, of course, adopted and aggressively voiced the Confederate argument. On March 10, Steele reprinted a long article from the *Richmond Dispatch* that extensively quoted the documents reportedly found on Dahlgren's corpse, especially a written "Address to the Officers and Men," in which the colonel explained his plan to free the prisoners on Belle Isle, "exhorting the released prisoners to destroy the hateful city, and do not allow the rebel leader Davis and his traitorous crew to escape."

The *Intelligencer* editor reinforced the Richmond paper's article with one of his own, declaring, "Our President—Commander-in-Chief of our army—was to be killed. His cabinet were to share his fate." Steele concluded that Ulric Dahlgren had gotten his just reward. As for the men he led who were now in Richmond prisons, they were "murderers, incendiaries, outlaws," undeserving of the treatment customarily accorded to prisoners of war.[5]

A measure of the strength of the North/South argument over Colonel Dahlgren's raid and papers (atrocity?/forgery?) was the speed with which charge and countercharge made their ways into early histories of the war.

Edward Pollard, the vitriolic associate editor of the *Richmond Examiner*, turned out his *The Lost Cause; A New Southern History of the War of the Confederates* in 1867. In it Pollard printed Dahlgren's memorandum to his officers and men as reported in the Southern press ("destroy and burn the hateful city, and do not allow the rebel leader Davis, and his traitorous crew to escape" appeared in italics). "The authenticity of 'the Dahlgren Papers'... is probably no longer a question with the intelligent," Pollard judged. To support his conclusion, Pollard printed the lengthy statement of Edward Halbach on how he and William Littlepage had obtained the papers on the battlefield and sent them up through the Richmond channels.

The Northern riposte appears in W. O. Blake's *Pictorial History of the Great Rebellion*, published in 1866. Blake charges that after Dahlgren's death, Rebels had planted on his body forged orders for "all kinds of atrocities in Richmond." But they blundered, Blake charges, "by misspelling Colonel Dahlgren's name, in a place where they pretended it was written by himself."[6]

Sometime in mid-March 1864, Secretary Benjamin directed the Confederate topographical department to photograph fifty sets of Dahlgren's documents. A decade after the war, the officer in charge of the production, Maj. Albert H. Campbell, sent a picture of Dahlgren's instructions for his men to the Southern Historical Society in Richmond. Campbell pointed out that the apparent signature of "Dalhgren" was caused by ink bleeding through the paper from its other side. Five years later, ex-Confederate general Jubal Early, who apparently had gotten one of the fifty sets, also sent a copy to the *Southern Historical Society Papers*, making the same observation: "it is the tail of the 'y' [in '"destroying" on the page's first side] which at first sight gives to the 'l' in his name [on the second side] the appearance of an 'h.'"[7]

Northerners were not swayed by this sharp-eyed sleuthing by ex-Rebels, so the intense, competing positions prevailed through the years, with historians struggling to reach consensus. In 1955, the South's argument received scientific support from historian Virgil Carrington Jones, who was working on a book about the Kilpatrick-Dahlgren raid. Jones obtained the National Archives copy of the disputed paper bearing the colonel's name, studied it in magnification and under special lighting, and—like Major Campbell and General Early—noticed that ink bleeding through the paper from its obverse side had led to the "Dahlgren" reading. He therefore concluded that Southerners were right: Ulric Dahlgren had wanted to burn the Rebel capital and kill the Confederacy's political leaders. Since that time, the scholarship supporting the South's position about the Dahlgren documents has only grown and solidified. In 1999 historian James O. Hall had handwriting experts examine the evidence at the National Archives. They found that the sensational statements about burning and killing were in fact scrawled by Ulric Dahlgren.[8]

History is written by the victors, as the saying goes, so it is quite unusual that the South's take on the Dahlgren Raid has made its way into modern texts. Thus also has John Steele been vindicated for the accusations that appeared in the *Intelligencer* on March 6, 1864. Two weeks later, the editor contemplated the situation, remarking upon it rather darkly. The fact that "this attempt on the part of the Yankees," he observed, "the destruction of Richmond, the murder of the citizens, including the President and his cabinet, was not carried out," he argued, reflected "the providential hand of God." But their very intent, he warned, demonstrated that Northerners intended to wage war as it was "conducted before the dawn of civilization." Against this, he warned, the Southern people must resolve to fight fire with fire.

> Let us, regardless of censure, give back barbarity for barbarity, commit murder for murder, incendiarism for incendiarism, outrage for outrage, and leave it to posterity to decide whether the provocation did not warrant the retaliation. And if future ages should not do us justice by declaring that our sufferings and the inhumanity of our enemies were sufficient causes, the God who judges mankind rightfully, will so declare it, and judge us by such declaration.[9]

NOTES

1. "Richmond, March 4 . . . ," *ADI*, March 6, 1864.
2. V. C. Jones, "The Kilpatrick-Dahlgren Raid: Boldly Planned . . . Timidly Executed," *Civil War Times Illustrated*, vol. 4, no. 1 (April 1965), 13–14; Virgil Carrington Jones, *Eight Hours Before Richmond* (New York: Henry Holt, 1957), 37–38; Emory M. Thomas, "The Kilpatrick-Dahlgren Raid—Part I," *Civil War Times Illustrated*, vol. 16, no. 10 (February

1978), 4–6, 8; Elizabeth R. Varon, *Southern Lady, Yankee Spy: The True Story of Elizabeth Van Lew, A Union Agent in the Heart of the Confederacy* (New York: Oxford University Press, 2003), 115.

3. Edward G. Longacre, "Ulric Dahlgren" in Patricia L. Faust, ed., *Historical Times Illustrated Encyclopedia of the Civil War* (New York: Harper & Row, 1986), 202; Jones, *Eight Hours*, ix, 6, 33, 62–63; Jones, "Kilpatrick-Dahlgren Raid," 14, 16, 18–21; Emory M. Thomas, "The Kilpatrick-Dahlgren Raid—Part II," *Civil War Times Illustrated*, vol. 17, no. 1 (April 1978), 26–30; James O. Hall, "'The Dahlgren Papers: Yankee Plot to Kill President Davis," *Civil War Times Illustrated*, vol. 22, no. 7 (November 1983), 31.

4. Jones, "Kilpatrick-Dahlgren Raid," 19–21; Hall, "Dahlgren Papers," 38–39.

5. "From the Richmond Dispatch. MORE OF THE RAID" and "KILPATRICK'S CAMPAIGN," *ADI*, March 10, 1864.

6. Edward A. Pollard, *The Lost Cause; A New Southern History of the War of the Confederates* (New York: E. B. Treat, & Co., 1867), 502–506; W. O. Blake, *Pictorial History of the Great Rebellion* (Columbus OH: Gilmore & Segner, 1866), 533–34.

7. Hall, "Dahlgren Papers," 35; J. William Jones, comp., "The Kilpatrick-Dahlgren Raid Against Richmond," *Southern Historical Society Papers*, vol. 13 (1885), 558–59.

8. "Papers Found on Dahlgren's Body a Detective Story in Themselves," *Civil War Times Illustrated*, vol. 4, no. 1 (April 1965), 21; Sandy Prindle, *Booth's Confederate Connections* (Gretna LA: Pelican Publishing Company, 2019), 24–25.

9. "BARBARITY OF THE FEDERALS," *ADI*, March 19, 1864.

33. "Glorious Victories"

IN MID-FEBRUARY 1864 at Charleston there had occurred an event on which the *Intelligencer* reported belatedly: the sinking of a Northern warship by a Southern submarine.

The Confederate commander at Charleston, General P. G. T. Beauregard, sought to counter Northern naval power by encouraging experimentation with unconventional weapons. One of them was a small "torpedo ram," a semi-submerged vessel carrying an explosive mine on its spar. In October 1863 a "David," as it was called, exploded a torpedo against the hull of the *New Ironsides* in Charleston Harbor. The blast damaged the Northern vessel but did not sink her.

Five hundred miles away, Southerners were experimenting with a similar vessel; this one was called the *H. L. Hunley*, after its inventor. In August 1863 the *Hunley* was brought to Charleston. Six months later, on the night of Feb. 17, 1864, with Lt. George Dixon's crew of eight hand-cranking the propeller, the *Hunley* approached the U.S.S. *Housatonic*, a big wooden-hulled vessel in the harbor. The Confederates succeeded in detonating their powder charge and the *Housatonic* sank—but so did the *Hunley*.

The *Intelligencer* waited six weeks after the event, till March 31, to bring word of it to readers. "The particulars of one of the most brilliant and successful achievements of this war have been kept, till now, from the people under the impression that a publication might be prejudicial to our interests," the article began. But it explained that reporting about the *Hunley* and *Housatonic* appearing in Northern and Southern papers "render further secrecy unnecessary." The *Intelligencer* gave background, based on writing in the *Charleston Courier*. The *Housatonic* sank in twenty-eight feet of water. When she settled, the top of her rigging stood above water, allowing crew members to cling for safety. Northern casualties included five dead.

As for the *Housatonic*, the *Intelligencer* correctly concluded, "she is the first vessel destroyed by a contrivance of this character"—a first in worldwide naval history.[1]

At Richmond, among the scuttlebutt, rumors and official statements that he digested, "Clio," the *Intelligencer*'s correspondent, also gleaned material from Northern papers. But this was about to change in the spring of 1864, as "Clio's" writing gradually disappears in the *Intelligencer*. From his first appearance in the paper in November 1862 to his departure in June 1864, "Clio" sent more than 150 articles to the *Intelligencer*. This output, both in terms of quantity and the author's consistent quality of reporting and writing, should entitle "Clio" to a place in the top tiers of Confederate newspapermen. But because his identity at this time still remains unknown (he could have been a journalist in Richmond, who, like other professionals wrote for various Southern newspapers under different pen names to earn additional income), "Clio" is largely unheralded in the literature of Confederate journalism. Intriguingly, though, he was evidently well-known among other Southern newspaperman. Samuel Chester Reid, "290," divulged in the spring of 1863 that "Clio" was "an old acquaintance of mine."[2]

The departure of "290" in January 1864, and of "Clio" six months later, meant that editor Steele had to rely on "St. Clair" even more. On May 2, writing "from the front" in north Georgia, Alexander St. Clair Abrams reported on what was happening. Both sides were obviously preparing for the spring campaign, when Maj. Gen. William T. Sherman's Union forces were expected to launch an offensive aimed at Atlanta. The Federals were busy as they prepared to move against Gen. Joseph E. Johnston's lines near Dalton. Altogether the enemy's movements suggested to "St. Clair" that "the object of the Yankees is to divert attention from our extreme right and left flanks, on which points they are said to be moving with a view to turning them."

The field correspondent would be proven prescient.[3]

On April 6, the Press Association held its first annual meeting in Augusta. The *Intelligencer*, which was a P. A. member, publicized the event by publishing on March 2 the invitation from the association president, "R. W. GIBBES, M.D."—Robert W. Gibbes, Jr., Surgeon General of South Carolina during the war as well as owner of the *Columbia South Carolinian*—for all member newspapers to send an attendee.

On the appointed day, President Gibbes welcomed those present by recognizing their patriotic contributions to the Confederate war effort. Business matters were also discussed. The association was growing; Superintendent John Thrasher reported that since their last meeting eleven newspapers had applied for membership, in order to receive the P. A.'s daily telegraphic news articles as reported from the war-fronts.

Enough newspapermen attended the association meeting–the *Intelligencer* later reported that 28 of 46 member papers had been represented—for "Cousin Nourma," the correspondent who had written earlier pieces for the *Intelligencer*, to now contribute an article for the *Chattanooga Rebel* (then being published in Marietta, Ga., twenty miles northwest of Atlanta), which the *Intelligencer* reprinted. "MEIN HERR REBEL," the piece began, offering sketches of some of the journalistic luminaries whom "Nourma" had seen in Augusta, including Dr. Gibbes, William Tappan Thompson (editor of the *Savannah Morning News*), Joseph Clisby of the *Macon Telegraph* and John Dumble of the *Memphis Appeal*. Standing out in the middle of the long article is "Nourma's" notice of the *Intelligencer* and its editor. The Atlanta paper's political positions, particularly in support of Gov. Joseph E. Brown, came in for a compliment: "the tremendous sway which that journal holds over the political arrangements of this State, gives it an exalted and prominent position." As for John Steele, "He is a large, heavy built man, about six feet in height, well proportioned and has a very durable look about him. His step and movements are elastic, and a sprightly appearance generally remains on the surface. His head is large and expansive, covered with a great thatch of silver grey, which lends that dignity to hearty and hale age that is attractive and demands the respect always accorded him."

Steele could be a funny guy. "Nourma" declared that he was a good storyteller and was "inimitable in racy anecdote." He was in demand at parties, "enjoys the society of the young [and] is popular with ladies." He could be serious, too, especially in public speaking; he "enunciates distinctly and effectively, and never fails to command attention whilst repeating any gem which he fancies or his audience demands." Altogether, "Nourma" concluded, John Steele was "a fine specimen of the Georgia gentleman."[4]

"Cousin Nourma" had entitled his article "Editorial Brotherhood." In Atlanta that fraternity—the editors of the *Intelligencer, Southern Confederacy, Memphis Appeal* and *Knoxville Register*—had a chance to bond closer in April 1864 during a citywide printers' strike. Sylvanus Lines, president of the Atlanta Typographical Union, had called for a fifty percent increase in wages. When the papers' management refused, the printers walked off the job. The owners and editors were in a tight place. There were no scabs available to replace the striking union members; the *Macon Confederate* had recently reported that three-quarters of qualified newspaper printers had been, or were currently serving in the army.

For his part, John Steele resisted having to raise subscription prices again. A two-day printers' strike in July 1862 had forced the paper to announce a cost increase, but this was to only $7 *per annum*. Now, in April 1864, not even two years later, the annual subscription rate of the *Intelligencer* had risen more than eightfold, to $60 ($5 a month), due to paper and ink shortages, but most of all to wartime inflation in the Confederate South. On April 7, Assistant Editor Alexander St. Clair Abrams commented on the high prices Southern newspapers were charging for subscriptions by placing the general inflation in a personal context. "Where are we drifting?," he asked. The answer lay in the rent increase his landlady had recently imposed upon him. "We are drifting into a universal scale of high prices," he answered, "so high indeed, that the entire subscription price of a newspaper at fifty or sixty dollars a year, does not pay the expenses of a single man for *one week's boarding.*"

The editor may have been exaggerating the cost of a week's board, but he was right about his paper's pricing. The *Columbia South Carolinian* had recently remarked that the *Augusta Chronicle & Sentinel* had raised its subscription price to forty dollars a year; "the Atlanta journals are from forty to fifty!" "Bless your soul, man!," Steele exclaimed in approval. No wonder he and his journalistic confreres could not give in to the printers' demands.

The strike ended when the newspaper editors visited the city's conscript office and addressed the printers' status. They were exempt from the draft while working, the editors claimed; but now, as they were on strike, the officer was encouraged to draft them for army service. The conscriptor liked the idea—too well, according to one account.

> "Gentlemen," he said, "you are undoubtedly right. I will go to work at once, and as you are here, I will conscript you to begin with."
>
> "Conscript us!" exclaimed the editors.
>
> "Certainly. As you have no printers, you can't get out your papers. So you no longer belong to the exempted class."

The editors raced back to their respective offices and contacted the printers' union. In fifteen minutes everyone was back to work.[5]

During the week-long strike, the *Intelligencer* had missed issues of six days, Tuesday, April 12 through Sunday April 17 (the paper did not appear on Mondays). During its absence, though, Atlantans were not without a newspaper to read, as the editors of the four strike-stricken journals combined to put out the *Atlanta Daily Press* during April 12–15.[6] When the *Intelligencer* resumed operation on Tuesday, April 19, John Steele reminded readers that the Typographical Union had struck for fifty percent higher wages. "We will not dispute the necessity that prompted this act of theirs," the editor admitted; everyone was aware of the Confederacy's inflationary economy and that prices of life's necessities were going up. Rather, Steele objected to the fact that the printers "struck without giving the proprietor of this journal [Jared Whitaker] at least, notice" of their intent to walk off the job. It was the "manner, the abruptness, the want of courtesy that characterized the act"; with more time, Steele implied, Whitaker might have been able to negotiate a deal that might have saved everyone from an unsettling work shutdown.

The editor did not divulge any terms of the newspaper owners' discussions with the printers, only stating that "all difficulties [had been] amicably adjusted."[7]

Once the paper got back to reporting war news, there was plenty of it. In Virginia, the Union army was preparing to launch another "on to Richmond" movement. At Dalton the Army of Tennessee was preparing to contest the expected advance of Sherman's forces. "Lone Jack," a soldier correspondent for the *Augusta Chronicle & Sentinel* (as reported in the *Intelligencer* on April 1) mentioned all the soldiers' drilling underway in the army's encampments. Lt. Gen. John B. Hood had arrived from Richmond to take command of one of Johnston's infantry corps. Notwithstanding all the arduous drill, "Lone Jack" affirmed, "General Johnston and Hood are exceedingly popular."[8]

There could be little doubt as to Sherman's objective in the forthcoming campaign, as the *Intelligencer* of April 26 carried a long column titled, "The Importance of Atlanta." "We receive authentic intelligence that large bodies of Federal troops are being concentrated at Huntsville, Chattanooga and Cleveland [Tenn.], with the evident design of flanking General Johnston and compelling his abandonment of Dalton and retreat on Atlanta," the paper declared.

The stakes were high. "We find no event could be more disastrous to the Confederacy than the capture of Atlanta," the editor intoned. The city's extensive railroad connections alone made it an important strategic point. Atlanta's fate obviously rested with Johnston and his Army of Tennessee. The general's skill and experience were beyond doubt, but the real question was "whether the means at his disposal are adequate"—meaning, whether his army was strong enough to withstand Sherman's larger force. "Let it be strengthened," Steele warned, turning his advice to "those who hold the reins of power in their hands."[9]

Occasionally in his hortatory prose John Steele would invoke the name of the Almighty, but in this case he did not; it was the president of the Confederate States who did. On March 12, 1864, as he had done seven times before during the war, Jefferson Davis set aside Friday, April 8 as a "day of humiliation, fasting and prayer." And as it had done those seven previous times, the *Intelligencer* vigorously publicized Davis' proclamation by reprinting it—repeatedly. After its first appearance on March 20, the Atlanta paper republished the presidential call to worship more than a half-dozen times in the days leading up to the appointed holiday. And also as it had done previously, the *Intelligencer* issue on Friday morning, the 8th, announced that there would be no paper on Saturday—the staff had the day off so members could attend services at the various worship places in town.[10]

The number of those places increased in April 1864 when a new Episcopal church, St. Luke's, began offering services. Atlanta's population by late spring 1864, had grown by some estimates to 22,000. The city's sole Episcopal church, St. Philip's, located in the block north of City Hall (today's state capitol), was no longer able to accommodate its crowd of Sunday morning worshipers. The Rev. Charles T. Quintard, serving in Atlanta as chaplain-at-large for Johnston's army, secured permission from Bishop Stephen Elliott to start a new congregation. A church building, on Walton Street three blocks northwest of the Car Shed, was constructed by soldiers with donated materials. It was not nearly so impressive as St. Philip's; Quintard remarked that in its simplicity the structure was "somewhat 'Confederate' in style."

The *Intelligencer* announced on April 21 that church doors would open the following day for St. Luke's initial service, over which Bishop Elliott himself would be presiding.[11]

The worshipers had much to be grateful for, as Confederate forces that April had won several comparatively small, but for Southerners psychologically salving battlefield victories.

The *Intelligencer* summarized a couple of these in an editorial appearing on April 26.

> Reports of successes to our arms come in from every quarter and with great rapidity. The capture of Plymouth and its garrison as well as the sinking of two gunboats, is a brilliant feat and reflects the highest honor on Gen. Hoke, while the late information to be found in our telegraphic column, that Dick Taylor has captured seven thousand prisoners, four hundred wagons and nineteen pieces of artillery in

Louisiana, is another source of exultation for our people. If this last statement be true, it is evident that another battle has been fought and the result was a victory to our arms.

Thus has the spring campaign opened. From every part of the Confederacy the intelligence comes that Heaven has blessed the arms of our patriot soldiers with victory over their infamous and unscrupulous adversaries. The dark cloud over our political sky is being swiftly dispelled and the bright azure of peace and independence forms up before us. Thank God! we say.[12]

Located on the south bank of the Roanoke River near Albemarle Sound, Plymouth was a town in eastern North Carolina that had been occupied by Federals in the spring of 1862. Confederates had made several attempts to drive them away before Brig. Gen. Robert F. Hoke took command of the area in the spring of 1864. With three infantry brigades, a regiment of cavalry and five artillery batteries, Hoke approached the 2,400-man Federal garrison at Plymouth on April 17 and laid siege. A recently completed Confederate ironclad, the *Albemarle*, arrived the next day to sink one Northern steamer and drive off another. Hoke's troops advanced on the 19th while his guns shelled the Federal fortifications. The garrison commander, Brig. Gen. Henry W. Wessells, then surrendered his men, twenty-eight cannon, 500 horses, plus large quantities of pork, beef, flour and—a rare delight for Confederate soldiers—coffee. Hoke's smart little victory won him a joint resolution of thanks from the C.S. Congress and promotion to major general; at twenty-six he became the youngest officer to attain that rank.[13]

The *Intelligencer* celebrated the Confederate recapture of Plymouth with predictable enthusiasm. "ANOTHER GLORIOUS VICTORY," was the headline in the paper's "TELEGRAPHIC" column on April 24. As so often happened, subsequent articles exaggerated the scope of General Hoke's triumph. "THE PLYMOUTH 'PILGRIMS'" (*Intelligencer,* April 28) stated that 25,000—not 2,500—Union prisoners captured by Hoke were on their way to Charleston.[14]

> News from the West.
> Glorious from Trans-Mississippi
> The "Stonewall" of the West at Work.
> 7,000 Prisoners Captured by Taylor.
> 19 Pieces Artillery.
> 400 Wagons.

This was the headline in the *Intelligencer*'s "Telegraphic" news section on April 26, announcing the Confederate victory in a battle fought on April 8 at Mansfield, in northwest Louisiana. There Maj. Gen. Richard Taylor's Confederate forces defeated Maj. Gen. Nathaniel P. Banks' Union troops, who were marching from New Orleans up the Red River. Taylor ("the 'Stonewall' of the West"), with some 8,800 troops had thrashed Banks' army of 12,000. Casualties totaled 113 killed, 581 wounded, 1,541 missing/captured for the Federals, and some 1,000 killed and wounded among the Confederates. The *Intelligencer* headlines thus exaggerated the number of Union troops captured, and also the number of wagons taken (some 160, not 400). But it got the number of Northern field pieces rounded up; it was actually twenty guns. In their rout of the Federals, Taylor's troops had also gathered up a thousand horses and mules. Most importantly, the Confederate victory at Mansfield doomed Banks' Red River expedition. "The rout was complete, even outdoing Bull Run" the *Intelligencer* related on April 27, perhaps with some exaggeration; "the order was, every man for himself and the devil take the hindmost. . . . The expedition is a total failure."[15]

Then there was Fort Pillow.

In early April 1864, Confederate cavalryman Maj. Gen. Nathan Bedford Forrest had his headquarters at Jackson, Tenn., eighty miles northeast of Memphis. On April 10 he ordered Brig. Gen. James R. Chalmers to take two mounted brigades, some 1,500 men, to "attend to" Fort Pillow, an earthwork on the Tennessee side of the Mississippi forty miles above Memphis. There, under the command of Maj. Lionel F. Booth, were 557 officers and men: 295 whites of the Thirteenth Tennessee Cavalry (Union) and 262 U.S. Colored Troops—former slaves now fighting for the North.

On the morning of April 12, Chalmers' force arrived and quickly surrounded the Federal fort. In heavy skirmishing Major Booth was killed, Maj. William F. Bradford succeeded to command. Forrest arrived midmorning and directed his men to inch closer to the fort. Around 3:30 he sent in a demand for surrender, which Bradford refused. Forrest then ordered an assault. Confederates rushed forward and clambered over the dirt parapets into the fort. Some Federals tried to surrender, but the Southerners shot them down. Garrison members later recalled hearing cries of "No quarter! No quarter!," "Kill the damned niggers; shoot them down" and "Damn you, you are fighting against your master!" Panicked bluecoats ran down the river bank; they were shot in the back or drowned in the Mississippi waters.

When it was all over, 231 Federals were dead, a hundred more wounded. The rest were prisoners. Confederate casualties totaled 14 killed and 86 wounded.[16]

The *Intelligencer*'s telegraphed news section April 19 included a report on Fort Pillow that was both matter-of-fact and dramatic. "The Fort refused to surrender and was carried by storm"; Confederates rushed into the fort and "an indiscriminate slaughter followed." The short article declared, "one hundred prisoners and the balance slain. The Fort ran with blood.—Many ran into the river and were drowned or shot in the water. Over one hundred thousand dollars worth of stores were taken. We captured six guns."

This was the "great victory" described in the *Intelligencer* of April 22, reprinting an article from the *Mobile Tribune*. The piece included commentary from one Northerner who observed that the Confederate conquest of Fort Pillow "looks to me more like indiscriminate butchery than honorable warfare."[17]

This was an ominous hint that Northern newspapers were already circulating reports of a massacre perpetrated by Forrest's men. For their part, Confederate newspapers did not shy away from the high Union casualties at Fort Pillow, but there was no talk of a "massacre." For instance, another account of the battle appearing in the *Intelligencer* on May 4 forthrightly stated that "the force of white and black Yankees was 850, of which 600 were killed—70 wounded, and 180 captured—not one escaped." Indeed, there was more attention given to a report that several days after Fort Pillow General Forrest had been killed. It proved to be false, as the *Intelligencer* affirmed on April 21, and again the next day under the line, "GEN. FORREST NOT KILLED."

When the Southern press addressed the allegations of "indiscriminate butchery" at Fort Pillow, it sided with Forrest. On May 7 editor Steele acknowledged that "the Yankees object to Forrest's style of fighting," then went on to reprint from the *Savannah Morning News* a short treatise on the conventions of war: when a besieged garrison refuses to capitulate and invites an assault, the attacker is entitled to "putting the garrison to the sword." (Indeed, Forrest had warned in his note demanding the fort's surrender, "Should my demand be refused, I cannot be responsible for the fate of your command.") Thus, the *News* concluded (and so did the *Intelligencer*, by inference), "we believe that Forrest was justified by the usages of war in the signal punishment he visited upon the mongrel garrison of Fort Pillow."[18]

In this context, Fort Pillow joined Plymouth and Mansfield among the "glorious victories" that John Steele liked to report so glowingly. "At the rate our boys have been capturing Yankee troops, gunboats, artillery and wagons within the last few days in Louisiana, West Tennessee and North Carolina," the *Montgomery Advertiser* boasted in a short piece appearing the *Intelligencer* on April 28, "they will soon bag the whole [Yankee] army and spoil all the fun of Grant's Spring Campaign."

To this Steele jauntily replied, "We have not the slightest objection to seeing this 'fun' spoiled."[19] Indeed, the editor who had exulted "Thank God!" over news of Plymouth, who had gloried that the enemy's "rout was complete" at Mansfield, and who had not winced when Fort Pillow "ran with blood" was the same one who as late as May 1864 was predicting that the war would conclude with Confederate victory by the end of the year.

NOTES

1. Milton F. Perry, *Infernal Weapons: The Story of Confederate Submarine and Mine Warfare* (Baton Rouge: Louisiana State University Press, 1965), 63, 83–84, 97–107; R. Thomas Campbell, *The C.S.S. H. L. Hunley: Confederate Submarine* (Shippensburg PA: Burd Street Press, 2000), 55, 122; "DESTRUCTION OF THE YANKEE WAR STEAMER HOUSATONIC," *ADI*, March 31, 1864; "X," "AUTHENTIC ACCOUNT OF THE LOSS OF THE HOUSATONIC" (February 22), *ADI*, April 7.

2. "CLIO," "FROM RICHMOND (March 29), *ADI*, April 6, 1864; "290," "ARMY CORRESPONDENCE," *ADI*, May 31, 1863.

3. "ST. CLAIR," "ARMY CORRESPONDENCE" (May 2), *ADI*, May 4, 1864.

4. "PRESS ASSOCIATION," *ADI*, March 2, 1864; Risley, "Confederate Press Association," 234; van Tuyll and McNeely, "Robert W. Gibbes," 95–97; "Cousin Nourma," "EDITORIAL BROTHERHOOD," *ADI*, April 30.

5. Venet, *Changing Wind*, 141; "SCARCITY OF PRINTERS," *ADI*, April 28, 1864; "REVISED TERMS OF THE DAILY INTELLIGENCER," *ADI*, July 27, 1862; "WHERE ARE WE DRIFTING?," *ADI*, April 7, 1864; Brantley, *Georgia Journalism*, 98; Reed, *History of Atlanta*, 408; Malone, "Atlanta Journalism," 217–18.

6. Of the *Atlanta Press*, journalism scholar Henry T. Malone has written, "it was an indication of the determination on the part of Atlanta's editors to keep some sort of news before the public at all times." Decades ago, Confederate bibliographer Richard Barksdale Harwell saw a complete file of the *Atlanta Press* for these dates at the Boston Atheneum library.

Then something must have happened. After the *Press*' issue of April 15, Dr. Harwell attests that as of April 16 there was another intra-strike Atlanta paper, this one called the *Reveille*. Wallace Reed, the postwar Atlanta newspaperman, states that the *Reveille* was edited by S. D. Niles. Harwell could find only one issue of it (at Boston Atheneum). Yet the *Reveille* must have survived for a while after the printers' strike ended. A generation after the war the *Atlanta Constitution* reprinted long excerpts from the *Atlanta Reveille* of April

21, 1864. It noted that the issue was "five columns wide and . . . one sheet printed on both sides" (Malone, "Atlanta Journalism," 218; Harwell, "Atlanta Publications," 193–94; Reed, *History of Atlanta*, 185; van Tuyll, "Essential Labor," 80; "OLD NEWSPAPERS; RELICS OF THE WAR," *Atlanta Constitution*, July 20, 1898).

7. "RESUMED," *ADI*, April 19, 1864; Venet, *Changing Wind*, 141.

8. "THE ON TO RICHMOND MOVEMENT," *ADI*, April 22, 1864; "Lone Jack," "From the Chronicle & Sentinel. A LETTER FROM LONE JACK (NEAR DALTON, March 22, 1864)," *ADI*, April 1.

9. "THE IMPORTANCE OF ATLANTA," *ADI*, April 26, 1864.

10. "PROCLAMATION," *ADI*, March 20, 1864 (repeated March 23, 24, 26, 29, 30, 31 and April 1); "FASTING HUMILIATION AND PRAYER," *ADI*, April 8.

11. Davis, *What the Yankees Did to Us*, 27, 74; "The opening services . . . ," *ADI*, April 21, 1864.

12. "THE NEWS," *ADI*, April 26, 1864.

13. John G. Barrett, *The Civil War in North Carolina* (Chapel Hill: University of North Carolina Press, 1963), 123, 134–36, 157n., 213–20; Daniel W. Broadfoot, *General Robert F. Hoke: Lee's Modest Warrior* (Winston-Salem NC: John F. Blair, 1996), 130, 134–50.

14. "ANOTHER GLORIOUS VICTORY," *ADI*, April 24, 1864; "THE PLYMOUTH 'PILGRIMS,'" *ADI*, April 28.

15. "TELEGRAPHIC. News from the West," *ADI*, April 26, 1864; Ludwell H. Johnson, *Red River Campaign: Politics & Cotton in the Civil War* (Baltimore: Johns Hopkins Press, 1958), 140–41; Gary Dillard Joiner, *One Damn Blunder from Beginning to End: The Red River Campaign* (Wilmington DE. Scholarly Resources, 2003), 103; "R.," "[Special Dispatch to the Memphis Appeal.] THE FEDERAL DEFEAT IN LOUISIANA," *ADI*, April 27.

16. Henry, *"First With the Most" Forrest*, 249–50; Albert Castel, "The Fort Pillow Massacre: A Fresh Examination of the Evidence" in Castel, *Winning and Losing in the Civil War: Essays and Stories* (Columbia: University of South Carolina Press, 1996), 36–44.

17. "FROM FORT PILLOW," *ADI*, April 19, 1864; "From the Mobile Tribune. FORT PILLOW AFFAIR—GREAT VICTORY," *ADI*, April 22.

18. Cimprich, *Fort Pillow*, 87; Andrew Ward, *River Run Red: The Fort Pillow Massacre in the American Civil War* (New York: Viking, 2005), 306; "CAPTURE OF FORT PILLOW," *ADI*, May 4, 1864; "DISTRESSING RUMOR," *ADI*, April 19; "FORREST'S DEATH CONTRADICTED," *ADI*, April 21; "GEN. FORREST NOT KILLED," *ADI*, April 22; "GEN. FORREST'S STYLE," *ADI*, May 7; Richard L. Fuchs, *An Unerring Fire: The Massacre at Fort Pillow* (Rutherford NJ: Fairleigh Dickinson University Press, 1994), 56.

19. "At the rate our boys have been capturing . . . ," *ADI*, April 28, 1864

34. The Story Behind an Editorial

IN STUDYING THE *ATLANTA DAILY INTELLIGENCER* during the last year of the war, the challenge for present-day readers is to grapple with the question of how editor John H. Steele could continue to voice Confederate patriotism and wartime optimism when that cause was obviously weakening and that conflict was turning inexorably against the South.

In early 1864 the Confederacy was beset by a host of problems—indeed, crises.

At the war front, the chief concern was manpower. On December 31, 1863, Adjutant and Inspector General Samuel Cooper in Richmond reported to President Jefferson Davis that he counted 233,586 men present for duty. All knew that the Federal forces were far more numerous (in fact, on that same last day of December, they numbered 496,783).[1]

Another measure of the war's tide lay in all the Southern territory that had been conquered and was being occupied by Union forces. Of the 700,000 square miles of land in the eleven seceded states, perhaps a quarter of it was under Federal control at the end of 1863: all of Tennessee, almost all of Arkansas, half of Louisiana, a third of Mississippi and a quarter of Virginia, plus coastal pockets along the entire Confederate coast.[2]

Far beyond the borders of the Confederacy came another grim realization: all hope of foreign intervention on behalf of the South was gone. In August 1863 Secretary of State Judah Benjamin ordered his envoy in London, James Mason, to come home. Two months later Benjamin even expelled British consuls from the Confederacy. Earlier in the war, France had been more disposed to recognize the infant Southern republic, but after Gettysburg and Vicksburg, Napoleon III no longer showed such interest.[3]

The Confederacy's travails at the start of 1864 extended from the war front to the home front. Most families were experiencing shortages of essential goods, both agricultural and industrial. Food was being produced in sufficient quantity, but with Southern railroads worn out or broken by overuse, and many Southern rivers under enemy control, distribution of life's essentials was difficult and uneven.

The Confederacy's main financial problem was inflation. When goods were available, they were often set at such exorbitant prices as to be unpurchasable. At the start of the war, one could buy a dollar in gold for three Confederate ones. At the end of 1863, one had to pay twenty.[4]

If the South could be said to be fighting for the protection of slavery, its war was failing in that regard as well. Lincoln's Emancipation Proclamation did not nearly have the effect as the approach of Northern armies. "The slaves were constantly going over to them," writes historian William C. Davis. Tellingly, the waning of Southern slave power led to the waxing of Northern military power. Of 186,017 African Americans in the Union army, 104,387 were recruited in Confederate territory.[5]

Such were the negatives for the South as it entered the third year of the Civil War. Seeking to comprehend the sunny optimism of *Intelligencer* editor John Steele—at least as it was evident in his editorial writing in the spring of 1864—one must grapple with a number of factors, beginning with the glass half-full/half-empty metaphor. "In January 1864, the course of the war still seemed uncertain," judges Anne Sarah Rubin of the University of Maryland, "and either side could have won."

Actually, Confederates did not have to win so much as simply to hold out. 1864 was a presidential election year in the North, so Abraham Lincoln was up for re-election. The Democrat facing him, Southerners hoped, might come from the antiwar faction of the party, the so-called "Peace Democrats." If Lee's army in Virginia held onto Richmond, and Johnston's army held onto north Georgia, or at least kept the Federals from taking Atlanta, a Democrat might be elected to the White House on a platform of negotiating a truce with the Confederate States, one that recognized its independence.[6]

The call to hold out came from the top, when Jefferson Davis addressed Congress in early December 1863. In his speech, which the *Intelligencer* printed on December 15, the president called for the people to tighten their belts for more sacrifices ahead. The chief executive's warning, however, had little effect on those doing the most sacrificing—Southern soldiers at the front—because they were expressing their own confidence in the cause and in their prospects of success. "Every soldier feels as confident of success as if we had already achieved it," wrote a Virginia cavalryman in late April 1864 from Lee's army. Closer to home, this was the spirit demonstrated in Johnston's army when time came to re-enlist; many regiments did so *en masse,* passing bellicose resolutions that they would fight on for the duration of the war. . . . even longer. On April 10, John Steele celebrated this kind of fighting spirit. "We have the grim humor of those soldiers of the Confederacy who have enlisted 'for the war and three years of the next,'" the editor declared. "To the question, 'How long will the war last?,'" Steele continued, "it has but one answer to give, and that is 'it will last till we are free.'"[7]

Beneath these expressions of "true grit," there lay subtle psychological factors that affected civilians such as John Steele as much as the reenlisting soldiers. One had to do with inurement to defeat and hardship; Confederates who had gone through so many failures and reversals could convince themselves that they were able to withstand still more. Contributing to the resilience of Southern fighting men, and by extension to the civilians behind them, were the intertwined nineteenth-century concepts of honor, duty and manly pride—factors that made the specter of defeat by the North so humiliating. These were the same factors that made *subjugation* Confederates' favorite term for their fate if they were forced back into the Union (from the Latin, *put under the yoke*). In the same vein is longtime University of Georgia professor E. Merton Coulter's observation that by this time of the war, "the fear of being conquered and losing his dignity as a citizen" kept the Southern soldier going.[8]

Another element of Confederates' self-assurance, even after three years of war, was the Protestant religious faith shared by most white Southerners. "A cause so virtuous, for which so many devout had given their lives, surely would win the favor of the Old Testament's Jehovah," writes historian Frank E. Vandiver. Writing on "Southern invincibility," Wiley Sword affirms that "faith in divine Providence" was a key to Confederates' "strength of their endurance."[9]

Finally, as a means of understanding how John Steele of the *Intelligencer* could envision Confederate victory in 1864, is Charles Royster's keen observation that Southerners simply had no vocabulary for conceiving defeat. Writing in *The Destructive War* (1991), he declares that Confederates' "defiant new language included many superlatives to depict the South's unique greatness but no antonyms for those words, no way to conceive of a reality other than triumph." Royster quotes Jefferson Davis' statement to the Confederate Congress: "To speak of subjugating such a people, so united and determined, is to speak a language incomprehensible to them." More recently, Professor Anne Sarah Rubin has made the same point: "Confederates had no vocabulary for defeat, no way to fit it into their ideology of God-sanctioned nationhood. . . . To us this seems an exercise in self-deception and denial," she continues; "Confederates refused to admit that the war was drawing to a close because they didn't want to believe it."[10]

Thus we have it, the negatives and the positives. On one hand were a series of defeats that included Gettysburg and Vicksburg; mounting battlefield casualties and diminishing manpower; vast territorial areas and major cities lost; no hope of foreign help; pinched availability of food and consumer goods; rampant economic inflation; and existential threats to slavery.

In the face of such facts, the voicing of persistent Confederate optimism seems illogical. Yet that is precisely what John Steele did in his long editorial appearing in the *Intelligencer* on May 7, 1864. "We are at a loss what to say to our readers, to-day," it began.[11]

> The great heart of the country is occupied with the contemplation of the mighty struggles in Virginia and upon the Northwest borders of Georgia; and the indications, the prospects, and their probable results, have been stated and restated—turned over and over—by the minds of all who think, and another subject, just at this time, could hardly hope to gain a passing thought. There are times when we feel inclined to keep silent in the presence of great events transpiring around us, and quietly await their developments. The happiness or misery, the weal or woe, of the people of this Confederacy, are involved in the approaching struggles; and, indeed, we may say that the cause of civil and religious liberty is involved, for we hold that the people of the Confederate States are the custodians of those great principles for which patriots in all ages have struggled, and for which martyrs have sacrificed their lives. Infidelity, fanaticism in all its hideous forms, licentiousness in all its grossness, and cruelty and rapine, with all their horrors, will raise their disgusting forms and march boldly throughout our bright and sunny land, should our wicked foes triumph in the end, and succeed in doing what we think cannot be done, subjugating the South.
>
>   Johnston's repulse of the enemy in North Georgia[12]—Forrest's terrible defeat of Grierson and Smith in Mississippi[13]—the splendid victory at Olustee in Florida[14]— the overwhelming rout of the white and black abolitionists in Louisiana[15]—the glorious triumphs of our arms in West Tennessee and Kentucky, in the captures of Paducah[16] and Fort Pillow[17]— and the brilliant achievement of Hoke in the old North State in the capture of Plymouth,[18] are but so many striking evidences that the God of Battles is with us—that his arm has been interposed in our behalf, and that he will, if we but, as a people, put our trust in him, lead us safely through the troubles that have come upon us. Witness the alarms, the fears, the dissensions that are now agitating our proud and impious foes, and can you hesitate to believe

that they already see the hand-writing on the wall, and in it read their entire and utter destruction.—Our accounts from their armies inform us that their soldiers, whose time of enlistment expires in this month, are unwilling to continue any longer in their service, and many of them utterly refuse to engage in another fight. See the bold and defiant manner in which Long of Ohio,[19] Harris of Maryland,[20] Wood of New York,[21] and Rogers of New Jersey,[22] have come out in the House of Representatives at Washington in favor of Southern recognition, as it were, in the very face of the tyrant, usurper and despot, and can you longer doubt the fact that a great and salutary change is taking place in the land of our enemies? For saying less than these men, and hundreds of others have said, and are repeating daily, Vallandigham less than a year ago was banished from his home, his family and his friends, and doomed to languish in a foreign land;[23] but now the fiendish usurper, who has ruled that country with a rod of iron, dare not attempt to prevent these bold, but to him unwelcome, declarations of opinions and views. All these things indicate, as we think, the beginning of the end of this wicked war, and presage for us a triumphant conclusion of the sanguinary strife.

Be of good cheer, then, for though our hearts no doubt will be made to mourn, in the next few months, for many friends in battle slain, yet, we think it is safe to say, that putting our trust in God for deliverance, we will behold, before another year expires, the rainbow of peace spanning our Heaven-blessed land and hear our young men and maidens, and our little ones singing, "This cruel war is over!"

Consensus among historians is that the fall of Atlanta and Lincoln's re-election two months later were the events that extinguished Confederates' hopes for victory. Yet here we find it striking that as late as May of 1864 John Steele in Atlanta could write so optimistically of prospects for Southern success. He did so, we believe, honestly and without evident effort to deceive himself—or his readers.

NOTES

1. Steven H. Newton, *Lost For the Cause: The Confederate Army in 1864* (Mason City IA: Savas Publishing, 2000), 1; Albert Burton Moore, *Conscription and Conflict in the Confederacy* (New York: Hillary House, 1963 [1924]), 317.

2. Charles H. Wesley, *The Collapse of the Confederacy* (Columbia: University of South Carolina Press, 2001 [1937]), 37; Henry Steele Commager, ed., *The Defeat of the Confederacy* (Princeton NJ: D. Van Nostrand, 1964), 142.

3. Thomas, *Confederate Nation*, 243, 256.

4. Albert D. Kirwan, ed., *The Confederacy* (Cleveland: World Publishing Co., 1959), 129; Clifford Dowdey, *The Land They Fought For: The Story of the South as the Confederacy 1832–1865* (Garden City NY: Doubleday, 1955), 303.

5. William C. Davis, *Look Away! A History of the Confederate States of America* (New York: Free Press, 2002), 150–51; Clement Eaton, *A History of the Southern Confederacy* (New York: Free Press, 1954), 263.

6. Anne Sarah Rubin, *A Shattered Nation: The Rise and Fall of the Confederacy 1861–1868* (Chapel Hill: University of North Carolina Press, 2005), 105; McPherson, *Battle Cry*, 494, 506; Larry E. Nelson, *Bullets, Ballots, and Rhetoric: Confederate Policy for the United States Presidential Contest of 1864* (Tuscaloosa: University of Alabama Press, 1980), xi-xii.

7. Frank E. Vandiver, *Their Tattered Flags: The Epic of the Confederacy* (New York: Harper's Magazine Press, 1970), 268; "MESSAGE OF PRESIDENT JEFFERSON DAVIS," *ADI*, Dec. 15, 1863; J. Tracy Power, *Lee's Miserables: Life in the Army of Northern Virginia from the Wilderness to Appomattox* (Chapel Hill: University of North Carolina Press, 1998), 2; Keith S. Bohannon, "'Witness the Redemption of the Army': Reenlistment in the Confederate Army of Tennessee, January-March 1864" in Lesley J. Gordon and John C. Inscoe, eds., *Inside the Confederate Nation: Essays in Honor of Emory M. Thomas* (Baton Rouge: Louisiana State University Press, 2005), 112–113; "Duration of the War," *ADI*, April 10, 1864.

8. Clifford Dowdey, *The Land They Fought For: The Story of the South as the Confederacy, 1832–1865* (Garden City NY: Doubleday, 1955), 303; McPherson, *For Cause and Comrades*, 21–24; Coulter, *Confederate States of America*, 449.

9. Charles P. Roland, *The Confederacy* (Chicago: University of Chicago Press, 1960), 160; Frank E. Vandiver, *Basic History of the Confederacy* (Princeton NJ: D. Van Nostrand, 1962), 47; Wiley Sword, *Southern Invincibility: A History of the Confederate Heart* (New York: St. Martin's Press, 1999), 202.

10. Charles Royster, *The Destructive War: William Tecumseh Sherman, Stonewall Jackson, and the Americans* (New York: Alfred A. Knopf, 1991), 177–78; Rubin, *Shattered Nation*, 112.

11. "We are at a loss . . . ," *ADI*, May 7, 1864.

12. Near Dalton during Feb. 24–26, 1864, Federals tested the right of the Confederate line along Rocky Face Ridge and Crow Valley. "St. Clair" reported on their repulse on the 25th: "the battle, although not a general engagement, was nevertheless a brilliant affair" (Albert Castel, *Decision in the West: The Atlanta Campaign of 1864* [Lawrence: University Press of Kansas, 1992], 534; Robert D. Jenkins, "Dalton: The Opening of the Georgia Campaign," *Blue & Gray*, vol. 32, issue 1 [December 2015], 8, 12); "ST. CLAIR," "ARMY CORRESPONDENCE. THE ENGAGEMENT AT STONESIDE MOUNTAIN!," *ADI*, March 1, 1864).

13. On February 22, Bedford Forrest with 2,500 men, attacked Union Brig. Gen. William S. Smith's force of 6,600 near Okolona, in northeast Mississippi. The Confederates charged so fiercely that Smith's troops were sent fleeing back to Memphis. Forrest reported taking 162 prisoners and six cannon (Henry, *"First With the Most" Forrest*, 227–33). The *Intelligencer* covered the battle in its telegraphic column of February 27 ("completely routed them").

14. The *Intelligencer* printed Confederate Brig. Gen. Joseph Finegan's brief report of his victory of February 19 at Olustee, fifty miles west of Jacksonville, in its telegraphic news section on the 24th.

15. Maj. Gen. Nathaniel Banks' forces included a "Corps D'Afrique"—four regiments of U.S. Colored Troops. Under the command of Col. William H. Dickey, the brigade participated in the battle of Mansfield, April 8; the African Americans helped guard Banks' wagon train in the Federal retreat (James G. Hollandsworth, T*he Louisiana Native Guards: The Black Military Experience During the Civil War* [Baton Rouge: Louisiana State University Press, 1995], 90–91).

16. Forrest led a mounted column into Paducah, Ky., on March 25. While his men skirmished with a fortified Union garrison, others cleaned out the town of supplies (Wills, *Battle From the Start*, 176–77). The *Intelligencer* of April 6 reported the action in its "TELEGRAPHIC" column ("Forrest burnt all the Government stores").

17. On April 22, in the *Intelligencer*'s "telegraphic" column, appeared a short summary of Forrest's report, which had arrived at the War Department in Richmond: 500 of 700 Federals killed (Confederate casualties were twenty dead, sixty wounded); "over 100 citizens, who had fled to the fort from conscription, ran into the river and were drowned."

18. On April 28, the *Intelligencer* noted that during Hoke's investment of Plymouth, April 17–19, Col. John T. Mercer of the 21st Georgia had been killed ("VERY SINGULAR," *ADI*, April 28, 1864).

19. On April 8, 1864, Rep. Alexander H. Long gave a speech in the U.S. House of Representatives in which he expressed willingness to recognize Southern independence. Long was one of those antiwar Northerners who came to be derisively called "Copperheads" (Nelson, *Bullets, Ballots, and Rhetoric*, 4–5).

20. On April 9, the day after Long spoke, Benjamin Harris, another "peace Democrat," went so far as to announce to the House, "I am a peace man, a radical peace man; and I am for peace by the recognition of the South, for the recognition of the southern confederacy; and I am for acquiescence in the doctrine of secession" (Nelson, *Bullets, Ballots, and Rhetoric*, 6).

21. Fernando Wood, former mayor of New York, was elected to Congress in 1862 as a Peace Democrat who espoused a negotiated armistice with the South (Jerome Mushkat, "Fernando Wood" in John T. Hubbell and James W. Geary, eds., *Biographical Dictionary of the Union: Northern Leaders in the Civil War* [Westport CT: Greenwood Press, 1995], 599).

22. Andrew Jackson Rogers was elected to the U.S. House in October 1862 as a well-known critic of emancipation. He warned crowds that freed Negroes would swarm into New Jersey and soon would be "crawling into bed with your wives and daughters" (Daniel W. Crofts, "Andrew Jackson Rogers" in Hubbell and Geary, eds., *Biographical Dictionary of the Union*, 443).

23. Ohio Democrat Clement L. Vallandigham, congressman from Dayton, was a vocal critic of Republican war measures, including emancipation. On Jan. 14, 1863, he delivered his "peace speech," in which he called for an armistice and the withdrawal of Federal troops from the South. He was arrested in May 1863 for expressing sympathy for the Confederacy. After he was tried and found guilty, President Lincoln commuted his sentence from imprisonment to banishment into Confederate lines. After two weeks in the South, Vallandigham sailed to Bermuda, heading for Canada (Frank L. Klement, *The Limits of Dissent: Clement L. Vallandigham & the Civil War* [New York: Fordham University Press, 1998], 23, 91, 123–27, 154–55, 168, 175, 177, 211–12).

35. "General Johnston Is Falling Back"

WHEN PRESIDENT LINCOLN promoted Ulysses S. Grant and appointed him general-in-chief of the Union armies in March 1864, the new lieutenant general announced a plan that was new—and yet not-so-new. He ordered that for their spring campaigns, major Union armies would "move together and toward one common center." Two years earlier President Lincoln had tried to do the same, when he issued an order in January 1862 for his armies in Virginia and Kentucky to get moving on February 22 (Washington's birthday). Tellingly, however, his generals simply ignored it.

This time would be different. General Grant got his way, with a multi-front offensive to be launched in early May 1864.

Its centerpiece would be Maj. Gen. George G. Meade's Army of the Potomac. "Lee's army will be your objective," Grant wrote Meade on April 9; "wherever Lee goes, there you will go also." To make sure, Grant would accompany Meade into the field. Meade remained in command of the army, but Grant would call the shots.

When Meade advanced, Grant expected Maj. Gen. William T. Sherman to do so, too. With Grant's promotion, Sherman was given command of the "Military Division of the Mississippi"—all Union forces between the Appalachians and the Mississippi. Assembling three western armies into an "army group," Sherman would advance south from Chattanooga against Confederate Gen. Joseph E. Johnston's Army of Tennessee. "You I propose to move against Johnston's army, to break it up," Grant wrote his friend Cump on April 4, "and to get into the interior of the enemy's country as far as you can."

Grant's plan involved smaller armies as well. Maj. Gen. Benjamin F. Butler would advance from southeastern Virginia up the James toward Richmond, as Grant and Meade pressed Lee north of the Confederate capital. Maj. Gen. Nathaniel P. Banks, commanding at New Orleans, would lead a force against Mobile, the South's most important Gulf seaport.

Grant's fifth offensive prong involved Maj. Gen. Franz Sigel, commanding

Federal forces in the Shenandoah and western Virginia. Grant ordered Sigel to send two columns out of Beverly and Charleston (now West Virginia) to move southward against the Virginia and Tennessee Railroad, as he explained in a letter of April 4.

All in all, it was an ambitious plan, one which President Lincoln approvingly termed "Operation Crusher."

Unfortunately, Grant would be reminded that war is a highly fluid situation. Before the start of the five-front offensive, the Lincoln administration ordered General Banks to lead a force into northwest Louisiana, up the Red River. Banks started late, suffered defeat at Mansfield on April 8, and limped back to New Orleans, too late to move against Mobile.

Franz Sigel bollixed up the plan as well. He refused to allocate sufficient troops for the advance out of Beverly, and instead marshaled his forces for an advance he himself would lead up the Valley from Winchester to Staunton. (Some authorities mistakenly assume that Sigel's move up the Valley was part of Grant's original plan.) Sigel met defeat at New Market on May 15 and retreated. The next day, Ben Butler was beaten at Drewry's Bluff on the James; he also retreated. So much for "Operation Crusher."[1]

But at least Grant got going, though not very auspiciously.

On May 7, readers of the *Intelligencer* got their first news of fighting in Virginia from the paper's telegraphic dispatch column, on page three, under the headline, "BATTLE IN VIRGINIA COMMENCED." On Thursday, the 5th, troops of Confederate Lt. Gen. Richard S. Ewell's corps in Lee's army had engaged elements of the V Corps, Army of the Potomac. Below it the column featured General Lee's "official dispatch" on the fighting that day.

The ability of the *Intelligencer* to print Lee's dispatch about the engagement of May 5, appearing in its evening edition on the 7th, shows how fast important news could travel in the Press Association's wire service. Lee stated that the Federals had crossed the Rapidan and marched into the Wilderness, the vast woodland where he had won his Chancellorsville victory. "Two corps of this army moved to oppose them," Ewell's and Ambrose Powell Hill's. Lee elaborated: "A strong attack was made on Ewell, who repulsed it, capturing many prisoners and four pieces of artillery. The enemy subsequently concentrated upon Hill, who, with [Maj. Gen. Henry] Heth's and [Maj. Gen. Cadmus M.] Wilcox's divisions, successfully resisted and repulsed repeated desperate assaults. By the blessing of God, we maintained our position against every effort, until night, when the conflict ended." There was no report of casualties for this, the first day of the battle of the Wilderness, though Lee named Brig. Gen. John M. Jones as killed and Brig. Gen. Leroy A. Stafford mortally wounded.[2]

On May 8, "Further Particulars from Virginia" continued reporting of "the battle fought near Wilderness." "The attack of the enemy this morning," began the wire dispatch dated May 6, "was very violent, but was repulsed in every instance." Lt. Gen. James Longstreet was seriously wounded in the fighting, and Brig. Gen. Micah Jenkins killed. Then, under date of May 8 came the wire dispatch stating that Brig. Gen. John B. Gordon had turned the enemy's right flank, driving the Federals back. Ominously, though, as a sign that Grant was not retreating across the Rapidan (as Hooker had done the year before), the report added, "the enemy has abandoned Germanna Ford, and removed their Pontoon bridge towards Ely's Ford."[3]

This sparse news was at least accurate, yet it was not enough for John Steele, as he expressed on May 10. "The anxiety of everyone to hear further particulars of the bloody struggle being enacted on the Rapidan, has been most intense for the last two days," he wrote. Perhaps the wires were down in North Carolina, or Yankee raiders had cut them in Virginia. "Whatever the cause may be," the editor shrugged, "it will doubtless pass away." Then Steele expressed hope that the news from Virginia would be of "the grandest and most decisive victory of the war."[4]

The telegraph *was* working between Atlanta and Dalton, but Alexander St. Clair Abrams, the *Intelligencer*'s correspondent at Dalton in early May, writing as "St. Clair," had nothing to report. "The enemy and everything else is quiet to-day" (May 6).[5]

Then things started heating up.

At the start of his campaign "to get into the interior of the enemy's country as far as you can" (as Grant had instructed him on April 4), William Tecumseh ("Cump") Sherman enjoyed a significant numerical advantage over Joe Johnston. On April 30, the three armies over which he would exercise command had an effective strength in officers and men as follows:

- Maj. Gen. George H. Thomas' Army of the Cumberland: 61,600 infantry in the IV, XIV and XX Corps;
- Maj. Gen. James B. McPherson's Army of the Tennessee: 22,300 infantry in the XV and XVI Corps;
- Maj. Gen. John M. Schofield's Army of the Ohio: 9,200 infantry of the XXIII Corps;

12,400 cavalry, mostly in Thomas' army; and

4,500 artillerymen serving 254 guns (mostly smoothbore Napoleons but also a hundred 3-inch rifled guns, 10- and 20-pounder Parrott rifles).

In all, these totaled 110,000 officers and men.

Against this force Johnston's Army of Tennessee could muster no more than half that strength. On April 30 there were counted in Lt. Gen. William J. Hardee's infantry corps, 20,600 officers and men; Lt. Gen. John B. Hood's had 21,800. Maj. Gen. Joseph Wheeler commanded 7,800 cavalrymen. The artillery arm consisted of 144 guns manned by 3,200 cannoneers. When headquarters staff, generals' escorts and engineers were added in, there were 54,500 Confederates present for duty on April 30.

General Johnston did not know Sherman's precise strength, but he knew it was greater than his own. When the Federals advanced, he therefore intended to take a strong defensive stand on commanding ground, dig in, and hope that they attacked (and were repulsed). This was the aggressive (and sanguinary) tactical campaign being waged by Grant in Virginia, who resolved to use his numerical strength to hammer Lee's army and wear it down in continuous attacking battles, even at the cost of heavy Union casualties.

But Sherman would not so oblige Johnston. During the winter of '63-'64, Confederates had fortified a seven-mile line north and west of Dalton along the tall Rocky Face Ridge. Sherman's men observed the strength of the Rebels' position, and wondered if they would be ordered to attack it. Some saw buzzards roosting in the heights ahead of them. One Northerner asked a comrade what he thought the birds were doing; "counting us," came the reply.[6]

Unwilling to commit to a frontal assault against Johnston's line, Sherman resolved to flank it, especially since south of it were several gaps in Rocky Face through which he could send columns of troops. The Confederates held one of them, Dug Gap on the left of their line (the southern end), but five miles south of that General Thomas had learned of another gap, called Snake Creek, that in early May looked unguarded. Sherman planned to send McPherson's Army of the Tennessee through Snake Creek Gap, with the aim of swiftly covering the few miles between the gap and the Western & Atlantic Railroad, the supply line for Johnston's army. If McPherson's troops got on that road in Johnston's rear, the Confederates would have no choice but to give up their Dalton position and retreat southward.[7]

On May 6, McPherson's infantry started marching for Snake Creek Gap.

By the evening of the 8th, the Federals were a few miles from it. To divert Johnston's attention away from McPherson's maneuver, Sherman ordered Thomas and Schofield on May 9 to launch three attacks on the Confederate center and right. They did so, and the diversion worked, for not only were Johnston's eyes drawn to those sectors, but so were Alexander Abrams'. Late on the 9th he sent a telegram back to Atlanta (*Intelligencer*, May 11) reporting that all three assaults "were whipped back with great loss" to the enemy. Editor Steele exulted in an editorial on Wednesday, the 11th, expressing satisfaction that "on Monday the enemy was repulsed at all points."[8]

But the real story was taking place eight miles southwest of Dalton, where McPherson's troops on May 9 brushed aside some Confederate cavalry, pushed through Snake Creek Gap and headed for the railroad. The Federal advance caused Johnston to realize that he could no longer hold his Rocky Face line. On the 11th he began moving troops by rail to Resaca, a town sixteen miles to the south. The Confederate evacuation of Dalton was complete by nightfall of May 12.[9]

Then, for several days, the *Intelligencer* office in Atlanta encountered a news blackout, as it announced on May 15. "Our Special Reporter"—"St. Clair"—"has not been able for several days to communicate with us, either through the telegraph or by letter," the paper announced.

It was indeed true. Yet once again (as at Dalton), the *Intelligencer* editor, much like General Johnston, had not figured out Sherman's "game," which was to engage the Confederate lines with infantry sorties and artillery bombardments, while a Union column was marching stealthily beyond the Rebel left flank to get at the Western & Atlantic Railroad. At the start of May 13, Johnston's army held a strong position north and west of Resaca just north of the Oostanaula River.

Sherman brought his forces toward Resaca that day. He ordered his infantry to attack all along the front on the 14th, or at least to "demonstrate" while the infantry division of Brig. Gen. Thomas W. Sweeny marched south, well downriver from the Confederate left, to lay a pontoon bridge and get across the Oostanaula. This Sweeny did, though he failed to establish a strong beachhead on the south bank.[10]

With its focus on the battle lines, the *Intelligencer* attempted to report the fighting on Saturday, May 14. "Early in the morning a rapid engagement commenced along the entire line," the paper announced a few days later. The artillery firing was intense and the musketry incessant. Multiple Federal assaults "were repulsed with severe loss on their side and few casualties on our part."

After such a glowing report from Resaca, appearing on May 17, readers must have been quite surprised to see the very next day that Johnston's army had given up its Oostanaula lines and was retreating back via Adairsville toward Kingston. No reason was given for the retrograde, though we today know that Sherman had ordered Sweeny on May 15 to get across the river and push forward (which he did). This meant a continuation of the diversionary Northern infantry advances for this, the second day of the battle of Resaca. That night, informed of the Federal maneuver around his left, Johnston ordered his army to begin withdrawing.

The *Intelligencer* could not relate these details, but to try to explain the retreat it informed readers that Sherman's forces numbered 100,000 men, and that "it is the determination of General Johnston not to risk a general engagement until he has reached the ground he desires."

About that time Lt. Gen. Leonidas Polk's Army of Mississippi (three infantry divisions), plus troops from the garrisons of Charleston, Savannah and Mobile, had reinforced the Army of Tennessee to around 70,000 officers and men, making it at the time the largest field army in the Confederacy.

Still, it was the combination of heavy Yankee battalions and Joe Johnston's defensive predilections that had brought about the second Confederate retreat, not even two weeks after the start of the Georgia Campaign. Nevertheless, the *Intelligencer* continued to chirp bright sentiments. "Our army is in fine spirits and eager to fight.... Let our people be confident.... We will fight a general engagement before many days and then with the help of God and the valor of our troops VICTORY is certain to rest on our banners!"[11]

Alexander St. Clair Abrams accompanied Johnston's troops in their retreat from Resaca, and near Calhoun on the afternoon of May 16 was able to write a letter to the *Intelligencer* (published on the 18th). He related in considerable detail the two-day battle of Resaca, emphasizing Confederates' repulse of the numerous Federal assaults ("one thing is certain, that they were slaughtered by hundreds at every charge, and must have suffered severely"). But the *Intelligencer*'s assistant editor and special field correspondent was at a loss as to how to explain the army's retreat after its smart little defensive victory. "The chances are that we will continue our retreat to Adairsville, to-morrow," he observed. Then, a bit ominously he added, "the army is still in fine spirits"—the word *still* suggesting that retreating without being told why could have a dampening effect on the men's morale.[12]

The waning confidence that Abrams only faintly alluded to was confronted pointblank by John Steele in an editorial appearing on May 19, entitled "Long Faces.'" "We are stopped daily on the street almost at every step, by people who anxiously enquire the news," he wrote. "Some of them say to us, 'Why do you publish such flattering opinions about the situation? You know as well as I do that Johnston is falling back.'" The editor dignified them as "Mr. Grumbler," "Mr. Suspicious Patriot," "Mr. Subjugated" and "Mr. Despair," and then let them have it. "Yes! General Johnston is falling back. Yes! The enemy; the Yankees; the terrible, great big, bugaboo Yankees; the fellows with cerulean abdomens or *azure corporations,* as some of our compeers name them, are thundering at our gates." Facing such dire prospects, Steele offered them some advice: either get out of town or join the soldiers bravely facing the foe.[13]

After the Confederate army marched through Adairsville, Johnston laid a trap for Sherman's troops marching on Cassville that would involve a crushing flank attack by Hood's corps upon them. The commanding general was so hopeful of success that on the evening of May 18, he had a bellicose order drawn up to be read to the troops. "Soldiers of the Army of Tennessee," it began, "you will now turn and march to meet his advancing columns. . . . I lead you to battle." The Press Association telegraphic news article that appeared in the *Intelligencer* on May 20 related that "Gen. Johnston's battle order was read to the troops . . . and received with the wildest enthusiasm."

Yet Johnston's battle plan fell apart on the morning of May 19 when a large body of Union cavalry threatened the flank of the assault column, forcing Hood to call off the battle before it had even begun. Johnston reluctantly established a defensive line south of Cassville. That night Johnston's lead generals voted to retreat again.[14]

"St. Clair" digested all of this in a letter dated May 20. After fully quoting Johnston's "I lead you to battle" address, he commented, "it may seem strange, after reading the above, that the army should continue to retreat." But the Yankees had begun to cross the Etowah downstream and thus had compelled General Johnston to withdraw across that river as well; the army was now positioned near Allatoona, four miles south of the Etowah.[15]

In columns titled "The Situation," the *Intelligencer* informed readers of events occurring in the war's two major theaters, Georgia and Virginia. As for the latter, Lee and Grant had been locked in bloody combat in the Wilderness and at Spotsylvania Court House. The paper had to report grimly that the famed Maj. Gen. "Jeb" Stuart had been mortally wounded on May 12 in the battle of Yellow Tavern. The *Intelligencer* went on not even to wince at the reportedly huge size of the Army of the Potomac facing Robert E. Lee's Army of Northern Virginia. In his "The Situation" column of May 23, John Steele acknowledged that "all the resources of the north have been placed at the disposal of Grant," such that his forces could be currently numbering 200,000 men. But not to worry, he assured readers, as the "cerulean abdomens" (highfalutin' terminology for *bluebellies*) had been "gathered from all the purlieus of effete Europe and the North," and were thus a substandard species of soldiery: "Dutch immigrants, cheated Irishmen, bamboozled mongrels, miserable contrabands, miscegenating adults and brigades of silly youths with cerulean abdomens, and a sufficiency of yankees to leaven the whole mass with their accursed principles of injustice and wrong."[16]

Editor Steele took stock of the situation in an article printed May 23. Aware of the topographical strength of the Rebels' position at Allatoona, Sherman ordered his troops to ready enough supplies for twenty days. For the first time in the campaign, the Federal commander was prepared to depart from his logistical lifeline, the Western & Atlantic Railroad. His planned path would take his army group well to the southwest of Allatoona, where he figured that his march beyond Johnston's left flank would compel the Confederates to retreat from their mountain position.[17]

Almost as soon as Sherman started sidling away from the railroad, heading toward Dallas (fifteen miles southwest of Allatoona), Johnston got his army marching in that direction, too. The *Intelligencer* followed the shifting battle lines. "The main body of the enemy seems to have abandoned the line of the railroad, and are attempting to mass on our left," the paper reported on May 25. The next day, "The Situation" related that "the brave men of this army are again on the march."[18]

Alexander St. Clair Abrams travelled with Maj. Gen. Carter L. Stevenson's division of Hood's corps as Johnston's army formed a five-mile defensive line running from Dallas eastward to New Hope Church, a small Methodist meeting house. Hood's troops held the right around New Hope. In the afternoon of the 25th, Sherman ordered three divisions of Maj. Gen. Joseph Hooker's XX corps to advance against the Rebels in their front. The Federals were bloodily repulsed, with casualties totaling more than 1,650. That night "St. Clair" wrote that they "were fearfully cut up by our gallant men."[19]

On May 26, the day after the fight at New Hope Church, activity in the opposing armies was confined "entirely to skirmishing, and attempts of the enemy to feel our position," according to the Press Association report issued on the 27th (in the *Intelligencer* on May 29). Sherman's "feeling" of the Confederate lines continued on May 27, when he ordered his IV Corps commander, Maj. Gen. Oliver O. Howard, to head east in order to find the right flank of Johnston's line and attack it. Howard's troops marched toward their left that morning and into the afternoon, even as the Confederates were busy extending their line father eastward. By mid-afternoon Johnston's flank rested near Little Pumpkinvine Creek and the grist mill owned by the Widow Pickett. Howard was therefore never able to turn the Southerners' flank. Not only that, but Johnston's right was held by Maj. Gen. Patrick R. Cleburne's division, probably the toughest in the Army of Tennessee. The afternoon was slipping away when an impatient Sherman ordered Howard to attack, flank or no flank. The Federal infantry assault was thus a frontal one, against Cleburne's troops, who were ready for it. The predictable bloody repulse of the Northern charge was succinctly reported in the *Intelligencer* of May 31: "Gen. Cleburne says the enemy's dead are piled thicker than he ever saw before." The paper was on the mark regarding Confederate casualties (85 killed, 363 wounded), but exaggerated Howard's, which were 212 killed, 927 wounded and 528 missing for a total of 1,457 officers and men.

The eastward movement of Union troops on May 27 led General Johnston to infer that on the Union right, held by McPherson's Army of the Tennessee near Dallas, the Federal lines were weakening. He therefore ordered Maj. Gen. William B. Bate, whose division held the Confederate left, to test McPherson's strength. Bate's troops, in their resulting frontal attack on the 28th, found out quite decidedly that Johnston was wrong in suggesting "it is believed he is not in force." The *Intelligencer* of June 1 related that after the Federals in his front were found to be in full force, Bate countermanded his attack order, but the message failed to reach two of his brigades. When they sallied forth, the Southerners were repulsed with 600–800 casualties, to the Federals' 379 in this battle of Dallas, May 28.

Thus, in the fighting along the Dallas-New Hope-Pickett's Mill line, May 25–28, Confederates won two rounds and lost one. But Sherman had won the bigger tactical prize: he had maneuvered Johnston out of his Allatoona Mountain stronghold. On May 30, Schofield and Thomas began marching east back to the railroad; McPherson left Dallas the next day. Johnston on June 3 ordered his army to shift to the next good defensive position, Lost Mountain, six miles to the southeast.

"St. Clair," with the army in the field, reported on these events in letters to the *Intelligencer* sent every morning by courier. "Flanking and flank movements have been the prominent features of this campaign," he observed on May 28. A few days later he predicted that Sherman's march by his left would force Johnston to move correspondingly, "and consequently we will be nearer Marietta than before."[20]

Atlantans were understandably rattled by the approach of Sherman's forces, but at least they had been preparing for it. Confederate engineers had begun planning a complete ring of fortifications around the city in the summer of 1863. By mid-April of '64 a 10 ½-mile perimeter of continuous entrenchments, studded with two dozen artillery forts, ringed the city. It became apparent that they would soon be needed, when citizens heard the faint sounds of distant artillery on May 25 from New Hope Church.

After "Shadow," a reporter for the *Mobile Advertiser & Register*, writing on May 24, gloomily predicted the eventual fall of Atlanta, John Steele objected editorially. "Vivid imagination" and "hyperbolic assumptions," were the Atlanta paper's judgements of "Shadow's" pessimistic predictions. Editor Steele asserted, "Atlanta will not fall; nor is it our opinion; nor do the *citizens* of Atlanta believe it; nor are they so panic stricken as to believe it." As evidence, he pointed out that though "occasionally we can hear the booming of artillery. . . . in only a few cases have we noticed any preparation on the part of any of [the citizens] to leave for parts more distant from the enemy." Indeed, the editor welcomed the prospect of the decisive battle being fought "as well . . . on the Chattahoochee, as at Marietta, or at New Hope; as well fight the battle in Fulton as in Paulding [County, the area of New Hope Church]." When it occurred, "for the safety of Atlanta we have no fear."[21]

We've seen it before: John Steele, and plenty of other Confederate editors, putting the rosiest spin on untoward events in the Confederate war for independence. Here again is more of the same, as Sherman's hordes neared New Hope Church, just two dozen miles northwest of Atlanta.

NOTES

1. Grant to Meade, April 9, 1864, *OR*, vol. 33, 827–29; Grant to Sherman, April 4, *OR*, vol. 32, pt. 3, 245–46; Richard M. McMurry, *Atlanta 1864: Last Chance for the Confederacy* (Lincoln: University of Nebraska Press, 2000), 14–15, 54–55; T. Harry Williams, *Lincoln and His Generals* (Baton Rouge: Louisiana State University Press, Alfred A. Knopf, 1952), 306–307.

2. "TELEGRAPHIC. BATTLE IN VIRGINIA COMMENCED" and "OFFICIAL DISPATCH FROM GENERAL LEE," *ADI*, May 7, 1864; Noah Andre Trudeau, *Bloody*

Roads South: The Wilderness to Cold Harbor May–June 1864 (Boston: Little, Brown, 1989), 41–77.

3. "TELEGRAPHIC. Further Particulars from Virginia," *ADI*, May 8, 1864; Gordon C. Rhea, *The Battle of the Wilderness May 5–6, 1864* (Baton Rouge: Louisiana State University Press, 1994), 440; "TELEGRAPHIC. LATEST FROM VIRGINIA," *ADI*, May 10.

4. "THE NEWS," *ADI*, May 10, 1864.

5. "ST. CLAIR," "TELEGRAPH. LATEST FROM THE FRONT" (Dalton, May 6), *ADI*, May 8, 1864.

6. Stephen Davis, *A Long and Bloody Task: The Atlanta Campaign From Dalton through Kennesaw Mountain to the Chattahoochee River May 5–July 18, 1864* (El Dorado Hills CA: Savas Beatie, 2016), 13–15; "Abstract from returns showing the effective strength of the army in the field under Maj. Gen. William T. Sherman, during the campaign against Atlanta, Ga., 1864. April 30, 1864," *OR*, vol. 38, pt. 1, 11; "Strength of the Confederate Forces. April 30, 1864," *OR*, vol. 38, pt. 3, 675–76.

7. Stephen Davis, *Atlanta Will Fall: Sherman, Joe Johnston, and the Yankee Heavy Battalions* (Wilmington DE: Scholarly Resources, 2001), 34–36.

8. Stephen Davis, "Sherman in North Georgia: The Battle of Resaca," *Blue & Gray*, vol. 31, issue 4 (Summer 2015), 8; Jenkins, "Dalton," 16–17; "TELEGRAPHIC. Special Dispatch to the Intelligencer. Latest from Dalton" and "THE WORK GOES BRAVELY ON," *ADI*, May 11, 1864.

9. Davis, *Long and Bloody Task*, 10, 21, 23.

10. "FROM THE FRONT," *ADI*, May 15, 1864; William R. Scaife, *The Campaign for Atlanta* (Saline MI: McNaughton & Gunn, 1993), 27–34, f.p. 38–39; Richard M. McMurry, "Resaca: 'A Heap of Hard Fiten,'" *Civil War Times Illustrated*, vol. 9, no. 7 (November 1970), 7.

11. "FROM THE ARMY OF TENN.," *ADI*, May 17, 1864; "From Wednesday Morning's Edition. LATEST FROM THE FRONT. Our Army Fall[s] Back on Kingston," *ADI*, May 18; Philip Secrist, "Resaca: For Sherman a Moment of Truth," *Atlanta Historical Journal*, vol. 22, no. 1 (Spring 1978), 38; Davis, *Atlanta Will Fall*, 50–51.

12. "ST. CLAIR," "Special Correspondence of the 'Intelligencer,'" *ADI*, May 18, 1864.

13. "LONG FACES," *ADI*, May 19, 1864.

14. Stephen Davis, *Texas Brigadier to the Fall of Atlanta: John Bell Hood* (Macon: Mercer University Press, 2019), 141–44; "TELEGRAPHIC NEWS," Latest from the Front," *ADI*, May 20, 1864.

15. "ST. CLAIR," "Special Correspondence to the Atlanta 'Intelligencer'" (May 20), *ADI*, May 21, 1864.

16. "THE SITUATION" and "TELEGRAPHIC. LATEST FROM VIRGINIA," *ADI*, May 23, 1864; "VIRGINIA NEWS. THE YELLOW TAVERN FIGHT," *ADI*, MAY 25.

17. Stephen Davis, "No Hope of Success," *Civil War Times*, vol. 57, no. 2 (April 2018), 36.

18. Davis, *Long and Bloody Task*, 49–50; "TELEGRAPHIC. Latest from the Front" (May 23), *ADI*, May 25, 1864; "THE SITUATION. ARMY OF TENNESSEE," *ADI*, May 26, 1864.

19. "ST. CLAIR," "Special Correspondence to the Atlanta 'Intelligencer'" (New Hope Church, May 25), *ADI*, May 28, 1864; Davis, "No Hope of Success," 37–40; "FROM THE FRONT," *ADI*, May 28.

20. "THRASHER," "TELEGRAPHIC. FROM THE FRONT" (May 27), *ADI*, May 29, 1864; Davis, *Long and Bloody Task*, 55–59, 61; "Latest from the Front (New Hope via Marietta, May 28," *ADI*, May 31; Stephen Davis, "Simply Criminal," *America's Civil War*, vol. 32, no. 2 (May 2019), 37; "TELEGRAPHIC. Latest from the Front (New Hope, May 29, via Marietta, 30)" and "ST. CLAIR," "Special Correspondence to the Atlanta 'Intelligencer'" (May 28 and 29), *ADI*, June 1; "ST. CLAIR," "Special Correspondence to the Atlanta 'Intelligencer'" (May 30), *ADI*, June 3.

21. Davis, *What the Yankees Did to Us*, 58–63, 70–71; Davis, *Atlanta Will Fall*, 3; "SHADOW," *ADI*, June 1, 1864; "OUR CITY—ITS SAFETY," *ADI*, June 1.

36. Kennesaw Mountain

IN EARLY JUNE 1864, the *Intelligencer* signaled its readers that events in Sherman's campaign for Atlanta were happening quickly. A regular column entitled "The Situation" appeared almost every day in the paper, offering editor John Steele and his correspondent in the field, Alexander St. Clair Abrams, a chance to offer updates and commentary.[1]

As they advanced, the *Intelligencer* forecast that Yankee soldiers would supplement their rations by foraging off the countryside—in other words, by taking what the people had to eat. The paper warned Georgians living between the Union forces and the defenses of Atlanta to prepare for a quick evacuation of their property in case of an enemy advance. Indeed, it warned that "if the cerulean abdomens besiege our city, no family, no people can live securely anywhere near them."[2]

The other "situation" involved Lee's Army of Northern Virginia facing the advance of Grant's/Meade's Army of the Potomac. Throughout May and early June, Grant directed his troops from the Wilderness (May 5–7), then southeast to Spotsylvania Court House (May 7–19), and farther still, toward Richmond *via* the North Anna River (May 23–26), with Lee masterfully moving his troops to stay ahead of the enemy. The Federals then marched to Cold Harbor, just ten miles northeast of the Confederate capital. On June 3, Grant unwisely ordered a frontal attack on Lee's fortified lines that cost 7,000 Union casualties in a half-hour.[3]

As for "The Situation" in Georgia, on June 7 the *Intelligencer* affirmed that "our army has been gradually retiring before the advance of Sherman." As the Federal forces marched east from Dallas to the Western & Atlantic, Johnston sidled that way, too, keeping his troops between Sherman's and Marietta (the railroad town some twenty miles northwest of Atlanta). By June 5, Johnston had taken up a new defensive line, this one anchored at Lost Mountain on the left (Hardee's corps) and Brush Mountain on the right (Hood's). In his letter of June 5, "St. Clair" reported that the new Confederate line ran from

Lost Mountain eastward across the Western & Atlantic to about three miles south of Big Shanty (now Kennesaw). In the middle, about a mile in front of the Confederates' main defenses, Maj. Gen. William B. Bate's division held an eminence, Pine Mountain, in a forward position unconnected by trenches to the army's fortified line. Some wag said that this exposed salient was intended as a trap for the Yankees, and that the Confederate force holding it was the "Bate."[4]

On June 10, Sherman got his army group marching southward, aiming to dislodge Johnston from his mountain line. During the next several days the Northerners sparred with Bate's troops with artillery and musket fire, while Sherman's columns gradually maneuvered to the east of Pine Mountain. General Hardee started to worry that Bate's salient might be enveloped by the Federals, so on the evening of June 13 he asked General Johnston to ride to the top of the mountain the next morning to take a long look at the situation. General/Bishop Polk was to go along, too.

On the morning of June 14, the generals rode to the top of Pine Mountain. There they dismounted and began surveying the Federals' position below them. General Sherman happened to be riding along his lines that morning when he noticed the Rebel officers on the summit. He ordered nearby artillerymen to lob some shots at the group. Atop the mountain, shells started whizzing and bursting. One struck Polk, killing him instantly as it passed through his chest, breaking both arms. A mortified Johnston and Hardee knelt grieving beside the bishop's mangled body.

The *Intelligencer* reported the news of Polk's death in a long tribute to the man published on June 16. "A martyr to the noble cause of the Southern Confederacy," it affirmed, "his name will be immortalized as one of its great lights; one of its noblest defenders; one of the most glorious soldiers of the nation." The article informed readers that the bishop/general's body would lie in state at St. Luke's that afternoon, before being borne to the Car Shed for train transport to Augusta.[5]

"Yesterday (Wednesday) was the first day of the battle of KENNESAW MOUN-TAIN," the *Intelligencer* announced on Friday, June 17. Actually, it was not, at least geographically speaking. After Bate's division withdrew from its Pine Mountain salient in the night of June 14–15, Sherman ordered Thomas to press the Confederate line in a reconnaissance-in-force. The ensuing combat on June 15 constituted the small engagement of Gilgal Church, fought five miles to the west of Kennesaw Mountain. Maj. Gen. Patrick Cleburne's infantry handily repulsed the Federals' advances, leading the *Intelligencer* to remark that among the troops, "the most unbounded confidence exists in General Johnston and our leaders." "St. Clair" echoed the sentiment in a letter he wrote late on the 15th: "So far as the situation is concerned, there is no apprehension on the part of this army, that the enemy will be able to carry our position by assault."[6]

Alexander St. Clair Abrams would be proven correct, but Sherman's assaulting was not the issue; it was his flanking. Schofield's maneuvering around his left led Johnston on June 16 to order a nighttime withdrawal of Hardee's corps on that flank, back a few miles from Lost Mountain and Gilgal Church but still connecting with Polk's (now Maj. Gen. William W. Loring's) troops in the Confederate center and Hood's on the right. Sherman kept up the pressure. "The second day of the battle of Kennesaw opened with heavy cannonading far off to the left," the *Intelligencer* announced on June 18. But the skirmishing and cannonading fell far short of the big, decisive battle that many Confederates were hankering for. "St. Clair" was among them. "The battle for the preservation of your city," he addressed readers in Atlanta on June 18, "*must* be fought on this side of the river [meaning the north bank of the Chattahoochee] and I believe it will come off in front of Marietta."

Notwithstanding this prediction, the *Intelligencer* editor on June 22 had to inform his readers that for a while the previous day, Brig. Gen. Marcus J. Wright, post commandant of the city, had taken its African American pressmen to work on Atlanta's fortifications. Not just newspaper laborers, but black men in all walks were being commandeered; according to one complaint, "negro drivers were taken from carriages, and wood wagons and drays, leaving the vehicles in the street." Word of all this activity seeped through the lines, as attested by a Union corporal's letter of July 7 claiming (doubtless with exaggeration) that according to one black man, "there had bin four thousand negroes working for six weeks making stockades." John Steele's paper may have been predicting that the campaign's decisive battle would be fought north of the Chattahoochee, but General Johnston was taking no chances.[7]

By now in the campaign, Joe Johnston had figured out that Sherman's continued threats to his flanks would necessitate yet another retreat, so he had directed his engineers to lay out a new line a few miles to the rear. This one hinged at its center on the almost seven hundred-foot- high Kennesaw Mountain. The new line extended westward seven miles from near the W. & A., over Big Kennesaw and Little Kennesaw Mountains, to a little tributary, Olley's Creek (some 3½ miles southwest of Marietta). Confederate infantrymen occupied their new line during the night of June 18–19. Late on the 19th, "St. Clair" recorded that "heavy skirmishing continued all day. The enemy shelled furiously and persistently along the entire line during the day, but without important results occurring."

During the next week the Federal commander drew up his forces to confront the Confederate position. The *Intelligencer* kept up with the action—or absence of it. "They shelled the summit of Kennesaw furiously" (June 21); "fighting between batteries and our advance lines was furious" (June 22); "skirmishing and cannonading continued" (June 23); "heavy artillery firing continued" (June 24). When Schofield on the 24th reported that he could not maneuver farther to the right, Sherman began thinking of an assault against several points in Johnston's line. The attack was to be made on the morning of June 27. When the time came, Union artillery opened up at 6 a.m. Two hours later, three blue-coated brigades advanced against the Southerners holding Little Kennesaw Mountain and nearby Pigeon Hill. Two miles to the south another five Federal brigades launched an assault against Rebels commanded by Pat Cleburne and Maj. Gen. Benjamin Franklin ("Frank") Cheatham. At all points were the Northerners repulsed in this battle of Kennesaw Mountain, which was over before 11 o'clock. Of the more than 14,000 Union soldiers who had fought in it, a fifth (2,900 officers and men) were killed, wounded or missing. Confederate casualties numbered about 600.[8]

Reports of Johnston's smart defensive victory were slow to reach John Steele's editorial desk on Whitehall Street. The paper's daily update, entitled "The Position" (formerly "The Situation") on June 28 related only what had been learned as of noon the preceding day (the very day of the battle). "Early in the day the enemy opened with terrific cannonading on our lines and at this moment . . . doubtless a battle is raging severely between the opposing armies." Late on the 27th, "St. Clair" sent a telegram from Marietta with a few particulars of the fight at Kennesaw. The Federals had opened with artillery that morning. Then they launched infantry charges against Cleburne's and Cheatham's divisions toward the left of the Confederate line (which came to be called Cheatham's Hill). "At one time they came within 30 yards of the line but were everywhere repulsed by our gallant men," Abrams wrote. "Enemy's loss very heavy. Our loss small." Still later he sent another short wire, adding that to the north of Cleburne and Cheatham, Maj. Gen. Samuel French's division at Little Kennesaw Mountain had also been attacked; the Federals were "gallantly repulsed by the Missourians and Mississippians."[9]

On June 29, the *Intelligencer* printed the letter that its correspondent in the field, Alexander St. Clair Abrams, had written on the night of the battle. On Cleburne's and Cheatham's front, he heard that in their charge "the Yankees planted several stand of colors on our entrenchments" before the bearers were shot down; three Northern flags had thus been captured. Taking all this in, John Steele summarized the fighting in his "The Position" column on June 29: "The enemy . . . were hurled back with great loss, and . . . they finally retreated in utter confusion and with immense loss. Our casualties are comparatively small."

What the *Intelligencer*'s editor could not report was that in the Civil War, defensive victories (Confederates entrenched, Federals attacking) such as at Kennesaw Mountain generally had little tactical impact on the military situation. A classic example of this was Lee's defensive victory at Fredericksburg a year and a half before: Burnside's army was bloodily repulsed but merely retreated across the river; Federal forces hovered near Fredericksburg for months. Moreover, Kennesaw Mountain was on a comparatively small scale. Sherman's eight assault brigades totaled 15,000 troops; three weeks before, at Cold Harbor, Grant had committed fully 40,000 men in his assault, which had also lasted just three hours. Casualties were thus proportional in the two uneven battles: Sherman's on June 27 were 2,900; Grant's on June 3 totaled 6,500–7,000.

Kennesaw Mountain was therefore a "morning dash," in Sherman's deprecating words after the battle (to wife Ellen, June 30). It would have little effect on Sherman's push toward Atlanta. At best, it bought Joe Johnston a few days before the Union commander resumed his combination of skirmishing and shelling on the two armies' front lines, while sending flanking columns around Johnston's left to force yet another retreat by the Confederate army. In other words, John Steele and his editorial confreres who dreamed of the Yankees being hurled back into Tennessee would continue to be disappointed.[10] Among the Confederate casualties in the fighting was a former employee of the *Intelligencer*.

William M. Rantin, a Charlestonian, was working as a printer in the *Intelligencer* office when, in March 1862, he volunteered for the army. Rantin had not joined in the initial rush of enlistments in the summer of 1861, perhaps because of his elderly age—in its article on Rantin, the paper noted that he had fought in the Mexican War of 1846–48. Yet at some point he had entered the ranks. As a private in Company I, 42nd Georgia, he had fought in Bragg's army during the Kentucky campaign in the fall of 1862. He was part of the Vicksburg garrison when it was surrendered in July 1863. After exchange he returned to the Army of Tennessee, and followed it in the 1864 campaign from Dalton to Marietta.

At the latter place on June 18 he was so severely wounded in the left shoulder that his arm had to be amputated. He was admitted to the Academy Hospital, an army facility that had moved from Marietta to east Atlanta by mid-June. "The operation proved more than his system, already worn down, could bear," the *Intelligencer* stated, "and on the 24th his spirit returned to God who gave it."

The article concluded by noting that the Atlanta Typographical Union—the workers who had struck for higher wages just two months before—saw to William Rantin's burial in the City Cemetery.[11]

NOTES

1. "THE SITUATION," *ADI*, June 4, 1864.
2. "THE SITUATION," *ADI*, June 5, 1864.
3. Jeffry D. Wert, "Overland Campaign" in Patricia L. Faust, ed., *Historical Times Illustrated Encyclopedia of the Civil War* (New York: Harper & Row, 1986), 551.
4. "THE SITUATION" and "ST. CLAIR," "SPECIAL CORRESPONDENCE TO THE 'INTELLIGENCER'" (June 5), *ADI*, June 7; Davis, *Long and Bloody Task*, 62.
5. Davis, *Long and Bloody Task*, 63–65; Joseph H. Parks, *General Leonidas Polk C.S.A.: The Fighting Bishop* (Baton Rouge: Louisiana State University Press, 1962), 170, 374, 378; Cheryl H. White, *Confederate General Leonidas Polk: Louisiana's Fighting Bishop* (Charleston: History Press, 2013), 102–104; "LIEUT. GEN. LEONIDAS J. [sic] POLK," *ADI*, June 16.
6. "THE POSITION. IN GEORGIA," *ADI*, June 17, 1864; Davis, *Atlanta Will Fall*, 79; "ST. CLAIR," "Special Correspondence of the 'Intelligencer'" (June 15), *ADI*, June 17.
7. Davis, *Long and Bloody Task*, 69; "THE POSITION. IN GEORGIA," *ADI*, June 18, 1864; "ST. CLAIR," "Special Correspondence of the 'Intelligencer'" (June 16), *ADI*, June 18; "OUR READERS," *ADI*, June 22; Davis, *What the Yankees Did to Us*, 86; William C. Niesen, "'The Consequences of Grandeur': A Union Soldier Writes of the Atlanta Campaign," *Atlanta History*, vol. 33, no. 3 (Fall 1989), 8.
8. Davis, *Long and Bloody Task*, 69, 72–76; "ST. CLAIR," "Special Correspondence of the 'Intelligencer'" (June 19), *ADI*, June 21, 1864; "THE POSITION. IN GEORGIA," *ADI*, June 21; "THE POSITION. IN GEORGIA," *ADI*, June 22; "TELEGRAPHIC," *ADI*, June 23; "THE POSITION," *ADI*, June 24; Davis, *Atlanta Will Fall*, 86–87.
9. "THE POSITION. IN GEORGIA," *ADI*, June 28, 1864; "ST. CLAIR," "TELEGRAPHIC" (Marietta, June 27) and "Very Latest From the Front" (June 27) *ADI*, June 29.
10. "ST. CLAIR," "Special Correspondence of the 'Intelligencer'" (June 27) and "THE POSITION," *ADI*, June 29, 1864; Jeffry D. Wert, "Fredericksburg Campaign" in Patricia L. Faust, ed., *Historical Times Illustrated Encyclopedia of the Civil War* (New York: Harper & Row, 1986), 290; Earl J. Hess, *Kennesaw Mountain: Sherman, Johnston, and the Atlanta Campaign* (Chapel Hill: University of North Carolina Press, 2013), 152–53; Wert, "Cold Harbor" in Faust, ed., *Encyclopedia*, 150; Ernest B. Furgurson, *Not War But Murder: Cold Harbor*

1864 (New York: Alfred A. Knopf, 2000), 278; Brooks D. Simpson and Jean V. Berlin, eds., *Sherman's Civil War: Selected Correspondence of William T. Sherman, 1860–1865* (Chapel Hill: University of North Carolina Press, 1999), 660.

11. "DEATH OF A PRINTER," *ADI*, June 28, 1864; "MARIETTA CAMP HOSPITALS," *ADI*, June 12; Henderson, *Roster Confederate Soldiers*, vol. 4, 603.

37. The Newspapers Leave Town

IT WAS NOT OFTEN that John Steele had to apologize for one of his own pages. But that is precisely what he did in the *Intelligencer* of June 22, 1864.

"In the 'EXTRA' which was issued at this office yesterday," the editor began, "a paragraph appeared in an article headed, 'THE POSITION,' which, referring to the success of GEN. LEE in Virginia, seemingly reflects upon GEN. JOHNSTON's movements at the front." The offending paragraph was this: "The *great* secret of *their success* (Lee's army) seems to be in the fact that General Lee always fights the enemy when he gets opportunity, and never permits his men to become dispirited by the disorganizing influences of retreat—a movement, however, which that great General does not seem to understand."

The "great General" was Joseph E. Johnston, whose handling of Sherman's Atlanta Campaign the *Intelligencer* writer was contrasting with Robert E. Lee's handling of Grant's Overland Campaign in Virginia. The author of the offending article—an educated guess points to Isaac Pilgrim, the paper's foreman who occasionally wrote for the *Intelligencer*—was obliquely criticizing Johnston both for his lack of battlefield aggressiveness and for his willingness to retreat, giving up territory and demoralizing his troops. While Lee had been exacting huge casualties in Grant's advance upon Richmond, Johnston's small defensive victories (New Hope Church, Pickett's Mill, Kennesaw Mountain) had not significantly slowed Sherman's approach to Atlanta.

Regardless of its intent, the article prompted a quick backtrack from the editor on the 22nd. Steele had not seen the offending paragraph until it appeared in print, he explained, as he added a strong defense of General Johnston. "Not a solitary movement which he has made, nor a battle which he has fought," the editor declared, deserved any criticism. Indeed, Steele professed "renewed confidence in the great Chieftain, to whom the fate of Atlanta is entrusted."[1]

On the other hand, the great chieftain on whom the fate of Richmond rested, was about to face one of his toughest challenges.

After his bloody repulse at Cold Harbor on June 3, Grant determined upon a new tactical gambit: a swift, secret crossing of the James River and a fast march on Petersburg, twenty-three miles south of Richmond. The city was an important rail hub, through which supplies poured to sustain Lee's army and the people living in the capital. If the Federals captured Petersburg, Lee could no long feed his men. At Petersburg, Gen. P. G. T. Beauregard had only a few thousand troops when the Federals began attacking his fortified lines on June 15. Beauregard barely held on till Lee sent him reinforcements, enough to defeat further Northern attacks in the next several days.[2]

The *Intelligencer* reported these events as the telegrams came in from Virginia. "GRANT AGAIN CHANGING HIS BASE" (June 13); "Grant's exact whereabouts or intentions not ascertained" (June 14); "Grant's exact whereabouts and intentions are still undefined" (June 15); "nothing authentic from Petersburg to-day (June 16); "it is believed that the enemy's forces are massed in front of Petersburg" (June 17); "some fighting near Petersburg" (June 18); "Grant's whole army in front of Petersburg" (June 19).[3]

True, Lee's and Beauregard's troops had repulsed every assault launched by Grant and Meade at Petersburg. But the bigger picture offered an ominous outlook: a semi-siege of Petersburg by Federal forces, who aimed to cut Lee's railway supply route. This was the grim prospect that Lee feared: a static trench war that he was bound to lose.

In late June 1864, William T. Sherman's and Joseph E. Johnston's armies remained locked in their Kennesaw lines. On the second of July the *Intelligencer* reported an incident of the opponents' trench warfare. A week earlier the men of Brig. Gen. John K. Jackson's brigade were under artillery fire when a Northern shell struck the Confederates' earthen parapet, skipped over it and fell into their trench. With the fuse smoking, the men scattered, expecting an explosion. One of them, however, Sgt. Isaac P. Collier of Company C, 5th Georgia, grabbed the projectile and threw it out of the ditch.

Sergeant Collier's bravery was witnessed by a half-dozen comrades. They apparently sent word of it through the ranks to General Jackson, who immediately promoted Sergeant Collier to lieutenant. "This is a case which calls for the exercise of the power of appointment for 'acts of distinguished valor,'" according to the general order drawn up by Jackson's assistant adjutant general (which the *Intelligencer* printed).

The story did not end there, for Collier respectfully declined the promotion. "In throwing the shell from the ditch," he explained in a note to his captain, "I am conscious of having done nothing but my duty, in attempting to save my life, and the lives of the men around me." Collier went further: "I prefer to remain in my company, with my comrades, with whom I left home on the 7th day of May, 1861."[4]

Meanwhile, the *Intelligencer*'s assistant editor was getting it right, even as its editor was not. In a letter written at Marietta on June 29, Alexander St. Clair Abrams observed, "whether we will assume the offensive or not, is a question of much doubt, for I do not believe General Johnston favors any aggressive movement just now." "St. Clair's" letter appeared in the newspaper on July 1. The next day, in his "The Position" article, John Steele observed that "the enemy seems to be somewhat confounded in his plans." Sherman's "furious and persistent sallies" had been bloodily repulsed; his "triumphant flank marches" had been "utterly thwarted." That very day, July 2, however, Federal columns were marching beyond Johnston's left flank, compelling the Confederate commander to order a nocturnal abandonment of his Kennesaw position and a retreat to yet another line that had already been staked out seven miles to the south.[5]

As Sherman's forces on July 3–4 pushed toward Johnston's new line, centered at Smyrna Station (less than twenty miles by railroad northwest of the Car Shed), the *Intelligencer* reminded readers of Atlanta's importance as a Confederate military administrative center. In its "City Military Directory," which appeared regularly in the newspaper, three dozen separate offices were listed: quartermasters; commissary, ordnance and conscript officers; headquarters for engineers, paymasters and surgeons; offices for Confederate Maj. Gen. Howell Cobb (commanding the District of Georgia and Florida); even one for the C.S. Navy. Many of them were located in buildings in the city's downtown business district, along the Whitehall-Peachtree axis over the railroad, which was a busy place.

Atlanta's streets were still not paved, which meant that pedestrians, horseback riders, wagons and mule teams stirred up a lot of mud and other stuff, which hot summer weather rendered into an olfactory offense. Occasionally, the *Intelligencer*'s "The City" column called attention to the need of authorities to address the downtown mire, especially where Whitehall and Peachtree Streets crossed the railroad, not a block from the newspaper's office. "The Whitehall railroad crossing must be repaired and made passable," the paper asserted on June 28, pointing to officers of the four railroads serving the city to lead the way. Yet the editor despaired of any action being taken until "one or more of the honorable members of the city council were lost, completely immured in the mud-hole."[6]

Then there was the stink. "The City" on July 2 charged that "seventy truly and well defined stinks are appreciable to the obfactory [sic] of our citizens." More than the number of the malodorous sites was their odor, which the columnist seemed to have had a bit of fun describing. "In numerous places there are scents as though the triple distilled extract of the quintessence of stink was being brewed there." Backyards and gutters filled with garbage and waste were the chief offenders, but there was also the railroad crossing at Whitehall Street, where the *Intelligencer* writer claimed that "even the rats have become disgusted with the filth and stench that has accumulated beneath those horrible planks and abandoned the neighborhood." The *Intelligencer* beseeched the city fathers to clean up the offending places "and abate their malignance and dangerous poisonous exhalations." Lest he be misunderstood with the use of "that last big word," the writer spelled it out: "its definition is unhealthy, sickness breeding stink; stinking stink k k k."[7]

Such levity took newspaper readers away from the war front, which had its own dangerous places. Nighttime artillery bombardments of the Confederate entrenchments in the vicinity of Smyrna, of which the *Intelligencer* took notice on July 3, kept Johnston's soldiers from sleeping in their camps and alarmed the citizens in Atlanta. To be sure, the paper continued to publish by-now familiar poetic exhortations ("They [Federals] say Atlanta they will have,/By the fourth of this July/But, brave soldiers, don't you know/It's nothing but a lie?"). Yet undeniable facts could not be ignored. When Schofield's infantry succeeded in outflanking the left of Johnston's Smyrna line, the Confederate commander again ordered a nocturnal withdrawal, July 4–5, to a fortified line his engineers had already built barely a mile from the Chattahoochee River (and less than ten miles from downtown Atlanta). Laced with three dozen log-and-dirt forts called "Shoupades" after the army's chief of artillery, Brig. Gen. Francis A. Shoup, Johnston's river line meant that the Confederates had virtually backed up to the water's edge. "Speculation was rife . . . to establish the reason for our retreat," the *Intelligencer* declared on July 5; "to-day it is more eagerly agitated—what will we do next? Our street Generals have it that we will be flanked to the Gulf and then to Richmond."[8]

On July 5, John Steele offered readers a piece that served up what was just about as close to an *Intelligencer* staff directory as the paper would offer. Titled "olla podrida"—a spicy stew consisting of assorted vegetables and meats—the editor likened the diversity of his employees' surnames to "a varied *mélange* of names in Natural Sciences." With a vein of humor, therefore, he wrote of himself, "our chief is a Steele from which many a brilliant spark has been struck during the forty years of his editorial life." The firm's treasurer, John Smith, "hammers out the cash"; as for "St. Clair," "our Ab-rams round considerably" securing war news. Mention was also made of the foreman Isaac Pilgrim. After that, the newspaper's staff is hard to figure out from the last names offered: Patton, Fitz (subscription collections), Christian, Holmes, Nelms, Hale, Reynolds, and Thrower. William G. Knox was a pressman for the paper, as listed in Atlanta's 1859 directory. Of him, the article remarked "a (Kn)ox's pressing tread mill work finishes the pages." Counting proprietor Whitaker, more than a dozen individuals are named—and this was likely without reference to African Americans working in the press room.[9]

In other words, the *Intelligencer* was doing pretty well.

The war news that "Ab-rams" was ramming around for ceased about this time, as "St. Clair" no longer appeared in the *Intelligencer* after late June 1864. Consequently, editor Steele relied more heavily than ever on dispatches telegraphed by the Press Association. As Sherman's troops slowly pushed toward the Southerners' river line, the telegraphic report appearing in the *Intelligencer* on July 5 declared, "there is nothing new." "No change of any material importance," the paper's "The Situation" column announced on the 7th. "There has been little fighting and really less skirmishing than usual," the paper affirmed on the 8th.[10]

Then the situation changed dramatically.

Thus far in the campaign, Cump Sherman had shown himself to be the superior general to Joe Johnston. He had shrewdly used his numerical superiority to conduct successive flanking movements that forced Johnston to retreat time after time. "I can find no mode of preventing this," the Confederate commander had glumly wired Richmond at one point. Other evidences of good generalship are tactical foresight and confidence—qualities that Sherman possessed in abundance. On April 10, 1864, before the campaign had even begun, Sherman had written General Grant, "should Johnston fall behind the Chattahoochee I would feign to my right, but pass to the left"—in other words, make Johnston believe that he was going to get across the river from the Federal right flank against the Confederate left, Indeed, this was what Sherman had been doing ever since Dalton: moving around the Rebel left flank to threaten Johnston's railroad. But now, with the Army of Tennessee backed up to the banks of the last river barrier before Atlanta, Sherman was going to fake right but move left, sending diversionary columns downriver to get Johnston's attention, while stealthily marching troops to Chattahoochee crossing points upriver, north of Atlanta.[11]

Sherman's plan unfolded July 8–9. To keep Johnston guessing about his intended beachheads, the Union commander spread his forces out for thirty miles along the Chattahoochee's north bank. McPherson's Army of the Tennessee demonstrated noisily downstream as Union cavalry pretended to be looking for fording places there. Meanwhile, well upriver, Schofield's Army of the Ohio located points where pontoons could be built and shallow places where the men could wade across. A half-dozen miles upstream from Johnston's right, Federals drove off Southern cavalry and laid a floating bridge that allowed Jacob Cox's infantry to start marching across. Farther still toward the east, Northern soldiers found a rock fish dam and literally walked across the water without a shot being fired. The next day, July 9, Federal horsemen crossed at a shallow ford. A fourth bridgehead was established when some Union horsemen dismounted, stripped down to hats, rifles and cartridge boxes and waded in. The few Southerners on the other bank laughed at this display of raw courage, then skedaddled.

Once again, Joe Johnston had no choice but to call for another nocturnal retrograde to the south side of the Chattahoochee River. It would be his last, as it would turn out, as commander of the army charged with defending Atlanta. He informed Richmond of his retreat by telegraph on July 10.[12]

The *Intelligencer* was slow to report these events. "Sherman has sent a large force to threaten our left," it noted on July 9, while acknowledging that "it seems to be a determined policy with Sherman not to fight a regular battle, but to take this city by strategy." The next day, "The Position" announced simply, "we do not think it would be valuable information to our readers to publish the present Position."[13]

This was the last word issued by the *Intelligencer* for a good while, because after its issue of July 10, John Steele and his staff packed up, boarded the Macon train and left town. Word that Johnston's army had retreated across the Chattahoochee spread through the city on the 10th, electrifying everyone. "The city has been in a complete swarm all day," Sam Richards, the downtown bookseller, recorded in his diary, "adding that Johnston's order of July 5 for hospitals and munitions works to be packed up and moved out of Atlanta had also upset the populace. "Of course the citizens are alarmed and many have left and others are leaving," Richards acknowledged.

Atlanta's "*corps* editorial" (as John Steele liked to call it) joined in this exodus.

In some cases, it already had. The *Chattanooga/Marietta Rebel* had moved to Griffin, Georgia (forty-four miles by rail south of the Car Shed) when Federal forces were still north of Pine Mountain. It was back in business by June 8, the day that the *Intelligencer* editor announced, "we are delighted to find the Rebel on our table this morning." On June 14, the *Intelligencer* announced that the *Knoxville/Atlanta Register* would be relocating in Charlotte, North Carolina. Yet the paper stayed awhile more in Atlanta; on June 25 the *Intelligencer* announced that the humorous writer from Rome, "Bill Arp" (Charles H. Smith), had signed on as assistant editor of the *Register*. The paper apparently cleared out in early July, relocating not in Charlotte, but Augusta. The *Constitutionalist* in that city stated that the *Augusta Register*'s first issue appeared on August 29.

July 10 seems to be the date that both the *Atlanta Intelligencer* and the *Atlanta Southern Confederacy* left Atlanta. The latter paper had editorialized on July 9, "we shall not attempt to lull into fancied security the readers of the Confederacy by the declaration that Atlanta is not in imminent peril." That peril apparently prompted a move; the *Macon Telegraph* of July 19 noticed the *Confederacy* was in town. The city's fourth daily, the migratory *Memphis Appeal*, stayed in Atlanta until July 22, when it packed its big Hoe press onboard a train and chugged out to Montgomery, Alabama.

Because of Federal forces' advance into Confederate territory and capture of key Southern cities, migration was a necessity for many newspapers, if their proprietors and editors were determined to stay in operation. The Memphis "moving Appeal" took the cake, with five moves during the war (to Grenada, Jackson, Meridian, Atlanta and Montgomery). The *Knoxville Register* made two leaps (to Atlanta, then Augusta); the *Chattanooga Rebel* likewise jumped twice. The *Atlanta Intelligencer*'s migratory pattern (to Macon and back five months later) seems comparatively modest.[14]

There is some uncertainty as to when the *Intelligencer*, reestablished in the Telegraph building at Third and Cherry Streets, resumed publication. The *Augusta Chronicle & Sentinel* of Wednesday, July 27, stated the "the first number of the Intelligencer was issued on Saturday last," which would have been July 23. The *Columbus Enquirer* of July 30 notes the resumption of the *Intelligencer*'s activity in Macon; that day it reprinted John Steele's "The Position in Georgia" article ("Atlanta Intell., 24th"). "The Position" appeared as far away as in the *New York Times* of August 16, which stated that it had lifted the article from the *Intelligencer* of July 26.[15]

July 24? July 26? July 27? Regardless of resumption date, when the *Intelligencer* re-emerged in Macon, earthshaking events had occurred: Northern artillery had begun bombarding Atlanta on July 20, the Confederate Army of Tennessee had gained a new commanding general as of July 18, and hard-fought battles had been fought just outside the city.

The war had finally come to Atlanta.

NOTES

1. "EXPLANATION," *ADI*, June 22, 1864.
2. Stephen Davis, "Lee, Hood and the Fog of War," *Civil War News*, vol. 43, no. 9 (September 2017), 20–22.
3. "GRANT AGAIN CHANGING HIS BASE" (Richmond, June 13), *ADI*, June 15, 1864; "CAVALRY FIGHT IN VIRGINIA" (Richmond, June 14), *ADI*, June 16; "CAVALRY FIGHT IN VIRGINIA" (Richmond, June 15), *ADI*, June 17; "TELEGRAPHIC. Richmond, June 16th," *ADI*, June 18; "Latest from Petersburg" (Petersburg, June 17), *ADI*, June 19; "THE LATEST FROM PETERSBURG. GRANT'S WHOLE ARMY IN FRONT OF PETERSBURG," *ADI*, June 19; "Official from Gen. Lee," *ADI*, June 21.
4. "MODEST MERIT," *ADI*, July 2, 1864.
5. "Special Correspondence of the 'Intelligencer'" (Marietta, June 29), *ADI*, July 1, 1864; "THE POSITION," *ADI*, July 2.
6. "City Military Directory," *ADI*, July 2, 1864; Davis, *What the Yankees Did to Us*, 29–30; Robert Scott Davis, *Civil War Atlanta* (Charleston: History Press, 2011), 34–37; Garrett, *A & E*, vol. 1, 590–93; "THE CITY," *ADI*, June 28.
7. "THE CITY," *ADI*, July 2, 1864.
8. "THE POSITION" and "V. D.," "TO THE PETS" (poem), *ADI*, July 3, 1864; Davis, *Long and Bloody Task*, 83–84; William R. Scaife, "The Chattahoochee River Line: An American Maginot," *North & South*, issue #1 (November 1997), 45–46; "THE POSITION," *ADI*, July 5.
9. "OLLA PODRIDA," *ADI*, July 5, 1864; Williams, *Directory*, 111.
10. "FROM THE FRONT" (Marietta, July 2), *ADI*, July 5, 1864; "THE SITUATION—THE RESPONSIBILITY," *ADI*, July 7; "THE POSITION," *ADI*, July 8.
11. Stephen Davis, "A Reappraisal of the Generalship of John Bell Hood in the Battles for Atlanta" in Theodore P. Savas and David A. Woodbury, eds., *The Campaign for Atlanta & Sherman's March to the Sea* (Campbell CA: Savas Woodbury Publishers, 1994), 54–57; Davis, *Long and Bloody Task*, 11.
12. Davis, *John Bell Hood*, 206 207; Gould Hagler, "Crossing the Hooch without a Hitch," *Civil War News*, vol. 43, no. 9 (September 2019), 26–27; "Raw Courage," *Civil War Times Illustrated*, vol. 13, no. 4 (July 1974), 46; Richard M. McMurry, ed., "More on 'Raw Courage,'" *Civil War Times Illustrated*, vol. 14, no. 6 (October 1975), 36–38; Davis, *Long and Bloody Task*, 89–90.
13. "THE POSITION," *ADI*, July 9, 1864; "THE POSITION," *ADI*, July 10.
14. Ellis, *Moving Appeal*, 162, 188, 223, 226, 324; Franc M. Paul, "*The Chattanooga Rebel*" in

Tennessee Old and New, 2 vols. (Nashville: Tennessee Historical Commission, 1947) vol. 2, 277.

15. Davis, *What the Yankees Did to Us*, 77, 81, 483–84; Venet, ed., *Sam Richards' Diary*, 227; "THE REBEL," *ADI*, June 8, 1864; "NEWSPAPER REFUGEEISM," *Columbia Daily South Carolinian*, July 8; "KNOXVILLE REGISTER," *ADI*, June 14; "Editorial Accession," *ADI*, June 25; "THE ATLANTA REGISTER," *Augusta Constitutionalist*, August 30; "The Defense of Atlanta," *Atlanta Southern Confederacy*, July 9; "THE SOUTHERN CONFEDERACY," *Macon Telegraph*, July 19; "THE NEWSPAPERS," *Augusta Chronicle & Sentinel*, July 27; "THE ATLANTA INTELLIGENCER" and "The Position in Georgia . . . Atlanta Intell., 24th," *Columbus Enquirer*, July 30; "THE POSITION IN GEORGIA," *New York Times*, August 16 (also in the *Macon Telegraph* of July 26 and the *Augusta Constitutionalist*, July 29).

38. A City Under Shellfire

BETWEEN THE TIME that the *Intelligencer* left Atlanta around July 10 and when it resumed operation at Macon later in the month, the Confederate Army of Tennessee got a new commanding general.

Jefferson Davis had already begun to consider firing Joe Johnston before he learned on July 11 that the army had retreated across the Chattahoochee. Nonetheless, the president took a full week consulting with General Lee, his Cabinet and the senior senator from Georgia before he relieved Johnston on the 17th. At the same time, Richmond also sent a telegram informing Lt. Gen. John B. Hood, corps commander, that he had been promoted to the rank of full general and placed in army command. Hood officially took over the next day, July 18.[1]

The newly-minted general faced a daunting situation on July 18. With some 59,000 troops manning the fortifications surrounding Atlanta, he faced Sherman's infantry—seven corps, 88,000 officers and men—who were all south of the Chattahoochee, five miles from the city and on the move. They were spread out in a ten-mile arc that stretched from the Chattahoochee to Decatur, the town a half-dozen miles east of Atlanta: George Thomas' army nearest the river, James McPherson's marching through Decatur, and John Schofield's in between.

Even with his numerical abundance, that meant there were gaps in Sherman's front. This gave General Hood an idea for an attacking battle. Between the left flank of Thomas' army bearing down on Atlanta from the north and Schofield's right there existed a two-mile gap, which General Wheeler's cavalry discovered as it countered the Union infantry's advances. Therefore, in his first full day as leader of the Army of Tennessee, Hood ordered an attack against Thomas for July 20. The assault that day, delayed by several hours' maneuvering, launched forth between 3 and 4 p.m. Some parts of Thomas' line had prepared slight breastworks, but for the most part the Federals were unready for the Confederate attack. That led to some limited and partial gains for the Southerners, but at the end of the day, the battle of Peachtree Creek was a repulse and defeat for Hood's troops. Casualties for the battle on July 20 numbered some 1,780 Federals and from 2,300 to 2,500 Confederates.

On July 21, McPherson's three corps were bearing down upon Atlanta so speedily from the east that Hood had to send reinforcements to help Wheeler hold them back. That afternoon Southern horsemen discerned that McPherson's left flank was unguarded by cavalry and therefore open to a surprise attack, which Hood promptly planned. During the night of the 21st-22nd Hardee's corps marched wearily toward their attack position east of the city. The Confederates did not begin their assault until noon on July 22. By then General McPherson had sensed danger and deployed for battle. In its opening hour, "Mac" (as Sherman liked to call him) rode toward the fighting, encountered the advance of Maj. Gen. Patrick Cleburne's division and was shot and killed. In their ensuing advance, Southern troops gained some ground and captured a dozen pieces of artillery. But the Federals held their lines and by nightfall the Confederates retired back to their start-off positions. In this, the so-called battle of Atlanta, Hood's losses totaled 5,500; McPherson's 3,700, including McPherson himself, the commander of the Union Army of the Tennessee and the highest-ranking Federal combat casualty in the war. Sherman named Maj. Gen. Oliver O. Howard to replace him.[2]

By this time Union forces marching in from the east had gotten to within two miles of downtown—effective range for Northern artillery with rifled barrels, their longest-range field pieces. Sherman ordered them to open fire, sending shells indiscriminately into the city of Atlanta. Despite the departure of many residents, at least several thousand civilians remained. Now, as so often happened in war, they fell victim to hostile cannon fire when on the afternoon of the 20th, Capt. Francis DeGress' Illinois battery (twenty-pounder Parrott rifled guns) fired three shells into the center of the city. Sherman's bombardment of Atlanta would last from July 20 to August 25, thirty-seven days of intermittent but deadly cannonading. When it was over, no one knew how many people had lost their lives, but most counts place the death toll at about twenty souls (including a free African American barber, Solomon Luckie).[3]

W. T. Sherman was too smart to waste his numerical strength in frontal assaults on Hood's army entrenched in Atlanta's defensive perimeter. Instead, he adopted the grand tactical plan of extending his lines so as to cut the railways supplying the Confederate forces.

Four railroads ran into Atlanta. The Western & Atlantic, to Chattanooga, was by now firmly in Sherman's possession, hauling food, forage and ammunition for the Union commander's men, horses and mules. The three others extended like wheel-spokes: the Georgia Railroad to Augusta, the Atlanta & West Point eventually to Montgomery, Alabama, and the Macon & Western to Macon, 103 railroad miles south of Atlanta and to points beyond.

Actually, two of these roads had been cut even before John Bell Hood took charge of the Army of Tennessee on July 18. That very day Union cavalry and infantry struck the Georgia road east of Decatur and had started tearing up track. Also, during July 17–19, Northern mounted troops tore up fully twenty-six miles of the Montgomery line in east central Alabama. Hood's army and Atlanta's remaining populace thus had only the Macon & Western to bring in supplies. For the duration of his campaign to capture Atlanta, Sherman focused on getting his troops astride the Macon road. If and when they did so, Hood and his army would have to abandon the Confederacy's prize city.[4]

After the battle fought on July 22 east of the city, Sherman—maintaining the initiative in his semi-siege of Atlanta—on July 27 swung Howard's army around by its right, to the north and then west of the city so as to threaten the Macon railroad. Confederate cavalry picked up on the movement, which Hood was determined to block. By this time Lt. Gen. Stephen D. Lee had arrived from Mississippi to assume command of Hood's old infantry corps, and it was to Lee that Hood assigned the task: marching west of the city on July 28 and seizing the important crossroads at Ezra (Methodist) Church. When Howard's troops came up, Lee would hold the road until, presumably on the 29th, Stewart brought his infantry out of the city, behind Lee and in a wide swing to catch Howard in (another) flank attack. The plan went awry on July 28 when Howard's Federals reached Ezra Church before the Southerners. Encountering them, without notifying Hood's HQ, Lee committed to piecemeal frontal assaults as his troops came up. The Confederates' predictable repulse in the battle of Ezra Church yielded 3,100–3,300 Southerners killed, wounded and missing to Howard's 600–620.[5]

Then Sherman turned to Civil War generals' usual method of getting at the enemy's railroads: he sent off his cavalry. On July 27, two mounted columns under Maj. Gen. George Stoneman and Brig. Gen Edward McCook rode out in separate directions, 5,100 strong. Both were heading to cut the Macon & Western at Lovejoy's Station, two dozen miles south of Atlanta. McCook got there and tore up a few miles of track before riding back to join Sherman's forces at Atlanta. (Southerners repaired the damage in two days.) Stoneman's troopers never even reached the Macon railroad. Confederate cavalry chased down both columns and in two separate battles, fought July 30–31, severely cut up the bluecoats. McCook's and Stoneman's men limped back to Sherman having lost half of their combined strength—2,559 officers and men. Among the missing was General Stoneman himself, the highest-ranking Union officer taken prisoner during the entire war.[6]

The defeat of the McCook-Stoneman raid encouraged Hood to do the same thing: send Wheeler and half of the army's cavalry on August 10 raiding into north Georgia, with the aim of cutting Sherman's railway supply line. (Wheeler failed to wreck more than a few miles of track, which were quickly repaired by Union engineers.)

After the McCook-Stoneman fiasco, Sherman settled down to extending his lines farther and farther south, toward the railroad hub called East Point (which was actually southwest of Atlanta, but was the eastern terminus of the Atlanta & West Point Railroad running to the Alabama line). Hood responded by stretching his troops out in a line of entrenchments protecting the track. Near a place called Utoy Creek, a few miles southwest of Atlanta's fortified perimeter, Federals tested the Confederate works and found them strong indeed. Meanwhile, skirmishing and cannonading all along the contested lines brought as many casualties as in a big battle. Confederate Maj. Gen. Carter Stevenson's division, for example, lost in six weeks of skirmishing more men than in the battle of Resaca three months before.[7]

This was the situation when the *Atlanta Daily Intelligencer* resumed publication at the city of Macon in the last days of July.

In his "The Position" column appearing on August 3, editor John Steele gloated over the capture of Stoneman and the defeat of the Federal cavalry raiders. "Their capture marks an important epoch in the history and operations of our army," the editorial proclaimed. "When Sherman finds his finest body of picked cavalry lost," it predicted, he would have to look to his rear, which "is now at our mercy." Maybe Sherman would launch a battle; perhaps he would retreat. "In either event, he will not accomplish the original object of the campaign," which was the seizure of Georgia's Gate City. "We are very certain that the Yankee forces will disappear from before Atlanta, before the end of August," the paper boasted; "our confidence in the prowess of General Hood and his invincible army of veterans is unabating."[8]

"Late yesterday afternoon heavy skirmishing occurred along the centre of the lines, which continued till after nightfall," read a report telegraphed from Atlanta on August 4 to the relocated *Intelligencer*. "The city was vigorously shelled," it continued, "and during the night one young lady was killed by a piece of shell." The alleged victim went unnamed, as would others in telegraphic reports reaching Macon. Yet John Steele was fortunate to have a man-on-the-scene: thirty-two-year-old Isaac Pilgrim.

Born in central Georgia in August 1832, Pilgrim devoted himself to a career in journalism. After editing a small paper in Lawrenceville, northeast of Atlanta, he had moved to the city by 1859; Atlanta's directory of that year listed him as a printer who was boarding downtown. At this point in the war, Pilgrim was John Steele's foreman and sometime contributing writer. When the *Intelligencer* moved to Macon, Pilgrim stayed behind. As John Steele's eyes and ears, he wrote articles on the goings-on around him and put them on the train to Macon, where they were published in the paper.

"Uncle Ike" was probably the author of "The Position" article that evidently appeared in the *Intelligencer* in late July and was reprinted in other Georgia newspapers. The enemy, Pilgrim wrote, "amuses himself by shooting shot and shell over the entire surface of the city, so that no spot is sacred or safe. Many buildings have been torn and defaced by the missiles.... A great many houses on Peachtree street have been completely torn to pieces."

Then there were the people. "A great many women and children remain in its limits, and are exposed to the enemy's fire. They however do not seem to be much disturbed by their dangerous position, for the women walk the streets as indifferently, even more so than the soldiers do, and the children make a business of picking up the fragments of the impotent shells, to keep as playthings, or perhaps for sale as relics."

Pilgrim was particularly interested in shell-casualties. "Several persons have been killed and wounded by these explosions," he declared; "on Friday [which would have been July 22] a white man and a mule were killed and two negroes wounded on the street [Alabama] before Franklin Printing Office." Yet the reporter strained for levity in his observations: "on Saturday a soldier was walking in the passenger depot with a sack of corn on his back. A shell entered the sack and exploded, without injury to the man. A friend remarked to us—that shell went against the *grain*—dreadful!"[9]

Besides this kind of reporting, Ike Pilgrim enhanced his role as chronicler of Sherman's bombardment in another way. After the *Memphis Appeal* moved to Montgomery in late July, its editor, John Dumble, stayed in Atlanta, and with Pilgrim's assistance composed articles and set type for a single-page broadside that they cranked out on a hand press every afternoon at the Franklin Printing House. These "extras," carrying a regular column called "The City," were placed on the train to Macon, where Steele got and reprinted their news. One article, from the *Appeal* "Extra" of August 2, appeared in the *Intelligencer* two days later. The piece reported "considerable shelling at various points during the day" and also another casualty: "the killing of an old lady residing in a little house at the extreme north end of Marietta street."[10]

Probably Pilgrim's most illustrious writing and reporting came as result of his having walked up and down the streets of Atlanta, recording shell damage to buildings he could see from the sidewalk. "Mr. Pilgrim made a complete tour of the city," the editor proudly announced in the *Intelligencer* of August 6, "and being an old resident of the city and perfectly acquainted with it, he has reported to us accurately the damage he discovered."

It was already extensive, even though the Federals' bombardment was barely two weeks old. Northwest Atlanta was hardest hit; "there is not a house on Marietta street to the Gas Works but what has been struck." The printer/foreman/reporter/writer obviously had talked with residents: Thomas Kile's grocery store downtown "had a shell to explode in a room, which entered the roof, but doing little damage." Sherman's shells showed little respect for holy places: "Wesley Chapel . . . is horribly mutilated." The landscape also showed its wounds. At John Peel's house on Spring Street, besides five shells to strike the house, others "cut down the shade trees in the yard, tear up the fencing and yard, making a wreck of the whole premises."

At the same time, the *Intelligencer*'s foreman-turned-reporter was beginning to suspect that stories of bombardment casualties in the city were . . . well, stories. "I hear of a great many persons being killed," he wrote, "though I cannot trace them to any person who actually knows it to be a fact. On my arrival I learned that a lady had been killed by a shell. I called on the lady's sister, who is an acquaintance of mine, and she informed me that it was news to her as her sister was in the city of Macon."[11]

Sherman's shelling of Atlanta and its civilian population lasted thirty-seven days, from July 20 to August 25, when he gave up his semi-siege and began marching most of his infantry well south of the city, heading toward Jonesboro.

A number of Southern cities came under Northern artillery fire during the war. Charleston endured the longest bombardment, intermittently between August 1863 and February 1865. Petersburg suffered the second-longest (June '64-April '65). But Atlanta has the "distinction" of the most civilian casualties, about twenty killed, as best as we can figure. Historians of Grant's siege of Vicksburg, which also came under cannonfire, estimate five to ten people dead; similarly, a half-dozen residents of Petersburg were killed.

A less gruesome statistic, but an equally telling one, is the tonnage of Sherman's shells. We know that the Federals brought in 4.5-inch rifled cannon that fired thirty-pound projectiles. We also know that these big guns fired more than 4,500 rounds into the city—by General Sherman's specific orders—some 68 tons of metal.

Sherman had a hundred other rifled cannon that could reach the center of the city. We estimate that the number of shot and shell fired into Atlanta could be as many as 27,000. Each of those rounds weighed from ten to twenty pounds.

And we're still finding them. Many shells fired never exploded. And because Union cannoneers aimed their guns indiscriminately toward the center of the city, Northern metal continues to be dug up in downtown Atlanta, carefully taken outside the city, and exploded by bomb crews.[12]

Atlantans' awareness of the everlastingness of Sherman's shelling fits in with Robert Penn Warren's famous observation that "the Civil War is our only felt history—history lived in the national imagination."[13]

NOTES

1. Stephen Davis, "'Far Better in the Present Emergency': John Bell Hood Replaces Joseph E. Johnston" in Chris Mackowski and Kristopher D. White, eds., *Turning Points of the American Civil War* (Carbondale: Southern Illinois University Press, 2018), 195–201.

2. Stephen Davis, *All the Fighting They Want: The Atlanta Campaign from Peachtree Creek to the City's Surrender, July 18-September 2, 1864* (El Dorado Hills CA: Savas Beatie, 2017), 9–10, 15, 22–27, 37–48; Davis, *Atlanta Will Fall*, 132; Robert D. Jenkins, *The Battle of Peach Tree Creek: Hood's First Sortie 20 July 1864* (Macon: Mercer University Press, 2013), 397.

3. Stephen Davis, "'A Very Barbarous Mode of Carrying on War': Sherman's Artillery Bombardment of Atlanta," *Georgia Historical Quarterly*, vol. 79, no. 1 (Spring 1995), 61–63, 78–80; Stephen Davis, "How Many Civilians Died in Sherman's Bombardment of Atlanta?," *Atlanta History*, vol. 45, no. 4 (2003), 20.

4. Davis, *All the Fighting*, 11–13; David Evans, *Sherman's Horsemen: Union Cavalry Operations in the Atlanta Campaign* (Bloomington: Indiana University Press, 1996), 78, 80–81, 137, 156, 166.

5. Davis, *All the Fighting*, 59–63; Earl J. Hess, *The Battle of Ezra Church and the Struggle for Atlanta* (Chapel Hill: University of North Carolina Press, 2015), 19–24; Gary Ecelbarger,

Slaughter at the Chapel: The Battle of Ezra Church 1864 (Norman: University of Oklahoma Press, 2016), 184–85.

6. Davis, *All the Fighting*, 67–73.

7. Stephen Davis, "Hood Fights Desperately: The Battles for Atlanta—Events from July 10 to September 2, 1864," *Blue &Gray*, vol. 6, issue 5 (August 1989), 36, 39, 46.

8. "THE POSITION. IN GEORGIA," *ADI*, Aug. 3, 1864.

9. "TELEGRAPHIC," *ADI*, Aug. 5, 1864; *Williams Directory*, 126; Davis, *What the Yankees Did to Us*, 161; "THE POSITION IN GEORGIA," *Macon Telegraph*, July 26.

10. Davis, *What the Yankees Did to Us*, 126–27; "The Army News" (*Memphis Appeal*, August 2) and "THANKS," *ADI*, Aug. 4, 1864.

11. "P." [Isaac B. Pilgrim], "The Houses Shelled in Atlanta" (August 4), *ADI*, Aug. 6, 1864; Davis, *What the Yankee Did to Us*, 161–66.

12. Stephen Davis, *What the Yankees Did to Us*, 248–49; Stephen Davis, "Sherman's Bombardment of Atlanta July 20-August 25, 1864," *The Artilleryman*, vol. 39, no. 2 (Spring 2018), 34; "West End Thinks Japs Are Here When Civil War Shell Explodes," *Atlanta Journal*, April 22, 1942; Bill Hendrick, "Treasure beneath Rich's Revealed in Bits, Pieces," *Atlanta Constitution*, Aug. 30, 1994; Hendrick, "Digging into Downtown's History," *Atlanta Constitution*, Dec. 24, 1994.

13. Robert Penn Warren, *The Legacy of the Civil War: Meditations on the Centennial* (New York; Random House, 1961), 4.

39. The Fall of Atlanta

THE UNION BOMBARDMENT of Atlanta in the summer of 1864 forced residents to seek shelter in cellars, bombproof dugouts covered with dirt and logs, sometimes in others' homes or in sturdy business buildings. Confederate soldiers and Atlanta citizens learned to listen for the missiles—"ferruginous conchology," as one newspaper reporter phrased it—and to conduct their day-to-day business as best they could. Sadly, however, some fell victim to the bombardment. A widely publicized shell-tragedy involved Joseph F. Warner, former superintendent of the city's gas works, and his ten-year-old daughter Elizabeth; both were killed in the night of August 3.[1]

During August the *Intelligencer* reported on the shelling and skirmishing occurring in the entrenched lines outside the city. Hood's army held the fortified perimeter encircling Atlanta up to 1 ½ miles from the downtown Car Shed. A half-mile or so farther out, Sherman's forces had constructed an entrenched line that ran from northeast of the city to its southwest, and then farther in that direction to parallel the Confederates' "railway defense line" guarding the train route leading toward East Point, seven miles southwest of the Car Shed.

Because the Federals did not completely encircle the city, their position is properly termed a *semi*-siege, characterized by both sides' swapping of artillery and rifle fire. As August wore on, the *Intelligencer* reported on this activity—or lack of it. Indeed, there was little variation in the daily "Telegraphic" reports issued by the Press Association, whose superintendent John Thrasher was staying in Atlanta: "brisk skirmishing" (August 5); "last night and this morning passed without any demonstration on the part of the enemy" (August 9). The *Memphis Appeal* "Extra" offered updates from "the immediate front": "the last twenty-four hours has been tolerably quiet" (August 6); "during the past twenty-four hours the firing, both of artillery and by the pickets, has been very desultory" (August 9).[2]

"Desultory" was not enough activity for General Sherman, who was becoming frustrated at his inability to outflank Hood's railway defense line or to break it somewhere. Sherman wired Grant on August 4 that Hood "shows a bold front wherever I get at him." For his part, Hood was content to keep his troops busy strengthening their fortifications. This was the "bold front" that was exasperating Sherman. As a demonstration of his pique (if for no other reason), the Northern commander ordered that all cannon capable of reaching downtown Atlanta should open fire on August 9, with each gun to fire fifty rounds. Sherman's artillery arm had a hundred rifled field pieces—three-inch rifles, ten- and twenty-pounder Parrotts—that could send shells flying for two miles or more. "Let us destroy Atlanta and make it a desolation," Sherman wrote General Howard in early August. When the commanding general was in such a frame of mind, officers saw that orders would be obeyed to the letter. As a result, some 5,000 shells rained down upon Atlanta on August 9 alone.

"Heaviest Shelling of the City Yet," headlined the *Intelligencer*'s "Telegraphic" column on the 11th. The short article gave few particulars, only that one citizen had been killed and a child wounded in the cannonade, noting that it was "the heaviest yet experienced" in the city, with "many buildings being struck."[3]

Even under such duress, hope springs eternal, as the English essayist Alexander Pope wrote, and as the Atlanta editor John Steele echoed. Upon rumor that President Davis intended that the Army of Tennessee "will be abundantly supported in both front and rear," Steele jumped to the assumption that Hood's army was to be reinforced. "The sooner this is done," he asserted, "the sooner Sherman will be flying before the Army of Tennessee, routed, 'horse, foot, and dragoons,' Georgia be saved, and Tennessee redeemed." He went further still: "Grant is already defeated by Lee"—actually he was not—"Sherman, defeated and routed by Hood, will end the summer's campaign in Virginia and Georgia so disastrously to Lincoln that we shall look confidently to his defeat in the coming presidential election, and the triumph of the peace party in the North." Then there would be no further Northern prosecution of the war, "and soon the independence of the Confederate States will be acknowledged by all in the world!," Steele exclaimed.[4]

Meanwhile, Sherman stuck to his plan of trying to take Atlanta by cutting the railroad to Macon. "The enemy continues massing on his right and endeavoring to extend their lines in the direction of the West Point road," the Press Association's telegraphic news article stated in the *Intelligencer* on August 12. "The enemy is still massing towards his right," the *Intelligencer* declared the next day, quoting the *Memphis Appeal* of the 9th—"his right" meaning the Union line's flank southwest of the city. "It is reported that the enemy is still massing on the [Confederate] left, but making no efforts to extend their lines," the P. A. reported from Atlanta on August 12.[5]

This was correct. "I do not deem it prudent to extend more to the right," Sherman wrote General Halleck in Washington on August 7, "but will push forward daily by parallels, and make the inside of Atlanta too hot to be endured." This latter remark referred to the ongoing bombardment of Atlanta and Sherman's hope that incessant shelling might compel Hood to abandon the city. (It would not.) But it did give Ike Pilgrim more to write about. Over the name "MIRGLIP," he described further evidence of the damage to buildings in the city caused by the Northern projectiles. Not content with the work of his 10- and 20-pounder rifled guns, Sherman had ordered up four 4.5-inch rifles, and after their arrival toward mid-August they added the weight of their thirty-pound shells (eventually, 4,526 of them, more than seventy tons of metal) to the Union cannonade.

One of these monsters struck the Intelligencer building at the foot of Whitehall Street, as "MIRGLIP" related: "A thirty-two pounder came over from the western portion of the city, and struck the Intelligencer building on the roof, over the news room, passing through the roof and the wall into the passage, where it lodged without exploding. I went over and saw it. The shell is now in possession of the Atlanta Fire Battalion, and I intend to bring it down when I come."

The *Intelligencer* related this on August 18. A few days before, it also printed excerpts of the letter from "a friend" in which the writer declared, "you can find evidence of the enemy's barbarity"—meaning building shell-holes, blasted trees, etc.—"in almost every home or lot in the city," including newspaper offices. "I have a fragment of a shell which I picked up on the floor of your old sanctum" on Whitehall Street. "It passed in at the window, breaking a pane of glass, and slightly injuring the plastering on the opposite side of the room. I was standing in Whitehall street when it went in, and immediately went up and found it. Should I go to Macon soon, I will have it with me, as a memento of the love that is borne for us by our Northern brethren."[6]

Further news came from the war front just a few miles outside of Atlanta, the itinerant *Intelligencer*'s former home. And to wherever his readers now were, the transplanted newspaper's editor continued to voice optimism that Sherman could still be foiled in his efforts to capture the Confederacy's (by now) second-most important city. "The condition and prospects of the Army of Tennessee, are more hopeful at the present hour than they have been since that sore trial of the evacuation of Kennesaw Mountain occurred," the editor wistfully imagined. John Steele had sharp words indeed for the Yankees and their city-shelling. "The enemy does not abate his daily amusement, of exhibiting pyrotechnic displays, by day and night. The pastime has become a chronic necessity, to appease the insatiate man of murder and destruction, for which, Sherman and his minions have come barbarously notorious. Their success in battering to pieces the impenetrable fortress Atlanta, must have given them great satisfaction. The murder of women and children, by fragments of their barbarous shells, will be a gory blot on the savage and unsoldierlike campaign of Sherman the flanker."[7]

In late August, realizing that even with his superior strength, he could not extend his right flank sufficiently southward to get around Hood's left (as he had so often done against Joe Johnston), Sherman determined upon a bold deviation from his previous tactics: he would lead most of his army—six of his seven infantry corps, 56,000 strong—in a wide march south of Atlanta, swinging then east, aiming at the Macon & Western Railroad well south of East Point. Maj. Gen. Henry Slocum's XX Corps was to withdraw to the Chattahoochee crossings, if only to pose a continuing threat against the city. Hood would be forced to stretch his already overstretched army both to guard Atlanta and somehow parry Sherman's massive lunge at the railroad. Worse for Hood, he did not know where the Federals would strike the Macon road; it could be anywhere between East Point and, say, Jonesboro, a stretch of track sixteen miles long.

Sherman delivered his orders on August 23. His troops commenced marching in the night of the 25th-26th. While Wheeler was off raiding (by now in Tennessee), Confederate cavalry under Brig. Gen. William H. ("Red") Jackson stayed ahead of the Federal infantry column, keeping Hood in Atlanta abreast of their advance.

The *Intelligencer* was slow to catch onto Sherman's gambit. On August 26, it ran the *Appeal*'s "Immediate Front" column, which stated that the Yankees were showing "an indecision and uncertainty of purpose." Yet the *Intelligencer*'s telegraphic news column that day announced, "for some cause the Federal batteries are silent this morning." A Press Association dispatch sent from Atlanta on the 26th declared that Union troops had disappeared from their lines north and east of the city, but held onto its sector west of town; "this movement is interpreted as a concentration upon our left." Another P. A. report from Atlanta on August 30 correctly stated that Sherman's troops were on the railroad to

West Point tearing up track, but there was no indication of where they would next be heading.[8]

Editor Steele began to catch on, as he indicated in a piece, "The Situation in Front," that appeared on August 31. Sherman seemed to be engaged in "a bold move," he declared, aimed at the railroad, "thus cutting off our communications and forcing an evacuation of Atlanta.... If we should be correct in our surmise twenty-four, or forty-eight hours at most, will determine the fact."

So true. On September 2, the *Intelligencer* reported that on August 31, "the Yankees effected a lodgment on the Macon & Western Railroad, between Rough & Ready and East Point Stations." While Generals Hardee and S. D. Lee, shunted south of Atlanta to deal with the approach of O. O. Howard's three corps toward Jonesboro, were preparing to attack there on mid-afternoon of the 31st, eight miles to the north troops of John Schofield's XXIII Corps reached the railroad and began tearing it up. Within a few hours Hood knew this, and began issuing orders for the abandonment of Atlanta the next day, September 1.[9]

Along with the Confederate troops marching south out of the city there fled a number of civilians, Isaac Pilgrim among them. On September 2, he was at Barnesville, fifty miles to the south, from where he sent a short telegram that did not mention the loss of Atlanta. Neither did a report in the *Chattanooga/Griffin Rebel* of the 2nd that appeared in the *Intelligencer* on September 4. Finally, two days later, the *Intelligencer* came face-to-face with the facts, based on a brief dispatch sent out on Sunday, September 4, by the Press Association from Lovejoy's, south of Atlanta: "the Federals entered Atlanta in column by the Peachtree road on Friday morning [September 2] nine o'clock... They took possession of the city very quietly and orderly, and citizens who remained were unmolested." Actually, with only a few Confederate cavalrymen still in the city, it fell upon Mayor James Calhoun to surrender it. With a group of citizens he rode out on Marietta Street the morning of the 2nd and formally surrendered it to the first Federal officer he encountered, Col. John Coburn.

Dr. I. E. Nagle had been listed as a newspaper staff member in Steele's "Olla Podrida" article of July 5. On September 4, the editor announced he was leaving Macon due to a "serious family affliction." He added that he would leave the paper in the hands of Nagle, "with whose labors as our ASSOCIATE our readers have been familiar during the several months past.") In an editorial probably written by the paper's new associate editor, the *Intelligencer* dealt with the news of Atlanta's fall in one of its "The Position" articles appearing on September 6.

The position in Georgia, the article began, "presents a decidedly uncomfortable aspect." After that gigantic understatement, the piece related the fighting at Jonesboro, August 31-September 1. The writer, without blaming Hood by name, criticized the command decision that essentially had divided Hood's army into two parts (Hardee's and Lee's corps at Jonesboro, Peter Stewart's at Atlanta): "the mistake culminated in the evacuation of Atlanta and the unnecessary destruction of immense stores," especially ammunition packed on railroad cars east of downtown and blown up in the night of September 1–2. Hood's ordnance officers came in for criticism for having allowed "such an enormous amount of material" to remain in the city until it was too late to get it out. Then, too, President Davis came in for a share of the blame, especially as he had promised the people that Atlanta would not fall. "Perhaps he would have taken measures that would have prevented the terrible and irremediable catastrophe," the paper charged, going so far as to declare that "the South West" (meaning Georgia, Alabama and Mississippi) "is too far off for him to pay the special attention to its needs and wants that its *importance* demands." Then, for good measure, there was an indirect poke at the president for having relieved Johnston and appointing Hood a month and a half before.

> When favoritism ceases to enlarge his pets and to sustain his incompetents. When wisdom clears from the rubbish of his prejudices his love for senseless officers, and men who are really soldiers are placed in their proper spheres, then we may expect that the ARMY OF TENNESSEE will become the terrible engine of power and the tower of strength that it can be made.[10]

Over the past several decades, historians have gone back and forth on the importance of Atlanta's fall in connection with Abraham Lincoln's re-election as U.S. president. The traditional view has been expressed by Albert Castel in *Decision in the West* (1992): Sherman's capture of Atlanta led to Lincoln's re-election and thus to the collapse of the Confederacy. Richard McMurry makes the same point, that Confederates' last hope for independence rested with their holding onto Atlanta (*Last Chance for the Confederacy*, 2000).[11]

The argumentative swirl hinges on the assumption that Lincoln's Democratic opponent, Union Maj. Gen. George B. McClellan, if elected, would have acted on his party's platform, which called for an armistice and negotiated peace with the Rebels.

Those historians seeking to counter Castel and McMurry make a couple of worthwhile points. Larry J. Daniel argues that the importance of Sherman's capture of Atlanta has been exaggerated: "the capture of Atlanta, though significant, was thus far from being the turning point of the Civil War. . . . there is much evidence that . . . Lincoln would have won anyway." Daniel compares the states Lincoln won in 1860 with those he took four years later; Abe carried every state that he won in his election and added just two (Maryland and Missouri). In other words, states that were Republican in '60 were just as Republican in '64. By this measure, Atlanta didn't matter.[12]

In 1996 William C. Davis argued strongly against the traditional hypothesis that Lincoln's re-election was the final turning point of the war. "The notion of Lincoln's loss leading directly to Confederate independence is but a fable," he asserted. He reminded us that in the nineteenth century, American presidents' terms ended on March 4, four months after the November election. In that time span, even as a lame-duck president, Lincoln would have ordered Grant to press a winter campaign against Lee and Richmond. Grant would have brought Sherman and the bulk of his army to Virginia to help him (instead of agreeing to Sherman's idea of a march across Georgia with his 60,000 troops). Against such colossal Federal strength, "Lee, his army, and Richmond as a result would inevitably have fallen before March 4."[13]

All of this academic discussion shouldn't cloak how Confederates at the time felt about the fall of Atlanta. When she wrote in her diary, "since Atlanta I have felt as if I were dead within me, forever," Mary Boykin Chesnut was speaking for hundreds of thousands of fellow Southerners.[14]

NOTES

1. Davis, *What the Yankees Did to Us*, 132, 138–45, 151–58.

2. Wilbur G. Kurtz, "Map of Atlanta as of 1938 Showing the Field and Fortified Lines of the Confederate Forces, Together with Those of the Federal armies—Also the Fields of the Three Major Engagements, During the Summer of 1864" (Atlanta Chamber of Commerce, 1938), copy in Kurtz Collection, MSS 100, FF 148, T2, folder 2, Atlanta History Center; Davis, *All the Fighting*, 75–77; "TELEGRAPHIC" (Atlanta, August 5), *ADI*, Aug. 6, 1864; "TELEGRAPHIC" (Atlanta, August 9), *ADI*, August 10; "THE IMMEDIATE FRONT" (*Appeal*, August 6), *ADI*, August 9; "THE IMMEDIATE FRONT" (*Appeal*, August 9), *ADI*, August 11.

3. Davis, *All the Fighting*, 77, 82–83; "LATEST FROM ATLANTA. Heaviest Shelling of the City Yet" (Atlanta, August 10), *ADI*, Aug. 11, 1864.

4. "A GLEAM OF HOPE," *ADI*, Aug. 11, 1864.

5. "TELEGRAPHIC" (Atlanta, August 11), *ADI*, Aug. 12, 1864; "THE IMMEDIATE FRONT" (*Appeal*, August 9) and "TELEGRAPHIC' (Atlanta, August 12), *ADI*, August 13.

6. Davis, *All the Fighting*, 82; Sherman to Halleck, Aug. 7, 1864, *OR*, vol. 38, pt. 5, 408; "MIRGLIP," "For the Intelligencer. SPECIAL CORRESPONDENCE," *ADI*, Aug. 18, 1864; Davis, "Sherman's Bombardment," 68; "ATLANTA," *ADI*, August 13.

7. "THE POSITION. IN GEORGIA," *ADI*, Aug. 18, 1864; Davis, *All the Fighting They Want*, 87–89.

8. Davis, *All the Fighting*, 101–107; "THE IMMEDIATE FRONT" (*Appeal*, August 23) and "TELEGRAPHIC," *ADI*, Aug. 26, 1864; "TELEGRAPHIC. FROM ATLANTA" (August 26), *ADI*, August 27; "TELEGRAPHIC. FROM ATLANTA" (August 30), *ADI*, August 31.

9. "THE SITUATION IN FRONT," *ADI*, Aug. 31, 1864; "THE POSITION. IN GEORGIA," *ADI*, September 2; Davis, *All the Fighting*, 109–111.

10. Isaac B. Pilgrim, "TELEGRAPHIC" (Barnesville, September 2), *ADI*, Sept. 3, 1864; "AFFAIRS IN THE FRONT" (*Rebel*, September 2), *ADI*, September 4; "Lovejoy's, Sept. 4," *ADI*, September 6; Davis, *What the Yankees Did to Us*, 261–62; "THE POSITION. IN GEORGIA," *ADI*, September 6; "OUR ABSENCE," *ADI*, September 4.

11. Castel, *Decision in the West*, 480; McMurry, *Atlanta 1864*, 207–208.

12. Larry J. Daniel, "The South Almost Won by Not Losing: A Rebuttal," *North & South*, no. 3 (February 1998), 47, 50–51.

13. William C. Davis, *The Cause Lost: Myths and Realities of the Confederacy* (Lawrence: University Press of Kansas, 1996), 139–41.

14. C. Vann Woodward, ed., *Mary Chesnut's Civil War* (New Haven: Yale University Press, 1981), 648.

40. The *Intelligencer* Takes on President Davis

RICHMOND, September 4.—The following official dispatch from General Hood on the 3d inst., states that on the evening of the 30th ult. the enemy made a lodgment across Flint river near Jonesboro. We attacked them there on the evening of the 30th ult. with two corps, but failed to dislodge them. This made it necessary to abandon Atlanta, which was done on the night of the 1st inst.

AS A MEANS OF CONVEYING BAD NEWS, this Press Association dispatch (in the *Intelligencer* of September 6) was about as laconic as it gets. It is also a misleadingly simplified version of what had happened south of Atlanta on "the 31st ult." (*ult.* meaning *last month*). True, Hardee and S. D. Lee had attacked Howard's army at Jonesboro and had been repulsed. But their defeat did not cause Hood in Atlanta to issue the evacuation order; it was the Federals' cutting of the railroad eight miles north of Jonesboro that did it. The news spread fast. Confederate Maj. Gen. Samuel French, a division commander in Stewart's corps, recorded in his diary on August 31, "the railroad to Macon was cut to-day." The Federals also cut the telegraph, so it was not until the next day (the "1st inst., meaning the *present month*) that Hood's headquarters knew of the repulse at Jonesboro. By that time, Confederates and the Georgia Militia were already taking steps to destroy the army's ordnance train, burn the big rolling mill east of Atlanta and spike cannon that could not be rolled away.[1]

At least General Hood did not blame the Confederate government for the loss of Atlanta; that was for the *Intelligencer's* associate editor, I. E. Nagle, to do. Nagle had already criticized Davis in the paper's "The Position" article of September 6, when he accused the president of indifference to the military situation in "the South West" (meaning Georgia, Alabama and Mississippi), and of poor judgment in replacing General Johnston with Hood. "When... men who are really soldiers are placed in their proper spheres," Nagle wrote, "then we may expect that the ARMY OF TENNESSEE will become the terrible engine of power and tower of strength that it can be made."

Dr. Nagle piled on in another piece two days later. "MR. DAVIS RESPONSIBLE FOR THE FAILURES IN THE WEST" proclaimed the headline of his editorial appearing on September 8 (during John Steele's three-week absence, ca. September 5–26). Nagle gave three reasons. First, "he has placed men who had no prestige of success, name, or capacity in positions of great trust." Presumably this meant the promotion of Hood to command the Army of Tennessee, which brought up the second accusation: "instead of making our Army of Tennessee effective and the powerful and invincible engine of war that it is capable of being, he has permitted unwarrantable interference, incapacity and inefficiency to dissipate its strength." The third charge went further: the *Intelligencer* accused the president of actually harboring "an antagonism against this State," though without explaining why or how.[2]

The associate editor went even further on September 13. A day after the fall of Atlanta, Hood had wired General Bragg, calling for reinforcements to his army. Once this message reached the president's desk, Davis on September 5 could only reply that all available troops had already been sent. Then when General Hardee reinforced Hood's plea with his own telegram (apparently sent at Hood's request), Davis responded the same: "no other resource remains. It is requisite that . . . the means in hand be used with energy proportionate to the country's need." Word of this correspondence apparently reached the *Intelligencer*, for Nagle blistered Jefferson Davis on the 13th by repeating his accusation that the Confederate president was acting in "antagonistic opposition to the vital interests of the State of Georgia." Davis' inability/refusal to send Hood reinforcements, the paper declared, was tantamount to his telling the state's *"suffering women and children,* Georgia must defend herself." (After his return to Macon, John Steele later referred to the author of this article by stating that it was composed by "a writer for this paper," who could only have been his associate editor, Dr. Nagle.) In his editorial of September 13, Nagle urged Davis not only to "put aside his prejudices and save the southwest," but also to effect "a radical change in the appointment and conduct of the army"—this latter being another veiled plea to relieve Hood and replace him with someone better.[3]

More explicit was the long editorial, "A General for the Army of Tennessee," appearing in the *Intelligencer* on September 14. "So many indefinite rumors come to us that the Army of Tennessee will have a new commander," it began, "that there seems to be no doubt that a change will be made." The piece, again written by Dr. Nagle, included his earlier phrasing about "the engine of power and success" that the Army of Tennessee could be. A good replacement for

Hood, he suggested, would be a general "who knows how to render the army competent and effective."

As for the broader question of command of Hood's army in Georgia, the paper welcomed the prospect of change, though without mentioning Hood's name and without suggesting who that replacement might be. One name being kicked around in Confederate newspapers was Gen. Pierre Gustave Toutant Beauregard, then in charge of defenses in the area of Petersburg, south of Richmond.

In truth, no less than Robert E. Lee was suggesting that Jefferson Davis relieve Hood and replace him with Beauregard (though the *Intelligencer*'s staff did not know it at the time). "Mr. President," Lee wrote Davis on September 19, "I have had a conversation with General Beauregard with reference to the army and operations in Georgia. . . . he says he will obey with alacrity any order of the War Department placing him in command of that army." Indeed, that same day Beauregard drafted and gave to Lee a memorandum attesting his interest in assuming "command of that army," meaning the one in Georgia currently under Hood. Somehow word of Lee's and Beauregard's communications got out and became gossip items in the Southern press, which the *Intelligencer* picked up. Under the heading of "General Beauregard," the paper declared, "the opinion generally prevails that it is the intention of the President to place this distinguished General at the head of the Army of Tennessee." It also reprinted a short piece from the *Savannah Republican* about how the *Charleston Mercury*, based on "a source deemed unquestionable," had learned that "President Davis has tendered to Gen. Beauregard the command of the Army of Tennessee. The result, it learns, has been brought about by the earnest intervention and counsel of General Lee." Actually, despite Lee's intervention, Jefferson Davis was not planning to do so. Instead, he envisioned creating a "Military Division of the West," that would have authority over both the Army of Tennessee (then currently under Hood in Georgia) and Confederate forces in Alabama and Mississippi (under Lt. Gen. Richard Taylor). This was the post that Davis would offer Beauregard in the fall of 1864.[4]

Hood's army in the second week of September was near Lovejoy's Station, twenty-five miles south of Atlanta. Sherman had concentrated his forces in and around the city, where in the first weeks of the Federal occupation there were still perhaps three thousand civilians, for whom Sherman did not care to provide. So on September 4, he issued an order kicking them all out. "I propose to remove all inhabitants of Atlanta, sending those committed to our cause to the rear, and the rebel families to the front," he explained to General Halleck (who did not object). He then arranged a ten-day truce with Hood, September 12–21. During it those civilians choosing to go south could take a few possessions and would be transported to Rough and Ready, the point where under flag of truce they were to be received into Confederate lines. From there they were to be borne farther south to Macon by conveyances arranged by Hood. The night before the truce began, a Confederate commissary officer, Benedict Semmes, observed, "the wagons, some 400 four- and six-mule teams, are now collected in front of my quarters, to go forward to bring down the unfortunate people of Atlanta." Eventually, Federal officers counted 1,651 people expelled into Confederate lines. Probably as many were sent by train to Chattanooga, Nashville and points farther north. The *Intelligencer* of September 17 related, "about one half of the population elected to go to Tennessee."[5]

The *Intelligencer* tracked these events, especially when the Atlanta exiles began arriving in Macon. "Trains have gone forward for the purpose of bring[ing] down exiles from Atlanta," it announced on September 13.[6]

The first train of Atlanta exiles arrived in Macon on the morning of September 14, the *Intelligencer* observed; "they were stripped by the Yankees of everything but a single change of clothing, and are in a deplorable condition." The arrival of the Atlantans in Macon prompted editorial expressions of empathy: "the citizens who came south are not permitted to bring any household stuff of any consequence, the quantity being very limited, whilst those who have chosen to go North carry what they wish," the paper asserted on September 15.[7]

It became apparent that a large number of the exiles were indigent—people too poor to have had a place to go while Hood fought to hold Atlanta and in the first days of the Federal occupation. "Numbers of the families are very poor," the *Intelligencer* declared on September 17, "and having been denied the privilege of bringing even what they had at home, they are now in a most primitive condition of want." Fortunately, the paper noted, the people of Macon were stepping forth with offers of assistance. The *Intelligencer* supported these gestures with appeals for the Macon citizenry to donate money for the recently arrived needy families. Another problem was shelter: the influx of hundreds of homeless strained the capacity of the middle Georgia city to take them all in. The *Intelligencer* suggested that a number of the Atlantans should continue their flight to towns farther south. Then, after Georgia's Quartermaster General, Col. Ira Foster, announced that the state would erect cabins for the exiles in the area of Gordon, twenty miles east of Macon, the paper on September 28 applauded the news, to the point of suggesting that the new settlement be called Fosterville. A month later, the *Intelligencer* congratulated state authorities for having created shelter for some 300 women and children.[8]

On September 23, there had been called a meeting for 11 a.m. at Macon's downtown Baptist church for citizens to discuss means of further helping the exiles, when word arrived that the city suddenly had a distinguished visitor: Jefferson Davis. The president was on his way from Richmond to visit Hood and his army, then at Palmetto (twenty miles southwest of Atlanta); he arrived in Macon by train from Savannah early that morning. City fathers quickly invited him to address the gathering. Davis had been giving speeches along the way, but when he arrived at the meeting, the president had a prepared text. The *Intelligencer* obtained the speech and printed it on the 25th; so did Macon's other two dailies, the *Telegraph* and the *Confederate* (which were actually one by this time, as noticed by the *Intelligencer* on September 20 in an article titled, "Newspaper Nuptials").

After being introduced by General Howell Cobb, in his remarks Davis put on a show of resolve and optimism for his listeners. "Let us with one arm and one effort endeavor to crush Sherman," he declared; "Sherman cannot keep up his long line of communication, and retreat sooner or later he must. And when that day comes, the fate that befell the army of the French Empire and its retreat from Moscow will be reacted." Davis carried this historical metaphor further when he predicted, "our cavalry and our people will harass and destroy his army as did the Cossacks that of Napoleon, and the Yankee General, like him will escape with only a bodyguard."

As he usually did in his orations, the president extolled the patriotic sacrifices being made by Southern women even as he urged that all soldiers absent from Hood's army return to the ranks. Then came this: "It has been said that I abandoned Georgia to her fate. Shame upon such a falsehood. . . . Miserable man. The man who uttered this is a scoundrel."

In a short piece on Sunday, the 25th, John Steele ("after an absence of some three weeks from his post, having just returned to resume his duties"), promised to offer comment on the president's speech in the paper's next issue. He kept his word. In the *Intelligencer* of Tuesday, September 27, Steele wrote an extensive article on the speech, and also on the situation of the Army of Tennessee and the administration's policy toward Georgia. In it the editor expressed his concern that Davis had not done enough to prevent the fall of Atlanta in the first place, and now was not doing enough to save the rest of Georgia from Sherman's threatened advance. He particularly accused Davis of paying more attention to the safety of the Confederate capital, Richmond, than of Tennessee, Alabama and Georgia. "The 'Great West' of the Confederacy has been sacrificed, that Richmond might be saved," he charged, emphasizing Georgia, "the great *centre* of the Confederacy. . . . Let him save the State from desolation," he exclaimed. "It is his *duty* to do so!"[9]

Davis' Macon address was reprinted widely in the Confederate press, as noted by the *Intelligencer*. On September 29 the paper printed a brief commentary about the speech from the *Charleston Mercury*, in which the *Mercury* expressed "our profound regret that such a speech should have been said to have been delivered by the Chief Magistrate of the Confederate States"—though it did not offer reasons for that "profound regret." The *Intelligencer* also reprinted an article from the *Montgomery Mail*, which had also published the president's text. This one was a lot longer and much more blistering in its criticism. In fairness to Davis, the *Mail* expressed hope that the text it had received reflected the "rambling, desultory character" of offhand remarks, rather than the studied writing of a prepared address. The *Mail* elaborated its criticisms. For one, in reviewing the course of the Atlanta Campaign, Davis had made remarks not very kind to General Johnston (referring to Johnston's retreats through north Georgia, he said, "I even heard that I had sent Bragg with pontoons to cross into Cuba. But we must be charitable"). As for appointing Hood to lead the army, Davis asserted, "I then put a man in command who I knew would strike an honest and manly blow for the city." To the contrary, the Montgomery paper charged that "had Gen. Johnston been retained in command of the Tennessee Army, Atlanta would not only have been saved, but Sherman's hosts would have been destroyed." "Periodical interferences of the President," such as the firing of Joe Johnston, "are fast bringing us to grief," the *Mail* argued. Worse, the Montgomery paper had learned that Davis was heading toward a conference with Hood and his generals at Palmetto, from which more "interferences" might be predicted. "May God deliver us this time from that dispensation which the past teaches us to anticipate," the *Mail* concluded.

The *Mercury* and *Mail* were not alone. A week after Davis' address in Macon, the *Intelligencer* informed readers that "thus far we have seen in but one of our exchanges any complimentary allusion to the President's speech in this city." The lone dissenter was the *LaGrange* (Georgia) *Reporter & Bulletin*, which Steele accused of "obsequiousness" to the nation's chief executive.

The *Intelligencer* editor took particular notice that the press in Georgia was buzzing about President Davis' "scoundrel" remark ("It has been said that I abandoned Georgia to her fate. Shame upon such a falsehood. . . . Miserable man. The man who uttered this is a scoundrel").

On October 4, Steele addressed the topic in an editorial titled, "THE PRESIDENT'S SPEECH IN MACON—HIS WAR POLICY." Davis had evidently obtained the *Intelligencer* of September 13, or someone must have told him about the paper's article accusing the president of the Confederacy of telling Georgia's "*suffering women and children,* Georgia must defend herself."

> Some of our exchanges appear to be greatly exercised as to whom the President, in his speech in this city, designed to apply the term *"scoundrel,"* for having stated that he had abandoned Georgia to her fate; some contending that he designed to apply it to Governor Brown, and others to a writer for this paper. That *he did not* design to apply it to Governor Brown we are as confident as we are that he *did* design to apply it to the gentleman who wrote an article for this paper, in which the charge, so galling to the President, was made, and which had the effect, we are sorry to say, of exasperating and seducing him from his propriety. Perhaps the charge that was made, needed some qualification. In *words* the President, we are free to admit, as far as our knowledge extends, did not say "he abandoned Georgia to her fate." In his *acts* it has looked very much like he had done so. His *policy* in our weak judgment indicated this, and it really matters not who said he had done so, or thought he had done so, *provided* always that he had not charged the President with *saying* he had done so.

So much for Steele's "qualification." But who was the "scoundrel"? "We are certain Governor Brown made no such charge and he is therefore not obnoxious to the term 'scoundrel' which the President, in his wrath, and at the expense of the dignity of his position, bestowed upon the mistaken individual who did. Our contemporaries, therefore, of the Augusta *Chronicle & Sentinel,* and the *Constitutionalist* need dispute no more upon the question, 'who the individual was the President aimed at?' It was doubtless the one we indicate—the writer of an article in this paper, whose good name has not and will not be tarnished by the opprobrious epithet uttered by our then wrathful President."

So associate editor I. E. Nagle had stepped out of line ("mistaken individual") during the time the editor was away on family business—sort of. In a bald demonstration of support for his associate's take on the military situation, Steele in his article elaborated further criticisms of Jefferson Davis' "war policy": "we assert that the war policy of the administration viewed in the light of history, and our resources, is incomprehensible." Steele particularly blamed Davis for Lee's disastrous Pennsylvania campaign of the year before; at the same time, "the sad story of Vicksburg was added to that of Gettysburg." With its limited resources, Steele (assuming something of the role of military theorist) argued that the Confederacy had to shift its troops for "*concentration* of numbers and *celerity* of movement." After Lee's victory at Chancellorsville in May 1863, he argued, a part of his army could have been sent west to help save Vicksburg. Instead, "the administration's policy was to send Gen. Lee a great distance into the enemy's country." Similarly, if Forrest had been sent to help Johnston in the spring of 1864, "he *would have* saved Atlanta"; this was another example of "the want of concentration." Resources then existed in the Trans-Mississippi that were conducting isolated and ineffectual operations. Even as he wrote, "the enemy . . . are transferring their strength to this side, while we leave ours to operate in a manner that can have no effect on the final result."

The editor then concluded, "we have no time to lose and must act speedily. But, in our judgment, action will avail us nothing, unless the President will change his war policy."[10]

Editor John Steele and Associate Editor I.E. Nagle had thus crossed the President of the Confederate States of America. Their criticisms had come to Davis' attention, and in a speech delivered in the very city where the *Intelligencer* was quartered he had termed the writer "a scoundrel." Historians have been aware of Davis' Macon speech for a long time, but the literature is silent on both Nagle's identity and the name of his offending newspaper.[11]

After his speech in Macon on September 23, Davis made a roundabout train trek to get to Palmetto and Hood's army encampments on the afternoon of the 25th. The next morning the president conducted a review of the troops, who had formed for the occasion, standing at attention. The Press Association telegram about it, as printed in the *Intelligencer*, stated that Davis "was received by the men with great applause and made them a speech."

That was not the whole story. On September 30, the *Intelligencer* ran the P. A. dispatch, but added no editorial comment on the president's review. It soon explained why. While some of the Tennessee army's soldiers had hallooed vociferously when Davis, Hood, and other officers rode before them, bowing and touching their hats, others very much had not. Years later, South Carolinian Arthur Manigault, a brigadier in the Army of Tennessee, remembered of Davis' review that in his part of the line "no cheers saluted him, countenances were depressed and sullen.... 'Give us Johnston! Give us our old Commander!,'" they yelled. The occasion made a mark on Manigault's memory, writing several years after the war. "This happened in many brigades," he recalled. "Arrests and threats of punishment alone prevented the cry from becoming loud and general," Manigault wrote; "one could not help remarking the expression of President Davis's countenance as he passed by. He looked thin, care-worn, and angry."

The *Intelligencer* on October 1 announced that it was aware of this information, "but declined to lay it before our readers." Now, though, because it had "got into the papers and as it will 'go the rounds' of them, ... we give publicity of it also more, however, for the purpose of expressing our regret at the occurrence, than from any other motive. Differing as we do from the President, we do not approve such manifestations of disapprobation to him. They were not calculated to remedy the evil complained of. No one regrets Gen. Johnston's displacement from the command of the Army of Tennessee more than we do, but it were better no such demonstrations of dissatisfaction had been made."[12]

Handing off the newspaper's day-to-day operation to I. E. Nagle would come back to haunt John Steele yet another time in late September 1864.

The Confederate press had begun discussing the possibility of actually enlisting enslaved African Americans as armed soldiers in the Confederate forces. In Georgia the subject was discussed in Augusta and Macon newspapers, including the *Intelligencer* on September 29: "A portion of the Southern press have agitated the policy of placing our slaves in the army as soldiers. We have long since decided that the policy is a good one, and it has been a source of much wonder to us that our government has not made arrangements to carry out the idea."

That was on September 29. In the *Intelligencer*'s issue of the very next day, Friday, the 30th, John Steele strove to set the record straight.

NEGRO SOLDIERS.

Under this heading, our Associate on yesterday wrote an article advocating the arming of negroes, and placing them in the field against the enemy. To this making soldiers of our negroes we totally dissent, and cannot advocate such a policy in this journal. Nor shall we in any wise discuss it. Suffice it to say, we object to it for many reasons; deem it unwise, impolitic, and dangerous. If we cannot win our independence without imitating the Yankee nation in the use he makes of the negro, we are in a worse condition than we believe we are.

To emphasize its opposition to the idea of arming slaves as Confederate soldiers, the *Intelligencer* ran a long editorial on the subject in its issue of Oct. 26, 1864. Moreover, Steele made sure that the opinion piece reflected the view of both the paper's owner, Jared Whitaker, and himself as editor. Such a proposal, if enacted, Steele declared, would be "destructive to the relation between master and slave, and to the distinction between the white and negro race which exists in the South."

The editor then continued more broadly with a statement about the institution of slavery in the South, and its political consequences. "Since African slavery was introduced into it," he maintained, slavery was responsible for "all that has been done to civilize and Christianize the negro." Indeed, the editor trotted out that old saw so frequently expressed by slavery's antebellum defenders: "we, of the South, religiously believe that existing relations between the white man and the negro, are promotive of the happiness of both."

Moreover, it was slavery, Steele argued, that had brought on the current disruption of the Union. "No financial, commercial, or manufacturing policy, pursued or adopted by the old Government, has had so much to do with its disruption, as the negro question; the question of the abolition of slavery. . . . All others were but trifling adjuncts to the disruption, when compared with it; and to preserve the distinction between master and slave, the South has been forced into the present unnatural and most cruel war."

This was just about as open an admission of slavery as the fundamental cause of the Civil War as one would see in the *Intelligencer*—or any other Confederate newspaper, for that matter. "We may be forced to yield up slavery," Steele concluded, "but we will fight on to maintain it as long as we have the power to do so."[13]

NOTES

1. "TELEGRAPHIC. RICHMOND, September 4," *ADI,* Sept. 6, 1864; Davis, *John Bell Hood: Texas Brigadier,* 431–32; Samuel G. French, *Two Wars: An Autobiography* (Huntington WV: Blue Acorn Press, 1999 [1901]), 222.

2. "THE POSITION. IN GEORGIA," *ADI,* Sept. 6, 1864; "MR. DAVIS RESPONSIBLE FOR THE FAILURES IN THE WEST" and "THE POSITION IN GEORGIA," *ADI,* September 8; "Our Absence," *ADI,* September 4; "THE PRESIDENT—HIS VISIT TO THE ARMY OF TENNESSEE—HIS SPEECH IN MACON—HIS WAR POLICY," *ADI,* September 27.

3. Hood to Bragg, Sept. 3, 1864; Hardee to Davis, September 4; Davis to Hood,

September 5; and Davis to Hardee, September 5, *OR,* vol. 38, pt. 5, 1016, 1018, 1021; "GEORGIA AND THE PRESIDENT," *ADI,* Sept. 13, 1864; "THE PRESIDENT'S SPEECH IN MACON—HIS WAR POLICY," *ADI,* October 4.

4. "A GENERAL FOR THE ARMY OF TENNESSEE," *ADI,* Sept. 14, 1864; Lee to Davis, Sept. 19, 1864, *OR,* vol, 39 pt. 2, 846; Roman, *Beauregard,* vol. 2 , 275; Stephen Davis, "Would P.G.T. Lead the A. o. T.?," *Civil War Times,* vol. 56, no. 2 (April 2017), 39–40; "GENERAL BEAUREGARD," *ADI,* September 30.

5. Davis, *What the Yankees Did to Us,* 290–96, 316, 324; Anderson Humphreys and Curt Guenter, *Semmes America* (Memphis: Humphreys, Ink, 1989), 357–58; "FROM THE FRONT. LOVEJOY STATION, Sept. 14, 1864," *ADI,* September 17.

6. "TELEGRAPHIC" (Macon, September 12), *ADI,* Sept. 13, 1864.

7. "TELEGRAPHIC" (Macon, September 14) and "THE EXILES," *ADI,* Sept. 15, 1864; Davis, *What the Yankees Did to Us,* 312.

8. "THE POSITION. IN GEORGIA," *ADI,* Sept. 17, 1864; "THE EXILES," *ADI,* September 20; "SUGGESTIONS TO THE EXILES," *ADI,* September 22; "A HOME FOR THE EXILES," *ADI,* September 28; "HOME FOR THE EXILES," *ADI,* October 30.

9. Cooper, *Jefferson Davis,* 489; Michael B. Ballard, "Breakdown in Macon," *Civil War Times Illustrated,* vol. 19, no. 6 (October 1980), 31; Crist, *et al.,* eds., *Papers of Jefferson Davis,* vol. 11, 61–63; "PRESIDENT DAVIS IN MACON" and "PRESIDENT DAVIS IN MACON" *ADI,* Sept. 25, 1864; "THE PRESIDENT—HIS VISIT TO THE ARMY OF TENNESSEE—HIS SPEECH IN MACON—HIS WAR POLICY," *ADI,* September 27.

10. "THE PRESIDENT'S SPEECH," *ADI,* Sept. 29, 1864 (from the *Charleston Mercury*); "THE PRESIDENT AT MACON," *ADI,* September 30 (from the *Montgomery Mail*); "Solitary and Alone," *ADI,* October 1; "THE PRESIDENT'S SPEECH IN MACON—HIS WAR POLICY," *ADI,* October 4.

11. An example is Professor van Tuyll's essay, "'We Have Spoken for Public Liberty': The Press, Dissent, and the Failure of Confederate Nationalism," which treats leading Confederate newspapers that voiced opposition to Davis' policies, without mentioning the Nagle/ Steele/ *Intelligencer* incident of September 1864 (David B. Sachsman, ed., *A Press Divided: Newspaper Coverage of the Civil War* [New Brunswick NJ: Transaction Publishers, 2014], 307–32).

12. Steven E. Woodworth, *Jefferson Davis and His Generals: The Failure of Confederate Command in the West* (Lawrence: University Press of Kansas, 1990), 291; "TELEGRAPHIC" (Griffin, September 26), *ADI,* Sept. 30, 1864; Arthur M. Manigault, *A Carolinian Goes to War: The Civil War Narrative of Arthur Middleton Manigault Brigadier General, C.S.A.,* ed. by R. Lockwood Tower (Columbia: University of South Carolina Press, 1983), 256; "THE ARMY OF TENNESSEE AND THE PRESIDENT," *ADI,* October 1.

13. Phillip D. Dillard, "The Confederate Debate Over Arming Slaves: Views from Macon and Augusta Newspapers," *Georgia Historical Quarterly,* vol. 79, no. 1 (Spring 1995), 119–22; "NEGRO SOLDIERS," *ADI,* Sept. 29, 1864; "NEGRO SOLDIERS," *ADI,* September 30; "ARMING THE NEGROES," *ADI,* October 26.

41. Hood Moves North

IN EARLY OCTOBER 1864, readers of the *Intelligencer* gradually learned that General Hood and his army were on the march into north Georgia.

The commander of the Confederate Army of Tennessee had really only one strategic option after the fall of Atlanta. With Sherman securely ensconced in the Atlanta fortifications that Hood himself had strengthened, there was no chance of trying to attack him there. And with his own army depleted in strength and shaken in morale, he could not stay inactive south of Atlanta waiting for Sherman to do something. As historian Thomas Robson Hay has written, Hood's army, if left idle, "would soon be reduced to a mere corporal's guard by desertions, by men gone off to visit their homes, and by expiring enlistments." All of this left but one option for Hood and his army: to maneuver north, around and behind Sherman, strike at the Western & Atlantic Railroad supplying the Federals from Chattanooga, and hope to force him to give up Atlanta in order to secure his rear.

There was something beyond that, too. Considerable evidence exists that during his time, September 25–27, with Hood and the army at Palmetto (twenty-five miles southwest of Atlanta) President Davis discussed strategy with the commanding general and that the two eventually agreed that not only would Hood take the offensive, marching his troops into north Georgia to wreck the Western & Atlantic Railroad and disrupting the flow of supplies to Sherman's troops in Atlanta, but that he would also keep marching into Tennessee (as a further means of drawing Sherman back from Atlanta). Such conversations took place late on the 25th, after Davis' train reached Palmetto, at least according to some of Hood's soldiers. In his postwar memoir (1882), Sam R. Watkins of the 1st Tennessee recalled that in his review of the troops on the morning of September 26, Davis stopped before the Tennesseans and announced, "Soon we commence our march to Kentucky and Tennessee. Be of good cheer, for within a short while your faces will be turned homeward, and your feet will press Tennessee soil." Just a few days later, Alabama captain

Ben Lane Posey wrote the *Mobile Advertiser & Register* that on the evening of September 26, Davis addressed some soldiers at Hardee's headquarters, telling them that "we [would] sweep over Tennessee, and finally bear our banners to the Ohio." Sumner Cunningham, of the 41st Tennessee, was at the same fireside gathering, and remembered that Davis told the men, "the army will go into Tennessee for victory."[1]

Davis left Palmetto on September 27, headed for Alabama. Today we know what eventually happened in the campaign that the president had been talking about: Hood marched into north Georgia in late September, knocked out Sherman's railroad for a while, continued into north Alabama and tarried there more than a month before entering Tennessee in the last half of November 1864. The bloody Confederate charge at Franklin, Tenn. (November 30) and the disastrous rout of Hood's army at Nashville (December 16) loomed ahead as well.

But that is what *we* know, thanks to hindsight. The readers of the *Intelligencer* had to learn about all this as their newspaper reported it . . . rather haphazardly, as it turns out.

Part of this was intentional. On September 24, the *Intelligencer* informed readers that it was not publishing news, much less rumors, about the Army of Tennessee, at least partly so as not to divulge information possibly useful to the enemy. "We make this statement in deference to the request and wishes of our readers," the editor explained, "who anxiously await the explanations of the position, and who inquire of us so often why we do not tell the movements of the army."[2]

The army did indeed begin to move on September 29. That was the day that the Army of Tennessee—4,455 officers and 42,976 men present for duty, as counted the week before (with 124 guns in thirty-two batteries)—started crossing the Chattahoochee River north of Palmetto on pontoon bridging laid down by the engineers. Lt. Gens. Peter Stewart's and Stephen Lee's infantry got across that day; on the 30th the other corps started. It was now under the command of Maj. Gen. Benjamin Franklin ("Frank") Cheatham, who had succeeded Lieutenant General Hardee. Hardee had long chafed at having to serve under Hood, and during the Atlanta Campaign had asked President Davis to be transferred. Davis had talked him out of it until the president's arrival at Palmetto, where he finally acceded. The *Intelligencer* announced on October 1 that Hardee would take charge of the Charleston-Savannah area. The next day it published some of his farewell remarks to the troops before departing: "he told them the commanding General would, in a few days, cross the army over the Chattahoochee on an offensive campaign, the plan of which he knew to be excellent." Hardee elaborated on this plan a few days later when, on his way to the coast, he stopped in Augusta and addressed impromptu a throng that had gathered to hear President Davis as well. Hardee declared that before he left Palmetto, General Hood had told him that soon "he hoped to lay his claws upon the State Road [the Western & Atlantic], and having once fixed them there, it was not his intention to let them loose [sic] their hold." Addressing the same audience, Davis went further—and farther. According to the *Intelligencer*'s article, "President Davis' Speech at Augusta" (October 7), the chief executive declared, "we must beat Sherman, we must march into Tennessee—there we will draw from 20,000 to 30,000 to our standard, and so strengthened, we must push the enemy back to the banks of the Ohio."[3]

This was tall talk indeed from the president who just the month before had fended off Lee's suggestion that John B. Hood be relieved of command. And needless to say, there was a lot of ground to cover between the Chattahoochee and Ohio Rivers. But at least the first part of Hood's plan was working out— getting his "claws" upon the Western & Atlantic. "All accounts agree that Gen. Hood's army is well in the rear of Atlanta," the *Intelligencer* stated on October 5, "and it is reported positively that we hold the Railroad between Vining [sic] and Marietta." Two days later the paper printed a dispatch seen in the *Memphis Appeal*, in which a soldier-correspondent, writing from "the Georgia front" on October 2, reported that "our cavalry has possession of the railroad between Marietta and Atlanta, and are destroying it as rapidly as possible." Also on the 7th, the *Intelligencer* printed an update taken from the *Columbus Sun* of October 5: "our forces are in possession of the State road from a little below Marietta to Acworth."[4]

What the *Intelligencer* and the other Georgia newspapers eager for news about Hood's advance could not report was just how much track the Confederates were tearing up. On October 3, Hood ordered Lieutenant General Stewart's corps to march to the railroad and start wrecking it. That day Maj. Gen. Samuel French's infantry division struck the Western & Atlantic at two places, Big Shanty (now the city of Kennesaw) and a place called Moon's Station, a couple of miles to the north. At each place Stewart's troops bagged a small Union garrison. On the 4th, Maj. Gen. William W. Loring's division reached Acworth, north of Moon's, and captured some 250 Federals. In the customary fashion of rail-wreckers on both sides during the Civil War, the men pried up the rails, stacked up the wooden ties and set them afire, then laid on the iron rails, heating them at the center so that when red-hot they could be twisted around trees or telegraph poles. When they were through with this work by mid-afternoon, October 4, the Southerners had destroyed between eight miles (General French's guess) and up to twelve miles (Stewart's) of track. In the capture of the three Federal garrisons they had lost little more than a dozen casualties.[5]

Union cavalry, hovering close to Hood's army, kept Sherman back at Atlanta informed of all this. The Federal commander decided that he would march north with most of his infantry, not so much in hot pursuit of Hood, but more as a means of keeping up with his movements and making sure he was heading out of Georgia. The infantry of Sherman's army group was by now down to six corps, after he dismantled the XVI Corps. On October 3, Sherman issued orders for five of these corps (IV, XIV, XV, XVII and XXIII) to pack ten days' rations and head out of Atlanta to cross the Chattahoochee and get ready to march farther north. Sherman would leave Maj. Gen. Henry Slocum's XX Corps to garrison and guard Atlanta. (When he decided that Hood was heading for Tennessee, in late September Sherman ordered Major General Thomas to go there with an infantry division. In the next five weeks he ordered the IV and XXIII Corps to Tennessee as well.)

Readers of the *Intelligencer* were able to keep up with at least the bare outlines of Sherman's "pursuit." "Three corps of Sherman's army are reported to have left Atlanta, moving in the direction of Hood," the paper reported from Macon on October 8. In that same issue, the *Intelligencer* was able to relate, "there was but one Corps—the 20th of the Yankee army, remaining in Atlanta on Friday [October 7]. Sherman is making a movement with the balance of his troops . . . it would seem to be his intention to 'demonstrate' against the present position of the ARMY OF TENNESSEE."[6]

The *Intelligencer* at this time—as so many Confederate newspapers had done, or were doing—was publishing on a "half sheet," the front and back of a single page. On September 10, the paper announced that it was compelled to issue only a half sheet due to shortage of paper (more was expected soon). It voiced hope that the shrunken editions would only be issued "a few days," although they continued to be printed for the rest of September and throughout October.[7]

This meant that the editor was cramming everything into half of his usual space, as one could have seen in the *Atlanta/Macon Intelligencer* of Sunday, October 9, 1864.

The most important element—then and now—was the news. At the time, Maj. Gen. Sterling Price was leading a Confederate force into Missouri, fighting at Pilot Knob, as the paper reported. Telegraphic news in the *Intelligencer* of October 9 also included word that the *Richmond Enquirer* was "pained at the tone of the President's address to the people of Georgia"—Davis' speech at Macon on September 23 was still being kicked around in the Confederate press.

Then came editorials; Steele noticed that the *Albany* (Georgia) *Patriot* had issued "a fierce denunciation of this journal and Gov. Brown, and a defence of President Davis," probably over the kerfuffle between Steele and Nagle *vs.* the president about his "scoundrel" remark in Macon.

Advertisements have always been a newspaper staple. On the 9th, one Joel D. Simms of Opelika, Ala., posted a $500 reward for the return of a runaway slave named Henry; the "boy" (in his twenties) was described as of "dark copper color." Simms disclosed, "I have reason to believe he was decoyed off by some white man." The slaveowner offered $200 for his property and $300 for the thief.

Exchanges, particularly with Virginia papers, on this day brought information from the *Petersburg Express* about a battle fought between Lee's and Grant's forces at a place called Peeble's farm; "an entire corps of infantry, well supplied with artillery, fell upon our works . . . and by force of numbers, succeeded, after a sharp engagement, in dislodging our troops."

Southern newspapers sharing exchange arrangements with the *Intelligencer* also carried advertisements that occasionally caught the eye of the editor. One such was this "Splendid Advertisement," introduced by the editor:

> We clip the following elegant advertisement from an exchange. Verily the literary excellence of the land arises from every walk and circle and condition of society:
> A CARD.
> Mansion dining room waiting man, of handsome and graceful demeanor, master of his business, and in every way just the servant for a household in generous living, or an officer to make himself comfortable in camp, at private sale by
>
> THOS. W. MORDECAI,
> Registered Auctioneer and Commercial Broker.

Patriotic expressions, big and small, were always to be seen in Confederate newspapers. The *Intelligencer* on October 9 opined that for Americans, "reconstruction will only occur between the blood divided sections of their continent,

'When wrapped in flames the realm of ether glow,/And heaven's last thunder shakes the world below.'"

Public notices included a call from a Confederate quartermaster in Columbus for hides of slaughtered animals, presumably for use in shoe factories. The *Intelligencer* of October 9 featured poetry, too. "I Dream of Home," unsigned by its composer, offered up a tender remembrance of his/her childhood home: "Once more in the old home I stand/And see those dear familiar faces,/The pressure of my mother's hand,/I feel her warm embraces." But, alas, the writer seems to have lost this lovely home, or at least contact with it, for the poem ends, "The verdant lawn, the tranquil lake,/I see in blest moonlight sleeping,/The vision vanishes—I wake/To pass the night in weeping."

Another staple of mid-nineteenth century newspapers—those of all eras, really—was the correspondence received from readers and contributors. The *Intelligencer* of the 9th printed the outraged communication sent in by "SOLDIER" about a Confederate officer in Hood's army—wounded six times previously in the war—who had been seriously wounded in the battle of Jonesboro, shot through the lung. Luckily, he survived and was brought to a Macon hospital, where his wife arrived to help in his convalescence. Medical officers transferred him to a local boardinghouse that he might have more peace and quiet than in the bustling hospital wards. Finally, when allowed to go home for further recovery, the officer and his wife were presented by the boardinghouse keeper with a bill based on *per diem* charges of $20 per day. Was this the price for patriotic sacrifice, the outraged "SOLDIER" asked?

Finally, there were entertainments to be had. The *Intelligencer* on October 9 featured a big notice for a "glorious bill" to be performed at a local theater, featuring "the great drama of THE RENT DAY!," "SINGING AND DANCING," as well as "the Negro Burlesque of Manager in Distress or Talent on a Bust."

And, of course, came the little literary diversions, such as "Fetid. Pedal extremities in old boots," a wry dictionary definition. Not to be overlooked was the odd characterization of wind as "a musician by birth." Finally, there came from the *Troy* (N.Y.) *Whig* the story of the child who talked at birth ("there are numbers who have seen the talking child and insist upon the truth of the stories").[8]

And all this for 25 cents at the *Intelligencer*'s Macon office, Cherry and Third Streets! (By the way, the *Macon Telegraph* is still there now.)

It has been said that Sherman's capture of Atlanta was a severe blow to the Southern people's war-spirit and morale. So it was, as least on the short term.

More durable, as a counterweight, was the continued propagandistic capacity of the Confederate press to vilify the enemy, conjuring up especially odious images of Northern soldiers as destroyers of civilians' homesteads and loathsome despoilers of fair Southern womanhood.

Such is the imagery of a letter first published in the *Columbus* (Georgia) *Times,* and reprinted in the *Intelligencer* of October 25. The writer, a Confederate soldier in Hood's army at Jonesboro, began, "If every man in the Confederacy could look back upon the desolation and ruin that mark the pathway of the Yankee army as they advance, we could then have a spirit of true harmony"—meaning, unity of resolve in the war-torn Confederate States—"and the foul breath that lisps that awful word, 'reconstruction'"—meaning, reunion with the United States—"would be hushed." The soldier referred to "desolated homes and fields" left behind by Northern armies marching through the South, and "the desecrated altars from which thousands of women and children have been ruthlessly driven out upon the world, penniless—homeless."

Then there was "one more spectacle which the fiendish hearts of our invaders have wrought," the blood-chilling scene that the writer stated was just six miles from where he sat. There an elderly mother and father sat drooped with grief in their little cottage, "once the scene of happiness—now misery." Sitting beside the parents, as described by the *Columbus Times'* contributor, was "a young girl, aged about seventeen years." She had been raped by Union soldiers, "the victim of the hellish appetite of these more than devils." The writer had apparently heard the parents' story about the Yankees: "three of them, in broad day light, before the face of these aged parents, outraged her" (*rape* was a word seldom used in Victorian America). The soldier-correspondent concluded that one had only to see "the maniac gaze" of the troubled rape victim, to dismiss any thought of "reconstruction or union with such people."[9]

"Most extraordinary news from Augusta" headlined the *Intelligencer*'s "Telegraphic" column on October 9 (except that the events being reported were not happening at Augusta; in the Press Association's roundabout routing of its wire dispatches, the telegraphed articles received by the *Intelligencer* office in Macon usually carried the names of the cities where they were received by the P. A., and then forwarded on to other subscribing newspapers). In this case, Sherman was following Hood with three corps (it was really five). The article stated that Hood's destination was unknown (true: Hood was heading for Tennessee, but he did not yet know where he would cross the formidable Tennessee River); four Yankee corps were said to be in Atlanta (it was just one); "Federal officers say Sherman will soon move for Macon or Augusta" (this would also prove incorrect). But included was the encouraging news that Hood's wrecking of rails north of Atlanta was having effect: "deserters from Atlanta say no trains have arrived for eight days," which meant that Slocum's garrison there was going hungry. And word was getting out, after the gossip that General Beauregard would be replacing Hood, that instead, Davis was creating a super-department in the West. Borrowing from the *LaGrange* (Ga.) *Reporter and Bulletin*, the *Intelligencer* on October 22 announced that the Creole general "has been placed in command of the two departments of Gen. Hood and Gen. Dick Taylor." It even correctly reported that Beauregard "has the privilege of commanding, *in person,* any portion of the army in this department whenever he chooses." The president had authorized the Military Division commander to take over any field forces in which he was personally present.[10]

But where was Hood going? On October 11, the *Intelligencer* reported that the Army of Tennessee on the 7th had occupied Cartersville and Kingston (35 and 45 miles northwest of Atlanta, respectively). Reports had it that General Beauregard was with Hood's army and was "doubtless directing its movements." This was not quite true. To be sure, on the evening of October 9, the new Military Division commander caught up with Hood at Cave Spring, Ga., thirty miles west of Allatoona and just a few miles from the Alabama line. In their discussions Beauregard allowed Hood to lay out his ideas for the next phase of his campaign, which was to return to the Western & Atlantic and tear it up from Kingston to Tunnel Hill, a train station ten miles south of the Tennessee line.

The *Intelligencer*'s "Telegraphic" columns followed the march of Hood's troops in north Georgia, as well as the unsuccessful attack of French's division on October 5 against Federal troops holding Allatoona Pass. It was hard keeping up with these developments, though, as the *Intelligencer* confessed on October 14. "The utmost secrecy" seemed to surround Hood's army, while "the Yankees also seem to be enveloped in a cloud that hides them from our view." Four days later, readers were told the same: "from the 'Army of Tennessee' we have nothing that we deem reliable to communicate."[11]

Then came word that Hood had indeed struck the Western & Atlantic. The *Intelligencer,* based on telegraphed news from Richmond, announced on October 21 that Hood's men had torn up fifteen miles of track north of Resaca, and then had marched westward. Actually, the Confederates had done more than that: between Resaca and Tunnel Hill, on October 12–13, they had ruined twenty to twenty-five miles of railway before withdrawing from the W. & A. toward Alabama, with Sherman none too aggressively following. By October 15, Hood's forces were at Gaylesville, Alabama, and Sherman was at Dalton. Five days later, Hood was at Gadsden (where General Beauregard joined him) and Sherman at Gaylesville.[12]

Hood's march into north Alabama was being followed by Sherman's rather indifferent "pursuit"—really, he was just chasing Hood's army out of Georgia, to be dealt with by Thomas' forces in Tennessee, so he could return to Atlanta and from there set out on his march toward Savannah. John Steele did not know this, of course, and on the basis of the information before him in the last week of October, as he so often did, the *Intelligencer* editor waxed optimistic. "The masterly strategy on the part of our commander and the activity with which his army answered to the requirements made upon it," he boasted, "is unparalleled in the history of war." Indeed, given Hood's wrecking of the Western & Atlantic and his apparent course toward Tennessee, Steele loftily predicted "the complete evacuation of Georgia by the Yankees, and ere another month shall have passed, our hearts will be gladdened by the joyful tidings that the hated foe will not be in possession of any point South of Chattanooga."[13]

On November 1, the *Intelligencer* stated that the Georgia General Assembly would convene in a couple of days at Milledgeville. It noted that since the previous legislative session, Atlanta and a third of the state had fallen under Federal occupation. As it announced that A. E. Marshall was returning as its legislative reporter at the state capital, the paper also voiced hope that the General Assembly "will resolve and legislate, to make every sacrifice to rescue that portion of our State in possession of the enemy."

John Steele—any Georgian, for that matter—could not have known that within just a few weeks, not only would Sherman's forces not be driven from north Georgia, but that Union soldiers would actually be sitting in the halls of the Capitol at Milledgeville, holding a mock legislative session and repealing Georgia's ordinance of secession.[14]

Worse for the Confederacy, Sherman's 60,000 men would be marching through Georgia virtually unopposed. The main reason was that President Davis and General Hood, conferring at Palmetto September 25–27, had conceived the plan of the Army of Tennessee marching into Sherman's rear, breaking his supply line, and perhaps compelling the Yankees to withdraw from Atlanta. Sherman refused to take the bait, however, and after he had secured Washington's permission to make his march, he waited until Hood had headed into north Alabama before making his preparations to head for Savannah and the sea.

After the war, Jefferson Davis denied having discussed Hood's incursion into Tennessee, but the number of Confederates who remembered that he announced such a campaign during the Palmetto review suggests otherwise. Moreover, after his Palmetto conference with Hood, Davis informed General Bragg, his advisor in Richmond, and Lt. Gen. Dick Taylor, his commander in Montgomery, of the proposed raid; both objected.

In this context, one should recall General Lee's suggestion in mid-September that the president should replace Hood with Beauregard as commander of the Army of Tennessee. (Davis did not.)[15]

In such a setting, omens were bleak for Hood's march into Tennessee.

NOTES

1. Thomas Robson Hay, *Hood's Tennessee Campaign* (Dayton OH: Press of Morningside Bookshop, 1976 [1929]), 19; Sam R. Watkins, *Co. "Aytch" Maury Grays, First Tennessee Regiment or, a Side Show of the Big Show*, ed. by Ruth Hill Fulton McAllister (Franklin TN: Providence House Publishers, 2007 [1882]), 239; Ben Lane, "Letter from the Army of Tennessee" (September 28), *Mobile Advertiser & Register*, Oct. 6, 1864; S. A. Cunningham, "Events Leading to the Battle," *Confederate Veteran*, vol. 18, no. 1 (January 1910), 17; [Sumner A. Cunningham], "Disastrous Campaign in Tennessee," *Confederate Veteran*, vol. 12, no. 7 (July 1904), 338; John A. Simpson, *S. A. Cunningham & the Confederate Heritage* (Athens: University of Georgia Press, 1994), 41.

2. John E. Stanchak, "Franklin and Nashville Campaign, Tenn. (Hood's Tennessee Campaign)" in Patricia L. Faust, ed., *Historical Times Illustrated Encyclopedia of the Civil War* (New York: Harper & Row, 1986), 285–86; "THE POSITION. IN GEORGIA," *ADI*, Sept. 24, 1864.

3. Abstract for Sept. 20, 1864, *OR*, vol. 3, pt. 1, 805; Larry J. Daniel, *Cannoneers in Gray The Field Artillery of the Army of Tennessee 1861–1865* (University: University of Alabama Press, 1984), 167; Connelly, *Autumn of Glory*, 480; Hughes, *Hardee*, 243–48; "LIEUT.-GEN. HARDEE," *ADI*, Oct. 1, 1864; "LIEUT. GENERAL HARDEE," *ADI*, October 2; "GEN. HARDEE'S SPEECH" and "PRESIDENT DAVIS' SPEECH AT AUGUSTA," *ADI*, October 7. :

4. Davis, "Would P. G. T. Lead the A. of T.?," 41; "Telegraphic" (Griffin, October 4), *ADI*, Oct. 5, 1864; "B.," "FROM THE GEORGIA FRONT" and "THE FRONT" (from *Columbus Sun*, October 5), *ADI*, October 7.

5. Brad Butkovich, *The Battle of Allatoona Pass: Civil War Skirmish in Bartow County, Georgia* (Charleston: History Press, 2014), 60–64; William R. Scaife, *Allatoona Pass: A Needless Effusion of Blood* (n.p.: Etowah Valley Historical Society, 1995), 9; French, *Two Wars*, 225;

Phil Gottschalk, *In Deadly Earnest: The Missouri Brigade* (Columbia: Missouri River Press, 1991), 414.

6. Davis, *What the Yankees Did to Us*, 345; Welcher, *Union Army*, vol. 2, 300; Special Field Orders No. 83, October 3, 1864, *OR,* vol. 39, pt. 3, 43; "TELEGRAPHIC. Special to the Memphis Appeal" (Newnan, October 5) and "There was but one Corps—the 20th . . . ," *ADI,* Oct. 8, 1864.

7. "OUR PAPER," *ADI,* Sept. 10, 1864.

8. "TELEGRAPHIC" (Mobile, October 7); "TELEGRAPHIC. . . . The Enquirer is pained"; "THE ALBANY PATRIOT"; "Runaway or Stolen. $500 Reward"; "THE SOUTH SIDE" (*Petersburg Express*); "SPLENDID ADVERTISEMENT"; "RECONSTRUCTION"; "CHIEF QUARTERMASTER'S OFFICE"; "I DREAM OF HOME"; "COMMUNICATED. MR. EDITOR"; "THEATRE"; "Fetid"; "THE WIND AS A MUSICIAN" and "A CHILD THAT TALKED AT BIRTH," all in *ADI,* Oct. 9, 1864; Charles L. Misulia, *Columbus Georgia 1865: The Last True Battle of the Civil War* (Tuscaloosa: University of Alabama Press, 2010), 31.

9. "THE SPIRIT OF THE ARMY" (*Columbus Times*), *ADI,* Oct. 25, 1864.

10. "TELEGRAPHIC: Most extraordinary News from the Front. Via Augusta" (Augusta, October 9) and "GEN. BEAUREGARD," *ADI,* Oct. 11, 1864; Williams, *Beauregard,* 241.

11. "THE POSITION. IN GEORGIA," *ADI,* Oct. 11, 1864; William R. Scaife, *Hood's Campaign for Tennessee* (Kennesaw GA: Kennesaw Mountain Historical Association, 2011 [1986]), f.p. 19; Alfred Roman, *The Military Operations of General Beauregard in the War Between the States 1861 to 1865,* 2 vols. (New York: Harper & Brothers, 1884), vol. 2, 280–81; "Telegraphic" (LaGrange, October 11), *ADI,* October 12; Butkovich, *Allatoona Pass,* 95–132; "THE POSITION. IN GEORGIA," *ADI,* October 14; "THE SITUATION," *ADI,* October 18.

12. "TELEGRAPHIC" (Richmond, October 20), *ADI,* Oct. 21, 1864; Davis, *What the Yankees Did to Us,* 345.

13. "THE POSITION," *ADI,* Oct. 26, 1864; Davis, *What the Yankees Did to Us,* 360–62.

14. "LEGISLATIVE PROCEEDINGS," *ADI,* Oct. 30, 1864; "THE LEGISLATURE," *ADI,* November 1; James C. Bonner, *Milledgeville: Georgia's Antebellum Capital* (Macon: Mercer University Press, 1978), 187.

15. Stephen Davis, *Into Tennessee and Failure: John Bell Hood* (Macon: Mercer University Press, 2020), 32–35, 44, 47–48.

42. Lincoln Is Re-Elected

IN EARLY NOVEMBER 1864, John B. Hood's Army of Tennessee was encamped in north Alabama, waiting to begin its march into Tennessee. At the same time, Robert E. Lee's Army of Northern Virginia was settling into winter quarters at the Petersburg-Richmond front. With both theaters virtually static, editor John Steele was forced to gather war news from a lot of different places to fill his newspaper, even though it was continuing to be published as a half-sheet. On November 3, it printed a letter written by Confederate lieutenant Bennett H. Young on how, October 19, he had led twenty men in a daring raid from Canada against St. Albans, Vt., a town of some 5,000 residents about sixteen miles south of the U.S. border. Young explained that "I went there for the purpose of burning the town and surrounding villages, in retaliation for the recent outages committed in the Shenandoah Valley" by Union Maj. Gen. Philip Sheridan's soldiers. In early October the Federals burned barns, mills, crops and slaughtered livestock in what Valley inhabitants came to call "The Burning."[1]

Young was more than a freelance marauder (unlike, say, William Quantrill, who with his guerrillas had led a bloody, destructive raid on Lawrence, Kansas a year before). Young's mission of attacking and burning New England towns near Canada's border had been approved by no less than Confederate Secretary of War James A. Seddon. "It is but right," Seddon had instructed, "that the people of New England and Vermont especially, some of whose officers and troops have been foremost in these excesses and whose people have approved of their course, should have brought home to them some of the horrors of such warfare." Indeed, after Young robbed the St. Albans banks, sacked and burned the town, Seddon suggested that Burlington, Vt., be his next target.

On the night of October 18, Young and twenty men slipped into St. Albans and checked into hotels. The next afternoon they gathered in the street, took off their overcoats to show Confederate uniforms, and proclaimed that they were taking possession of the town in the name of the Confederate States. While some men robbed banks and rounded up horses, others set fires with glass jars of Greek fire, the igneous liquid. With $20,000 in their saddlebags, Young and his cohorts rode out of town, burning a bridge to halt a small group of Federal pursuers.

This was the exploit referred to by Lieutenant Young in his *Intelligencer* article, which was reprinted from a Canadian newspaper, the *Evening Telegraph*. "I am a commissioned officer of the Provisional Army of the Confederate States, and have violated no laws of Canada," he explained. In Canada, though, Young and five of his men were captured by some angry residents of St. Albans, who had the Southerners put in jail. U.S. authorities requested their extradition, but the Canadian government refused. They were ultimately released.[2]

In its "Telegraphic" news column of November 4, the *Intelligencer* related from New York and Baltimore papers that Lincoln had declared Nevada as a state, newly admitted to the Union. It was all about politics. The year of 1864 was election time in the United States, and President Lincoln worried after the Democrats nominated a popular Union general, George B. McClellan, as their candidate that he might lose. The Democratic platform played to many Northerners' war weariness, which Southerners picked up on. Confederates hoped for McClellan's election and the possibility that as president he might work for a truce to end the bloodshed—which might in turn lead to recognition of the Confederates States. Lincoln feared that the North's antiwar sentiment might defeat him. Indeed, on August 23, he wrote a memo predicting his defeat, which he asked his cabinet members to sign sight unseen. But then Atlanta had fallen, and Sheridan had defeated Confederate Lt. Gen. Jubal Early's forces in the Valley at Winchester, September 19. Lincoln accordingly believed his re-election prospects were brighter, and in the first week of October listed the states he thought he would win, and also listed those he believed would go to McClellan. Beside them he added up their electoral votes: "Genl. McClellan 114"; "Abraham Lincoln, 117." This was obviously a razor-thin margin of victory, so Old Abe pulled something from his bag of tricks. Despite Nevada Territory's population of only 20,000 whites—the Northwest Ordinance of 1787, which had allowed admission of Ohio, Indiana and other "northwestern" states, called for an adult male population of 60,000 in each territory—Lincoln rushed Nevada's admission of the Union on Oct. 31, 1864, a week before the election. (A hastily drafted state constitution was telegraphed to Washington at a cost of $3,000.) In the end, Lincoln handily won re-election, carrying 212 electoral votes to McClellan's 21. "Little Mac" had taken just three states (New Jersey, Kentucky and Delaware), not the eight that Lincoln had guessed a month earlier.[3]

After the fall of Atlanta, Confederates realized that Hood's failure to hold the city had strengthened Lincoln's re-election prospects. The *Richmond Examiner*, as early as September 5, opined that the loss of Atlanta "will render incalculable assistance to the party of Lincoln, and obscures the prospect of peace, late so bright." It was in this spirit—acceptance of the inevitable—that just before the Northern election results were known, the *Intelligencer* tried to downplay the likelihood of Lincoln's re-election. In an editorial entitled, "Election Day at the North," the paper braced readers for the untoward outcome: "we venture confidently to predict that Lincoln will be the successful candidate." Not only that, but the editorial declared, "Be it so!"—or, in today's parlance, "bring it on!" The election of Lincoln obviously meant a prolongation of the war, "more treasure wasted, more widows and orphans made, more blood to drench the earth! Well, we again say, be it so!" The *Intelligencer* urged Southerners to resolve to continue fighting; "let us teach our enemy, that until the independence of the South is recognized we shall never, no *never*, lay down our arms!"[4]

After this, the confirmation of Lincoln's electoral victory was almost anticlimactic, as the *Intelligencer* reported during the second week of November. In a New York newspaper was to be seen, "The Herald editorially announces the re-election of Lincoln." The *New York Tribune* was able to list the states the Republican had won; this was in the *Intelligencer* on November 13. And on the 15th the *Intelligencer* could also name the three states that had gone for McClellan.[5]

So the prospects for peace, brought about by a possible armistice negotiated with a Democratic president, were dashed, and a protracted war lay ahead. Echoing the *Intelligencer*'s editorial of November 9, the *Richmond Examiner* two days later observed, "the Yankee nation has committed itself to a game of all or nothing; and so must we."

Confederates' mortification over Lincoln's electoral win is well known. Less recognized is the spirit of gritty determination voiced by the *Intelligencer* at the prospect of a continued and exhausting war.

At the same time, cheering news could be had closer to home. On November 6, the *Intelligencer* announced that on the previous day, a gentleman had visited its Macon office, at Cherry and Third, and said that he wanted to buy twenty-one three-month subscriptions. This was indeed a "substantial compliment to the INTELLIGENCER," the paper proudly declared. It was more than that: the purchaser paid cash on the spot, which at $5 a month, came to $315. In celebrating this "highly complimentary and cheering" news, the *Intelligencer* graciously expressed its wish that someone would pay "so handsome a compliment" to its two competitors in Macon, the *Confederacy* and the *Telegraph and Confederate*.[6]

Little could editor John Steele predict that within a fortnight the *Intelligencer* would no longer be publishing in Macon.

NOTES

1. "LETTER FROM THE COMMANDER IN THE ST. ALBANS EXPEDITION," *ADI*, Nov. 3, 1864; Jeffry D. Wert, "Sheridan's Shenandoah Valley Campaign" in Patricia L. Faust, ed., *Historical Times Illustrated Encyclopedia of the Civil War* (New York: Harper & Row, 1986), 677–78.

2. Herman Hattaway, "Raid on Lawrence, Kans." in Patricia L. Faust, ed., *Historical Times Illustrated Encyclopedia of the Civil War* (New York: Harper & Row, 1986), 427; Oscar A. Kinchen, *General Bennett H. Young Confederate Raider and a Man of Many Adventures* (West Hanover MA: Christopher Publishing House, 1981), 39; Oscar A. Kinchen, *Confederate Operations in Canada and the North: A Little-Known Phase of the American Civil War* (North Quincy MA: Christopher Publishing House, 1970), 128–29; John W. Headley, "The Confederates Raid Vermont" in Philip Van Doren Stern, ed., *Secret Missions of the Civil War* (New York: Bonanza Books, 1959), 245–46.

3. "TELEGRAPHIC," *ADI*, Nov. 4, 1864; Harold Holzer, *The Civil War in 50 Objects* (New York: Viking, 2013), 292, 294; James West Davidson and Mark H. Lytle, *The United States: A History of the Republic* (Englewood Cliffs NJ: Prentice-Hall, 1981), 148 (Northwest Ordinance); Josephy, *Civil War in the West*, 262; Allan Nevins, *The War for the Union: The Organized War to Victory 1864–1865* (New York: Charles Scribner's Sons, 1971), 140; Robert E. Lowe, "Lincoln, the Fall of Atlanta, and the 1864 Presidential Election," *Georgia Historical Quarterly*, vol. 100, no. 3 (2016). 260–89.

4. Nelson, *Bullets, Ballots, and Rhetoric*, 126; "ELECTION DAY AT THE NORTH," *ADI*, Nov. 9, 1864.

5. "TELEGRAPHIC," *ADI*, Nov. 13, 1864; "TELEGRAPHIC," *ADI*, November 15.

6. John C. Waugh, *Reelecting Lincoln: The Battle for the 1864 Presidency* (New York: Crown Publishers, 1997), 358; "AN INCIDENT—CHEERING AND COMPLIMENTARY," *ADI*, Nov. 6, 1864.

43. The *Intelligencer* Returns to a Ruined City

TO OUR PATRONS.

In a few days we will again in this city resume the regular daily and weekly publication of the Intelligencer. Nearly all the material for the same has arrived. Until then we will give them only a synopsis daily of current events.

WITH THIS ANNOUNCEMENT on Dec. 10, 1864, the *Atlanta Daily Intelligencer* informed readers that it had returned to its home town.

Its last issue in Macon was that of November 18, when the paper reported that Sherman and his army had left Atlanta and were marching in a southeasterly direction across Georgia. A few days before, on the 15th, the *Intelligencer* reported ominously that "on last Thursday" (November 10), Federal soldiers in Atlanta "had been engaged during several days in destroying all articles and material that they could not carry with them." This was astute reporting on two major developments: 1) that Sherman had ordered the destruction in Atlanta of everything that could be used by Confederates when they returned—factories, railroad roundhouses and workshops, not to mention the train track itself; and 2) that the Federal army was then going to abandon Atlanta (though the newspaper could not predict where it was going). "The evidences that they were evacuating the place were very plain," the *Intelligencer* claimed. Among those evidences was that the few Union sympathizers—maybe a couple hundred—who had been allowed to stay in the city were now taking the last trains north. "Dunning, Schofield, Markham, Stone and all the rest of the mongrel curs took their departure last week," the paper snarled, referring to the prominent Northern sympathizers James L. Dunning, Lewis Scofield, William Markham and Amherst Stone.

Then the *Intelligencer* added a bleak prediction about the once-proud Gate City of the South: "the Yankees have informed those from whom we get the information, that they will blow up that portion of the city that they cannot burn."[1]

The paper was definitely onto something. Sherman had conceived the idea for his next campaign: after sending enough infantry back to Maj. Gen. George Thomas at Nashville to deal with Hood's army, he proposed to Grant, Halleck and even Lincoln that he would "destroy Atlanta and then march across Georgia to Savannah and Charleston, breaking roads and doing irreparable damage," as he wrote Grant on October 1. "I can make the march, and make Georgia howl," he boasted. After the Washington authorities had given their consent, Sherman wrote Grant on November 6 that before he set out, he would see that "Atlanta itself is utterly destroyed."

By November 11, satisfied that Hood intended to march into Tennessee where Thomas was gathering forces to meet him, Sherman and his troops in north Georgia started marching back toward Atlanta. On that day he directed his chief engineer, Capt. Orlando Poe, to begin the destruction in the city that had been previously planned. Northern engineers and pioneer troops (those designated for special labor) then began knocking down factories such as Winship's Foundry, burning the suburban gas works, and destroying downtown railway facilities, such as the Car Shed, machine shops and freight houses. Sherman's soldiers, marching into the city from northwest Georgia, saw that "the pioneers were having all the fun," and started setting fires of their own. The first unauthorized arson occurred on November 11. Four days later, on the 15th—the day of the heaviest burning—the 7th Illinois was marching into the city; Surgeon E. P. Burton observed that "many houses had been burned and all day long the fires kept increasing in number." Capt. James R. Ladd was entering *via* Marietta Street on the 15th. "We arrived in the suburbs of Atlanta at 2 p.m.," he recorded in his diary; "no sooner did we arrive than the boys commenced burning every house in part of the town [in the area of today's Georgia Tech campus]. The wind was blowing hard at the time and soon that part of the city was gone." There was more destruction downtown as well: a map prepared by the 33rd Massachusetts, one of the three provost guards regiments occupying Atlanta, showed that the brick business district lining both sides of Whitehall and Peachtree Streets was marked for burning; Sherman wanted no brick structures left that the returning Confederates could use. This included the Intelligencer building in the block of Whitehall south of the railroad; the newspaper offices ceased to exist in the fires of November 15, 1864.

The commanding general himself had ridden into Atlanta the day before. From his downtown quarters the next night he could see the red glow from all the fires raging in the city. On the morning of the 16th Sherman rode out to begin leading his 60,000 veterans across the state. In his memoirs he recalled looking back and seeing what was left of Atlanta, "smouldering and in ruins, the black smoke rising high in the air, and hanging like a pall over the ruined city."[2]

Maj. Gen. Joseph Wheeler's cavalry had been watching all of this activity, and on November 17 Southern horsemen rode into a wrecked and depopulated Atlanta. Then looters arrived, people living nearby who came to see what they could make off with. Eventually more respectable citizens returned and restored order.

This was the situation when John Steele rode into Atlanta, probably in the first days of December, after word had reached Macon that people were coming back. He evidently brought with him a small hand press, paper, ink, type and compositors' equipment, the "material" that the issue of December 10 mentioned as nearly all having arrived. As for staff, Steele may have brought workers who had helped him during the paper's Macon sojourn, July–November 1864; he may also have hired new employees (in March 1865, the *Intelligencer* mentioned "our Pressman," one William Whitmire).

The contents of that first "extra"—front-only, on untinted paper, measuring 11 ¾" by 16 ¾"—showed just how quickly the *Intelligencer* was able to return to its familiar, if less lengthy, look. There were public service announcements: the city postmaster, "Col. Howard," announced that mail service would soon be restored. Also, telegraphic connection with Macon was predicted in ten or twelve days; railroad linkage to Augusta was forecast in forty. Official documents lined the right side of the sheet, headed by Capt. Thomas L. Dodd's declaration, dated December 5, that he had "assumed the duties of Provost Marshal of this Military Post," another signal that order was being restored in Atlanta.[3]

Surely the most remarkable article in the *Intelligencer Extra* of Dec. 10, 1864, was its almost street-by-street description of the destruction that Sherman's soldiers had wreaked in Atlanta before they left. The piece detailed both destruction ("Whitehall street from Roark's corner up to Peachtree street is one entire mass of ruins") and structural survival ("on Pryor street the buildings from Hunter street are all standing"). "All the churches with the exception of the Episcopal Church, on Walton street, are preserved"—referring to St. Luke's, which had been built in the spring of 1864 by Confederate chaplain Charles Quintard, and which occupying Federals had called "the Rebel church." To be sure, all the downtown railroad facilities had been wrecked. The article concluded with a mixed message: "To our absent citizens we would say return as soon as possible, and with one mind commence to extricate ourselves from the ruin detailed upon us by the God-forsaken, miserable and deluded Yankee crew."[4]

In another instance of notable journalism, the *Intelligencer Extra* of December 10 managed to summarize accurately Sherman's order to his troops about how their upcoming campaign was to be conducted. On November 16, in one of its last issues at Macon, the *Intelligencer* cited the *Chicago Times* for the news regarding Sherman that "after gathering sufficient supplies, he will start with five corps on a winter tour through the cotton States, leaving a force to look after Hood." In its "Extra" of December 10, the *Intelligencer* did not specify where the Union army's "tour through the cotton States" would take it, but based on an account in the *New York Herald*, the paper correctly reported that four Federal infantry corps, split into two wings commanded by Maj. Gens. Oliver O. Howard and Henry A. Slocum, would be marching along parallel routes, covering fifteen miles a day. The cavalry, commanded by Brig. Gen. Judson Kilpatrick "will forage on the country and not destroy property in localities where they are unmolested," the *Intelligencer* announced; "horses, mules, wagons, and able-bodied negroes will be appropriated freely."[5]

Sherman's "march to the sea" would have enormous impact on Georgians. Some of his troops were in motion on November 15, but the operation may be said to have begun the next morning when the commanding general rode out of a devastated Atlanta. The Federals' four corps consisted of 55,255 infantry, 4,500 cavalry and 1,750 artillery (with 68 guns), totaling 61,500 troops. Against them, scattered Confederate forces numbered no more than 8,500—Wheeler's cavalry, some state militia and local defense units. They could only harass Sherman's inexorable advance to Savannah, which eventually became evident as his objective. The city-by-the-coast was some 225 miles southeast of Atlanta by direct line, and much longer by march route. Rather, *routes*, for the four Federal corps advanced in as many columns on a front fully fifty miles wide. The left wing (XIV and XX Corps) and right (XV, XVII) took only a week to reach Milledgeville, back then the state capital. The only "battle" along the way occurred at a place called Griswoldville, ten miles east of Macon. There some 2,300 poorly armed old men and boys were imprudently ordered to charge 1,500 veteran Northern infantry prepared to meet them. The Southerners were predictably repulsed with equally predictably lopsided casualties: 473 C.S., 94 U.S.

Ninety miles east of Griswoldville is the town of Millen, which Sherman entered on December 3. The next day the Federals resumed their march to Savannah. The *Intelligencer* kept up with these events as best it could. A letter received from Savannah, dated December 10, had been printed by the *Macon Telegraph and Confederate*, from which the *Intelligencer* stated that the Yankees were fifteen miles from Savannah "and still advancing." On December 13, Sherman's forces established communication with Union vessels offshore. They then began a siege of Savannah, whose defenses were manned by some 10,000 Confederates under Lieutenant General Hardee, formerly corps commander in Hood's army. Given the two forces' numerical disparity, the outcome of the operation was never in doubt. For instance, on December 13, a Federal division of 1,500 stormed and took Fort McAllister, an earthwork on the Ogeechee River fourteen miles south of Savannah, which was manned by just 150 Confederates. Casualties in the brief fight numbered 16 killed and 54 wounded among the garrison (with the rest captured), and 24 killed and 110 wounded among the attackers (mostly from land mines the Southerners had planted).

The *Intelligencer* reported McAllister's fall on December 17, again borrowing from the *Macon Telegraph and Confederate*. That day John Steele published an editorial that can be seen as a sign both of stubborn optimism and reality-blindness. With Sherman twenty miles from Savannah, and Hood's army having fought a very bloody battle at Franklin, Tennessee, south of Nashville, the *Intelligencer*'s editor launched forth with one of his most preposterous propositions. Referring to Sherman and his "worse than vandal hordes," Steele declared, "If the God of battles shall favor us highly, and deliver into our hands these vile marauders, who have committed such waste and destruction, and been guilty of unparalleled outrages, in passing through our State, and then the noble State of Tennessee shall be redeemed by the gallant Hood and his brave troops, as the latest information from the West would seem to promise, we shall close the year 1864 with a chapter of greater success than was ever before vouchsafed to any people on earth, notwithstanding some sad reverses which we have endured."

Alas, the God of battles did not cooperate. Hardee's troops evacuated Savannah on the night of December 21; Federals entered Savannah the next day. On the 22nd, Sherman sent President Lincoln a short telegram: "I beg to present you, as a Christmas gift, the city of Savannah, with 150 heavy guns and plenty of ammunition, and also about 25,000 bales of cotton" (it was actually more than 38,000 bales).[6]

News from Tennessee was even bleaker. In the last week of November, Hood's army marched into Tennessee heading toward Nashville. First they encountered Maj. Gen. John Schofield's small army at Franklin, eighteen miles southwest of Nashville. Determined to thrash Schofield before he could slip north and join George Thomas' larger force in the Tennessee capital, on November 30 Hood ordered a frontal assault against Schofield's fortified lines.

The *Intelligencer* picked up this news in snippets. On December 12, the paper abruptly reported, "the fight at Franklin is confirmed, and our army on the 3d instant was within six miles of Nashville." Apparently some very bloody fighting had occurred, as this short piece continued: ". . . the casualties not stated, except the death of the following General officers: Gens. Cleburn [*sic*], Strahl, Granberry [*sic*], Gist, John Adams; and Gens. John Brown, Canty [*sic*], Manigault, Quarles, Cockerille [*sic*] and Scott, wounded; and General Gordon captured. At last accounts our cavalry were pursuing the enemy."

This was a brutally brief glance at one of the war's bloodiest battles. As historian Thomas Robson Hay counts them, Hood's infantry at Franklin numbered 20,087 against Schofield's 22,830, who had the advantage of fighting behind breastworks. The Confederates charged desperately, reaching the Federals' earthworks and at places pouring over them, but by the end of the five hours' engagement they were repulsed. Their courage and determination, however, were attested by the *Intelligencer*'s listing of general officer casualties, which was unusually accurate.

In relating all of this carnage, the *Intelligencer* erred only once: Brig. Gen. James Cantey was not at Franklin (home, ill). But the most tragic element of the Confederate casualty count came from the number of killed and wounded among officers of lesser rank and the enlisted men themselves. A recent writer on the battle of Franklin, Eric Jacobson, tallies up 1,750 Southerners killed, 3,800 wounded and another 700 captured for at least 6,250. Schofield's losses came to 189 killed, 1,033 wounded and 1,104 missing for a total of 2,326.[7]

The irony of Hood's bloody repulse at Franklin was that the next morning, December 1, his troops actually commanded the battlefield. During the night, Schofield's troops quietly slipped back, crossed the Harpeth River and withdrew toward Nashville. Hood followed and south of the capital established a defensive line, essentially daring George Thomas to come out and attack him, despite the weakened state of his army. The *Intelligencer*, which re-established its "TELEGRAPHIC ITEMS" column on December 12, was able to relate a little of all this. From the *New York Herald*, "the rebels . . . fought with the desperation of demons"; from a Richmond dispatch, "Schofield's troops fell back to a point three miles south of Nashville. The bridges across the Harpeth were burned"; "New York and Baltimore papers . . . contain additional details of the battle at Franklin, in which a repulse of Hood, with heavy loss, is reiterated."[8]

While struggling to stay abreast of these events, the *Intelligencer* related the steps by which Atlantans were trying to reestablish their city. First need was food. "To our country friends who have been fortunate enough to escape the clutches of the Yankee hordes," it suggested on December 10, "we would advise them to bring it in, as there is a great scarcity of everything in the city." The paper repeated its call for provisions ten days later in an article titled "to our country friends." It began by reminding readers that the *Intelligencer* had returned to Atlanta "after its temporary exile," and that it would continue to promote the best interests of the city's citizens. In that promotion, the paper again urged "our up country friends" to help out "by bringing in such provisions as they can spare." It added that the Confederate commandant in Atlanta, Col. Luther J. Glenn, promised that authorities would not interfere with the people's horses or mule teams—the kind of expropriation of animals that was said to have occurred in the last days that Confederate troops were stationed in the city.

There were indeed more mouths to feed; the *Intelligencer* announced on December 12, "the city is fast filling up." On December 16, it reported that the evening before, Jared Whitaker, the newspaper's proprietor, had returned to the city, bringing his family. "Many of our old citizens are coming in to make arrangements for the return of their families," it added, predicting confidently that "soon all the houses left in our ruined city will be occupied."[9]

Atlanta had always been a railroad town, so news about the repair of its rail linkages was an important index of a city rebuilding. The *Intelligencer* of December 14 publicized the departure and arrival times of the Macon train. The next day an issue announced that a railroad superintendent predicted that the Atlanta and West Point line, which had been torn up by Sherman's troops in late August, would be repaired by January 10. Meanwhile, because the Federals had destroyed the Western & Atlantic railroad bridge before they left, the *Extra* on December 16 stated that Green & Howell's ferry over the Chattahoochee was the only one operating on the river between Warsaw and Campbellton—a distance of almost forty miles by crow's flight.

As a sign of the *Intelligencer*'s own status, the paper on December 16 informed readers "we are now prepared to do Book and Job Work of every description, and also Ruling and Binding." It was thus evident that the enterprise had definitely set up shop in Atlanta, though it did not divulge the location of its new office in the city. "Our Exchanges will please send us their papers to Atlanta instead of Macon," the *Intelligencer* declared on December 17. Below this request, as further evidence of just how important newspaper exchanges were, was the question directed to "our contemporaries why they do not send us their papers?" The rationale was obvious: "with our railroads torn up and the telegraph wires down, we have but little chance to hear what is going on in the great outside world."[10]

The *Intelligencer*'s issue of December 20 was printed in its pre-Maconian four-page layout. On its front page was a report by Georgia militia general William P. Howard to Governor Brown (taken from the *Macon Telegraph and Confederate*) on the structural damage he had observed in Atlanta. Much of page two was filled with a long article, "Atlanta—Her Past, Her Present, and Her Future," which reviewed the city's origins and prewar growth, its contributions to the Confederacy, as well as its current ruined condition. Yet if her citizens "put their own shoulders to the wheel," the paper predicted that Atlanta would rise "to her former greatness." On the third page was another infomercial for Robert Crawford, the slave dealer who had moved his operations to Macon. "Thoroughly posted in the question of supply and demand—candid and fair in all his dealings—courteous in his manners, and obliging in his deportment," the paper cooed (and mind you, it was describing someone who bought and sold African American human beings as "property"). The *Intelligencer* advised that "those who wish to purchase or sell will find it to their advantage to give him a call." Finally, on the back page, usually the place for ads, there was a long one for the *Intelligencer*'s own Book and Job Office.[11]

But the increase in size and content came at a higher price. On December 16, the paper had proudly reprinted a statement from the *Albany* (GA) *Patriot* that the *Intelligencer* was returning to Atlanta and that "its rates we suppose will be as formerly—$5.00 per month." They were not. On the front page of its issue of December 20 was posted the new subscription rate of $6 per month ($12 for two months, $18 for three).[12]

Having demonstrated its resilience, the newspaper took a few days off. On Christmas morning, Sunday, December 25, the *Intelligencer* announced that its staff would be taking vacation on the next Tuesday, returning to work Wednesday, so that an issue would be put out on Thursday morning, the 29th. Then the editor indulged in a little Christmas cheer. "The usual merry greetings, notwithstanding the ruins by which we, in Atlanta, are surrounded," John

Steele predicted, "will prevail, innocent and cheering as they are to both old and young." He reminded readers that this was "a Christian's Sabbath" and urged its observance by the faithful. Besides, in the city, though the enemy had "rioted within its limits, and then attempted to destroy it," there was still much to be grateful for. "Be not despondent or cast down, but fail not especially on this day, to give thanks to HIM who saved so much for our once proud and prosperous city from the destructive element which a fierce and cruel foe invoked to destroy it," Steele urged.

"It will again rise from the ashes!"[13]

In 1887 Atlanta's City Council changed its official seal by removing the rather graceless locomotive it had adopted in 1854. In its place it conceived a broad-winged phoenix, the legendary mythical eagle rising out of flames. Two dates were added, *1847* and *1865*: the former was the year of Atlanta's incorporation, and the latter was the beginning of a massive rebuilding of the ruined city. More important, replacing *City Council* was *Resurgens*, the Latin participle for "rising again."

With its editorial of Dec. 25, 1864, the *Intelligencer* beat the city fathers by two decades.

NOTES

1. "TO OUR PATRONS," *ATLANTA DAILY INTELLIGENCER—EXTRA*, Dec. 10, 1864; "FROM THE FRONT IN GEORGIA," *ADI*, November 18; "FROM ATLANTA," *ADI*, November 15; Thomas G. Dyer, *Secret Yankees: The Union Circle in Confederate Atlanta* (Baltimore: Johns Hopkins University Press, 1999) 109, 111, 197.

2. Davis, *What the Yankees Did to Us*, 360–62, 365, 370–71, 378, 389, 391, 393, 397, 402.

3. Davis, *What the Yankees Did to Us*, 404, 412–14; "TO OUR PATRONS," "THE MAILS," "TELEGRAPH," "GEORGIA RAILROAD," "PROVOST MARSHAL'S OFFICE" and "NORTHERN ITEMS," *ADI EXTRA*, Dec. 10, 1864.

4. "THE CITY," *ADI EXTRA*, Dec. 10, 1864; Davis, *What the Yankees Did to Us*, 405–406, 409, 414.

5. "TELEGRAPHIC," *ADI*, Nov. 16, 1864; "MOBILE, Dec. 3 . . . ," *ADI Extra*, December 10; Alan Bussel, "The Atlanta *Daily Intelligencer* Covers Sherman's March," *Journalism Quarterly*, vol. 51, no. 3 (Autumn 1974), 410.

6. William R. Scaife, *The March to the Sea* (Saline MI: McNaughton & Gunn, 1993), 19, 35, 39, 50–51, 55–56, 60, 70, 85, 112; William Harris Bragg, "Griswoldville" in John C. Inscoe, ed., *The Civil War In Georgia* (Athens: University of Georgia Press, 2011), 97; "FROM SHERMAN'S ARMY" ("Tel. & Confed."), "SAVANNAH" and "THE SITUATION," *ADI EXTRA*, December 17; "FROM HOOD'S ARMY" AND "TELEGRAPHIC

ITEMS," *ADI EXTRA*, December 12; Lawrence, *Present for Mr. Lincoln*, 184–86, 199, 208; Derek Smith, *Civil War Savannah* (Savannah: Frederic C. Beil, 1997), 205.

7. Richard M. McMurry, *John Bell Hood and the War for Southern Independence* (Lexington: University Press of Kentucky, 1982), 170–77; "FROM HOOD'S ARMY," *ADI EXTRA*, Dec. 12, 1864; Hay, *Hood's Tennessee Campaign*, 246 n.40, 41; James Lee McDonough and Thomas L. Connelly, *Five Tragic Hours* (Knoxville: University of Tennessee Press, 1983), 129, 136, 139, 147, 149; James Dinkins, *1861 to 1865 Personal Recollections and Experiences in the Confederate Army By an Old Johnnie* (Dayton OH: Press of Morningside Bookshop, 1975 [1897]), 237–38; Eric A. Jacobson and Richard A. Rupp, *For Cause & for Country: A Study of the Affair at Spring Hill and the Battle of Franklin* (Franklin TN: O'More Publishing, 2008), 417.

8. James R. Knight, *Hood's Tennessee Campaign: The Desperate Venture of a Desperate Man* (Charleston: History Press, 2014), 89–90; "TELEGRAPHIC ITEMS" (Richmond, December 4 and 5), *ADI EXTRA*, Dec. 12, 1864.

9. "To our country friends . . . ," *ADI EXTRA*, Dec. 10, 1864; "TO OUR COUNTRY FRIENDS," *ADI*, December 20; "PERSONAL," *ADI EXTRA*, December 12; "We were pleased . . . ," *ADI EXTRA*, December 16.

10. "The Macon & Western R.R. mails . . . ," *ADI EXTRA*, Dec. 14, 1864; "ATLANTA AND WEST POINT RAILROAD," *ADI EXTRA*, December 15; Davis, *What the Yankees Did to Us*, 385; "We are requested to state. . . . " and "We are now prepared . . . ," *ADI EXTRA*, December 16; "Our Exchanges will please. . . . " and "We are under obligations . . . ," *ADI EXTRA*, December 17.

11. W. P. Howard, "From the Telegraph and Confederate. ATLANTA AS LEFT BY THE ENEMY," "ATLANTA—HER PAST, HER PRESENT, AND HER FUTURE," "COL. ROBERT A. CRAWFORD" and "BOOK AND JOB OFFICE," *ADI*, Dec. 20, 1864.

12. "ATLANTA INTELLIGENCER," *ADI EXTRA*, Dec. 16, 1864; "SUBSCRIPTION RATES," *ADI*, December 20.

13. "In order that the Employees. . . . " and "CHRISTMAS," *ADI*, Dec. 25, 1864; Garrett, *A & E*, vol. 2, 131.

44. The Debate to Arm the Slaves

FOLLOWING THE BATTLE AT FRANKLIN, the *Intelligencer* had traced Hood's advance on Nashville and his establishment of a defensive line south of the Tennessee capital. The Southern press speculated on his next move. On December 25, the *Intelligencer* reprinted an article from the *Griffin Rebel* pondering the question of whether Hood would attack the Federal garrison in an attempt to capture Nashville. (No, it counseled; the place was well fortified, too many men would be lost, and the city was not that important anyway.) A few days later the *Intelligencer* offered its guess that Hood would make no attempt to take Nashville, but would fall back upon a defensive line near Franklin or Murfreesboro, south of the capital, and there go into winter quarters while preparing for an attack by Thomas' Federal forces. "What is Nashville, or its possession, to us," the paper asked, "compared to the cost of taking and holding it?" It echoed a point made in the *Rebel*: "the preservation of our armies is more now to be considered than the occupation of any city."[1]

Then disturbing reports started coming in. On December 29, the *Intelligencer* stated that according to Northern newspapers perused at Richmond, General Thomas' Union army had driven Hood from Nashville to Franklin and that "Hood's army [was] completely demoralized." Two days later the paper offered the brief statement, "Nashville telegrams report that Hood continues to retreat, pursued by Thomas." News continued to dribble in from Tennessee. From the *Selma Reporter* came this, as related in the *Intelligencer* on January 5: "Gen. Hood, on the eve of withdrawing from before Nashville, was attacked vigorously by the enemy, who massed a heavy force and threw it upon his centre, composed of Cheatham's and Bate's divisions.—Those veterans gave way. Hood then moved on Columbia where he was at latest dates."

This was as close to conceding defeat as the Confederate press could offer. After Thomas notified Washington of his victory over Hood at Nashville, Northern papers were quick to celebrate it, and Southern papers had to take notice. According to the *Intelligencer* of January 5, the *Mobile Advertiser & Register* drew from St. Louis papers of December 20–21 the following:

> The battle commenced on the 15th. The first day Thomas succeeded in driving Hood from his entrenchments, capturing 18 pieces of artillery and 1500 prisoners—the loss on both sides being very heavy.
>
> During the night Hood constructed a new line of earthworks, from which he was driven on the 16th, losing 4000 prisoners and half his artillery.
>
> He continued to fall back, closely pursued by Thomas, who telegraphs that he had captured about five thousand prisoners. . . . Hood is trying to cross Duck river. His army is completely demoralized. Heavy rains have checked pursuit.[2]

The St. Louis papers, the *Intelligencer*'s indirect source for this account of the battle of Nashville, had gotten the story pretty accurately.

George Thomas had earned the nickname of "Rock of Chickamauga" after he had saved Rosecrans' army in September 1863. There was a downside to that lapidary strength, however, and it was reflected in another sobriquet Thomas had acquired: "Old Slow Trot." In early December, with General Grant pressing him to move against Hood, Slow Trot patiently amassed his forces until he had some 55,000 troops—more than twice the size of Hood's 23,000. Finally, on December 15 he gave the order to advance. That afternoon the Federal assault overwhelmed Hood's left, where Confederate resistance crumbled and Southern soldiers ran for the rear. Darkness ended the Union pursuit as Hood shored up another defensive line a mile to the south. Thomas attacked that point on the 16th, and once more the Federal assault crushed the Confederate left. Again, Southern soldiers ran from the field, throwing down their weapons in utter rout while officers vainly called on them to rally. Thomas' cavalry pursued as Hood's army retreated back toward Franklin.

When the battle of Nashville, Dec. 15–16, 1864, was toted up, Hood's losses came to 1,500 killed/wounded, but 4,500 officers and men captured (including three generals), more than a quarter of the army's strength. Moreover, Hood had to admit the loss of fully fifty-four pieces of artillery, the second largest battlefield cannon-haul during the entire war (Rosecrans gave up sixty-six guns at Chickamauga).

Hood's rout at Nashville was worse than Bragg's at Missionary Ridge the year before. The simple reason was that after it had ended its retreat at Corinth in north Mississippi by January 10, the Army of Tennessee had ceased to exist as a cohesive fighting force. Confederates themselves admitted this. "Hood is a compleet [*sic*] failure," George W. Peddy, surgeon for the 56th Georgia, wrote his wife two days after Christmas; "we have nothing left but a remnant of a demoralized army." Another Southerner, W. H. Reynolds, wrote his wife on January 15 about the condition of his comrades, "it seems that they are not going to get over it Soon, especially if Gen. Hood remains in command."

Reynolds had sensed the situation. John Bell Hood submitted his resignation on January 13, 1865, just before General Beauregard arrived at Corinth to relieve him from command.[3]

Atlantans in January 1865 would not have been privy to all of this narrative. Besides, there were immediate concerns closer to home—such as rebuilding their city after Sherman left. "It will again rise from its ashes!" the *Intelligencer* had predicted on Christmas Day 1864. Actually, by a long view, the city of Atlanta had always been a-buildin'. As early as 1847 a resident observed that the place was "full of trade and bustle." During the Civil War this bustle had been maintained, leading an observer to remark on the city's "goaheadativeness," perhaps coining a word that later chambers of commerce would relish.[4]

A city on the mend deserved a good daily newspaper. The *Intelligencer*'s chief competitor, the *Southern Confederacy*, never returned from Macon; its last issue appears to be dated Feb. 8, 1865. Having itself returned to Atlanta, the *Intelligencer* just before Christmas 1864 had declared a price increase of a dollar, to $6 per month. But that was evidently not enough, for as of Jan. 1, 1865, the paper's new price was a hefty $10 a month. At the start of the war the *Daily Intelligencer* had cost $6 *a year*. In other words, with this, its eighth rate hike in two and a half years, regular subscribers were paying sixteen times more for their daily news and features.

The paper also solicited advertisers, as it did on January 27, 1865: "We desire to call the attention of merchants, traders, and business men generally, to the fact that the ATLANTA INTELLIGENCER furnishes peculiar advantages to them in advertising. Having a large circulation in every portion of the State, it is the only paper published in Atlanta, and is the only medium, through which access can be had to command that important and interesting portion of the State known as North Georgia; and we are satisfied that businessmen will find it to their interest to make themselves known through its columns. A hint to the wise is sufficient."

In justifying its price jump, the *Intelligencer* promised readers that once all its typesetters had returned to work, it would "contain more reading matter than any daily paper in the Confederacy." That was a tall order, especially as the

Intelligencer office in Atlanta was having trouble receiving its exchanges. "We are compelled again to call the attention of our brethren of the Press to the fact that we are in Atlanta, and much in need of our Exchanges," it repeated in late January, more than a month after it had resumed operation with its single-sheet "EXTRA" of December 10. "Please forward direct by way of Macon," it advised, referring to the Macon post office. That turned out to be part of the problem for editor John Steele, who criticized the Macon facility for failing to forward mail to his relocated office. "No through mail from Macon to-day, sir," he kept hearing, "hence we are deprived of our *exchange papers,* and, as to-day, have to 'make up' our paper with odds and ends from a few old scattering ones that we can pick up about our office."[5]

That same spirit of resolve and certainty had been evident in John Steele's editorial three months before, when he addressed the issue of arming slaves to fight alongside Confederate soldiers ("destructive to the relation between master and slave, and to the distinction between the white and negro race which exists in the South"). So it must have been with some degree of mortification that the *Intelligencer* editor watched as the Confederate Congress began debate on that very issue.

With its telegraphic news service restored, the *Intelligencer* was able to report Congressional discussions taking place in Richmond on how to employ blacks amidst the Confederacy's shrinking manpower. First came the House's vote on January 29 merely to use slaves as fortification workers (which had been done throughout the war, but Congress was taking baby-steps). On February 4, the paper related that a Virginia representative had called for a cessation of talk about negro troops, "a measure which has already divided public sentiment and produced much despondency," he argued. Yet Congress talked on, and on. "The negro bill was further discussed," the *Intelligencer* stated on February 7, until the House went into secret session. In the Senate two members voiced opposition to arming blacks, while another declared he would favor the measure if it helped bring about Southern independence. The chamber then voted to table the whole thing.[6]

On February 10, Texas senator Williamson Oldham and Mississippi congressman Ethelbert Barksdale introduced matching pieces of legislation in their respective chambers that authorized President Davis to "ask for and accept from the owners of slaves, the services of such number of able-bodied negro men as he may deem expedient, for and during the war, to perform military service." (The bills left it to the states to deal with the question of eventual emancipation for those blacks who served in the army.) Two days later Representative Barksdale wrote Gen. Robert E. Lee, asking his views on the matter. The congressman must have been pleased by Lee's reply, which came within a week. "In my opinion," the general wrote, "the negroes, under proper circumstances, will make efficient soldiers.... Under good officers and good instructions, I do not see why they should not become soldiers. They possess all the physical qualifications, and their habits of obedience constitute a good foundation for discipline." Barksdale, probably with Lee's permission, gave the letter to the Richmond papers. Its publication helped persuade members of the Confederate House of Representatives to pass Barksdale's bill on February 20, by a vote of 40 to 37. In the Senate, the vote in favor of Oldham's bill was even closer, nine to eight.

Dated March 13, 1865, the law permitted at least a few African Americans to be recruited. In less than a month, however, the war was over. The Confederacy had dealt with its military manpower issue too late.[7]

In voting to arm black men as soldiers, the Confederacy had come a long way from the time of its creation, even if the *Intelligencer* had not. "Every negro in Georgia should have a master," the paper had editorialized in January 1860. Then, during the war, the *Intelligencer*'s attitude toward arming blacks became somewhat slippery. "We must 'fight the devil with fire,' by arming our negroes to fight the Yankees," it had asserted in May 1862, after some in the North began suggesting such a source of new manpower for Federal armies. Then two years later, in September 1864, during a period of John Steele's absence, Associate Editor Nagle had written a piece endorsing "the policy of placing our slaves in the army as soldiers." The returning editor contradicted his associate the very next day: "to this making soldiers of our negroes we totally dissent, and cannot advocate such a policy in this journal."

Not content with this affirmation, Steele several weeks later declared, "we may be forced to yield up slavery, but we will fight on to maintain it as long as we have the power to do so."[8]

To those today who contend that the Civil War had nothing to do with slavery, we'd advise them to check out the pages of the *Atlanta Daily Intelligencer*.

NOTES

1. "From the Rebel. NASHVILLE—WILL IT BE CAPTURED," *ADI*, Dec. 25, 1864; "THE POSITION IN TENNESSEE," *ADI*, December 29.
2. "From the Southern Confederacy. Latest from the North," *ADI*, Dec. 29, 1864;

"LATER FROM THE NORTH," *ADI*, December 31; "News from Middle Tennessee" and "Special Dispatches to the Mobile Register," *ADI*, Jan. 5, 1865.

3. Benson Bobrick, *The Battle of Nashville: General George H. Thomas & the Most Decisive Battle of the Civil War* (New York: Alfred A. Knopf, 2010), 94–97; Brian Steel Wills, *George Henry Thomas: As True as Steel* (Lawrence: University Press of Kansas, 2012), 23, 64; Stanley F. Horn, *The Decisive Battle of Nashville* (Baton Rouge: Louisiana State University Press, 1956), 74; Stanley F. Horn, "Nashville: The Most Decisive Battle of the Civil War," *Civil War Times Illustrated*, vol. 3, no. 8 (December 1964), 6; 31–36; James Lee McDonough, *Nashville: The Western Confederacy's Final Gamble* (Knoxville: University of Tennessee Press, 2004), 273–74; George W. Peddy, *Saddle Bag and Spinning Wheel: Being the Civil War Letters of George W. Peddy, MD Surgeon 56th Georgia Volunteer Regiment, C.S.A.* Ed. by George W. Cuttino (Macon: Mercer University Press, 1981), 204; McMurry, *Hood*, 182.

4. "CHRISTMAS," *ADI*, Dec. 25, 1864; Davis, *What the Yankees Did to Us*, 3.

5. "IMPORTANT DECISION," *ADI*, Jan. 6, 1865 (referring to "the Macon *Southern Confederacy*"); "NEW RATES," *ADI*, January 5; "THE MACON POST OFFICE" and "Our Paper as an Advertising Medium," *ADI*, January 27.

6. "CONGRESSIONAL," (Richmond, January 29), *ADI*, Feb. 2, 1865; "CONFEDERATE CONGRESS" (Richmond, February 1), *ADI*, February 4; "CONFEDERATE CONGRESS" (Richmond, February 3), *ADI*, February 7.

7. Robert F. Durden, *The Gray and the Black: The Confederate Debate on Emancipation* (Baton Rouge: Louisiana State University Press, 1972), 202–203, 206; Yearns, *Confederate Congress*, 97–98; Stephen E. Ambrose, "By Enlisting Negroes, Could the South Still Win the War?," *Civil War Times Illustrated*, vol. 3, no. 9 (January 1965), 21.

8. Hart, "Mood of Atlanta," 26; "MOVEMENTS AND SPIRIT OF THE WAR," *ADI*, May 16, 1862; "NEGRO SOLDIERS," *ADI*, Sept. 29 and 30, 1864; "ARMING THE NEGROES," *ADI*, October 26.

45. Nearing the End

IN A LETTER CARRIED by a prestigious Northern officeholder, Francis P. Blair, President Lincoln invited President Davis to send envoys to meet with him and discuss possibilities for "securing peace to the people of our common country." That phrase should have alerted Southern leaders to Lincoln's position, but the idea of peace talks of any kind was too important to pass up. Davis accordingly appointed as his commissioners Vice President Alexander H. Stephens, Assistant Secretary of War John A. Campbell and Robert M. T. Hunter, president *pro tem* of the C.S. Senate. The Confederates, of tall cotton themselves, met with taller still, for joining them were no less than Abraham Lincoln, President of the United States, and his Secretary of State, William H. Seward.

The two sets of ambassadors—if that is the right word—met onboard the *River Queen,* a steamboat moored at Hampton Roads, the Atlantic port in southeastern Virginia. Leading the Confederate delegation was Vice President Stephens—"Little Aleck," as he was called, not so much because of his height, which was five-foot-ten, but more for his scrawny torso, whose weight was under a hundred pounds. Little Aleck was removing several scarves as he prepared to take his seat in the ship's saloon, where the meeting was held. Observing this, Lincoln commented that he had never seen such a small nubbin come out of such a big shuck.

Then came the conversation, friendly at first. Abe and Aleck reminisced about old times (the two had served in Congress in the 1840s). It was the Confederate Vice President who brought up the subject of the meeting: peace. Lincoln quickly made clear that he would never consent to the Southern states' severance from the Union. Secretary Seward broke the news that just a few days before, the U.S. Congress had passed a thirteenth amendment to the Constitution, abolishing slavery wherever it existed in the United States.

So that was it: no Southern independence, no Southern slavery. R. M. T. Hunter protested this all-or-nothing "negotiation." He dredged forth the history lesson that even Charles the First, the English monarch, in the midst of his own civil war, had entered into agreements with rebels, suggesting that Lincoln was being too heavy-handed. "I do not profess to be posted in history," the president is said to have replied; "all I seem to recall about the case of Charles I, is, that he lost his head" (the monarch was beheaded in 1649).

The talks were over and the Southerners walked out.[1]

The *Intelligencer* actually found good news in the outcome of the Hampton Roads Conference. "If the South were not satisfied before, they must be now, that under no circumstances will the people of the North consent to a division of the country," the paper opined on March 2. Lincoln ("the tyrant and usurper") had announced to the Southern commissioners that "the only means by which we could obtain peace, consisted in an unconditional surrender to the authority of the United States, and an approval or acceptance, upon our part, of his unconstitutional proclamations and outrageous usurpations . . . by which all our property rights would be destroyed." These terms, the *Intelligencer* editorialized on March 12, "have exerted a most happy influence upon the popular heart." Notwithstanding the fall of Atlanta, Sherman's march and Hood's disastrous Tennessee campaign, Southerners could now see that nothing remained for them but a firmer adherence to the Confederate cause, a resolve to carry on the fight—"a settled determination to achieve our Independence or perish in the attempt," as the paper put it. With such spirit, the *Intelligencer* looked forward (as it had so many times before) to "a brilliant victory."[2]

Even Abraham Lincoln's second inaugural, March 4, 1865, which also portended a longer war, served to steel Confederate hearts. A writer signing himself "H. St. P." for the *Mobile Advertiser & Register* (his letter was reprinted in the *Intelligencer* of March 15) termed the occasion "the elevation to power of one of the lowest specimens of humanity." Writing evidently the day after the inauguration in Washington, "H. St. P." affirmed, "yesterday has simply opened to us a harder, but no less sure path to final independence." Indeed, he exulted, "God be praised!"[3]

Meanwhile, William Tecumseh Sherman was marching through the Carolinas.

After spending more than a month in Savannah, Sherman led his army of 60,000 veterans into South Carolina, with the intent of making for Goldsboro, North Carolina, 300 miles to the northeast. The Federals were opposed by only 9,000 Confederates under General Hardee near Charleston, to whom were soon added a division of veterans from Hood's wrecked army in north

Mississippi. In overall charge in South Carolina was Gen. P. G. T. Beauregard, who pleaded to Richmond for reinforcements. (There were none to be sent.)

South Carolina suffered more at the hands of Sherman's soldiers than had Georgia. At Barnwell, a town seventy-five miles north of Savannah, Federals killed animals, looted residents' houses, then set them on fire. Union cavalry commander Brig. Gen. Judson Kilpatrick sent a message to Sherman: "we have changed the name of Barnwell to Burnwell."[4]

It was even worse in Columbia, the state capital, which Northern troops entered on February 17. Two days before, General Beauregard had ordered all cotton in the city to be burned before the Yankees arrived. But on the morning of the 17th, newly-promoted Confederate Lt. Gen. Wade Hampton worried that the strong winds prevailing would spread the flames to buildings. They did. Fires were fanning when Northern troops began marching in around 10:30 a.m. Some Federals chanced upon a cache of whiskey, and drunkenness led to deteriorating discipline and still more fires. Fine houses fell victim to deliberate arson, even as some Federals tried to snuff out the flames. Before the conflagration subsided about 8 p.m., 265 residences and 193 business and public structures, virtually Columbia's entire business district, had been wiped out.[5]

"The 15th corps reached Columbia on Friday, the 17th inst.," the *Intelligencer*'s "TELEGRAPHIC" column reported on March 2, "and while the soldiers were drunk they sacked and pillaged the city, burning every house on Main street, and the cotton they found." The column continued: "every article of the people's subsistence was carried off. The cellars and every part of buildings were thoroughly searched by them." On March 2 the *Intelligencer* also reported that on February 17, Confederate forces had evacuated Charleston and that the Federals had marched in.[6]

Commenting on the burning of Columbia, the *Intelligencer* editorialized on March 3 that "the atrocities committed by the enemy there, make the blood curdle in our veins." Though the editor did not raise the point, it was obvious that Confederate forces were inadequate to prevent Sherman's progress through Carolina and his troops' further atrocities. So he turned to the Almighty: "may the *vengeance* of the Lord fall heavily upon them!"[7]

This is the same kind of righteous indignation that animated Confederate General Hampton when he went after Cump Sherman.

The Union general started it. On February 24, Sherman composed a letter to Hampton, who was commanding Confederate cavalry in the Carolinas.

Sherman came right to the point: soldiers in his army out on foraging expeditions—in his orders for the march he had encouraged his troops to live off the land—had been found dead with signs on their bodies reading "death to foragers." He gave two such instances: a lieutenant and seven men found thus near Chesterville, and twenty more found near a place called Feasterville. Sherman informed Hampton that foraging was a long-accepted practice in war and that soldiers so engaged should not be murdered as criminals. He then pointedly stated, "I have ordered a similar number of prisoners in our hands to be disposed of in like manner"—in other words, he would retaliate for his soldiers' deaths.

Hampton got Sherman's letter on the 27th and immediately composed a long reply. First, the retaliation threat: for every Confederate soldier murdered at Sherman's order, Hampton would have two killed, "giving in all cases preference to any officers who may be in my hands." Then, the foragers: he had given no orders for the killing of prisoners, and he knew nothing of the two alleged incidents. But that did not really matter, as Hampton blamed Sherman's foragers for setting fire to civilians' homes. "It is a part of the system of the thieves whom you designate as your foragers to fire the dwellings of those citizens whom they have robbed," he charged. Hampton declared that he had instructed his troops to shoot on sight any house-burning Federals they encountered.

Not content with that, Hampton went on to accuse Sherman for having fired artillery into the city of Columbia without giving warning to its residents, and for having "laid the whole city in ashes, leaving amidst its ruins thousands of old men and helpless women and children, who are likely to perish of starvation and exposure." Then came the accusation of rape: "in more than one household there is now an agony far more bitter than that of death," he explained, using the customary Victorian euphemism.

Evidently Hampton gave South Carolina newspapers his and Sherman's letters, which would explain how the *Intelligencer* was able to print them fully in its issue of March 22, probably from one of its Carolina exchanges. The correspondence led Steele to comment thus:

> Our readers will find an interesting correspondence between Sherman and Gen. Wade Hampton in our paper to-day. It seems that Sherman has been informed that some of his white-livered, blackhearted thieves, robbers and house-burners, had been killed by Hampton's men after they had surrendered, and he was disposed to complain of such treatment and threatened to retaliate upon prisoners in his

hands.—Gen. Hampton's reply is just such as might have been expected from a gentleman so high minded and a soldier so bold and chivalrous; and must have made even Sherman feel that the manner in which he is conducting this war, is disgraceful and violative of all the usages observed by civilized nations. We will not detain the reader from the letter by further remarks.[8]

Here it was, three weeks before the end of the American civil war (Lee's surrender), and *Intelligencer* editor John Steele was still fulminating against the Yankees and celebrating the courage of Confederate military heroes. As an index of how or why the Confederacy held out for so long, now four years later, in a failing war effort, the *Intelligencer*'s editorial of March 22, 1865, stands in the forefront of Confederate journalistic literature.

South Carolina's two largest cities had fallen to Union troops on February 17, within the same twenty-four hours, yet these setbacks failed to dampen John Steele's war ardor. Not even a rumor that Lee had been forced to abandon Richmond ("we doubt the correctness of the same") did not faze the editor, who on March 2 issued another saber-rattler. "Our cities may all fall into the hands of the enemy," he reasoned, "and the South be as far from conquered as the colonies under Washington were, when the British held every city of importance in them during the first revolution." There was too much Confederate territory still to be conquered by Federal forces, Steele contended; "time will as surely exhaust our enemies. . . . This, with our gallant armies, backed by the stern resolve of our people at home, not to be subjugated, render us invincible in defence, and is a guaranty that independence will come as surely as we be true to the cause of which so much blood had been shed."[9]

To his editorial role as Confederate propagandist, which John Steele had been practicing for some time, was added a relatively new one, that of civic cheerleader. "Each returning day increases our population," he stated in an "Our City" editorial that appeared in the *Intelligencer* on April 1. "Every train that arrives is crowded," he observed. To accommodate the returnees, especially those of the working class, the editor noted "many small cheap houses . . . are being erected." Stores and marts in the city were "tolerably well supplied" with food and other items, though at times the prices were a little high. Another index of recovery: church services. The *Intelligencer* reminded readers that Sunday rites were being conducted at five different sanctuaries in town. With all of this activity, the paper boasted—in true chamber-of-commerce manner—"thus will our 'Gate City' rise from the ashes. . . . At present, all is life, and energy, and enterprise.... *Onward* seems to be the motto of our people, and ONWARD we feel confident, will be the progress of the 'Gate City' of the South."

In the *Intelligencer* of March 7 was the encouraging news that the Atlanta & West Point Railroad was now operating, with trains coming and going daily (the first one entered on March 5, 1865). The Macon & Western, which Sherman's troops had also torn up, was being repaired, too, and in about two weeks its last stretch, the several miles south of East Point, was expected to be finished, allowing a return of full railroad service between Atlanta and Macon (it would resume on March 27). Accommodating this traffic was "a vast car-shed," according to a letter to the paper written by "Atlantanian"; it had been rebuilt on the site of the one destroyed by Sherman's engineers. The writer also commented that "a broad and stable iron bridge" had been built over the railroad, allowing traffic to pass between Peachtree and Whitehall Streets. As for the latter, "Atlantanian" commented that Whitehall had been widened considerably, with other thoroughfares similarly improved. Atlanta's iron link to Augusta, the Georgia Railroad, was predicted to be operable by April 20. Repairs to "the State Road," the Western & Atlantic to Chattanooga, would take longer, however. Federal troops had wrecked eighty-four miles of track between Atlanta and Resaca, and they had taken up another twenty miles of rails north of Resaca. But the *Intelligencer* voiced optimism that "time and energy will restore the broken link."

Even little improvements mattered. The *Intelligencer* on March 10 announced that city authorities had rebuilt a bridge over Peachtree Creek, which would allow "our up country friends" more easily to bring "their Irish potatoes, apples and other supplies" for sale to Atlanta's returning population. As for the city's overall rebuilding, "the work of her redemption may be slow, but it is sure," the paper observed. Similarly, the return of businesses to the city was something of which to take note. The *Intelligencer* of March 9 informed readers that the commission and produce merchant firm of Winter & Pittman had opened at Roark's Corner (Whitehall and Mitchell Streets). Ten days later there appeared brief mention of a new dining place in town, the Rebel Restaurant. "We call special attention to the notice of this new Eating Saloon in our city," the paper declared, "and doubt not its Proprietors will make it a place where something good can be had." The paper of April 2 announced that G. W. Jack's Bakery, which had been located downtown on Decatur Street (and thus had not survived Sherman's fires) was returned and back in operation. After two hotel keepers renovated the old Gate City Hotel on Alabama Street and reopened it as the Exchange, the *Intelligencer* called attention to the new hotel, advising "our country friends" that the facility offered market space so they could sell their food and wares.¹⁰

In the reconstructing city John Steele and his staff could not return to their pre-Sherman offices at the foot of Whitehall Street—that and other downtown blocks had been swept by flames on November 15, 1864. (In a letter to the editor printed in the *Intelligencer* on April 7, "Atlantanian" wrote, referring to Whitehall Street near the railroad, "that old and annoying portion of it on which your office, and those of two of your contemporaries, stood, had disappeared.") After its return to the city, though, where the *Intelligencer* had set up shop could not be discerned in the newspaper's pages during the winter of 1865. A recurring notice simply advised, "all persons writing to this Office, will please address Intelligencer, Atlanta, Ga." (Looking ahead, we know that the postbellum *Intelligencer* sank roots in its old neighborhood once it was rebuilt; the 1867 city directory states that the *Daily Intelligencer* was headquartered on "w s Whitehall, b RR and Alabama"—in other words, directly across the street from its pre-Sherman location.)

The newspaper office, wherever located, was a busy place. In mid-March the *Intelligencer* announced, "In answer to numerous inquiries, we would state that we are now publishing the WEEKLY INTELLIGENCER and sending it to all the offices in the country that can be reached by mail." Nevertheless, the same problems that throughout the war had dogged John Steele (indeed all of his editorial *confreres* around the country)—printing expenses, scarcity and cost of paper and ink—caused him to announce on March 14 that the *Intelligencer* would henceforth be issued as "half a sheet," meaning the front and back of a single page. The alternative would have been to raise subscription prices, which were already high at $10 a month. "We hope our friends will interest themselves in our behalf," the editor entreated, "and give us all the aid and encouragement in their power; for we assure them that we have been for months laboring under many difficulties in keeping the banner of the INTELLIGENCER unfurled."¹¹

After Gen. John B. Hood's resignation as commander of the Army of Tennessee, Lt. Gen. Richard Taylor had assumed command of what was left of it. Returns of Jan. 20, 1865 showed only 18,708 officers and men in an army that a few months before had numbered 35,662 present for duty.¹²

But Taylor's army was being dismantled. Some 3,500 Trans-Mississippi and Tennessee troops were furloughed (unlikely ever to return). Another 4,000 were sent to Mobile, which was facing the advance of newly aggressive Federal forces.

As for deserters, there could be no reliable count. Thus when the Confederate War Department ordered all available troops eastward to help Joe Johnston face Sherman in North Carolina, only about 5,000 were left to make the journey. As the *Intelligencer* reported on March 12, by February 23 Johnston had taken charge of all troops in the Department of South Carolina, Georgia and Florida, and at once assumed command of what was left of the Army of Tennessee.

The *Intelligencer*'s "TELEGRAPHIC" column still bore the heading of "REPORTS OF THE PRESS ASSOCIATION," but the P. A. was a shadow of its former self, if only because of the deterioration of the wartime South's telegraphic network. Superintendent John S. Thrasher had migrated to Macon with Atlanta's press corps in the summer of 1864. In early September he traveled afar, across the Mississippi to Texas, his prewar home. During his absence John Graeme, the Association's Richmond agent, directed its work. Thrasher returned to Richmond in January 1865. In mid-March he was passing through Augusta, as the *Intelligencer* noted on the 17th: "Col. J. S. Thrasher, who has just arrived from Richmond, reports that the confidence of the people is strong, everything becoming more hopeful." That it was still in operation (if perhaps feebly) was evidenced by the letter of Henry L. Flash, editor of the *Macon Telegraph and Confederate,* appearing in the *Intelligencer* on April 8, concerning the fees being charged by the P. A. At this time Southern telegraph service was troubled, and in the shrinking Confederacy there were fewer newspapers subscribing to the Association's news services. This led Flash, "in view of the present exigencies, and diminished number of Associates of the Press Association," to ask whether other papers would join him in asking Superintendent Thrasher to continue to offer P. A. news "at a cost which will not exceed an extra assessment of five hundred dollars on each associate for the present month."[13]

The telegraph then brought news of an important engagement in North Carolina. Sherman's army began marching into North Carolina on March 1, heading northeast. On the 13th it was at Fayetteville, wrecking the Confederate arsenal and armory there. To oppose it General Johnston had no more than 25,000 troops scattered widely across North Carolina: Lt. Gen. Wade Hampton's 6,000, Lt. Gen. William J. Hardee's 8,000, Army of Tennessee diehards (5,000), and 6,000 under Gen. Bragg from Wilmington (the city had fallen on March 21). This disparate force was desperately inadequate to meet Sherman.

As two of Sherman's four corps marched toward Bentonville, thirty-five miles southeast of Raleigh, Johnston saw a chance to pounce. On March 19 with some 15,000 troops Johnston laid an ambush for the 20,000 Federals heading his way. The Northerners believed the Rebels ahead of them were retreating, so they were not ready for the mid-afternoon flank attack that sent many of them fleeing the field. This was the action that the *Intelligencer* reported on March 23: "General J. E. Johnston reports that about 5 o'clock, 19th inst., he attacked the enemy near Bentonville, routed him, and captured three guns. . . . This morning he is entrenched. Our troops behaved admirably."[14]

The *Intelligencer* editor jumped on this good news, a rarity these days. "The tidings from the scene of conflict in North Carolina are encouraging," John Steele observed on March 24. This rather reserved statement would have been all right had not the editor once more slipped into the guise of Confederate cheerleader. "They are but the harbingers of great and glorious victories that await our arms in that direction." In fact, they were not. After a couple of days of skirmishing and small-scale fighting, as the Federals called in reinforcements from the rest of Sherman's forces, Johnston and his small army slipped away. Casualties at Bentonville, March 19–21, amounted to approximately 3,500 for the Confederates (including some 1,500 captured) and 1,500 for the Federals. Rather than a harbinger "of great and glorious victories," Bentonville would in fact prove to be Johnston's last battle with Sherman. At Goldsboro, Maj. Gen. John M. Schofield was waiting with enough troops to bring Sherman's total force to 90,000 men—an army that Joe Johnston would have found it impossible to confront, much less defeat.[15]

After the telegraphed dispatch about the Bentonville fighting on March 19, the *Intelligencer* waited anxiously for more news. The wires were down somewhere, it announced to readers on the 26th, "and consequently [we] are without any additional information in reference to the situation in North Carolina." Downed wires meant there was also no news from Virginia, where Lee's army held its Richmond-Petersburg lines. Absence of news did not dissuade John Steele from expressing yet again (for the umpteenth time) an optimistic editorial. In an article titled "One Year Ago," the editor opined on April 2, "when we review the events of the last twelve months . . . we fail to discern any evidence of the suppression of the rebellion, of a people subdued and conquered. . . . On the contrary, the spirit and determination of the people, and particularly of our armies, to fight on until our independence is established and acknowledged, is stronger to-day than it was twelve months ago, if such a thing is possible."[16]

Then came the news that Richmond had fallen.

There had been little warning. The *Intelligencer* on April 2, in its "TELEGRAPHIC" column, related a dispatch from Petersburg that there had been fighting "in

Dinwiddie, near Hatcher's Run, eight miles from Petersburg." Only with a good map of Virginia could a reader discern that Grant's troops were testing Lee's defensive lines with assaults southwest of Petersburg. Grant's objective was to cut the South Side Railroad, Lee's last supply line. He had placed his cavalry chief, Maj. Gen. Philip Sheridan, in charge of the effort, and reinforced Sheridan's horse soldiers with lots of infantry. Lee had put Maj. Gen. George Pickett in charge of guarding the South Side. The Federals attacked him on April 1 at a place called Five Forks and overwhelmed Pickett's troops, exposing the railroad. The next day, April 2, an all-out Union attack against Lee's whole line broke it so decisively that Lee had to warn President Davis that he could no longer defend the capital.

"The evacuation of Richmond commenced on Sunday afternoon [April 2]," the *Intelligencer* laconically announced on April 6, based on a dispatch sent out on the 4th. After receiving word from General Lee that he was uncovering the city, President Davis moved swiftly to get government officials onboard southbound trains. The capital citizenry caught on and panic ruled the streets as everyone sought conveyances to clear out. After Confederate troops began burning military supplies, the arsenal and railroad bridges, the fires got out of hand. After officers dumped barrels of whiskey into the street, rioters drank it in the gutters. Amid this mayhem the last Confederate soldiers left the city. On the morning of April 3, Federal troops entered Richmond. Mayor Joseph Mayo surrendered the city to the first high-ranking Federal officer he encountered, Maj. Gen. Godfrey Weitzel.

On April 6 the *Intelligencer* disclosed that Jefferson Davis and his Cabinet members were fleeing to Danville, 125 miles southwest of Richmond. "The position of our army now is unknown," the paper's telegraphed dispatch added. It soon developed, though, that Lee was marching his army westward as well, with the *Intelligencer* reporting Lee heading to Farmville, fifty-five miles west of Petersburg, with Grant's forces pursuing closely.[17]

As it had done so many times before, the *Intelligencer* took the calamitous news of Richmond's fall with an editorial shrug. "We doubt not that almost every true Southron will feel a momentary depression of spirits, when first he hears that the Capital of the Confederacy has been left open to an enemy," editor Steele declared on April 7. And as it had also done so many times, the paper chose to look on the bright side of events: General Lee's army was no longer pinned down in the Richmond-Petersburg fortifications. "Liberated," it could now "strike whenever and wherever its blows can be most effective in beating back and destroying the enemy."[18]

John Steele was not alone in continuing to voice confidence in the cause. Alexander St. Clair Abrams, the *Intelligencer*'s former assistant editor and, as "St. Clair," its field correspondent with the Army of Tennessee, came out of retirement long enough to write a saber-rattling letter to the *Intelligencer*. Abrams echoed Davis' talk of "a new phase of the struggle" when he wrote, "Mr. Editor, with the fall of our Capital the struggle for liberty commences anew. If, as it has been said, we were formerly fighting for the slavery of our negroes, let us now fight for the preservation of our independence.... We must never be subjugated. Our fair women must never be placed in the power of the North, so that the beastly doctrine of miscegenation shall be forced upon them. We must *fight*, FIGHT, FIGHT."[19]

In 1966, J. Cutler Andrews wrote, "During 1864 and early 1865 the disparity between the image of the military situation presented in the Confederate press and the real situation became, if anything, greater, in some instances assuming the proportions of sheer fantasy." More recently Charles Royster has framed Confederate pugnacity in a different light, suggesting that wartime Southerners could not conceive of defeat, hence they developed no vocabulary for it. He quotes Jefferson Davis: "To speak of subjugating such a people, so united and determined, is to speak a language incomprehensible to them."[20]

Only in this context can the *Intelligencer*'s exhortation for Southerners to "*fight*, FIGHT, FIGHT"—published two days before Lee's surrender, mind you—be understood.

NOTES

1. McPherson, *Ordeal by Fire*, 470; Current, *Lincoln Nobody Knows*, 243–47; E. Ramsay Richardson, *Little Aleck: A Life of Alexander H. Stephens The Fighting Vice-President of the Confederacy* (Indianapolis: Bobbs-Merrill Company, 1932), 18; Schott, *Alexander H. Stephens*, 81; Harry J. Maihafer, *War of Words: Abraham Lincoln and the Civil War Press* (Washington: Brassey's, 2001), 233–34.

2. "THE PEACE CONFERENCE," *ADI*, March 2, 1865; "THE PROSPECT," *ADI*, March 12.

3. "From the Register & Advertiser. THE FOURTH OF MARCH," *ADI*, March 15, 1865.

4. Stanley P. Hirshson, *The White Tecumseh: A Biography of William T. Sherman* (New York: John Wiley & Sons, 1997), 277; James Lee McDonough, *William Tecumseh Sherman: In the Service of My Country—A Life* (New York: W. W. Norton, 2016), 598; Burke Davis,

Sherman's March (New York: Random House, 1980), 149; "THE YANKEES AT BARNWELL, S.C.," *ADI,* March 2, 1865.

5. Marion Brunson Lucas, *Sherman and the Burning of Columbia* (College Station: Texas A & M University Press, 1976), 64, 67, 76, 128.

6. "What the Yankees did in South Carolina," *ADI,* March 2, 1865.

7. "THE ENEMY AT COLUMBIA," *ADI,* March 3.

8. "CORRESPONDENCE BETWEEN GEN. SHERMAN AND GEN. HAMPTON" and "Our readers will find . . . ," *ADI,* March 22, 1865.

9. "THE EVACUATION OF RICHMOND," *ADI,* March 2, 1865.

10. "OUR CITY," *ADI,* April 1, 1865; "OUR 'GATE CITY,'" *ADI,* April 12; "RAILROAD AND TELEGRAPH," *ADI,* March 7; "ATLANTANIAN," "A LETTER ABOUT ATLANTA," *ADI,* April 7; Franklin M. Garrett, "The Phoenix Begins to Rise: The *Atlanta Daily Intelligencer* Announces the Return of the Railroads," *Atlanta History,* vol. 37, no. 4 (Winter 1994), 5–8; Davis, *What the Yankees Did to Us,* 386–87, 418; "BRIDGE OVER PEACH TREE CREEK," *ADI,* March 10; "By reference to our advertising columns . . . ," *ADI,* March 9; "'REBEL RESTAURANT,'" *ADI,* March 19; "JACK'S BAKERY," *ADI,* April 2; Franklin M. Garrett, "Civilian Life in Atlanta," *Civil War Times Illustrated,* vol. 3, no. 4 (July 1964), 30; EXCHANGE HOTEL," *ADI,* April 19.

11. "ATLANTANIAN," "A LETTER ABOUT ATLANTA," *ADI,* April 7, 1865; "All persons . . . ," *ADI,* March 12; *Barnwell's 1867 Atlanta City Directory,* 133; "WEEKLY INTELLIGENCER," *ADI,* March 15; "OUR PAPER," *ADI,* March 14.

12. Stephen Davis, *Into Tennessee and Failure: John Bell Hood* (Macon: Mercer University Press, 2019), 237–38; "Abstract . . . November 6, 1864," *OR,* vol. 40, pt. 1, 678; "Consolidated abstract from returns of the Confederate Army on or about December 31, 1864," *OR,* Ser. 4, vol. 3, 989.

13. Horn, *Army of Tennessee,* 422–23; Herman Hattaway, *General Stephen D. Lee* (Jackson: University Press of Mississippi, 1976), 152; Larry J. Daniel, *Conquered: Why the Army of Tennessee Failed* (Chapel Hill: University of North Carolina Press, 2019), 325; "TELEGRAPHIC. FROM AUGUSTA" (March 8), *ADI,* March 12, 1865; T. Michael Parrish, *Richard Taylor: Soldier Prince of Dixie* (Chapel Hill: University of North Carolina Press, 1992), 430; "TELEGRAPHIC. The Enemy Crosses the Pedee" (Augusta, March 15), *ADI,* March 17; Wilken, "As the Telegraph Saw It," iii; "TELEGRAPHIC. . . . Macon, April 6," *ADI,* April 8.

14. Wilson Angley, Jerry L. Cross and Michael Hill, *Sherman's March through North Carolina* (Raleigh: North Carolina Division of Archives and History, 1995), 1, 23–24; Edward G. Longacre, *Gentleman and Soldier: A Biography of Wade Hampton III* (Nashville: Rutledge HillPress, 2003), 225–26, 230–31; Symonds, *Joseph E. Johnston,* 344–45; Roger Behrens, *Total War in Carolina: Sherman's 1865 Carolinas Campaign* (Mahomet IL: BPC Publishers, 1992), 65–67; "TELEGRAPHIC. Richmond, March 20 . . . ," *ADI,* March 23, 1865.

15. "THE SITUATION," *ADI,* March 24, 1865; Nathaniel Cheairs Hughes, Jr., *Bentonville: The Final Battle of Sherman and Johnston* (Chapel Hill: University of North Carolina Press, 1996), 219; Donald B. Connelly, *John M. Schofield and the Politics of Generalship* (Chapel Hill: University of North Carolina Press, 2006), 160.

16. "WIRES DOWN," *ADI*, March 26, 1865; "ONE YEAR AGO," *ADI*, April 2.

17. "TELEGRAPHIC. Petersburg, March 30," *ADI*, April 2, 1865; Noah Andre Trudeau, *The Last Citadel: Petersburg, Virginia, June 1864–April 1865* (Boston: Little, Brown, 1991), 358; Bruce Catton, "Sheridan at Five Forks," *Journal of Southern History*, vol. 21, no. 3 (August 1955), 307, 311; "TELEGRAPHIC. Evacuation of Richmond," *ADI*, April 6; Emory M. Thomas, "Wartime Richmond," *Civil War Times Illustrated*, vol. 16, no. 3 (June 1977), 47; "TELEGRAPHIC. DANVILLE," April 9," *ADI*, April 11; "LEE'S ARMY," *ADI*, April 14; Burke Davis, *To Appomattox: Nine April Days* (New York: Rinehart, 1959), 4–5.

18. "THE EVACUATION OF RICHMOND" and "TELEGRAPHIC" (Danville, April 5) *ADI*, April 7, 1865.

19. "St. Clair," "For the Intelligencer. ATLANTA, GA., April 5, 1865," *ADI*, April 7, 1865.

20. Andrews, "Confederate Press and Public Morale," 454; Royster, *Destructive War*, 177–78.

46. Surrender

DURING APRIL 1865, on just about every front, the Confederacy was falling apart. On the 10th Sherman began leading his army from Goldsboro northwest toward Raleigh. Johnston, powerless to resist, retreated ahead of him. At Mobile Bay, Union Maj. Gen. Edward R. S. Canby's troops pressured Confederate Maj. Gen. Dabney H. Maury's forces to abandon the several forts guarding the city; Maury evacuated Mobile on the morning of April 12. Only the sluggishness of the Confederate postal system prevented the *Intelligencer* from reporting these events in a timely manner. (A *Columbus Enquirer* correspondent's letter from Mobile dated March 29 was not published in the *Intelligencer* until April 16.)[1]

On March 22, nearly 13,500 Union cavalrymen under Brig. Gen. James H. Wilson rode out from northwest Alabama on a huge raid that would sweep across Alabama and into middle Georgia. Eight days later the Federals rode into Elyton (today's Birmingham). On April 1 at a place called Ebenezer Church, Wilson defeated Forrest in what some say was the Confederate cavalry wizard's only defeat in the war. The next day the Federals beat the outnumbered defenders of Selma, an important ordnance manufacturing center. Ten days later Montgomery fell to Wilson's troopers after Confederates burned more than 80,000 bales of cotton (worth some $40 million in gold). The raiders then rode east to Columbus, Georgia. There on April 16, Yanks and Rebs fought what has been called the last battle of the Civil War. Again, after taking the town, Union horsemen burned everything of use to the Confederates in their fast-collapsing war effort.

In Atlanta the *Intelligencer* tried to keep up with Wilson's whirlwind. It reported the fall of Selma on April 6, and after that the advance of "the Selma and Montgomery raiding party" (it still did not know its commander's name). When Wilson's raiders crossed the Chattahoochee for Columbus, the paper observed, "the enemy has again entered Georgia; and is now doubtlessly advancing on Macon" (it was correct). Then, echoing the call to arms it had so often sounded, the *Intelligencer* once more exhorted, "Let every inch of the march be disputed! Let it not be said that he was permitted to pass over our state and devastate our cities, without blows being struck in their defence!"[2]

A half-year before, after Jefferson Davis in Macon had predicted that eventually Sherman would be forced to retreat back through north Georgia in a march as humiliating as that of Napoleon from Moscow, General Grant is said to have asked who would furnish the snow for Sherman's retreat.[3] Likewise, with John Steele of the *Intelligencer* bellowing about "blows being struck," the question for readers was, who would strike them?

Already rocked by these reportorial thunderbolts, the *Intelligencer*'s editor then had to deal with rumors that Gen. Robert E. Lee had surrendered the Army of Northern Virginia.

Predictably, when newspapers in Union-controlled cities carried the story, Steele dismissed it. "Nashville papers state that Gen. Lee capitulated with, and surrendered his army to Gen. Grant on the 9th instant," he wrote on April 18; "we place no confidence in these statements, viewing them as base fabrications of an unscrupulous foe."

Then the *Chattanooga Gazette* on April 11 actually published what appeared to be three letters exchanged between General Grant and Lee concerning the Confederate army's surrender; the *Intelligencer* published them on April 19. The three missives were undated. One, Lee to Grant, mentioned an earlier note from the Union commander concerning the surrender of the Confederate army. Second was Grant to Lee, proposing terms: officers to give their parole not to take up arms against the U.S. government before being properly exchanged; regimental commanders to sign for their men; all arms to be handed over, except officers' side arms; private horses and baggage to be retained; the men would be free to return to their homes. Finally was Lee's note to Grant accepting these terms.

In his attempt to disbelieve this first-hand evidence, however, Steele essentially conducted a word-content analysis to argue that "such a correspondence never transpired between the two commanders of the respective armies in Virginia." To make his case that "General Lee *has not surrendered nor capitulated*," Steele contended that Lee's purported missives used language that the editor claimed the general did not regularly employ. "We say this is not characteristic of Gen. Lee's style, in closing his official communications," he asserted; hence he viewed the correspondence picked up from the Chattanooga paper as "spurious." This in turn allowed him to "doubt the genuineness of the 'correspondence'" and to conclude that the whole thing was "a *bogus* affair." The next day the *Intelligencer* was still at it: "the story of Gen. Lee's surrender of his gallant army to Grant" was based on reports in Northern-controlled newspapers. The purported letters between the two generals had been doctored, perhaps even fabricated, the editor argued, "a bogus correspondence between the two commanders."[4]

Steele's linguistic calisthenics, however, could not cloud the arrival of further information that confirmed the "Yankee report" when a Confederate newspaper carried it. On April 23 the *Intelligencer* reprinted from the *Augusta Constitutionalist*, "THE CAPITULATION OF GEN. LEE," which had appeared two days before: "Rumors of a very painful and depressing character have been prevalent in our city the past day or two, involving the loss by capture of a portion of the gallant Army of Northern Virginia, and the capitulation of the heroic General Lee to the enemy." The editor confessed that he was reluctant to believe these disastrous stories. After recounting the march of Lee's army from Petersburg westward, the article concluded that Lee, hemmed in by Grant's superior forces, had no option. "It is, however, no longer the part of wisdom or prudence to withhold the facts of the case, so far as they have reached us":

> The melancholy office of surrendering the army was tendered to Gen. Longstreet, but he declined and Gen. Lee performed the graceless office with the elevated dignity of his grand nature. He was immediately paroled, and given liberty to go either North or South. One report states that he proceeded to Richmond where his family is; and another that he is at Greensboro', North Carolina.
>
> The facts are received from an officer of the army who reached here yesterday, and entire reliance may be placed in the statement. They are confirmed by dispatches received through official channels, as well as by Northern papers which have come to hand.[5]

So it could not be denied. On the 25th, the *Intelligencer* was compelled to relate the particulars coming in from the paper's various exchanges, under a headline that blared, "Capitulation of Gen. Lee's Army! ["Surrender" was too loaded a term.] SAD DETAILS!!/GEN. LEE'S FAREWELL ADDRESS!" From the *Newberry* (S.C.) *Herald* of April 20 was taken information about the situation leading up to Sunday, the 9th of April: having reached Appomattox Court House, Lee's army was surrounded. By this time, it had only 5,000–8,000 effective soldiers with muskets, though without much ammunition.

Still, Lee ordered one last attempt to break out, which failed. Then under truce flag Union Brig. Gen. George Custer brought a note that eventually led to a meeting of Generals Lee and Grant on the morning of the 9th. Then came this, as printed in the *Intelligencer* of April 25:

> General Lee tendered his sword to Grant in token of surrender. That officer, however, with a courtesy for which we much accord him due respect, declined to receive it, or receiving, declined to retain it, and accompanied its return with substantially the following remarks: "Gen. Lee keep that sword. You have won it by your gallantry. You have not been whipped, but overpowered, and I cannot receive it as a token of surrender from so brave a man." The reply of Gen. Lee, we do not know. But Grant and himself are said to have been deeply affected by the solemnity of the occasion and to have shed tears. The scene occurred between ten and eleven o'clock a.m.

When word spread among Lee's officers and men of the capitulation, "some among the veterans wept like children," the *Intelligencer* added. Some men stole into the woods rather than surrender. Then occurred the parole exercises for the estimated 23,000 Confederates, after which the Southerners slowly dispersed, walking away toward home. The Federals perambulating the Confederates' camps gave no shouts of joy or jeers of contempt; "on the contrary, every symptom of respect was manifested."

The *Intelligencer* was even able to print Robert E. Lee's farewell address to his army, with its famous first sentence: "After four years of arduous service, marked by unsurpassed courage and fortitude, the army of Northern Virginia has been compelled to yield to overwhelming numbers and resources."[6]

In the midst of all this arrived word of the death of Abraham Lincoln.

Just the week before, the *Intelligencer* had called the president a "bloody tyrant"—one of the milder epithets that the paper had applied to Lincoln during the war. All of that changed when the *Chattanooga Gazette* of April 16 related what had occurred in Washington on the evening of the 14th, Good Friday. The *Intelligencer* on April 21 reprinted the *Gazette*'s long article under the bold headline, "THE DEATH OF LINCOLN! Great Tragedy in Washington!!" The article began with several brief dispatches out of the capital: "the President was shot in the Theatre to-night"; "the President is not expected to live through the night"; "Secretary Seward was also assassinated, but no arteries were cut."

The *Gazette* related that the president and Mrs. Lincoln were attending a performance of "Our American Cousin" at the city's Ford's Theatre and that a gun shot was heard during the play's third act. J. Wilkes Booth was named as Lincoln's assailant; after firing his pistol and dropping it on the floor of the Lincolns' private box, Booth jumped to the stage shouting, "*Sic semper tyrannis!*"

(Latin, "thus always to tyrants," Virginia's state motto). The assassin then ran across the stage and out of the theatre.

"The screams of Mrs. Lincoln first discovered the facts to the audience," the article stated; "after a hasty examination, it was found that the President had been shot through the head above and back of the femoral bone, and that some of the brain was oozing out." Lincoln was carried to a house across the street where surgeons rushed to help. "The President was in a state of syncope," the paper explained, "totally insensible, and breathing slowly.—The blood oozed from the wound at the back of his head. The Surgeons used every possible effort in medical skill, but all was gone."

Then came the final dispatches: "WASHINGTON, April 15, 1865. Abraham Lincoln died this morning at twenty-two minutes after seven o'clock" and "Vice President Andrew Johnson was sworn in as President of the United States, at 11 o'clock this morning."

The *Intelligencer*, quoting the *Gazette* article, was also able to recount the attack, evidently by one of Booth's accomplices, upon Secretary of State William H. Seward at his Washington home. Around 10 p.m. on April 14, a man rang the bell at Seward's residence. The secretary was in an upstairs bedroom recovering from a recent carriage accident. Claiming he had a doctor's note about Seward's medicines, the stranger strode past the servant at the door and rushed upstairs. When confronted by Seward's son Frederick, he knocked him forcefully on the head. Then, storming into the secretary's room, the stranger stabbed him three times in the neck, "severing, it is thought and hoped, no arteries, though he bled profusely," the article stated. "The assassins have not yet been discovered," it concluded (Seward's attacker was later identified as Lewis Payne, who, like Booth, made his escape).[7]

The day after the *Intelligencer* printed this article, editor Steele could only muse upon "The Tragedy at Washington" and its senselessness: "truly the mysterious workings of Providence are past all human comprehension." Several days later Steele—the same John Steele who once had characterized the Northern president as "the inhuman monster who now rules the North with more despotic sway than any autocrat ever ruled of whom history writes"—editorialized on Lincoln's assassination and the attempt on Seward's life, declaring, "a more appalling tragedy has not transpired in centuries."[8]

All eyes were now on Sherman's and Joe Johnston's armies in North Carolina. On April 13, the *Intelligencer* reported on Sherman's march through the state. It could not have reported that on that very day, Union troops entered

Raleigh—the ninth Confederate state capital to fall, and the third in the single month of April 1865. During the second week of April, Sherman's forces were concentrated around Raleigh, and Johnston's near Hillsboro, 35 or 40 miles northwest of the state capital. By this time Davis and his six Cabinet members, with other officials and aides, had travelled by rail from Richmond through Danville, in southwestern Virginia, to Greensboro, arriving there on the morning of April 11. On the 11th Johnston received word that Davis wished to meet with him at Greensboro. The general quickly boarded the train and on the morning of the 12th arrived there, three dozen miles to the west.

That evening in a private home President Davis, Generals Johnston and Beauregard convened with six Cabinet members: Judah Benjamin (State), Maj. Gen. John C. Breckinridge (War, since late January), George Trenholm (Treasury), George Davis (Attorney General), Stephen Mallory (Navy) and John Reagan (Postmaster General). Davis announced that even though they had just learned of Lee's surrender, he still planned to continue the war, saying, "I think we can whip the enemy yet if our people will turn out"—meaning all the soldiers absent without leave—by this time there were at least a hundred thousand of them. Johnston, however, disagreed and remarked (according to Secretary Mallory's diary): "My views, sir, are that our people are tired of the war, feel themselves whipped, and will not fight."

Johnston won out after Beauregard and all the Cabinet save Judah Benjamin supported his view. By the end of the meeting Davis had dictated a note that Johnston signed and that was to be carried to Sherman, proposing a meeting to discuss an armistice that would lead to an end of the war.

The general returned to his army that same night. After getting Johnston's note, Sherman sent one back agreeing to a meeting at some point between the lines in order to talk truce. The place eventually chosen was Durham, halfway between Hillsboro and Raleigh, and the residence of James and Nancy Bennett. Johnston and Sherman met on April 17, with the Union commander offering Johnston the same terms Grant had given Lee, including the key provisions: Southerners would give up their arms and go home on parole.

The discussions continued the next day, the 18th. This time Secretary of War Breckinridge attended, as the two generals had begun to broaden their conversation into one about making permanent peace between the U.S. and C.S. governments (and Breckinridge could represent that of the Confederacy). The secretary, fond of Kentucky bourbon, was delighted when Sherman produced a bottle of it and offered each general a drink. When Johnston proposed an agreement that would entail all remaining Confederate forces, Sherman worried that this surpassed his authority. Deep in thought, he wandered over to his saddlebag, again brought out the bottle and poured himself another drink, though without offering one to Johnston and Breckinridge. This led the outraged Kentuckian to complain to Johnston, "General Sherman is a hog. Yes, sir, a hog. Did you see him take that drink by himself?"[9]

Johnston and Sherman finally agreed upon a document that both thought would end the war. Within a week news of the armistice had reached Atlanta, with the *Intelligencer* reporting it on April 23. Two days later the paper reported that when Wilson's raiders approached Macon, Confederate Maj. Gen. Howell Cobb informed him of the armistice (General Beauregard had telegraphed him) and declared that his command, under Beauregard's authority, was therefore bound by it. John Steele confessed that all of this was too much to take:

> The public mind had hardly recovered from the shock it sustained in consequence of the evacuation of Richmond, when it was again surrounded by the intelligence that the gallant Army of Northern Virginia had been surrendered by Gen. Lee—again by the announcement that Lincoln had met with a terrible and bloody end—and now again that an armistice with a view to peace has been agreed upon between Gen. Johnston and Gen. Sherman. . . . The fall of Richmond told indeed of "coming events," but how sad some of them have been to us, and how unexpected. Truly, "the ways of Providence are past finding out!"[10]

But then General Grant, who had travelled to North Carolina, told Sherman that the deal was off; in arranging for the capitulation of Confederate forces beyond his immediate front, he had exceeded his authority. On April 24, Sherman thus informed Johnston that the armistice had been annulled and would expire in a few days. He then suggested another meeting. This time Johnston and Sherman reconvened at the Bennett house on the 26th and quickly agreed on a surrender of just the troops under Johnston's command.

Within a week the *Intelligencer* was able to report on the capitulation of the second Confederate army. (Actually, it was all the Southern forces in the Carolinas, plus the Army of Tennessee's remnant—a total of 39,012 officers and men, a considerably larger number than Lee had surrendered at Appomattox.) First came the rumor that Johnston had surrendered, which the paper related on April 30. Then, on May 2 (from the *Augusta Constitutionalist*) it published Johnston's general orders to his troops about how they would disband.[11]

And so the war was lost, as the *Intelligencer* acknowledged in remarkably speedy fashion. On May 4, in an editorial titled, "Adversity—How To Bear It," the paper offered its readers a colloquy on manly fortitude, reaching back to Roman history for precedents and encouraging "the humblest citizen of our land" to face the future with bravery. Even more than this, recall that the *Intelligencer* during the war had rattled its journalistic sword against "the Northern Goths and Vandals"; had defined the Yankee as "a cold-blooded, hypocritical, mean, underhand, cowardly fellow"; had editorialized against "Lincoln's minions"; and had repeatedly warned of the consequences of subjugation. Now, in a conversion every bit as dramatic as that of Saul of Tarsus, the *Intelligencer* counseled Georgians to accept subjugation under their former foes, and to do it in an orderly and peaceful manner as well:

> And now that adversity has overtaken the South; now that we have become a people overpowered in a contest long, and bloody, and fearful; now that great suffering, even for food to feed the women and children whom we are bound to protect and support, has become our fate; what becomes our duty? Yield to despair? NO!—Rather let us exercise fortitude; to "Caesar render that which is Caesar's, and to God that which is God's." Politically and religiously, this becomes our duty. In no slavish spirit, with no timid or fearful feeling with regard to coming consequences, do we arrive at this conclusion. What we have been during the great struggle the South has had with the North, we have been. Nothing have we to palliate or to deny; nothing to beseech mercy for. But we have now a future to pass over, a future that demands as much from us as the past, and so has every son of the South. Adversity is upon us and upon our people, and we and they must bear it with manly fortitude. Our armies have been surrendered and dispersed. The brave men who composed them have returned to their families and their homes. The fight is done. We have become an overpowered and an armless people, and our political, like our military leaders, are dispersed no more to be united in struggling against what seems to be our fate. Truly we are in a state of adversity, and in it let prudence and wise counsels prevail. The extent and nature of the terms upon which *peace* is to succeed *war*, we know not. Powerless to resist, whatever these may be, let us be orderly and peaceful, obeying the laws prescribed for our government, and leave the rest to the wise dispensation of HIM, who had we better served, might have given to the South that victory which he has withheld from it, and too surely bestowed upon another.[12]

As early evidence of postwar reconciliation, the *Intelligencer*'s advice to its readers on how they should face adversity is as eloquent a piece of consoling counsel as one is likely to find in the post-Appomattox South.

NOTES

1. Barrett, *Civil War in North Carolina*, 368–69; Sean Michael O'Brien, *Mobile, 1865: Last Stand of the Confederacy* (Westport CT: Praeger, 2001), 208–10.

2. James Pickett Jones, *Yankee Blitzkrieg: Wilson's Raid through Alabama and Georgia* (Athens: University of Georgia Press, 1976), 28, 33, 58, 69–71, 89–90, 111; Misulia, *Columbus Georgia*, 243; "Fall of Selma," *ADI*, April 6, 1865; "LATEST FROM THE SELMA AND MONTGOMERY PARTY" AND "THE EVACUATION OF MONTGOMERY," *ADI*, April 18; "THE ENEMY IN GEORGIA," *ADI*, April 20.

3. Horace Porter, *Campaigning with Grant* (Bloomington: Indiana University Press, 1961 [1897]), 313.

4. "CAPITULATION OF GEN. LEE," *ADI*, April 18, 1865; "YANKEE REPORT OF THE SURRENDER OF GEN. LEE'S ARMY," *ADI*, April 19; "GEN. LEE'S CAPITULATION TO GRANT," *ADI*, April 20.

5. "FROM THE AUGUSTA Constitutionalist 21st. THE CAPITULATION OF GEN. Lee," *ADI*, April 23, 1865.

6. "Capitulation of Gen. Lee's Army! SAD DETAILS!! Gen. Lee's Farewell Address!," *ADI*, April 25, 1865.

7. "THE EVACUATION OF RICHMOND," *ADI*, April 11, 1865; "DEATH OF LINCOLN!," *ADI*, April 21; W. Emerson Reck, *A. Lincoln: His Last 24 Hours* (Columbia: University of South Carolina Press, 1987), 92, 132–34.

8. "THE TRAGEDY AT WASHINGTON," *ADI*, April 22, 1865; "THE IRREPRESSIBLE CONFLICT," *ADI*, Oct. 5, 1862; "MORE PARTICULARS OF THE TRAGEDY AT WASHINGTON," *ADI*, April 25, 1865.

9. "THE LATEST NEWS," *ADI*, April 13, 1865 Angley, Cross and Hill, *Sherman's March*, 63–67; Symonds, *Joseph E. Johnston*, 353–56; William C. Davis, *Breckinridge Statesman Soldier Symbol* (Baton Rouge: Louisiana State University Press, 1974), 479; Joseph T. Durkin, *Confederate Navy Chief: Stephen R. Mallory* (Columbia: University of South Carolina Press, 1969 [1954]), 340; Davis, *Into Tennessee and Failure*, 39 n.22.

10. "Armistice Between Generals Johnston and Sherman. Suspension of Hostilities," *ADI*, April 23, 1865; "GEN. COBB'S NOTIFICATION OF THE ARMISTICE TO GEN. WILSON," "MACON SURRENDERED," "TELEGRAPHIC. The Enemy Occupy Macon" and "COMING EVENTS CAST THEIR SHADOWS BEFORE THEM,'" *ADI*, April 25.

11. Symonds, *Joseph E. Johnston*, 357; "Tabular statement of officers and men of the Confederate Army paroled at Greensborough, N.C., and other points, in accordance with the military convention of April 26, 1865," *OR*, vol. 47, pt. 1, 1066; "RUMORS AFLOAT," *ADI*, April 30, 1865; "OUR CONDITION—WHAT IS IT?," *ADI*, May 3; Joseph E. Johnston, *Narrative of Military Operations* (New York: D., Appleton, 1874), 415–16.

12. "ADVERSITY—HOW TO BEAR IT," *ADI*, May 4, 1865; "Our War Policy," *ADI*, April 15, 1861; "What Constitutes a Yankee?," *ADI*, Aug. 24, 1861; "Sacrilege," *ADI*, March 12, 1862; "ENCOURAGEMENT FOR THE TIMID FROM THE LESSONS OF HISTORY," *ADI*, May 15, 1862.

Epilogue. After the War

AT THE END OF THE CIVIL WAR the *Atlanta Daily Intelligencer,* like Scarlett O'Hara in the famous novel, had done something notable: it had survived. More than half of the approximately sixty daily and weekly newspapers publishing at the start of the war had ceased doing so at its end.

As with all Georgians, and with ex-Confederates particularly, the *Intelligencer* struggled not only to stay afloat financially, but to cope with the shifting political winds during the first years of reconstruction and Federal military occupation. After Whitehall Street south of the railroad was rebuilt, the paper set up its offices directly across the street from where it had been located before Sherman's fires. An issue from July 1868 stated that it was located in the "Muhlenbrink Building, west side of Whitehall street," using the prewar name for the stretch of Whitehall that derived from Hansa Muhlenbrink's cigar store (which had literally gone up in smoke during the Federal occupation).

The newspaper's durability was evident in mid-1868 with the *Intelligencer's* return to its conventional four-page format—a big sheet, 24 inches tall and 34 inches wide, folded down the middle. Moreover, in Atlanta's "normalized" postwar economy, subscription prices had dropped. In September 1868, a year's-worth of the *Intelligencer* cost $10; in January 1865, that much money (mind you, in Confederate currency) would have bought just one month of the daily.

It was not economics, though, that threatened the *Intelligencer,* Atlanta's oldest daily newspaper. It was politics. In the immediate years after the war, the *Intelligencer* shared the city with another appropriately-named daily, the *New Era.* Yet the real competition came in 1868—the year Atlanta became the state capital—when the *Atlanta Constitution* was founded. The new paper became the voice of the Democratic Party, as John Steele's editorial voice grew weaker.

Indeed, that voice silenced altogether when the *Intelligencer's* longtime editor passed away on January 11, 1871. Just a few months later, the owner of the newspaper, Jared Whitaker, sold all of his printing equipment for $4,000 in a public auction (the *Constitution* bought it).

DRAMATIS PERSONAE

SAMUEL CHESTER REID, the "290" who switched over to the *Knoxville/Atlanta Register* in January 1864, ceased writing six months later due to a rheumatic attack. He recovered and resumed the practice of law in 1865. The next year he got married and started raising a family. He died in Washington, D.C., in 1897.

After the war ALEXANDER ST. CLAIR-ABRAMS, the *Intelligencer*'s "St. Clair," moved to New York and joined the staff of James Gordon Bennett's *New York Herald*. Onset of bad health brought him back to Atlanta. There he founded another newspaper, the *Daily Herald* (of which Henry W. Grady became editor). In 1880, after moving to Florida, he bought land and helped found the town of Tavares (now an exurb of Orlando). By the turn of the century, Abrams had moved to Jacksonville. He died there in 1931 at the age of 86.

ISAAC BOWEN PILGRIM, foreman of the wartime *Intelligencer*, returned to Atlanta after the war. He resumed his position as a typesetter at the *Intelligencer* until the paper folded. Then he worked for a decade as a printer for the *Constitution*. He died in 1917 at the age of 85, and is buried in Atlanta's Oakland Cemetery with his wife Nancy and their daughter Honolulu Pilgrim Harris.

JOHN H. STEELE held the position of editor of the *Daily Intelligencer* from March 21, 1863, to his death on January 11, 1871. He is buried in Oakland Cemetery with his wife Mary Ann.

JARED IRWIN WHITAKER, longtime *Intelligencer* owner, led a life of distinction (grandson of a Georgia governor, attorney, state legislator, mayor of Atlanta, state commissary general). He was also no stranger to tragedy. His first wife, Susan, died before the war at the age of 22. During the war he lost three of his five brothers as well as an infant son. By the time of his death in 1884 at the age of 65, Whitaker's decline had become a matter of public record. Author of an early history of Georgia (1881), Isaac W. Avery wrote of Whitaker, "illy fitted to be a poor man, taking to drink, falling lower and lower, drifting down socially and pecuniarily, he is to-day to those who knew him in his better days a sad spectacle, seedy, impecunious and pitiful." Whitaker is buried in Oakland Cemetery alongside his wife Nannie beneath a headstone that reads:

JARED IRWIN
WHITAKER
MAY 4, 1818.
MAY 3, 1884.

Works Cited

Adolphson, Steven J. "An Incident of Valor in the Battle of Peachtree Creek, 1864." *Georgia Historical Quarterly*, vol. 57, no. 3 (Fall 1973). 406–20.
Alexander, Bevin. *Lost Victories: The Military Genius of Stonewall Jackson*. New York: Henry Holt, 1992.
Alexander, Thomas B. and Richard E. Beringer. *The Anatomy of the Confederate Congress*. Nashville: Vanderbilt University Press, 1972.
Allen, Richard Michael, comp. *The 7th Georgia Volunteer Infantry Regiment, 1861–1865: A Biographical Roster*. El Dorado Hills, CA: Savas Beatie, 2018.
Ambrose, Stephen E. "By Enlisting Negroes, Could the South Still win the War?" *Civil War Times Illustrated*, vol. 3, no., 9 (January 1965). 16–21.
———. "Fort Donelson: A 'Disastrous' Blow to the South." *Civil War Times Illustrated*, vol. 5, no. 3 (June 1966). 4–13, 42–45.
———. "The Struggle for Vicksburg." *Civil War Times Illustrated*, vol. 6, no. 4 (July 1967). 4- 26, 43–46, 48–55, 60–65.
Ames, William F. *A History of the National Intelligencer*. Chapel Hill: University of North Carolina Press, 1972.
Andrews, J. Cutler. *The North Reports the Civil War*. Pittsburgh: University of Pittsburgh Press, 1955.
———. *The South Reports the Civil War*. Princeton: Princeton University Press, 1970.
———. "The Southern Telegraph Company, 1861–1865: A Chapter in the History of Wartime Communication. *Journal of Southern History*, vol. 30, no. 3 (August 1964). 319–44.
Angley, Wilson, Jerry L. Cross and Michael Hill. *Sherman's March through North Carolnia*. Raleigh: North Carolina Division of Archives and History, 1995.
Arnold, James R. *Grant Wins the War: Decision at Vicksburg*. New York: John Wiley & Sons, 1997.
Ash, Steven V. *When the Yankees Came: Conflict and Chaos in the Occupied South, 1861–1865*. Chapel Hill: University of North Carolina Press, 1995.
Ashby, Thomas A. *Life of Turner Ashby*. New York: Neale Publishing, 1914.
Baker, B. Kimball. "The Memphis Appeal." *Civil War Times Illustrated*, vol. 18, no. 4 (July 1979). 32–39.
Ballard, Michael B. "Breakdown in Macon." *Civil War Times Illustrated*, vol. 19, no. 6 (October 1980). 31–33
———. *Pemberton: A Biography*. Jackson: University Press of Mississippi, 1991.

Barnwell, Valentine T. *Barnwell's Atlanta City Directory*. Atlanta: Atlanta Intelligencer Book and Job Office, 1867.
Barrett, John G. *The Civil War in North Carolina*. Chapel Hill: University of North Carolina Press, 1963.
Basler, Roy P., ed. *The Collected Works of Abraham Lincoln*. 9 vols. New Brunswick, NJ: Rutgers University Press, 1953.
Bates, Samuel P. *The Battle of Chancellorsville*. Gaithersburg MD: Ron R. VanSickle Military Books, 1987 [1882].
Bearss, Edwin C. "Benjamin Henry Grierson." In John T. Hubbell and James W. Geary, eds., *Biographical Dictionary of the Union: Northern Leaders of the Civil War*. Westport, CT: Greenwood Press, 1995. 214–15.
———. "Earl Van Dorn." In William C. Davis, ed., *The Confederate General*. 6 vols. Harrisburg, PA: National Historical Society, 1991. Vol. 6, 71–75
———. "Engagement at Raymond," "Grierson's Raid" and "Raid on Holly Springs, Miss." In Patricia L. Faust, ed., *Historical Times Illustrated Encyclopedia of the Civil War*. New York: Harper & Row, 1986. 617, 326, 365–66.
———. "Tullahoma Campaign." In Patricia L. Faust, ed., *Historical Times Illustrated Encyclopedia of the Civil War*. New York: Harper & Row, 1986. 764–65.
Bearss, Edwin C. and Howard P. Nash. "Fort Henry." *Civil War Times Illustrated*, vol. 4, no. 7 (November 1965). 8–15.
Bearss, Edwin Cole. *The Campaign for Vicksburg*. 3 vols. Dayton, OH: Morningside, 1985–86.
Beck, Brandon H. *Streight's Foiled Raid on the Western & Atlantic Railroad: Emma Sansom's Courage and Nathan Bedford Forrest's Pursuit*. Charleston, SC: History Press, 2016.
Behrens, Roger. *Total War in Carolina: Sherman's 1865 Carolinas Campaign*. Mahomet, IL: BPC Publishers, 1992.
Bergeron, Arthur W., Jr. "Danville Leadbetter." In William C. Davis ed., *The Confederate General*. 6 vols. Harrisburg: National Historical Society, 1991. Vol. 4, 30–31.
Bill, Alfred Hoyt. *The Beleaguered City: Richmond 1861–65*. New York: Alfred A. Knopf, 1946.
Blair, William A. "Barbarians at Fredericksburg's Gate: The Impact of the Union Army on Civilians." In Gary W. Gallagher, ed., *The Fredericksburg Campaign: Decision on the Rappahannock*. Chapel Hill: University of North Carolina Press, 1995. 142–70.
Blake, W. O. *Pictorial History of the Great Rebellion*. Columbus, OH: Gilmore & Segner, 1866.
Blondheim, Menahem. *News over the Wires: The Telegraph and the Flow of Public Information in America, 1844–1897*. Cambridge: Harvard University Press, 1994.
Bobrick, Benson. *The Battle of Nashville: General George H. Thomas & the Most Decisive Battle of the Civil War*. New York: Alfred A. Knopf, 2010.
Bogle, James G. "The Great Locomotive Chase, or the Andrews Raid." *Blue & Gray*, vol. 4, no. 6 (July 1987). 8–19, 22, 24, 46–54, 58–59, 62.
Bohannon, Keith S. "'Witness the Redemption of the Army': Reenlistment in the

Confederate Army of Tennessee, January-March 1864." In Lesley J. Gordon and John C. Inscoe, eds., *Inside the Confederate Nation: Essays in Honor of Emory M. Thomas*. Baton Rouge: Louisiana State University Press, 2005. 111–127.

Bollet, Alfred Jay. *Civil War Medicine: Challenges and Triumphs*. Tucson: Galen Press, 2002.

Bond, Bill, "Abrams Made mark on County, State." *Orlando Sentinel*, Jan. 28, 1987.

Bonds, Russell S. *Stealing the General: The Great Locomotive Chase and the First Medal of Honor*. Yardley, PA: Westholme, 2007.

Bowers, John. *Stonewall Jackson: Portrait of a Soldier*. New York: William Morrow, 1989.

Bragg, Diane. "An Affair of Words: Tennessee's Civil War Press and the Confederate Nation." In David B. Sachsman, ed., *A Press Divided: Newspaper Coverage of the Civil War*. New Brunswick, NJ: Transaction Publishers, 2014. 115–140.

Bragg, William Harris. "Griswoldville." In John C. Inscoe, ed., *The Civil War in Georgia*. Athens: University of Georgia Press, 2011. 97–98.

Brantley, Rabun Lee. *Georgia Journalism of the Civil War Period*. Nashville: George Peabody College for Teachers, 1929.

Brewer, James D. *The Raiders of 1862*. Westport, CT: Praeger, 1997.

Broadfoot, Daniel W. *General Robert F. Hoke: Lee's Modest Warrior*. Winston-Salem, NC: John F. Blair, 1996.

Brooksher, William Riley. *Bloody Hill: The Civil War Battle of Wilson's Creek*. Washington: Brassey's, 1995.

Brown, D. Alexander. *Grierson's Raid*. Dayton, OH: Press of Morningside Bookshop, 1981 [1954].

———. "Pea Ridge." *Civil War Times Illustrated*, vol. 6, no. 6 (October 1967). 4–11, 46–48.

Brown, Dee Alexander. *The Bold Cavaliers: Morgan's 2nd Kentucky Cavalry Raiders*. Philadelphia: Lippincott, 1959.

Brown, Jack I. *The Shade of the Trees: A Narrative Based on the Life and Career of Lieutenant General Thomas Jonathan "Stonewall" Jackson*. Great Neck, NY: Todd & Honeywell, 1988.

Brown, Kent Masterson. *Retreat from Gettysburg: Lee, Logistics, and the Pennsylvania Campaign*. Chapel Hill: University of North Carolina Press, 2005.

Bryan, Charles F., Jr. "The Siege of Yorktown Part I." *Civil War Times Illustrated*, vol. 21, no. 4 (June 1982), 8–15.

———. "The Siege of Yorktown Part II." *Civil War Times Illustrated*, vol. 21, no. 5 (September 1982). 18–25, 28–29.

Bryan, T. Conn. *Confederate Georgia*. Athens: University of Georgia Press, 1953.

Bulla, David W. and Gregory A. Borchard. *Journalism in the Civil War Era*. New York: Peter Lang, 2010.

Burton, E. Milby. *The Siege of Charleston 1861–1865*. Columbia: University of South Carolina Press, 1970.

Bussel, Alan. "The Atlanta *Daily Intelligencer* Covers Sherman's March." *Journalism Quarterly*, vol. 51, no. 3 (Autumn 1974). 405–10.

Butkovich, Brad. *The Battle of Allatoona Pass: Civil War Skirmish in Bartow County, Georgia*. Charleston: History Press, 2014.
Butler, Benjamin F. *Butler's Book*. Boston: A. M. Thayer, 1892.
Byrd, Joseph P., IV. *Confederate Sharpshooter: Major William E. Simmons*. Macon: Mercer University Press, 2016.
Campbell, R. Thomas. *The C.S.S. H. L. Hunley: Confederate Submarine*. Shippensburg, PA: Burd Street Press, 2000.
Campbell, R. Thomas and Alan B. Flanders. *Confederate Phoenix: The CSS Virginia*. Shippensburg, PA: Burd Street Press, 2001.
Carter III, Samuel. *The Final Fortress: The Campaign for Vicksburg 1862–1863*. New York: St. Martin's Press, 1980.
Casdorph, Paul D. *Prince John Magruder: His Life and Campaigns*. New York: John Wiley & Sons, 1996.
Castel, Albert. *Civil War Kansas: Reaping the Whirlwind*. Lawrence: University Press of Kansas, 1997 [1958].
———. *Decision in the West: The Atlanta Campaign of 1864*. Lawrence: University Press of Kansas, 1992.
———. "The Fort Pillow Massacre: A Fresh Examination of the Evidence." In Castel, *Winning and Losing in the Civil War: Essays and Stories*. Columbia: University of South Carolina Press, 1999. 35–50.
———. *General Sterling Price and the Civil War in the West*. Baton Rouge: Louisiana State University Press, 1968.
———. "Victory at Corinth." *Civil War Times Illustrated*, vol. 17, no. 6 (October 1978). 12–22.
Catton, Bruce. *The American Heritage Picture History of the Civil War*. New York: American Heritage Publishing Co., 1960.
———. "Sheridan at Five Forks." *Journal of Southern History*, vol. 21, no. 3 (August 1955). 305–15.
Chambers, Lenoir. *Stonewall Jackson*. 2 vols. New York: William Morrow, 1959.
Chernow, Ron. *Grant*. New York: Penguin Press, 2017.
Cimprich, John. *Fort Pillow, a Civil War Massacre, and Public Memory*. Baton Rouge: Louisiana State University Press, 2005.
Cohen, Stan and James G. Bogle. *The General & the Texas: A Pictorial History of the Andrews Raid, April 12, 1862*. Missoula, MT: Pictorial Histories Publishing, 1999.
Coleman, Kenneth, ed. *A History of Georgia*. Athens: University of Georgia Press, 1999 [1997].
Collins, Darrell L. *The Battles of Cross Keys and Port Republic*. Lynchburg, VA: H. E. Howard, 1993.
Commager, Henry Steele, ed. *The Defeat of the Confederacy*. Princeton, NJ: .D. Van Nostrand, 1964.
Connelly, Donald B. *John M. Schofield and the Politics of Generalship*. Chapel Hill: University of North Carolina Press, 2006.

Connelly, Thomas L. *Civil War Tennessee: Battles and Leaders.* Knoxville: University of Tennessee Press, 1979.

Connelly, Thomas Lawrence. *Army of the Heartland: The Army of Tennessee, 1861–1862.* Baton Rouge: Louisiana State University Press, 1967.

———. *Autumn of Glory: The Army of Tennessee, 1862–1865.* Baton Rouge: Louisiana State University Press, 1971.

Connelly, Thomas Lawrence and Archer Jones. *The Politics of Command: Factions and Ideas in Confederate Strategy.* Baton Rouge: Louisiana State University Press, 1973.

Conti, Gerald. "Seeing the Elephant." *Civil War Times Illustrated,* vol. 23, no. 4 (June 1984). 19.

[Cooke, John Esten]. *The Life of Stonewall Jackson.* New York: Charles B. Richardson, 1864 [1863].

Cooling, Benjamin Franklin. *Forts Henry and Donelson: The Key to the Confederate Heartland.* Knoxville: University of Tennessee Press, 1987.

Coombe, Jack D. *Thunder Along the Mississippi: The River Battles That Split the Confederacy.* New York: Bantam Books, 1998 [1996].

Cooney, Charles F. "First to Fall." *Civil War Times Illustrated,* vol. 20, no. 6 (October 1981), 26- 27.

Cooper, William J. *Jefferson Davis, American.* New York: Alfred A. Knopf, 2000.

Cottrell, Steve. *Civil War Tennessee.* Gretna, LA: Pelican Publishing, 2001.

Coulter, E. Merton. *The Confederate States of America 1861–1865.* Baton Rouge: Louisiana State University Press, 1950.

Cozzens, Peter. *The Darkest Days of the War: The Battles of Iuka & Corinth.* Chapel Hill: University of North Carolina Press, 1997.

———. *General John Pope: A Life for the Nation.* Urbana; University of Illinois Press, 2000.

———. *The Shipwreck of Their Hopes: The Battles for Chattanooga.* Urbana; University of Illinois Press, 1994.

———. *This Terrible Sound: The Battle of Chickamauga.* Urbana: University of Illinois Press, 1992.

Craven, Avery. *The Coming of the Civil War.* Chicago: University of Chicago Press, 1957 [1942].

Crist, Lynda Lasswell, *et al.,* eds. *The Papers of Jefferson Davis.* 14 vols. *Volume 7: 1861.* Baton Rouge: Louisiana State University Press, 1992.

Crofts, Daniel W. "Andrew Jackson Rogers." In John T. Hubbell and James W. Geary, eds., *Biographical Dictionary of the Union : Leaders in the Civil War.* Westport, CT: Greenwood Press, 1995. 443.

Crook, D. P. *Diplomacy During the American Civil War.* New York: John Wiley and Sons, 1975.

Cunningham, Horace H. *Field Medical Services at the Battles of Manassas (Bull Run).* Athens: University of Georgia Press, 1968.

Cunningham, S. A. "Events Leading to the Battle." *Confederate Veteran,* vol. 18, no. 1 (January 1910). 17–20.

[Cunningham, Sumner A.] "Disastrous Campaign in Tennessee." *Confederate Veteran*, vol. 12, no. 7 (July 1904). 338–41.

Current, Richard N. *The Lincoln Nobody Knows*. New York: McGraw-Hill, 1958.

Dabney, R. L. *Life and Campaigns of Lieut.-Gen. Thomas J. Jackson, (Stonewall)*. New York: Blelock & Co., 1866.

Dabney, Virginius. *Pistols & Pointed Pens: The Dueling Editors of Old Virginia*. Chapel Hill: Algonquin Books of Chapel Hill, 1987.

Daniel, Larry J. *Battle of Stones River: The Forgotten Conflict between the Confederate Army of Tennessee and the Union Army of the Cumberland*. Baton Rouge: Louisiana State University Press, 2012.

———. *Cannoneers in Gray: The Field Artillery of the Army of Tennessee 1861–1865*. University: University of Alabama Press, 1984.

———. *Conquered: Why the Army of Tennessee Failed*. Chapel Hill: University of North Carolina Press, 2019.

Daniel, Larry J., and Lynn N. Bock. *Island No. 10: Struggle for the Mississippi Valley*. Tuscaloosa: University of Alabama Press, 1996.

Davidson, James West and Mark H. Lytle. *The United States: A History of the Republic*. Englewood Cliffs, NJ: Prentice-Hall, 1981.

Davis, Burke. *Sherman's March*. New York: Random House, 1980.

———. *They Called Him Stonewall: A Life of Lt. Gen. T. J. Jackson, C.S.A.* New York: Holt, Rinehart and Winston, 1964.

———. *To Appomattox: Nine April Days*. New York: Rinehart, 1959.

Davis, James A. *Maryland, My Maryland: Music and Patriotism during the American Civil War*. Lincoln: University of Nebraska Press, 2019.

Davis, Michael. *The Image of Lincoln in the South*. Knoxville: University of Tennessee Press, 1971.

Davis, Robert Scott. *Civil War Atlanta*. Charleston: History Press, 2011.

Davis, Stephen. *All the Fighting They Want: The Atlanta Campaign from Peachtree Creek to the City's Surrender, July 18-September 2, 1864*. El Dorado Hills, CA: Savas Beatie, 2017.

———. *Atlanta Will Fall: Sherman, Joe Johnston, and the Yankee Heavy Battalions*. Wilmington, DE: Scholarly Resources, 2001.

———. "An Avalanche of Wounded: Atlanta's Confederate Hospitals and the Challenge of Chickamauga, Fall 1863." *Atlanta Medicine*, vol. 78, issue 3 (2005). 5–11

———. "The Conductor versus the Foreman: William Fuller, Anthony Murphy, and the Pursuit of the Andrews Raiders." *Atlanta History*, vol. 34, no. 4 (Winter 1990–91). 39–55.

———. "'Far Better in the Present Emergency': John Bell Hood Replaces Joseph E. Johnston." In Chris Mackowski and Kristopher D. White, eds., *Turning Points of the American Civil War*. Carbondale: Southern Illinois University Press, 2018. 186–206.

———. "How Many Civilians Died in Sherman's Bombardment of Atlanta?" *Atlanta History*, vol. 45, no. 4 (2003). 5–23.

———. *Into Tennessee and Failure: John Bell Hood.* Macon: Mercer University Press, 2019.
———. "Lee, Hood and the Fog of War." *Civil War News*, vol. 43, no. 9 (September 2017). 20–22.
———. *A Long and Bloody Task: The Atlanta Campaign From Dalton through Kennesaw Mountain to the Chattahoochee River May 5–July 18, 1864.* El Dorado Hills, CA: Savas Beatie, 2016.
———. "No Hope of Success." *Civil War Times*, vol. 57, no. 2 (April 2018). 34–40.
———. "A Reappraisal of the Generalship of John Bell Hood in the Battles for Atlanta." In Theodore P. Savas and David A. Woodbury, eds., *The Campaign for Atlanta & Sherman's March to the Sea.* Campbell, CA: Savas Woodbury Publications, 1994. 49–95.
———. "Riding with Sheridan." *Civil War News*, vol. 43, no. 12 (December 2017). 32–33.
———. "Sherman in North Georgia: The Battle of Resaca." *Blue & Gray*, vol. 31, no. 4 (Summer 2015). 6–9, 17–28 42–50.
———. "Sherman's Bombardment of Atlanta July 20-August 25 1864," *The Artilleryman*, vol. 39, no. 2 (Spring 2018). 32–39.
———. "Simply Criminal." *America's Civil War*, vol. 32, no. 2 (May 2019). 28–37.
———. *Texas Brigadier to the Fall of Atlanta: John Bell Hood.* Macon: Mercer University Press, 2019.
———. "'A Very Barbarous Mode of Carrying on War': Sherman's Artillery Bombardment of Atlanta." *Georgia Historical Quarterly*, vol. 79, no. 1 (Spring 1995). 57–90.
———. *What the Yankees Did to Us: Sherman's Bombardment and Wrecking of Atlanta.* Macon: Mercer University Press, 2012.
———. "Would P. G. T. Lead the A. o. T?" *Civil War Times*, vol. 56, no. 2 (April 2017). 36–41.
Davis, Steve. "Another Look at Civil War Medical Care: Atlanta's Confederate Hospitals. *Journal of the Medical Association of Georgia*, vol. 88, no. 2 (April 1999). 9–23.
Davis, William C. *Battle at Bull Run: A History of the First Major Campaign of the Civil War.* Garden City, NY: Doubleday, 1977.
———. *Breckinridge Statesman Soldier Symbol.* Baton Rouge: Louisiana State University Press, 1974.
———. *Jefferson Davis: The Man and His Hour.* New York: HarperCollins, 1991.
———. *Look Away! A History of the Confederate States of America.* New York: Free Press, 2002.
Deberry, J. H. "Kirby Smith's Bluegrass Invasion." *America's Civil War*, vol. 10, no. 3 (March 1997. 54–60, 88, 90.
DeRosa, Marshall L. *The Confederate Constitution of 1861: An Inquiry into American Constitutionalism.* Columbia: University of Missouri Press, 1991.
Derry, Joseph T. *Georgia.* Vol. 6 of Clement A. Evans, ed., *Confederate Military History.* Atlanta: Confederate Publishing Co., 1899. 12 vols.

Detlefson, Ellen Gay. "Printing in the Confederacy, 1861–1865: A Southern Industry in Wartime. Ph.D. dissertation, Columbia University, 1975.

Detzer, David. *Allegiance: Fort Sumter, Charleston, and the Beginning of the Civil War.* New York: Harcourt, 2001.

Dillard, Phillip D. "The Confederate Debate Over Arming Slaves: Views from Macon and Augusta Newspapers. *Georgia Historical Quarterly*, vol. 79, no. 1 (Spring 1995). 117–46

Dinkins, James. *1861 to 1865 Personal Recollections and Experiences in the Confederate Army By an Old Johnnie.* Dayton OH: Press of Morningside Bookshop, 1975 [1897].

Dolan, Mark K. "Samuel Chester Reid, Jr.: A Professional Goes to War." In Patricia G. McNeely, Debra Reddin van Tuyll and Henry H. Schulte, eds., *Knights of the Quill: Confederate Correspondents and their Civil War Reporting.* West Lafayette, IN: Purdue University Press, 2010. 247–64.

Dowdey, Clifford. *The Land They Fought For: The Story of the South as the Confederacy, 1832- 1865.* Garden City, NY: Doubleday, 1955.

Dufour, Charles. *The Night the War Was Lost.* New York: Doubleday, 1960.

Duncan, Russell. *Where Death and Glory Meet: Colonel Robert Gould Shaw and the 54th Massachusetts Infantry.* Athens: University of Georgia Press, 1999.

Durden, Robert F. *The Gray and the Black: The Confederate Debate on Emancipation.* Baton Rouge: Louisiana State University Press, 1972.

Durkin, Joseph T. *Confederate Navy Chief: Stephen R. Mallory.* Columbia: University of South Carolina Press, 1969 [1954].

Dyer, John P. *The Gallant Hood.* Indianapolis: Bobbs-Merrill, 1950.

Dyer, Thomas G. *Secret Yankees: The Union Circle in Confederate Atlanta.* Baltimore: Johns Hopkins University Press, 1999.

Eaton, Clement. *A History of the Southern Confederacy.* New York: Free Press, 1954.

Ecelbarger, Gary. *Slaughter at the Chapel: The Battle of Ezra Church 1864.* Norman: University of Oklahoma Press, 2016.

Ellis, B. G. *The Moving Appeal: Mr. McClanahan, Mrs. Dill, and the Civil War's Great Newspaper Run.* Macon: Mercer University Press, 2003.

Ellis, Barbara G. and Steven J. Dick. "Who Was "Shadow"?'The Computer Knows: Applying Grammar-Program Statistics in Content Analysis to Solve Mysteries about Authorship." *Journalism & Mass Communication Quarterly*, vol. 73, no. 4 (Winter 1996). 947–62.

Engle, Stephen D. *Struggle for the Heartland: The Campaign from Fort Henry to Corinth.* Lincoln: University of Nebraska Press, 2001.

Esposito, Vincent J., ed. *The West Point Atlas of American Wars.* 2 vols. New York: Frederick A. Praeger, 1979.

Evans, David. *Sherman's Horsemen: Union Cavalry Operations in the Atlanta Campaign.* Bloomington: Indiana University Press, 1996.

Everett, Donald E., ed. *Chaplain Davis and Hood's Texas Brigade.* Baton Rouge: Louisiana State University Press, 1999 [1863].

Farwell, Byron. *Stonewall: A Biography of General Thomas J. Jackson.* New York: W. W. Norton, 1992.

Feldman, Ruth Elaine. "A Checklist of Atlanta Newspapers, 1846–1948." Master's thesis, Emory University, 1948.
Ferris, Norman B. *The Trent Affair: A Diplomatic Crisis.* Knoxville: University of Tennessee Press, 1977.
Frank, Joseph Allan and George A. Reaves. *"Seeing the Elephant": Raw Recruits at the Battle of Shiloh.* Westport, CT: Greenwood Press, 1989.
Franklin, John Hope. *The Militant South 1800–1861.* Cambridge: Harvard University Press, 1956.
Frazier, Donald S. *Blood & Treasure: Confederate Empire in the Southwest.* College Station: Texas A & M University Press, 1995.
———. *Lee's Lieutenants: A Study in Command.* 3 vols. New York: Charles Scribner's Sons, 1942–44.
———. *R. E. Lee: A Biography.* 4 vols. New York: Charles Scribner's Sons, 1934–35.
Freemon, Frank R. *Gangrene and Glory: Medical Care during the American Civil War.* Madison, NJ: Fairleigh Dickinson University Press, 1998.
French, Samuel G. *Two Wars: An Autobiography.* Huntington, WV: Blue Acorn Press, 1999 [1901].
Fuchs, Richard L. *An Unerring Fire: The Massacre at Fort Pillow.* Rutherford, NJ: Fairleigh Dickinson University Press, 1994.
Fullenkamp, Leonard, Stephen Bowman and Jay Luvaas, eds. *Guide to the Vicksburg Campaign.* Lawrence: University Press of Kansas, 1998.
Furgurson, Ernest B. *Ashes of Glory: Richmond at War.* New York: Alfred A. Knopf, 1996.
———. *Chancellorsville 1863: The Souls of the Brave.* New York: Alfred A. Knopf, 1992.
———. *Not War But Murder: Cold Harbor 1864.* New York: Alfred A. Knopf, 2000.
Gallagher, Gary W. "The Yanks Have Had a Terrible Whipping: Confederates Evaluate the Battle of Fredericksburg." In Gallagher, ed., *The Fredericksburg Campaign: Decision on the Rappahannock.* Chapel Hill: University of North Carolina Press, 1995. 113–141.
Galloway, Tammy Harden, ed. *Dear Old Roswell: The Civil War Letters of the King Family of Roswell, Georgia.* Macon: Mercer University Press, 2003.
Garrett, Franklin M. *Atlanta and Environs: A Chronicle of Its People and Events.* 2 vols. New York: Lewis Historical Publishing, 1955.
———. "Civilian Life in Atlanta." *Civil War Times Illustrated,* vol. 3, no. 4 (July 1964). 30–33.
———. "The Phoenix Begins to Rise: The *Atlanta Daily Intelligencer* Announces the Return of the Railroads." *Atlanta History,* vol. 37, no. 4 (Winter 1994). 5–8.
Garrison, Webb. *The Encyclopedia of Civil War Usage.* Nashville: Cumberland House, 2001.
Gay, Mary A. H. *Life in Dixie During the War.* Atlanta Charles F. Byrd, 1897, third edition [1892].
Gott, Kendall D. *Where the South Lost the War: An Analysis of the Fort Henry-Fort Donelson Campaign, February 1862.* Mechanicsburg, PA: Stackpole Books, 2003.

Gottfried, Bradley M. *The Maps of Fredericksburg.* El Dorado Hills, CA: Savas Beatie, 2018.

Gottschalk, Phil. *In Deadly Earnest: The Missouri Brigade.* Columbia: Missouri River Press, 1991.

Govan, Gilbert E. and James W. Livingood. *A Different Valor: The Story of General Joseph E. Johnston, C.S.A.* Westport, CT: Greenwood Press, 1973 [1956]).

Grant, Alfred P. *The American Civil War and the British Press.* Jefferson, NC: McFarland, 2000.

Griffith, Louis Turner and John Erwin Talmadge. *Georgia Journalism 1763–1950.* Athens: University of Georgia Press, 1957.

Grimsley, Mark. *The Hard Hand of War: Union Military Policy Toward Southern Civilians 1861–1865.* New York: Cambridge University Press, 1995.

———. "Rear Guard at Williamsburg." *Civil War Times Illustrated,* vol. 24, no. 3 (May 1985), 10–13, 27–30.

Guelzo, Allen C. *Lincoln's Emancipation Proclamation: The End of Slavery in America.* New York: Simon & Schuster, 2004.

Gwynne, S. C. *Rebel Yell: The Violence, Passion, and Redemption of Stonewall Jackson.* New York: Scribner, 2014.

Hagler, Gould. "Crossing the Hooch without a Hitch." *Civil War News,* vol. 45, no. 9 (September 2019). 26–27.

Hall, James O. "The Dahlgren Papers: Yankee Plot to Kill President Davis." *Civil War Times Illustrated,* vol. 22, no 7 (November 1983). 30–39.

———. "The Spy Harrison." *Civil War Times Illustrated,* vol. 24, no. 10 (February 1986). 19–25.

Hall, Martin Hardwick. *Sibley's New Mexico Campaign.* Austin: University of Texas Press, 1960.

Hamlin, Augustus C. *The Attack of Stonewall Jackson at Chancellorsville.* Fredericksburg VA: Sergeant Kirkland's, 1997 [1896].

[Hanleiter, Cornelius Redding]. "C. R. H." "A History of Newspaper Enterprises in Atlanta." *Atlanta Southern Confederacy,* July 14, 1861.

Hardy, Michael C. *The Capitals of the Confederacy: A History.* Charleston: History Press, 2015.

Harrington, Fred Harvey. *Fighting Politician: Major General N. P. Banks.* Westport, CT: Greenwood Press, 1970 [1948].

Harris, Brayton. *Blue & Gray in Black & White: Newspapers in the Civil War.* Washington: Brassey's, 1999.

Harrison, Lowell. "Perryville: Death on a Dry River." *Civil War Times Illustrated,* vol. 18, no. 2 (May 1979). 4–6, 8–9, 44–47.

Harrison, Lowell H. *The Civil War in Kentucky.* Lexington: University Press of Kentucky, 1975.

Hart, Donald S. "The Mood of Atlanta 1850–1861." *Atlanta Historical Bulletin,* vol.15, no. 2 (Summer 1970). 22–41.

Hartje, Robert G. *Van Dorn: The Life and Times of a Confederate General.* Nashville: Vanderbilt University Press, 1967.

Harwell, Richard B. "Civilian Life in Atlanta, 1862." *Atlanta Historical Bulletin*, vol. 7, no. 29 (October 1944). 212–19.

———. ed. *The Confederate Reader*. New York: David McKay Company, 1976 [1957].

Harwell, Richard Barksdale. "Atlanta Publications of the Civil War." *Atlanta Historical Bulletin*, vol. 6, no. 25 (July 1941).165–200.

Hattaway, Herman. *General Stephen D. Lee*. Jackson: University Press of Mississippi, 1976.

———. "Raid on Lawrence, Kans." In Patricia L. Faust, ed., *Historical Times Illustrated Encyclopedia of the Civil War*. New York: Harper & Row, 1986. 427.

Hawkins, J. D.R. *Horses in Gray: Famous Confederate Warhorses*. Gretna, LA: Pelican Publishing Co., 2017.

Hay, Thomas Robson. *Hood's Tennessee Campaign*. Dayton, OH: Press of Morningside Bookshop. 1976 [1929].

———, ed. *Cleburne And His Command, by Capt. Irving A. Buck and Pat Cleburne Stonewall Jackson of the West by Thomas Robson Hay*. Jackson, TN: McCowat-Mercer Press, 1959.

Headley, John W. "The Confederates Raid Vermont." In Philip Van Doren Stern, ed., *Secret Missions of the Civil War*. New York: Bonanza Books, 1959.

Hearn, Chester G. *The Capture of New Orleans 1862*. Baton Rouge: Louisiana State University Press, 1995.

———. *When the Devil Came Down to Dixie*. Baton Rouge: Louisiana State University Press,1997.

Hebert, Keith S. *The Long Civil War in the North Georgia Mountains: Confederate Nationalism, Sectionalism, and White Supremacy in Bartow County, Georgia*. Knoxville: University of Tennessee Press, 2017.

Henderson, G.F.R. *Stonewall Jackson and the American Civil War*. New York: David McKay, 1961 [1898].

Henderson, Lillian, comp. *Roster of the Confederate Soldiers of Georgia 1861–1865*. 7 vols. Hapeville, GA: Longino and Porter, 1959–64.

Henderson, Lindsey P., Jr. *The Oglethorpe Infantry: A Military History*. Savannah: Civil War Centennial Commission of Savannah and Chatham County, 1961.

Hennessy, John. *The First Battle of Manassas: An End to Innocence, July 18–21, 1861*. Lynchburg, VA: H. E. Howard, 1989.

———. *Return to Bull Run: The Campaign and Battle of Second Manassas*. New York: Simon & Schuster, 1993.

Henry, Robert Selph. *"First With the Most" Forrest*. Jackson, TN: McCowat-Mercer Press, 1969 [1944].

Hess, Earl J. *Banners to the Breeze: The Kentucky Campaign, Corinth and Stones River*. Lincoln: University of Nebraska Press, 2000.

———. *The Battle of Ezra Church and the Struggle for Atlanta*. Chapel Hill: University of North Carolina Press, 2015.

———. *Braxton Bragg: The Most Hated Man of the Confederacy*. Chapel Hill: University of North Carolina Press, 2016.

———. *Kennesaw Mountain: Sherman, Johnston, and the Atlanta Campaign.* Chapel Hill: University of North Carolina Press, 2013.

———. *Pickett's Charge—The Last Attack at Gettysburg.* Chapel Hill: University of North Carolina Press, 2001.

Hewitt, Lawrence Lee. *Port Hudson: Confederate Bastion on the Mississippi.* Baton Rouge: Louisiana State University Press, 1987.

Hicks, Brian and Schuyler Kropf. *Raising the Hunley: The Remarkable History and Recovery of the Last Confederate Submarine.* New York: Ballantine Books, 2002.

Hilde, Libra R. *Worth a Dozen Men: Women and Nursing in the Civil War South.* Charlottesville: University of Virginia Press, 2012.

Hill, Louise Biles. *Joseph E. Brown and the Confederacy.* Westport, CT: Greenwood Press, 1972 [1939].

Hirshson, Stanley P. *The White Tecumseh: A Biography of William T. Sherman.* New York: John Wiley & Sons, 1997.

Hoehling, A. A. *Vicksburg: 47 Days of Siege.* Englewood Cliffs, NJ: Prentice Hall, 1969.

Holland, Cecil Fletcher. *Morgan and his Raiders: A Biography of the Confederate General.* New York: Macmillan Company, 1942.

Hollandsworth, Jr., James G. *The Louisiana Native Guards: The Black Military Experience During the Civil War.* Baton Rouge: Louisiana State University Press, 1995.

Holzer, Harold. *The Civil War in 50 Objects.* New York: Viking, 2013.

Horn, Huston. *Leonidas Polk: Warrior Bishop of the Confederacy.* Lawrence: University Press of Kansas, 2019.

Horn, Stanley F. *The Army of Tennessee: A Military History.* Indianapolis: Bobbs-Merrill, 1941.

———. "The Battle of Perryville." *Civil War Times Illustrated,* vol. 4, no. 10 (February 1966). 4- 11, 42–47.

———. *The Battle of Stones River.* Gettysburg: Historical Times, 1972.

———. *The Decisive Battle of Nashville.* Baton Rouge: Louisiana State University Press, 1956.

———. "Nashville: The Most Decisive Battle of the Civil War. *Civil War Times Illustrated,* vol. 3, no. 8 (December 1964). 4–11, 31–36.

———, comp. *Tennessee's War 1861–1865 Described by Participants.* Nashville: Tennessee Civil War Centennial Commission, 1965.

Howe, Daniel Walker. *What Hath God Wrought: The Transformation of America, 1815–1848.* New York: Oxford University Press, 2007.

Hubbell, Jay B. *The South in American Literature 1607–1900.* Durham: Duke University Press, 1954.

Hudson, Carson O., Jr. *Civil War Williamsburg.* Williamsburg, VA: Colonial Williamsburg Foundation, 1997.

Hughes, Nathaniel Cheairs, Jr. *Bentonville: The Final Battle of Sherman and Johnston.* Chapel Hill: University of North Carolina Press, 1996.

———. *General William J. Hardee: Old Reliable.* Baton Rouge: Louisiana State University Press, 1965.

Humphreys, Anderson and Curt Guenter. *Semmes America.* Memphis: Humphreys, Ink, 1989.
Hurst, Jack. *Nathan Bedford Forrest: A Biography.* New York: Alfred A. Knopf, 1993.
Iobst, Richard W. *Civil War Macon: The History of a Confederate City.* Macon: Mercer University Press, 1999.
Jacobson, Eric A. and Richard A. Rupp. *For Cause & for Country: A Study of the Affair at Spring Hill and the Battle of Franklin.* Franklin, TN: O'More Publishing, 2008.
Jamieson, Perry D. *Death in September: The Antietam Campaign.* Fort Worth TX: Ryan Place Publishers, 1995.
Jenkins, Robert D. *The Battle of Peach Tree Creek: Hood's First Sortie, 20 July 1864.* Macon: Mercer University Press, 2013.
———. "Dalton: The Opening of the Georgia Campaign." *Blue & Gray*, vol. 32, issue 1 (December 2015). 6–9, 19–27, 41–50.
John, John E. *Florida During the Civil War.* Gainesville: University of Florida Press, 1963.
Johnson, Ludwell H. *Red River Campaign: Politics & Cotton in the Civil War.* Baltimore: Johns Hopkins University Press, 1958.
Johnston, Joseph E. *Narrative of Military Operations.* New York: D. Appleton, 1874.
Joiner, Gary Dillard. *One Damn Blunder from Beginning to End: The Red River Campaign of 1864.* Wilmington, DE: Scholarly Resources, 2003.
Jones, Howard. *Union in Peril: The Crisis over British Intervention in the Civil War.* Chapel Hill: University of North Carolina Press, 1992.
Jones, J. B. *A Rebel War Clerk's Diary At the Confederate States Capital.* Ed. by James I. Robertson, Jr. 2 vols. Lawrence: University Press of Kansas, 2015.
Jones, J. William, comp. "The Kilpatrick-Dahlgren Raid Against Richmond." *Southern Historical Society Papers*, vol. 13 (1885). 515–60.
Jones, James Pickett. *Yankee Blitzkrieg: Wilson's Raid through Alabama and Georgia.* Athens: University of Georgia Press, 1976.
Jones, Terry L. "Lucius Jeremiah Gartrell." In William C. Davis, ed., *The Confederate General.* 6 vols. Harrisburg, PA: National Historical Society, 1991.
Jones, V. C. "The Kilpatrick-Dahlgren Raid: Boldly Planned...Timidly Executed.." *Civil War Times Illustrated*, vol. 4, no. 1 (April 1965). 12–21.
Jones, Virgil Carrington. *Eight Hours Before Richmond.* New York: Henry Holt, 1957.
———. "Vicksburg." In Patricia L. Faust, ed., *Historical Times Illustrated Encyclopedia of the Civil War.* New York: Harper & Row, 1986. 784.
Jordan, Mildred. "Georgia's Confederate Hospitals." Master's thesis, Emory University, 1962.
Joslyn, Mauriel Phillips. "An Open, Stand Up Affair: Cleburne's Defense at Ringgold Gap." In Joslyn, ed., *A Meteor Shining Brightly: Essays on Maj. Gen. Patrick R. Cleburne.* Milledgeville GA: Terrell House, 1997. 113–42.
———, ed., *Charlotte's Boys: Civil War Letters of the Branch Family of Savannah.* Gretna, LA: Pelican Publishing, 2010.
Keely, Alfred H. and Winfred S. Harbison. *The American Constitution: Its Origins and Development.* New York: W. W. Norton, 1963.

Keller, Allan. *Morgan's Raid.* New York: Collier Books, 1962 [1961].
Kelly, Dennis. "The Second Battle of Manassas." *Civil War Times Illustrated,* vol. 22, no. 3 (May 1983). 9–44.
Kinchen, Oscar A. *Confederate Operations in Canada and the North: A Little-Known Phase of the American Civil War.* Quincy, MA: Christopher Publishing House, 1970.
———. *General Bennett H. Young, Confederate Raider and a Man of Many Adventures.* West Hanover, MA: Christopher Publishing House, 1981.
Klein, Frederic S. "Engagement at Front Royal." In Patricia L. Faust, ed., *Historical Times Encyclopedia of the Civil War.* New York: Harper & Row, 1986. 293.
Klein, Maury. *Days of Defiance: Sumter, Secession, and the Coming of the Civil War.* New York: Alfred A. Knopf, 1997.
Klement, Frank L. *The Limits of Dissent: Clement L. Vallandigham & the Civil War.* New York: Fordham University Press, 1998.
Knight, James R. *Hood's Tennessee Campaign: The Desperate Venture of a Desperate Man.* Charleston: History Press, 2014.
Koch, Adrienne and William Pederson. *The Life and Selected Writings of Thomas Jefferson.* New York: Modern Library, 1944.
Kreiser, Christine M. "Showdown in Mexico." *America's Civil War,* vol. 25, no. 6 (January 2013), 44–47.
Krick, Robert K. "The Smoothbore Volley That Doomed the Confederacy." In Gary W. Gallagher, ed., *Chancellorsville: The Battle and Its Aftermath.* Chapel Hill: University of North Carolina Press, 1996.
———. *Stonewall Jackson at Cedar Mountain.* Chapel Hill: University of North Carolina Press, 1990.
Kundahl, George G. *Alexandria Goes to War: Beyond Robert E. Lee.* Knoxville: University of Tennessee Press, 2004.
Kurtz, Wilbur G. "The Andrews Railroad Raid." *Civil War Times Illustrated,* vol. 5, no. 1 (April 1966). 8–16, 38–43.
———. "Map of Atlanta as of 1938 Showing the Field and Fortified Lines of the Confederate Forces, Together with Those of the Federal Armies Also the Fields of the Three Major Engagements, During the Summer of 1864." Atlanta Chamber of Commerce, 1938. Kurtz Collection, MSS 100, FF 148, T2, folder 2, Atlanta History Center.
Lack, Paul D. "Law and Disorder in Confederate Atlanta." *Georgia Historical Quarterly,* vol. 66, no. 2 (Summer 1982). 171–95.
Lee, Alfred McClung. *The Daily Newspaper in America: The Evolution of a Social Instrument.* New York: Octagon Books, 1973.
Lee, James Melvin. *History of American Journalism.* Boston: Houghton Mifflin, 1923.
Lee, Thomas Amory. *Colonel William Raymond Lee of the Revolution.* Salem, MA: Essex Institute, 1917.
Livermore. Thomas L. *Numbers and Losses in the Civil War in America: 1861–1865.* New York: Kraus Reprint Co., 1969 [1900].

Livingood, James W. "The Chattanooga Rebel." *East Tennessee Historical Society's Publications,* no. 39 (1967). 42–55.
Longacre, Edward G. *Gentleman and Soldier: A Biography of Wade Hampton III.* Nashville: Rutledge Hill Press, 2003.
———. *Lee's Cavalrymen: A History of the Mounted Forces of the Army of Northern Virginia.* Mechanicsburg, PA: Stackpole Books, 2002.
———. *Mounted Raids of the Civil War.* Lincoln: University of Nebraska Press, 1994 [1975].
———. "Siege and Evacuation of Battery Wagner, S.C." In Patricia L. Faust, ed., *Historical Times Illustrated Encyclopedia of the Civil War.* New York: Harper & Row, 1986. 46.
———. *A Soldier to the Last: Maj. Gen. Joseph Wheeler in Blue and Gray.* Washington: Potomac Books, 2007.
Lonn, Ella. *Salt as a Factor in the Confederacy.* University: University of Alabama Press, 1965.
Losson, Christopher. *Tennessee's Forgotten Warriors: Frank Cheatham and His Confederate Division.* Knoxville: University of Tennessee Press, 1989.
Lowe, Robert E. "Lincoln, the Fall of Atlanta, and the 1864 Presidential Election." *Georgia Historical Quarterly,* vol. 100, no. 3 (2016). 260–89.
Lucas, Marion Brunson. *Sherman and the Burning of Columbia.* College Station: Texas A & M University Press, 1976.
Luvaas, Jay and Harold W. Nelson, eds., *The U.S. Army War College Guide to the Battles of Chancellorsville & Fredericksburg.* Carlisle, PA: South Mountain Press, 1988.
Mahin, Dean B. *One War at a Time: The International Dimensions of the American Civil War.* Washington: Brassey's, 1999.
Maier, Larry B. *Gateway to Gettysburg: The Second Battle of Winchester.* Shippensburg, PA: White Mane, 2002.
Maihafer, Harry J. *War of Words: Abraham Lincoln and the Civil War Press.* Washington: Brassey's 2001.
Malone, Henry T. "Atlanta Journalism During the Confederacy." *Georgia Historical Quarterly,* vol. 37, no. 3 (September 1953). 210–219.
———. "The Weekly Atlanta Intelligencer As a Secessionist Journal." *Georgia Historical Quarterly,* vol. 37, no.4 (December 1953). 278–86.
Manigault, Arthur M. *A Carolinian Goes to War: The Civil War Narrative of Arthur Middleton Manigault Brigadier General C.S.A.* Ed. By R, Lockwood Tower. Columbia: University of South Carolina Press, 1933.
Markle, David E., ed. *The Telegraph Goes to War: The Personal Diary of David Homer Bates, Lincoln's Telegraph Operator.* Hamilton, NY: Edmonston Publishing, 2003.
Martin, David G. *Jackson's Valley Campaign November 1861–June 1862.* Conshohocken, PA: Combined Books, 1994.
———. *The Second Bull Run Campaign July-August 1862.* Conshohocken, PA: Combined Publishing, 1997.
Massey, Mary Elizabeth. *Ersatz in the Confederacy: Shortages and Substitutes on the Southern Homefront.* Columbia: University of South Carolina Press, 1952.

McCabe, James Dabney. *The Grayjackets; and How They Lived, Fought and Died, for Dixie.* Dahlonega GA: Confederate Reprint Co., 2009 [1867].

McCash, William B. *Thomas R. R. Cobb: The Making of a Southern Nationalist.* Macon: Mercer University Press, 1983.

McDonough, James Lee. *Nashville: The Western Confederacy's Final Gamble.* Knoxville: University of Tennessee Press, 2004.

———. *Stones River: Bloody Winter in Tennessee.* Knoxville: University of Tennessee Press, 1980.

———. *War in Kentucky: From Shiloh to Perryville.* Knoxville: University of Tennessee Press, 1994.

———. *William Tecumseh Sherman: In the Service of My Country—A Life.* New York: W. W. Norton, 2016.

McDonough, James Lee, and Thomas L. Connelly. *Five Tragic Hours.* Knoxville: University of Tennessee Press, 1983.

McKee, John Miller. "The Evacuation of Nashville." In Edwin L. Drake, ed., *The Annals of the Army of Tennessee and Early Western History.* Nashville: A. D. Hughes, 1878. 219–29.

McKinney, Joseph W. *Brandy Station, Virginia, June 9, 1863: The Largest Cavalry Battle of the Civil War.* Jefferson, NC: McFarland, 2006.

McKitrick, Eric L., ed. *Slavery Defended: The Views of the Old South.* Englewood Cliffs NJ: Prentice-Hall, 1963.

McMillan, Malcolm C., ed. *The Alabama Confederate Reader.* Tuscaloosa: University of Alabama Press, 1963.

McMurry, Richard M. *Atlanta 1864: Last Chance for the Confederacy.* Lincoln: University of Nebraska Press, 2000.

———. *John Bell Hood and the War for Southern Independence.* Lexington: University Press of Kentucky, 1982.

———, ed. "More on Raw Courage." *Civil War Times Illustrated*, vol. 14, no. 6 (October 1975). 36–38.

———. "Resaca: 'A Heap of Hard Fiten.'" *Civil War Times Illustrated*, vol. 9, no. 7 (November 1970). 4–12.

McNeely, Patricia G. "Bartholomew Riordan: Spying on Washington, D.C." In McNeely, Debra Reddin van Tuyll and Henry H. Schulte, eds., *Knights of the Quill: Confederate Correspondents and their Civil War Reporting.* West Lafayette, IN: Purdue University Press, 2010. 127–39.

McPherson, James M. *Abraham Lincoln and the Second American Revolution.* New York: Oxford University Press, 1990.

———. *Battle Cry of Freedom: The Civil War Era.* New York: Oxford University Press, 1988.

———. *Embattled Rebel: Jefferson Davis as Commander in Chief.* New York: Penguin Press, 2014.

———. *For Cause and Comrades: Why Men Fought in the Civil War.* New York: Oxford University Press, 1997.

———. *The Negro's Civil War: How American Negroes Felt and Acted During the War for the Union.* New York: Pantheon Books, 1965.

———. *Ordeal by Fire: The Civil War and Reconstruction.* Second Edition. New York: McGraw-Hill, 1992 [1982].

McWhiney, Grady. "General Beauregard's 'Complete Victory' at Shiloh: An Interpretation." *Journal of Southern History,* vol. 49, no. 3 (August 1983). 421–34.

Misulia, Charles L. *Columbus Georgia 1865: The Last True Battle of the Civil War.* Tuscaloosa: University of Alabama Press, 2010.

Mixon, Wayne: "Joel Chandler Harris." In Kenneth Coleman and Charles Stephen Gurr, eds., *Dictionary of Georgia Biography.* 2 vols. Athens: University of Georgia Press, 1983. Vol. 1, 400–402.

Mohr, Clarence L. *On the Threshold of Freedom: Masters and Slaves in Civil War Georgia.* Athens: University of Georgia Press, 1986.

Moore, Albert Burton. *Conscription and Conflict in the Confederacy.* New York: Hillary House, 1963 [1924].

Moore, Frank, ed. *The Rebellion Record: A Diary of American Events.* 12 vols. New York: Arno Press, 1971 [1861–1868].

Morris, Roy: "The Chattanooga Daily Rebel." *Civil War Times Illustrated,* vol. 23, no. 7 November 1984). 16, 18, 20–24.

Mott, Frank Luther. *American Journalism: A History of Newspapers in the United States Through 250 Years, 1690 to 1940.* New York: Macmillan, 1941.

Mushkat, Jerome. "Fernando Wood." In John T. Hubbell and James W. Geary, eds., *Biographical Dictionary of the Union: Northern Leaders in the Civil War.* Westport, CT: Greenwood Press, 1995. 599–600.

National Archives and Records Administration. *Atlanta Intelligencer.* Confederate Citizens' File, Business Document no. 3, M346, Roll 28.

Nelson, Larry E. *Bullets, Ballots, and Rhetoric: Confederate Policy for the United States Presidential Contest of 1864.* Tuscaloosa: University of Alabama Press, 1980.

———. *The War for the Union: The Organized War to Victory 1864–1865.* New York: Charles Scribner's Sons, 1971.

Newton, Steven H. *Lost For the Cause: The Confederate Army in 1864.* Mason City, IA: Savas Publishing, 2000.

Niesen, William C. "'The Consequences of Grandeur': A Union Soldier Writes of the Atlanta Campaign." *Atlanta History,* vol. 33, no. 3 (Fall 1989). 5–19.

Noe, Kenneth W. *Perryville: This Grand Havoc of Battle.* Lexington: University Press of Kentucky, 2001.

Nye, Russel Blaine. *Society in America, 1830–1860.* New York: Harper & Row, 1974.

O'Brien, Sean Michael. *Mobile, 1865: Last Stand of the Confederacy.* Westport, CT: Praeger, 2001.

Osthaus, Carl R. *Partisans of the Southern Press: Editorial Spokesmen of the Nineteenth Century.* Lexington: University Press of Kentucky, 1994.

Owsley, Frank Lawrence. *State Rights in the Confederacy.* Gloucester, MA: Peter Smith, 1961 [1925].

Page, Dave. *Ships versus Shore: Civil War Engagements along Southern Shores and Rivers.* Nashville: Rutledge Hill Press, 1994.

Paludan, Phillip Shaw. *The Presidency of Abraham Lincoln.* Lawrence: University Press of Kansas, 1994.

"Papers Found on Dahlgren's Body a Detective Story in Themselves." *Civil War Times Illustrated,* vol. 4, no. 1 (April 1965). 21.

[Parham, Louis L., ed.]. *Pioneer Citizens' History of Atlanta 1833–1902.* Atlanta: Byrd Printing Co., 1902.

Parks, Joseph H. *General Edmund Kirby Smith C.S.A.* Baton Rouge: Louisiana State University Press, 1954.

———. *General Leonidas Polk C.S.A.: The Fighting Bishop.* Baton Rouge: Louisiana State University Press, 1962.

———. *Joseph E. Brown of Georgia.* Baton Rouge: Louisiana State University Press, 1972.

Parrish, T. Michael. *Richard Taylor: Soldier Prince of Dixie.* Chapel Hill: University of North Carolina Press, 1992.

Parton, James. *General Butler in New Orleans.* New York: Mason Brothers, 1864.

Paul, Franc M. "*The Chattanooga Rebel.*" In *Tennessee Old and New,* 2 vols. Nashville: Tennessee Historical Commission, 1947), vol. 2, 273–79.

Payne, George Henry. *History of Journalism in the United States.* New York: D. Appleton, 1920.

Peddy, George W. *Saddle Bag and Spinning Wheel: Being the Civil War Letters of George W. Peddy, MD Surgeon 56th Georgia Volunteer Regiment, C.S.A.* Ed. by George W. Cuttino. Macon: Mercer University Press, 1981.

Perry, James. M. *The Civil War Correspondents: Mostly Rough, Sometimes Ready.* New York: John Wiley & Sons, 2000.

Perry, Milton F. *Infernal Weapons: The Story of Confederate Submarine and Mine Warfare.* Baton Rouge: Louisiana State University Press, 1965.

Pfanz, Donald C. *Richard S. Ewell: A Soldier's Life.* Chapel Hill: University of North Carolina Press, 1998.

Pfanz, Harry W. *Gettysburg: Culp's Hill and Cemetery Hill.* Chapel Hill: University of North Carolina Press, 1993.

———. *Gettysburg: The First Day.* Chapel Hill: University of North Carolina Press, 2001.

———. *Gettysburg: The Second Day.* Chapel Hill: University of North Carolina Press, 1987.

Pickenpaugh, Roger. *Rescue by Rail: Troop Transfer and the Civil War in the West 1863.* Lincoln: University of Nebraska Press, 1998.

Pollard, E. A. *The Lost Cause: A New Southern History of the War.* New York: E. B. Treat & Co., 1867.

Pollard, Edward A. *The First Year of the War.* Richmond: West & Johnston, 1862.

Porter, Horace. *Campaigning with Grant.* Bloomington: Indiana University Press, 1961 [1897].

Power, J. Tracy. *Lee's Miserables: Life in the Army of Northern Virginia from the Wilderness to Appomattox.* Chapel Hill: University of North Carolina Press, 1998.

The Press Association of the Confederate States of America. Printed by Order of the Board of Directors. Griffin GA: Hill & Swayze's Printing House, 1863.

Prindle, Sandy. *Booth's Confederate Connections.* Gretna LA: Pelican Publishing Co., 2019

Rable, George W. *Fredericksburg! Fredericksburg!* Chapel Hill: University of North Carolina Press, 2002.

———. *God's Almost Chosen Peoples: A Religious History of the American Civil War.* Chapel Hill: University of North Carolina Press, 2010.

Ramage, James A. *Rebel Raider: The Life of General John Hunt Morgan.* Lexington: University Press of Kentucky, 1986.

Ratner, Lorman A. and Dwight L. Teeter, Jr. *Fanatics and Fire-Eaters: Newspapers and the Coming of the Civil War.* Urbana: University of Illinois Press, 2004.

"Raw Courage." *Civil War Times Illustrated,* vol. 13, no. 4 (July 1974). 46.

Rawlings, Kenneth W. "Statistics and Cross-Sections of the Georgia Press to 1870." *Georgia Historical Quarterly,* vol. 23, no. 2 (June 1939). 177–87.

Reck, W. Emerson. *A. Lincoln: His Last 24 Hours.* Columbia: University of South Carolina Press, 1987.

Reed, Wallace P. *History of Atlanta, Georgia.* Syracuse NY: D. Mason, 1889.

Rhea, Gordon C. *The Battle of the Wilderness May 5–6, 1864.* Baton Rouge: Louisiana State University Press, 1994.

Rhoades, Jeffrey L. *Scapegoat General: The Story of Major General Benjamin Huger, C.S.A.* Hamden CT: Archon Books, 1985.

Richards, William E. "'We Live Under a Constitution': Confederate Martial Law in Atlanta." *Atlanta History,* vol. 33, no. 2 (Summer 1989). 26–35.

Richardson, E. Ramsay. *Little Aleck: A Life of Alexander H. Stephens The Fighting Vice-President of the Confederacy.* Indianapolis: Bobbs-Merrill Company, 1932.

Richardson, James D. *A Compilation of the Messages and Papers of the Confederacy including the Diplomatic Correspondence 1861–1865.* 2 vols. Nashville: United States Publishing Co., 1906.

Risley, Ford. *Civil War Journalism.* Santa Barbara CA: Praeger, 2012.

———. "The Confederate Press Association: Cooperative News Reporting of the War." *Civil War History,* vol. 47, no. 3 (September 2001). 222–39.

———. "Wartime News over Southern Wires: The Confederate Press Association." In David B. Sachsman, S. Kittrell Rushing and Roy Morris Jr., eds., *Words at War: The Civil War and American Journalism.* West Lafayette IN: Purdue University Press, 2008. 149–64.

Risley, J. Ford. "Georgia's Civil War Newspapers; Partisan, Sanguine, Enterprising." Ph.D. dissertation, University of Florida, 1996.

Robertson, James I., Jr. *Civil War Virginia: Battleground for a Nation.* Charlottesville: University Press of Virginia, 1991.

———. *Soldiers Blue and Gray.* Columbia: University of South Carolina Press, 1988.

———. "Stonewall in the Shenandoah: The Valley Campaign of 1862." *Civil War Times Illustrated*, vol. 12, no. 2 (May 1972). 3–49.

———. *Stonewall Jackson: The Man, the Soldier, the Legend*. New York: Macmillan, 1997.

Roland, Charles P. *Albert Sidney Johnston: Soldier of Three Republics*. Austin: University of Texas Press, 1964.

———. *The Confederacy*. Chicago: University of Chicago Press, 1960.

Roman, Alfred. *The Military Operations of General Beauregard in the War Between the States 1861 to 1865*. 2 vols. New York: Harper & Brothers, 1884.

Rose, Michael. *Atlanta: A Portrait of the Civil War*. Charleston, SC: Arcadia Publishing, 1989.

Rose, Willie Lee. *Rehearsal for Reconstruction: The Port Royal Experiment*. Indianapolis: Bobbs Merrill, 1964.

Rosen, Robert N. *Confederate Charleston: An Illustrated History of the City and the People During the Civil War*. Columbia: University of South Carolina Press, 1994.

Rosen, Robert N. and Richard W. Hatcher III. *The First Shot*. Charleston, SC: Arcadia Publishing, 2011.

Rottman, Gordon L. *The Great Locomotive Chase: The Andrews Raid 1862*. New York: Osprey Publishing, 2009.

Royster, Charles. *The Destructive War: William Tecumseh Sherman, Stonewall Jackson, and the Americans*. New York: Alfred A. Knopf, 1991.

Rubin, Anne Sarah. *A Shattered Nation: The Rise and Fall of the Confederacy, 1861–1868*. Chapel Hill: University of North Carolina Press, 2005.

Russell, James Michael. *Atlanta 1847–1890: City Building in the Old South and the New*. Baton Rouge: Louisiana State University Press, 1988.

Scaife, William R. *Allatoona Pass: A Needless Effusion of Blood*. N.p.: Etowah Valley Historical Society, 1995.

———. *The Campaign for Atlanta*. Saline MI: McNaughton & Gunn, 1993.

———. "The Chattahoochee River Line: An American Maginot." *North & South*, Issue #1 (November 1997). 42–48.

———. Hood's Campaign for Tennessee. Kennesaw GA: Kennesaw Mountain Historical Association, 2011 [1986].

———. *The March to the Sea*. Saline MI: McNaughton & Gunn, 1993.

Scaife, William R. and William Harris Bragg. *Joe Brown's Pets: The Georgia Militia, 1861- 1865*. Macon: Mercer University Press, 2004.

Scales, John R. *The Battles and Campaigns of General Nathan Bedford Forrest, 1861–1865*. El Dorado Hills CA: Savas Beatie, 2017.

Schiller, Herbert M. *Sumter is Avenged! The Siege and Reduction of Fort Pulaski*. Shippensburg, PA: White Mane, 1995.

Schlesinger, Arthur M., Jr. "War and the Constitution: Abraham Lincoln and Franklin D. Roosevelt." In Gabor S. Boritt, *Lincoln the War President: The Gettysburg Lectures*. New York: Oxford University Press, 1992.

Schott, Thomas E. *Alexander H. Stephens of Georgia: A Biography.* Baton Rouge: Louisiana State University Press, 1988.

Schroeder-Lein, Glenna R. *Confederate Hospitals on the Move: Samuel H. Stout and the Army of Tennessee.* Columbia: University of South Carolina Press, 1994.

Schwarzlose, Richard A. *The Nation's Newsbrokers. Volume 1: The Formative Years, from Pretelegraph to 1865.* Evanston, IL: Northwestern University Press, 1989.

Sears, Stephen W. *Gettysburg.* Boston: Houghton Mifflin, 2003.

———. *Landscape Turned Red: The Battle of Antietam.* New Haven: Ticknor & Fields, 1983.

———. *To the Gates of Richmond: The Peninsula Campaign.* New York: Ticknor & Fields, 1992.

Secrist, Philip. "Resaca: For Sherman a Moment of Truth." *Atlanta Historical Journal,* vol. 22, no. 1 (Spring 1978). 9–41.

Shackelford, George Green. *George Wythe Randolph and the Confederate Elite.* Athens: University of Georgia Press, 1988.

Shea, William L. *War in the West: Pea Ridge and Prairie Grove.* Fort Worth: Ryan Place Publishers, 1996.

Shea, William L. and Earl J. Hess. *Pea Ridge: Civil War Campaign in the West.* Chapel Hill: University of North Carolina Press, 1992.

Silver, James W. *Confederate Morale and Church Propaganda.* Tuscaloosa: Confederate Publishing Co., 1957.

Simkins, Francis Butler and James Welch Patton. *The Women of the Confederacy.* Richmond: Garrett & Massie, 1936.

Simpson, Brooks D. and Jean V. Berlin, eds. *Sherman's Civil War: Selected Correspondence of William T. Sherman, 1860–1865.* Chapel Hill: University of North Carolina Press, 1999.

Simpson, Harold B. *Hood's Texas Brigade: A Compendium.* Hillsboro, TX: Hill Jr. College Press, 1977.

Simpson, John A. *S. A. Cunningham & the Confederate Heritage.* Athens: University of Georgia Press, 1994.

Singer, Ralph Benjamin, Jr. "Confederate Atlanta." Ph.D. Dissertation, University of Georgia, 1973.

Smith, Derek. *Civil War Savannah.* Savannah: Frederic C. Beil, 1997.

Smith, Gerald J. *"One of the Most Daring of Men": The Life of Confederate General William Tatum Wofford.* Murfreesboro TN: Southern Heritage Press, 1977.

Smith, Timothy B. *Grant Invades Tennessee: The 1862 Battles for Forts Henry and Donelson.* Lawrence: University Press of Kansas, 2016.

———. *The Real Horse Soldiers: Benjamin Grierson's Epic 1863 Civil War Raid Through Mississippi.* El Dorado Hills CA: Savas Beatie, 2018.

Stackpole, Edward J. *Chancellorsville: Lee's Greatest Battle.* Harrisburg, PA: Stackpole Co., 1958.

———. *Drama on the Rappahannock: The Fredericksburg Campaign.* Harrisburg: Stackpole Company, 1957.

Stanchak, John E. "Battle of Chickamauga." In Patricia L. Faust, ed., *Historical Times Illustrated Encyclopedia of the Civil War*. New York: Harper & Row, 1986. 136–37.

———. "Battle of Port Gibson" and "Second Vicksburg Campaign." In Patricia L. Faust, ed.., *Historical Times Illustrated Encyclopedia of the Civil War*. New York: Harper & Row, 1986. 595–96; 781–84.

———. "Franklin and Nashville Campaign, Tenn. (Hood's Tennessee Campaign)." In Patricia L. Faust, ed., *Historical Times Illustrated Encyclopedia of the Civil War*. New York: Harper & Row, 1986. 285–86.

Starr, Louis M. *Bohemian Brigade: Civil War Newsmen in Action*. New York: Alfred A. Knopf, 1954.

Stevenson, Alexander F. *The Battle of Stone's River near Murfreesboro', Tenn. December 30, 1862 to January 3, 1863*. Dayton, OH: Press of Morningside Bookshop, 1983 [1884].

Stewart, George R. *Pickett's Charge: A Microhistory of the Final Attack at Gettysburg, July 3, 1863*. Dayton OH: Press of Morningside Bookshop, 1980 [1959].

Stout, Harry S. *Upon the Altar of the Nation: A Moral History of the American Civil War*. New York: Viking, 2006.

Strode, Hudson. *Jefferson Davis Confederate President*. New York: Harcourt, Brace, 1959.

Styple, William B., ed. *Writing & Fighting the Confederate War: The Letters of Peter Wellington Alexander Confederate War Correspondent*. Kearny, NJ: Belle Grove Publishing Co., 2002.

Suhr, Robert Collins. "Attack Written Deep and Crimson." *America's Civil War*, vol. 4, no. 1 (September 1991), 46–52.

Sullivan, James R. *Chickamauga and Chattanooga Battlefields*. Washington: Government Printing Office, 1956.

Sutherland, Daniel E. *The Emergence of Total War*. Fort Worth: Ryan Place Publishers, 1996.

———. *Fredericksburg and Chancellorsville: The Dare Mark Campaign*. Lincoln: University of Nebraska Press, 1998.

Swanberg, W. A. *First Blood: The Story of Fort Sumter*. New York: Charles Scribner's Sons, 1957.

Sword, Wiley. *Southern Invincibility: A History of the Confederate Heart*. New York: St. Martin's Press, 1999.

Sydnor, Charles H. *The Development of Southern Sectionalism 1819–1848*. Baton Rouge: Louisiana State University Press, 1948.

Symonds, Craig L. *Joseph E. Johnston: A Civil War Biography*. New York. W. W. Norton, 1992.

Tanner, Robert G. *Stonewall in the Valley: Thomas J. "Stonewall" Jackson's Shenandoah Valley Campaign, Spring 1862*. Garden City NY: Doubleday, 1976.

Tate, Allen. *Stonewall Jackson: The Good Soldier*. New York: Minton, Balch, 1928.

Taylor, William R. *Cavalier & Yankee: The Old South and American National Character*. New York: Harper & Row, 1969 [1961].

Temple, Sarah Rockwell Gober. *The First Hundred Years: A Short History of Cobb County, Georgia*. Atlanta: Walter W. Brown Co., 1935.

Thomas, Emory. "The Peninsula Campaign: Part I." *Civil War Times Illustrated*, vol. 17, no. 10 (February 1979), 4–6, 8–9, 40–45.

———. "The Peninsula Campaign, Part II." *Civil War Times Illustrated*, vol. 18, no. 1 (April 1979). 28–35.

———. "The Peninsula Campaign Part III." *Civil War Times Illustrated*, vol. 18, no. 2 (May 1979). 13–18.

———. "The Peninsula Campaign, Part IV." *Civil War Times Illustrated*, vol. 18, no. 3 (June 1979). 10–17.

———. "The Peninsula Campaign, Part V." *Civil War Times Illustrated*, vol. 18, no. 4 (July 1979). 14–18, 20–24.

Thomas, Emory M. *Bold Dragoon: The Life of J. E. B. Stuart*. New York: Harper & Row, 1986.

———. *The Confederate Nation 1861–1865*. New York: Harper & Row, 1979.

———. *The Confederate State of Richmond: A Biography of the Capital*. Baton Rouge: Louisiana State University Press, 1988.

———. "The Kilpatrick-Dahlgren Raid—Part I." *Civil War Times Illustrated*, vol. 16, no. 10 (February 1978). 4–9, 46–48

———. "The Kilpatrick-Dahlgren Raid—Part II." *Civil War Times Illustrated*, vol. 17, no. 1 (April 1978). 26–33.

———. "Port Hudson, La." In Patricia L. Faust, ed., *The Historical Times Illustrated Encyclopedia of the Civil War*. New York: Harper & Row, 1986. 596–97.

———. "Wartime Richmond." *Civil War Times Illustrated*, vol. 16, no. 3 (June 1977). 2–47, 50.

Thomason, John W., Jr. *Jeb Stuart*. New York: Charles Scribner's Sons, 1930.

Thompson, W. Fletcher, Jr. *The Image of War: The Pictorial Reporting of the American Civil War*. New York: Thomas Yoseloff, 1959.

Tice, Douglas O. "'Bread or Blood!': The Richmond Bread Riot." *Civil War Times Illustrated*, vol. 12, no. 10 (February 1974). 12–19.

Trudeau, Noah Andre. *Bloody Roads South: The Wilderness to Cold Harbor May–June 1864*. Boston: Little, Brown, 1989.

———. *Gettysburg: A Testing of Courage*. New York: HarperCollins, 2002.

———. *The Last Citadel: Petersburg, Virginia, June 1864–April 1865*. Boston: Little, Brown, 1991.

———. *Like Men of War: Black Troops in the Civil War 1862–1865*. Boston: Little, Brown, 1998.

Tucker, Glenn. *High Tide at Gettysburg: The Campaign in Pennsylvania*. Indianapolis: Bobbs-Merrill, 1958.

Tucker, Ruby Florence. "The Press Association of the Confederate States of America in Georgia." Master's thesis, University of Georgia, 1950.

U.S. Federal Census Slave Schedules, 1860. Atlanta History Center.

U. S. War Department. *The War of the Rebellion: A Compilation of the Official Records of the Union and Confederate Armies*. 128 vols. Washington: Government Printing Office, 1880–1901.

Vandiver, Frank. *Basic History of the Confederacy.* Princeton, NJ: D. Van Nostrand, 1962.
———. *Mighty Stonewall.* New York: McGraw-Hill, 1957.
———. *Their Tattered Flags: The Epic of the Confederacy.* New York: Harper's Magazine Press, 1970.
Van Tuyll, Debra Reddin. "Beyond the Household Gate: Women War Correspondents in the Confederacy." In David B. Sachsman, ed,. *A Press Divided: Newspaper Coverage of the Civil War.* New Brunswick, NJ: Transaction Publishing, 2014. 163–87.
———. *The Confederate Press in the Crucible of the American Civil War.* New York: Peter Lang, 2012.
———. "Essential Labor: Confederate Printers at Home and War." *Journalism History,* vol. 31, no. 2 (Summer 2005). 75–87.
———. "'We Have Spoken for Public Liberty': The Press, Dissent, and the Failure of Confederate Nationalism." In David B. Sachsman, ed., A Press Divided: Newspaper Coverage of the Civil War. New Brunswick, NJ: Transaction Publishers, 2014. 307–32.
Van Tuyll, Debra Reddin and Patricia G. McNeely, "Robert W. Gibbes: The 'Mind' of the Confederacy." In Patricia G. McNeely, Debra Redin van Tuyll and Henry G. Schulte, eds., *Knights of the Quill: Confederate Correspondents and their Civil War Reporting.* West Lafayette, IN: Purdue University Press, 2010. 95–103.
Venet, Wendy Hamand. *A Changing Wind: Commerce and Conflict in Civil War Atlanta.* New Haven: Yale University Press, 2014.
———, ed. *Sam Richards's Civil War Diary: A Chronicle of the Atlanta Home Front.* Athens: University of Georgia Press, 2009.
Voegeli, V. Jacques. *Free but Not Equal: The Midwest and the Negro during the Civil War.* Chicago: University of Chicago Press, 1967.
Von Abele, Rudolph. *Alexander H. Stephens: A Biography.* New York: Alfred A. Knopf, 1946.
Wade, Richard C. *Slavery in the Cities: The South 1820–1860.* New York: Oxford University Press, 1964.
Walker, Mary Hubner. *Charles W. Hubner: Poet Laureate of the South.* Atlanta: Cherokee Publishing, 1976.
Walker, Peter F. *Vicksburg: A People at War, 1860–1865.* Chapel Hill: University of North Carolina Press, 1960.
Ward, Andrew. *River Run Red: The Fort Pillow Massacre in the American Civil War.* New York: Viking, 2005.
Warner, Ezra J. and W. Buck Yearns. *Biographical Register of the Confederate Congress.* Baton Rouge: Louisiana State University Press, 1975.
Watkins, Sam R. *Co. "Aytch" Maury Grays, First Tennessee Regiment or, a Side Show of the Big Show.* Ed. By Ruth Hill Fulton McAllister. Franklin, TN: Providence House Publishers, 2007 [1882].
Waugh, John C. *Reelecting Lincoln: The Battle for the 1864 Presidency.* New York: Crown Publishers, 1997.

Weisberger, Bernard A. *The American Newspaperman*. Chicago: University of Chicago Press, 1961.

Welcher, Frank J. *The Union Army, 1861–1865: Organization and Operations*. 2 vols. Bloomington: Indiana University Press, 1989, 1993.

Welsh, Jack D. *Medical Histories of Confederate Generals*. Kent, OH: Kent State University Press, 1995.

Wert, Jeffry D. "Battle of Chantilly (Ox Hill) Va." In Patricia L. Faust, ed., *The Historical Times Encyclopedia of the Civil War*. New York: Harper & Row, 1986. 129–30.

———. "Battle of McDowell, Va." In Patricia L. Faust, ed., *The Historical Times Illustrated Encyclopedia of the Civil War*. New York: Harper & Row, 1986. 460.

———. "Chancellorsville Campaign" and "Battle of Chancellorsville." In Patricia L. Faust, ed., *The Historical Times Illustrated Encyclopedia of the Civil War*. New York: Harper & Row, 1986. 126–29.

———. "Cold Harbor." In Patricia L. Faust, ed., *Historical Times Illustrated Encyclopedia of the Civil War*. New York: Harper & Row, 1986. 149–50.

———. "Fredericksburg Campaign." In Patricia L. Faust, ed., *Historical Times Illustrated Encyclopedia of the Civil War*. New York: Harper & Row, 1986. 288–90.

———. "Overland Campaign" in Patricia L. Faust, ed., *Historical Times Illustrated Encyclopedia of the Civil War*. New York: Harper & Row, 1981. 551.

Wesley, Charles H. *The Collapse of the Confederacy*. Columbia: University of South Carolina Press, 2001 [1937].

Wesley, Charles H. and Patricia W. Romero. *Negro Americans in the Civil War: From Slavery to Citizenship*. New York: Publishers Company, 1967.

Whan, Vorin E., Jr. *Fiasco at Fredericksburg*. Gaithersburg MD: Butternut Press, 1986 [1961].

White, Cheryl H. *Confederate General Leonidas Polk: Louisiana's Fighting Bishop*. Charleston: History Press, 2013.

Wiley, Bell Irvin, ed. *Why Georgia Should Commemorate the Civil War*. Atlanta: Department of State, 1960.

Wilken, William Herbert. "As the *Telegraph* Saw It: A Study of the Policy of the Macon *Daily Telegraph (And Confederate)*, 1860–1865." Master's thesis, Emory University, 1964.

Wilkinson, Warren and Steven E. Woodworth. *A Scythe of Fire: A Civil War Story of the Eighth Georgia Infantry Regiment*. New York: William Morrow, 2002.

Williams, T. Harry. *Lincoln and His Generals*. New York: Alfred A. Knopf, 1952.

Williams' Atlanta Directory, City Guide, and Business Mirror. Atlanta: M. Lynch, 1859.

Wills, Brian Steel. *A Battle from the Start: The Life of Nathan Bedford Forrest*. New York: HarperCollins, 1992.

———. *George Henry Thomas: As True as Steel*. Lawrence: University Press of Kansas, 2012.

Wilson, Quintus C. "Confederate Press Association: A Pioneering News Agency." *Journalism Quarterly*, vol. 26 (June 1949). 160–66.

Winschel, Terrence J. *Triumph and Defeat: The Vicksburg Campaign.* El Dorado Hills, CA: Savas Beatie, 1999.

Winters, John D. *The Civil War in Louisiana.* Baton Rouge: Louisiana State University Press, 1963.

Wise, Stephen R. *Lifeline of the Confederacy: Blockade Running During the Civil War.* Columbia: University of South Carolina Press, 1988.

Wittenberg, Eric L. and Scott L. Mingus. *The Second Battle of Winchester: The Confederate Victory that Opened the Door to Gettysburg.* El Dorado Hills, CA: Savas Beatie, 2016.

Wood, Janice Ruth. "John S. Thrasher: Journalistic Revolutionary and Reformer." In Patricia G. McNeely, Debra Reddin van Tuyll and Henry H. Schulte, eds., *Knights of the Quill: Confederate Correspondents and their Civil War Reporting.* West Lafayette, IN: Purdue University Press, 2010. 362–75, 658–61.

Woodworth, Steven E. *Davis and Lee at War.* Lawrence: University Press of Kansas, 1995.

———. *Jefferson Davis and His Generals: The Failure of Confederate Command in the West.* Lawrence: University Press of Kansas, 1990.

———. *Six Armies in Tennessee: The Chickamauga and Chattanooga Campaigns.* Lincoln: University of Nebraska Press, 1998.

Worsham, John H. *One of Jackson's Foot Cavalry.* Ed. by James I. Robertson, Jr., Jackson, TN: McCowat-Mercer Press, 1964.

Wortman, Marc. *The Bonfire: The Siege and Burning of Atlanta.* New York: Public Affairs, 1999.

Yearns, Wilfred Buck. *The Confederate Congress.* Athens: University of Georgia Press, 1960.

Young, Robert W. *Senator James Murray Mason: Defender of the Old South.* Knoxville: University of Tennessee Press, 1998.

Zaworski, Robert E. *Confederate Sections at Oakland Cemetery Atlanta Georgia: History and Restoration.* 2 vols. Privately printed, 1996.

Index

"A," correspondent for *Mobile Tribune,* 302
Abbeville (SC) *Press,* 23
Abolition/Northern war aim, 41, 206, 225
Abrams, Alexander St. Clair, "A. S. A.": *ADI* Assistant Editor, 343–44, 347; author of *The Siege of Vicksburg,* 348; believes Johnston not aggressive, 398; field correspondent for *ADI,* 342, 360; 348, 350, 362, 379, 400; leaves *ADI,* 400; postwar, 486; reports on Atlanta Campaign, 381–85, 389, 391–93; writes *A Review of the War,* 348–49; writes *ADI* on Richmond's fall, 473; writes "President Davis and his Administration," 349
Academy Hospital, Marietta, 394. *See also* Female Academy Hospital
Acquia Creek, VA, 239
Acton, T. M., 348
Acworth, GA, 127, 434
Adair, George W., 11, 64, 126, 259–61, 196, 319
Adairsville, GA, 382
Adams, Jacob, execution reported in *ADI,* 289–91
Adams, John, 452
Adams press, 25
Adjutant General's Office, Richmond, 216
"Adversity—How to Bear It," Steele editorial, 482
Advertisements: as newspapers' revenue source, 19, 28, 210, 346, 436; in *ADI,* 52, 67, 71, 224–25, 231, 288, 436; of slave traders, 224–25; relegated to back pages, 33
Aereopagetica, 6
African Americans: *ADI* claims slavery beneficial to, 167–68; *ADI* publicizes hospital directors' need for, 106; as *ADI* workers, 25, 30, 48, 400; as "contrabands," 172; as Federal soldiers, 140–41, 198, 316, 371; as fortification workers, 30; as hospital workers, 105–6; as possible Confederate soldiers, 140, 429; capturing a Yankee, 172; laborers on Atlanta defenses, 391; number in city (1850), 5; owned by Gaulding and Whitaker, 7; shell casualty in Atlanta, 406; sold as slaves, 202, 224, 288–89, 454; support women's hospital aid society, 120; travel restricted in Atlanta, 150
African Methodist Church, 105
Alabama, secession of, 9–10
Alabama Street, 6, 20, 42, 45, 101, 151, 153, 225, 409, 468–69
Alabama troops, 21st Infantry Regiment, 121
"Alabama" writes to *ADI,* 331
Albany (GA) *Patriot,* 436
Albemarle, C.S.S., 365
Albemarle Sound, NC, 365
Albuquerque, NM, 114
Alexander, Peter W., "P. W. A.," 217, 219, 236; on Atlanta's press fraternity, 343–44; reports Gettysburg, 311–12
Alexandria, VA, 116, 205, 224
Allatoona, GA, 127, 383, 385, 439
Alleged Northern outrages, 135
Allen's Farm, VA, battle at, 182
American Revolution, 19
American Telegraph Company, 26, 262
Americus, GA, 334
"An Old Soldier" writes to *ADI,* 43
Anderson, Robert, 13, 15–16, 20
Andrews, J. Cutler, 19, 27, 33, 236, 473
Andrews, James J., 126–29; hanged, 158
Andrews, L. F. W., 259
Andrews railroad raid, 143–45, 169, 179

Angel Daughter, The, 29
Announcements, *ADI*'s: Alexis E. Marshall as associate editor, 271; citizens' meeting, 99; "Clio" as Richmond correspondent, 235; evening edition, 76; George Hathaway's enlistment, 47; fall of Nashville, 93; Female Institute Hospital, 324; influx of sick and wounded soldiers, 101; Lincoln's election, 20; St. Luke's Church, 364; Steele as editor, 191; subscription rate increase, 210; *The Soldier's Friend,* 249; Van Dorn's death, 288; "victory" at Fort Donelson, 89, 91, 93; Virginia's secession, 52. See also *Atlanta Daily Intelligencer*
Antietam, battle of. *See* Sharpsburg, MD, battle of
Antietam Creek, MD, 217–18
Appalachian Mountains, 93, 377
Appomattox, VA, 141; Lee surrenders, 478, 482, 485
Army group, Sherman's, strength mid-July 1864, 379, 405
Army of Mississippi, C.S., 382
Army of Northern Virginia, C.S., 48, 163, 168, 171, 177, 185, 279; reorganized, 306–7, 308–9, 384, 389, 443; surrenders, 477–78
Army of Tennessee, C.S., 153; and Hood's Tennessee Campaign, 433, 439–41, 443; at Murfreesboro 245–46, 269, 315, 326, 328, 332, 335, 342–43, 347–48, 350–51, 363; in Atlanta Campaign, 377, 382, 385, 393, 400, 403, 405, 407, 414–19, 421–23, 425, 429, 432, 470; destroyed at Nashville, 458; diehards, 470, 482; marches into Tennessee, 435; May 1864 strength, 380; medical director, 100; new commander, 446, 448; ordnance blown up, 418; re-enlistments in, 408; strength, September 1864, 433; strength, January 1865, 469; visited by Davis, 428
Army of the Cumberland, U.S., 245, 285, 315, 338, 379
Army of the Gulf, U.S., 300
Army of the Ohio, U.S., 228, 379, 401
Army of the Potomac, C.S., 163
Army of the Potomac, U.S., 163, 178, 190, 196, 203, 236, 240, 274, 276, 309, 338, 353, 377–78, 384, 389
Army of the Tennessee, U.S., 291, 379–80, 385, 401, 406
Army of Virginia, U.S., 196, 203–4
Ashby, Turner, 163
Atheneum concert hall, 23, 46, 99, 106
Athens, GA, 62
Athens Banner, 91
Atlanta, 11, 30–31, 40, 46, 56–57, 73, 98–99, 101, 103, 118, 125–26, 141–42, 150–51, 159, 176, 185, 195, 211, 215–16, 219, 231, 235, 24, 259, 280, 285–86, 297, 312, 318, 324–27, 332–33, 346, 361, 371, 379, 386, 389, 393, 399, 401, 406–9, 415, 434–35, 437, 440, 447, 450, 454, 469; as Confederate hospital center, 99, 106, 152, 231; as Confederate supply center, 106; as manufacturing center, 106; as military administrative center, 398; as possible Confederate capital 12, 21; as railroad center, 106, 363; becomes state capital, 485; bombarded by Northern artillery, 403, 410–11, 413; bread riot, 270; City Hall, 13, 41, 99, 103, 149, 202, 364; civilians expelled by Sherman, 424; damaged by Sherman, 447–48; fall of, 417–19, 421–22, 425, 432, 444–45, 464; fortifications, 386, 413; headquarters, Press Association, 261; importance of to Confederacy, 106, 415; Jefferson Davis visits, 14, 248; and Lincoln's re-election, 374, 418; mayor's election of 1861, 9, of 1862, 81; military post, 148; name changed from Marthasville, 5; newspapers in, 351; Northern migrants to, 136; population in 1850, 5; population in 1860, 28, 118; population in 1864, 364; rebuilds, 459, 468; site of editorial convention, 79, 133; soldiers in Virginia, 63; unpaved streets, 398
Atlanta, battle of (July 22), 406
Atlanta Amateurs, 46, 103
Atlanta & West Point Railroad, 407–8, 414; repaired, 468; wrecked, 453
Atlanta Cadets, 41, 45
Atlanta Campaign of 1864, 426, 433
Atlanta City Council, 7, 12–13, 50, 73, 150;

514 INDEX

changes City Seal, 455; expands City Cemetery, 154; thanks Forrest, 287–88
Atlanta City Court, 316
Atlanta Commonwealth, 11, 32, 64, 211, 259–60; joins Press Association, 262; member of the P.A., 319
Atlanta Confederate Volunteers, 55
Atlanta Constitution, 485
Atlanta Daily Intelligencer, 51, 53, 74, 85, 105, 116, 120, 129, 131–32, 144, 148, 167, 177, 184, 190, 211, 217, 220, 226, 231, 235–36, 238, 240, 248, 267, 322, 327–28, 333, 351, 360, 433, 446, 470; Abrams as associate editor, 343; accuses Northerners of outrages, 135; admits fall of Atlanta, 417; advertisements for slave traders, 224–25; advertisements in, 32, 33, 52, 288–89; advertises for printer, 24; advertising rates, 38, 71; advises on how to bear Confederate defeat, 482–83; advocates arming blacks, 140, 429; advocates for Southern schoolteachers, 61–62; advocates for women workers, 151; afternoon edition, 27; and Butler's "woman order," 147; and U.S. presidential election of 1860, 8; appeals for subscribers to pay, 13; articles reprinted, 291; as Confederate propagandist, 34, 38, 146; as daily, 28; as morning paper, 5; assists Press Association, 297; "Atlanta—Her Past, Her Present, and Her Future," 454; becomes daily, 5; blames Davis for fall of Atlanta, 421; blasts Ben Butler, 146; blockade, 88; boasts circulation, 15; boasts staying power, 78; boasts telegraphic news, 39; Book and Job Office, 6, 25, 29, 34, 48; bulletin board in front of office, 27, 29; calls for citizens' meeting, 99; calls for increased corn production, 266; calls for martial law, 118–19, 214–15; calls for retaliation, 201; calls Lincoln "Baboon Lincoln," 202; calls Lincoln "bloody tyrant," 479; calls Lincoln "King Abe," 201, 206; castigates Butler, 198–99; celebrates Gaines' Mill, 181; celebrates Jackson's victories, 163; celebrates Second Manassas, 205–6; celebrates victory at Mansfield, 366; celebrates victory at Plymouth, 364–65; characterizes Lincoln as baboon, 227; characterizes Yankees, 176; circulation 1850, 9; circulation 1863, 25, 28, 235, 298; circulation 1864, 346, 459; cites *Chicago Times*, 450; claims slavery beneficial to blacks, 167–68; claims victory at Fort Donelson, 97–98; "Clio's" letters, 269, 335; closes on presidential fast days, 209; commends Stuart, 204; commends women's aid societies, 171; comments on citizens' hospital committees, 278; complains of mail service, 267, 460; complains of "sickening effluvia," 150, 399; complains of telegraphic news service 142, 471; compliments Davis, 10; "counting room," 29; "Cousin Nourma," 330; covers Andrews railroad raid, 125–26, 128, 158–59; criticizes Davis, 418, 426; criticizes Johnston, 396; Davis' inauguration, 104; deals with reverses, 109; defends Davis, 349; denies news of Lee's surrender, 527; denounces "Yankee lies," 141, 188–89; derides McClellan's "change of base," 182; derides Yankees, 166, 176; describes damage in city, 449; dismisses Northern accounts of Shiloh, 124; downplays Lincoln's re-election, 445; editorial of March 22, 1865, 467; editorializes against Yankees, 262; editorializes/follows Vicksburg news, 326–27, 330–31; editorializes on Confederate strength, 145; editorializes on fall of Norfolk, 165; editorializes on printing war news, 368; editorializes on reconstruction with North, 436–37; editorializes on war, 73–74, 253; editorials reprinted, 320, 351; employees of, 35, 86, 150; encourages Southern people, 96, 143, 300; endorses Davis' Fast Day, 317; estimates number of soldier patients in city, 153; eulogizes fallen soldiers, 71; evening edition, 114, 132; exchanges in, 26–27, 76, 84, 87, 93, 132, 460; excoriates Lincoln, 186, 253; exhorts people to fight on, 254; expenditures, rise in, 86; "extra" editions, 279, 453; extra of Dec. 10, 1864, 449–50, 460; falsely reports Confederate victory at Gettysburg, 310; falsely

INDEX *515*

Atlanta Daily Intelligencer (*continued*) reports Hood's death, 325; financial status, 79, 131, 346; flatters Beauregard, 254; foreman Isaac Pilgrim, 152; gas blackout, 298; Gate City Guards' departure, 48; gives printers New Year's Day off, 78; *habeas corpus,* 216; hails Whitaker's election, 9; "half sheet," 409, 435; Hampton-Sherman correspondence, 466; hospitalized soldier and patient names, 152, 327; inflation, 362; infomercial for Winship's Iron Works, 67; insists correspondents sign their letters, 239; issue of Oct. 9, 1864, 435–37; issues extras, 32; joins Press Association, 262; last issue in Macon, 447; layout of four pages, 31, 38, 58, 75, 79, 205, 288; Lee's Farewell Address, 478–79; lists hospitals in city, 101; lists newspaper staff, 347, 399–400; member of Press Association, 319; minimizes Perryville, 230; misleads readers on Vicksburg, 300; morning and evening issues, 31, 45, 84, 132; moves to Macon, 402, 408, 437; moves to Whitehall and railroad, 34; news blackout, 381; newsboys, 131; Northern press, 188; observes Fast Days, 115, 167; office burned by Federals, 469; office of (Whitehall Street), 52, 151, 276, 286, 288, 392, 398; office relocated, 469; office struck by shell, 415; opposes arming African Americans, 509; "Our City" column, 319; overly sanguine reporting of Vicksburg, 301; paper, newsprint, changes in color, 317; participates in editorial convention, 87; pleas to subscribers, 150; Pollard's *First Year of the War,* 384; Pope's vindictive orders, 198; postwar activity, 536; praises Atlanta Grays, 46; praises Johnston, 391; predicts Atlanta's future greatness, 454; predicts Confederate victory, 5, 80, 177, 223, 464; predicts Lincoln's use of force, 11; predicts peaceful secession, 9; press, printing room, 30; Press Association member, 360; price of, 40, 46, 131; printers' strike, 211, 362; prints articles by "290," 346, 349, 373; prints Conscription Act, 134; prints Davis' address to Congress, 371; prints Davis' Macon speech, 425; prints Governor Brown's proclamation, 97–98; prints Governor's proclamation, 97–98; prints Lincoln's call for troops, 39; prints names of soldiers deceased in city hospitals, 105, 152–54; prints Northern stories, 191; prints on half-sheet, 435, 443; prints poetry by Abrams, 343; prints Press Association reports, 326; prints Reid/"290," 326, 331, 338–39; prints Richmond telegraphic dispatches, 53; prints rumors, 85; prints soldiers' letters, 26, 170, 262; prints W. H. Nesbit's letter, 313; prints W. R. Lee/R. E. Lee/O. A. Bull correspondence, 193–95; prints war news rumors, 64, 93, 143; procures agent in Newnan, 71; profit from publishing, 131; promotes Abrams' *Siege of Vicksburg,* 348; promotes Atlanta as Confederate capital, 12–13; promotes Brown's fast day, 97; promotes local musical performance, 482; promotes "Morgan's Capture and Escape" (Abrams), 350–51; promotes Southern literature, 62; promotes Southern manufactures, 68; propagandizes, 62, 187, 385; proposes terms for Southern independence, 187; protests hanging of Mumford, 201; provides war news, 62; publicizes call for conscription, 152–53; publicizes citizens' meeting, 149; publicizes entertainments, 437; publicizes presidential fast days, 31, 49–50, 69, 97, 167, 209, 267, 364; publishes Abrams' *Review of the War,* 348–49; publishes Abrams' *The Trial of a Soldier's Wife,* 350; publishes articles by "290," 315; publishes Bragg's battle order, 323; publishes Campbell County property value, 202; publishes Davis' inaugural address, 96–97, 278; publishes Dr. Pim's order, 101, 105; publishes E. M. Seago, 47; publishes letters only from named contributors, 145; publishes poetry, 62, 81–82, 177, 437; publishes soldiers' letters, 57, 437; publishes Thrasher's articles, 318, 332; publishes Vardy Sisson, 50, 63; publishes war news, 69, 75, 150–51; quotes *New York Herald,* 301; racism in, 82; rails against Emancipation Proclamation 225; raises subscription and advertising prices, 249, 271–72, 316, 362, 454; rarely prints illustrations, 63–64; reading room, 29; receives soldiers' letters, 31; relates fortifying of city, 391; relates Morgan's escape, 350; relates soldier's anecdote, 267; relocates to Macon, 401–3, 405; resumes publication in Atlanta, 447, 449; retaliation, 338; Richmond Bread Riot, 270; salaries, 30; scolds *Atlanta Southern Confederacy,* 368; "scoundrel" imbroglio with Davis, 422–28; "Situation," "Position," military news reports, 389, 392, 400; six-day work week, 5, 30, 131, 249, 279, 310; size of pages, 27, 485; softens news of Sharpsburg, 218, 220; solicits subscribers, advertisers, 33, 298, 459; Southern industries, 74; Southern schoolteachers, 68; spars with *Southern Confederacy,* 188, 259, 319; staff gets day off, 5, 248, 364, 454; staff of, 131, 310; steam power press, 29, 297; subscription rates, 103, 131, 210, 316–17, 445, 454, 459, 485; suggests arming slaves, 140–41; suggests replacing Hood, 422–23; supports Atlanta Grays, 65; supports Bragg, 36; supports Confederate troops, 72; supports Davis' and Stephens' election, 72; supports editorial convention, 79; supports George W. Lee, 170; supports Governor Brown, 64–65, 72, 106, 114, 266, 334, 361; supports martial law in Atlanta, 242; supports Press Association, 346; supports slavery, 461; supports women's hospital societies, 120; survives war, 485; telegraphic column, 15–16, 20, 79, 400; telegraphic news service, 133–34; thanks city physicians, 102; urges Atlantans' support for troops, 43; urges citizens to return, 450; urges corn production, 267; urges disloyalists to leave town, 118; urges food be brought to city, 453; urges help for poor, 49; urges Southerners to fight on, 445; urges subscribers to pay, 9; urges voters to polls, 72; uses exchanges, 21, 40, 83, 134; uses Hoe cylinder press, 25; uses Northern newspapers, 308; vilifies Lincoln, 464; vilifies Yankees, 438, 483; voices confidence in victory, 83, 177, 382; warns against fires in city, 74; warns of false rumors, 142; warns of Federals' depredations, 389; warns of harsh war, 239; warns of spies and traitors, 118; warns of Yankee subjugation, 165, 168; Whitaker's mayoralty election, 13; "Wit and Humor," 336; withholds military intelligence, 478; without "special" correspondent in the field, 25, 32, 50, 204; worries about Federals' approach, 149; Yankee barbarity, 154; Yankee lies, 161. See also Announcements, ADI's; News coverage, *ADI*'s; Reprints, *ADI*'s

Atlanta Daily Press, 362
Atlanta *Examiner,* 5
Atlanta Female Institute, 34, 43
Atlanta Fire Battalion, 415
Atlanta Gas Works, 410, 413
Atlanta Grays, 41–42, 44, 46, 50–51, 53, 55, 63–65
Atlanta Hospital Association, 102, 104–5
Atlanta Medical College, 7, 101. *See also* Medical College Hospital
Atlanta Southern Confederacy, 11–13, 28, 32, 39, 64, 73, 79, 83, 138, 188, 211, 259–61, 319–20, 351, 385, 397, 446, 491; and Andrews railroad raid, 125–26; criticizes *ADI* on martial law, 119, 214, 216; criticizes Davis, 335; leaves for Macon, 402; member of Press Association, 262, 319; never returns to Atlanta, 459
Atlanta Typographical Union, 361, 363, 394
Atlanta Weekly Intelligencer, founded 9, 24, 33
"Atlantanian," writes *ADI,* 468–69
Augusta, GA, 14, 21, 23, 26, 32, 79, 132, 230, 248, 271, 429, 434, 438–39, 468, 470; bread riot, 270; site of Press Association meeting, 360–61
Augusta Chronicle & Sentinel, 21, 23, 28, 132, 260, 289, 362–63, 402, 407, 427
Augusta Constitutionalist, 21, 23, 133, 29, 272, 427, 478
"Azure corporations," "bluebellies," 389

"B.," writes to *ADI,* 66
Bagby, George W., 29, 33, 82, 134, 168 ("Hermes")
Ball's Bluff, battle of, 68–69, 76
Baltimore, MD, 117, 217, 312; newspapers, 444, 453
Baltimore Sun, 49, 90
Bank Hospital, 105

INDEX   517

Bank of Fulton, 7
Banks, Nathaniel P., 159; as "Jackson's Commissary," 161–62, 203; at Port Hudson, 300–302, 366, 377–78
Banner and Baptist, 231
Bannockburn Scotland, 166
Baptist Church, Macon, 425
"Bar room generals," 332
Barksdale, Ethelbert, 460–61
Barksdale, William, 241
Barnes, William H., 46
Barnesville, GA, 417
Barnwell, SC, 465
Bartlett, Frederick, 5
Bartow, Francis S., 54, 56, 103
Bartow County, GA, 103
Bassford, William B.: Associate Editor *ADI*, 9, 15–16, 38–39, 149; leaves, 53, 92; predicts Confederate independence, 41–42, 50
Bate, William B., 385, 390, 457
Bath, SC, paper mill, 32, 271
Baton Rouge, LA, 148, 287, 294, 300
Battery Wagner, Charleston, 316, 318
"Battle-Eve Dreams" (Abrams), 343
Batty, W. H., 150
Baylor, C. G., 24
Beall, W. T., 33
Beauregard, P. Gustave T., 13–14, 16–17, 20, 25, 53, 55, 57, 113, 397; appointed commander of Military Division of the West, 439, 459, 465, 481–82; at Shiloh, 121–25, 127, 143, 148–49, 170, 177, 226, 343, 359; rumored as Hood's successor 423, 439
"Beauregard," poem, 177
Beaver Dam Creek, VA, 179–80
Bee, Barnard E., 54–55
Bell, John, 8
Bell, Marcus Aurelius, 7
Belle Isle, Richmond, 353, 355
Benjamin, Judah P., 97, 355–56, 370, 481
Bennett, James A., 57, 481–82
Bennett, Nancy, 481–82
Bentonville, NC, battle of, 470–71
Berkeley, VA, 204
Bermuda, 81

"Beta," writes to *ADI*, 213
Beverly, WV, 378
Big Bethel, VA, 52, 124
Big Black River, MS, battle at, 293, 299, 301
Big Shanty, GA, Kennesaw, 108, 126–27, 390, 434
"Bill Arp," Charles H. Smith, 402
Biloxi, MS, 136
Birth, J. W., 288
"Black Republicans," 16, 20, 38–39
Blair, Francis P., 463
Blake, W. O., 356
Blockade, Northern, 31, 81, 83, 131, 266
Blockade runners, 81
Bloodworth, W. L., 24
Blue Ridge Mountains, VA, 306, 308
Boatswain's Creek/Swamp, VA, 180
Bohnefield's Coffin Shop, 346
Bolivar, TN, 288
Bombardment: casualties, 409–11, 413–14; damage to city, 406; effect on civilians, 413; shell tonnage, 411, 414–15
"Bombproofs," 456
Book and Job Office, *ADI*, 454
Book of Common Prayer (Episcopal), 115–16
Booth, John Wilkes, 479
Booth, Lionel F., 402
Boston, MA, 19, 21, 75
Boston Atheneum, 27
Bowen, John S., 292
Bowling Green, KY, 85, 93
Bracken, Peter, 128
Bradford, William F., 366
Bragg, Braxton, 209, 227–30, 261, 269, 287, 315, 322–24, 327–28, 331, 355, 393, 426, 458, 470; and quarrel with his generals, 332–35; at Chattanooga, 339–41, 350; at Murfreesboro, 245–48; Davis advisor, 441; expels reporters, 325–26; imposes martial law in Atlanta, 214–16; resigns, 341–43; succeeds Beauregard, 177
Bragg, Walter L., 106
Branch, Hamilton, 51
Branch, John, 51
Branch, L. O'Brien, 218

Brandy Station, VA, battle of, 307
Brantley, William, 210
Braumuller, H., 52, 67
Bread Riot, Richmond, 269–70; in Atlanta and other cities, 270–71
Breckinridge, John C., 8, 481–82
Bridgeport, AL, 141, 144
British government, and *Trent* affair, 75–76
British West Indies, 75
Brown, John C., 452
Brown, Joseph E., 28, 47, 51, 56; and "scoundrel" incident, 427, 436; calls for volunteers, 97–98, 119; proclaims fast day, 97, 115, 143, 216, 235, 266, 454; re-elected, 64–65, 73–76; re-election, 334
Brunswick, GA, 74
Brush Mountain, GA, 389
Buchanan, John F., *Intelligencer* treasurer, 24, 342, 347
"Bucking and gagging," 268
Buckner, Simon B., 91–92, 333, 335
Buell, Don Carlos, 93, 122–23, 148, 228–30
Buena Vista, battle of, 49
Bull, Gustavus A., 193–95
Bull, Orville A., 193–95
Bull Run, VA, 134. *See also* Manassas, battle of; Manassas, Second, battle of
Bulletin board in front of *ADI* office, 27, 29, 249
Burke, J. Edmund, Associate Editor, *ADI*, 7
Burkesville, KY, 79
Burlington, VT, 443
Burnside, Ambrose E., 204, 240–42, 274, 331
Burt, E. R., 68
Burton, E. P., 448
Butler, Benjamin F. ("Beast"), 137, 172, 198, 354, 377–78; hanging of Mumford, 199; "Picayune Butler," 201; Special Order No. 150, 198; vilified in *ADI*, 184; "woman order," 147

"C.," writes to *ADI*, 184
Cabinet, British, 83
Cabinet, C.S., 14, 355; flees Richmond, 472, 481
Cabinet, U.S., 38, 67, 176, 444
Cacoethes scribendi, 26
Cain, Jeff, 126–28

Cairo, IL, 21, 86
Calhoun, James M., mayor of Atlanta, 80–81, 99–100, 107–8, 111, 115–16, 119, 169, 215, 316; surrenders city, 417
Calhoun, GA, 128, 382
Camp McDonald, Marietta GA, 98
Campaign from Texas to Maryland, The (Davis), 263
Campbell, Albert H., 356–57
Campbell, John A., and Hampton Roads Conference, 463
Campbell County, GA, 104; value of slaves in, 202
Campbellton, GA, 184, 453
Canby, Edward R. S., 114, 476
Cantey, James, 452
Car Shed (Union Depot), 10, 20, 101, 105, 216, 247–48, 324, 364, 390, 398, 402, 413; destroyed, 443
Car Shed Committee, 327
Carlisle PA, 309, 336
Carondelet, U.S.S., 89
Carter, Mrs. E. F., 247
Cartersville, GA, 439
Carthage Africa, 308
Cass County, GA, 103
Cassville, GA, Johnston's planned battle, 383
Castel, Albert, 60–61, 418
Casualties, *ADI* reports: Atlanta (July 22), 406; Ball's Bluff, 68; Battery Wagner, 316; Bentonville, 471; Big Black River, 293; Brandy Station, 307; Cedar Mountain, 203; Champion's Hill, 293; Chancellorsville, 275, 280; Chickamauga, 323, 326; Cold Harbor, 393; Corinth, MS, 227; Cross Keys, 162; Dallas, 385; Ezra Church, 407; Fort McAlister, 451; Fort Pillow, 367; Franklin, 452; Fredericksburg, 242; Front Royal, 161; Gaines' Mill, 180–81, 183; Gettysburg, 311–12; Griswoldville, 450; in Civil War battles, 393; Kennesaw Mountain, 392–93; Logan's Cross Roads, 80; Malvern Hill, 185; Manassas, 55–57; Mansfield, 366; McDowell, 160; Mechanicsville, 179–80; Murfreesboro, 247; Nashville, 458; New

INDEX *519*

Casualties, *ADI* reports (*continued*)
   Orleans, 137–38; Pea Ridge, 111; Perryville, 229; Port Gibson, 292; Oak Grove, 178; Peachtree Creek, 406; Pickett's Mill, 385; Port Republic, 162; Richmond, KY, 209; Ringgold Gap, 341; Savage's Station, 182; Second Manassas, 206; Seven Days' Battles, 189; Seven Pines, 169; Sharpsburg, 219; Springfield, 63; Valverde, 114; Williamsburg, 165
Catlett's Station, VA, 204, 223–24
Cave Spring, GA, 439
Cedar Mountain, VA, battle of, 203
Cemetery Hill, Gettysburg, 312
Cemetery Ridge, Gettysburg, 311
Censorship by military officers, 324
Census, U.S., (1860), 28, 211
Central Presbyterian Church, 210
"Cerulean abdomens," bluebellies, 389
Chalmers, James R., 366
Chambersburg, PA, 308–9
Champion's Hill, MS, battle at, 293
Chancellorsville, VA, battle of, 274–82, 306–7, 349, 378, 428
Chantilly, VA, fight at, 206
"Characteristics and Capabilities of the Negro Race," 82
Charles I, English monarch, 464–64
Charleston, SC, 13–16, 19–22; Great Fire, 74, 75; naval battle, 270, 289–90, 315, 317–18, 320; shelled, 339, 359, 382, 410, 433; "stone fleet," 81, 87, 93, 143, 220, 226–27, 239, 269
Charleston Courier, 20–21, 33, 49, 82, 147, 169, 269, 289–90, 359
Charleston Mercury, 20, 28–29, 55–56, 82, 133–34, 168, 189, 217, 317, 339; on Davis' Macon speech, 426
Charlotte, NC, 402
Chattahoochee River, 31, 103, 386, 391, 399–401, 405, 416, 433–35, 453, 476
Chattanooga, TN, 92, 124, 126–28, 141, 143–44, 149, 158; abandoned, 323, 326, 331–32, 338; battle at, 340–41, 377, 406, 424, 440, 468; shelled, 159, 176, 319, 214, 223, 228–29, 269, 285, 315, 319

Chattanooga Advertiser, 259
Chattanooga Daily Rebel, 214, 246, 296, 315, 319, 361, 402, 417
Chattanooga Gazette: prints Lee-Grant correspondence, 477; reports Lincoln's assassination, 479–80
Cheatham, Benjamin Franklin, 333, 392–93, 433, 457
Cheatham, Richard, 93
Cherokee Artillery, 56
Cherokee Block, 288
Cherokee Indians, 110
Cherry Street, Macon, 402, 437, 445
Chesnut, James, 17, 332
Chesnut, Mary Boykin, 419
Chesterville, SC, 466
Chicago, IL, 90
Chicago Times, 450
Chickahominy River, VA, 163, 168–69, 171, 178–79, 182, 201–3, 205
Chickamauga, battle of, 287, 322–23, 326–28, 330–34, 349, 458
Chickamauga, GA, 340
Chickasaw Bluffs, MS, 291
Chivalry, 218
Church of the Holy Trinity, Nashville, 115
Cincinnati, OH, 91, 217
Cincinnati Commercial, 213
Cincinnati Enquirer, 213
Circulation, of Confederate newspapers, 28
Citizens' hospital committees, 248
"City, The," *ADI* column, 398–99
"City, The," in *Memphis Daily Appeal Extra*, 410
City Cemetery (Oakland), 64, 105; expanded, 154, 158, 247, 394
City Hall, New Orleans, 147
City Hotel Hospital, 113, 121, 171, 173
City Light Guards, 41
City Military Directory, in *ADI*, 398
Clapp, Joseph, 5
Clarke, R. M., 225
Clarksville, TN, 86
Clayton County, GA, 195
Cleburne, Patrick R., 340; "Stonewall of Our Army," 341, 385, 390, 392–93, 406; killed, 452

"Clint," *Advertiser & Register* correspondent, 300
"Clio," *ADI* correspondent, 150; articles by, 235–36, 238, 276–77, 360; ceases to write for *ADI*, 360; mentions Richmond Bread Riot, 270; not identified, 346; on Brandy Station, 307; on Chancellorsville, 278–79, 281; on Pennsylvania campaign, 308–9, 312; on possible foreign recognition, 237; predicts Lee's Pennsylvania offensive, 306; reports Fredericksburg, 239–41; reports from Richmond, 315; writes on Vicksburg, 302, 320
Clisby, Joseph, 83, 260, 296, 361
Cobb, Howell, 398, 425, 482
Cobb, Thomas R. R., 62, 98, 241
Cobb County, GA, 47, 186, 224
Coburn, John, 417
Cockrell, Francis M., 452
Cockspur Island, GA, 119–20
Cohen, Solomon, 225
Cold Harbor, VA, battle of, 389, 393
College of William and Mary, 66
Collier, Isaac P., 397
Colquitt, Alfred, 48
Columbia, SC, burns, 465–66
Columbia Daily South Carolinian, 217, 261, 296, 360, 362
Columbus (GA) *Sun*, 434
Columbus (GA) *Times*, 20, 438
Columbus, GA, 73, 79; bread riot, 270, 437
Columbus, KY, 112
Columbus, OH, 350
Columbus Enquirer, 132, 402
Commissary General of Georgia Army, 73–74, 346
Commission merchants, 211, 224, 288
Commonwealth, Atlanta, 44, 349
Compositors/typesetters, 29, 212
Concert Hall, 7, 47, 69
Confederate Continentals, 47
Confederate Military History, 55
Confederate Shoe Blacking Company, 288
Confederate States of America: allows soldier voting, 334; election day 1861, 71; enacts newspaper copyrighting, 318

Confederate Territory of Arizona, 114, 116
Confederate Volunteers 47, 57
Confiscation Bill, U.S., 201
Congress, C.S., 21, 45, 71, 216, 248, 270, 276; authorizes soldier voting, 335; belated arming of blacks, 141; commends Cleburne, 341; commends Hoke, 365; debates arming African Americans, 460–61; enacts Conscription, 133
Congress, U.S.: encourages newspapers' use of mails, 21, 238, 463; passes XIII Amendment, 463
Congress, U.S.S., 109–10
Conscription, C.S.: newspapermen's exemption from, 27; for others, 98, 133–34, 248
Constitution, C.S., 71, 96, 334
Constitution, Georgia, 334
Constitution, U.S., 41, 201, 225, 334; XIII Amendment, 463
Constitutional Union Party, 8
Contrabands, 172, 201, 204
Cooper, Mark 47, 67
Cooper, Samuel, 121–22, 200, 216, 241, 340, 370
Cooper, Thomas L., 41, 46
Coosa River, GA, 286
Copyright law, C.S., 318
Copyright law, U.S., 21, 318
Corinth, MS, 121–25, 148–49, 176–77, 196; battle at, 227, 458–59
"Corps editorial." *See* editorial fraternity
Correspondence, letters received by *ADI*, 31
Correspondents, "specials," 25, 37
Cossacks, 425
Cotton Spinners' convention, 289
Coulter, E. Merton, 372
"Cousin Nourma," 330, 361
Covington, KY, 217
Coweta County, GA, 71
Cox, Jacob D., 401
Cozzens, Peter, 227
Crawford, Frazer & Co.: *ADI* infomercial for, 289; slave merchants and advertiser in *ADI*, 288–89
Crawford, George W., 143
Crawford, J. T., 280

Crawford, Robert, 288; infomercial for, 454
Crawley, R. L., 225
Crimean War, 75
Crittenden, George B., 80
Cross Keys, VA, battle at, 162–63
Crutchfield, Stapleton, 279
Cuba, Davis' quip about, 426
Culbertson, Jacob, 87
Culpeper County, VA, 198
Culpeper Court House, VA, 198, 203, 306–8, 354
Culp's Hill, Gettysburg, 312
Cumberland, U.S.S., 126–27
Cumberland Gap, TN, 144, 229
Cumberland River, 86, 91
Cunningham, Sumner, 433
Curtin, Andrew, 308
Curtis, Samuel R., 111
Custer, George A., 478
Cuthbert, GA, 104

Da Ponte, Durant, 231
Dahlgren, John, 353, 355
Dahlgren, Ulric, raid of, 353–57
Dallas, GA 423; battle of, 385, 389
Dalton, GA, 128, 191, 231, 259, 333, 341–43, 348, 350, 360, 363, 379, 381, 393, 400, 440
Daniel, John M., 262, 268
Daniel, Larry J., 418
Danielly, Laura V., 104
Danville, KY, 86
Danville, VA, 472, 481
David, submarine, 359
Davies, Americus C., 153
Davis, George, 481
Davis, Jefferson, 49, 51, 64, 123, 144, 164, 168, 177–78, 188, 190, 199–200, 205, 212, 216, 226, 236, 238, 263, 277–78, 282, 290, 293, 311, 339, 340–42, 349–50, 441, 460, 463, 473; addresses Congress, 371–72; and Bragg imbroglio, 332–35; and Dahlgren plot, 353, 355–56, 370; and Fort Sumter, 13–14; and *Intelligencer* imbroglio, 422–28; and Richmond Bread Riot, 270; announces Hood's Tennessee advance, 432–34; appoints Beauregard to Military Division of the West, 439; appoints Hood to army command, 405; approves Lee's Pennsylvania campaign, 306; becomes Confederate president 10–11, 96; calls for Conscription, 133; creates Military Division of the West, 423, 439; criticized by Pollard, 349; criticizes Johnston in Macon, 426; declares Butler war criminal, 199; defends appointing Hood, 426; defends himself in speech, 427; elected popularly, 71, 96; flees Richmond, 472, 481; inaugural address, 96; proclaims fast days, 31, 69, 97, 167–68, 209, 267, 317 364; relieves Beauregard, 177, 254; relieves Johnston, 405; "scoundrel" remark, 425, 436; speaks in Macon, 425–28; transfers Hardee, 433; visits Atlanta, 10, 42, 248; visits Hood in Palmetto, 428–29, 432–33, 440
Davis, Nicholas A., 263–64
Davis, William C., 55, 371, 419
Davis Infantry, 41, 47, 53
De Fontaine, Felix, "Personne," 217, 269
Decatur, AL, 286
Decatur, GA, 62, 106, 405, 407
Decatur Street, 102, 105, 468
Decision in the West (Castel), 418
Deck headline, 51, 121
DeGress, Francis, 406
DeKalb County GA 8, 47, 186
Democratic Party, Northern, 8, 165; 1862 elections, 238; "peace Democrats," 145, 371, 418, 444; postwar, 485
Den Corput, Maximilian Van, 56
Denny, Thomas, 109, 117
Department No. 2, C.S., 214
Department of South Carolina, Georgia and Florida, C.S., 470
Department of the West, C.S., 293
Derry, Joseph T., 55
Desertion, C.S. troops', 290–91
Destructive War (Royster), 372
Devil's Den, Gettysburg, 312
DeWitt, A. H., 52
Dick, Stephen J. 236
Dill, C. W., 288
Dinwiddie, VA, 472

Diplomatic recognition, European 266, 349
Directory, City Guide, and Business Mirror, Atlanta, 1859, 6, 409; 1867 *Directory,* 469
Disease, in ranks, 66, 100, 115–16
Dispatches from Richmond, *ADI* use of, 68, 123, 160, 163, 169–70, 177, 179, 185, 187, 218, 439
District of Georgia and Florida, C.S., 398
Dixon, George, 359
Dodd, Thomas L. 449
Dods, J. Bovee, 48
Dolan, Mark K., 318
Donelson, Daniel S., 86
Douglas, Stephen A., 8
Drewry's Bluff, VA, 167, 378
Dry Tortugas, 187
Duck River, TN, 458
Dug Gap, GA, 380
Dumble, John, 361, 409
Dumfries, VA, 153
Duncan, Johnson K., 137
Dunning, James L., 447
Durham, NC, 481
Dyer, Thomas G., 214

Early, Jubal A., 356–57; defeated by Sheridan, 444
East Point, GA, 408, 413, 416–17, 468
East Tennessee & Georgia Railroad, 231
Eatonton, GA, 103, 143
Ebenezer Church AL, battle at, 476
Editorial convention, calls for, 77, 132; in Atlanta, 133, 142; in Augusta, 249, 260–61; in Macon, 249, 260
Editorial fraternity, 212, 214, 231, 296, 346, 361; "corps editorial," 401
Editors' work, 22–23, 27, 29, 34, 212, 346; as Confederate propagandists, 27, 347; minimize Southern defeats, 112
Eighth Congressional District/Georgia 79–80
El Paso, TX, 21
Election, Confederate presidential, 96
Election, of 1860, U.S., 8; 1862 Northern, 238–39; presidential election of 1864 in North, 334, 371, 418–19, 445
Elkhorn Tavern, AR, battle of, 110–11

Elliott, Stephen, 364
Ellis, Barbara G., 236
Ellis' Ford, VA, 277
Ellis Street, 324
Ells, James N., 231
Ely's Ford, VA, 379
Elyton, Birmingham, AL, 476
Em, typesetters' measurement, 30
Emancipation Proclamation, 225, 238, 289
Empire House Hotel, 121; Hospital, 105, 152, 154, 324
Empire State, 5
Employees, newspaper, salaries 30; types of, 30
England, C.S. diplomat to, 75; possible recognition of Confederacy, 83, 237
Ericsson, John, 110
Etowah Iron Works 46, 67
Etowah River, GA, 383
Etowah Station, GA, 127
European intervention, 251
Eutaw (AL) *Whig and Observer,* 268
Evans, Nathan G., 69
Ewell, Richard S., 162–63, 306–9, 311, 378; anecdote about, 336
Exchange Hotel, 469
Exchanges, *ADI* use of, 21, 40, 83, 134, 142, 160, 193, 213–14, 242, 262, 281, 299, 320, 339, 346, 436, 454, 466; newspapers' use of, 19, 21, 34
Execution, of C.S. deserters, 316
Executive Aid Committee 359
"Extra," issued by *Richmond Dispatch,* 278
"Extras," issued by *ADI,* 32, 396
Ezra Church, battle of, 407
Ezzard, William L., 9, 42, 64

Fair Ground, 47, 277
Fair Ground Hospital, 152, 247, 324, 324, 327
Fair Oaks Station, VA, battle at, 169, 193–95
Fairbanks, G. R., 327
Falmouth, VA, 240
Farewell Address, Lee's, 478–79
Farmville, VA, 472
Farragut, David G., 136–37, 146, 148
Fast day, proclaimed by Governor Brown, 96, 115

Fast days, proclaimed by President Davis, 31, 49, 69, 97, 167, 209, 267, 317
Fayetteville, AR, 112
Fayetteville, NC, 470
Feasterville, SC, 466
Female Academy, Institute, Hospital, 324, 327
"Ferruginous conchology," 413
Fillion, Leon, 290
Fire companies in Atlanta, 43, 64
First Baptist Church, 231
1st Georgia Hospital, Richmond, 169
First Presbyterian Church, 210
First Year of the War, The (Pollard), 349
Fitts, R. C., 24
Five Forks, VA, battle at, 472
Flash, Henry L., 470
Flint River, GA, 421
Florida, secession of, 9–10; number of troops, 98
Floyd, John B., 89, 91–92
Floyd County, GA 56
"Foot Cavalry," Jackson's infantry, 162, 204
Foote, Andrew H., 86–88. 91, 113
Foragers, execution of, 514–15
Ford's Theatre, Washington, 479
Foreacre, Greenberry J., 47, 55, 150, 186
Foreign recognition, Confederate hopes for, 370
Forrest, Nathan B., 223, 277; and Streight's raid, 285–87; at Fort Pillow, 366–67, 428; Atlantans give "Highlander" to, 286–87, 291
Forsyth, John, 268
Forsyth, GA, 104
Fort Bliss, NM, 114
Fort Craig, NM, 114
Fort Donelson, TN, 86–89; fall of, 90–93, 99, 112, 121, 196
Fort Henry, TN, 86; falls, 87–88, 93, 112, 196
Fort Jackson, LA, 136–37
Fort Lafayette, IN, 115
Fort McAllister, GA, 451
Fort Monroe, VA, 134, 163, 172
Fort Pillow, TN, 113, 147–48; battle at, 366–68
Fort Pulaski, GA, 48, 119–20
Fort St. Philip, LA, 136–37

Fort Sumter, SC, 5, 11, 13–16, 23, 25, 28, 31, 34, 39–40, 109, 133, 316, 318, 320, 338, 353
Fort Wagner, SC. *See* Battery Wagner, Charleston
Foster, Ira, 424
"Fosterville," 425
4.5-inch rifled cannon, 415
France, C.S. diplomat sent to, 75; possible recognition of Confederacy, 83, 237, 370
Frank Leslie's Illustrated Newspaper, 63
Frankfort, KY, 223, 228–29
Franklin, TN, battle of, 433, 451–53, 457–58
Franklin, WV, 160
Franklin Building, 225
Franklin Printing House, 42, 409–10
Frayser's Farm, VA, battle of, 182
Frederick, MD, 217
Fredericksburg, VA, 239–40; shelled by Federals, 241; battle of, 241–42, 274–78, 306
Free Masons, 186
Freeman, Andrew F., 103, 105
Fremont, John C., 160–63, 201
French, Samuel G., 392, 421, 434–35, 439
Front Royal, VA, battle at, 161–62
Full and Detailed History of the Siege of Vicksburg, A (Abrams), 342, 348
Fuller, William A., 125–29
Fulton Blues, 41, 45, 64
Fulton County, GA, 44, 47; Militia Regiment, 98, 106, 186, 248, 386
Fulton Dragoons, 41
Furlough, Timothy M., 334

Gadsden, AL, 440
Gadsden, James, 22
Gaines, R. C., 101
Gaines' Mill, battle at, 180–81
Gallatin, TN, 224
Galloway, M. C., 212
Galveston, TX, 81
Gardner, Franklin, 302
Garner, George G., 214
Garnett's Farm, VA, fight at, 182
Garrett, Franklin M., 41
Gartrell, Henry Clay, 55–56

524   INDEX

Gartrell, Lucius J., 43, 47, 53, 55, 71–73
Gaskill, Varney A., 16
"Gate City," Atlanta, 11–12, 68, 408, 447, 467
Gate City Guardian, 11–12
Gate City Guards, 41–42, 44
Gate City Hospital, 101, 105, 154, 324, 327
Gate City Hotel, as Atlanta telegraph office 20; as hospital site, 105, 468
Gaulding, Archibald A., 38–39, 50, 53, 57, 66, 68, 74, 82, 102, 106, 115, 118–19, 134, 143, 149, 184, 213, 240; acknowledges fall of Fort Donelson, 91; acknowledges fall of Fort Henry, 88; advocates arming blacks, 141; advocates for women workers, 151; aids medical care for soldiers, 122; and Andrews railroad raid, 125–28; and soldiers' hospitals, 152; appointed Georgia surveyor general, 73; as *ADI* editor, 23; as Atlanta attorney, 6, 27; asks readers to be patient, 183; at editorial convention, 133; belittles Federal battle accounts, 80; boasts *ADI* staying power, 76; calls for careful reporting, 124–25; calls for Confederate offensive, 190; calls for martial law, 118–19, 128–29; cautions against news rumors, 111, 123, 125; celebrates Confederate victories, 110, 180, 183; commends G. W. Lee, 150; commends John Leonard, 10; complains about rumors, 163; complains about Yankee lies, 141, 188; complains of delayed exchanges, 22, 162; complains of Pritchard's news service, 86–87, 132; complains of slow telegraphic service, 78–79, 132; compliments women for medical care, 152; co-proprietor of *ADI* with Whitaker, 24–25, 27, 33, 40, 65, 109, 126, 131, 143, 146, 165, 167; criticizes *Southern Confederacy*, 119; deals with letter-writers, 131; defends slavery, 7; denounces speculators, 137; dismisses Yankee lies, 90–92 170; disregards unverifiable dispatches, 141; doubts rumors, 85; editor of *ADI*, 6, 8, 15, 20; editorializes on causes of war, 44; editorializes on Seven Days' Battles, 185, 187–88, 190; editorializes on shelling of Chattanooga, 159; employees paid Saturday, 9; encourages people, 97; favors conscription, 152; hails Davis, 11, 72, 96; hails Shiloh "victory," 123; income, 27; on Ball's Bluff, 68; on battle of Mill Springs, 88; on loss of New Orleans, 138; on Shiloh, 122–24; on Yankee barbarity, 191; on Yankee greed, 187; praises volunteers, 99; predicts Confederate victory, 66–67; predicts long war, 66; prints rumors, 57, 128, 184; prints soldiers' letters, 26, 177; promotes Fast Days, 167; promotes Southern literature, 61; propagandizes, 177; protests hanging of Mumford, 147; publisher of *ADI*, 5–7; publishes letters only from named contributors, 144, 184–85; publishes names of soldiers deceased in city hospitals, 152; rallies Atlantans for soldiers' medical care, 152; reports Manassas, 54, 58; reports Peninsula Campaign, 135; resigns as *ADI* editor, 191, 198; sells half-interest in *ADI* to Whitaker, 191, 319; slaveowner, 7; spins Confederate retreats, 163–64; supports Conscription, 133; supports editorial convention, 87; supports Governor Brown, 28, 64–65, 72; thanks subscribers, 28; urges people's sacrifices for victory, 34, 88; urges subscribers to pay, 131; urges support of Southern manufactures, 67; uses exchanges, 21; vilifies Lincoln, 116; warns against hoping for European intervention, 81; warns of traitors in Atlanta, 128, 141; worries over Atlanta's safety, 149, 159, 176

Gay, Mary A. H., 62, 106
Gaylesville, AL, 440
Gazette, 319
General (locomotive), 125–26, 128, 149
General Assembly, Georgia, calls for Georgia secession convention, 9, 73, 235, 266–67, 271, 485
General Order No. 1, of G. W. Lee, 150
General Orders, Pope's punitive, 196
General Orders No. 2, Leyden's, 150
George III, 186
Georgia, 13, 47, 52; allows soldier voting, 334; 8th Congressional District, 71; "Empire State," 377; Governor's election of 1863, 334; newspapers in, 28; secession 9–11, 45, 61, 440; troops for Lee's army, 201
Georgia Air Line Railroad, 7

INDEX 525

Georgia Citizen, 260
Georgia Commissary Department, 131
Georgia Historical Quarterly, 215
Georgia Institute of Technology, 448
Georgia Journalism (Griffith and Talmadge), 146
Georgia Legion, 62
Georgia Railroad, 21; cut by Federals, 407; repaired, 468
Georgia Railroad Bank Agency, 7
Georgia State Senate, 7
Georgia troops: First Georgia Regulars, 106; 1st Infantry Regiment, 53, 231; 4th Infantry Regiment, 195; 5th Infantry Regiment, 397; 7th Infantry Regiment, 47, 53–57, 71, 186; 8th Infantry Regiment, 50–51, 53–54, 56, 59, 63; 9th Infantry Regiment, 50, 340; 10th Infantry Regiment, 66, 280; 13th Infantry Regiment, 280; 19th Infantry Regiment, 48, 169, 242, 281; 35th Infantry Regiment, 193–95; 42nd Infantry Regiment, 393; 46th Infantry Regiment, 289–90; 56th Infantry; government's call for, 105–6; number of, 65, 97–98, 224; State Militia, 98, 106, 114, 421; State Troops, 74
Georgia Volunteers, 41, 46–48
"Georgian," writes to *ADI,* 346
Germanna Ford, VA, 379
Gettysburg, PA, battle of, 309–13, 317, 327, 370, 373, 428
Gibbes, Robert W., 261, 296, 360–61
Gilgal Church, GA, fight at, 390–91
Gilmer (TX) *Patriot,* 21
Gilmer, Jeremy, 87
Gist, States R., 452
Glasgow Scotland, 237; newspapers, 290
Glendale, VA, battle of, 182
Glenn, Luther J., 453
Goldsboro, NC, 464, 471, 476
Gordon, GA, 424
Gordon, George W., 452
Gordon, John B., 379
Gordonsville, VA, 203
Gorgas, Josiah, 325
"Goths," Northern troops, 5, 135
Grace Street, Richmond, 280

Graeme, John, 470
Granbury, Hiram B., 452
Grand Junction, TN, 291
Grant, Ulysses S., 86, 88–89, 122–23, 148, 331, 339–40, 378–80, 419, 458, 482; and Lee's surrender, 477–78; at Petersburg, 472; becomes general-in-chief, 377; campaigns against Vicksburg, 291–94, 301–4, 342, 411, 436; captures Fort Donelson, 91–92; in Overland Campaign, 383, 389, 393, 396, 400, 414
Grates, Jacob, 241
Great Smoky Mountains, 86
Green, Benjamin, 259
Green, Duff, 259
Green & Howell's ferry, 453
Greencastle, PA, 308
Greensboro, NC, 48, 478, 481
Grenada, MS, 214, 280, 296, 402
Grierson, Benjamin, 287, 301
Griffin, GA, 5, 98, 327, 402, 417
Griffin, S. H., 224
Griffin Empire State, 143
Griffin Rebel, 457
Griffith, Louis, 146
Griswoldville, GA, battle of, 450
Groveton, VA, battle at, 204
Gubernatorial election, GA, 71–72
Guerrillas, 196
Guiney Station, VA, 279–80
Gulf of Mexico, 399
Gwinnett County, GA, 16

"H. St. P.," writes to *Mobile Advertiser & Register,* 464
Habeas corpus, writ of, 119, 216, 326
Hagerstown, MD, 21, 217, 310–11
Halbach, Edward W., 355–56
Half-sheets, *ADI* resists, 211; reverts to, 297, 435, 443, 469
Hall, James O., 357
Halleck, Henry W., 86, 113, 148, 176–77, 199, 240, 423, 448
Hambleton, James B., 11
Hambricht, H.A., 180
Hamilton, Markey and Joyner's drugstore, 150

Hammond, Amos W., 53
Hampton, Wade, 193, 465, 470; and Sherman correspondence, 465–67
Hampton Legion, 195
Hampton Roads, VA, naval battle at, 109–10, 116, 512; Conference, 463–64
Hanleiter, Cornelius R., 11, 42, 64
Hanleiter, Josephine, 42
Hanover Court House, VA, 171–72
"Hard war," 196, 206
Hardee, William J., 52, 212, 228–29, 343, 380, 389–91, 406, 417–18, 421, 433–34; succeeds Bragg temporarily, 342; transferred, 433
Hardee's Tactics, 52
Harpers Ferry, VA, 50–51, 162, 308
Harper's Weekly, 63
Harpeth River, TN, 452–53
Harris, George C., 115
Harris, Isham G., 86, 93
Harris, Joel Chandler, 32
Harris Street, 105
Harrisburg, PA, 217, 309
Harrison, Henry, 309
Harrisonburg, VA, 163
Harrison's Landing, VA, 188
Harwell, Richard Barksdale, 29
Harwood, Edward, 135
Hatcher's Run, VA, 472
Hathaway, George, 47–48, 53; writes *ADI*, 169–70
Havana Cuba, 75
Hawes, Richard, 229
Hawks, Wells J., 282
Hay, Thomas Robson, 432, 452
Hayden's Hall, Hospital, 101, 105
Hayne Street, Charleston, 320
Hebert, Louis, 112
Heery, Daniel, 101, 154
Heery's Hospital, 154
Heimstreet's Inimitable Hair Restorative, *ADI* advertiser, 34
Helm, Ben H., 325
Henderson, G. F. R., 275
"Hendrick Conscious," 61
Hennessy, John, 55, 204

Henry, African American, 436
Henry, Gustavus A., 86
"Hermes" (George Bagby), 168
Herring, W. R., 74
Heth, Henry, 277–78, 378
"Highlander," Forrest's horse, 287
Hill, Ambrose Powell, 178–79, 240, 277–78, 306–9, 311, 378
Hill, Benjamin, 214
Hill, Daniel Harvey, 178, 181–83, 185, 241, 332–33
Hill, H. S., 259
Hill, Joshua, 334
Hillsboro, NC, 481
Hillview Cemetery, LaGrange, GA, 195
Hindman's Hall Hospital, 105
Hines, T. Henry, 350
Hoe, Richard M., 25
Hoe Steam Cylinder Press, 25, 30, 402
Hoke, Robert F., 364–65
Holbrook, J. M., 52, 61
Holbrook's Hat Manufactory, 52, 61, 67
Holcombe, William H., 82
Holland Hall Hospital, 105, 153
Holland's Hall, 105
Holley, Samuel, 135
Holly Springs, MS, 291
Hood, John B., 153, 286, 311–12, 363, 406, 424–25, 437, 440, 444, 450–51, 464; advances into Tennessee, 432–33, 438, 440–41, 443, 448; aims for Western & Atlantic, 434–35, 439–40; appointed army commander, 405, 407, 421–22; asks for reinforcements, 422; Atlanta Campaign, 380, 383–84, 391, 413–16, 418, 421; attack at Franklin, 451–52; defeated at Nashville, 458, 464; leg amputated, 325; orders Atlanta evacuated, 417; resigns, 459, 469; rumored dead, 325; sends Wheeler raiding, 408; visited by Davis, 428
Hooker, Joseph, 274–75, 278, 307, 310, 341, 379, 384, 389; relieved, 309
Hornaday, Henry C., 231
Hospital, 1st Georgia, Richmond, 190
Hospitals, Atlanta soldiers', 152, 324; deaths in, 153, 259, 277

Housatonic, U.S.S., 359
House of Representatives, C.S., 460–61; Judiciary Committee, 318
House of Representatives, U.S., 26
Houston, TX, 114
Houston Street, 155
Howard, Oliver O., 274, 384, 417, 421, 450; assumes command of Army of the Tennessee, 406; at Ezra Church, 407
Howard, Thomas C., Atlanta postmaster, 297, 449
Howard, William P., 34, 98, 114, 454
Howell's Hall Hospital, 105
Hoyle, Eli W., 186
Huger, Benjamin H., 165, 182
Hughey, W. Proctor, 186
Humboldt, TN, 291
Hunley, C.S.S., 359
Hunter, David, 140, 201
Hunter Robert M. T., and Hampton Roads Conference, 463
Huntsville, AL, 126, 142, 149, 319
Huntsville Confederate, 319
Hurlbut, Stephen A., 287
Hutcheson, M. W., 319, 351

Illinois troops, 7th Infantry Regiment, 448
"In for the War," writes to *ADI*, 335
Indiana troops, 51st Infantry Regiment, 285
Indianapolis, IN, 63
Inflation, 210–11, 320, 362; as Confederate national problem, 371
Ink, newspapers' need for, 32; cost of, 279; shortage, 362, 469
Instant ("this month"), 217, 421
Institute Hospital. *See* Atlanta Female Institute
Intelligencer Job and Book Bindery, 30
Intelligencer Steam Press, 367, 386
Iroquois, U.S.S., 148
Irwin, Jared, 7
Island No. 10, 112–13, 147, 196
Iuka, MS, 143

Jack, G. W., 468
Jack's Bakery, 468

Jackson, Andrew, 119, 252
Jackson, John K., 397
Jackson, Thomas J.: at Chancellorsville, 274–79; burial, 306; death of, 274, 279, 306, 325; in Shenandoah Valley Campaign, 159–63, 171, 177–79, 182, 184, 196; in Second Manassas Campaign, 204–5; 209, 213, 240–42; marches against Pope, 203; "Stonewall" nickname, 54–55, 159
Jackson, Mary, 270
Jackson, MS, 214, 248, 287, 289, 292–93, 296, 299, 301–3, 402
Jackson, TN, 241
Jackson, William H. ("Red"), 416
Jackson Guards, 170
Jackson Mississippian, 292, 300
Jacobson, Eric, 452
James River, VA, 134, 164–67, 203–4, 353–55, 377–78, 397
Jefferson, Thomas, 6
Jenkins, Micah, 379
Jim, enslaved black, 224
"John Bull," 76
"Johnny Reb," humor of, 267
Johnson, Andrew, 480
Johnson, Bushrod R., 91–92
Johnson, John M., 106, 121, 153
Johnson, Richard, 224
Johnston, Albert Sidney, 85, 93, 100–101; killed at Shiloh, 121–22; 153, 214
Johnston, F. M., 271
Johnston, Joseph E., 48, 54–55, 66, 122, 134, 165, 177–78, 190, 261, 293, 343, 363–64, 371, 385–86, 389–93, 396–401, 416, 428–29, 470–71; Cassville, 382; evacuates Yorktown, 163–64; in Atlanta Campaign, 360, 377, 379–82; in Mississippi, 298–99, 301–3; relieved, 405, 418, 42, 426; retreats before Sherman, 476, 480–81; succeeds Bragg, 342; surrenders, 481–82; wounded, 168–69
Jones, Benjamin O., 100
Jones, David R., 218
Jones, John A., 72
Jones, John Beauchamp, 203, 325
Jones, O. H., 328

Jones, Virgil Carrington, 357
Jonesboro, GA, 410; battle of, 417–18, 421, 437; Sherman's march toward, 416
Juniper Street, 158

Kelly, Elijah, 330
Kelly Farm, Chickamauga, 330
Kenly, John R., 161
Kennesaw, GA, 103, 126, 390, 434. *See also* Big Shanty, GA, Kennesaw
Kennesaw Mountain, fighting at, 390–93, 396–98, 416
Kentucky, allows soldier voting, 335; anti-Lincoln politicians, 145
Key West, FL, 187
Kile, Thomas, grocery, 410
Kilpatrick, Judson, 353–55, 450, 465; Kilpatrick-Dahlgren raid, 354, 357
King George III, 165
Kingston GA, 127, 382, 439
Knox, William G., 400
Knoxville, TN, 143–44, 158, 209, 231, 335, 339; falls, 322, 332–33
Knoxville Daily Register, 112, 228, 338, 361, 402; arrives in Atlanta, 322, 351; hires "290," 351
Krick, Robert K., 203, 275

Lack, Paul, 214–15
Ladd, James R., 448
Ladies' Soldiers' Relief Society, Atlanta, 43, 65, 101–3
Ladies' Soldiers' Relief Society, Lafayette AL, 103
Ladies' Soldiers' Relief Society, Macon, 103
"Lady Davis" Hospital, 101
Lafayette, GA, 323
LaGrange, GA, 193–94, 324, 327
LaGrange, TN, 287
LaGrange Reporter, 193, 195
LaGrange Reporter and Bulletin, 439; on Davis' Macon speech, 426
Last Chance for the Confederacy (McMurry), 418
Latane, William, 171
Lawrence, KS, 443
Lawrenceville, GA, 409

Lawrenceville News, 409
Lawshe & Purtell, clothiers, 150–51
Lawton, Alexander R., 149, 218
Lawton, W. J., 150
Leadbetter, Danville, 141, 159
Lebanon, TN, 223
Lee, George Washington, 41–42, 149–50, 214–16, 231, 248, 288
Lee, Robert E., 163–64, 168, 177–78, 199–200, 209, 212–13, 217, 224, 236–37, 239, 428, 436, 443; abandons Richmond, 467; and Seven Days' Battles, 179–87, 189–90, 193–94, 196; at Chancellorsville, 274–79; at Fredericksburg, 240–42, 393; at Petersburg, 290, 471–72; at Sharpsburg, 218–20, 223; in Overland Campaign, 383; "King of Spades," 171; on arming slaves, 461; Pennsylvania campaign and Gettysburg, 306–12, 323, 325, 332, 342, 355, 371, 377–78, 380, 383, 389, 396–97, 405, 414, 419, 428; Second Manassas Campaign, 203–5; suggests Beauregard to command Army of Tennessee, 423; suggests Hood be relieved, 423, 434, 441; surrenders, 141, 467, 473, 477, 482; takes command of Army of Northern Virginia, 168; terms Pope "miscreant," 203
Lee, Stephen D., 17, 417–18, 421, 493; and Ezra Church, 407
Lee, W. Raymond, 193–95
Lee, William G., 20
Lee's Volunteers, 44
Leesburg, VA, 68–69
Leonard John W., Associate Editor, 7; quits, 10
Leonidas, Greek warrior, 341
Letcher, John, 45–46, 263, 269, 279
Letters, soldiers' use by *ADI,* 134, 212, 262
Lewis, George C., 237
Lewis, J. T., 65
Lex Talionis (law of retaliation), 200
Lexington (VA) *Gazette,* 55
Lexington, KY, 209, 223, 228
Lexington, VA, 281–82
Leyden, Austin, 170
Libby Prison, Richmond, 353
"Light-wood knotboy," anecdote in *ADI,* 83

INDEX 529

Lin, Susan, 109, 117
Lincoln, Abraham, 30, 36, 47, 64, 73, 83, 89, 132–33, 140, 153, 160, 165, 169, 183, 189, 225, 308, 312, 338, 341, 368, 371–72, 378, 383, 448, 479; and Fort Sumter, 13; announces blockade, 83; approves Kilpatrick raid, 353; assassinated, 479–80; calls for 75,000 volunteers, 15–16, 30, 36, 39, 45; confiscation order, 201; declares Nevada statehood, 444; decried in *ADI*, 44; derided by Steele, 202; 1860 election, 8–9, 20; emancipation policy, 201, 206, 225, 239; Hampton Roads Conference, 463–64; hard war, 201; in 1864 re-election, 371, 414, 418–19, 444–45; inaugurated, 11; removes Hooker, 309; removes McClellan, 236; second inaugural, 464; *Trent* affair, 75–76; "tyrant and usurper" in *ADI*, 464
Lincoln, Mary Todd, 479–80
"Lincolnites," 167
"Lincoln's minions," 533
Linebaugh, John, 268; arrested by Bragg, 326
Lines, Sylvanus, 361
Little Pumpkinvine Creek GA, 385
Little Rock, AR, 63
Little Round Top, Gettysburg, 312
Littlepage, William, 354–56
Livermore, Thomas L., 19
Liverpool England 75, 81; newspapers, 290
Logan, J. P., 247–48, 324
Logan's Crossroads, KY, battle of, 80
London England, 370; newspapers, 290
"Lone Jack," correspondent for *Augusta Chronicle & Sentinel*, 399
Longstreet, James, 185, 189, 203–5, 239–41, 306–9, 311–12, 323, 325, 330, 332–33, 335, 339, 363, 478; wounded in Wilderness, 378
Lookout Mountain, TN, 338; battle at, 339–40
"Loomis," writes to *ADI*, 163–66
Loring, William W., 391, 434
Lost Cause, The (Pollard), 356
Lost Mountain, GA, 385, 389–91
Loudon, KY, 229
Louisiana, secession of, 10
Louisiana C.S.S., 155–56

Louisiana troops, 1st Infantry Regiment, 139, 201–2
Louisville, KY, 26, 227–28
Louisville Courier-Journal, 236
Louisville Daily Journal, 161
Lovejoy's Station, GA, 407, 417, 423
Lovell, Mansfield, 155, 227
Lowe, Thomas F., 73
Loyd Street, 113, 121
Luckie, Solomon, 406
Lynchburg Republican, 263
Lynchburg Virginian, 181
Lyon, Nathaniel, 63
Lyons, Richard, 75

Macfarlane & Ferguson, 82
Mackall, William, 130
Macon, GA, 64, 67, 73, 99, 107, 111, 115, 219, 224, 249, 261, 415, 417, 421, 429, 435, 437, 439, 449–50, 454, 460, 470, 476, 482; as new home for *ADI*, 401, 405, 407, 409–10; bread riot, 270; hosts Davis' visit, 425; receives expelled Atlantans, 424
Macon & Western Railroad, 99, 115, 407, 416; cut by Federals, 417, 421; repaired, 468
Macon Citizen, 30
Macon Daily Confederate, 259, 361; prints Davis' Macon speech, 425
Macon Telegraph, 20, 23, 30, 82, 161, 212, 260, 296, 361, 402; prints Davis' Macon speech 425, 437
Macon Telegraph and Confederate, 425, 446, 451, 470
Maddox, Robert F., 98
Madison, GA, 334
Madison, VA, 22
Magruder, John B., 153–54, 184–86, 231
Mahone, William, 276
Mail, newspapers' source of material, 19, 153, 267; *Intelligencer* use of, 28
Main Street, Richmond, 269
Mallory, Stephen R., 185, 481
Malvern Hill, VA, battle of, 204
Manassas, battle of, 54–57, 63–64, 69, 97, 105, 111, 119, 140, 142, 153, 180, 226, 349

Manassas, Second, battle of, 204–6, 209, 212, 223
Manassas, C.S.S., 155
Manassas Junction, VA, 53, 56, 65–66, 100, 108, 116, 204, 206
Manchester Guardian, 49
Manigault, Arthur M., 428–29, 452
Manning, Van H., 218
Manpower, Confederate, 370
Mansfield, LA, battle at, 365–68, 378
Manufactories, *ADI* counts in South, 67
March to the Sea, Sherman's, 440, 451, Federal strength, 450
Marietta, GA, 32, 98, 106, 144, 361, 386, 389, 391–93, 398, 402, 434
Marietta Paper Mill, 31–32
Marietta Street, 110, 118, 288, 410, 417, 448
Markham, William, 447
Markham's Building, 171
Marshall, Alexis E., 235; *ADI* legislative reporter, 347, 440; associate editor, 271, 347; leaves *ADI*, 347
Marshall, Charles, 218–21
Marshall, Humphrey, 143; sword manufacturer, 17
Marshall Street, Richmond, 191
Marthasville, GA, 5
Martial law: *ADI* calls for, 136, 214–15; imposed in Atlanta, 214–16
Maryland, Jackson rumored to enter, 184
Mason, James M., 75, 78, 237, 370
Masonic Hall, 74
Masons, 64
Massachusetts troops, 20th Infantry Regiment, 193, 195; 33rd Infantry Regiment, 448; 54th Infantry Regiment, 316
Massey, Mary Elizabeth, 83, 262
Maury, Dabney H., 476
Mayo, Joseph, 270, 472
McCall, George, 20
McClanahan, John R., 296, 319
McClellan, George B. ("Young Napoleon"), and Peninsula Campaign, 153, 161, 180, 182–85, 189, 191–92, as practitioner of "soft war," 195–96, 199, 203–4; at Antietam, 218–19, 236–37; in 1864 election, 418, 444

McClernand, John A., 292
McCook, Edward, and McCook-Stoneman raid, 407–8
McDowell, Irvin, 53–54, 56, 66
McDowell, VA, battle at, 181
McGowan, Samuel, 278
McLaws, Lafayette, 66, 311–12
McMurry, Richard M., 418
McNaught, Ormond and Company, 67
McPherson, James, bookseller, 52
McPherson, James B., 292, 379–81, 386, 401; killed, 406
McPherson, James M., historian, 166
McPherson's bookstore, 48
Meade, George G., 242, 309–10, 312, 338, 353, 355, 377, 389, 397
Mechanics' Fire Company No. 2, 43
Mechanicsville, VA, battle of, 179–80
Medical College Hospital, 105, 324, 327
Memphis, TN, 22, 79, 86, 93, 287, 366; surrender of, 213
Memphis and Charleston Railroad, 162
Memphis Avalanche, 213
Memphis Daily Appeal, 22, 128, 130, 136, 291, 315, 326, 351, 361, 434; "extra," 409–10, 413–14, 434; member of Press Association, 319; moves to Atlanta, 296; moves to Montgomery, 402, 409
Meridian, MS, 287, 402
Meridian Clarion, 348
Merrimack. See *Virginia*, C.S.S.
Mesilla Arizona Territory, 21
Mesilla Valley (AZ) *Times*, 21
Mexican War, 11, 20, 43, 49, 209, 393
"Miasmatic effluvia," 100
Military Division of the Mississippi, U.S., 377
Military Division of the West, C.S., 423, 439
Militia, Georgia. See Georgia troops
Militia law, exempts printers from conscription, 74
Mill Springs, KY, battle of, 79–80, 83, 85
Milledgeville, GA, 9, 29, 73, 97, 150, 171, 235, 266–67, 271, 347, 440
Milledgeville Southern Federal Union, 64
Millen, GA, 450

Miller, James I., 6–7; sells interest in *ADI,* 40
Milroy, Robert H., 181
Milton, John, 6
Minnesota, U.S.S., 126–27
Minute Men of Fulton County, 8–9
Miscegenation, Southerners' fear of, 473
Missionary Ridge, TN, 332, 338–39, 458; battle at 340–41, 349
Mississippi, C.S.S., 155–56
Mississippi, secession of, 9–10; legislature, 278
Mississippi River, 86, 126, 129–30, 133, 155, 167–68, 317–18, 366, 377
Mississippi troops, 17th Infantry Regiment, 68; 18th Infantry Regiment, 68
Missouri State Guard, 63, 85
Mitchel, Ormsby M., 144, 161, 163, 169, 180
Mitchell Street, 468
Mobile, AL, 81, 139, 168, 229, 239, 248, 269, 293, 299, 301, 318, 377–78, 382, 470; abandoned, 476
Mobile & Ohio Railroad, 291
Mobile Daily Advertiser & Register, 136, 139–40, 236, 268–69, 300, 315, 330, 348, 386, 433, 458, 464
Mobile Daily Tribune, 61, 143, 155, 297, 302, 305, 316–17
"Model," writes to *ADI,* 12
Monitor, U.S.S., 110
Montgomery, AL, 16, 42, 45, 79, 104, 269, 407, 409, 441, 476; and Confederate convention 10, 12, 14, 17; Confederate capital, 13, 96
Montgomery Daily Advertiser & Register, 21, 143, 260, 299, 368
Montgomery Mail, on Davis' Macon speech, 426
Moon's Station, GA, 145, 434
Moore, Thomas, 168
Moran, Hannah, 316
Mordecai, Thomas W., 436
Morgan, John H., 223–24, 350
"Morgan's Capture and Escape" (Abrams), 351
Morgan's raid, 350
Morris, William S., 26
Morris Island SC, 316, 320
Morse, Nathan G., 26

Morse, Samuel F., 19
Moscow Russia, 425, 477
Muhlenbrink, Hansa, 485
Mumford, William B., 199, 201
Murfreesboro, Stones' River, battle of, 245–46, 269, 315, 324, 328, 342
Murfreesboro, TN, 93, 100, 275, 291, 457
Murphy, Anthony, 143–46

Nagle, I. E., *ADI* associate editor, 417; as "scoundrel,"427; criticizes Davis' administration for Atlanta's fall, 421–22, 428; favors African Americans as Confederate soldiers, 429, 461; postwar, 486; suggests replacing Hood, 422–23
Napoleon, Louis, 237
Napoleon Bonaparte, 425, 477
Napoleon smoothbore cannon, 380
Nashville, TN, 22, 26, 79, 86–88, 91–92; battle of, 433, 457–58; Confederate evacuation, 93–94; 99–100, 125, 213, 223, 228, 245, 315, 424, 448, 451–53
Nashville Banner, 74
Nashville Union and American, 33
Natchez, MS, 168, 291
National American, 11
National Archives, 24, 355, 357
Navy, C.S., 398
Navy, U.S., 81
Neal, James H., 170, 242, 281
Neal, John, 170
Neisbet, J. W., 313
Neisbet, W. H., 313
Nevada, statehood declared, 444
New England, derided by *ADI,* 61
New Era, 485
New Hope Church, GA, battle of, 384, 386, 396
New Ironsides, U.S.S., 359
New Madrid, MO, 112–13
New Market, VA, battle of, 378
New Mexico Territory, 113–14
New Orleans, LA ("Crescent City"), 22, 26, 81, 136; loss of, 155–57, 221; 160, 166–68, 206, 342, 366, 377
New Orleans Delta, 231

New Orleans Picayune, 346
New York, NY, 16, 19–20, 26, 81; newspapers, 444, 453
New York Associated Press, 26
New York Herald, 20, 91, 170, 213, 228, 445, 450, 452
New York Times, 20–21, 160; reprints from *ADI,* 402
New York Tribune, 281, 445
New York World, 238
Newberry (SC) *Herald,* 478
Newnan, GA, 33, 71, 324
Newport, KY, 217
News coverage, *ADI*'s: arrival of Atlanta exiles in Macon, 424; arrival of Yankee prisoners, 247; Atlanta bread riot, 270; Atlanta Campaign, 381–94, 396–99, 401, 414, 416; Atlantans rebuilding, 468; Atlantans' vote, 72–73; battle of Ball's Bluff, 68–69; battle of Bentonville, 471; battle of Cedar Mountain, 203; battle of Chickamauga, 323–24, 331; battle of Corinth, 227; battle of Elkhorn Tavern, 112; battle of Franklin, 452; battle of Frayser's Farm, 206; battle of Fredericksburg, 241–42; battle of Manassas, 54, 57; battle of Mechanicsville, 202–3; battle of Mill Springs, 87–88; battle of Murfreesboro, 245–47, 349; battle of Nashville, 505; battle of New Orleans, 137–38; battle of Pea Ridge, 111–12; battle of Perryville, 228–29; battle of Pickett's Mill, 385; battle of Richmond, KY, 209; battle of Seven Pines, 169; battle of Shiloh, 121–23; battle of Springfield, 70; battle of Valverde, 113–14; battle of Wilderness, 378–79; Beauregard and Military Division of the West, 439; bombardment of Atlanta, 409, 413–14; burning of Columbia, 465; capture of Fort Pulaski, 119–20; Chancellorsville, 276–81, 291; Dahlgren's raid, 353–57; Davis' creation of Military Division of the West, 439; Davis' visit to Army of Tennessee, 428–29; Davis' visit to Atlanta, 332; death and funeral of Jackson, 303–6; destruction of *Virginia,* 165; engagement at Island No. 10, 113; evacuation of Richmond, 472; fall of Fort McAllister, 451; fall of Jackson, 293; fall of Memphis, 159; fight at Williamsburg, 164–65; fighting at Chattanooga, 339–40; Fort Henry and Donelson, 86–88, 91; Fort Pillow, 367; Fort Sumter, 14; Gettysburg, 309–11; Hampton Roads Conference, 464; hanging of Mumford, 199; Hood's advance into Tennessee, 432–34, 439, 457; *Hunley* submarine, 359; Island No. 10, 113; Jackson's death, 279; Jackson's Shenandoah Valley Campaign, 160–63; Johnston's retreats, 429, 441; Johnston's surrender, 532–33; Lee's surrender, 528–29; Lincoln's assassination, 479–80; Lincoln's call for troops, 19, 45; Lincoln's election, 8; local news, 40; loss of New Orleans, 136; military news, 109; naval battle at Hampton Roads, 110; naval battle at Memphis, 180; occupation of Alexandria, 133; occupation of Nashville, 132; on Port Hudson, 301; Overland Campaign in Virginia, 396–97; Peninsula Campaign, 163, 168, 184; Polk's death, 390; Pope's orders, 197; repair of railroads, 468; Second Manassas, 203, 205–6; Sergeant Collier's bravery, 397–98; Sequestration Act, 71; Seven Days' Battles, 179–89; Sharpsburg, 244–46; shell damage to Atlanta, 410, 415; shelling of Chattanooga, 159; shelling of Vicksburg, 291; Sherman's march to the sea, 447, 450–51; Sherman's movements, 417, 435; St. Albans raid, 443–44; Streight's raid, 285–87; Stuart's raid, 171, 223; train wreck on W. & A., 190–91; *Trent* Affair, 75–76; Vicksburg Campaign, 291–94, 298–99, 302; volunteering in city, 41, 44; Wilson's raid, 476. See also *Atlanta Daily Intelligencer*

News reports: *ADI*'s delay in receiving, 18, 151; costs for, 90

Newspaper office layout, 34–35

Newspaper staff, volunteers for army, 28, 90

Newspapers: as publishers of poetry and essays, 19, 62; functions of, 126, 241; number in U.S., 1830s, 19; profitability of, 27; size of, 26; struggle for subscribers and advertisers, 82

Newspapers, Confederate, 259; and military news, 141; number at end of war, 485; number in 1864, 381; overly sanguine, 300, 303
Newspapers, Northern, 21; celebrate Thomas' victory, 457; derided by *ADI*, 68, 213
Newton Station, MS, 287
Nisbet, Eugenius, 64–65, 73
Norfolk, VA, 23, 90, 164
North Anna River, VA, 389
North Carolina, secession of, 45
Northwest Ordinance, 444

Oak Grove, VA, battle of, 178–79
Oakland Cemetery. *See* City Cemetery (Oakland)
Ogeechee River, GA, 451
Oglethorpe Light Infantry, 56
O'Hara, Scarlett, 485
Ohio River, 86, 217, 433–34
Ohio State Penitentiary, 350
O'Keefe, Daniel, 191
Oldham, Williamson, 460
"Olla podrida," staff list in *ADI*, 399–400, 417
Olley's Creek, GA, 391
Olmstead, Charles H., 120
Olustee, FL, battle at, 410
Oostanaula River, GA, 146, 381–82
Opelika, AL, 436
"Operation Crusher," Lincoln's term, 378
"Ora." *See* Reid, Samuel Chester
Ormond, James, 242
Orchard Knob, Chattanooga, 340
Ordnance Bureau, C.S., 325
Orr, Gustavus, 63
Osterhaus, Peter, 341
"Our American Cousin," 479
"Our City": *ADI* column, 319, 327; boasts Atlanta's resurgence, 467
Overland Campaign, 389, 396

"P. W. A." *See* Alexander, Peter W.
Page, newspaper size of, 82–83
Palmerston, H. J. T., 237
Palmetto GA, 425–26, 428, 432–34, 440–41
Paper: changes in color, 83; cost of, 82, 150, 210, 317; mill at Bath SC, 271; mills, number in South, 31, 82; mills, number in US, 31; shortage of, 31, 297, 317, 362, 435, 469
Parrott rifled cannon, 331, 380, 406, 414–15
Pascagoula, MS, 301
Passenger Depot. *See* Car Shed (Union Depot)
Patterson, Robert, 54
Paul, Franc M., 214, 296, 319
Paul, Gabriel R., 311
Paulding County GA, 386
Paxton, Elisha F., 277
Pay, C.S. soldiers', 98
Payne, Lewis, 480
Payne, Rice W., 56
Pea Ridge AR, battle of, 110–12
Peach Orchard, Gettysburg, 312
Peachtree Creek, 468; battle of, 405–6
Peachtree Street, 7, 45, 47, 64, 71, 247, 288, 324, 327, 398, 417, 448–49, 468
"Peculiar institution," Southern slavery, 48, 202, 236, 289
Peddy, George W., 459
Peeble's Farm, VA, fight at, 436
Peel, John, 410
Pemberton, John C., 261; and Vicksburg Campaign, 291–93, 299, 302–4, 342, 468
Peninsula Campaign, 163
Pennsylvania State University, 28
Pensacola, FL, 42, 44, 46
Perryville, KY, battle at, 229–30, 328, 342
"Personne." *See* De Fontaine, Felix
Peters, George B., 288
Peters, Jessie, 288
Petersburg, VA, 239, 262, 397; bombarded, 410–11, 466; siege of, 397, 423, 443, 472, 478
Petersburg Express, 142–43, 154, 162, 181, 222, 436
Peterson, J. S., 11, 259, 319
Philadelphia, PA, 21, 308
Philadelphia Inquirer, 187
Phillips, Eugenia, 223–24
Phillips, Henry, 207
Physicians, care for soldiers in Atlanta, 49
Pickett, George E., 310, 312, 472
Pickett, Martha, 385
Pictorial History of the Great Rebellion (Blake), 356

Pigeon Hill, Kennesaw, 392
Pike County, GA, 5
Pilgrim, Isaac B.: *ADI* foreman, 30, 172–74, 347, 396, 400; flees Atlanta, 417; postwar, 486; writes on Federals' shelling, 409–10, 415
Pillow, Gideon J., 91–92
Pilot Knob, MO, fight at, 436
Pim, Lewis T., 100, 113–14, 116–18, 121–22, 173
Pine Mountain, GA, 390, 402
Pittsburg Landing, TN, 139–40
Pleasonton, Alfred, 335–36
Plymouth, NC, battle at, 365, 367–68
Poe, Orlando M., 448
Poetry in *ADI*, 62, 89
Polk, Leonidas, 257, 332–33, 382 killed, 390–91
Pollard, Edward A., 22, 285, 291, 349–50, 356
Ponder, Ellen, 120
Pope, Alexander, 414
Pope, John, 129–30; in Second Manassas Campaign, 204–6, 223–24; "Proclamation Pope," 201; soldiers destroy Virginians' property, 198; vindictive orders of, 197–200, 203
Port Gibson, MS, battle of, 292
Port Hudson, LA, 262; siege of, 300–302
Port Republic, VA, battle at, 183–84
Port Royal, SC, 160
Port Royal, VA, 240
Porter, David D., 155–56, 292
Porter, Fitz John, 202–4, 206
Posey, Ben Lane, 433
"Position," column in *ADI*, 392–93, 396, 398, 401–2, 408–9, 417, 421
Postal service, C.S., 22, 50, 76, 211–12, 238, 476
Postal service, U.S., 19
Potomac River 57, 217–19, 224, 308, 311
Powell, Thomas S., 171
Prentiss, Benjamin M., 139–40
"President Davis and His Administration" (Abrams), 349–50
Press, Confederate on Yankee barbarity, 154; on Pope's orders, 222
Press Association of the Confederate States of America, 152, 297, 318, 326, 332–33, 335, 343, 361, 470; announces death of Hood and recants, 325; annual meeting, 360–61; Board of Directors, 296, 318; copyrights telegraphic dispatches, 318; founded, 261; prices and fees, 238, 470; reports Atlanta Campaign, 384, 414–16; reports Chickamauga, 323; reports Davis' visit to Hood's army, 428; reports Federal occupation of Atlanta, 417, 421; telegraphic dispatches as *ADI* news source, 318, 339, 378, 383, 400, 438, 470
Price, Sterling, 63, 85, 127–28, 227; *ADI* reports Missouri raid, 436; "Old Pap," 268
Prices: in Atlanta, 270; leather, 346; of food, 351
Prince, Henry, 203
Printers: exempted from conscription, 74; strike, 211, 361–62; volunteer for army, 82, 361
Printing press: hand press, 19, 25; steam powered, 25
Prisoners, Union, in Atlanta, 277
Pritchard, William H., 26, 151–52, 162, 214; editors' complaints against, 78–79, 262
Pritchard, William H., Jr., 162
Propaganda, Confederate newspapers' role in, 38, 81–82, 141, 165–66, 186, 214, 438
Provost Marshal, Atlanta, 21, 215, 449
Proximo, ("next month"), 317
Pryor Street 20, 449

"Q," writes *ADI*, 224
Quantrill, William, 443
Quarles, William A., 452
Quartermaster General, GA, 424
Quintard, Charles T., 364, 449

Racism, in *ADI*, 82
Radicals, Northern, 201
Railroads, Confederate, 82; in disrepair, 370
Raleigh, NC, 470, 476; falls, 481
Raleigh Register, 49
Raleigh Standard, 27
Raleigh State Journal, 28
Randall, B.A., 32
Randolph, George W., 185–86, 224, 243
Rantin, William M., *ADI* printer, 393–94
Rape, allegations of by Federals, 154, 438, 466
Rapidan River, VA, 378–79

Rappahannock River, VA, 204, 236, 239–41, 274–77, 306–7
Rasberry, R. A., 74
Rawson, Edward E., 74
Raymond MS, battle of, 293, 299
Reading rooms, at newspaper offices, 34
Reagan, John H., 76, 481
"Reason," writes to *ADI*, 137
Rebel Restaurant, 468
Receiving & Distributing Hospital, 324, 327
Red River LA, 366, 378
Reed, Wallace P., 32, 41
Reid, Samuel Chester "Ora," "290," "Sparta," 333, 338–39, 342, 347, 350, 360; as *ADI* special correspondent, 338; hired by Steele as "290," 269, 280, 289, 346–49, 351, 354; leaves *ADI*, 351; "Morgan's Capture and Escape," 350–51; postwar activity, 486; reports fighting at Chattanooga, 339–41; writes from Charleston, 315–18, 320
Reid, Samuel G., 283
Religious faith, among Southern soldiers, 372
Reprints, *ADI*'s: editorials, 320, 351; from *Athens Banner*, 83; from *Augusta Chronicle & Sentinel*, 113, 281, 399; from *Augusta Constitutionalist*, 478, 482; from *Charleston Courier*, 21, 79, 169; from *Charleston Mercury*, 56, 76, 168, 189, 217, 339, 426; from *Chattanooga Gazette*, 479–80; from *Columbus Enquirer*, 476; from *Columbus Times*, 438; from *Griffin Rebel*, 457; from *Knoxville Register*, 228, 338; from *Lynchburg Republican*, 263; from *Lynchburg Virginian*, 160, 281; from *Macon Journal & Messenger*, 105; from *Macon Telegraph and Confederate*, 454, 470; from *Memphis Appeal*, 416; from *Mesilla Valley Times*, 21; from *Milledgeville Recorder*, 224; from *Mobile Advertiser & Register*, 198–99, 300; from *Mobile Tribune*, 61, 136; from *Montgomery Advertiser*, 21, 125, 368; from *Montgomery Mail*, 426; from *Nashville Banner*, 74; from *New Orleans Delta*, 147; from *New York Herald*, 452–53; from *New York Times*, 140; from *Petersburg Express*, 197; from *Philadelphia Inquirer*, 166;
from *Richmond Dispatch*, 124, 181, 197–98; from *Richmond Enquirer*, 110, 116, 187, 237, 281; from *Richmond Examiner*, 124, 171, 197, 205, 279; from *Richmond Whig*, 172, 309; from *Savannah Republican*, 124, 219, 311–12; from *Selma Reporter*, 457; from *Vicksburg Daily Citizen*, 262; from *Western Carolinian*, 166; from *Wilmington Journal*, 124. See also *Atlanta Daily Intelligencer*
Republican Party, 66; in 1860 election, 8
Resaca, GA, 146, 408, 439, 468; battle of, 381–82
Retaliation, *ADI* urges, 201
Review of the War, A (Abrams), 348
Reynolds, John F., 204, 311
Reynolds, T. S., envelope manufacturer, 171
Reynolds, W. H., 459
Richards, Jabez, 249
Richards, Samuel, 210, 249, 441
Richmond, KY, Confederate victory at, 209
Richmond, VA, 22, 29, 44, 50–51, 53–54, 56–57, 78–79, 90, 93, 96–98, 104, 126–27, 129, 140–41, 153, 162, 168, 181, 184–92, 203, 205–6, 213, 217–18, 228, 235, 237–41, 245, 260, 262–63, 276–77, 279–80, 289, 301–3, 306–8, 310, 312, 318, 320, 332, 335, 338, 340, 346, 349, 353–56, 360, 363, 370–71, 377, 389, 396–97, 399–401, 405, 419, 421, 423, 425–26, 439, 443, 453, 457, 460, 465, 470, 478; becomes Confederate capital, 21, 45; Bread Riot, 269–70; falls, 471
Richmond Associated Press, 260
Richmond Bread Riot, 292–93
Richmond Dispatch, 27, 55, 141–42, 204, 222–23, 348, 355; as *ADI* exchange, 69
Richmond Enquirer, 23, 127, 133; as *ADI* exchange, 69; on Davis' Macon speech, 436; predicts Confederate victory, 210–11; 213, 218, 237, 242, 260, 277, 280; reports Hood dead, 325
Richmond Examiner, 22, 142, 152, 192, 213, 229, 239, 268, 279, 308, 311; vilifies Yankees, 263
Richmond Sentinel, 260
Richmond Whig, 192, 309
Ringgold, GA, 146, 323, 328; battle at Gap, 340–41
Rio Grande River, 81, 131

Riordan, Bartholomew R., 318
Ripley, Roswell S., 218
Risley, J. Ford, 28, 31, 33, 82, 220, 281
Rival Administrations, The (Pollard), 349
River Line, Confederate defenses at Chattahoochee, 400
River Queen, 463
Roanoke River, NC, 365
Roark's Corner, 449, 468
Robinson, Martin, 354
Rocky Face Ridge, GA, 380–81
Rodes, Robert E., 267–68, 308
Rolling Mill, Atlanta, 421
Rome, GA, 56, 285–86, 402
Rome Courier, 28
Rosecrans, William S., 227, 245–47, 269, 285, 287, 315, 319, 338, 458; at Chickamauga, 322–23, 328, 330–32
Roswell, GA, 31–32, 67
Roswell Manufacturing Company, 111, 119, 327
Rough and Ready GA, 417, 424
Rowland, John, 111, 119
Royster, Charles, 372, 473
Rubin, Anne Sarah, 371–72
Rumors, printed in *ADI*, 57, 85, 128, 141–42, 213; readers warned against, 217
Russell, Lord John, 237

Salem Church, VA, 275
Salt, Georgians' need for, 81
Salter, George, 20
San Francisco, CA, 19
San Jacinto, U.S.S., 75
Sanctum/editor's office, 29, 282, 300, 305, 317, 324, 415
Sandersville Central Georgian, 23
Savage's Station, VA, battle of, 182
Savannah, GA, 20–21, 42, 44, 56, 79, 81, 98, 106, 137–38, 219, 239, 382, 425, 433, 440–41, 448, 451, 465; Federal siege and occupation, 464
Savannah Morning News, 20, 154–55, 361, 367
Savannah Republican, 20–21, 137–38, 141, 152, 217, 219, 236, 311, 317
Savannah River, 271

Schenck, Robert C., 181
Schofield, John M., 379, 381, 385, 391–92, 399, 401, 405, 417; at Franklin, 452–53, 471
Schott, Thomas E., 215
Scofield, Lewis, 447
Scott, Albert, 231
Scott, Thomas M., 452
Scott, William J., 179
Scott, Winfield, 14, 58
"Scoundrel," Davis' accusation against Nagle, 425, 427
Scruggs, William L., joins *ADI* staff, 163–64
Seabrook's Warehouse, Richmond, 280
Seago, E. M., 47
Seal, Confederate, 276
Sears, Stephen W., 219
"Second American Revolution," 165, 350
Second Baptist Church, 210
Seddon, James A., 332, 443
Sedgwick, John, 275
"Seeing the elephant," 50–51, 58
Selma, AL, 79, 112, 120, 268, 476
Selma Reporter, 291, 457
Seminole Indians, 43
Semi-siege, Sherman's, of Atlanta, 407, 413
Semmes, Benedict, 424
Senate, C.S., 300, 460, 463
Senate, U.S., 10
"Senex," writes to *ADI*, 164–65
Sequestration Act, 71
Seven Days' Battles, 178–90
Seven Pines, VA, 184; battle of, 189–91, 193–95
Seward, Frederick, 480
Seward, William H., 1; and Hampton Roads Conference, 463; and *Trent* affair, 75; assassination attempt, 479–80
Seymour, Horatio, 238
"Shadow." *See* Watterson, Henry
Sharpsburg, MD, battle of, 217–19, 225, 237
Shaw, Robert, 316
Shenandoah River, VA, 180
Shenandoah Valley, VA, 53–54, 180; "lower" and "upper," 183–84, 203, 219, 281, 306–8, 378; ravaged by Sheridan, 449
Shepherdstown, MD, 218

Sheridan, Philip H., 443, 472; defeats Early, 444
"Sheriff's Sale Day," 202
Sherman, Ellen, 393
Sherman, William T., 32, 48, 291, 339–40, 419, 426, 434, 439, 470, 477; accepts Johnston's surrender, 481–82; aims to cut Macon & Western R.R., 406–8, 416–17; and Atlanta Campaign, 360, 379–82, 384–85, 389–93, 396–98, 400, 414; appoints Howard to succeed McPherson, 448; arranges truce with Hood, 424; captures Atlanta, 418, 423, 437; correspondence with Hampton, 465–67; departs Atlanta, 450; expels Atlanta residents, 423; flanking tactics, 416; follows Hood northward, 435, 438, 440; heads Military Division of the Mississippi, 377; issues orders for march to sea, 450; march across Georgia, 440–41, 447–48, 464; marches through Carolinas, 465, 470, 480–81; marches through north Georgia after Hood, 435; orders destruction in Atlanta, 448; orders march toward Jonesboro, 410, 416; reported killed, 301; sends IV and XXIII Corps north, 435; sends Lincoln "Christmas gift" of Savannah, 451; sends Thomas to Tennessee, 435; shells Atlanta, 403, 406, 409, 411, 414–15; troops burn parts of city, 449, 485
Shields, James, 183–84
Shiloh, TN, battle of, 138–42, 168, 246, 342, 349
Ship Island, MS, 155, 223
Shortages, in Confederacy, 370
Shoup, Francis A., 399
"Shoupades," 399
Shreveport, LA, 301
Sibley, Henry H., 130–31
Sickles, Daniel E., 278, 312
Siege of Vicksburg, The (Abrams), 348
Sigel, Franz, 63, 353, 377–78
Silver, James W., 49
Silver Grays, 43
Silvey and Dougherty's dry goods store, 110, 118
Simms, Joel D., 436
Singer sewing machines, 288

Sisson, Vardy P., 50–51, 63, 65
"Situation, The," column in *ADI*, 383–84, 400
Slavery, *ADI* references to, 48, 188, 225; as cause of the war, 430; Steele defends, 430
Slidell, John, 75, 78
Slocum, Henry, 416, 450; XX Corps as Atlanta garrison, 435, 439
Smith, Bartley M., 64
Smith, Charles H, "Bill Arp," 402
Smith, Edmund Kirby, 143, 209, 217, 227, 229–30, 268, 301
Smith, Ephraim Kirby, 209
Smith, Gustavus W., 189
Smith, J. B. & Co., 231
Smith, J. Henly, 64, 144, 259, 319
Smith, John T., *Intelligencer* cashier, 24; mail manager, 235; treasurer, 400
Smith, Preston, 325
Smith, Timothy, 87
Smith, William S., 410
Smyrna, GA, 398–99
Snake Creek Gap, GA, 380–81
Snodgrass house, Chickamauga, 330
"Soft war," 196
"Soldier," writes to *ADI*, 437
Soldier-correspondents, 50
Soldier's Friend, The, 249
Soldiers Relief Society, Athens, GA, 112, 120
Soldiers' Relief Society, Forsyth, GA, 120
Somerset, KY, 80
Sope Creek, GA, 31
South Carolina, secession 9–10, 227
South Carolina troops, 1st Infantry Regiment, 290
South Side Railroad, VA, 472
Southern Associated Press, 132, 260
Southern Confederacy Publishing Company, 13
Southern Field and Fireside, 69
Southern Historical Society, 356
Southern Historical Society Papers, 356
Southern Illustrated News, 64
Southern Literary Messenger, 82
Southern Miscellany, 5
Southern Telegraph Company, 26, 152, 260
Southwestern Telegraph Company, 26, 262, 318

Sparta, GA, 211
Sparta Greece, 42
"Specials," field correspondents and paid reporters for newspapers, 32–33, 219, 338
Spotsylvania Court House, VA, battle at, 383, 389
Spratt, Leonidas W., 55
Spring Street, 410
Springfield, MO, battle of, 62–63, 69, 76, 96
St. Albans, VT, 443–44
St. Louis, MO, 63, 85–86, 129, 458
St. Luke's Episcopal Church, 364, 390, 449
St. Paul's Episcopal Church, Alexandria, 133
St. Paul's Episcopal Church, Richmond, 238
St. Philip's Episcopal Church, 110–11, 117–20, 364
St. Philip's Hospital Society, 109, 111–12
Stafford, Leroy A., 379
Stanton, Edwin M., 185, 225
Starke, William E., 218
Stars and Bars, 46
Staunton, VA, 180–81, 183, 417
"Stay-at-home-patriots," 331
Steele, John H., 201, 212, 217, 219, 224, 226, 228, 230–31, 235, 238–39, 240–41, 260–63, 269, 276, 291, 296, 308, 317, 322, 326, 332–33, 335, 342, 347, 349, 351, 364, 391–20, 402, 446, 454–55; absent Sept. 5–26, 1864, from *ADI* and hands *ADI* to Nagle, 421, 429, 461; addresses inflation, 320; adds A. E. Marshall as associate editor, 271; *ADI* editor, 378, 400; advocates for women, 232, 271; and editorial fraternity, 213; and Maryland Campaign, 218–19; announces printers' strike, 237; announces subscription price hike, 249, 316; apologizes for anti-Johnston editorial, 396; appearance described, 361; as Confederate propagandist, 351, 467; assumes Hood will be reinforced, 414; becomes *ADI* editor, 191; boasts *ADI* circulation, 235; calls for increased corn production, 289; calls for "Lex Talionis," 200; calls for martial law, 215–16; calls for war of extermination, 201; calls Lincoln "inhuman monster," 480; cautions readers against over-optimism, 251; celebrates Second Manassas, 205–6; celebrates Southern victories, 216, 367–68, 381; cheers people, 322–23; commends "290" (Samuel C. Reid), 269, 315–17; commends Bragg, 245–46, 328; commends Forrest, 286; commends women hospital workers, 327; comments on Hampton-Sherman correspondence, 466–67; comments on Northern treatment of C.S. prisoners, 277; comments on Second Manassas, 230; complains about reprinting of his work, 268; complains against telegraph operators, 258; complains of mail service, 297; complains of sparse news, 379; complains of telegraph service, 260; compliments ladies, 319; compliments Southern reporters, 291–92; conceals identity of "290," 338; conceals identity of "Clio," 236; conceals identity of "Shadow," 326; Confederate cheerleader, 471; consoles readers, 299; continues to voice optimism, 371; counsels patience, 230; counsels readers on Confederate defeat, 482–83; criticizes Davis, 425, 427–28; Davis' Macon speech and "scoundrel incident," 425, 427; deals with rumors of Lee's surrender, 477; defends Johnston, 396; defends slavery, 226, 430, 460; denies Union victory at Gettysburg, 311; denounces Butler, 198; denounces Pope, 203; denounces Sherman's shelling, 416; denounces Yankees, 384; disbelieves news of Vicksburg's fall, then admits it, 303; dismisses Corinth defeat, 227; dismisses defeat at Chattanooga, 341; editorial work of, 285, 333, 346; editorializes and follows Vicksburg news, 300, 302; encourages Atlantans to take in wounded, sick, 248; encourages readers' optimism, 471; excerpts "Ora" from *Mobile Tribune*, 317; exhorts against discouragement, 220; explains Johnston's retreats, 383; explains Murfreesboro, 246; explains skimpy news, 217; explains subscription rate hike, 271; expresses confidence in Hood, 440; fulminates against Yankees, 467; gloats over Stoneman's capture, 408; hails victory at Winchester, 307; helps needy Atlantans,

Steele, John H. (*continued*)
294; hires Samuel C. Reid ("290"), 292; "indisposed," 231; joins *ADI* staff, 162–63, 169; leaves *ADI* in Nagle's hands, 417, 422; lists *ADI* staff, 347, 399–400, 417; "Long Faces" editorial, 383; misleads readers, 304; objects to "Shadow's" prediction of Atlanta's fall, 386; observes presidential fast day, 210; on Chancellorsville, 304–5; on Confederate defeat at Corinth, 255; on Dahlgren raid, 355–57; on Davis' visit to Atlanta, 332; on Emancipation Proclamation, 254; on Fredericksburg, 241–42; on Gettysburg, 312; on inflation, 362; on Jackson's death, 279; on martial law, 22–43; on Murfreesboro, 275–76; on Northern emancipation policy, 201–2; on Northern mid-term elections, 267; on "Sherman the flanker," 416; opposes African Americans as Confederate soldiers, 429–30, 460; "Our Prospects Bright," 223; personality described, 397; postwar, 486; predicts Atlanta's rise from ashes, 455; predicts Confederate independence, 252, 414; predicts Confederate victory, 386; printers' strike, 363; prints letters from "290," 315; protests Yankees' shelling of Charleston, 320; publishes Bragg's battle order, 323; publishes letters only from named contributors, 212–13; publishes W. H. Nesbit's letter, 313; quotes *Richmond Enquirer*, 309; quotes *Richmond Examiner*, 311; rails against enemy, 242, 351; raises money for Forrest's horse, 286–87; rallies Georgians, 343, 347; refuses Northern papers' news of Lee's surrender, 478; relocates to Macon, 401; remains optimistic, 371; reports battle of Sharpsburg, 217–19; reports Davis' speech in Atlanta, 248; reports Perryville, 228; reports Sherman's movements, 417; reports train wreck on W. & A., 214; reprints from *Lynchburg Republican*, 263; reprints from *Memphis Appeal Extra*, 410; reprints from *Richmond Dispatch*, 355; reprints from *Richmond Examiner*, 308; reprints from *Savannah Morning News*, 367; resists issuing half-sheet editions, 238; returns to Atlanta from Macon, 449; Richmond's fall, 472; sides with Forrest on Fort Pillow, 367; spars with *Southern Confederacy*, 259, 335; spins untoward events, 386; staff of, 347; standing as editor, 268; supports Davis, 349; supports editorial convention, 249, 260; supports Fast Days, 267; urges corn planting, 266; urges reinforcement of Johnston, 363; urges retaliation, 201, 309; urges voter turnout, 334; uses exchanges, 242; vilifies "King Abe," 202; vilifies Lincoln, 226, 480; visits City Barracks jail, 247; visits hospitals, 248; voices Confederate patriotism and war optimism, 370, 372–74, 451, 473, 477; warns of fall of Atlanta, 363; warns of strangers in city, 319; warns of Yankee subjugation, 226, 304; warns readers of rumors, 217; welcomes papers to Atlanta, 319, 322; works to fill *ADI* pages, 443; writes on fighting at Chattanooga, 340–41; writes "Situation in Front," 384; writes "The Position" column, 392–93, 398, 402

Steinwehr, Adolph von, 224–25
Stephens, Alexander H., 10; and Hampton Roads Conference, 463–64; elected popularly, 71, 96, 214, 216; visits Atlanta, 42
Stephens Rifles, 43
"Stephens Rifles," poem, 62
Stevenson, Carter L., 340, 384, 408
Stewart, Alexander Peter, 340, 421, 433–35
Stewart, K. J., 133
Stone, Amherst, 447
"Stone fleet," 81
Stone Mountain, GA, 12, 41, 210
Stoneman, George, 307; and raid with McCook, 407–8
Stones River, TN, battle of. *See* Murfreesboro, Stones' River, battle of
Stout, Harry S., 69
Stout, Samuel H., 324, 327
Stoy, F. S., 47–48
Strahl, Otho F., 452
Strasburg, VA, 182–83
Strawberry Plains (TN) College, 163
Streight, Abel, raid of, 285–87, 353

Strike, *ADI* printers', 237–38, 394
Stuart, James E. B. ("Jeb"), 192–93, 204, 223–24, 308–9; at Brandy station, 307; mortally wounded, 383
Subjugation to Yankees, 165–66; and Southerners' dread of, 304, 372, 467, 483
Subscription fees: as newspapers' revenue source, 19, 28; rates for *ADI,* 211, 249, 271
Subscription number, for Confederate newspapers, 32–33
Sumner, Edwin V., 239–40
Sweeny, Thomas W., 381–82
Sword, Wiley, 372
Swords, James M., 262

Talmadge, John, 166
Tattnall, Josiah, 186
Taylor, Jesse, 95
Taylor, Richard, 364, 423, 441, 469; "Stonewall of the West," 365–66; wins at Mansfield, 366
Taylor, Zachary, 163
Telegraph: arrives in Atlanta, 24; invention of, 24; office in Atlanta, 75, 86; operators, 212
Telegraphic news dispatches, 22, 32, 34, 39, 45, 53–54, 68, 85; column in *ADI,* 51, 76, 89, 93, 153, 187–88, 203, 212, 216–17, 230, 241, 276–78, 293; cost of, 37, 93, 261; cut off by North, 26; delay in receiving, 86–87, 150, 152; dispatches as news source for *ADI,* 30, 45–46, 58, 60, 64, 75, 82, 84, 93, 97, 205, 298, 300, 302–3, 308–9, 318, 416, 436, 438–39, 444, 452, 460, 465, 470, 472; of Press Association, 413; on Confederate defeats, 87; poorly handwritten, 20, 212
Tennessee, secession of, 52
Tennessee River, 86–87, 161, 322, 438
Tennessee troops: 1st Infantry Regiment, 432; 41st Infantry Regiment, 433
Texas (locomotive), 145
Texas: allows soldier voting, 335; secession of, 10
Texas troops: 4th Infantry Regiment, 286; 5th Infantry Regiment, 173; 10th Infantry Regiment, 280; Texas Brigade, 173
Thermopylae Greece, 341
Third Street, 179
Third Street, Macon, 402, 437, 445

Thomas, George H. ("Rock of Chickamauga"), 80, 338–39; at Chickamauga, 323; defeats Hood at Nashville, 457–58; in Atlanta Campaign, 379, 381, 385, 390, 405, 440, 448, 452; sent to Nashville, 435
Thomas, Thomas L., 80
Thompson, William Tappan, 361
Thrasher, John J. ("Cousin John"), 261
Thrasher, John S., P. A. Superintendent, 261–62, 296–97, 323–26, 332, 335, 360, 413; announces copyrighting, 318; relationship with *ADI,* 346; travels west, 470
Tilghman, Lloyd, 86–87, 283
Tilton, GA, 146
Timrod, Henry, 23, 33
Tracy, Edward D., 292
Train depot, Atlanta. *See* Car Shed (Union Depot)
Trans-Mississippi Department, C.S., 428, 469
Trenholm, George, 481
Trent, H.M.S., 75
Trent affair, 76, 78, 237
Trials of a Soldier's Wife, The (Abrams), 350
Trinity Methodist Church, 210
Trout House, 10, 74–75
Troy (NY) *Whig,* 437
Truitt, Ann, 112, 120
Tullahoma, TN, 246, 269
Tunnel Hill, GA, 439
Tupelo, MS, 169
Turner, D. R., 224
Tuscumbia, AL, 286
"290." *See* Reid, Samuel Chester
Tybee Island, GA, 81, 138
Tyler, Nathaniel, 28
Typesetters and compositors, salaries for, 30

Ultimo ("last month"), 217, 421
Union City, TN, 291
Union Depot. *See* Car Shed (Union Depot)
Union troops, Army of the Potomac, 203; I Corps, 311; III Corps, 312; IV Corps, 379, 385; V Corps, 309, 378; VI Corps, 275; XI Corps, 274–75, 311; XIII Corps, 292; XIV Corps, 379, 435, 450; XV Corps, 292, 379,

Union troops, Army of the Potomac (*continued*) 435, 450, 465; XVI Corps, 379, 435; XVII Corps, 292, 435, 450; XX Corps, 341, 379, 384, 416, 435, 450; XXIII Corps, 379, 417, 435
United States Telegraph, 259
University of Georgia, 220, 372
University of Maryland, 371
Upson County, GA, 112, 120, 248
Utoy Creek, GA, 408

Valley Campaign, Shenandoah, 180–84
Valverde, NM, battle of, 130–31
Van Dorn, Earl, 127–29, 227, 287–88, 291
Van Lew, Elizabeth, 353
Van Tuyll, Debra Reddin, 22–23, 27, 32
Vandiver, Frank E., 372
Vicksburg, MS, 31, 79, 210, 262, 276, 287, 317, 342, 370, 373, 428; falls, 303, 349, 393; Grant's campaign against, 291–94, 298–302; shelled, 291, 302, 411
Vicksburg Mississippian, 168
Vicksburg Whig, 342
Vinings, GA, 434
Virginia, C.S.S., 109–10; destruction of, 164
Virginia, secession of, 29, 45; Georgia troops in, 65
Virginia and Tennessee Railroad, 387
Virginia Central Railroad, 203
Virginia troops: 8th Infantry Regiment, 68, 98; government's call for, 105
"Volunteer City," Atlanta nickname, 68
Volunteer companies, in Atlanta, 40, 67

Walker, Mrs. E. B., 102
Walker, Leroy P., 16–17, 42
Wallace, Alexander M., 41
Walton Spring, 50
Walton Street, 364, 449
"War and Its Horrors," 220
War Department, C.S., 14, 16, 46, 98, 105, 203, 216, 226, 270, 332, 355, 423, 470
Warner, Elizabeth, 413
Warner, Joseph F., 413
Warren, Robert Penn, 411
Warrenton, VA, 56, 218

Warsaw, GA, 453
Warwick, VA, 135
Washington, DC, 13–15, 24, 26, 43, 45, 53, 57, 66, 153, 163, 199, 203, 217, 259, 290, 312, 355, 440, 444, 448, 457, 480
Washington, George, 96–97, 276, 317
Watkins, E. P., 7
Watkins, Sam R., 432
Watterson, Henry, "Shadow," 265; predicts Atlanta will fall, 386
Waynesboro (GA) *News,* 22
Wayside, Distributing Hospital, 248
Wayside Hospital Committee, 327
Weekly Intelligencer, 469
Weitzel, Godfrey, 472
Wesley Chapel, 102, 410
Wesley Chapel Ladies Hospital Association, 102
Wessels, Henry W., 365
West Point, NY, 193
Western & Atlantic Railroad ("State Road"), 6, 126–27; Confederates tear up track, 434–35, 439–40; Federals' damage repaired, 453, 468; train wreck on, 190–91, 210, 285–87, 332, 380–81, 389–91, 406, 432
Western Carolinian, 187
Western Flotilla, Foote's, 86
Westmoreland, John, writes to *ADI*, 66
Westmoreland, Maria, 43, 65–66, 102–3
Westmoreland, Willis F., 66, 100
Wheatfield, Gettysburg, 312
Wheeler, Joseph, 247, 380, 405–6, 449–50; raids north Georgia, 408, 416
Whitaker, Edwin, 280
Whitaker, Jared I., 6, 10, 12, 56, 64, 68, 100 108, 304, 347–48, 386, 398–99; and election of 1860, 8; announces John Steele as *ADI* editor, 191; announces subscription rate hike, 279; as Atlanta mayor, 13, 43, 53; as Georgia Commissary General, 73–74, 150, 171, 235, 346; co-proprietor of *ADI*, 7, 24–25, 27, 33, 40, 53, 65, 67–68, 73, 83, 116, 126, 150, 163, 165, 186, 188; elected Atlanta mayor, 9; postwar, 486; resigns as mayor, 73; returns to Atlanta, 453; sells *ADI,* 485; slaveowner,

7; sole proprietor of *ADI,* 191, 235, 249, 271, 280, 316–17, 319, 346–47, 363, 400, 453; supports fast day, 50; supports Governor Brown, 28, 64
Whitaker, Jared Irwin (son), 174
Whitaker, Nannie, 68, 175
Whitaker, Richard, 280
Whitaker, Samuel H., 280
Whitaker and Gaskill law firm, 6
Whitaker Volunteers 67–68, 74
White House, VA, 203
White House, Washington, 353, 371
White Oak Swamp, VA, battle of, 206, 20
Whitehall Street, 6, 45, 52, 67, 110, 113, 118, 121, 170–71, 173–74, 225, 249, 261, 270, 276, 288, 332, 398, 415, 448–49, 468–69; *ADI* office, 29, 392; postwar *ADI* office, 485
Whitmire, William, *ADI* pressman, 449
Wilcox, Cadmus M., 378
Wilderness, VA, 274, 277; battle of, 378–79, 383, 389
Wilkes, Charles, 75
Wilkes County, GA, 248
William R. Smith (locomotive), 145
Williams' Drug Store, Charleston, 320
Williamsburg, VA, 66, 100, 154, 354; battle at, 185–86
Williamsburg Road, Richmond, 190, 201
Williamsport, MD, 311
Williford, Benjamin, 271
Willingham, Charles H. C., 218–19
Wilmington, NC, 81, 470
Wilmington Journal, 142
Wilson, James H., 476, 482
Wilson, W. T., Mrs., 65
Wilson's Creek, MO, 62. *See also* Springfield, MO, battle of
Winchester, VA, 53–54, 180, 182–83, 219, 307, 313, 378, 444

Winder, Charles S., 203
Winship, Isaac, 113, 121
Winship, Martha, 110–13, 118–21
Winship and Blackie Hospital, 324, 327
Winship's Iron Works and Foundry, 67, 448
Winslow's Soothing Syrup, *ADI* ad, 33
Winter & Pittman, commission merchants, 468
Wise, Jennings, 23
Wittgenstein's liquor store, 29
Women: aiding wounded soldiers, 102–6, 324, 327; as hospital workers, 105; sewing for soldiers, 72
Woodcut illustrations, in *ADI,* 70–71
Woodson, Will, 325–26
Working class, Northern, 188
Worrell, A. S., 249
Wounded soldiers arrive in city, 100–103, 247, 327
Wright, Marcus J., 324, 391
Wyly, A. C., commission merchant, 211

"X.," writes to *Richmond Enquirer,* 277, 280

Yandell, David W., 100, 116
"Yankee Doodle," 46, 76, 223
"Yankee lies," in *ADI,* 98–99, 170, 213, 301
Yankees, *ADI* disdain for, 56, 80, 263–64, 320
Yellow Tavern, VA, battle of, 383
York River, VA, 165
York River Railroad, 180
Yorktown, VA, 163–64
Young, Bennett H., and St. Albans raid, 443–44

Zollicoffer, Felix K., 79–80

www.ingramcontent.com/pod-product-compliance
Lightning Source LLC
Chambersburg PA
CBHW030507080526
44586CB00011B/107